Hong Kong
and Macau

THE ROUGH GUIDE

There are more than one hundred Rough Guide titles
covering destinations from Amsterdam to Zimbabwe

Forthcoming titles include
Bangkok • Barbados • Central America
Israel • Japan • Jordan • New Zealand • Syria

Rough Guide Reference Series
Classical Music • European Football • The Internet • Jazz
Opera • Reggae • Rock Music • World Music

Rough Guide Phrasebooks
Czech • French • German • Greek • Hindi & Urdu • Hungarian • Indonesian
Italian • Japanese • Mandarin Chinese • Mexican Spanish • Polish
Portuguese • Russian • Spanish • Thai • Turkish • Vietnamese

Rough Guides on the Internet
http://www.roughguides.com

Rough Guide credits

Text Editor:	Jo Mead
Series Editor:	Mark Ellingham
Editorial:	Martin Dunford, Jonathan Buckley, Samantha Cook, Ann-Marie Shaw, Paul Gray, Amanda Tomlin, Kate Berens, Sarah Dallas, Chris Schuler, Helena Smith, Caroline Osbourne, Kieran Falconer, Judith Bamber, Olivia Eccleshall, Orla Duane, Andrew Rosenberg (US)
Online:	Al Spicer (UK), Geronimo Madrid (US)
Production:	Susanne Hillen, Andy Hilliard, Melissa Flack, Judy Pang, Link Hall, Nicola Williamson, Helen Ostick, James Morris
Finance:	John Fisher, Celia Crowley, Catherine Gillespie, Neeta Mistry
Marketing & Publicity:	Richard Trillo, Simon Carloss, Niki Smith (UK); Jean-Marie Kelly, SoRelle Braun (US)
Administration:	Tania Hummel, Alexander Mark Rogers

Acknowledgements

Special thanks to Michael Mackey, whose diligent research, assistance, and unrivalled knowledge of Southeast Asian cakes and taxis is greatly appreciated. Thanks, also, to Jo Evans, for graciously putting up with a body on the floor. At Rough Guides, I'm grateful to Jo Mead for her encouragement and patient editing; Sam Kirby for the maps; Gareth Nash for proofreading; Kathryn at Book Trust; and Carol Pucci and Anne Dehne for research in the US and Australia.

For other assistance, thanks to Andrew Hoskins and the MTIB (in London and Hong Kong) for their generous help in Macau; and to Robert Anderson for regular political updates.

At home, Katie hardly complained once when she couldn't come on holiday and gets a big kiss; as do Ken, Jean and Joanna Brown, and my friends Greg Ward and Sam Cook. Regards, as ever, to Anna Hanley, Alan Brooks and Cheryl Taylor, and hello to little Lachlan. Sadly, Capt. I. Little was swept away by a freak wave during his attempt to make a single-handed voyage across the Pacific by coracle; his constant interference in matters of which he displayed a supreme ignorance will be sorely missed.

This third edition published September 1996 by Rough Guides Ltd, 1 Mercer Street, London WC2H 9QJ. Reprinted in December 1996 and March 1998.

Distributed by the Penguin Group:

Penguin Books Ltd, 27 Wrights Lane, London W8 5TZ

Penguin Books USA Inc., 375 Hudson Street, New York 10014, USA

Penguin Books Australia Ltd, 487 Maroondah Highway, PO Box 257, Ringwood, Victoria 3134, Australia

Penguin Books Canada Ltd, 10 Alcorn Avenue, Toronto, Ontario, Canada M4V 1E4

Penguin Books (NZ) Ltd, 182–190 Wairau Road, Auckland 10, New Zealand

Printed in the United Kingdom by Cox and Wyman Ltd (Reading).
Typography and original design by Jonathan Dear and The Crowd Roars.
Illustrations throughout by Edward Briant.

432pp. Includes index.

A catalogue record for this book is available from the British Library.

ISBN 1-85828-187-3

Hong Kong
and Macau

THE ROUGH GUIDE

Written and researched by
Jules Brown

With additional research by
Michael Mackey

Contents

List of Maps

MAP SYMBOLS

▭▭▭	Railway		◆	Point of interest
▭▭	Main road		⚱	Garden
▭	Minor road		▲	Mountain peak
- - - -	Path		◠	Cave
▬	River		≋	Rocks
- - - -	Ferry route		ⓘ	Tourist office
▬▪▬▪	National boundary		✉	Post office
▬ ▬ ▪	Chapter division boundary		☆	Bus stop
✕	Airport		▮	Building
◉	Hotel		▨	Park
♠	Temple		⊹	Cemetery
◮	Monastery		⬚	Beach
♦	Museum		▨	Reclaimed land

Introduction

Hong Kong is a beguiling place to visit: a land whose aggressive capitalistic instinct is tempered by an oriental concern with order and beauty. Indeed, whatever you've heard about it, the most important thing to remember is that Hong Kong is, and always has been, Chinese. Despite over 150 years of British colonial rule, modern Hong Kong has a cosmopolitan veneer through which shines the inescapable fact that the vast majority of its people and customs are thoroughly Chinese. The ultra-modern skyline imitates others throughout the world; the largest department stores are Japanese-owned; you can take English high tea to the accompaniment of a string quartet; there's cricket and horse-racing, pubs and cocktail lounges. But for most of the Chinese locals – 98 percent of the six-million-strong population – life still follows a pattern that many of the mainland Chinese would recognize as their own: food from teeming markets and street stalls; hard work and cramped housing; a polytheistic religion celebrated in the home and in smoky temples; annual, intense, stylistic festivals. Above all, for visitors new to the scene, there's the bizarre juxtaposition of the all-consuming noise and smell of the East in one of the world's most clinically up-to-date cities.

In recent years, Hong Kong has been undergoing its last painful manoeuvres under colonial rule, and each political push and shove in the run-up to the **handing back of the territory** to China has been front-page international news. The British have been here since 1841 and have found it difficult to fulfil their obligations to the citizens of this vibrant, thriving colony; the Chinese government, for its part, hasn't yet discovered the key to reassuring Hong Kong that there's a place for its naked free enterprise economy in a largely unreconstructed state-socialist society. Caught between these two stools, the people of Hong Kong are variously worried, or angry, or unconcerned as long as the dollars keep flowing in. Visitors to Hong Kong should find little change once the handover takes place on June 30, 1997. The Chinese have pledged to retain the existing system for the next fifty years, as Hong Kong becomes a Special Administrative Region of China, and many practical matters – such as entry requirements for visitors – shouldn't be affected. For full details see the relevant *Basics* sections and see "History" (pp.379–386) for a comprehensive account of the minutiae of the handover.

Because all that's Chinese is found in Hong Kong, you need have no fear that a visit to the territory is somehow second-best to seeing China itself. Most people, in fact, do make at least a day trip to neighbouring Guangzhou (Canton), and all the necessary transport and visa details are contained in the guide, but it's not an essential requirement. More important is that you throw away any preconceived notion that all there is to do in Hong Kong is go shopping while on the way to more exciting parts of Asia. The city is dense with interest: the **architecture** is an engaging mix of styles, from stunning, modern banks to ramshackle town housing and centuries-old Chinese temples; the markets and **streetlife** are always compelling; the **shopping** – if no longer the bargain it once was – is eclectic, from open-air stalls to glittering, hi-tech malls. Hong Kong is also *the* place in the world to eat **Chinese food** (and a good many other cuisines besides), while the Western influence on the territory throws up a mean selection of **bars and nightspots**. If there's a downside, it's that straightforward consumption tends to dominate life: **cultural** matters have been less well catered for, though a superb Cultural Centre, several new museums, and an increasing interest in and awareness of the **arts** – both Chinese and Western – are changing even that.

Outside Hong Kong, the obvious move is the sixty-kilometre trip west across the Pearl River estuary to **Macau**, which makes Hong Kong look like the gaudy *arriviste* colony it is, the Portuguese having arrived in southern China in the early sixteenth century, setting up base here in 1557. This gave the Portuguese almost three hundred years start on the British, and although Hong Kong and its harbour soon surpassed the older territory in terms of trading importance, Macau absorbed its Portuguese links and culture in a way that Hong Kong never did with Britain.

On a much smaller scale than its better-known neighbour, Macau is more immediately attractive, and though it, too, is due to be handed back to China (though not until 1999), for the time being it remains a fascinating contrast to the madness across the way in Hong Kong. It's one of Asia's most enjoyable spots for a short visit, its Chinese life tempered by a Catholic, almost Mediterranean, influence, manifest in the ageing churches, hilltop fortresses and a grand seafront promenade. Of course, like Hong Kong, Macau is Chinese, and 95 percent of its population speak Cantonese. All the temples and festivals of southern China are reproduced here, but few come to Macau to pursue them, believing – perhaps rightly – that such things are done bigger and better in Hong Kong. Instead, two main draws bring tourists to Macau: the food and the gambling. **Eating** in Macau is one of the highlights of any trip to the region, so much so that, even with only a couple of days in Hong Kong, it's worth taking the jetfoil over for a meal: Macanese food is an exciting combination of Portuguese colonial cooking, with dishes and ingredients taken from Portugal itself, Goa, Brazil, Africa and China, washed down with very cheap, imported Portuguese wine, port and brandy. And with gambling illegal in Hong Kong, except for horse-race betting, the Hong Kong Chinese look to Macau's several **casinos** to cater to their almost obsessive interest in the matter.

When to go

Hong Kong and Macau's **climates** are broadly similar – subtropical in character, which means that apart from a couple of months a year when the weather is reliably good, it's generally unpredictable and often downright stormy. The heat is always made more oppressive by the **humidity**: in very humid weather you'll get hot and sticky very quickly, and will find your strength sapped if you try to do too much walking around. You'll need air-conditioning in your hotel room, or – at the very least – a fan. Macau, though, does have the bonus of the cool breeze off the sea in summer, which makes nursing a beer on the waterfront the pleasant experience it rarely is in Hong Kong.

The best time is undoubtedly the **autumn**, when the humidity is at its lowest, and the days bright, clear and hot without being stifling. In **winter**, things get noticeably cooler (you'll need a jacket) and though the skies do often stay clear, there'll be periods of wind and mist – don't expect constant decent views from The Peak at this time. **Spring** sees a rise in temperature and humidity, but there's little improvement as far as the skies go; they stay grey and there are frequent showers and heavier rain. The **summer** is dramatically different: it's terribly hot and humid (about the worst possible time for extended walking in either territory, in the city or countryside); you'd be wise not to come at this time. If you do visit in the spring or summer, you'll need an umbrella; raincoats are hot and aren't much use in heavy downpours.

The summer also sees the **typhoon season**, which lasts roughly from July to September. Getting stuck in a typhoon can be quite an experience. The word comes from the Chinese *dai foo*, or "big wind", an Asian hurricane, and over the years typhoons whistling through Hong Kong have had a devastating effect – scores of people dead and millions of dollars' worth of damage. Listen to the radio or TV weather broadcasts to find out what's happening and check the box below for Storm Signal details.

Average Temperatures and Humidity

Note that the figures below are *averages*. In summer, the temperature is regularly above 30°C, and the humidity over 90%. The winter is comparatively chilly, but the temperature rarely drops below 15°C.

	Average Temperature °C (°F)	Average Humidity	Monthly Rainfall (mm)
Spring (March to May)	18 (70)	84%	137
Summer (June to mid-Sept)	28 (82)	83%	394
Autumn (mid-Sept to mid-Dec)	23 (73)	73%	43
Winter (mid-Dec to Feb)	16 (60)	75%	33

Storm Signals

Once a typhoon is in full swing (after the no. 8 signal has been announced), planes will start to be diverted, local transport (like the buses and cross-harbour ferries) will eventually stop running, and you would be wise to stay indoors and away from exposed windows.

Storm Signal 1 means a tropical cyclone (and thus the wind, or typhoon, associated with it) is within 800km of Hong Kong.

Storm Signal 3 indicates winds are expected across Hong Kong of 60km/hr, with gusts up to 110km/hr. This generally means a typhoon is on its way: you're supposed to tie things down on balconies and rooftops, and check transport availability.

Storm Signal 8 means be prepared for storm force winds of between 63 and 117km/hr and gusts up to 180km/hr.

Storm Signal 9 indicates storm force winds are set to increase significantly.

Storm Signal 10 means there will be a hurricane of 118km/hr and upwards, with gusts up to and above 220km/hr.

Help Us Update

We've endeavoured to make this guide as up to date as possible, but it's inevitable that some of the information will become inaccurate between now and the preparation of the next edition. All suggestions, comments or corrections are much appreciated and we'll send a copy of the next edition (or any other Rough Guide, if you prefer) for the best letters. Please mark all letters "Rough Guide to Hong Kong and Macau Update" and send to:

Rough Guides, 1 Mercer Street, London WC2H 9QJ
or
Rough Guide, 375 Hudson Street, 9th Floor, New York NY10014
or
HongKong@roughtravl.co.uk

Thanks

Many thanks to the readers who wrote in following the second edition of this book: Patrick D'Haese, Sian and Hal Carroll, Tristan Pollard, Donna Hughes, Don W. Joe, Maxine Patel, Mary Winterburn, Warren Dunn, Betty R. Ciaffone, Barbara E. Haines, P. J. Ayling, Mike Higginbottom, S. Honeybone, Alison Dunimer, Douglas Evans, Eleanor Christie, David Hall, Alan Forbes, Dorothy Patterson, Dan Colwell.

Basics

Getting There from Britain

The simplest way to reach either Hong Kong or Macau from Britain is to fly. All the main routings are to Hong Kong in the first instance, from where it's around an hour by boat to Macau; for details of travel on to Macau from Hong Kong, see pp.314–315. Macau's international airport is operational, but isn't yet served by direct flights from Europe. However, there are direct services to Macau from Singapore and Kuala Lumpur; for more details on approaching the region from elsewhere in Southeast Asia see p.6. There's also the possibility of following one of the world's classic overland trips, by train from London, through Russia and Mongolia to China, and from there to the end of the line in Hong Kong. Travelling this way takes at least twelve to fourteen days and requires making the necessary travel and visa arrangements well in advance, but as a route it has few equals. See p.7 for more details.

Flights from Britain

The least demanding way to reach Hong Kong is to **fly non-stop** with one of the three major airlines – just under a thirteen-hour flight **from London** Heathrow. British Airways flies non-stop twice daily; Cathay Pacific and Virgin both have a once-daily non-stop service. Prices, though, are high. With the cheapest fares, you must stay a minimum of seven days and a maximum of three months, and there's a penalty payment for changing your flights. Low-season fares (Oct–Feb) cost from around £650 return, shoulder season around £780, while in high season (mid-June to Sept, Christmas, New Year and Easter), you'll pay around £950.

Of the big three only Cathay Pacific flies **from Manchester** (once daily via Amsterdam or Paris), with fares starting at around £770 return, rising to just under £1100 in high season. For flights from Ireland see pp.7–9.

Several **other airlines** fly to Hong Kong (from London and Manchester) but touch down two or three times on the way, sometimes giving the opportunity of a stopover: the Middle East and Southeast Asia are standard stops, while Air China (China's national airline) flies via Beijing. These flights are cheaper than non-stop services but can take sixteen to twenty hours. Depending on the time of year, they cost from around £550–650 return, though seats at Christmas, Chinese New Year and Easter are hard to come by: try and book well in advance.

Buying a ticket

You can try the airlines direct (see box) for their current prices and special offers: some don't sell tickets directly to the public and will point you in the direction of their appointed agent. Generally you're best off booking through an established **discount agent** which can usually undercut airline prices by a significant amount. See the box on p.5 for a list of recommended agents or check the ads in the national Sunday newspapers, in the weekly London listings magazine *Time Out* or London's *Evening Standard*; and in Manchester's weekly listings magazine *City Life*. If you are a **student or under 26**, you may be able to get further discounts on flight prices especially through agents such as *Campus Travel, Council Travel* and *STA Travel* – prices can sometimes go as low as £500 return.

Most of the specialist agents will also be able to sell you a **Round-the-World** ticket, routed out of London, which often includes Hong Kong in the itinerary. These are, of course, much more expensive – the current cheapest including a stop in Hong Kong costs around £1100 – but, as they're usually valid for six to twelve months, they're just the thing if your Hong Kong visit is part of a longer world trip.

Package tours

The other option is to travel to Hong Kong on an inclusive **package tour**, something that can be very good value out of season. For a week (2 nights on a plane and 5 nights in Hong Kong), including flights and three-star hotel accommodation, you can expect to pay from around £700 per person. Obviously, the price goes up in the high season (mid-June to Sept and Christmas), and according to which class of hotel you choose to stay in – at peak times, the same holiday will be more like £1000. However, all the hotels used are more than adequate and you can sometimes get

extremely good deals for a stay in the very best hotels; in low season some operators can get you a return flight and five nights in a five-star hotel for around £750. If you want to stay longer, all operators offer a daily add-on charge starting at around £40.

See the box opposite for suggested **tour operators**. Packages to Hong Kong are fairly standardized and the operators listed all offer holidays based on three- and five-star hotels on Hong Kong Island and in Kowloon, with various add-on local tours. If you have a particular hotel in mind, mention it when making enquiries. For longer holidays incorporating travel into China, *CTS* and *Magic of the Orient* are good first calls. For details of *China Travel Service*'s Trans-Siberian Express package to Moscow, Beijing, Guangzhou and Hong Kong, see "Overland by Train", p.7.

Airlines

Air China
c/o *CTS*, 7 Upper St Martin's Lane
London WC2 ☎0171/836 9911
Good deals on flights to Beijing, where you can change for Hong Kong.

Air India
17 New Bond St, London W1 ☎0171/491 7979
Stopovers in Delhi/Bombay.

Biman Bangladesh
17 Conduit St, London W1 ☎0171/629 0252
Flies via Dacca; no direct sales to the public.

British Airways:
156 Regent St, London W1
146 New St, Birmingham
19–21 St Mary's Gate, Market St, Manchester
64 Gordon St, Glasgow
32 Frederick St, Edinburgh
All enquiries ☎0345/222111
Direct from London Heathrow.

Cathay Pacific
52 Berkeley St, London W1 ☎0171/747 8888
Non-stop from London Heathrow; from Manchester via Amsterdam or Paris.

China Airlines
41 Piccadilly, London W1 ☎0171/434 0707
Flies via Amsterdam, Bangkok and Taipei. No direct sales to the public.

Emirates Airlines
125 Pall Mall, London SW1 ☎0171/930 5356
Flies via Dubai; possible stopovers in Bangkok.

Gulf Air
10 Albemarle St, London W1 ☎0171/408 1717
Usually among the cheapest flights; stopovers in Bahrain, Muscat and Bangkok.

Qantas
182 The Strand, London W1 ☎0345/747767
Flies via Bangkok.

Royal Brunei
49 Cromwell Rd, London SW7 ☎0171/584 6660
Flies via Brunei. No direct sales to the public.

Thai International
41 Albemarle St, London W1 ☎0171/491 7953
Flies via Bangkok.

Virgin Atlantic
Sales office, Virgin Megastore
Tottenham Court Rd
London W1 ☎01293/747747
Direct from London Heathrow.

Agents and Operators

DISCOUNTED FLIGHT AGENTS

Campus Travel
52 Grosvenor Gardens
London SW1 ☎0171/730 8111

541 Bristol Rd, Selly Oak
Birmingham ☎0121/414 1848

61 Ditchling Rd, Brighton ☎01273/570226

39 Queen's Rd, Clifton
Bristol ☎0117/929 2494

5 Emmanuel St, Cambridge ☎01223/324283

53 Forest Rd, Edinburgh ☎0131/668 3303

166 Deansgate, Manchester ☎0161/833 2046

105–106 St Aldates, Oxford ☎01865/242067
*Student youth travel specialists with branches
also in YHA shops and on university campuses
all over Britain.*

Council Travel
28a Poland St, London W1 ☎0171/437 7767
Specialist in student discounts.

Crystal Travel
9 Rathbone Place, London W1 ☎0171/830 0600
Discounted flights agent.

Far East Travel Centre
33 Maddox St, London W1 ☎0171/414 8844

2 Gerrard Place, London W1 ☎0171/437 8164
*Flight and package tour agent, with lots of
options to Hong Kong.*

Globepost Ltd
324 Kennington Park Rd
London SE11 ☎0171/587 0303
Flight agent specializing in Hong Kong.

STA Travel
86 Old Brompton Rd, London SW7

117 Euston Rd, London NW1

38 Store St, London WC1 ☎0171/361 6262

25 Queens Rd, Bristol ☎0117/929 4399

38 Sidney St, Cambridge ☎01223/366966

75 Deansgate, Manchester ☎0161/834 0668

88 Vicar Lane, Leeds ☎0113/244 9212

36 George St, Oxford ☎01865/792800
*Worldwide specialists in low-cost flights and
tours particularly for students and under-
26s. Branches on university campuses
nationwide.*

Trailfinders
42–50 Earls Court Rd
London W8 ☎0171/938 3366

194 Kensington High St
London W8 ☎0171/938 3939

58 Deansgate, Manchester ☎0161/839 6969

254–284 Sauchiehall St
Glasgow ☎0141/353 2224

22–24 The Priory, Queensway
Birmingham ☎0121/236 1234

48 Corn St, Bristol ☎0117/929 9000
*One of the best-informed and most efficient
agents.*

Travel Bug
597 Cheetham Hill Rd
Manchester ☎0161/721 4000
Large range of discounted tickets.

TOUR OPERATORS

British Airways Holidays
Atlantic House, Hazelwick Ave,
Crawley, West Sussex RH10 ☎01293/613777

China Travel Service (*CTS*)
7 Upper St Martin's Lane
London WC2 ☎0171/836 9911

Far East Travel Centre
see above

Globepost Ltd
see above

Jade Travel
1st Floor, 5 Newport Place
London WC2 ☎0171/494 2461

Kuoni Worldwide
Kuoni House, Dorking
Surrey RH5 4AZ ☎01306/740500

Magic Of The Orient
2 Kingsland Court,
Three Bridges Rd, Crawley,
West Sussex RH10 1HL ☎01293/537700

Thomas Cook Holidays
PO Box 36, Thorpe Wood
Peterborough PE3 ☎01733/332255

Travelling via Southeast Asia and China

With more time on your hands, you could see Hong Kong and Macau as part of a longer, Southeastern Asian trip or use the territories as the start or end points of a trip further into China. Moreover, since certain Southeast Asian countries (Thailand in particular) have opened up as long-haul package destinations from Europe and North America, flight prices to some cities are markedly cheaper than those to Hong Kong.

Flights via Southeast Asia and China

At most times of the year you should be able to find a flight from London to Bangkok, Singapore or Kuala Lumpur for around £380–480 return. Once there, **discounted air tickets to Hong Kong** are no problem, available from most local travel agencies and tour operators. For one-way flights you can expect to pay in the region of £80/US$120 from Bangkok, and £100/US$150 from Singapore. There are also now non-stop services **to Macau** from Kuala Lumpur (with *MAS*) and Singapore (*Singapore Airlines*), with several departures a week. Official prices, booked through the airlines, are high, but agents should be able to undercut them substantially: in the end though, since the two territories are only an hour apart by hydrofoil, you'd probably do best to take the cheapest available Hong Kong flight.

Another alternative is to fly first to **China**, specifically to Beijing, and travel on to Hong Kong from there, either overland (2–3 days by train) or by air. The best deals are with *Air China* (booked through the *China Travel Service*) whose return fares from London to Beijing start at around £400

SOUTHEAST ASIA

Beijing · NORTH KOREA · JAPAN

CHINA · Seoul · SOUTH KOREA · Tokyo

BANGLADESH

INDIA

Shanghai

EAST CHINA SEA

N

MYANMAR (BURMA) · Guangzhou · Taipei · TAIWAN

Hanoi · Macau · Hong Kong

LAOS

THAILAND · *SOUTH CHINA SEA* · THE PHILIPPINES · *PACIFIC OCEAN*

Bangkok · VIETNAM · Manila

CAMBODIA

Ho Chi Minh City

MALAYSIA · BRUNEI · Sabah

Kuala Lumpur

SINGAPORE · Sarawak

0 ____ 1000 km

Jakarta · INDONESIA · PAPUA NEW GUINEA

in low season, rising to £500 in summer. The train journey from Beijing to Hong Kong (via Guangzhou) costs around £50.

Overland by train

The **overland train route from London** passes through eastern Europe, Russia and Mongolia to China and Beijing, from where trains run south to the end of the line in Hong Kong. It's a supremely satisfying – though exacting – journey, but it doesn't save you any money; count on £300–400 one-way, just for the Moscow to Beijing route. Fares are highest from June to September. You'll have to plan the necessary visas and prepare for a very long haul: from London to Moscow is two days, Moscow to Beijing takes a week, and it's at least another two days from there to Hong Kong. There's no direct train service between Beijing and Hong Kong – you have to change in Guangzhou – though a direct service is planned for the future. Note that while the cheapest Moscow–Beijing train ticket costs just under £300 for a four-berth hard sleeper, but this proves to be intolerably uncomfortable over a six-night journey; the two-berth so-called "1st-class deluxe" is no such thing, but at £375 it's not a lot extra to pay for the possibility of sleep during the week's travel.

If this doesn't put you off, you'll have to decide upon the route and train you want to take – services are operated by both the Russians and Chinese, either passing through, or bypassing, Mongolia (for which you need a separate visa). To sort it all out, talk to *STA Travel* (see Discounted Flight Agencies and Tour Operators box), or to the *China Travel Service*, either of which sell train tickets to independent travellers and can arrange a cheap flight back to London. The Russian State travel agency, *Intourist* (☎0171/538 3203) can also advise about the Russian route, though dealings with them are notoriously convoluted. *CTS* also offers a 22-day organized trip from London, which starts at about £1500 per person (more if you're travelling on your own) – this includes travel to Moscow, six nights on the train to Beijing, accommodation in Beijing (4 nights), Xian (3), Guangzhou (2) and Hong Kong (2), and a flight back to London.

Getting There from Ireland

The smoothest route from Ireland to Hong Kong is to fly with *British Airways* **from Belfast** via Heathrow, giving an optimum flight time of around fifteen hours – though this stretches depending on how long you have to wait in London for the connection. Fares start at around £800 in low season, rising to around £1100 between mid-June and September. Tickets are valid for a minimum of seven days and a maximum of three months. A specialist agent like *USIT* (see box below for address) can often find students and under-26s better deals than this – though you're still looking at return fares of around £650 from Belfast (and not much scope for changing departure times or dates).

From Dublin, the problem is that most international flights are routed in the first instance to Gatwick, meaning you have to switch airports to make the Hong Kong leg of the journey. Through-flight prices from Dublin are prohibitively expensive, and even though *Cathay Pacific* in London can arrange an add-on Dublin–London fare with another airline in conjunction with their regular London–Hong Kong flights, these are usually much higher than the budget fares that you yourself can book with a variety of airlines, *Ryanair, Aer Lingus,* and *British Midland* among them – the cheapest cost from around IR£69 return. You may want to consider taking advantage of these discounted air fares between Ireland and Britain and picking up an onward flight from London

---

Airlines and Agents

AIRLINES

Aer Lingus
46 Castle St, Belfast BT1 1HB	☎01232/314844
40 O'Connell St, Dublin 1	☎01/844 4777
2 Academy St, Cork	☎021/327155
136 O'Connell St, Limerick	☎061/474239

Air UK ☎0345/666777

British Airways
9 Fountain Centre
College St, Belfast BT1 6ET	☎0345/222111
Dublin reservations	☎1800/626747

British Midland
Belfast reservations	☎0345/676676
Dublin reservations	☎01/283 8833

Malaysia Airlines
20 Upper Merrion St, Dublin 2	☎01/676 2131

Ryanair
3 Dawson St, Dublin 2	☎01/677 4422

Singapore Airlines
Third Floor, 29 Dawson St
Dublin 2	☎01/671 0722

Virgin Atlantic
30 Lower Abbey St
Dublin 1	☎01/873 3388 USA/Far East; ☎01/844 5566 London flights

DISCOUNTED FLIGHT AGENCIES

Apex Travel
59 Dame St, Dublin	☎01/671 5933

Flight Finders International
13 Baggot St Lower, Dublin	☎01/676 8326

Inflight Travel
92–94 York Rd
Belfast	☎01232/740187 or 743341

Joe Walsh Tours
8–11 Baggot St, Dublin	☎01/676 3053

Student & Group Travel
71 Dame St, Dublin	☎01/677 7834

Stranmillis Travel
84 Stranmillis Rd, Belfast	☎01232/681457

Twohigs
8 Burgh Quay, Dublin	☎01/677 2666
13 Duke St, Dublin	☎01/670 9750

USIT
Fountain Centre, Belfast	☎01232/324073
10–11 Market Parade Patrick St, Cork	☎021/270900
33 Ferryquay St, Derry	☎01504/371888
Aston Quay, Dublin 2	☎01/679 8833
Victoria Place Eyre Square, Galway	☎091/565177
Central Buildings O'Connell St, Limerick	☎061/415064
36–37 Georges St Waterford	☎051/72601

Williames
18–20 Howard St, Belfast	☎01232/230714

World Travel Centre
35 Pearse St, Dublin	☎01/671 7155

TOUR OPERATORS

Liffey Travel,
Abbey Mall
13 Lower Liffey St, Dublin 1	☎01/873 4900

Package tour specialists.

Thomas Cook
11 Donegall Place, Belfast	☎01232/554455
118 Grafton St, Dublin	☎01/677 1721

Package holiday and flight agent, with occasional discount offers.

---

with another airline (see "Getting There from Britain", above), though you'll need to plan connections carefully.

If you intend to see Hong Kong as part of a wider **Southeast Asian** trip, you may well find that you can turn up cheaper flights to destinations like Kuala Lumpur, Singapore and Bangkok, all of which will be routed through London in the first instance. Talk to a specialist travel agent for the best deals; and see p.6 for more details on travel from the region to Hong Kong.

Alternatively, check on details of **package holidays**, on which the Ireland–Britain section of your trip will be included in the overall price. A one-week holiday (2 nights on a plane, 5 nights in Hong Kong), staying in a three-star hotel, costs around IR£1100 in peak summer season, with add-on nights possible for another IR£40 or so. In the low season (Oct–Feb, excluding Christmas and New Year), you'll find you can get much better deals than this, either shaving ten to fifteen percent off the price or substituting a five-star hotel for around the same price.

Getting There from the US and Canada

There are any number of possible routes to Hong Kong from North America, with a wide variation in fares. In particular, the recent influx of Hong Kong Chinese into Vancouver has prompted a surge in competition and discounted fares from Canada. Check the ads in newspaper travel sections, and shop around, being aware that discount travel agents who deal with consolida-

tors can almost always quote you a fare $200–250 lower than the airlines' discounted rates.

Shopping for tickets

Barring special offers, the cheapest fare is usually an **Apex** ticket, although this will carry certain restrictions: you have to book – and pay – at least 21 days before departure, spend at least seven days abroad (maximum stay 3 months), and you tend to get penalized if you change your schedule. Some airlines also issue **Special Apex** tickets to people younger than 24, often extending the maximum stay to a year. Many airlines offer youth or student fares to **under-25s**; a passport or driving licence are sufficient proof of age, though these tickets are subject to availability and can have eccentric booking conditions. It's worth remembering that most cheap return fares will only give a percentage refund if you need to cancel or alter your journey, so make sure you check the restrictions carefully before buying a ticket.

You can normally cut costs further by going through a **specialist flight agent** – either a **consolidator**, who buys up blocks of tickets from the airlines and sells them at a discount, or a **discount agent**, who wheels and deals in tickets offloaded by the airlines, and often offers special student and youth fares and a range of other travel-related services such as travel insurance, car rentals and tours. Bear in mind, though, that penalties for changing your plans can be stiff. Remember too that these companies make their money by dealing in bulk – don't expect them to answer lots of questions. Some agents specialize in **charter flights**, which may be cheaper than anything available on a scheduled flight, but again departure dates are fixed and withdrawal penalties are high (check the refund policy). If you travel a lot, **discount travel clubs** are another option – the annual membership fee may be worth it for benefits such as cut-price air tickets and car rental.

A further possibility is to see if you can arange a **courier flight**, although the hit-or-miss nature of these makes them most suitable for the single traveller who travels light and has a very flexible schedule. In return for shepherding a parcel through customs and possibly giving up your baggage allowance, you can expect to get a deeply discounted ticket. See below or, for more options, consult *A Simple Guide to Courier Travel* (Pacific Data Sales Publishing).

Regardless of where you buy your ticket, the fare will depend on the **season**. Fares are highest in December, June, July and August. and fares during these months can cost between $100 and $200 more depending on the airline. Flying

---

Airlines

Air Canada
USA ☎ 1-800/776 3000
Canada for local toll-free number call ☎ 1-800/555 1212
Non-stop flights from Vancouver and from Montréal and Toronto via Vancouver.

Asiana Airlines
☎ 1-800/227 4262
Hong Kong via Seoul from Seattle, Los Angeles, Honolulu, New York and Vancouver.

Canadian Airlines
Canada ☎ 1-800/665 1177
USA ☎ 1-800/426 7000
Non-stop from Vancouver and Toronto and direct from Montréal.

Cathay Pacific
USA ☎ 1-800/233 2742
Canada for local toll-free number call ☎ 1-800/555 1212
Non-stop flights from Vancouver, Los Angeles; direct flights from New York via Vancouver and Toronto via Anchorage.

China Airways
☎ 1-800/227 5118
From Los Angeles, San Francisco, Honolulu and Anchorage via Taipei, and from Vancouver via Los Angles and Taipei.

EVA Airlines
☎ 1-800/695 1188
Flights from New York via Seattle and Taipei and from San Francisco and Los Angeles via Taipei.

Japan Airlines
☎ 1-800/525 3663
Los Angeles, San Francisco, New York and Vancouver to Hong Kong via Tokyo.

Korean Airlines
☎ 1-800/438 5000
To Hong Kong via Seoul from New York, San Francisco, Los Angeles and Vancouver.

Northwest Airlines
☎ 1-800/447 4747
Seattle, New York, Los Angeles, San Francisco and Chicago via Tokyo.

Singapore Airlines
☎ 1800/742 3333
Non-stop from San Francisco; direct from Los Angeles, San Francisco and New York via Frankfurt.

Thai International
USA ☎ 1-800/426 5204
Canada ☎ 1-800/668 8103
Los Angeles to Hong Kong.

United Airlines
☎ 1800/538 2929
Daily flights from major US and Canadian cities to New York and Los Angeles. Non-stop service to Hong Kong from Los Angeles and San Francisco, Direct service from New York via Tokyo or San Francisco.

---

on weekends can add $100 to the cost of a round-trip ticket: prices quoted in the sections below assume midweek travel.

Flights from the US

Singapore Airlines, *Cathay Pacific* and *United Airlines* fly **non-stop to Hong Kong** from the **West Coast** in fifteen hours. In addition, *Northwest* has a direct flight from Seattle three times a week. Other airlines, such as *China Airlines*, *Japan Airlines* and *Singapore Airlines*, make connections from Los Angeles or San Francisco via Tokyo, Seoul and Taipei. Round-trip fares for these flights are around $800 (low season) and $1240 (high).

Discounters can often find good deals for travellers from Seattle on *Canadian Airlines'* non-stop flight from Vancouver – as low as $700 round-trip including the connecting flight from Seattle to Vancouver.

The cheapest way to reach Hong Kong from the West Coast is on *Asiana Airlines*, a Korean carrier, which makes connections via Seoul. Figure on the total flight time being around nineteen hours, the longer journey time being compensated for by the cheap fare; discount travel agents can quote round-trip fares on *Asiana* as low as $550 from West Coast cities.

From the **East Coast**, *Cathay Pacific* offers daily direct service from New York via Vancouver, while *United* offers daily flights via San Francisco or Tokyo (20hr). *EVA Airlines* flies from New York through Seattle and Taipei, and *Korean* and *Asiana Airlines* fly via Seoul with a stop in Anchorage (23hr). *Singapore Airlines* offers the eastern route via Frankfurt in 21 hours. Round-trip fares range from $1000 (low season) to $1600 (high), with discounters offering round-trip fares from $800.

Many airlines offer a **stopover in Hong Kong** for $50–75 extra on a round-trip fare to another city in Asia. This is ideal if Hong Kong is not your only destination. *Thai International*, for instance, allows a stop in Hong Kong for $75 more on flights to Bangkok, while *Singapore Airlines* charges $50 to stop in Hong Kong on routes to Singapore.

Flights from Canada

Vancouver is a growing gateway to Asia. *Canadian Airlines* offers daily non-stop service to Hong Kong from Vancouver (13hr) and Toronto,

and a direct service form Montréal (15hr). *Cathay Pacific* also flies daily non-stop from Vancouver and has direct flights five days a week from Toronto via Anchorage. *Air Canada* flies non-stop four to five times a week (depending on season) from Vancouver, and also offers a service to Hong Kong from Montréal and Toronto via Vancouver. *China Airlines* makes a connection to Hong Kong from Vancouver via Los Angeles and Taipei. Round-trip fares range from CDN$1265 (low season) to $1865 (high) for Vancouver departures and from CDN$1730 to $2090 for Toronto–Montréal departures. Round-trip fares as low as CDN$825 are available through discounters on *Asiana's* daily flights from Vancouver with connections through Seattle and Seoul.

Round-the-World tickets and courier flights

Round-the-World (RTW) and **Circle-Pacific** tickets with a stop in Hong Kong are offered by *Airbrokers International* or *High Adventure Travel* for $1100–$1450. A good way to get familar with routes and fares is to check out *High Adventure's* World Wide Web site whch lists hundreds of possible combinations and sample fares: http://www.highadv.com.

Round-trip **courier flights** to Hong Kong are available for around $350, with last-minute specials as low as $150 (a flight booked within three days of departure). For information about courier flights contact the *Air Courier Association*, 191 University Blvd, Suite 300, Denver, Col 80206 (303/279 3600); *Discount Travel International*, 169 West 81st Street, New York, NY 10024 (212/362 3636); or *Now Voyager*, 74 Varick St, Suite 307, New York, NY (212/431 1616).

Packages and organized tours

Air/hotel packages and tours are available for Hong Kong alone or as part of a trip to China and other parts of Asia. The vacation divisions of the major airlines offer a range of **city holidays**, which can be good value depending on what time of year you travel and what kind of hotel you want. *United Air Vacations* offers six nights in Hong Kong including air fare, airport transfers and a half-day sightseeing tour for £1630 (West Coast departures) and $1850 (East Coast). *Cathay Pacific Holidays* has similar packages starting at $949 (West Coast departures)

Agents and Operators

DISCOUNT AGENTS

Air Brokers International
323 Geary St,
Suite 411
San Francisco, CA 94102 ☎1-800/883 3273
Consolidator and specialist in RTW tickets.

Council Travel in the US
205 E 42nd St
New York, NY 10017 ☎212/822 2700
and branches in many other US cities.
Discount travel agent and student discounts.

Educational Travel Centre
438 N Frances St
Madison, WI 53703 ☎1-800/747 5551
Student/youth discounts.

High Adventure Travel Inc
253 Sacramento St,
Suite 600
San Francisco, CA 94111 ☎1-800 428 8735
Discounted and RTW tickets.

Last Minute Travel
132 Brookline Ave
Boston MA 02215 ☎1-800/LAST-MIN
Discount air fares and hotel packages.

Overseas Tours
475 El Camino Real, Room 206
Millbrae CA 94030 ☎1-800/323 8777
Discount air tickets and tours.

STA Travel
10 Downing St
New York, NY 100143 ☎1-800/777 0112
and branches in many other US cities.
Discounts for students under 25.

Travel CUTS
187 College St
Toronto, Ontario, M5T 1P7 ☎416/979 2406
and other branches all over Canada.
Student travel organization.

TOUR OPERATORS

Asian Pacific Adventures ☎213/935 3156
Interesting range of China-wide tours with Hong Kong stopovers.

Cathay Pacific Holidays ☎1-800/762 8181
City breaks.

Mir Corps ☎1-800/424 7289
Packages and train tickets for the Trans-Siberian Express.

TBI Tours ☎415/668 0964
General Asian tour operator with stopovers in Hong Kong.

TEI Tours ☎1-800/435 4334
Trans-Siberian Express packages.

United Air Vacations ☎1-800/328 6877
City breaks.

---

and $1259 (East Coast) for three nights (4 days) including air fare, transfers, hotel, and a half-day tour.

From Canada, *Canadian Holidays*, through travel agents, has similar six-night stays in Hong Kong for CAN$2000 (departing Vancouver; allow an extra $200–250 for Toronto or Montréal).

Many broader **Asian tours** offer stopovers in Hong Kong. *TBI Tours*, which partners with *United, Northwest, JAL, United Air* and *Malaysia Airlines*, operates a variety of tours in Asia which include several nights in Hong Kong. For example, their fourteen-day China tour includes three nights in Hong Kong starting at $3,325 (West Coast departures). *Asian Pacific Adventures* are worth checking out for their wide range of tours including women-only trips, and a fourteen-day bike trip through Southwest China including a

Hong Kong stopover for $3,295 (excluding flights; bike included).

A trip on the **Trans-Siberian Express** between Moscow and Beijing, then onto Hong Kong is a great way to arrive in the city (see p.7 for more details). Train tickets can be purchased from agents in the US and package tours including overnight stays in Beijing and Moscow are available. *Mir Corp* in Seattle offers ten different tour packages starting at $475 per person for six nights on the Trans-Siberian Express, plus a night in Moscow. First and second class tickets for the train ride only can also be purchased from *Mir*. *TEI Tours* offers twelve-day tours between Moscow and Beijing from $1500 including two nights in Beijing plus sightseeing tours, six nights on the train, sightseeing tours along the way and one night in Moscow.

Getting There from Australia and New Zealand

The most convenient way to travel between Australasia and Hong Kong, is to fly direct with *Qantas*, *Cathay Pacific*, *Ansett* or *Air New Zealand*. However, practically all the Southeast Asian airlines fly to Hong Kong via their home airports and you'll find cheaper fares on some of these routes. Prices for flights and flight/accommodation packages vary from week to week, depending on the season and on demand, and you should always check out what the specialist **independent travel agents** have on offer (see box below). Look, too, in the travel sections of the weekend newspapers, which carry adverts for agents and their special offers. Fares are highest during December and through until January 15 (Jan 31 with some airlines).

From Australia

From Australia, *Qantas* flies **direct to Hong Kong** daily from Sydney, Melbourne and Perth, with less frequent flights from Brisbane, Adelaide and

---

Airlines

Air New Zealand
5 Elizabeth St, Sydney   ☎ 02/9223 4666
Quay St, Auckland   ☎ 09/357 3000

Ansett
501 Swanston St
Melbourne local-call rate   ☎ 13 1300
50 Grafton Rd, Auckland   ☎ 09/796409

Cathay Pacific
Level 12, 8 Spring St, Sydney   ☎ 02/931 5500
11f Arthur Andersen Tower
205–209 Queen St, Auckland   ☎ 09/379 0861

Garuda Indonesian
175 Clarence St, Sydney   ☎ 02/334 9900
120 Albert St, Auckland   ☎ 09/366 1855

JAL
Floor 14, Darling Park
201 Sussex St, Sydney   ☎ 02/9283 1111
Floor 12, Westpac Tower
120 Albert St, Auckland   ☎ 09/379 9906

Korean Airlines
36 Carrington St, Sydney   ☎ 02/9262 6000
7–9 Falcon St, Parnell
Auckland   ☎ 09/307 3687

MAS Malaysian Airlines
16 Spring St, Sydney   ☎ 02/364 3500;
local-call rate ☎ 13 2627
Floor 12, Swanson Centre
2–26 Swanson St, Auckland   ☎ 09/373 2741

Philippine Airlines
49 York St, Sydney   ☎ 02/9262 3333

Qantas
Chifley Square,
cnr Hunter and Phillip streets
Sydney   ☎ 02/957 0111
Qantas House, 154 Queen St
Auckland   ☎ 09/357 8900

Royal Brunei
Level 9, 25 Mary St, Brisbane   ☎ 07/3221 7757

Singapore Airlines
17–19 Bridge St
Sydney   ☎ 02/9236 0144;
local-call rate 13 1011
Lower ground floor,
West Plaza Building cnr Customs and Albert
streets, Auckland   ☎ 09/379 3209

Thai Airways
75–77 Pitt St, Sydney   ☎ 02/844 0999;
toll-free ☎ 1800/422 020
Kensington Swan Building
22 Fanshawe St, Auckland   ☎ 09/377 3886

Cairns, for around A$1400 return high season (A$1200 low season); it's a couple of hundred dollars cheaper from Perth. Youth/student fares offer a slight saving on these prices. *Ansett* flies daily from Sydney and *Cathay Pacific* serves Sydney and Melbourne daily, with less frequent services from the other main cities. Fares are comparable with *Qantas*.

There's a wide choice if you want to fly **via an Asian stopover city**. However, fares with *Thai International*, *Singapore Airlines*, *Malaysian* and *Garuda Indonesian* via their home ports are little different from those on the direct services. To save money, look at *Philippine Airlines*, which flies several times weekly from Sydney, Melbourne and Brisbane to Hong Kong for A$1240 high

season (A$940 low season), and *Royal Brunei* which flies twice weekly from Darwin and Perth via Brunei for A$1140 high season (around $1000 low season). The hitch with this route is that you have to spend two nights in Brunei at your own expense before getting your connecting flight.

If Hong Kong is your only destination, an **all-inclusive package** could well be the best deal. You should be able to find a package giving return airfare form Sydney or Melbourne including transfers, five nights' accommodation and a half-day sightseeing tour for around A£1700 high season (A$1300 low season). *Qantas, Cathay Pacific,* and *Ansett* all sell package trips.

If Hong Kong is part of a longer world trip, it's worth looking at **one-way fares** and **Round**

Discounted Flight Agents

Accent on Travel
545 Queen St, Brisbane ☎ 07/3832 1777

Anywhere Travel
345 Anzac Parade,
Kingsford, Sydney ☎ 02/663 0411

Asian Travel Centre
3rd Floor, 126 Russell St
Melbourne ☎ 03/9654 8277

Budget Travel
16 Fort St, Auckland ☎ 09/366 0061;
toll free 0800/808040

Destinations Unlimited
3 Milford Rd, Milford, Auckland ☎ 09/373 4033

Flight Centres
Australia
Circular Quay, Sydney ☎ 02/9241 2422
Bourke St, Melbourne ☎ 03/9650 2899
plus other branches nationwide.

New Zealand
National Bank Towers,
205 Queen St, Auckland ☎ 09/209 6171

Shop 1M, National Mutual Arcade
152 Hereford St, Christchurch ☎ 09/379 7145

50–52 Willis St, Wellington ☎ 04/472 8101
other branches countrywide.

Harvey World Travel
Princess Highway,
Kogarah, Sydney ☎ 02/567 6099
Numerous branches throughout Australia

Northern Gateway Travel
22 Cavenagh St, Darwin ☎ 08/8941 1394

STA Travel
Australia
732 Harris St, Ultimo, Sydney ☎ 02/9212 1255;
toll free 1800/637 444

256 Flinders St, Melbourne ☎ 03/9654 7266
other offices in Townsville, Cairns, state capitals and at major universities.

New Zealand
Traveller's Centre,
10 High St, Auckland ☎ 09/309 4058

233 Cuba St, Wellington ☎ 04/385 0561

90 Cashel St , Christchurch ☎ 03/379 9098
other offices in Dunedin, Palmerston North and Hamilton and at major universities.

Taking Off Tours
Suite 3/618 St Kildo Rd
Melbourne ☎ 03/9510 9382

Topdeck Travel
65 Glenfell St, Adelaide ☎ 08/8232 7222

Tymtro Travel
428 George St, Sydney ☎ 02/9223 2211

UTAG Travel
122 Walker St, North Sydney ☎ 02/9956 8399
numerous branches nationwide

---

the-World (RTW) tickets. The cheapest one-way fare is with *Royal Brunei* from Darwin for around A$500. RTW tickets are based on mileage: you are allowed a number of stopoffs (usually six) within a maximum number of miles. For example you should be able to put together a Sydney–Hong Kong–London–New York–Los Angeles–Honolulu–Sydney ticket with *Qantas/ British Airways* for around A$2500 low season (A$2800 high season), but its worth shopping around.

From New Zealand

From New Zealand, *Air New Zealand* flies **direct** from Auckland to Hong Kong three times a week, while *Cathay Pacific* goes four times a week.

Fares are around NZ$1500. You won't save any money going via another carrier's home city: *Korean Airlines* via Seoul, *Japan Airlines* via Tokyo and Garuda Indonesian via Bali are about the same, while *Qantas* via Australia, *Singapore Airlines* via Singapore and Malaysian Airlines via Kuala Lumpur are all more expensive. There are currently no flight/accommodation packages on offer with the airlines or specialist operators, but it's worth checking when you book, as these can work out to be a very good deal.

Round-the-World fares from New Zealand are not particularly cheap. Figure on around NZ$3150 for Christchurch–Australia–Hong Kong–London–New York–Los Angeles–Christchurch in high season (NZ$2750 low season).

Visas and Red Tape

Most people need only a valid passport to enter Hong Kong or Macau. Depending on your nationality, you'll be allowed to stay for various periods, from three days to a year without a visa. There are not expected to be any changes to the various entry requirements **following the handover** to the Chinese in mid-1997. Under the terms of the agreement, the existing framework is to be retained, though since entrance regulations can be politically sensitive, it's recommended that you check first with the relevant authorities in

your own country before travelling. Your foreign office, state department or embassy should have the latest details. A further source of information will be the **new British Consulate General in Hong Kong**, due to be in place by 1 July 1997. At the time of writing, its exact address and telephone number was not available.

Hong Kong

British citizens will be given a stamp in their passports on entry allowing them to stay for up to one year. Citizens of **Eire, Canada, Australia, New Zealand**, all other **Commonwealth** passport holders and citizens of most **European** countries also do not require a visa and can stay for up to three months. **American** citizens can stay for up to thirty days, as can South African, Japanese, German and Greek passport holders.

Everyone else should consult the relevant British Embassy, Consulate or High Commission in their country of origin for visa requirements; some are listed over the page. If in any doubt, contact the **Immigration Department**, Wan Chai Tower, 7 Gloucester Rd, Wan Chai, Hong Kong ☎ 2829 3000.

There shouldn't be any trouble with the **immigration officers**, all of whom speak English. You

British Embassies and Consulates Abroad			
Australia		Unter den Linden 32–34	
Commonwealth Avenue		Berlin 1080	☎ 220 2431
Yarralumla, Canberra, ACT 2600	☎ 06/270 6666	**Ireland**	
		31–33 Merrion Rd, Dublin 4	☎ 01/269 5211
Canada			
Room 901, 1155 University St		**Netherlands**	
Montréal H3B 3A7	☎ 514/866 5863	General Koningslaan 44	
80 Elgin St, Ottawa K1P 5K7	☎ 613/237 1530	1075AE Amsterdam	☎ 020/676 4343
China		Lange Voorhout 10	
11 Guang Hua Lu	☎ 532 1961, ☎ 532 1930	2514ED Den Haag	☎ 364 5800
Jian Guo Men Wai	or ☎ 532 1938	**New Zealand**,	
Beijing 100600		44 Hill St, Wellington 1	☎ 472 6049
244 Yong Fu Lu, Shanghai 20031	☎ 4330 508	**Singapore**	
Denmark		Tanglin Rd, Singapore 1024	☎ 473 9333
Kastelsvej 36–40		**USA**	
DK-2100, Copenhagen	☎ 35 26 46 00	3100 Massachusetts Ave NW	
Germany		Washington DC 20008	☎ 202/462 1340
Friedrich-Elbert-Allée 51		845 Third Ave	
53113 Bonn 1	☎ 23 40 61	New York 10022	☎ 212/745 0202

may be asked how long you intend to stay and, if it's for a fairly lengthy period, for referees in Hong Kong and to prove that you can support yourself without working. Remember that the questions are designed to see if you're intending to work in Hong Kong: if you are, and you don't have an employment visa (see p.35), on no account say so.

Given the length of time most people are allowed to stay in Hong Kong, you shouldn't need to **extend your stay** if you're just a tourist: in any case, go to Macau or China for the weekend and come back, and nine times out of ten you'll just get another period stamped in your passport. If you want to ensure a longer stay, though, you'll need to apply for a visa from the Immigration Department (see above); as you will if you're intending to stay on and work in the territory, for details of which see "Staying On", pp.34–36.

If you're in trouble or lose your passport, or you want details of the visas necessary for travel on to neighbouring countries, consult the relevant **foreign consulate in Hong Kong** – there's a list on p.304. And for specific visa requirements for **travel to China**, see p.58.

Customs

You're allowed to bring the following **duty-free goods** into Hong Kong: 200 cigarettes (or 50 cigars or 250g of tobacco), 1 litre of wine, 60ml

of perfume and 250ml of toilet water. Apart from spirits, which are all taxed, you can take most other things into Hong Kong with little difficulty. **Prohibited items** include all firearms and fireworks, and if you're caught carrying any kind of illegal **drugs** you can expect very tough treatment. Indeed, if you're arriving from anywhere in Southeast Asia that has a high drugs profile, and are young and scruffy, or have long hair, your baggage might come in for some extra attention.

Macau

Macau isn't due to be handed back to China until 1999, until which time the following entry requirements are still in place. Citizens of Britain, Ireland, Australia, New Zealand, Canada, USA and most European countries need only a **valid passport** to enter Macau, and can stay up to twenty days; Hong Kong residents can stay for ninety days. Most other nationals can buy an **individual visa** on arrival, valid for twenty days. If you're a national of a country which doesn't have diplomatic relations with Portugal, you need a visa in advance from an **overseas Portuguese Consulate** – for the address of the Portuguese Consulate in Hong Kong, see p.305.

If you need to extend your stay, the simplest thing is to return to Hong Kong and re-enter Macau at a later date.

You'll barely notice the **customs** officials as you arrive in Macau, though there might be the odd spot check, with the same severe penalties as Hong Kong for any drugs or firearms offences. Otherwise, the only thing to watch for is when returning to Hong Kong: there's no export duty on goods taken out of Macau, though the Hong Kong authorities will only allow you to bring in one litre of the cheap wine (or spirits) sold in Macau, and fifty cigarettes.

Insurance

A good **travel insurance** policy is vital for anyone travelling abroad. It's worth noting that bank and credit cards often have certain levels of medical or other insurance included, especially if you use them to pay for your trip. This can be quite comprehensive, anticipating anything from lost or stolen baggage and missed connections to charter companies going bankrupt; however, certain policies (notably in North America) only cover medical costs.

Medical services, particularly in Hong Kong, are good, but you'll have to pay for all your treatment on the spot (and it can be enormously expensive). Make sure that the medical cover is high enough – ie sufficient to get you home under supervision if you fall really ill – and that there is a 24hr emergency contact number.

For medical treatment and drugs, keep all the **receipts** so that you can claim the money back later. If you have anything stolen, register the loss immediately with the **police**, since without their report, you won't be able to claim. For the address of the main **police stations** in Hong Kong, see p.307, in Macau, p.367.

British and Irish cover

Most travel agents and tour operators will offer you insurance when you book your flight or holiday, and some will insist you take it. These policies are usually reasonable value, though as ever, you should check the small print. If you feel the cover is inadequate, or you want to compare prices, any travel agent, insurance broker or bank should be able to help. If you have a good "all risks" home insurance policy it may well cover your possessions against loss or theft even when overseas, and many private medical schemes also cover you when abroad – make sure you know the procedure and the helpline number.

In **Britain and Ireland**, travel insurance schemes are sold by various specialist companies. A couple of weeks' cover for Hong Kong and Macau starts at around £35, a month at around £42.

North American cover

Before buying an insurance policy, check that you're not already covered. **Canadians** are usually covered for medical mishaps overseas by their provincial health plans. Holders of official **student/teacher/youth cards** are entitled to accident coverage and hospital in-patient benefits. **Students** will often find that their student health coverage extends during the vacations and for one term beyond the date of last enrollment. **Homeowners' or renters'** insurance often covers theft or loss of documents, money and valuables while overseas, though conditions and maximum amounts vary from company to company.

After exhausting the possibilities above, you might want to contact a specialist **travel insurance** company; your travel agent can usually

Travel Insurance Companies

AUSTRALIA AND NEW ZEALAND

AFTA 144 Pacific Hwy
North Sydney   ☎ 02/956 4800

Cover More Level 9,
32 Walker St, North Sydney   ☎ 02/9202 8000;
                    toll-free ☎ 1800/251 881

Ready Plan 141–147 Walker St
Dandenong, Victoria   ☎ 1800/337 462
10th Floor, 63 Albert St
Auckland   ☎ 09/379 3208

UTAG
347 Kent St, Sydney   ☎ 02/9819 6855;
                    toll-free ☎ 1800/809 462.

BRITAIN AND IRELAND

Campus Travel
see p.5

Columbus Travel Insurance
17 Devonshire Square
London EC2   ☎ 0171/375 0011

Endsleigh Insurance
97–107 Southampton Row
London WC1   ☎ 0171/436 4451

Frizzell Insurance Frizzell House, County
Gates Bournemouth, Dorset   ☎ 01202/292 333

STA
see p.5

USIT in Ireland
see p.8

NORTH AMERICA

Access America
PO Box 90310
Richmond, VA 23230   ☎ 1-800/284 8300

Carefree Travel Insurance
PO Box 310, 120 Mineola Blvd
Mineola, NY 11501   ☎ 1-800/645 2424

International Student Insurance Service
(ISIS) *sold by STA Travel, which has several
branches in the US; see p.12*

Travel Assistance International
1133 15th St NW, Suite 400
Washington, DC 20005   ☎ 1-800/821 2828

Travel Guard
1145 Clark St
Stevens Point, WI 54481   ☎ 1-800/826 1300

Travel Insurance Services
2930 Camino Diablo, Suite 300
Walnut Creek, CA 94596   ☎ 1-800/937 1387

recommend one, or see the box above. Policies are comprehensive (accidents, illnesses, delayed or lost luggage, cancelled flights, etc.), but maximum payouts tend to be meagre. Premiums vary, so shop around. The best deals are usually to be had through student/youth travel agencies and start at around $65 for a two-week trip and $85 for three weeks to a month.

Most North American travel policies apply only to items lost, stolen or damaged while in the custody of an identifiable, responsible third party – hotel porter, airline, luggage consignment, etc. Even in these cases you will have to contact the local police within a certain time limit to have a complete report made out so that your insurer can process the claim. Note also that very few insurers will arrange on-the-spot payments in the event of a major expense or loss; you will usually be reimbursed only after going home.

Australian cover

Travel insurance is put together by the airlines and travel agent groups in conjunction with insurance companies. They are all comparable in premiums and coverage. For Hong Kong (and the rest of Southeast Asia), a typical comprehensive insurance policy will cost about A$140/NZ$180 for a month.

Health Matters

You don't need to have any inoculations to enter Hong Kong or Macau. The only stipulation is that if you've been in an area infected with cholera and typhoid during the fourteen days before your arrival, you'll need certificates of vaccination against the two diseases. These requirements might change, so ask your doctor if you're unsure about what constitutes an infected area. If you're travelling elsewhere in Asia or China, before or after Hong Kong and Macau, it's a good idea to make sure that all your inoculations (against typhoid, cholera, tetanus, polio and hepatitis) are up to date.

Medical Resources for Travellers

BRITAIN

Most general practitioners in the UK have a travel surgery from which you can obtain advice and certain vaccines on prescription, though they may not administer some of the less common immunizations. For up-to-the-minute information, contact one of the following organizations:

Hospital for Tropical Diseases, *St Pancras Hospital, 4 St Pancras Way, London NW1* (Mon–Fri 9am–5pm; ☎0171/530 3454). *This also operates a recorded message service on* ☎0171/530 3429 *which gives hints on hygiene and illness prevention as well as listing appropriate immunizations.*

British Airways Travel Clinic, 156 Regent St, London W1 (Mon–Fri 9am–4.15pm, Sat 10am–4pm; ☎0171/439 9584). *This can be visited without an appointment; there are also appointment-only branches at 101 Cheapside, London EC2 ☎0171/606 2977 and at the BA terminal in London's Victoria Station ☎0171/233 6661. BA also operates regional clinics throughout the country (call ☎0171/831 5333 to discover the one nearest to you). All these clinics sell travel associated accessories, including mosquito nets and first-aid kits.*

MASTA (Medical Advisory Service for Travellers Abroad), London School of Hygiene and Tropical Medicine ☎0891 224100. *Operates a Travellers' Health Line 24 hours a day, 7 days a week, giving written information tailored to your journey by return of post.*

IRELAND

All of these places offer medical advice before a trip and medical help afterwards in the event of a tropical disease.

Travel Medicine Services, P.O. Box 254, 16 College St, Belfast 1 ☎01232/315220.

Tropical Medical Bureau, Grafton St Medical Centre, Dublin 2 ☎01/671 9200.

Tropical Medical Bureau, Dun Laoghaire Medical Centre, 5 Northumberland Ave, Dun Laoghaire, Co. Dublin ☎01/280 4996.

NORTH AMERICA
International Association for Medical Assistance to Travellers (IAMAT), 417 Center St, Lewiston, NY 14092 ☎716/754 4883 and 40 Regal Rd, Guelph, ON N1K 1B5 ☎519/836 0102. *A non-profit organization supported by donations, it can provide a list of English-speaking doctors, climate charts and leaflets on various diseases and inoculations.*

International SOS Assistance, PO Box 11568, Philadelphia, PA 19116 ☎1-800/523 8930; in Canada, ☎1-800/363 0263. *Members receive pre-trip medical referral info, as well as overseas emergency services designed to complement travel insurance coverage.*

Medic Alert, 2323 Colorado Ave, Turlock, CA 95381 ☎1-800/432 5378; in Canada, ☎1-800/668 1507. *Sells bracelets engraved with the traveller's medical requirements in case of emergency.*

Travel Medicine, 351 Pleasant St, Suite 312, Northampton, MA 01060 ☎1-800/872 8633. *Sells first-aid kits, mosquito netting, water filters and other health-related travel products.*

Travelers Medical Center, 31 Washington Square, New York, NY 10011 ☎212/982 1600. *Consultation service on immunizations and treatment of diseases for people travelling to developing countries.*

Health problems

You shouldn't encounter too many problems during your stay. The **water** is fit for drinking everywhere (except from old wells on some of Hong Kong's outlying islands), though bottled water always tastes nicer. Other than washing or peeling fruit and vegetables from the market, you needn't worry about the **food** either: Cantonese food is usually so fresh it's alive, and the only real problem is with shellfish that's often dredged out of the sometimes less-than-clean bays and waters around the islands.

The **heat** is more likely to lay you low. Hong Kong and Macau can be terribly humid and hot, and skin rashes are not uncommon, something you can combat by showering often and using talcum powder, renting a room with air-conditioning and wearing light cotton clothing. If you come down with **stomach trouble**, the best advice is not to eat anything for 24 hours, drink lots of water or weak tea, and take it easy until you feel better. Once on the mend, start on foods like soup or noodles, though if you don't improve quickly, get medical advice.

While **AIDS** is not as prevalent in the territories as in some other Southeast Asian places such as Bangkok, there's a growing awareness of the threat caused by the virus, and TV advertising campaigns and educational programmes have been set in motion. As the posters in Hong Kong have it: "Condoms: Less Risky, More Happy!"

Pharmacies, doctors and hospitals

Pharmacies can advise on minor ailments and will prescribe basic medicines: they're all registered, will often employ English speakers (especially in the centre of Hong Kong, less so in Macau), and are generally open daily 9am–6pm.

At some stage, even if it's just to look, go into one of the **Chinese herbal medicine shops**, found throughout Hong Kong and Macau, which are stacked from floor to ceiling with lotions, potions and dried herbs. The people in these shops are less likely to speak English, but if you can describe your ailment they'll prescribe and mix for you a herbal remedy that might or might not cure it. Opinions – Western opinions certainly – divide on whether or not the herbal cures really work. On balance, though, there's a strong case to be made for the holistic approach of Chinese medicine. Nevertheless, remember that Chinese herbalists need no formal training to set up shop and are not registered.

Turn to the appropriate pages for details and addresses for the following **medical services**.

Hong Kong

Contraception	p.305
Dentists	p.305
Doctors	p.305
Hospitals	p.306
Pharmacies	p.307
Vaccination Centres	p.309

Macau

Doctors	p.367
Hospitals	p.367
Pharmacies	p.367
Vaccination Centre	p.368

For a **doctor**, look in the local phone directories' Yellow Pages (under "Physicians and Surgeons" in Hong Kong; "Medicos" in Macau), or contact the reception desk in the larger hotels. Most doctors have been trained overseas and often speak English. You'll have to pay for a consultation and any medicines they prescribe; ask for a receipt for your insurance.

Hospital treatment is infinitely more expensive, which makes it essential to have some form of medical insurance. Casualty visits are free, however, and hospitals in both territories have 24-hour casualty departments. Finally, both doctors and **dentists** are known as "doctor" in Hong Kong, so be sure you're not wasting your time at the wrong place. Having dental work done costs a lot, so if you possibly can, wait until you get home for treatment.

A Travellers' First-aid Kit

First aid items are readily available in Hong Kong. If you're planning to travel on into China, or elsewhere in Southeast Asia, a useful kit might include:

Antiseptic cream.
Plasters/band aids.
Lints and sealed bandages.
Knee supports.
A course of flagyl antibiotics.
Imodium (Lomotil) for emergency diarrhoea treatment.
Paracetamol/aspirin.
Multi-vitamin and mineral tablets.
Rehydration sachets.
Hypodermic needles and sterilized skin wipes.

Travellers with Disabilities

There are **organized tours and holidays** specifically for people with disabilities – the contacts in the box will be able to put you touch with any specialists for trips to Hong Kong. If you want to be more independent, it's important to become an authority on where you must be self-reliant and where you may expect help, especially regarding transport and accommodation. It is also vital to be honest – with travel agencies, insurance companies and travel companions. Read your travel **insurance** small print carefully to make sure that people with a pre-exisiting medical condition are not excluded. And use your travel agent to make your journey simpler: airline or bus companies can cope better if they are expecting you, with a wheelchair provided at airports and staff primed to help. A **medical certificate** of your fitness to travel, provided by your doctor, is also extremely useful; some airlines or insurance companies may insist on it. Make sure that you have extra supplies of drugs – carried with you if you fly – and a prescription including the generic name in case of emergency. Carry spares of any clothing or equipment that might be hard to find; if there's an association representing people with your disability, contact them early in the planning process.

Hong Kong

Physically disabled travellers, especially those reliant upon wheelchairs, will find **Hong Kong** easier to manage than they might have imagined. There are special access and toilet facilities at the airport, as well as on the main Kowloon–Canton

■ CONTACTS FOR TRAVELLERS WITH DISABILITIES

Contacts for Travellers with Disabilities

AUSTRALIA
ACROD
PO Box 60, Curtin, ACT 2605 ☎ 06/682 4333

Barrier Free Travel
36 Wheatley St
North Bellingen, NSW 2454 ☎ 066/551733

BRITAIN
Holiday Care Service
2nd floor, Imperial Building,
Victoria Rd
Horley, Surrey RH6 9HW ☎ 01293/774535
Information on all aspects of travel.

RADAR
12 City Forum, 250 City Rd
London EC1V 8AS ☎ 0171/250 3222
Minicom ☎ 0171/250 4119
A good source of advice on holidays and travel abroad.

IRELAND
Disability Action Group
2 Annadale Ave,
Belfast BT7 3JH ☎ 01232/91011
Information about access for disabled travellers abroad.

Irish Wheelchair Association
Blackheath Drive Clontarf,
Dublin 3 ☎ 01/833 8241
A national voluntary organization working with people with disabilities with related services for holidaymakers.

NEW ZEALAND
Disabled Persons Assembly
PO Box 10-138, The Terrace
Wellington ☎ 04/472 2626

NORTH AMERICA
Directions Unlimited
720 N Bedford Rd
Bedford Hills, NY 10507 ☎ 1-800/533 5343
Tour operator specializing in custom tours for people with disabilities.

Information Center for People with Disabilities
Fort Point Place, 27–43 Wormwood St,
Boston, MA 02210 ☎ 617/727-5540;
TDD ☎ 617/345-9743
Clearing house for information, including travel, primarily in Massachusetts.

continued overleaf

Contacts for Travellers with Disabilities (continued)

Jewish Rehabilitation Hospital
3205 Place Alton Goldbloom
Montréal, PQ H7V 1R2 ☎514/688 9550, ext 226
Guidebooks and travel information.

Kéroul
4545 Ave. Pierre de Coubertin,
CP 1000, Station M
Montréal, PQ H1V 3R2 ☎514/252 3104
Organization promoting and facilitating travel for mobility-impaired people, primarily in Quebec.

Mobility International USA
PO Box 10767, Eugene,
OR 97440 Voice and TDD ☎503/343-1284.
Information and referral services, access guides, tours and exchange programs.

Society for the Advancement of Travel for the Handicapped (SATH)
347 5th Ave,
New York, NY 10016 ☎212/447 7284.

Non-profit travel-industry referral service that passes queries on to its members as appropriate; allow plenty of time for a response.

Travel Information Service
Moss Rehabilitation Hospital,
1200 W Tabor Rd,
Philadelphia, PA 19141 ☎215/456 9600
Telephone information and referral service.

Twin Peaks Press
Box 129, Vancouver,
WA 98666 ☎206/694 2462
or 1-800/637 2256
Publisher of the Directory of Travel Agencies for the Disabled, listing more than 370 agencies worldwide; Travel for the Disabled; the Directory of Accessible Van Rentals and Wheelchair Vagabond, loaded with personal tips.

Railway (KCR) and LRT system, and at some MRT stations, though other forms of public transport – particularly buses and trams – are virtually out of bounds. However, wheelchairs are able to gain access to the lower deck of cross-harbour and outlying island ferries, taxis are usually obliging, and there's a special bus service, *Rehabus*, which operates on a dial-a-ride system – see p.305 for details. There are fewer facilities for visually disabled visitors, though assistance is offered by braille signage in KCR elevators and clicking poles at the top and bottom of escalators.

All other facilities for the disabled in public buildings, hotels, restaurants and recreational buildings are listed in a very useful and comprehensive free booklet, **A Guide for Physically Handicapped Visitors to Hong Kong**, distributed by the Hong Kong Tourist Association.

On the whole you'll find people willing to help as you go. If you can, use the telephone numbers given in the text to phone ahead if you think there's likely to be a problem with access at any hotel, restaurant or public building. There's a list of **useful numbers** given on p.305 if you require more information when in Hong Kong.

Macau

Macau is far less easy to negotiate for most physically disabled travellers. The streets are older, narrower, rougher and steeper, and there isn't the same hi-tech edge – overhead rampways, wide, modern elevators, etc – that makes Hong Kong relatively approachable. Visitors in wheelchairs will first have to contact the *STDM* office in Hong Kong (in the Shun Tak Centre; see p.000), which can assist with travel arrangements on the Jetfoils. Some of the larger hotels are also geared towards disabled visitors; contact the MTIB for more information.

Information and Maps

Both Hong Kong and Macau maintain tourist offices in several cities abroad, where you can pick up information, maps, brochures and leaflets before you go. Don't go mad, though: once you're there, you'll get better, more detailed information from **local tourist offices**. For addresses and opening hours, see Hong Kong, p.46, Macau, p.317.

Of the many Internet sites covering Hong Kong (mostly geared to the upmarket business traveller) the Hong Kong Tourist Association's site is one of the most detailed and up to date, featuring festivals, weekly events, shopping, food and entertainment listings with a new, visually tempting "Wonder of the Day" idea every day: http://www.hkta.org.

Tourist Offices Abroad

HONG KONG TOURIST ASSOCIATION (HKTA)

Australia
Level 5, 55 Harrington St
The Rocks, Sydney, NSW 2000 ☎ 02/251 2855

Canada
Suite 909, 347 Bay St
Toronto, Ontario M5H 2R7 ☎ 416/366 2389

France
53 rue François 1er, 8th Floor
75008 Paris ☎ 47/20 39 54

Germany
Humboldt Str. 94, D-60318 ☎ 069/9591290

New Zealand
PO Box 2120, Auckland ☎ 09/575 2707

Singapore
10 Collyer Quay, No. 13-08 , 13th Floor,
Ocean Building , Singapore 0104 ☎ 65/532 3668

UK
3rd Floor, 125 Pall Mall
London SW1 ☎ 0171/930 4775

USA
Suite 200, 610 Enterprise Drive, Oakbrook
Chicago IL 60521 ☎ 708/575 2828

590 Fifth Ave, 5th Floor
New York, NY 10036 ☎ 212/869 5008

10940 Wilshire Blvd, Suite 1220
Los Angeles, CA 90024 ☎ 310/208 4582

MACAU TOURIST INFORMATION BUREAU (MTIB)

If your country has no representation, contact the relevant Portuguese National Tourist Office for information.

Australia
449 Darling St, Balmain
Sydney, NSW 2041 ☎ 02/555 7548

Canada
Suite 157, 10551 Shellbridge Way
Richmond, BC, V6X 2W9 ☎ 604/231 9040;

13 Mountalan Ave
Toronto, Ontario, M4J IH3 ☎ 416/466 6552

Germany
Shafergasse 17
D-60313 Frankfurt-Am-Main ☎ 69/234094

New Zealand
PO Box 42-165, Orakei
Auckland 5 ☎ 09/575 2700

Singapore
11-01A PIL Building , 140 Cecil St
Singapore 069540 ☎ 65/225 0022

UK
6 Sherlock Mews,
Paddington St
London W1M 3RH ☎ 0171/224 3390

USA
Suite 2R, 77 Seventh Ave
New York, NY 10011 ☎ 212/206 6828

3133 Lake Hollywood Drive
PO Box 1860
Los Angeles, CA 90078 ☎ 213/851 3402

toll-free information ☎ 800/331 7150

Map Outlets

AUSTRALIA

Adelaide
The Map Shop, 16a Peel St
SA 5000 ☎08/231 2033

Brisbane
Hema, 239 George St
QLD 4000 ☎07/221 4330

Melbourne
Bowyangs, 372 Little Bourke St
Melbourne, VIC 3000 ☎03/670 4383

Perth
Perth Map Centre, 891 Hay St
Perth, WA 6000 ☎09/322 5733

Sydney
Travel Bookshop, 20 Bridge St
Sydney, NSW 2000 ☎02/241 3554

BRITAIN

London
Daunt Books,
83 Marylebone High St, W1 ☎0171/224 2295

National Map Centre,
22–24 Caxton St, SW1 ☎0171/222 4945

Stanfords,
12–14 Long Acre, WC2 ☎0171/836 1321
52 Grosvenor Gardens, SW1W 0AG
156 Regent St, W1R 5TA

The Travel Bookshop, 13–15 Blenheim
Crescent, W11 ☎0171/229 5260

Glasgow
John Smith and Sons,
57–61 St Vincent St, G2 ☎0141/221 7472

Maps by **mail or phone order** are available from
Stanfords; ☎0171/836 1321

CANADA

Montréal
Ulysses Travel Bookshop,
4176 St-Denis ☎514/289 0993.

Toronto
Open Air Books and Maps,
25 Toronto St, M5R 2C1 ☎416/363 0719

Vancouver
World Wide Books and Maps,
736A Granville St, V6Z 1G3 ☎604/687 3320

IRELAND

Easons Bookshop,
40 O'Connell St, Dublin 1 ☎01/873 3811

Fred Hanna's Bookshop,
27–29 Nassau St, Dublin 2 ☎01/677 1255

Hodges Figgis Bookshop,
56–58 Dawson St, Dublin 2 ☎01/677 4754

Waterstone's, Queens Bldg,
8 Royal Ave, Belfast BT1 ☎01232/247355

USA

Chicago
Rand McNally,
444 N Michigan Ave,
IL 60611 ☎312/321 1751

New York
British Travel Bookshop,
551 5th Ave, NY 10176 ☎1-800/448 3039
or ☎212/490 6688

The Complete Traveler Bookstore,
199 Madison Ave, NY 10016 ☎212/685 9007

Rand McNally, 150 E 52nd St,
NY 10022 ☎212/758 7488

Traveler's Bookstore,
22 W 52nd St, NY 10019 ☎212/664 0995

San Francisco
The Complete Traveler Bookstore,
3207 Fillmore St, CA 92123 ☎415/923 1511

Rand McNally, 595 Market St,
CA 94105 ☎415/777 3131

Santa Barbara
Pacific Traveler Supply,
529 State St, 93101 ☎805/963 4438;
phone orders ☎805/965 4402

Seattle
Elliot Bay Book Company,
101 S Main St, WA 98104; ☎206/624-6600

Washington DC
Rand McNally,
1201 Connecticut Ave NW,
Washington DC 20036 ☎202/223 6751

Note: *Rand McNally* now has more than 20
stores across the US; call ☎1-800/333 0136 (ext
2111) for the address of your nearest store, or
for **direct mail** maps.

Maps

The **street plans** given away by the tourist offices are fairly good, but if you want more detailed **regional maps** of Hong Kong and Macau or Southeast Asia, visit one of the map outlets listed in the box opposite. If you're in Hong Kong for any length of time, you'll need a detailed street **gazetteer**, which names all the streets and buildings in English as well as Chinese: the *Hong Kong Guidebook* (Universal Publications) is a reliable one. Good travel bookshops and map stores should stock them, and they're also available in Hong Kong; see p.288 for local bookshops.

Costs and Money

It's difficult to pinpoint an average daily cost for staying in Hong Kong and Macau, though it's broadly true to say that both places come more expensive than most other Southeast Asian destinations in terms of food and accommodation. If you've just come from China or Thailand, for instance, you're in for a substantial increase in your daily budget. The details below should help you plan exactly how much to allow for.

The easiest and safest way to carry your money is as **travellers' cheques**, available for a small commission (usually 1–2 percent of the amount ordered) from any bank, whether or not you have an account, and from branches of *American Express* and *Thomas Cook*. Make sure to keep the purchase agreement and a record of cheque serial numbers safe and separate from the cheques themselves. In the event that cheques are lost or stolen, the issuing company will expect you to report the loss forthwith to their office; most companies claim to replace lost or stolen cheques within 24 hours.

You can use all major **credit cards** in Hong Kong in return for goods and services. However, watch out for the three to five percent **commission** that lots of travel agencies and shops add to the price. It's illegal, but there's not much you can do about it except shop around: always ask first if there's an extra commission charge with a credit card. And inform your credit card company when you get home.

In addition, *American Express*, *Mastercard* and *Visa* cardholders can use the **automatic teller machines** (ATMs) at various points in both territories to withdraw local currency; details from the companies direct. Make sure you have a personal identification number (PIN) that's designed to work overseas. Remember that all **cash advances** are treated as loans, with interest accruing daily from the date of withdrawal; there may be a transaction fee on top of this.

If you need to **transfer money from overseas**, go to one of the major international banks (preferably one which is linked with your bank back home) and get them to have your bank telex the money to a specific branch in Hong Kong. This will probably take a day or so, and you'll be charged a small handling fee. Or you can use **Western Union Money Transfer**, which typically charges eight to ten percent of the sum transfered to effect a money transfer to Hong Kong. For addresses and contact numbers in Hong Kong see "Directory", p.304 and p.309.

For **banking information and opening hours** in both territories, see Hong Kong, p.304, Macau, p.366.

Hong Kong

The vast consumer choice in Hong Kong leads to a few contradictions in terms of how much things cost. There is no limit to the amount of money you could spend; certain hotels, restaurants and shops are among the priciest in the world. But the overwhelming majority of the population doesn't command the same income as the super-rich, and consequently it's possible to survive as they do: eating well and cheaply, travelling for very little and staying in low-cost accommodation.

At the bottom end of the scale, staying in hostels and dormitories costs around £7/US$10.50 a night, and cheap Chinese meals at street stalls and in cafés go for another £2–3/$3–4.50 a time. **Living frugally** this way, for a fairly short time, you could survive on around £13/$20 a day.

Eat out more in fancier restaurants, take a taxi or two, have a drink in a bar, and an average day easily costs £25–30/$38–45 or more. Upgrade your accommodation to a room with en-suite facilities, eat three meals a day and don't stint on the extras and this figure at least doubles: a reasonable estimate for a good time in the territory, without going over the top, is anything from **£40–60/$60–90 a day**. Obviously, if you're planning to stay in one of the very expensive hotels, this figure won't even cover your room – but then you probably won't be bothered about sticking to any kind of budget.

The bonus of Hong Kong is that once you've accounted for your room and a decent meal every day, most of the extras are very cheap: snacking as you go from the street, or lunching on *dim sum*, is excellent value; public transport costs are among the lowest in the world; the museums and galleries are mostly free; and the active, colourful street life doesn't cost a cent either.

Currency

The unit of **currency** is the Hong Kong dollar, often written as HK$, or just $, and divided into 100 cents (written as c). Bank notes are issued by the *Hongkong and Shanghai Banking Corporation*, the *Standard Chartered Bank* and the *Bank of China*, and are of slightly different design and size, but they're all interchangeable. **Notes** come in denominations of $10, $20, $50, $100, $500 and $1000; there's a nickel-and-bronze $10 coin; **silver coins** come as $1, $2 and $5; and **bronze coins** as 10c, 20c and 50c. It's a good idea to buy at least a few Hong Kong dollars from a bank before you go; that way you don't have to use the airport exchange desk (which has poor rates) when you arrive.

The current **rate of exchange** fluctuates around $11–12 to the pound sterling/$7.50–8 to the US$. There's no black market and money can be freely taken in and out of the territory.

Macau

You'll find **living costs** in Macau similar to those in Hong Kong, though there are significant differences. You'll pay slightly more for the very cheapest beds, but will get much better value in the larger hotels – which drop their prices even further in midweek; it's always worth shopping around. Meals, too, are particularly good value: wine and port is imported from Portugal and untaxed, and an excellent three-course Portuguese meal with wine and coffee can be had for as little as £10/$15. Transport costs are minimal, since you can walk to most places, though buses and taxis are in any case extremely cheap. All in all, you can live much better than in Hong Kong on the same money, or expect to be around ten to twenty percent better off if you watch your budget.

The unit of **currency** is the *pataca*, made up of 100 *avos*. You'll see prices written in several ways, usually as M$100, MOP$100 or 100ptcs (as in this book), all of which mean the same thing. **Coins** come as 10, 20 and 50 *avos*, and 1 and 5ptcs, **notes** in denominations of 10, 50, 100, 500 and 1000ptcs.

The *pataca* is pegged to the Hong Kong dollar (see above), though officially worth roughly three percent less. In practice, **you can use Hong Kong dollars (notes and coins) throughout Macau** to pay for anything, on a one-for-one basis, though you can't use *patacas* in Hong Kong – in fact, you'll find them almost impossible to get rid of there, so spend all your *patacas* before you leave Macau.

Opening Hours, Holidays and Festivals

Hong Kong has a fairly complicated set of different opening hours for different shops and services. Generally, **offices** are open Monday–Friday 9am–5pm, Saturday 9am–1pm; **banks**, Monday–Friday 9am–4.30pm, Saturday 9am–noon; **shops**, daily 10am–7/8pm, though later in tourist areas (see p.285 for more details); and **post offices**, Monday–Friday 8am–6pm, Saturday 8am–2pm. **Museums** are open various hours, but are usually closed one day a week; check the text for exact details. **Temples** often have no set hours, though are usually open from early morning to early evening; again, the text has full details.

In **Macau**, opening hours are more limited, with government and official offices open Monday–Friday 8.30/9am–1pm and 3–5/5.30pm, Saturday 8.30/9am–1pm. Shops and businesses are usually open throughout the day and have slightly longer hours.

On **public holidays** and some religious festivals (see below) most shops and all government offices in both territories will be closed. Annual public holidays in Hong Kong and Macau are listed below; Macau has several more than Hong Kong, due to its Portuguese (and consequently Catholic) colonial heritage.

Festivals

You're in luck if you can time a visit to coincide with one of the many **festivals** that bring whole streets or areas in both Hong Kong and Macau to a complete standstill. At the most exuberant festival of all – Chinese New Year – the entire population takes time out to celebrate. With roots going back hundreds (even thousands) of years, many of the festivals are highly symbolic and are often a mixture of secular and religious displays and devotions. Each has its own peculiarities and attractions: not all are as vibrant and lively as New Year, but each offers a unique slice of Hong Kong and Macau and, by extension, China.

Confusingly, not all the festivals are also public holidays, when most things will be closed. But all mean a substantial increase in the number of people travelling on public transport, higher prices for certain services and large crowds in the festival centres. Also, as the Chinese use the lunar **calendar** and not the Gregorian calendar, many of the festivals fall on different days, even different months, from year to year. The likely months are listed below, but for exact details contact the HKTA or MTIB. And for a description of what happens at each major festival in each territory, turn to p.281 (Hong Kong) and p.319 (Macau).

> **Chinese Festivals**
>
> **January/February**: Chinese New Year; Yuen Siu (Lantern Festival).
> **April**: Ching Ming Festival.
> **April/May**: Tin Hau Festival.
> **May**: Birthday of the Lord Buddha; Tai Chiu Festival.
> **June**: Tuen Ng (Dragon Boat Festival).
> **July**: Birthday of Lu Pan.
> **August**: Maiden's Festival; Yue Lan Festival.
> **September**: Mid-Autumn (Moon Cake) Festival; Birthday of Confucius.
> **October**: Cheung Yeung Festival.

Public Holidays

HONG KONG

It's likely that some of Hong Kong's public holidays will change in time as China jettisons the old colonial holidays in favour of its own celebrations, but, for now, the following public holidays are still observed.

January 1: New Year.

January/February: three days' holiday for Chinese New Year.

March/April: Easter (holidays on Good Friday and Easter Monday).

April: Ching Ming Festival.

June: Dragon Boat Festival.

June: Queen's Birthday (public holidays on a Sat and following Mon).

August: Liberation Day (public holidays on Sat preceding last Mon in Aug, and on last Mon in Aug itself).

September: Mid-Autumn Festival.

October: Cheung Yeung Festival.

December 25 and 26: Christmas.

MACAU

January 1: New Year.

January/February: three days' holiday for Chinese New Year.

March/April: Easter (holidays on Good Friday and Easter Monday).

April: Ching Ming Festival.

April 25: anniversary of the 1974 Portuguese revolution.

May 1: Labour Day.

June 10: Camões Day and Portuguese Communities Day. Commemorating Portugal's national poet.

June: Dragon Boat Festival; also Feast of St John the Baptist.

September: Mid-Autumn Festival.

October 5: Portuguese Republic Day, to mark the establishment of the Portuguese Republic in 1910.

October: Cheung Yeung Festival.

November 2: All Souls' Day.

December 1: Portuguese Independence Day.

8: Feast of Immaculate Conception

22: Winter Solstice.

25 and 26: Christmas.

Communications

As befits one of the world's greatest business centres, Hong Kong's communications are fast and efficient. The phones all work and the postal system is good, sending mail home is quick and relatively cheap, and the poste restante system is well organized. Macau is slightly more laid back, but you should have few problems getting in touch.

Hong Kong

Post offices throughout the territory are open Monday–Friday 8am–6pm, Saturday 8am–2pm. Letters sent **poste restante** will go to the GPO building in Central (see p.307 for address) – take your passport along when you go to collect them. Letters and cards sent **airmail** take five days to a week to reach Britain or North America. **Surface mail** is slower, in weeks and not days; the rates are listed in a leaflet available from most post offices.

If you're sending **parcels** home, they'll have to conform with the post office's packaging regulations, so take your unwrapped parcel along to a main post office – together with your own brown paper and tape – and follow their instructions. It's a good idea to **insure** your parcels, too: the post office will have the relevant forms, as well as the **customs declaration** form that you must fill in for all goods sent abroad by post. Your parcel will go by surface mail unless you specify otherwise – and the price obviously increases the bigger the parcel and the further it has to go.

The Hong Kong **telephone** system – operated by *Hongkong Telecom* – works well, perhaps

inspired by the fact that everybody, roadmenders to millionaires, seems to have their own portable phone. Making a **local call** from a private phone, which means throughout the territory of Hong Kong, is free. Public **Coinphones** cost HK$1 for an unlimited call, while there are also **Creditcard phones** and **Cardphones**. You'll find phones at MTR stations, ferry terminals, in shopping centres and hotel lobbies, while most shops and restaurants will let you use the phone for free. You can buy **phone cards** from *HK Telecom Service Centres* (see below) and from tourist offices and *7-Eleven* stores; they come in units of $50, $100, $200 and £300; some are specifically for use when calling overseas.

Making a call is easy: on every pay and card phone there are instructions in English – the ringing, engaged and number-unobtainable tones are similar to those used in Britain and America. All telephone numbers contain eight digits and there are no area codes. For **long distance** (ie, international) calls, use the International Direct Dialling (IDD) phones found around the territory, or go to one of the several **Hong Kong Telecom Service Centres** throughout the territory; there's a list of the central ones on p.308. Here you can

---

Telephone Numbers

The Hong Kong Chinese consider certain phone **numbers** to be unlucky, principally because the words for some of the numbers sound like more ominous words, for example, 4 (*sei*), which sounds like the Cantonese word for "death". Lots of people won't accept the private numbers they're allocated by the telephone company for this reason, and there's a continuous struggle to change numbers. Conversely, other numbers are considered lucky because they sound fortuitous – particularly 3 (longevity), 8 (prosperity) and 9 (eternity) – and people will wheedle, pay or bribe to have these included in their telephone number. The same applies, incidentally, to car number plates: each year there's a government auction of the best ones, some of which fetch thousands of dollars.

make overseas calls, including **reverse-charge** ("collect") calls, and send telexes and faxes. Another method of making cashless international calls is to use Hong Kong's **Home Direct** service (see box above), which gives you access to an operator in the country you're calling, who can either charge calls collect or to an **overseas telephone card**. These include the **BT Chargecard** and the card issued by **AT&T Direct Service**. Both cards are free and they work in the same way – just ring the company's international operator, who will connect you free of charge and add the cost of the connected call to your domestic bill.

For a list of **useful telephone numbers** in Hong Kong, see p.308.

Macau

The main **post office** in Macau (see p.367 for address) is open Monday to Friday 9am–1pm and 3–5.30pm, Saturday 9am–12.30pm. Otherwise little booths all over Macau sell **stamps**, as do the larger hotels, and there's a post office on each of the two outlying islands, Taipa and Coloane. Letters and cards sent from Macau to Europe and North America take around the same time as from Hong Kong – between five days and a week.

The Macanese **telephone system** is operated by *Companhia de Telecomunicações de Macau* (*CTM*). **Local phone calls** from a pay phone cost 1ptca, though like in Hong Kong, local calls are free from a private phone or from the courtesy phones in shops and restaurants. There are no area codes; just dial the five- or six-figure number

given. Instructions on most phones are in English, as well as in Portuguese. You can make **international calls** from the telephone office at the back of the main post office; some of the staff there speak English. As in Hong Kong, there's a **Home Direct** service (*Pais Directo*), which gives you access to an operator in the country you're calling, who can either charge calls collect or to your overseas phone card (see "Hong Kong" above). For a round-up of **useful and emergency telephone numbers** in Macau, see p.367.

Police and Trouble

Hong Kong and Macau are both relatively safe places for tourists, certainly compared to other Asian cities. The only thing to be really concerned about is the prevalence of **pickpockets**: the crowded streets, trains and buses are the ideal cover for them. To guard against being robbed in this way, keep money and wallets in inside pockets, sling bags around your neck (and not just over your shoulder) and pay attention when getting on and off packed public transport.

Apart from this, **avoiding trouble** is a matter of common sense. Most of the streets are perfectly safe, as is Hong Kong's MTR underground system, which is clean, well lit and well used at night. Taxis, too, are reliable, though it's still wise to take precautions: try not to travel on your own at night and only use registered taxis from proper taxi ranks.

In both territories, it's rare that you'll be wandering around areas of the city at night that are a bit dodgy and if you are, there's nothing you can do to avoid standing out. The best advice if you're lost, or somewhere vaguely threatening, is to look purposeful, don't dawdle, and stick to the main roads. If you are **held up and robbed** – an extremely unlikely event – hand over your money and *never* fight back: local villains have large knives which they have few compunctions about using.

More common problems are those associated with **drunkenness** in Hong Kong. If it's your scene, be careful in bars where the emphasis is on buying hugely expensive drinks for the "girls": if you get drunk and can't/won't pay, the bar gorilla will help you find your wallet. And unless you like shouting and fighting, try to avoid the bars when the sailors of various fleets hit the city.

Police and offences

Probably the only contact you'll have with the green- or blue-uniformed **Hong Kong Police** (who are armed) is if you have something stolen, when you'll need to get a report for your insurance company. On the street, police officers who speak English wear a red flash under their shoulder number. Otherwise, contact one of the police stations, whose addresses are given on p.307. In **Macau**, police wear a dark blue uniform in winter, and sky-blue shirts and navy blue trousers in summer. The main police station, where you should go in the event of any trouble, is listed on p.367.

There are a few **offences** you might commit unwittingly. In Hong Kong, you're required to carry some form of **identification** at all times: if you don't want to carry your passport around, anything with your photograph will do, or your driving licence. Residents (and those thinking of staying and working in Hong Kong) need a special ID card – see p.36 for details of how to get one. It's not likely that you'll be stopped in the street and asked for ID, though you might be involved in the occasional police raid on discos and clubs, when they're usually looking for known Triad members, illegal immigrants and drugs. They'll prevent anyone from leaving until they've taken down everyone's details from their ID.

Buying, selling or otherwise being involved with **drugs** is extremely unwise. If you're caught in possession, no one is going to be sympathetic, least of all your consulate.

> ### Emergencies
>
> In both **Hong Kong and Macau,** dial ☎999 for any emergency service (police, ambulance or fire).

Other than these things, you'll be left pretty much alone, though don't think of **bathing topless** on any of Hong Kong or Macau's beaches: you'll draw a lot of attention to yourself, offend some people and in any case it's illegal.

Sexual harassment

As a **woman travelling in Hong Kong and Macau**, you're more likely to be harassed by sexist foreign expats than by Chinese men, which at least has the advantage of being more familiar and so easier to deal with. You're not likely to mistake unwelcome advances from a Westerner as cultural inquisitiveness, and the same tactics as at home are the ones to use to get rid of creeps. To minimize what physical risks there are, try to avoid travelling alone late at night in taxis and on Hong Kong's MTR; don't be tempted by any work offers as "hostesses" (see "Staying On", p.35); and generally use your common sense. For local womens' organizations in Hong Kong, see p.309.

Organized crime: the Triads

Much of the lurid crime you read about every day in Hong Kong's English-language newspapers is related to the **Triads**. The historical reasons for the existence of these organized crime societies (similar to the Mafia) is discussed in "History" (p.379), but at street level they're directly and indirectly responsible for all the drug dealing, prostitution, corruption and major crime in the territory. Needless to say, the average visitor won't come into contact with any of this, though the drug addicts support their habit by pickpocketing and mugging, and the shop you bought your camera from almost certainly pays protection money to one Triad society or another.

Religion

Most major **religions** are represented in Hong Kong and Macau, though it's the three Chinese and Eastern ones – Taoism, Confucianism and Buddhism – that are of most interest to visitors. Everywhere, you'll come across temples and shrines, while many of the public holidays are connected with a particular religious occasion. The whole picture is further confused by the contemporary importance attached to superstition and ancestor worship. The information below should help sort out some of the main themes, and add some interest as you look around the temples and shrines covered in the book.

The religions

The main local religion, **Taoism**, dates from the sixth century BC. A philosophical movement, it advocates that people follow a central path or truth, known as *Tao* or 'The Way', and cultivate an understanding of the nature of things. This search for truth has often expressed itself in Taoism by way of superstition on the part of its devotees, who engage in fortune telling and the like. The Taoist gods are mainly legendary figures, with specific powers – protective or otherwise – which you can generally determine from their form: warriors, statesmen, scholars, etc. Taoist temples are generally very colourful, hosting the rowdiest of the annual festivals.

Confucianism also began as a philosophy, based on piety, loyalty, education, humanitarianism and familial devotion. In the 2500 years since Confucius died, these ideas have permeated every aspect of Chinese social life, and the philosophy has acquired the characteristics of a religion. However, it's the least common of the Eastern religions in Hong Kong, with few temples and fewer regular observances. Rather it's a set of principles, adhered to in spirit if not in practice.

Also represented in Hong Kong and, to a lesser extent, Macau, is **Buddhism**, which isn't Chinese at all, but originally came from India to China in the first century AD. It recognizes that there is suffering in the world, which can be relieved only by attaining a state of personal enlightenment, *nirvana*, or extinction, at which point you will find true bliss. The method of finding this enlightenment is by meditation. There are lots of different Buddhist sects following slightly different practices, and in Hong Kong the situation is made more complicated by the way in which deities from various religions are worshipped in each other's temples – it's common for Buddhist deities to be worshipped in Taoist temples, for example. Buddhist temples are relaxed places, less common and less bright than Taoist, but often built in beautiful, out-of-the-way places and with resident monks and nuns.

Gods and Goddesses

You'll find further information about the following **deities** throughout the text, usually under the entry for the main temple in which they're worshipped. For the most part, the Chinese gods and goddesses honoured in Macau are the same as in Hong Kong, with occasional variations in spelling and importance. One to watch for is A-Ma, celebrating the goddess of the sea, who corresponds exactly to Hong Kong's Tin Hau.

Tin Hau: goddess of the sea, and one of the most popular deities, unsurprising in a land where fishing has always been important; known as A-Ma in Macau.

Kuan Ti (or Kuan Yue): god of war; a warrior.

Kuan Yin (or Kwun Yum): Buddhist goddess of mercy.

Pak Tai: god of order and protection; also known as Emperor of the North.

Pao Kung: god of justice.

Wong Tai Sin: a god who cures illness and brings good fortune.

Sui Tsing Paak: a god who cures illness; also known as the "Pacifying General".

Tai Sui: a series of sixty different gods, each related to a year in the Chinese calendar.

Shing Wong: a city god, who's responsible for people living in a certain area.

Inside a temple: the deities

You'll find descriptions of many Chinese temples in Hong Kong and Macau throughout the text, and as the majority are Taoist what goes on inside is fairly similar everywhere. Most temples are **open** from early morning to early evening and people go in when they like, to make offerings or to pray; there are no set prayer and service times.

The **roofs** of Taoist temples are usually decorated with colourful porcelain figures from Chinese legend, while inside you'll find stalls selling joss sticks, and slow-burning **incense** spirals which hang from the ceiling. In most temples there's a stall or special room for **fortune telling**, most commonly achieved by shaking sticks in a cylinder until one falls out: there's a fortune paper attached to the stick, which has to be paid for and interpreted by the fortune teller at the stall. Go with someone who can speak Chinese if you want to try this, or visit Hong Kong's massive Wong Tai Sin temple in Kowloon (see p.139), where fortune telling takes place on a much more elaborate scale: here you'll find lots of long-established fortune tellers, as well as palmists and phrenologists, who are used to foreign tourists, and lots of explanatory notes.

Obviously, coinciding with one of the main religious **festivals** (see "Opening Hours, Holidays and Festivals", above) is an invigorating experience, and this is when you'll see the various temples at their best: lavishly decorated and full of people. There'll be dances, Chinese opera displays, plenty of noise and a series of **offerings** left in the temples – food, and paper goods which are burned as offerings to the dead.

Staying on: Working and Living in Hong Kong

Hong Kong is – and always has been – full of foreigners working and living in the territory. As ties with the UK weaken, fewer of them are British and these days the biggest immigrant group in Hong Kong is from the Philippines, mostly women who come here to work as servants and house maids (*amahs*). What European expatriate workers (expats) there are tend more and more to have been posted to the territory by their company, or have applied for jobs with Hong Kong firms from abroad. That said, the dream still persists with many travellers that they can turn up, find work and make their fortune; and you *can* find work and accommodation in Hong Kong. However, mostly you'll need to lower your sights and be aware that you're in competition with six million other people.

Hong Kong isn't an easy place to live, job or no job. It's crowded, hot and humid, with few prospects of getting away from it all and all the frustrations of living in a country where you don't speak the native language. You'll find the basic rules below, together with ideas about how to get a job and somewhere to live. However, there are no short-cuts to making the kind of money Hong Kong is famous for – though you can be happy with the thought that it's several times easier to become a Hong Kong dollar millionaire than a sterling or US dollar millionaire.

Finding work

Currently, British citizens get an automatic year-long stamp in their passport and don't require an **employment visa**. Everyone else needs a visa, which you have to apply for at any British Embassy or Consulate, before you arrive. Any general enquiries should be addressed to the **Immigration Department**, Wan Chai Tower, 7 Gloucester Rd, Wan Chai, Hong Kong ☎ 2829 3000. Staying and working longer than six months, you'll also need an ID card (see below).

The kind of work where vacancies are currently on offer is **skilled, professional work**: there's a brain drain occurring right now from the territory, due to uncertainty about Hong Kong's future, and there's never been a better time to look to plug the gaps, provided you aren't worried about what Chinese rule will bring. Flick through the *South China Morning Post* and its jobs pages – it's on sale in foreign Chinatowns – and you might be able to apply before you leave. Note, though, that if you need an employment visa and find a job while you're a visitor in Hong Kong, you'll have to leave the territory and apply for a visa before being allowed to take up the position.

If you don't want to apply for anything specific, you can always try **writing and ringing around** once you're in Hong Kong. Ideally, you'll need a base (your own or someone else's flat and phone), plenty of experience in the field you're trying to bust into, and lots of time. Bring copies of all relevant qualifications. You can get a free list of many different Hong Kong companies from the **Employment Services Division**, Labour Department, 17th Floor, Harbour Building, 38 Pier Rd, Central.

Failing that, the other option is to look for **semi- and unskilled work**, which is more widely available, but has the disadvantage of being fairly badly paid. Some ideas are listed below and though you'll make enough to live on with most of the jobs, you're in competition with young Chinese people, who are mostly well-educated, bilingual and prepared to accept lower wages than you'd expect for the same job.

Employment agencies

Employment agencies are listed in the Yellow Pages. Most will ask to see your CV/résumé before registering you. And the longer you plan to work, the more chance you have of getting a job – you might need to be economical with the truth about the length of time you intend to spend in Hong Kong. The following agencies will register people looking for as little as six weeks' clerical work:

Adia Personnel Services Ltd, Room 1103, Wilson House, 19–27 Wyndham St ☎ 2525 1257.

Drake International, 18th Floor, Peregrine Tower, Lippo Centre, Drake St, Admiralty ☎ 2848 9288.

Swift Recruitment Ltd, Room 504, Luk Yu Building, 24–26 Stanley St, Central ☎ 2845 3280.

Career opportunities

• **Bar and restaurant work**. Poorly paid – around $35 an hour plus tips – but there are always vacancies in English and Australian pubs and often in non-Chinese restaurants. Ask around the bars, look in windows for notices of "help wanted", check the noticeboard in the *Travellers' Hostel*, Chungking Mansions.

• **Film extras**. Hong Kong is a huge film-making centre and there are jobs going as extras for films and commercials, paying around $250 a day. Watch noticeboards and newspapers.

• **Hostess/modelling/escort work**. You might see adverts seeking any of these three categories of people, though in general they're worth avoiding. At best, hostessing/escort work consists of drinking lots of champagne with fat old businessmen; at worst it consists of sleeping with them as well.

• **Hotel work**. Fairly hard to come by for foreigners, but watch out for advertising by the big hotels for cleaning, kitchen and desk staff. Some of the hostels in Chungking Mansions also occasionally take on helpers; ask at the ones used to Western travellers, like the *Travellers' Hostel*.

• **Office work**. The Hong Kong papers are full of office jobs – clerking, dogsbodies, gofers and sales people – but you'll often need to speak Cantonese. Law companies are among the few businesses which employ only English-speaking people; phoning them direct can be very effective. Reckon on earning from $6000 a month and upwards, not a fortune by any means, though many jobs also offer commission.

• **Smuggling**. The noticeboards at the *Travellers' Hostel* and elsewhere sometimes advertise for people to take items – electronic gear and the like – to other countries, where it can be sold at a premium. You'll get the air ticket for your trouble, and maybe paid too, but if customs stamp the gear in your passport you'll be expected to have it when you leave the country you've brought it into – and if you don't know exactly what it is you're taking, or haven't checked the goods, it could well be drugs. Not at all recommended.

• **Teaching**. Eminently possible, though again not brilliantly paid (around $70–100 an hour). However, you don't always need experience or a TEFL qualification. Look in the *South China Morning Post* for jobs in private and government schools, or for people wanting private tuition; or advertise yourself. The language schools listed in the Yellow Pages are worth checking.

Finding an apartment

If you're staying in Hong Kong for any length of time, you'll need to get out of your hostel or hotel and into an apartment. Space is at a premium in the territory and rents aren't cheap, nor will you get the same space for your money as at home. But as long as you don't want to live on Hong Kong Island itself, you should be able to find somewhere that's reasonably priced, especially if you can share accommodation with someone else.

If you've been sent to Hong Kong by your company, or have come for a job that's been offered to you by a large company, then you won't pay most or all of your rent: your initial hotel bills should be paid, too, while you look for apartments on **Hong Kong Island** – perhaps in the nice areas on the south side by the beaches, or in Mid-Levels above Central. If you *are* paying your own rent, however, these places are likely to be way out of your price range. A flick through the papers at the property pages will show you that you're talking telephone numbers, and living on The Peak itself has always been reserved for the phenomenally wealthy. Mere mortals will have to look elsewhere for accommodation; generally, the further out of Kowloon you get, the cheaper it becomes. The **New Territories** towns are good places to look: Sha Tin is probably the closest place you'll be able to afford, only a quick train ride from Kowloon Tong; Tsuen Wan and Tuen Mun are further out and plagued by rush-hour congestion, but connected with Central by hoverferry. If you don't mind the travelling time,

and being fairly isolated as one of the few foreigners around, towns further up the KCR rail line are substantially cheaper: like Tai Po and developments in and around Fanling and Sheung Shui. Living on one of the **outlying islands** (Lamma, Cheung Chau or Lantau particularly) is popular with many foreigners and certainly it's quieter and often cheaper. But commuting in every day can be a real pain, and in typhoon season the ferry services are often suspended altogether.

You can start **to look** for apartments in the classified sections of the *South China Morning Post* and the *Hong Kong Standard*. Places are mostly rented unfurnished and are advertised by the square footage of the apartment; you'll soon work out what's big and what isn't. The price in dollars will be the monthly **rent** – around $10,000 and upwards for anything halfway decent – and you'll have to pay two months' rent as a deposit as well. If nothing comes up, or at the same time, look for lettings agencies in the Yellow Pages and have them put you on their lists. Or wander around the shopping centres in the New Territories towns, like Sha Tin, and go into the agents you see to ask about apartments: they're the shops with coloured cards in the windows, generally in Chinese, but with explicable square footage and price signs.

Once you're in your apartment, you'll be responsible for furnishing it and all the bills. Lots of the new buildings have security guards and video-protection services, but otherwise give some thought to **securing your apartment**: change the locks or get a steel door like everyone else.

ID cards

Every resident of Hong Kong has to have and carry an **identity card**, which you should get hold of as soon as possible; you use it often in everyday life. Technically, you're supposed to apply for one within thirty days of arrival if you're going to stay in Hong Kong.

ID cards are **issued** free of charge at the territory's Immigration Department at Wan Chai Tower, Gloucester Rd, Wan Chai ☎2829 3000. Take your passport, and a few dollars in change which you'll need for making photocopies and having a couple of photos taken. They'll take your name and address and you'll have to return about a month later to pick the card up. Lose it and a replacement costs $170.

Hong Kong

Chapter 1

Introducing Hong Kong

A mainland peninsula and 235 islands of assorted shape and size on the southeastern tip of China make up the **territory of Hong Kong**, which has a total land area of just under 1100 square kilometres. Over six million people live here, but despite the congestion on the roads and in the urban areas, it's fairly easy to get around: you could travel the 40km from the Chinese border in the north to the south coast of Hong Kong Island in a couple of hours or so. Indeed, it's compact enough to make seeing the whole territory in just a few days eminently possible – though the geographical and cultural diversity packed in between could take weeks of careful exploration if you have the time.

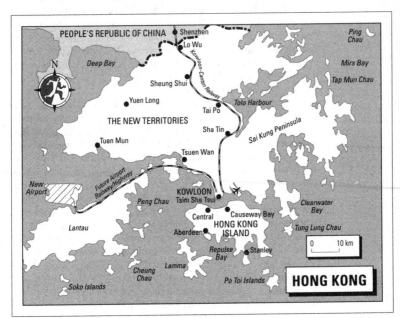

Hong Kong Island, which later gave its name to the entire territory, was the original British settlement – at its widest points, around 15km from east to west and 11km north to south. If you're on the island, you're "Hong Kong-side". The southern part of the Kowloon peninsula (just 12 square kilometres) was added in 1860, but this gave the British control of the deep-water harbour between the two: here, you're "Kowloon-side". At a certain point beyond Kowloon (actually, north of Boundary Street) lie the New Territories, acquired in 1898: they stretch right to the Chinese border and, together with the outlying islands, also added to the colony in 1898, make up the rest of Hong Kong. These distinctions will last only until July 1, 1997 when Hong Kong becomes a Special Administrative Region (SAR) of the People's Republic of China.

If your time is at all limited in Hong Kong, you'll do nearly all your sleeping, eating and sightseeing on the island or in Kowloon, crossing between the two on the cross-harbour ferries or on the MTR underground system. However, if you stay on the island and in Kowloon, you're only seeing a fraction of Hong Kong, and – arguably – little of the real Chinese part of the territory.

Orientation

Most visitors start with **Hong Kong Island** (Chapter 2), whose main business centre is called **Central**. To the west, it shades into the old **Western** district, around the area called Sheung Wan, while further west still, at the edge of the island, is **Kennedy Town**. Moving east from Central, the built-up areas change little in outer appearance as they run through **Wan Chai** to **Causeway Bay** and **Happy Valley**, though beyond here – certainly beyond the island's northernmost tip, **North Point** – things become more residential. South of Central the land becomes immediately steeper, rising through the **Mid-Levels** to the heights of **Victoria Peak**, usually just known as "The Peak". The island's **south side** is characterized by its bays and beaches, running from **Aberdeen** in the west, through **Deep Water Bay**, **Repulse Bay** and **Stanley**, around to **Shek O** and **Big Wave Bay** on the eastern side.

Cross to **Kowloon** (Chapter 3) and you leave the island geography firmly behind. The tip of the peninsula is known as **Tsim Sha Tsui** and it's here – along its spine, **Nathan Road** – that every consumer durable under the sun is sold, stolen or traded; here, too, that you're most likely to sleep and eat. To the east is **Tsim Sha Tsui East**, an area of flash hotels and shopping centres built on reclaimed land, and **Hung Hom** train station; while a couple of kilometres north of Hung Hom is **Kai Tak airport**. North of Tsim Sha Tsui, you head through crowded, gridded streets which become less recognizably Western and more recognizably Asian as you go: through noisy residential and shopping centres like **Yau Ma Tei** and **Mongkok**, 3km from Tsim Sha Tsui.

CENTRAL HONG KONG DISTRICTS

You should try and make at least one trip to the **outlying islands** (Chapter 5), the southwestern group especially – **Lamma, Lantau, Cheung Chau** and **Peng Chau** – only around an hour away from Central by ferry. But it's the **New Territories** (Chapter 4) that give an insight into the real Hong Kong: they feed the colony, and provide it with water, labour and enterprise. New towns, like **Sha Tin, Tsuen Wan, Tuen Mun** and **Yuen Long,** are all easily reached by public transport; or you can take the New Territories train line (the KCR) from Hung Hom to **Sheung Shui** and **Lo Wu** – the end of the line on the Hong Kong side of the border – for a fifty-minute tour through the region. To the east, the **Sai Kung peninsula** is a glorious region of country parks, islands, bays and beaches. In the west, traditional Chinese fishing villages, like **Lau Fau Shan,** are also easily reached on a good day out from central Hong Kong.

Arriving in Hong Kong

As most old hands will tell you, arriving in Hong Kong by air is one of travel's most thrilling experiences, the plane swooping down onto the city from over the South China Sea, skimming the high-rise buildings and pulling up quickly on a runway surrounded by water in the heart of Hong Kong. This will remain the most common approach for most visitors until the new airport on Chek Lap Kok, one of the outlying islands, is operational – that isn't expected to be until mid-1998. Sadly, arriving by ship from anywhere outside Southeast Asia is only for the spectacularly rich, with cruise ships docking at the ritzy Ocean Terminal, on the tip of Tsim Sha Tsui. However, there's a distinct chance that you'll arrive in Hong Kong by water if you're staying in the region for any length of time, as there are regular ferry connections with both Macau and China, while overland travellers can also arrive by train or bus from China.

By air

Planes touch down at **Hong Kong International (Kai Tak) Airport** (☎2769 7531), on the Kowloon peninsula about 5km from Tsim Sha Tsui. There's a foreign-exchange office in the Buffer Hall (with poor rates), a left-luggage office, as well as an office of the Hong Kong Hotel Association (see p.211), which can help you find somewhere to stay. The Hong Kong Tourist Association (see "Information and Maps", below) has an office too, and you'll be able to pick up a plastic bag full of tourist literature and brochures.

Helicopter arrivals from Macau with East Asia Airlines touch down on the helipad above the Macau Ferry Terminal (see "By sea" opposite), where you'll clear customs.

The cheapest way into the city (and to most hotels) is by bus. For the **Airbus**, follow the signs out of the terminal to the bus and taxi ranks: there are five routes, detailed below, all of which have very regular departures, and there's plenty of room for luggage. To use the cheaper **city buses**, take the footpath to the right after leaving the airport and follow the signs to Ma Tau Cheung Road – any of the double-deckers, including the #101 and #111, will take you to Central for around a third of the Airbus price (though using the city buses in the rush hour, with luggage, is madness).

Approximate **taxi** fares into the city are posted on boards at the taxi rank: the taxis themselves are metered and reliable (see "Getting Around", below, for more details). You might want to get the tourist office in the Buffer Hall to write down the name of your hotel or guest house in Chinese characters for the driver, though drivers will usually know the names of the big hotels in English. It costs roughly $50 to get to Tsim Sha Tsui or the hotels in Tsim Sha Tsui East, slightly more than twice that to reach Hong Kong Island, since you have to pay the cross-harbour tunnel toll on top. If you're **staying in New Kowloon or the New Territories**, take a taxi from the airport to Kowloon Tong, ten minutes west, a $35 ride, where you can change onto the underground (MTR) and overground (KCR) train systems; the #A7 Airbus runs here, too.

Note that **rush-hour traffic** can slow down journey times considerably, particularly if you're using the cross-harbour tunnel to Hong

Airbus Routes

Enquiry Hotline ☎2745 4466

- **#A1** to Tsim Sha Tsui via Nathan Road, stopping at the Kowloon-side Star Ferry terminal (daily 7am–midnight, every 10–15min; $12, under-12s $6). Travels via *Miramar Hotel, Mirador Mansions, Hyatt Regency, Chungking Mansions/Holiday Inn Golden Mile/Sheraton, YMCA/The Peninsula, Kowloon, New World/Regent.*

- **#A2** to Hong Kong Island via Wan Chai and Central, stopping at the Macau Ferry Terminal (daily 7am–midnight, every 10–15min; $17/$8.50). Travels via *Century Hotel, Luk Kwok, Grand Hyatt, Harbour View International House, Island Shangri-La/Conrad/Marriott, Furama Kempinksi, Ritz-Carlton, Mandarin Oriental.*

- **#A3** to Hong Kong Island, stopping in Causeway Bay (daily 7am–midnight, every 10–15min; $17/$8.50). Travels via *Excelsior, Park Lane Radisson, Charterhouse, South Pacific, New Cathay, Regal Hong Kong.*

- **#A5** to Hong Kong Island, stopping in Taikoo Shing, for City Plaza (daily 7am–11pm, every 10–15min; $17/$8.50).

- **#A7** to Kowloon Tong MTR Station (daily 8am–11pm, every 10–15min; $6.50/$3.25).

For the location of Airbus stops, see the Accommodation Maps on p.216 (Hong Kong Island) and p.219 (Tsim Sha Tsui). English-language announcements on board tell you where to get off for your hotel.

Kong Island. Depending on where you're aiming for, and the amount of luggage you're carrying, it's sometimes quicker to take a bus or taxi to the Star Ferry terminal on Kowloon-side and cross that way – or cross the water by MTR from Tsim Sha Tsui.

By sea

Almost all the various jetfoil and ferry services **from Macau** arrive at the **Macau Ferry Terminal**, in the Shun Tak Centre, 200 Connaught Road, Hong Kong Island. The MTR (from Sheung Wan station, accessed directly from the Shun Tak Centre) links with most places from there; or you can pick up Airbus #A2 from outside the centre if you're heading for hotels in Central and Wan Chai. Some services from Macau (hoverferries and Jetcats) dock instead at the **China Hong Kong Ferry Terminal** at 33 Canton Road, in Tsim Sha Tsui, behind Kowloon Park, from where it's walking distance to most of the area's accommodation, though taxis are available, too.

All sea arrivals **from China** dock at the China Hong Kong Ferry Terminal (see above). Services include the ferry and Jetcat services from **Guangzhou**, the hoverferry from **Shekou** (close to Shenzhen) and Whampoa, the Turbocat from **Fu Yong** Ferry Terminal (for Shenzhen airport), the catamaran service from **Zhuhai** (west of Macau), and ferry from **Shanghai**. For departure details, see the box on pp.58–59.

By train and bus

Express trains from Guangzhou arrive at **Hung Hom Railway Station** (train enquiries ☎2602 7799), east of Tsim Sha Tsui, also known as the **Kowloon–Canton Railway Station** (or KCR). Signposted walkways lead from here to an adjacent bus terminal, taxi rank and – ten minutes around the harbour – the Hung Hom Ferry Pier: for Tsim Sha Tsui, take bus #1K, #5C, #8 or #8A to the Star Ferry; for Hong Kong Island, take the cross-harbour ferry to Wan Chai or Central.

Local trains from Guangzhou drop you at the Chinese border city of Shenzhen, from where you walk across the border to Lo Wu on the Hong Kong side and pick up the regular KCR trains to Kowloon: it's a fifty-minute ride, the trains following the same length of track to Hung Hom station.

For details of travel into China from Hong Kong by train or bus, see the box on pp.58–59.

You might conceivably arrive **by bus** from a couple of Chinese cities, though the services are mostly used by the local Chinese. It's an easier and quicker route than it once was, since the opening of the Guangzhou–Shenzhen highway and will, in time, become an increasingly popular method of reaching Hong Kong. The main bus service, the *CTS* bus **from Guangzhou**, makes stops in Sheung Shui, Sha Tin and at Kowloon Tong MTR Station, before terminating at Hung Hom train station (though some services also run on to the *CTS* branch offices in Mongkok or Wan Chai). There's also an increasing number of minor routes and services. From Shenzhen, for instance, the *Citybus* stops at the corner of Middle Road and Kowloon Park Drive, Tsim Sha Tsui (behind the YMCA); whilst their service from Dongguan stops at Admiralty and China Hong Kong City.

Information, maps and addresses

At the **airport** HKTA assistants will sidle up to you and hand over a bag full of brochures. If you miss out, visit the HKTA **information office** in the Buffer Hall (daily 8am–10.30pm).

In **central Hong Kong** there are two more information centres: at Shop 8, Basement, Jardine House, 1 Connaught Place, Central (Mon–Fri 9am–6pm, Sat 9am–1pm); and at the Star Ferry Concourse, Tsim Sha Tsui (Mon–Fri 8am–6pm, Sat, Sun & public holidays 9am–5pm). They are both staffed by English-speakers and have a wealth of free printed information to dish out: transport timetables, accommodation brochures and sightseeing manuals. The most useful things to pick up are the magazine *Hongkong This Week*, which has "what's on" listings; the separate guides to Sightseeing and Culture, Shopping, and

---

There's a general, English-language **HKTA Telephone Information Service** on ☎2807 6177 (Mon–Fri 8am–6pm, Sat, Sun & public holidays 9am–5pm).

Dining and Entertainment; the factsheets on individual temples, sights and areas; and the monthly *Official Hong Kong Guide*, which changes its restaurant recommendations each month and covers current festivals and events.

Maps

Our maps of Hong Kong should be good enough for most purposes; taken together with the free HKTA map of Tsim Sha Tsui and Central to Causeway Bay, you shouldn't go far wrong. For anything more detailed you'll need one of the **commercial maps and gazetteers**, vital if you're intending to do any serious travelling around the territory. Best is the paperback format *Hong Kong Guidebook*, a couple of hundred pages of indispensable maps, street and building indexes, transport timetables and other listings. There are various editions, but you should pick one up for around $60 from large bookshops which sell English-language books (see p.288).

You might also want to visit the **Government Publications Centre**, in the Queensway Government Offices, Low Block, Ground Floor, 66 Queensway, Admiralty (Mon–Fri 9am–5pm, Sat 9am–1pm; ☎2537 1910). As well as government publications, this sells the *Countryside Series* of maps, which come in very useful if you plan to go hiking on the outlying islands or in the New Territories. They have various scales, with good inset maps of the smaller islands and areas.

Finding an address

Finding your way around Hong Kong isn't particularly difficult, though there are certain local peculiarities to be aware of. Addresses make great use of building names – often designated "Mansions" or "Plazas" – as well as street names and numbers, and usually specify whether the address is in Hong Kong (ie, on Hong Kong Island) or Kowloon. Abbreviations to note are HK (Hong Kong Island), Kow (Kowloon) and NT (New Territories).

The shop or office **numbering system** generally follows this format: no. 803 means no. 3 on the 8th floor; 815 is no. 15 on the 8th floor; 2212 is no. 12 on the 22nd floor, and so on. And floors are numbered in the British fashion: ie, the bottom floor is the ground floor.

To maximize the convenience of the guide, we've listed hotels and many of the restaurants and bars under subheadings which correspond to various districts covered in the guide, such as Tsim Sha Tsui, Central, Wan Chai, Causeway Bay. These are all served by **MTR underground stations** (see below), called by the same name, which is the easiest way to reach the various districts. Occasionally, a district has more than one MTR station – Tsim Sha Tsui is also served by Jordan MTR; Causeway Bay by Tin Hau MTR – so it's always worth checking which is the nearest. We've marked MTR exits and entrances on our maps.

Getting around

Hong Kong has one of the world's most efficient integrated **public transport** systems – from trams and buses to underground and overground trains and ferries – connecting almost every part of the territory. Moreover, services are extremely cheap and simple to use, which encourages you to roam far and wide. Two problems are universal, whatever type of transport you use. Travelling in the rush hour anywhere in the urban area is a slow and crowded business, worth avoiding; while travelling outside the urban areas, don't expect too many people to speak English – sorting out your route back in advance is a good idea.

The Mass Transit Railway (MTR)

Hong Kong's transport pride and joy, the **Mass Transit Railway** – always shortened to MTR – opened in 1979 and is in a state of constant, and speculative, expansion. It's the city's underground system, running on three lines for over 43km: the **Island Line**, which runs along the north side of Hong Kong Island; the **Tsuen Wan Line**, crossing under the harbour from Admiralty on the island and reaching out to Tsuen Wan in the western New Territories; and the **Kwun Tong Line**, linking Yau Ma Tei in Kowloon with Kwun Tong to the east, and then running back under the harbour to connect with Quarry Bay on Hong Kong Island. The latest plans are for links with the new transport termini associated with the airport at Chek Lap Kok, though these are not due to be operational until the airport comes on stream during 1998.

The MTR is the fastest means of public transport in the territory, and the most expensive – the harbour crossing, from Central or Admiralty to Tsim Sha Tsui costs around $9, considerably more than the Star Ferry. However, it is also air-conditioned, fully automated, sparkling clean and very easy to use: the **interchange stations** between lines are clearly marked on maps and boards at the stations and there's a handy interchange at Kowloon Tong (Kwun Tong Line) with the Kowloon–Canton Railway.

The MTR's **hours of operation** are daily from 6am to 12.30am, with trains running every few minutes; the first and last train times are posted on boards at the stations. The times to avoid travelling are the morning and evening **rush hours** (8–9.30am and 5.30–7pm); in the morning especially, the crowds piling onto the escalators and trains are horrendous, and the MTR authorities have taken to hiring people to "help" passengers onto trains and get the doors closed. Incidentally, don't even think about taking heavy luggage onto the train during the morning rush hour.

There's a **no smoking** policy on all trains; you're not supposed to eat anything either. There are also **no toilets** on any of the MTR platforms. However, everything is marked and signposted in

English, as well as in Chinese characters, so you shouldn't get lost. See the colour MTR map for all line and station details; for the **MTR** Passenger Information Hotline, call ☎2750 0170.

Tickets

Tickets cost from \$4 to \$11 for a one-way journey. There are no returns and tickets are only valid for ninety minutes, so don't buy one for your return journey at the same time. Feed the right amount (coins or notes) into the machines on the station concourse and you'll get your ticket, which looks like a plastic credit card. The machines don't give change (the next person gets any credit left), but there are small change machines in the stations, and you can change notes at the information desks. **Children** under 12 need a special Child Ticket from similar machines (\$3–5 depending on the route).

To **use the system**, you feed your ticket into the turnstile, walk through and pick it up on the other side. When you've completed your journey, the turnstile at the other end will retain the ticket.

For more than one journey, there's a souvenir MTR **Tourist Ticket**. It costs \$25, but gives only \$20 worth of travel on the system (it's valid on the KCR, too). Feed it into the turnstile and at the end of each journey the cost is deducted, the indicator showing how much money is left on the ticket, though for your last ride it doesn't matter how much is left – you'll get the ticket back to keep at the end of your last journey. The ticket is available from MTR stations, HKTA offices, the *Hang Seng* banks in the major stations and KCR stations.

You can also buy a **Common Stored Value Ticket**, available from station booking offices and automatic machines in units of \$70, \$100 and \$200. This is what the locals use, and works on exactly the same principle, with the same last ride bonus; with the \$100 and \$200 tickets you also get the small benefit of a few extra dollars' worth of journeys. They're worth buying if you're going to travel into the New Territories, since they're also valid on the KCR, but note that unused value on the tickets is non-refundable.

As everything is completely automated on the MTR, it seems simple enough to leap the turnstiles and **travel without a ticket** – which, indeed, is what you'll see some people doing. The stations, however, are patrolled by inspectors and swept by TV cameras, and there are fines of \$5000 if you're caught.

See the colour plates for a map of the MTR and KCR.

New Territories' trains

There are two **train networks** out in the New Territories, again referred to by acronyms – the KCR and the LRT. You'll have occasion to use them both, particularly the KCR, if you intend to do a bit of out-of-the-way sightseeing. Like the MTR, all stations, signs and trains are marked in English.

The Kowloon–Canton Railway (KCR)

The Kowloon–Canton Railway – the KCR (information on ☎2602 7799) – runs from the Hung Hom train station in Kowloon to the border with China at Lo Wu. Regular, electric stopping trains use the line, calling at various New Territory towns on the way – a fifty-minute journey – while some non-stop express trains run right the way through to Guangzhou (Canton). Even if you're only staying in Hong Kong, a ride on the KCR is thoroughly recommended, giving you a first-hand view of New Territories life.

More details on using the KCR to leave Hong Kong are given in "Onward Travel: Into China", p.59.

The ticketing and turnstile system is the same as that on the MTR. One-way tickets cost from $3.50 (the Kowloon Tong–Mongkok section) to $8 (for the journey from Kowloon to Sheung Shui). Children under 3 travel for free, those under 12 pay half-fare, and there's a first-class compartment, staffed by a guard, tickets for which are twice as much as ordinary tickets. You'll pay a $100 fine if caught travelling without a ticket, or travelling first-class with an ordinary ticket. The Tourist Ticket and Common Stored Value Ticket (see above) are both valid on the KCR, and are used in exactly the same way as on the MTR.

As far as the stations are concerned, Kowloon Tong is the interchange station for the MTR; just follow the signs to switch rail networks. More importantly, Sheung Shui is the last Hong Kong stop that you can get off at on the KCR. Although most trains run through to Lo Wu, which is still in Hong Kong, it's a restricted area and you'll need to have travel documents valid for entering China to alight here (and a special Lo Wu ticket, which costs $27 one-way from Kowloon).

The air-conditioned trains operate from around 6am to midnight, running every five to ten minutes or so. They're generally much less crowded than the MTR trains (except during rush hour at the Kowloon stations – Kowloon Tong and Mongkok), but be aware that pickpockets tend to ply their trade on this route. Again, there's no smoking and no eating on board, but there are toilets on all the station concourses.

The Light Rail Transit (LRT)

A second train system, the Light Rail Transit – LRT (information on ☎2468 7788) – links two towns in the western New Territories, Tuen Mun and Yuen Long (see map opposite). There are plans to extend the system further into the New Territories and possibly to link it up with the MTR and KCR networks in the future. At the moment, though, it's the rail system you're least likely to use.

The trains are electric, running alongside – and down the middle of – the New Territories' roads, and the system is zoned. Automatic ticket machines on the platforms tell you which zone your destination is in and how much it'll cost. Fares are comparable to the KCR, around $4–6 per journey; feed your money in and wait for your ticket. One branch of the line starts at Tuen Mun Ferry Pier, which

LIGHT RAIL
TRANSIT (LRT)
ROUTE MAP

LRT Enquiries ☎ 2468 7788

614 Terminal Stations

▬ ▬ ▬ Sam Shing - Sui Hong 505	▪▪▪▪▪▪ Tuen Mun - Yuen Long 614
▪▪▪▪▪ Ferry Pier - On Ting 506	───── Tuen Mun - Yuen Long 615
▬▪▬▪ Ferry Pier - Tin King 507	▬ ▪ ▬ ▪ On Ting - Tin Shui 720
▬▬▬ Ferry Pier - Yuen Long 610	▬▬▬ Tin Shui Wai - Yuen Long 721

you can reach direct by hoverferry from Central; the northernmost LRT station, **Yuen Long**, is connected by bus #76K and #77K to Sheung Shui (the end of the KCR line).

Buses

Double-decker buses are operated by three companies: on Hong Kong Island, the *China Motor Bus Company* (*CMB*; ☎2565 8556) runs the cream and blue buses, *Citybus* (☎2736 3888) the orange ones; while the *Kowloon Motor Bus Company* (*KMB*; ☎2745 4466) operates the cream and red ones in Kowloon and the New Territories. **Fares** are low – from $3 to around $10 a trip, depend-

---

Useful Bus Routes: Numbers and Terminals

Each double-decker bus is marked with the destination in English and a number. "K" after the number means that the bus links with a stop on the KCR line; "M"-suffixed buses stop at an MTR station; buses with an "R" only run on Sundays and public holidays; and "X" buses are express buses with limited stops.

Hong Kong Island
Central Bus Terminal (Exchange Square) to: Aberdeen #70; Airport #A2; Ap Lei Chau (Aberdeen) #90; Deep Water Bay #6A, #64 and #260; Mid-Levels #15; Ocean Park #90; The Peak #15; Repulse Bay #6, #6A, #61, #64, #66 (not Sun), #260; Stanley #6, #6A, #260; Taikoo Shing #21 and #721.

Central Piers Bus Terminal to: Aberdeen #7; Admiralty #11, #500 (not Sun) and #681; Causeway Bay #11 and #681; Central #11; Mid-Levels #12; Sheung Wan/Western #7; Wan Chai #681. Also *maxicabs* to Central/Shun Tak Centre #54 and #55.

City Hall (Edinburgh Place): *maxicabs* to Admiralty MTR #7 (not Sun); Happy Valley #7 (not Sun); Ocean Park #6 (not Sun); The Peak #1. Also *express bus* to Ocean Park; and free *shuttle bus* to Lower Peak Tram terminus.

Happy Valley (tram terminus) to: Admiralty/Central #5; Kennedy Town via Queen's Rd East, Des Voeux Rd, Connaught Rd & Des Voeux Rd West #5A; Mongkok/Sham Shui Po #117.

Macau Ferry Terminal to: Airport #A2; Causeway Bay #2; Shau Kei Wan #2; Wan Chai #2.

Rumsey St to: Cotton Tree Drive (Hong Kong Park) #3; Happy Valley #1; Lower Peak Tram Terminus #3; Wan Chai #1.

Kowloon
China Hong Kong Ferry Terminal (Canton Rd) to: Airport via Jordan Rd #14.

Jordan Road Ferry to: Airport #11; Sheung Shui #70; Star Ferry #8; Tuen Mun #60X; Wong Tai Sin temple #11; Yuen Long #68X.

KCR (Hung Hom) Station to: Kowloon Park #26; Mong Kok #1K; Star Ferry #1K, #5C, #8, #8A; Tsim Sha Tsui East #1K; Whampoa Gardens #8A.

---

ing on the route – and the amount you have to pay is posted at most bus stops and on the buses as you get on. Put the exact fare into the box by the driver; there's no change given, so always keep a supply of coins with you. The buses run on fixed **routes** from various terminals throughout the city, from around 6am to midnight: some of the main **bus terminals,** and the buses which depart from them, are detailed below; for more information check the text. Most buses are not air-conditioned (those that are cost more), not particularly well sprung, and can get very crowded during rush hour. However, on longer journeys, to the south of Hong Kong Island and out in the New Territories, they're an excellent way to see the countryside.

Star Ferry to: Airport #A1, #1A, #5C, #9; Jade Market #6, #6A, #7, #9; Jordan Rd Ferry #8; KCR station (Hung Hom) #2K, #5C, #8; Kowloon Park #1, #1A, #2, #6, #6A, #7; Lai Chi Kok #6A; Mongkok (up Nathan Rd) #1K; Science Museum #5, #5C, #8; Sung Dynasty Village #6A; Temple St Night Market #1, #1A, #2, #6, #6A, #7, #9; Waterloo Road (for YMCA) #7; Whampoa Gardens #8A. Also *maxicabs* to Tsim Sha Tsui East #1, #1M.

Cross-Harbour services
There are around a dozen **cross-harbour bus services**: ones you might use include the #170 (Ocean Park/Hennessy Rd/Causeway Bay/Waterloo Rd/Sha Tin KCR), #111 (Chatham Rd North/Wan Chai/Admiralty/Central/ Macau Ferry Terminal) and #103 (Waterloo Rd/Wan Chai/Admiralty/ Cotton Tree Drive). Otherwise, the two that use the cross-harbour tunnel all night are #121 (Macau Ferry Terminal–Choi Hung) and #122 (North Point Ferry Pier–So Uk).

New Territories
Choi Hung to: Clearwater Bay #91; Pak Tam Chung #96R; Sai Kung #92.

Fanling to: Hok Tau Wai #52K; Luen Wo Market and Sha Tau Kok #78K; Luk Keng #56K; Sheung Shui #78K.

Pak Tam Chung to: Wong Shek #95R.

Sai Kung to: Nai Chung #99; Pak Tam Chung #94; Sha Tin #299; Wong Shek #94.

Sha Tin to: Sai Kung, via Nai Chung #89R and #299.

Sheung Shui to: Fanling #78K; Jordan Road Ferry #70; Lok Ma Chau 76K or minibus #17; Luen Wo Market #70; Shau Tau Kok #78K; Yuen Long #76K and #77K.

Tai Po Market to: Kam Tin #64K; Tai Mei Tuk (for Plover Cove) #75K; Yuen Long #64K.

Tsuen Wan to: Kam Tin #51; Sham Tseng #34B or minibus #96M; Yuen Long, via Tuen Mun (for Ching Chung Koon Temple and Mui Fat Monastery) #68M.

Yuen Long to: Jordan Road Ferry #68 and #68X; Kam Tin #54; Lau Fau Shan #655; Sheung Shui (via Lok Ma Chau) #76K; Sheung Shui (via Kam Tin) #77K; Tai Po Market KCR #64K; Tuen Mun #68M.

Minibuses are red and yellow and seat 14–16 people. They run very regularly on fixed routes throughout the territory, but will stop (within reason) wherever you flag them down or ask to get off. As they're almost exclusively used by the locals, the destination card on the front of each one is in Chinese characters, with a tiny English version above it that is not always visible. Either make sure you know the number that you want to catch (given in the text where necessary) or flag them all down until you strike the one that you want. They're quicker than the double-deckers, the fares are roughly similar and posted inside the bus ($3–10; pay the driver when you get off), and they can be really useful for jumping short distances (up Nathan Rd, say) when you're in a hurry. When they want to get off, the Chinese shout *yau lok*; in practice, you can say almost anything as long as you make it clear you want to get off. On Sundays, public holidays, race days and when it's raining, the fares shoot up to around twice the normal rate. Hours of operation are from around 6am until well after midnight on some routes.

The green and yellow minibuses are called **Maxicabs**, seating the same number of people but running on fixed routes and stopping at marked maxicab stops. Some useful routes are given in the box, and detailed in the text, and the fares are fixed: again, from around $3 to $10 depending on distance, but paid to the driver as you get on. Operative hours are around 6am to midnight.

The HKTA puts out some very useful free **timetables** listing bus routes, frequencies, fares and the Chinese characters for all the major destinations on Hong Kong Island, in Kowloon and the New Territories. Timetables are also posted at most bus stops.

Trams

Rickety **trams** run along the north shore of Hong Kong Island, from Kennedy Town in the west to Shau Kei Wan in the east, via Western, Central, Wan Chai and Causeway Bay; some detour around Happy Valley; and there are plans to extend the system in the near future once the Central–Wan Chai land reclamation projects are complete. Not all of the trams run the full distance, so check the destination (marked in English) on the front and sides before you get on. From Central, east to Causeway Bay takes around 25 minutes, to Shau Kei Wan around fifty minutes, and west to Kennedy Town around half an hour.

Climb aboard at the back. If you're staying on for a long journey, head upstairs for the views. Otherwise, start working your way through to the front and when you get off, drop the **flat fare** ($1.20 for adults, 60c for senior citizens and children) in the box by the driver: there's no change given. Trams operate from 6am to 1am, though some routes finish earlier; avoiding the rush hours is essential if you actually want to see anything as you go – seats are in short supply. For travel **information**, call *Hong Kong Tramways* ☎2559 8918.

The most famous tram of all is the **Peak Tram**, not really a tram at all but a funicular railway, which climbs swiftly from the Lower Peak Tram Terminal on Garden Road to the Peak Tower on Victoria Peak; the journey takes eight minutes. Tickets cost $14 one-way, $21 return (children under 12, $4 and $7 respectively), and the service operates from 7am to midnight, every ten to fifteen minutes; see p.90 for more details. Information from *Peak Tramways* ☎2522 0922.

Ferries and hoverferries

The one enduring image of Hong Kong is that of the countless ferries and boats zipping across the harbour. The views are rightly lauded, and on a clear day the ferries provide an unforgettable first

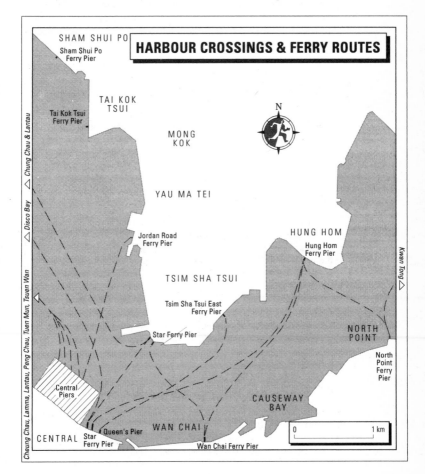

sight of Hong Kong Island. All the services are very cheap and reliable: the only days to watch out for are in **typhoon** season when the
crossings sometimes become very choppy, though at really blustery
times, they will be suspended altogether.

Of all the **cross-harbour ferry services**, the quickest and most
famous is the **Star Ferry** (information on ☎2366 2576), a seven-
minute crossing **between Tsim Sha Tsui and Central** on one of
the ten double-decker, green and white passenger ferries. The
service runs every three minutes at peak hours and operates from
6.30am to 11.30pm; it currently costs just $1.70 to travel on the
upper deck, $1.40 on the lower deck. Check you're in the right
channel at the ferry pier, feed your coins into the relevant turnstile
and join the waiting hordes at the gate, which swings open when
the ferry docks. It all looks chaotic, but the numbers allowed on
board are controlled, and if there are too many people you'll have
to wait for the next ferry – though this will never be more than a
few minutes behind.

Main Cross-Harbour and New Town Services

*The location of ferry piers is in a state of flux while land reclamation
work continues in Central, Hung Hom and West Kowloon (Jordan
Rd). Some services have already relocated to the new Central Piers;
others may follow or move elsewhere since even the Central Star
Ferry Pier is susceptible to redvelopment. Current departures are
listed below; for up-to-date information, contact the HKTA. Services
are daily unless otherwise stated.*

Hong Kong Island

From **Central Piers**: ferry to Jordan Road (6.15am–midnight, every 10–
20min); ferry (Mon–Fri 3 daily) and hoverferry (6.45am–8.30pm, every
10–20min) to Tuen Mun; ferry (Mon–Fri 4 daily) and hoverferry (7am–
6.30pm, every 15–20min) to Tsuen Wan.

From **Central Star Ferry Pier**: ferry to Tsim Sha Tsui (6.30am–11.30pm,
every 3–5min); ferry to Hung Hom (7am–7.20pm, every 10min); hoverferry to Discovery Bay, Lantau (24-hr service, every 20min at peak
times).

From **Queen's Pier**: hoverferry to Tsim Sha Tsui East (8am–8pm, every
20min).

From **Wan Chai**: ferry to Hung Hom (Mon–Sat 6.30am–9.45pm; every
15–30min); ferry to Tsim Sha Tsui (7.30am–11pm, every 10min).

Kowloon

From **Hung Hom Ferry Pier**: ferry to Central (7am–7.20pm, every
10min); ferry to Wan Chai (Mon–Sat 6.30am–9.45pm; every 15–30min);
ferry to North Point (6.15am–10.45pm, every 20min).

From **Jordan Road Ferry Pier**: ferry to Central Piers (6.15am–midnight,
every 10–20min).

From **Tsim Sha Tsui Star Ferry Pier**: ferry to Central (6.30am–11.30pm,
every 3–5min); ferry to Wan Chai (7.30am–11pm, every 10min).

There are several other cross-harbour ferry services, too, operated either by *Star Ferry* or the *Hong Kong and Yaumatei Ferry Company*, with regular services throughout the day. These include the fifteen-minute **Central–Hung Hom** crossing (for the KCR station); the **Tsim Sha Tsui–Wan Chai** and **Wan Chai–Hung Hom** runs; and the **Central–Jordan Road** route; there are also links from **North Point** to Hung Hom, Kowloon City and Kwun Tong. While you may have no real cause to use any of these services, they're worth thinking about simply as trips in their own right: splendid, cheap sightseeing.

Quicker harbour crossings are provided by a fleet of **hoverferries**, most usefully the one that links Central (Queen's Pier, in front of City Hall) with Tsim Sha Tsui East, stopping at the pier in front of the *Shangri-La Hotel*: this runs every twenty minutes or so, from 8am to 8pm, and costs $4.50. Hoverferries also run from Central to the **new towns** of Tsuen Wan and Tuen Mun, in the New Territories, and to Discovery Bay on Lantau, and details are given in the text. In addition, there's another series of ferries and hoverferries that serve the **outlying islands** from Central and elsewhere: all the details for those are given on pp.184–185.

Taxis

Hong Kong's **taxis** are relatively cheap: you can flag them down in the street, or pick one up at the **ranks** you'll find at major MTR and KCR stations, both Star Ferry terminals, the KCR train station, and Jordan Road Ferry Terminal. Look for a red "For Hire" flag in the windscreen; at night the "Taxi" sign on the roof is lit. Make sure the driver turns the meter on when you get in (though rip-offs are rare). On **Hong Kong Island** and **Kowloon**, taxis are red: minimum charge is $14 (for the first 2km) and then it's $1.20 for every 200m. In the **New Territories**, taxis are green and slightly cheaper. The island of **Lantau** has its own taxi service, though there's no taxi service on any other island.

Taxis can be extremely hard to come by when it rains, during typhoons, on race days, after midnight, and at driver changeover time (around 9.30am and again at 4pm). Many drivers don't speak English, although they'll know the names of major hotels – and they should have a card somewhere in the cab with major destinations listed in Cantonese and English. Otherwise you'll need to have someone write down where you're going on a piece of paper and show it to the driver.

Although the red taxis are supposed to work on Hong Kong Island and in Kowloon, drivers will often only pick up fares on one side or the other. In practice, this means that if you want to use the **cross-harbour tunnel**, the driver is allowed to charge you double the $10 toll (ie another $20 on top of the fare), since they assume they won't get a fare back. More annoying is the practice of drivers

Onward Travel: Into China

It's becoming ever easier to visit China from Hong Kong, with the nearest major Chinese city of note, **Guangzhou** (Canton) as little as two hours away by train. There are even organized bus tours starting at around HK$600 for a day-trip to Shenzhen – the nearest city – though more like $1100 for a day-trip to Guangzhou itself; details from any Hong Kong travel agent (see p.308 for list). But you won't see much of anything on a day trip. It's far better to allow at least one night in Guangzhou; all the details necessary to plan the trip yourself are given below; just make sure you avoid travelling at Chinese New Year or at at any other major festival time, when local transport in and out of China is packed solid.

Entry requirements, visas and money

To enter China you need a valid passport and a **visa** easily obtained in Hong Kong and generally valid for three months from the date of issue (*not* the date of entry); one-month extensions are available in China. As well as the two official visa-issuing organizations listed below, just about any travel agency in Hong Kong can arrange a visa for you, and can also sort out your transport to China and accommodation once there if you wish; for the visa only, take along two passport photographs. Currently, it takes one to three working days to get a single-entry visa, for which you'll pay around $160–300, depending on how quickly you need it. Same-day visas cost around $360–400. For a dual-entry visa, count on another $150. You'll still need a separate visa **after the Chinese takeover in 1997** and they should be available from the same sources – though don't be surprised if prices change.

At the border, **Chinese customs** will ask you to declare all your valuables (including things like personal stereos and cameras) and how much money and travellers' cheques you're carrying. This is entered onto a declaration form, which you keep until you leave China; don't lose it, as it's designed to prevent you selling such items in China. As always, don't carry anything through customs for anyone else, however innocent it may seem.

The unit of **currency** is the *yuan* (¥), which is divided into ten *jiao* (further divided into ten *fen*). You can now buy *yuan* in Hong Kong banks before your trip, and there are exchange offices at Shenzhen and Guangzhou train stations, but you'll find that Hong Kong dollars are freely accepted in Shenzhen (where it's legal currency) and for various services in Guangzhou.

Ministry of Foreign Affairs of the PRC

Visa Office, 5th Floor, Lower Block, 26 Harbour Rd, China Resources Building, Wan Chai ☎2827 1881; Mon–Fri 9am–12.20pm & 2–5pm, Sat 9am–12.20pm.

China Travel Service (*CTS*)

4th Floor, CTS House, 78–83 Connaught Rd, Central ☎2853 3533; 2nd Floor, China Travel Building, 77 Queen's Rd, Central ☎2525 2284; 1st Floor, Alpha House, 27–33 Nathan Rd, Tsim Sha Tsui ☎2721 1331; 10–12, 1st Floor, China Hong Kong City, 33 Canton Rd, Tsim Sha Tsui ☎2736 1863; all open Mon–Fri 9am–5.30pm, Sat 9am–5pm, Sun 9am–1pm & 2–5pm.

By local train
The cheapest route to Guangzhou, though a little time-consuming, is to take any of the **local KCR trains** from the Kowloon–Canton Railway Station, at Hung Hom, to the border station of **Lo Wu**; the one-way, fifty-minute trip costs $27. Lo Wu is on the Hong Kong side of the border but is a restricted area: you must be going on into China to come here. From here, follow the signs and walk across the border, through passport control and customs, into **Shenzhen**, the Chinese frontier city. From the new train station here, there are hourly trains to Guangzhou, which cost around $100. You can pay for your Guangzhou ticket in Hong Kong dollars, and the journey takes another two to three hours, depending on the train and the time of day. Note that the **last border-crossing train to Lo Wu** from Hung Hom is at around 10pm; the border closes before 11pm. This local route to Guangzhou is to be avoided at all costs on public and religious holidays, at Easter and at Chinese New Year, when most Hong Kong families decide to visit their relations over the border.

By express train
It's much easier to travel directly to Guangzhou by **express train**, with four daily services from the Kowloon–Canton Railway Station. Although the departure times occasionally change, there are usually two early morning and two early afternoon trains (with one extra daily service at Christmas); the standard trains take two hours forty minutes, while one service a day is designated High Speed and takes just two hours. Standard tickets cost $200 one-way ($240 at peak holiday periods); the High Speed service costs $220 or $250 in first class. Children pay half-fare on all services. You can buy tickets in advance from *CTS* offices in Hong Kong (see above for addresses), and at the office in the Kowloon–Canton Railway Station. Outside holiday times, it's generally not necessary to buy in advance.

By bus
There are plenty of local **bus** services into China's Guangdong province (which encompasses both Shenzhen and Guangzhou), the service to **Guangzhou** is straightforward enough, with nine *CTS* buses daily making the trip; the journey takes three hours and costs $185 one-way, $300 return. Tickets are available from *CTS* offices (see list opposite) and from Hong Kong travel agencies; departures are from the *CTS* branch in Wan Chai (side of Southorn Playground) or from the Hung Hom Coliseum, near the KCR Station. There's also a daily, non-stop *CTS* service to **Shenzhen**, which costs just $60 one-way (tickets and departures as above). From there, minibuses (outside Shenzhen train station; prices posted at the bus stop) or trains make the trip on to Guangzhou. Doing it this way costs around half the price of the direct bus, but takes at least twice as long. **Citybus** (☎2736 3888) also has similarly priced cross-border bus services from Hong Kong to Shenzhen (10 daily) and Guangzhou (5 daily); tickets and information from their office in China Hong Kong City, 33 Canton Road, Tsim Sha Tsui (Room 28, Lower Ground Floor).

By air
Flights from Hong Kong to China are competitively priced. To Guangzhou, it'll cost you about $500 one-way and the trip takes 35

continued over page

Onward Travel: Into China (continued)

minutes; there are direct services, too, to Beijing and Shanghai, with connections to most other Chinese cities. Various airlines (*Cathay Pacific* among them) serve each destination several times daily, and you can get more information from any of the travel agents listed on p.308 or at any *CTS* office. It's always worth shopping around since prices can vary sharply and even on the major airlines, special seasonal deals and discounts are often attractively priced.

By boat

The once-daily, overnight **ferry to Guangzhou** leaves from the China Hong Kong Ferry Terminal (Canton Rd, Tsim Sha Tsui) and costs around $250 one-way for a bed in a dormitory bunk or $300 for a bed in a small cabin. The journey takes eight to nine hours; there's no ferry on the last day of each month, and it's wise to book a few days in advance. The **Jetcat** service from the same terminal departs once daily (in the morning) and takes around three hours; the fare is $250. All tickets are available from *CTS* offices, most travel agents, or directly at the ferry terminal. There are also six daily catamaran services to **Shenzhen** ($175); **Shekou**, the port closest to Shenzhen, is served by hoverferry four times daily ($99); and there are six daily Turbocat services to **Fu Yong** Ferry Terminal (for Shenzhen airport; $175).

Other useful services from the China Hong Kong Ferry Terminal include boats to Zhuhai, Hainan Island, Shantou and Xiamen. Longer term China travellers might also consider the two-and-a-half-day ferry voyage to **Shanghai** (departures every week); or the ten-hour hovercraft link between Hong Kong and **Wuzhou** which means if you're heading ultimately for the Guilin area, you can cut out the long ferry ride from Guangzhou to Wuzhou. For current ticket prices and departure times, contact *CTS* or the ferry terminal.

For bus and ferry services to China from Macau, see p.366.

heading back to base and putting a sign in their window saying either "Hong Kong" or "Kowloon", depending on where they are; they'll only take you if you're headed their way, but more often than not will still charge you double the actual toll. Ask before you set off, and if they want $20 kick up a fuss and get out. On the subject of tolls, you'll also have to pay them on top of your fare at the other tunnels in the territory: the Aberdeen tunnel ($5) and the Lion Rock tunnel to Sha Tin ($6). You'll also have to pay an extra $5 for each piece of **luggage**.

There's a **Taxi Complaints Hotline** (☎2527 7177): take a note of the taxi number if you want to pursue a complaint.

Renting cars and bikes

There are comparatively few private cars in Hong Kong: only nineteen percent of the territory's vehicles are privately owned and run; the rest are public transport, goods' and works' vehicles. And you soon get an idea of who does drive when you look at the other figures: there are more Rolls Royces in Hong Kong per head of the population than anywhere else in the world, and more in number than everywhere except Britain and the US.

Accordingly, there isn't a circumstance when **renting your own car** in Hong Kong is a sensible idea. The public transport system is so good that it's rarely quicker to drive, and in any case, one dose of rush-hour traffic would put you off for ever. If you really need a car, out in the New Territories, say, or on Lantau, it's always cheaper just to take a taxi. There's also the problem of parking: finding a space in the centre is nigh impossible, and the multi-storey car parks are generally expensive and located where you least want them. If you're determined, turn to p.304 for the addresses of **car rental** agencies and central **car parks**.

Bike rental is a more likely possibility, though again, not in crowded central Hong Kong or Kowloon. There are several places in the New Territories where it's fun: there are cycle lanes around Sha Tin and stretching all the way along Tolo Harbour to Tai Po. To use these, go to Tai Wai KCR station and rent a bike from the open space next to the amusement park there; the cheapest are only a few dollars an hour (for more, see p.147). You can also rent bikes at the Plover Cove country park, near Tai Po; see p.155. The best places, though, for bikes are the less congested outlying islands: there are some for rent at Mui Wo on Lantau.

Walking and hiking

The best way of getting around much of the territory is **walking**. It's unavoidable on nearly all the outlying islands, good fun in the country parks of the New Territories and essential on the view-laden round-Peak tour. In the city, parts of Central and Western on the island, and Kowloon, are fascinating places to stroll around, and in Central there's a hi-tech edge to walking: step off the Star Ferry and head up the nearest set of steps and you don't need to touch the ground again for hundreds of metres as you walk above the traffic on **footbridges**, **escalators and moving walkways** – in fact, you can keep above ground right the way from the Star Ferry to the Macau Ferry Terminal in the west (and up to Mid-Levels via the Hillside Escalator Link, p.92) and Admiralty in the east.

All the possible **long-distance hikes** are also covered in the text. The three main routes are the **Lantau Trail** (p.195); the 100-kilometre **MacLehose Trail** in the New Territories (p.178), from Pak Tam Chung to Tuen Mun; and the **Hong Kong Island Trail** (p.68), which runs from east to west across Hong Kong Island.

Rickshaws and helicopters

Every time you step off the Star Ferry on Hong Kong Island, you'll pass the idle red **rickshaws** in the concourse, survivors of a trade that was once the only way around Hong Kong, certainly for the monied classes. The old men squatting next to their vehicles are touting for custom, though what this generally means is a photo-opportunity: bargain before you snap away and expect to pay around $50 for a picture. You can even ask them to take you around the block, something that with bargaining will cost around twice that. But try to get them to take you any further and, whatever you pay them, you could end up on manslaughter charges, as most of them don't look fit enough to blow their own noses.

If you're really intent on wasting your cash on frivolous transport, you could always charter a **helicopter** (for five people or less) for a jaunt over Hong Kong Island, Lantau or the New Territories. Prices start at $3370 for a fifteen-minute jaunt with *Heliservices* ☎2802 0200.

Organized tours

There are more **organized tours** of Hong Kong than you can shake a stick at and even if you have a general antipathy to this kind of operation, with only a couple of days in Hong Kong, some are worth considering – certainly the more exotic tram- and boat-related extravaganzas. Some of the better ideas are detailed below. Also, if you really can't bear to make your own arrangements, a whole range of companies will organize your trip to Macau or China, though this is so easy to do yourself these days it makes falling off a log look tricky. For more help, turn to the list of **travel agencies** on p.308.

China Travel Service (see box on pp.58–59 for locations.) Local tours and China trips with the Chinese state organization.

The Gray Line, 5th Floor, Cheong Hing Building, 72 Nathan Rd, Tsim Sha Tsui ☎2368 7111, fax 2721 9651. An international organization whose Hong Kong arm runs predictable coach tours ($220 upwards) plus longer trips to Macau and China.

Hong Kong Archeological Society, Block 58, Kowloon Park, Tsim Sha Tsui ☎2723 5765. Field trips, lectures and excavations. Contact the Honorary Secretary.

HKTA Any of the HKTA offices can book you onto one of their tours, which include everything from escorted visits to various attractions to harbour cruises and full-day New Territories tours. Some of the more offbeat itineraries include a *dim sum* lunch served on an antique tram; an evening cruise with unlimited free drinks; a Family Insight Tour, including a visit to a public housing estate; a day at the races; and a day's sport at the Clearwater Bay Golf and Country Club. From around $200–400 a head; more expensive China day-trips, too.

Watertours, 1018 Star House, 3 Salisbury Rd, Tsim Sha Tsui ☎2724 2856 or ☎2739 3302, fax 2735 1035. From around $200 for a two-hour harbour cruise. Most of their tours include at least a few drinks; the $500 ones come with dinner and unlimited booze.

Museums

The alphabetical list of Hong Kong's **museums** below includes full details of current opening hours, admission and concessionary prices, telephone contact numbers and public transport links. The page references refer to specific accounts of the particular museums. Note that on **public holidays** (there's a list on p.28), museums adopt Sunday opening hours, while most are closed for a few days over Christmas and Chinese New Year.

A special **Visitors' Pass** ($50) gives one month's unlimited admissions to the Museum of Art, Museum of History, Science Museum (excluding special exhibitions) and Space Museum (excluding Space Theatre). Buy it at any of the museums or from the HKTA.

Chinese University Art Gallery, Chinese University, Sha Tin, New Territories ☎2609 7416. Open Mon–Sat 10am–4.30pm, Sun 12.30–4.30pm; free. University KCR. See p.152.

Fung Ping Shan Museum, University of Hong Kong, 94 Bonham Rd ☎2859 2114. Open Mon–Sat 9.30am–6pm; closed Founder's Day (16 March); free. Bus #3. See p.86.

Lei Cheng Uk Museum, 41 Tonkin St, Sham Shui Po ☎2386 2863. Open Mon–Wed & Fri–Sat 10am–1pm & 2–6pm, Sun 1–6pm; free. Cheung Sha Wan MTR. See p.140.

Museum of Art, Cultural Centre Complex, 10 Salisbury Rd, Tsim Sha Tsui ☎2734 2167. Open Mon–Wed, Fri & Sat 10am–6pm, Sun 1–6pm; $10, children and senior citizens $5. Tsim Sha Tsui MTR. See p.123.

Museum of Chinese Historical Relics, 1st Floor, Causeway Centre, 28 Harbour Rd, Wan Chai ☎2827 4692. Open Mon–Sat 10am–6pm, Sun 1–6pm; free. Bus #10A or ferry to Wan Chai. See p.96.

Museum of History, Kowloon Park, Haiphong Rd, Tsim Sha Tsui ☎2367 1124. Open Mon–Thurs & Sat 10am–6pm, Sun 1–6pm; $10, children and senior citizens $5. Tsim Sha Tsui MTR. See p.129.

Museum of Teaware, Flagstaff House, Hong Kong Park, Cotton Tree Drive, Central ☎2869 0690. Open daily except Wed 10am–5pm; free. Admiralty MTR, bus #3. See p.78.

Police Museum, 27 Coombe Rd, Wan Chai Gap ☎2849 7019. Open Tues 2–5pm, Wed–Sun 9am–5pm; free. Bus #15. See p.94.

Railway Museum, On Fu Rd, Tai Po Market, New Territories ☎2653 3339. Open daily except Tues 9am–4pm; free. Tai Po Market KCR. See p.154.

Sam Tung Uk Museum, Kwu Uk Lane, Tsuen Wan, New Territories ☎2411 2001. Open daily except Tues 9am–4pm; free. Tsuen Wan MTR. See p.162.

Science Museum, 2 Science Museum Rd, Tsim Sha East ☎2732 3232. Open Tues–Fri 1–9pm, Sat & Sun 10am–9pm; $25, children and senior citizens $12.50. Minibus #1, buses #5, #5C, #8. See p.130.

Sheung Yiu Folk Museum, Pak Tam Chung, Sai Kung Country Park, New Territories ☎2792 6365. Open daily except Tues 9am–4pm; free. Choi Hung MTR, bus #92 to Sai Kung and then bus #94. See p.177.

Museums

Space Museum, Cultural Centre Complex, 10 Salisbury Rd, Tsim Sha Tsui ☎2734 2722. Open Mon & Wed–Fri 1–9pm, Sat & Sun 10am–9pm; $10, children & senior citizens $5. Tsim Sha Tsui MTR. See p.126.

Tsui Museum of Art, 11th Floor, Bank of China Building, 2 Des Voeux Rd, Central ☎2868 2688. Open Mon–Fri 10am–6pm, Sat 10am–2pm; $20, children & senior citizens $10. See p.74.

Chapter 2

Hong Kong Island

To many people – visitors and residents alike – **Hong Kong Island** *is* Hong Kong. Seized by the British in 1841, the colony took its name from the island (*Heung Gong* in Cantonese, or "Fragrant Harbour") and created its initial wealth here, despite Lord Palmerston's famous disappointment that all Britain had grabbed was a "barren rock" in the South China Sea. The rich, industrious and influential carried on their business around the enormous harbour, building warehouses, offices and housing, in support of which communications, roads and transport developed as best they could. The island still doesn't look planned, though it has taken a kind of mad, organizational genius to fit buildings into the space allowed by the terrain. First impressions are of an organic mass of concrete and glass, stretching back from the water to the encroaching green hills behind. This is **Central**, the economic hub of the island and territory. Like Manhattan, which it superficially resembles, film and TV familiarity does nothing to prepare you for the reality of a walk through Central's streets, which hold as tightly constructed a grouping of buildings as can be imagined: there's little available space to drive, walk or even breathe at ground level, and the only way left to build is up.

The wealth generated in this urban concentration is part of the reason that Hong Kong exists at all, and brash, commercial Central is interesting for just that – though the island also encompasses the more traditional districts of **Western** and **Wan Chai**, and the tourist

HONG KONG ISLAND: TOP TEN ATTRACTIONS	
Shopping in Causeway Bay (p.103)	Ocean Park theme park (pp.109–110)
Fung Ping Shan Museum (p.86)	The tram ride to The Peak (p.90)
The Hongkong and Shanghai Bank (pp.73–74)	Shek O Beach (p.116)
Hong Kong Park (p.78)	A walk around Sheung Wan (pp.79–83)
Man Mo Temple (pp.83–84)	Stanley village and market (pp.111–114)

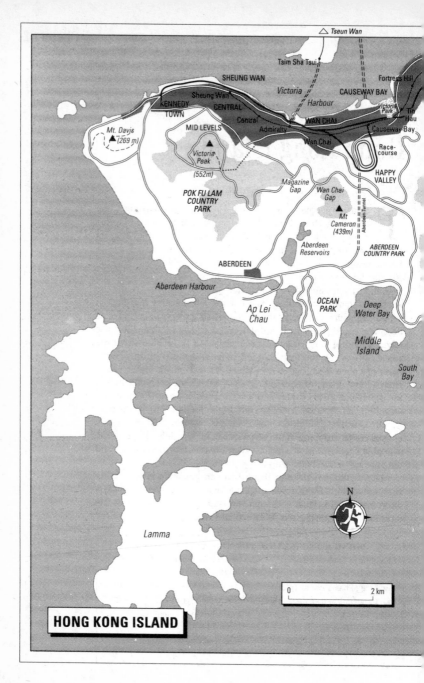

HONG KONG ISLAND

HONG KONG: CHAPTER 2

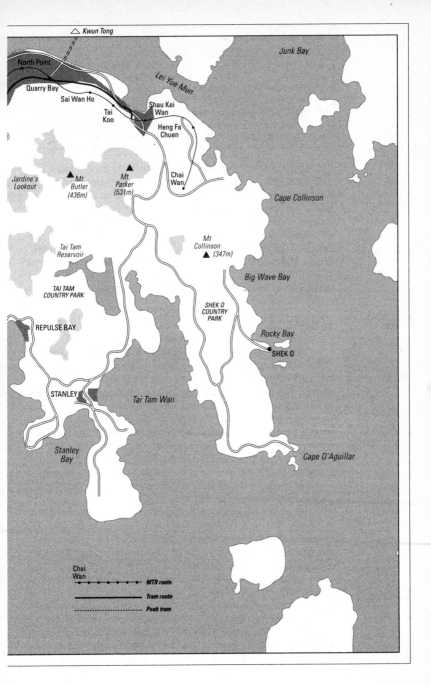

and shopping zone of **Causeway Bay**. There are rural pockets and
walks, too, that make Hong Kong Island an attractive target for a few
days' gentle sightseeing. Out from the city, half an hour's bus ride
leaves you on the island's **south side** or **east coast** with a diverse
series of attractions: beaches, small villages and seafood restaurants,
an amusement park, markets and walks. Closer to Central, you can
escape the city by getting on top of it, either by a walk through residential **Mid-Levels** or **Wan Chai Gap**, or by going one better and
scaling **Victoria Peak** itself, the highest point on the island, reached
by the famous Peak Tram, a perilously steep funicular railway.

Central

HONG KONG ISLAND

*See the colour
plates for a
map of Central.*

The financial, business and administrative heart of the territory,
CENTRAL, is crammed into a tight web of streets on the northern
side of Hong Kong Island. It forms the southern edge of Victoria
harbour and is just a few minutes from the mainland by ferry. Still
technically the "capital" of Hong Kong, the district was originally
named Victoria, following the planting of the Union Jack just to the
west of here in 1841, claiming the island for Britain. The name still
survives with the harbour, but the district's no-nonsense, latter-day
tag reflects what this part of Hong Kong has become in the last fifty
years: the most expensive bit of real estate in the world, supporting
a few of the planet's priciest (and most exciting) buildings and a
skyline for the twenty-first century.

Packed into a short stretch of land (much of it reclaimed over
the years) that only reaches a few blocks back from the harbour,
Central is emphatically a place to walk around. You can see much of
the area from elevated walkways and escalators that pass above the
snarling streets and construction jackhammers. This way, without
touching the ground, you can head along the harbour front or
through the shopping malls and lower floors of the skyscrapers that
stack back from the water. Nearly all the sights are contemporary,
relating to the buildings and views, shops and consumption. But it's
an appealing concoction: markets and street traders rub shoulders
with the monolithic financial slabs and towers; the **harbour** is a
mass of activity; while a few rare **colonial buildings** survive, one –

Flagstaff House – hosting Central's only **museum**. This lies within the boundaries of the highly attractive **Hong Park Park**, and it's here – and in the nearby **Zoological and Botanical Gardens** – that the district gets as close as Hong Kong ever does to winding down.

Around the Star Ferry Pier

The cheapest, greatest ferry ride in the world, the *Star Ferry* across the harbour from Tsim Sha Tsui, lands you right in Central at the **Star Ferry Pier**. If you're staying in Tsim Sha Tsui, make this seven-minute ride as soon as you can after arrival: the sight of Central's skyscrapers, framed by the hills and looming up as the ferry skips across the channel, is one of the most thrilling images of Hong Kong – one you're unlikely to forget in a hurry. The ferries themselves (so-called because each ferry is named after a star: "Morning Star", "Evening Star", etc) have been running since 1898, the diesel-operated, double-decker boats carrying around 100,000 passengers a day.

Step off the ferry onto the concourse and there's a huddle of buildings immediately to hand. City Hall (see below) is to the left past the car park; the long and low **General Post Office** (GPO) building is to the right of the pier; and, rising behind it, the white building with the hundreds of portholes is **Jardine House**, the head-quarters of the Jardine company. Built in 1972, within ten years it had been completely covered in aluminium, since the tiles from its original facing kept falling off. It's still marked on some maps with its old name, the Connaught Centre, and contains the main office of the **Hong Kong Tourist Association** (HKTA) in the basement (Shop 8; Mon–Fri 9am–6pm, Sat 9am–1pm).

Central Piers and Exchange Square

From the Star Ferry concourse, you can climb up to the **elevated walkway and footbridge** system that runs alongside the harbour and deeper into Central. Best for a first view of the city is the section that stretches for a half-kilometre or so above Connaught Road, west to the Macau Ferry Terminal, with offshoots crossing the road into various shopping centres. Keep going and eventually you'll reach Central Market and the starting-point of the Mid-Levels escalator (see p.92).

Heading west from the Star Ferry also provides access down to the massive land reclamation project that has provided space for **Central Piers** – a purpose-built wedge of land accommodating most of the ferry and hoverferry services that run in and out of Central (including the services to the outlying islands) and a new bus terminal. This part of the Central waterfront has changed unrecognizably in just a couple of years: Blake Pier and the old ferry piers, which you may still see marked on some maps, were all demolished and the harbour front suddenly jumped three hundred metres out into

Central

Details of ferry departures from Central Piers are given on p56; for bus routes from the Central Piers bus terminal and from Exchange Square bus terminal, see p.52.

the water. Buildings and support services associated with the new airport will be located on the rest of the land created by the scheme: at underground levels, a new MTR station and airport rail terminal are planned; above will be commercial and retail space, and harbour viewing decks.

While the construction continues, you get a good view of its scale from the terraces of the adjacent pastel-pink, marble and glass buildings which house Hong Kong's **Stock Exchange**, ranking behind New York, London and Tokyo in world importance. The territory's four exchanges were merged in April 1986 and found a new home in Swiss architect Remo Riva's **Exchange Square**, whose three towers, open spaces (with Henry Moore sculpture) and fountains add a rare touch of grace to the waterfront. Everything here is computer-operated: you can watch the latest gold prices on video screens, the buildings' environment is electronically controlled, and the brokers and others who work here whisk between floors in state-of-the-art talking elevators. There's exhibition space, too, inside **The Forum**, the restaurant and meeting area that splits the complex.

Underneath Exchange Square (reached by escalators) is Hong Kong's **Central Bus Terminal**, also referred to as Exchange Square Bus Terminal – a handy place to know about if you want to head further afield. Buses leave from here for Aberdeen, Stanley, Repulse Bay and The Peak among other places; see p.52 for details.

Victoria Harbour

Central is the best place to ponder the magnificent **Victoria Harbour**, one of the major reasons that the British took possession of Hong Kong Island in the first place. This was once the best and busiest deep-water harbour in the world, though the waterfront warehouses – or "godowns" – are long gone, and the money-making has shifted into the office buildings of Central, many of which are built upon land reclaimed from the sea. In 1840, the harbour was 2km wide: the latest reclamation project has added another 300m to the island's north shore, halved the original width of the harbour and drastically reduced its natural capacity for flushing itself. This could prove catastrophic since the harbour is already dangerously polluted, as a peer over the side of any *Star Ferry* will prove – 1.5 million cubic litres of untreated sewage are discharged here daily. It's still difficult to beat the thrill of crossing the harbour by ferry, but even that is at risk from a mooted plan to build a pedestrian footbridge from Central to Tsim Sha Tsui.

Apart from the *Star Ferry*, there are several other **ferry** routes and **harbour cruises** to take, and you get a fine sight of the capacity of the port every time you arrive by ferry from one of the outlying islands or Macau. Or simply park yourself on Central Piers or in front of the Stock Exchange and watch the comings and goings of the junks, ferries, motorboats, container ships, cruise liners, hoverferries and sailing boats. Twenty thousand ocean-going ships pass through the harbour every year, with scores of thousands of smaller boats heading from here on their way to the Pearl River Estuary and China.

City Hall to HMS Tamar

East of the Star Ferry Pier, the two blocks of the City Hall are a mean exercise in 1960s' civic architecture, given the grand mid-nineteenth-century French classical structure that was its forerunner – and which was knocked down with little care for aesthetics, like so much in Hong Kong. The Low Block, to the front, has a theatre and a concert hall (and a *dim sum* restaurant with harbour views), as well as an enclosed garden through which parade regular wedding parties. The High Block to the rear holds a succession of libraries, a recital hall and various committee rooms.

It's useful to know that the City Hall Low Block houses clean, free public toilets.

In front of City Hall, **Queen's Pier** has a hoverferry service across to Tsim Sha Tsui East. This is also where the corporate junks belonging to the local businesses tie up. If you're here at around 6pm on Friday and Saturday evening, the quayside is jammed with motorized yachts jockeying for position.

The area just to the east of here was once the site of the British Naval Headquarters – known as **HMS Tamar** after the naval supply ship that docked here in 1878 and became the Royal Navy's administrative HQ in 1897. The ship was scuttled during World War II, to prevent the Japanese getting their hands on it, but the name continued to be used. In 1993, the Navy moved to a new base on Stonecutter's Island, at the western end of the harbour, ostensibly because HMS Tamar and the adjacent naval dockyard form part of a planned land reclamation scheme. Indeed, reclamation of the dockyard has already started, but the real reason for the move was almost certainly to deprive the Chinese navy of a politically sensitive base in the heart of Central after 1997.

Transport: between City Hall and the adjacent Edinburgh Place car park, there's a free double-decker shuttle bus to the Lower Peak Tram Terminal; while the #1 minibus from the same place goes to The Peak.

From the Star Ferry to Statue Square

Follow the pedestrian underpass from the Star Ferry concourse and you emerge by the **Cenotaph** war memorial, which was decked in flowers, banners, letters and poems left by pro-democracy demonstrators after the massacre at Tiananmen Square in June 1989. The **Hong Kong Club**, a bastion of colonial privilege since Victorian times, still faces the Cenotaph, though it's no longer housed in the stately building that went up at the end of the nineteenth century, but instead occupies several floors of a modern tower. Opposite, the **Mandarin Oriental Hotel** was built in 1963, the first of the new wave of luxury hotels in Hong Kong and candidate for "best hotel in the world" almost every year since – though it hides its riches well inside a fairly dull box-like structure. Taking tea inside is one way for riff-raff to get a glimpse, or you can march in and use the toilets, almost the last word in urinary comfort.

Cross Chater Road and you're in **Statue Square**, the statue in question – typically – that of a banker, Sir Thomas Jackson, a manager of the Hongkong and Shanghai Bank in the nineteenth century. The square once gave Hong Kong its colonial focus, open down to the water, surrounded by fine buildings and topped with a statue of Queen

Hong Kong's Government

Under Hong Kong's **British colonial** structure, the head of government, the **Governor**, was appointed by the Queen and served in office without limit. Traditionally, the Governor was appointed from the ranks of senior British civil servants or diplomats. The last incumbent, Chris Patten, appointed in 1992, after the Conservative Party's general election victory – but following his own personal defeat in his British parlimentary seat – was unique in that he was the first career politician to hold the post.

The Governor was head of both the **Executive Council** (known as Exco), which wielded effective administrative power and advised the Governor on his day-to-day decisions, and of the **Legislative Council** (Legco), which formulated the territory's laws and controlled its expenditure. The only matters the Governor had no responsibilty for were defence and foreign relations, which until the handover to China remained in the hands of the British government. The other governmental body, the **Urban Council**, raises local taxes to finance municipal services like markets, sports and cultural faciltities.

In the past, both Exco and Legco were staffed solely by appointed and ex-officio members, approved by the Governor. Representative rule had never had any place in Hong Kong and there were no legal political parties until 1990. However, following direct **elections** in September 1991 – the territory's first – roughly a third of Legislative Council members were elected, most of them belonging to Hong Kong's main pro-democracy political party, the United Democrats (now the Democratic Party). The future of Legco's democratically elected members immediately became a point at issue between the Governor (and, by extension, Britain) and China, with Chris Patten making it clear that he regarded an extension of the franchise in Hong Kong as of paramount importance.

Victoria, but it's lost almost all its character to twentieth-century development. (Even a cricket pitch once adorned the square, but this, too, had to move.) There are plans to re-create the square's fomer grandeur as part of the city centre's development scheme, and it's hoped to restore the harbour views and harmonious lines at some point in the future. For now, the largely sterile square does at least come to life on Sunday, when it and the surrounding streets and spaces are packed with the territory's Filipina maids, who gather here on their day off. People from the Philippines form the largest immigrant grouping in Hong Kong and have been coming to the territory since the ending of Spanish colonial rule in their country a century ago. Most are women who come to work here as maids, sending money back home to support their families. They descend upon Statue Square at the weekend, setting out picnics on matting, and reading and singing – a scene Jan Morris likened, memorably, to an "assembly of starlings".

The Legislative Council

One of the most important of Central's surviving colonial buildings sits on the eastern side of Statue Square. Built in the first decade of dome and colonnade, is the only extant structure from earlier times

China, for its part, remained adamant that the democratic content of Hong Kong's "parliament" should be as muted as possible when it takes control of the territory. Despite this, the Governor pressed ahead with his proposals to increase the number of directly and indirectly elected Legco members and widen the franchise from around 200,000 voters to around 2.6 million, actions which prompted virulent verbal hostility from Beijing.

Further elections in September 1995 – the first time that each of Legco's sixty seats was contested – brought **more democracy** and more pro-democracy gains. Not all seats were decided by direct election, and only around forty percent of those eligible to vote actually voted, but that was almost twice as many as had ever voted previously in Hong Kong. After the results were declared, the Democratic Party could count on the support of around 28 of Legco's members, a number opposed in Legco, and outside, by the considerably less well-represented Democratic Alliance for the Betterment of Hong Kong, the biggest pro-China political grouping.

After 1 July 1997, when Hong Kong becomes a **Special Administrative Region** of the People's Republic of China, most of these manoeuvrings will become academic since the colonial political structure will disappear completely. Following the widening of the franchise in the territory, China always maintained that it would **dissolve Lecgo** as soon as the territory reverted to Chinese rule and has even proposed a "watering down" of the Bill of Rights, promulgated in 1991 as a confidence-building measure after the events of Tiananmen Square. Beijing announced a **Preparatory Committee** – effectively a government-in-waiting – in early 1996, charged with setting up Hong Kong's first "Chinese" government after the hand-over. In turn, the committee will recommend a **Chief Executive**, who will become, in effect, the first post-colonial Governor.

left in the square. It's as safe from future development as anything can be in Hong Kong, renovated since the Court moved to new, modern, premises nearby and now used as the meeting place of Hong Kong's **Legislative Council**. You can't go into what is effectively Hong Kong's parliament; nor, presumably, will you be able to do so in future, once China has decided exactly what political body will sit in the building.

The Hongkong and Shanghai Bank and around

Over Statue Square and crossing busy Des Voeux Road puts you right underneath one of Hong Kong's most extraordinary buildings, Norman Foster's headquarters for the **Hongkong and Shanghai Banking Corporation**, first opened in 1986. Depending on who you believe, it's the most expensive building in the world, costing around a billion US dollars to complete, although the structure itself is far more impressive than any statistics. Wearing its innards on the outside, the battleship-grey, ladder-like construction hangs from towers like a suspension bridge, the whole building supported on eight groups of four pillars. Walk under the glass canopy and you this century as the **Supreme Court**, the granite building, with its look up through the glass underbelly into a sixty-metre-high atrium, the floors linked by long escalators that ride through each storey, open offices ranged around the central atrium. No one minds you riding the first couple of escalators from the gallery underneath the bank to have a look.

On a less hi-tech note, all buildings in Hong Kong have to conform with the dictates of the geomancer, called in with the planning of every building to ensure that spirits aren't disturbed and that the building is favourably sited – and the Hongkong and Shanghai Bank is no exception. The stone lions guarding the entrance are from the bank's previous HQ, torn down to make way for this one, while even the angle of the escalators was fixed according to the instructions of the geomancer.

The Standard Chartered Bank and the Bank of China

Next door to the Hongkong and Shanghai Bank, the **Standard Chartered Bank** put up its own new headquarters, a fairly anonymous thin tower squeezed between opposing blocks that – by design – just topped out above the Hongkong and Shanghai's building.

But the only serious conceptual rival to Foster's creation is the Chinese-American architect I.M. Pei's **Bank of China Tower** further along, across Garden Road. Built in five years between 1985 and 1990 and at seventy storeys high (just over 300m), Pei's blue-trimmed, spear-like building was the territory's highest until Central Plaza went up in Wan Chai (see p.95). It's an engineering triumph since it has no internal columns and is supported by the remarkable strength of its glistening shaft walls. Yet for all that, it doesn't have the compelling interest of the Hongkong and Shanghai Bank, except in its complete domination of the Central skyline – a soaring advertisement for the strength of Communist China, which owns the bank.

The new tower succeeded a solid stone predecessor, built in 1950, and known as the **Old Bank of China** in a vain attempt to avoid confusion; it passes almost unnoticed, next to the Hongkong and Shanghai and opposite the Legco Building. Inside here, on the 11th floor, the **Tsui Museum of Art** (Mon–Fri 10am–6pm, Sat 10am–2pm; $20, children and senior citizens $10) is worth half an hour. There are three thousand pieces of Chinese art contained within, from ceramics – some of the best-presented in the territory – and bronzes to paintings and furniture.

Along Queen's Road and Des Voeux Road

Queen's Road is Central's main street, as it has been since the 1840s when it was just above the water and described by contemporaries as a "grand boulevard" (or *dai ma lo* in Cantonese, a name by which it's still known by the Chinese). Running west from **Chater Garden**, the first road to cross it is **Ice House Street**, named for a building that once stored blocks of ice for use in the colony's early hospitals, imported from the United States since there were no commercial ice-making facilities in Hong Kong. A wander up Ice House Street to the junction with Lower Albert Road gives you a view of a later storage building, the early twentieth-century **Old Dairy Farm Building**, in brown and cream brick, which today houses the Fringe Club (see "The Arts and Media", p.276) and the Foreign Correspondents' Club, a members-only retreat for journalists. On the way, opposite a hospital, you'll also pass two gas street lamps, almost miraculous survivors from earlier times.

To the west, beyond Ice House Street, Queen's Road and parallel **Des Voeux Road** take in some of the most exclusive of the territory's shops and malls, including **The Landmark**, on the corner of Pedder Street and Des Voeux Road. Open since 1980, this shopping complex has an impressive fountain in the huge atrium, and you'll doubtless pass through at some point since it's part of the **pedestrian walkway** system that cuts above this area of Central, linking all the major buildings with the Star Ferry and the harbour.

It's worth leaving the indoor galleries to reach **Pedder Street** itself at some stage – where the turn-of-the-century **Pedder Building**, filled with shops and businesses, is a solid old structure that's somehow escaped demolition over the years. Back across the street, between no. 3a and The Landmark, you should be able to make out a plaque which marks the line of the 1841 waterfront – a remarkable testament to the amount of land reclamation that has taken place since then.

West to Central Market

It doesn't matter which of the two main streets you follow west from Pedder Street, though it's useful to know that **trams** run straight down Des Voeux Road, either into Western or east into Wan Chai. Stay on foot, though, until you've walked the few hundred metres up to Central Market (see below), and you'll pass the parallel cross alleys of **Li Yuen Street East** and **Li Yuen Street West**, which run between the two main roads. Both are packed close with stalls touting clothes and accessories: the East alley sells mostly women's clothes, including silk wear, and accessories; the West alley has more of the same, as well as fabrics and kids' clothes. Emerge from Li Yuen Street East on Queen's Road and you're opposite the more upmarket shopping experience of **Lane Crawford**, one of the city's top – and most staid – department stores, with a smart café at the top and aisles full of heavily made-up charge-card queens.

A little further on, the district's western end is marked by **Central Market** (daily 6am–8pm), which – like all markets in Hong Kong – is about the best fun you can have outside a hospital operating room. Fish and poultry get butchered on the ground floor, meat on the first, with the relative calm of the fruit and veg selling taking place one floor higher. It's virtually all over by midday, so aim to get here early and (if you've the stomach for it) take a break at one of the food stalls inside. There's a shopping arcade on the upper floor, from where the **Central–Mid-Levels escalator link** takes off, snaking up the hill above street level (see p.92 for details).

South of Queen's Road: Lan Kwai Fong

There's a network of streets south of Queen's Road – Stanley Street, Wellington Street, D'Aguilar Street and Wyndham Street – that supports a fancy array of shops, galleries, restaurants and bars, in which the emphasis is firmly European and American. Sedan chairs and rickshaws used to park at the bottom of **Wyndham Street** as late as the 1950s; on foot, you can follow this street right the way up to the zoological gardens (see below).

Apart from the Luk Yu Teahouse (details on p.235), the other famous Cantonese restaurant in the area is the Yung Kee, 32–40 Wellington Street (p.235), a great spot for lunch.

Alternatively, try to grab a table in the **Luk Yu Teahouse** at 24–26 Stanley Street, a traditional Chinese tea house relocated here in 1975, using the lovely wooden furniture and decorations from the original building, which had stood on Wing Kut Street since the 1930s.

You may well find yourself eating and drinking in this area at other times, particularly off D'Aguilar Street on a sloping L-shaped lane known as **Lan Kwai Fong**. This once housed a major flower market, and a couple of florists still survive, but Lan Kwai Fong is known exclusively today for its burgeoning set of trendy pubs, bars, restaurants and clubs: full details are given in chapters 7 and 8. They're all late-opening – you can eat and drink here until 5am – and mostly frequented by expats and well-to-do Chinese yuppies (called, predictably enough, "chuppies"). Every year at the end of August, the area resounds with the sounds of the **Lan Kwai Fong Street Festival**: several days' worth of outdoor events, food promotions in the restaurants and general good times. During street celebrations in Lan Kwai Fong for New Year's Eve in 1992, panic set in among the twenty thousand or so people crowded into the area. In the ensuing crush, twenty people died, a sobering thought as you trawl around the various bars.

There is one small, traditional enclave amid this contemporary barrage of bars and restaurants. **Wo On Lane**, off the western side of D'Aguilar Street, retains an Earth God shrine, a couple of basic cafés and a working street-barber – a rare sight these days.

From the Zoological Gardens to St John's Cathedral

Buses #3 or #12 run directly to the gardens from stops along Connaught Rd; get off at the Caritas Centre.

Perching on the slopes overlooking Central are the two halves of the **Zoological and Botanical Gardens**, open since 1864 (daily 6am–7pm; free); the main entrance is on Upper Albert Road. The views of the harbour disappeared years ago, replaced by spectacular close-ups of the upper storeys of the Bank of China Tower and the Hongkong and Shanghai Bank. Early in the morning it's a favourite venue for people practising *tai chi*, a balletic discipline in which the protagonists are reminiscent of someone walking through treacle.

The Botanical Gardens, together with the aviary, are the nicest retreat, replete with pink flamingos, cranes, toucans and all kinds of ducks. Cross the road using the underpass and the Zoological section is much less worthy, its unhappy captives – including stir-crazy simians – sitting bored in cramped cages.

An exit through turnstiled gates from here and a right turn down the steep hill, followed by a left up a driveway, leads to the city's **Roman Catholic Cathedral**, finished in 1888 and financed largely by Portuguese Catholics from Macau. If it's open take a look around, particularly to see the stained-glass west windows, made in Toulouse.

Government House and the Cathedral

Beneath the gardens, on Upper Albert Road, **Government House** was the official residence of Hong Kong's colonial Governors since 1855. It's a strange conglomeration of styles, with several additions made over the years, the most unusual being those of a young Japanese architect who was commissioned to redesign the building during the Japanese occupation of Hong Kong in World War II.

The main building was retouched and the central Asian-influenced tower added, making it the one colonial building that's seen spirited adaptation rather than destruction. You can't normally get into the house (though public concerts are occasionally held here; watch the local press for details). One Sunday every spring, however, you're allowed to extend your tour through the Botanical Gardens to take in Government House's flowering gardens, famous for their rhododendrons and azaleas.

Government House is slated to become a salutory museum of Colonialism once the last British governor leaves.

Down Garden Road, past the **Lower Peak Tram Terminal** (see p.90), is the other dominant symbol of British colonial rule, the Anglican **St John's Cathedral**, founded in 1847 but damaged during World War II when the Japanese army took it over. Supposedly the oldest Anglican church in the Far East, it's been restored since and despite being dwarfed by almost everything around, its pleasant aspect gives you an idea of the more graceful proportions of colonial Hong Kong. The main doors, incidentally, were made from the wood of the supply ship *HMS Tamar*, which was docked down at the harbour for nearly fifty years until 1941 (see p.71), and which lent its name to the British Naval HQ.

You can regain Central's lower reaches by walking on down Garden Road, past the contorted towers of **Citibank Plaza**, towards the Bank of China, but it's rather more appealing to stroll across the small, leafy cathedral grounds to the early nineteenth-century redbrick building at the top of the hill, known as **Beaconsfield** after Disraeli, the Earl of Beaconsfield. This has had several uses: once the French Mission Building, for years it housed Victoria District Court, and now it's the Government Information Services Department. During business hours, if you want to see its original early twentieth-century interior, including a mosaic floor, you might ask someone inside to let you have a quick look. From Beaconsfield, a path drops down to Queen's Road and the Hongkong and Shanghai Bank building.

Hong Kong Park

Heading straight for the park, bus #3 from along Connaught Rd stops near the entrance; get off at the first stop on Cotton Tree Drive. From Admiralty MTR, head for Pacific Place and look for the sign to Hong Kong Park.

The other route from the Zoological Gardens is to branch to the right down **Cotton Tree Drive**, which sounds charmingly rural, but is in fact choked with traffic. However, beyond the Lower Peak Tram Terminal, on the eastern side of the drive, is the territory's newest urban park project, the remarkably attractive **Hong Kong Park** (daily 7am–11pm; free), which incorporates the colonial Flagstaff House and its museum of teaware (see below).

Opened in 1991, and beautifully landscaped in tiers up the hillside, the park contains an interesting **conservatory** with dry and humid habitats for its plants and trees, as well as a superb **aviary** (daily 9am–5pm; free) – an enormous mesh tent which incorporates a tropical rainforest and its attendant bird species. Wooden walkways lead you through and above the trees, bringing you face-to-face with exotically coloured hooting birds; signs point out which ones are currently rearing chicks. The rest of the park features ornamental lakes, a visual arts display centre, a children's playground and a bar-restaurant. It's also a popular wedding spot (there's a registry office inside the park), so bridal parties framed by Central's surrounding skyscrapers are a common sight.

Flagstaff House: the Museum of Teaware

Also within the park, in the northern corner, is **Flagstaff House**, in the lee of the massive Bank of China building. Built in 1844, this was the residence of the Commander of the British Forces in the territory for well over a century, and it survives as an impressive piece of colonial architecture – a cool, white, shuttered building, its simple pillars and surrounding garden an elegant contrast to the skyscrapers all around. That it still stands is down to the donation by one Dr. K.S. Lo of his fine teaware collection to the Urban Council, which promptly restored the house and opened the **Museum of Teaware** inside (daily except Wed 10am–5pm; free). The house alone – with high-ceilinged rooms and polished wooden floors – is worth seeing, but the displays of teaware and related items from China throughout the ages are engaging, too, and there are explanatory English notes.

Admiralty

Latterly, Central has expanded east, with a batch of striking new buildings down **Queensway**, beyond Hong Kong Park, in an area known as **ADMIRALTY**; all the buildings are connected by overhead walkways which you can join from the bottom of Cotton Tree Drive. Most of the land here was originally part of the old colonial Victoria

Barracks, which were decommissioned at the turn of the 1980s; Hong Kong Park, too, sits on former miltary turf.

The **Lippo Centre** is the most obvious structure, designed by American architect Paul Rudolph and formerly owned by the Australian entrepreneur Alan Bond (after whom it used to be named). Supported on huge grey pillars, interlocking steel and glass spurs trace their way up the centre's twin towers, while in the central lobby a ten-metre-high stone relief of a dragon and junk dominates. A time capsule placed behind the sculpture in 1988 is due to be opened in the year 2000, the next year of the dragon.

Admiralty MTR has several entrances in the neighbourhood, one at the Lippo Centre itself, another at Queensway Plaza.

Walkways connect the Lippo Centre to more office and retail buildings, like Queensway Plaza, the gold block of the **NEC** building (the one that looks like a giant cigarette lighter) and **Hutchison House**, from where you can get back to the other footbridges that lead around Central's office blocks. There are also walkways across Queensway to the Government Offices and the modern **Supreme Court** building – a disappointingly squat, grey block – and, along from it, to the vast development of **Pacific Place**, with yet more shops, offices, cinemas, restaurants and three luxury **hotels** – the *Island Shangri-La*, the *Conrad* and the *Marriott*.

Western District: Sheung Wan To Kennedy Town

HONG KONG ISLAND

The oldest settled parts of Hong Kong Island are all in **Western District**, which starts only a few hundred metres from the heart of Central's skyscrapers and office blocks. Not long after the seizure of the island, the British moved out of Western, leaving what was a malarial area to the Chinese, who have been living and trading here ever since. Full of traditional businesses, small temples and crowded residential streets and fronted by a working harbour, it has a claim to be the most characterful part of the island, but it's by no means a homogeneous mass, and encompasses several quite distinct areas.

Sheung Wan, closest to Central, is what's generally thought of as "Western", a web of street markets and traditional shops that unfolds back from the **Macau Ferry Terminal**. You can reach the terminal by the footbridge from Star Ferry in Central; Sheung Wan also marks the western end of the MTR Island Line. South of Sheung Wan, climbing up the island's hillside, **Hollywood Road** is one of the more important of the district's thoroughfares, where you'll find the famous **Man Mo Temple**; nearby, the **Tai Ping Shan** district conceals a set of lesser-known temples. Further west, you can skip the less appealing bits of Western by taking the bus to the **University of Hong Kong**, where there's the fine **Fung Ping Shan Museum** of Chinese art. Or take the tram direct to **Kennedy Town** – the island's westernmost point of interest – which retains much of its mid-nineteenth-century character in a series of streets and warehouses alive with the trade based around its harbour.

Sheung Wan

SHEUNG WAN begins immediately west of Central Market, its streets a Chinese mixture of traditional shops and merchants, tucked into the narrow lanes that run between the main roads. Some of the more fascinating trades have been lost recently as redevelopment rips out old alleys to replace them with new office and retail buildings. This is especially true of the nooks and crannies immediately west of Central Market, between Bonham Strand and Des Voeux Road, but you should still find enough to occupy a morning's stroll. You can follow the routes outlined below, or simply wander into the district: it's difficult to get lost since the main roads are always close by, and once you start climbing you know you're heading away from the harbour.

SHEUNG WAN

Tram route
⊗ MTR Station Entrance/Exit

0   100 m

N

◁ Kennedy Town

◁ Ko Shing St

Macau Ferry
Terminal

Bus
Terminal
for # 2
& Airport

CONNAUGHT ROAD WEST

Shun
Tak
Centre

NEW MARKET ST

WING LOK STREET

BONHAM STRAND WEST

Western
Market

TUNG LOI LANE

Car
Park

Central
Piers

◁ Tai Ping Shan Temples

West
Exchange Tower

DES VOEUX ROAD

Wing On
Centre

Bus Stop
for #1 & #3

PIER ROAD

Sheung Wan
Market

QUEEN'S ROAD WEST

WING LOK STREET

MAN WA LANE

CONNAUGHT ROAD CENTRAL

POSSESSION ST

MORRISON ST

BONHAM STRAND EAST

RUMSEY ST

Harbour
Building

TAI PING SHAN ST

JERVOIS ST

CLEVERLY ST

BURD ST

HILLIER ST

MERCER ST

Vicwood
Plaza

GILMAN'S ST

CENTRAL

PO HING KONG

TUNG STREET

LOK KU RD

HOLLYWOOD RD

SQUARE ST

Golden
Centre

WING KUT ST

WING LOK ST

GILMAN'S BAZAAR

WING ON ST

◁ Central

QUEEN'S ROAD CENTRAL

QUEEN'S ROAD CENTRAL

GOUGH ST

WELLINGTON ST

KING TUNG ST

LADDER ST

♛ Man Mo
Temple

HOLLYWOOD ROAD

ABERDEEN ST

PEEL STREET

GRAHAM ST

Central
Market

STANLEY ST

D'AGUILAR ST

JUBILEE ST

AL VICTORIA ST

BRIDGES STREET

SHING WONG ST

Central Mid-
Levels
Escalator

Mid-Levels ▽

From Central Market to Man Wa Lane

Heading down Des Voeux Road, a couple of blocks up on the left is **Wing On Street**, formerly known as "Cloth Alley" because of the fabric stalls that used to cluster here. They've all been relocated to Western Market, for which, see below. Neighbouring alleys are still devoted to various trades, though for how much longer is anyone's guess: **Wing Kut Street** features jewellery stores and stalls selling accessories, socks and scarves; in **Wing Wo Street** a few hardy traders have survived the encroaching redevelopment. Not so further up Des Voeux Road where Wing Sing Street, once the haunt of egg sellers, has disappeared completely under the construction.

Cut up Wing Lok Street and you'll happen across the stalls of **Man Wa Lane**, where another old Chinese trade is practised – carving seals, or "chops", as the carved name stamps they make here are called. They're used to tourists coming down here to get their personal chop made, and lots of the stalls have their methods and prices marked in English, so if you're tempted it's easy enough to arrange. The craftsmen will translate your name or message into Chinese characters, which are then carved onto the seal you've picked, usually made of wood, soapstone or porcelain. The process takes around an hour, making it possible to wander round the rest of Sheung Wan while you're waiting.

Around the Macau Ferry Terminal

Down at the waterfront, catamarans and jetfoils to Macau leave from the **Macau Ferry Terminal**, part of the massive, twin-towered **Shun Tak Centre**, a shopping mall and apartment complex built in 1986. The complex replaced "temporary" Macau ferry piers that had stood for over twenty years and its futuristic design, for once, doesn't yet appear dated. In a nice touch, the red trimming at base, middle and apex of both towers is echoed in the design colours of the Jetfoils which whip off to Macau from the parallel piers. If you want to circle back to Central from here, head inside up the main shopping level and from the eastern section an **elevated walkway** runs right the way along the harbour to the Star Ferry terminal, a fifteen-minute walk.

Across Connaught Road from the Shun Tak Centre, **Western Market** (daily 10am–7pm), built in 1906, retains its Edwardian shell but has undergone a marked interior transformation. A Chinese food market for over eighty years, much like Central Market to the east, it was renovated and in 1991 reopened as an arts and crafts centre – which means it has retained its fine original brick- and ironwork but replaced the noisy market with a two-floor shopping mall. Ground-floor stalls sell arts and crafts, while the first floor is devoted to the cloth shops that moved here from Wing On Street; the second floor is a galleried restaurant, *Mythical China* (which stays open until 11pm).

For a traditional Chinese market, you don't have to venture very far from Western Market. Head up Morrison Street and the large

If you're looking for a dim sum lunch, try Mythical China, *the restaurant on the top floor of Western Market (p.235).*

white complex on the right is the **Sheung Wan Market**, packed full of meat, fish, fruit and vegetable stalls. The second floor is a cooked food centre (open 6am–2am), with *dai pai dongs* in operation almost around the clock.

Wing Lok Street and Bonham Strand

There's more sustained interest in the long streets to the south and west, which provide glimpses of the trades and industries that have survived in this area since the island was settled. **Wing Lok Street**, in its lower reaches at least, and **Bonham Strand** retain some of their older, balconied buildings and a succession of varied shops and businesses that merit a browse. The *Lam Kie Yuen Tea Company*, at Bonham Strand East 105–107 features a variety of teas in boxes and tins, as well as ceramic tea pots and cups; there are more teastores at the Morrison Street end of the road, too. Along **Hillier Street**, stalls run a brisk business in street snacks, while the area around **Jervois Street** is the centre of the flourishing **snake shop business**, most in evidence from October through to February, when you're considered to need the extra strength that the snake products provide to live through the winter months. The snakes themselves lie coiled up in cages outside the shops, inside which you can buy a wine made out of snakes' gall bladders, and out of snake bile, too: the more poisonous the snake, the better it is for you. The restaurants around here serve snake soup in season.

This area of Sheung Wan is also known as **Nam Pak Hong** – "North–South Trading Houses" – and many of the businesses are herbal and medicinal wholesalers, with snake recipes just one of their many products. Glass cases fronting Bonham Strand contain a whole host of Chinese medicinal ingredients, of which **ginseng** is the most famous – and one of the most expensive. The root of a plant found in Southeast Asia and North America, there are over thirty different varieties of ginseng, including the pricey red from North Korea, white from the United States and wild from mountainous northeast China. It's prescribed for a whole host of problems, from saving those faced with imminent death by illness (which wild ginseng is purported to delay for three days) to curing hangovers (take white ginseng in boiled water). Some of the larger ginseng trading companies have their offices along **Bonham Strand West**, the most venerable ones boasting impressive interiors of teak and glass. Here you'll see people sorting through newly arrived boxes of ginseng root, chopping it up and preparing it for sale.

Bonham Strand West is quite a modern street, but at its western end **Ko Shing Street** is very different, the bustling artery of the wholesale medicinal trade. Great sacks and wicker baskets are taken off a line of trucks by men carrying a wicked hook in one hand: they spear the sacks and hoist them onto their shoulders, dumping them onto the pavements where others unload and sort their contents. The shops here, open to the street, display ginseng alongside antlers, crushed pearls, dried sea horses, birds' nests and all the assorted paraphernalia of Chinese herbalists. In keeping with the traditional nature of the trade, some of the names are straight from the nineteenth century – one company here has a sign proclaiming it to be the *Prosperity Steamship Company*.

Ko Shing Street bends back round to the main **Des Voeux Road** (along which the tram runs). The stretch between here and as far west as Centre Street is devoted to stores selling various grades of dried mushrooms, salted and preserved fish, dried squid, oysters, sea slugs, seahorses, sharks' fins, scallops and seaweed. They make for colourful displays, and even if the priciest goods are out of your range, you could always pick up a string of Chinese sausages or a bottle of oyster sauce.

Along and around Hollywood Road

Hollywood Road, running west from the end of Wyndham Street in Central, and the steep streets off it, form one of Western's most interesting areas, a run of secondhand and antique shops, curio and furniture stores. There's some wonderful Asian·applied art here – blackwood furniture, ceramics, painted screens, prints, figurines and statues – and although most of the shops are firmly geared towards tourists there are any number of smaller places that sell (basically) junk. Hollywood Road is also known for its coffin sellers, and there are a few surviving shops as well that sell funeral clothes for the dead, made from silk.

Man Mo Temple

Follow Hollywood Road west and just before the junction with Ladder Street is the **Man Mo Temple** (daily 7am–5pm), one of Hong Kong's oldest, built in the 1840s and equipped with impressive interior decorations from mainland China. It's dark and smoky, the hanging, pyramidal incense coils belching out scented fumes, but it's not intimidating and no one will mind you poking about the interior. It's generally busy, too, as plenty of people pop in to pay their respects to the two gods honoured here, while others have their fortunes told by shaking inscribed sticks out of bamboo cylinders. The name of the temple means "civil" (Man) and "martial" (Mo) and it's dedicated to these two characteristics which are represented by separate gods. The "civil" aspect belongs to the God of Literature, Man Cheong, who protects civil servants (he's the red-robed statue wielding a writing brush); the "martial" is that of the God of War, Kuan Ti (represented by another statue, in green, holding a sword). Kuan Ti, particularly, is an interesting deity, worshipped by both Buddhists and Taoists, and a protector of – among other things – pawn shops, policemen, secret societies and the military. Close to the main altar, the carved nineteenth-century sedan chairs in the glass cases were once used to carry the statues through the streets at festivals. The other altars in the temple are to Pao Kung, the God of Justice, and to Shing Wong, a God of the City, who protects the local neighbourhood.

Ladder Street to Possession Street

Outside the temple, Hollywood Road is crossed by **Ladder Street**, not so much a street as a steep flight of steps linking Caine Road with Queen's Road. Built to ease the passage of sedan-chair bearers as they carried their human loads up to the residential areas along Caine Road in the nineteenth century, it's the only surviving street of this kind, one of several that used to link Central and Western with Mid-Levels. It retains some of its older, shuttered houses, their balconies jutting over the steps.

Turn right, down the steps, and immediately on the left, **Upper Lascar Row** is what's left of the area known to the late nineteenth-century citizens of Hong Kong as "Cat Street". The names have various interpretations: "lascar" is an Urdu word, meaning an East Indian seaman, and the area is probably where these seamen lived, the "Cat Street" tag probably deriving from its consequent role as a red-light area. The other theory is that Cat Street was a "thieves' market", all the goods at which were provided by cat burglars. Whatever the derivation, these days Upper Lascar Row is mostly a small-scale flea market, with old banknotes, coins, jade, watches and jewellery spread out on the ground alongside broken TVs, chests and other junk. All the pricey antique stuff has shifted into the plush **Cat Street Galleries** (Mon–Sat 9am–6pm, Sun 11am–5pm), halfway along the Row, with antique and craft showrooms on several floors.

Hollywood Road continues west past **Possession Street**, where in 1841 the British landed, claiming the island by planting the Union Jack – though the street's name is the only reminder of this symbolic act. The only interesting thing about Possession Street, in fact, is how far inland it is today, land reclamation having pushed the shoreline hundreds of metres north over the years.

A little further on, Hollywood Road meets **Queen's Road West**, which carries another mix of age-old shops and trades. You can follow Queen's Road right back into Central, a long walk past wedding shops full of embroidered clothes and goods; shops selling paper offerings, burnt at various religious festivals; art supply shops, with calligraphy sets, paper and ink; teastores and all manner of other traditional trades, conducted from a variety of gleaming windows and dusty shop fronts.

Tai Ping Shan

Up Ladder Street from the Man Mo Temple and off to the right lies the district of **TAI PING SHAN** or "Peaceful Mountain". One of the earliest areas of Chinese settlement after the colony was founded, it was anything but peaceful, notorious for its overcrowded housing and outbreaks of plague, and known as a haunt of the early Hong Kong Triad societies. An exiled Chinese scholar, Wang Tao, took a walk through the district in the late-nineteenth century and was disappointed by the quality of the "singsong girls" available in the brothels, most of which had large feet instead of the "tiny bowed feet" he considered attractive.

Tai Ping Shan is a far less dramatic place these days, but it's worth a stroll down **Tai Ping Shan Street** itself, beyond Bridges Street, to see the neighbourhood's surviving temples, which cluster together at the junction with Pound Lane. Raised above the left-hand side of the street, the temples are easily missed, more like part of someone's house than a place of worship, an impression that persists until you see the incense sticks and get hassled for money by the old women sitting outside. First is the **Kuan Yin Temple**, the smallest, dedicated to the Buddhist Goddess of Mercy and reached by climbing the steps. The green-tiled **Sui Tsing Paak Temple**, next door, has a main hall whose altar holds a statue of the god Sui Tsing Paak, known as the "Pacifying General" and revered for his ability to cure illnesses: the statue was brought here in 1894 during a particularly virulent outbreak of plague. One of the rooms off the main hall is used by fortune tellers, and you should also look for the rows of *Tai Sui* in the temple – a series of statues of sixty different gods, each one related to a specific year in the sixty-year cycle of the Chinese calendar. In times of strife, or to avert trouble, people come to pray and make offerings to the god associated with their year of birth.

The most interesting temple is further down the street, past the little red Earth God shrine at the junction with Pound Lane, which protects the local community. The **Paak Sing** ("hundred names") ancestral hall was originally established in the mid-nineteenth century (and rebuilt in 1895 after the buildings in the area were razed because of plague), to store the bodies of those awaiting burial back in China, and to hold the ancestral tablets of those who had died in Hong Kong, far from their own villages. Usually such halls are for the sole use of one family or clan, but this one is used by anyone who wishes to have an ancestral tablet made for their relatives – there are around three thousand people commemorated here. Several small rooms hold the ancestral tablets – little wooden boards with the name and date of birth of the dead person written on them, and sometimes a photograph, too. Behind the altar there's a courtyard, whose incinerator is for burning the usual paper offerings to the dead, on the far side of which is a room lined with more tablets, some of them completely blackened by years of incense and smoke.

West to Kennedy Town

If you've followed the route through Western district this far, you won't want to **walk** on to Kennedy Town as it's a long haul from Central. Either head straight there on the tram, down Des Voeux

*You can also
reach the
museum direct
from Causeway
Bay on buses
#23 or #103;
it's much
quicker than
taking the
tram.*

Road, or follow the route outlined below, which takes you most of
the way there by **bus**, and allows you to stop off at a couple of
points of interest along the way.

The Fung Ping Shan Museum

Bus #3 from the stop in front of the Connaught Centre, on
Connaught Road Central, takes around ten minutes to run along
Caine Road and Bonham Road. Get off opposite St Paul's College, at
the university, and the **Fung Ping Shan Museum** is at 94 Bonham
Road (Mon–Sat 9.30am–6pm; free), opposite an old, yellow-
plastered house of the type that once lined this residential road.

An impressive museum of Chinese art, the Fung Ping Shan is a rare
find in Hong Kong, a quiet collection that's rich in interest. Certainly, it
will not be crowded, and its ceramics and bronzes especially are worth
the detour on the way to Kennedy Town – not to mention some interesting scroll paintings and character scrolls, and a set of inlaid, carved
chairs and tables, all beautifully and precisely executed.

The bronzes are on the **first floor**, including bronze mirrors from
the Early Warring States period (475–221 BC) through to the Tong
Dynasty (seventh to tenth century AD), and a large, impressive Six
Dynasties' bronze drum. There are also swords, vessels, bird figures
and decorative items, but the most remarkable exhibit here is a
unique group of Nestorian bronze crosses, relics of the Yuan Dynasty
(1271–1368 AD) from the Ordos region of northern China. There are
966 crosses in all, each just a few centimetres across and every one
different, though only a fraction of the collection is displayed here.
The bronzes were decorations for a heretic Christian group, which
had survived in central and east Asia since the fifth century AD, and
most are cruciform in shape, though a few are bird-shaped (also a
Christian symbol), star-shaped or circular, or use a swastika pattern.
Each has a flat back and a fixed loop, designed to be attached to a
leather thong and probably worn as a pendant.

Upstairs on the **second floor** is the ceramics collection, from
Neolithic pottery right through the Dynasties. Fine pieces here
include the three-coloured, glazed Tang pottery – dishes, jars, even
an arm rest and head rest. There's white ceramic ware from the Sui
to the Song Dynasties, too (like the delicate spittoons); a coloured
Tang camel, with arched neck; and Song Dynasty ceramic pillows,
one round and one rectangular and decorated with black and white
line drawings. More colourful are the polychromatic Ming Dynasty
bowls and dishes, displaying rich blues, greens and reds. Outside
China, the museum takes in ceramics from Vietnam, Thailand and
Korea as well, while contemporary work is represented by early
twentieth-century Buddhist monk figurines.

From the University to Lu Pan Temple

From the museum, you can walk up into the car park and through
the grounds of the **University of Hong Kong**, whose buildings have

stood here since its foundation in 1912, when it had less than a hundred students (today it has 8000, in 9 faculties). Architecturally, it's less than gripping, though you might as well walk around to Loke Yew Hall on your left, inside which some quiet cloisters planted with high palm trees make for a bit of a break from the traffic outside.

Follow the road through the grounds, cross Pokfulam Road by the footbridge and then walk up the right-hand side of Pokfulam Road (you'll have to dodge under a subway initially). A few hundred metres up, after no. 93, a flight of steps leads down on the right to a terrace overlooking the elaborate, multicoloured roof carvings of figures and dragons on top of the **Lu Pan Temple**. It's the only temple in Hong Kong dedicated to Lu Pan, the "Master Builder", blessed with miraculous powers with which (according to legend) he repaired the Pillars of Heaven and made carved birds which could float in the air. He's commemorated every year on the thirteenth day of the sixth moon (see "Festivals", p.283), when building and construction workers take some time off to have a feast and make offerings to him in the temple here. At most other times of the year it's dark and empty inside, but take a look at the interesting carvings on either side of the door and above the two internal doors.

From the temple's terrace, steps continue down and turn into a wide, stepped path, Li Po Lung Path, which descends to Belcher's Street, at which point you're in Kennedy Town.

Kennedy Town

Most people come out to **KENNEDY TOWN** for a ride on the tram, and then catch the first one back again to Central, which certainly gives you good enough views of the moored junks and warehouses. But it doesn't begin to give you the real flavour of the place, which is a sort of down-at-heel Sheung Wan, supporting a fascinating series of sea- and market-related businesses. Much of the district (named after Sir Arthur Kennedy, Governor from 1872–77) is built on reclaimed land, piled high with decrepit tenements, the streets busy with traders and jammed traffic. Since the mid-nineteenth century, it's seen its goods arrive and leave by sea, at a curved harbour that still retains its working edge, though like so many areas of the island's north coast it's threatened by planned land reclamation.

If you've walked down from the University, make for the **tram terminus**, which is away to your left at the end of Catchick Street. Here, where the trams turn round before heading back to Central, is the **Kennedy Town Wholesale Market**, the warehouses in the vicinity constantly busy between dawn and noon – one filled with coconuts, another occupied by men sorting and boxing fresh clams. The waterfront strip a couple of blocks down is known as the **Praya**, a Portuguese word (used more commonly in Macau) that's evidence of the once-strong Portuguese influence in the whole of the South

China Sea. The Praya is lined with ships unloading by crane into the waterfront **godowns** (warehouses), and there are scores of junks moored offshore, painted in traditional reds and greens. The tram runs back along part of the Praya, but before you go take a walk through the small streets back from the shore. One of them, **North Street**, has a lively food market, and everywhere there are loads of basic restaurants and cafés where you can get a cheap bowl of noodles or a plate of roast meat with rice.

Victoria Peak

HONG KONG ISLAND

As one of Hong Kong's main attractions, you have to visit **VICTORIA PEAK** (or simply "The Peak") sooner or later, and since you're going up primarily for the views, make sure you do so on a clear day. It's a fine ride up, by bus or tram, and the little network of paths and gardens at the top provides one of the world's most spectacular cityscapes – little wonder that this is *the* place to live in the territory, and has been since the mid-nineteenth century.

Yet even on the murkiest days The Peak is worth a journey. It's cooler up here, there's badly needed foliage and birdlife to immerse yourself in, and a series of paths gives you a choice of quiet, shady walks – both around The Peak and away from it. Bring a picnic and it easily beats struggling through the crowds below.

The Peak

The 550-metre heights of Victoria Peak give you the only perspective that matters in Hong Kong – down to the outlying islands, the towers of Mid-Levels and Central and the magnificent harbour that frames the island. It didn't take long for the new British arrivals to flee the malarial lower regions of Hong Kong Island and set up cool summer homes here. The first path up to The Peak, as everyone soon learned to call it, was made in 1859 and within twenty years it was a popular retreat from the summer diseases and heat below. Access was difficult at first, by sedan chair only, something that ensured it would remain the preserve of the colony's wealthy elite; and it originally had just the cool air to recommend it, since the bare rock was only gradually transformed by the planting of trees and shrubs. Things changed in 1888 with the opening of the Peak Tram, and the first road connection was made in 1924, since which time the territory's power brokers and administrators have settled it properly with permanent houses – and latterly, apartment buildings – that rival each other in terms of position, views and phenomenal rentable value. Along the racist lines of other British colonial haunts elsewhere in the world, the Chinese weren't allowed on The Peak, unless it was to carry up overweight Europeans and supplies on their backs, and it didn't see its first Chinese-owned house until well into modern times. Now, of course, money is the only qualification necessary for residence here. Among the super-rich currently maintaining houses up here are Martin Lee, barrister and leader of the Democratic Party; the chairman and deputy chairman of the Hongkong bank; members of the Hotung family, the first Chinese people to live on The Peak; and various Consul-Generals, businessmen and assorted celebrities. There are also official residences for Hong Kong's Chief Secretary, Attorney General and Chief Justice, and the Commander of the British forces – all of which will have new Chinese residents in the years to come.

Getting there: the Peak Tram and other routes

Since 1888, the **Peak Tram** – actually a funicular railway – has been transporting passengers from a terminal close to St John's Cathedral to the end of the line at Victoria Gap, close on a 1400-metre-long ride up to around 400m above sea level. It's an extraordinary sensation, the 27-degree gradient providing an odd perspective of the tall buildings of Central and Mid-Levels, which appear to lean in on the tram as it makes its speedy journey. The terminals at either end have been renovated over the years, and in 1989 there was a complete overhaul of the tram system itself, replacing the old cars with computer-controlled ones and increasing their capacity. Fundamentally, though, there's been little change in its operation: it's still the same route that was followed in the late nineteenth century and it's still reputed to be the safest form of transport in the world. There's never been an accident yet, and the track brakes fitted to the wheels can stop the tram on the steepest part of the system within six metres.

Most tourists take the tram right to the top, which disguises the fact that for the whole of its life it's been primarily a commuter system. There are four intermediate stops at which you can flag the tram down – at Kennedy, Macdonnell, May and Barker roads – but unless you've been up before and have time to explore on the way, stick with the journey, since the views are remarkable.

Catch the tram from the **Lower Peak Tram Terminal**, in Garden Road, just up from Citibank Plaza in Central. It runs daily from 7am to midnight, every ten to fifteen minutes, and **tickets** cost $21 return (under 12s, $7) and $14 one-way (under 12s, $4). If you've just come from the Star Ferry, rather than walk you can head over to the City Hall car park and catch the **free shuttle bus** from there to the Lower Terminal; it runs daily, every twenty minutes from around 9am to 7pm. Be warned that on Sundays and public holidays the queues at the terminal can be maddening: get there early.

You can also reach Victoria Gap by **bus**, a route worth considering in its own right, whatever the queues are like for the tram. Bus #15 runs from the Central Bus Terminal, underneath Exchange Square (every 15–30min; 6.15am–11pm), a splendid ride up the switchback road to The Peak and offering arguably even more spectacular views than those from the tram; it costs around half as much too, though count on the journey taking at least half an hour. The other service is the #1 minibus from the City Hall car park (Edinburgh Place), a slightly quicker bus ride, though a bit pricier. You can do the trip by **taxi** as well, though this costs around $60 from the Star Ferry.

Walks around The Peak

The trams pull up at the terminal in **Peak Tower**, which has a viewing point and various other facilities designed to delay you. There are more splendid views across the road from the upper terrace of the

Peak Galleria, a fancy complex with a synchronized perfoming fountain outside and high-class stores and two restaurants with views inside; buses and taxis stop at the ranks in the Galleria basement.

The first thing to know is that you're not yet at the top of The Peak itself. Three roads pan out from the tower, one of which, Mount Austin Road, leads up to the landscaped Victoria Peak Garden – all that remains of the old Governor's residence here which was destroyed by the Japanese during their occupation of the territory in World War II. It's a stiff climb, but is rewarded by more of those views that leave your stomach somewhere in Central.

Nearly everyone makes the circuit of The Peak, a circular walk that takes around an hour depending on how many times you stop for photo calls. Opposite Peak Tower, a noticeboard details the various possible walks: basically, you follow the green arrows up to Victoria Peak Garden, the blue arrows if you want to follow Old Peak Road down to May Road tram station, and the yellow arrows for the Harlech and Lugard Roads walk.

Start at Harlech Road and you'll get the very best views at the end. It's a shaded path for most of the route, barely a road at all, and you'll be accompanied by birdsong and cricket noises as you go: other wildlife is less conspicuous, certainly the mythical monkeys that are said to frequent the trees, but you might catch sight of the odd alarmed snake. First views are of Aberdeen and Lamma, and as you turn later into Lugard Road, eventually Stonecutter's Island, Kowloon and Central come into sight – with magnificent views of the latter especially, just before you regain the Peak Tower. It's a panorama that is difficult to tire of, and if you can manage it, come up again at night when the lights of Hong Kong transform the city into a glittering box of tricks, the lit roads snaking through the buildings and Kowloon glinting as gold in the distance.

The Cafe Deco Bar and Grill, *in Peak Galleria, is the spot for a coffee or meal, while* Peak Café, *opposite Peak Tower, is also a good place for lunch; see p.253 and p.254 for reviews.*

Walks from The Peak

More adventurous types can make one of several walks from The Peak which will take you down to both sides of the island in steep scrambles. Each one won't take more than a couple of hours, but you'll need to carry some water if you're going to tackle them during the heat of the day, as there are no facilities en route.

Head down Harlech Road from the Peak Tower and after about five minutes a signposted path runs down to Pok Fu Lam Reservoir, a couple of kilometres away to the south and a decent target for picnics and barbecues. You can reach the same place by way of Pok Fu Lam Reservoir Road, which starts close to the car park. Either way, once you're there, the path runs past the reservoir and joins the main Pok Fu Lam Road – from where you can catch any of several buses back to Central.

You could also do this walk and then catch a bus in the other direction, on to Aberdeen, but it's more fun to walk there direct from The Peak. To do this, follow Peel Rise (down, and then off, Peak Road) for around an hour, a lovely shaded – and signposted – walk down the valley, passing an immense cemetery on the way into Aberdeen. Huge swathes of graves are strung across the terraces, which are cut into the hillside above the town, and from here there are great views of the town's harbour.

Finally, if you follow Harlech Road to just past the junction with Lugard Road, **Hatton Road** makes a steep descent down to the streets above the **University of Hong Kong**, one possible approach to Kennedy Town (see "West to Kennedy Town" in the previous section) or Mid-Levels (see below).

HONG KONG ISLAND

Mid-Levels

The area halfway up The Peak, back from the flat strip around the harbour, is known – reasonably enough – as **MID-LEVELS**. Although a notch or two down the social scale from The Peak, it retains a definite cachet. A forest of swanky apartment buildings and the odd grand house line the leafy narrow roads which run across the hillside, and though Mid-Levels is only a short, steep climb from the crowded streets of Western, there's a world of difference in atmosphere in this mostly dull, if affluent, neighbourhood.

Easiest access to the area is by the **Central–Mid-Levels Escalator Link**, an eight-hundred-metre-long series of elevated walkways, escalators and travelators which cuts up the hillside directly above the streets. The starting point is Central Market (at the footbridge across Queen's Road, at the corner of Jubilee Street), from where it heads through Cochrane Street, Hollywood Road and Robinson Road to Conduit Road. It cost over HK$200 million, and is capable of carrying thirty thousand people a day on a one-way system, which changes direction during the day depending on the flow of passengers: uphill from 10.20am to 11pm, downhill from 6am to 10am. All told, it's a twenty-minute ride from bottom to top, passing very close to the attractions outlined below, though it's rather more impressive in conception than being of any great use. You get the feeling, as with so many structures in Hong Kong, that it was built simply because it was possible to do so.

Caine Road to Robinson Road

Mid-Levels begins just above **Caine Road**, which leads past the Roman Catholic Cathedral (p.77) to Shelley Street, a left turn up which – at no. 30 – is the **Jamia Mosque**, or Shelley Street Mosque, an important place of worship for the territory's fifty thousand Muslims. A mosque has stood on this site since the 1850s, though this building dates from 1915, a pale green structure, set in its own quiet, raised courtyard above the surrounding terraces. The cool interior isn't always open, but the courtyard behind should be accessible, flanked by three-storeyed houses with wooden, railed balconies strung across with drying washing. The Mosque and Islamic Society accounts are pinned to the doors, enabling the faithful to see how much has been spent on maintaining the hearse and sending the Imam on overseas trips.

This part of Mid-Levels is very peaceful, with plenty of incidental interest in the peeling residential terraces around. One of the terraces off the other side of Shelley Street is **Rednaxela Terrace**, an unlikely name even for Hong Kong until you reverse the letters – actually a misspelling of Alexandra and named after the wife of King Edward VII, Queen Victoria's son.

Go up Shelley Street to the top and follow the other streets around and you'll come out on busy **Robinson Road** with its prestigious apartment buildings. Head west along here and at no. 70 a driveway leads down to the **Ohel Leah Synagogue**, finished in 1902, the territory's only synagogue. The name means "Tent of Leah" and it was built by the wealthy Sassoon family in memory of their mother. It lurks in its own leafy hollow below the main road and there should be a door open into the quiet, oak-carved interior if you want to take a look.

Wan Chai Gap

HONG KONG ISLAND

The other hillside section of town, east of The Peak, is a better bet than Mid-Levels for an extended stroll: the tree-planted paths leading to **WAN CHAI GAP** offer some fine views and a couple of rather peculiar points of interest. As the approach to the walk is by the #15 bus, it's a tour you can make on your way back from The Peak if you wish.

Along Bowen Road

Get off the #15 bus on Stubbs Road at the stop closest to the *Highcliff Apartments* and *Monte Rosa*, two apartment buildings you can't miss if you're watching out for them. Steps opposite the apartments lead down to **Bowen Road**, which runs west above the city, right the way back to the Peak Tram line.

Just down from Stubbs Road, a red-railed path runs up to the right to an **Earth God shrine**, a painted red image on the rock below the road, fronted by a neat altar where there are usually incense sticks burning and small food offerings lying about. Protectors of the local community, Earth Gods have been worshipped for centuries on the mainland; in Hong Kong you still find them tucked into street corners and against buildings, but this is easily the most spectacularly sited, with views falling away over the Happy Valley racecourse below and the gleaming, teeming tower blocks beyond.

Wan Chai Gap

Keep on shaded Bowen Road – a marvellous walk at rooftop level – and after about fifteen minutes the so-called **Lover's Stone Garden** is home to more shrines, a steep landscaped area through which steps lead up past a motley succession of red-painted images, tinfoil windmills (representing a change in luck), burning incense sticks and porcelain religious figures. At the top is the **Yan Yuen Sek**, "Lover's Rock", a nine-metre-high rock pointing into the sky from the top of the bluff. It's one of several focuses of the Maiden's Festival, held in mid-August, and since the nineteenth century unmarried women, wives and widows have been climbing up here to pray for husbands and sons.

Beyond the garden, passing various other small shrines along the way, it's about another ten minutes to the junction with **Wan Chai Gap Road**, where a sharp right leads down into Wan Chai itself, past the Pak Tai Temple (p.97). The left turn heads back up to Stubbs Road to Wan Chai Gap proper, and the Police Museum.

The Police Museum

The #15 bus from Central Bus Terminal stops close to the Police Museum, at the junction of Stubbs Road and Peak Road.

Back up to Stubbs Road, a signpost points you to the **Police Museum** (Tues 2–5pm, Wed–Sun 9am–5pm; free), housed in the old Wan Chai Gap Police Station, 100m up Coombe Road at no. 27, on the hill to the right behind the children's playground. One room charts the history of the Royal Hong Kong Police Force, formed officially in 1844, though there was a volunteer force as early as the initial 1841 landing under the command of Captain William Caine, who was in charge of 32 ex-soldiers. The exhibition here displays lots of old photos, uniforms and guns, as well as police statements, seized counterfeit cash and a tiger's head (a beast shot in Sheung Shui in 1915). Another room displays every kind of drug you've ever heard of and shows you exactly how to smuggle them – hollowed-out bibles and bras and girdles stuffed with heroin are just some of the more obvious methods. There's also a mock-up of a heroin factory, and there's a Triad room, complete with ceremonial uniforms and some very offensive weapons retrieved by the police.

Back on Peak Road, you can hang around for the #15 bus up to The Peak, or follow Wan Chai Gap Road all the way down into Wan Chai. Coombe Road itself climbs on to **Magazine Gap**, another of the hillside passes, from where – if you've got a decent map and lots of stamina – you can eventually strike The Peak from another direction.

Wan Chai

HONG KONG ISLAND

East of Central, long, parallel roads run all the way to Causeway Bay, cutting straight through **WAN CHAI**, a district noted for its bars, restaurants and nightlife. Wan Chai first came to prominence as a red-light district in the 1940s, though its real heyday was twenty years later when American soldiers and sailors ran amok in its bars and clubs while on R&R ("rest and recreation") from the wars in Korea and Vietnam. Richard Mason immortalized the area in his novel, *The World of Suzie Wong*, later made into a fairly bad film, whose eponymous heroine was a Wan Chai prostitute. (Oddly, when the film was made in 1960, Wan Chai itself wasn't deemed to be properly photogenically sleazy, filming taking place around Hollywood Road instead.)

Set against those times, present-day Wan Chai is fairly tame, though its eastern stretch is still a decent venue for a night out – packed with places to eat and drink, from *dai pai dongs* on the street corners to restaurants and bars; full of local colour during the day and vibrant at night. However, the westernmost part of Wan Chai, beyond Queensway, belies its traditional, rather seedy good-time image. As the rents have increased in Central, the office blocks and businesses have moved into the area, giving the local yuppies the chance to tag it "East Central". It's a development that has acquired its own momentum since the opening of the enormous **Convention and Exhibition Centre** in 1988; the latest, spectacular addition is **Central Plaza**, currently Asia's tallest building (though soon to be eclipsed by Kuala Lumpur's latest skyscraper).

Walking through Wan Chai you can follow one of three parallel main roads – Lockhart Road, Jaffe Road or Hennessy Road – all of which reach down to Causeway Bay. If you're going by **tram**, note that it detours down Johnston Road instead, which is fine for the Pak Tai Temple and Queen's Road East, but not so handy if you're aiming for the Arts Centre, Convention and Exhibition Centre or the waterfront – for these, take the **#18 bus** (not Sun) from Connaught Road Central or the **Star Ferry** from Tsim Sha Tsui to Wan Chai Ferry Pier.

The tram from Central to Causeway Bay, via Wan Chai, follows this route: Des Voeux Rd, Queensway, Johnston Rd, Hennessy Rd, Yee Wo St.

The Arts Centre and Academy for Performing Arts

Since 1976 much of Hong Kong's arts and drama has been centred on the fifteen-storey **Hong Kong Arts Centre** at 2 Harbour Road, in Wan Chai. Despite the competition posed by the Cultural Centre in Tsim Sha Tsui (see p.123), it's still a leading venue for drama, film and various cultural events, and also contains the fifth-floor *Pao Sui Loong Galleries* (daily 10am–8pm; free), which maintain temporary exhibition space for contemporary art: local and international painting, photography and sculpture. It's always worth dropping in to see what's on, especially as you can take advantage of the Arts Centre's coffee shop or restaurant, which both feature views of the harbour.

Backtracking a little, to Gloucester Road, the building with the triangular windows houses the **Academy for Performing Arts** (APA). Here the majority of the productions are performed by the students themselves – local works to Shakespeare – though you'll also come across visiting shows, as well as modern and classical music and dance. Other than performances, the facilities are only

For events and box office details for the Arts Centre and Academy for Performing Arts, see pp.275–276.

open to the students, though once a year (usually May or June) an open day allows visitors to tour the wardrobe rooms, library and backstage areas.

The Convention and Exhibition Centre and around

Massive development over recent years has changed the Wan Chai harbour front. Enormous buildings loom over the water, grandest of all the gigantic **Convention and Exhibition Centre**, the largest of its kind in Asia, flanked by landscaped gardens. Remarkably, it's already outgrown its dimensions and land reclamation here will facilitate the adding of new wings to the centre. Other record-breaking claims include the building's use of the world's largest glass curtain wall – the centre's first five floors are open to view and cross-hatched by escalators which grant superb harbour views. The centre is topped by two luxury hotels, the ultra-flash *Grand Hyatt* and *New World Harbour View*, aimed firmly at the expense-account businesspeople here to wheel and deal at the centre's various trade exhibitions.

The Wan Chai Ferry Pier is across from the Convention and Exhibition Centre, for services to Tsim Sha Tsui (7.30am–11pm) or Hung Hom (6.20am–10pm)

Further east, there's the **China Resources Building**, over Harbour Road, worth walking through for its department store in the Low Block, which displays a grand mixture of Chinese arts and crafts. A little enclosed Chinese garden sits in the middle of the block, while the adjacent building, the Causeway Centre, has some interest in its **Museum of Chinese Historical Relics** (1st Floor, 28 Harbour Rd; Mon–Sat 10am–6pm, Sun 1–6pm; free), with changing exhibitions of Chinese painting and handicrafts, and usually plenty of rare historical pieces on display.

Central Plaza

With the completion of **Central Plaza** in October 1992, Hong Kong acquired the latest high-tech, high-profile addition to its already cluttered skyline. Sited across from the Convention and Exhibition Centre, at 18 Harbour Road, it pipped Central's Bank of China Tower by topping out at 78 storeys, to become Asia's tallest building and – for now at least – the fourth tallest building in the world. It's built of reinforced concrete (which, almost interestingly, makes it the world's tallest reinforced concrete building), though more impressive is its height – 374 metres to the top of its mast – and its extraordinary design and exterior cladding. Triangular in shape, it's topped by a glass pyramid from which a 64-metre mast protrudes: the locals, always quick to debunk a new building, promptly dubbed it "The Big Syringe". As if this wasn't distinctive enough, the American design team swathed the reflective glass curtain walls with luminous neon panels, while the glass pyramid shoots out computer-controlled light. At night, there's no question that Central Plaza is the dominant feature of the skyline, lit up like a beacon from almost anywhere you care to look.

You can go inside the split-level, thirty-metre-high lobby, whose marble and sandstone interior is enlivened by soaring palm trees; and from here, you're connected to the elevated walkways that run deep into Wan Chai and back to Central. To get back to Central by bus, take the #10A, #20, #21 or #104, which run from Gloucester Road, or alternatively walk back around to the water to the Wan Chai Ferry Pier, for ferry services to Tsim Sha Tsui and to Hung Hom.

Along Lockhart Road

If Wan Chai has a main street it's **Lockhart Road**, which runs west–east through the district and finishes up in Causeway Bay. For many, Lockhart Road epitomizes Wan Chai. The street's heady days as a thriving red-light district, throbbing with US marines on leave, are now behind it, but although the bite has gone out of Lockhart Road, that's not to say that the area has become gentrified, or anything approaching it. Lots of the bars and clubs still make a living from fleecing tourists, and a walk down the street at night is a fairly lively experience even now. Most of the **pubs and clubs** between Luard Road and Fleming Road are rowdy until the small hours, and it's easier to get a late meal in the hundreds of restaurants along and around Lockhart Road than anywhere else in Hong Kong. If there's a merchant or naval fleet in town, Wan Chai occasionally echoes with the sounds of yesteryear, though the most pleasant experience is to stroll down here on Sunday. This is a day off for the Filipina house-maids all over the territory, and after meeting in Central, many head for Wan Chai, where the bars and clubs around Lockhart Road open their doors early for some wild singing and dancing.

Queen's Road East and around

There's a more sustained pocket of interest in Wan Chai's southern streets, particularly around **Queen's Road East**, which you can reach from Central on buses #6, #260 or #15: get off at **Wan Chai Market**, another of the island's indoor municipal meat, fish, fruit and veg markets.

The Pak Tai Temple

From the market, Stone Nullah Lane ("nullah" is a ravine) leads uphill; off to the left, down Lung On Street, is the **Pak Tai Temple**, decorated with handmade, colourful roof pottery. The temple is dedicated to Pak Tai, the Military Protector and Emperor of the North, whose task it is to maintain harmony on earth, and he's represented inside the main hall by a tall, seventeenth-century copper statue, seated on a throne facing the door. Behind, four figures of warriors and scholars guard the ebony-faced and bearded god, who is resplendent in an embroidered jacket with a tiger-face motif. A room off to the left, as you leave the main hall, is one to linger in. Here you'll find

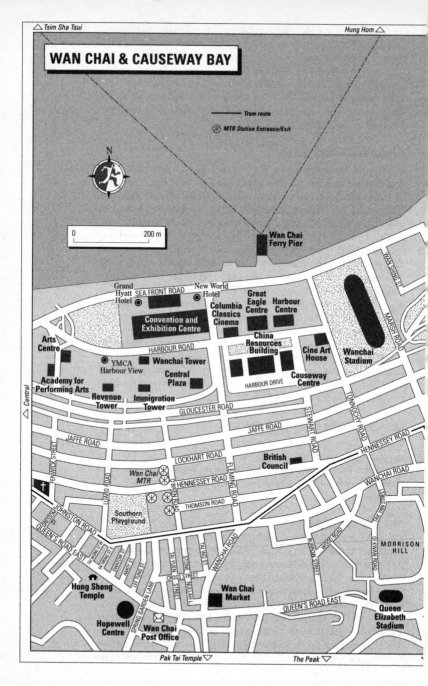

WAN CHAI & CAUSEWAY BAY

Tram route

MTR Station Entrance/Exit

N

0   200 m

Wan Chai Ferry Pier

Grand Hyatt Hotel

SEA FRONT ROAD

New World Hotel

Great Eagle Centre

Harbour Centre

Columbia Classics Cinema

Convention and Exhibition Centre

China Resources Building

Cine Art House

Wanchai Stadium

Arts Centre

HARBOUR ROAD

YMCA Harbour View

Wanchai Tower

Central Plaza

Causeway Centre

HARBOUR DRIVE

Academy for Performing Arts

Revenue Tower

Immigration Tower

GLOUCESTER ROAD

JAFFE ROAD

JAFFE ROAD

LOCKHART ROAD

British Council

HENNESSEY ROAD

STEWART ROAD

TONNOCHY ROAD

HENNESSEY ROAD

WANCHAT ROAD

Wan Chai MTR

O'BRIEN ROAD

THOMSON ROAD

Southorn Playground

FENWICK STREET

WARD ROAD

FLEMING ROAD

JOHNSTON ROAD

QUEEN'S ROAD EAST

BURROW STREET

WOOD ROAD

OI KWAN ROAD

MORRISON HILL

TAK HING STREET

Hung Sheng Temple

TAI WONG ST W

SWATOW ST

AMOY ST

LEE TUNG ST

SPRING GARDEN LANE

CROSS STREET

TAI YUEN STREET

STONE NULLAH

WANCHAI ROAD

Wan Chai Market

QUEEN'S ROAD EAST

Queen Elizabeth Stadium

Hopewell Centre

Wan Chai Post Office

△ Tsim Sha Tsui

Hung Hom △

◁ Central

Pak Tai Temple ▽

The Peak ▽

Hundred-Year-Old Eggs

In every Hong Kong market you can buy a variety of fresh eggs – from ducks, quails, pigeons and geese, as well as chickens – which are inspected under a light by the traders for their freshness. Most also contain a massive range of preserved eggs, including the so-called "hundred-year-old eggs" which have a complicated production process. Duck eggs are covered with a thick mixture of lime, ash and tea leaves, soaked for a month and then wrapped in ash and rice husks for around six months, when they are peeled and eaten with pickled ginger. They're an acquired taste: green and black inside, with a strong odour, they have a jelly-like consistency and a rich yolk. Salted eggs, too, are produced, covered with a black paste made from salt and burnt rice – in street markets you'll see men plunging the eggs into murky vats of the paste and stirring slowly. These eggs are Cantonese delicacies, which you can try in plenty of restaurants as an appetizer. Failing that, buy a moon cake during the Mid-Autumn Festival (see "Festivals", p.283), which uses the preserved yolk as a filling.

---

craftsmen practising an age-old Chinese art, making **burial offerings** from paper and bamboo, delicate works of art that are burned in order to prepare and equip the deceased for the afterlife. Around the walls hang half-finished and finished items: a car, an apartment building, houses, money, furniture and aeroplanes, all painted and coloured. From the temple, you can continue up to the main Kennedy Road, and take a left turn up Wan Chai Gap Road, to join the walk described under "Wan Chai Gap", above.

From Wan Chai Post Office to Johnston Road

Queen's Road East leads back towards Central, a route that traces the nineteenth-century shoreline. It's a good street for browsing with lots of the shops devoted to selling **rattanware** products, a tropical cane or palm used extensively here for making furniture. It's all fairly cheap, and often very elaborate. You'll soon pass the old, white-washed front of the **Wan Chai Post Office**, opened in 1915 and positively ancient by Hong Kong standards, before reaching the circular **Hopewell Centre**, once Hong Kong's tallest building; though it's dwarfed by more recent constructions, it's still worth taking the lift to the sixtieth floor, where there's a revolving *dim sum* restaurant.

A hundred metres or so further along, the **Hung Sheng Temple** at no. 131 is built right into the rocks that bear down upon Queen's Road East at this point, with boulders dotted among the altars inside. A long, narrow temple, with the room on the far right reserved for fortune tellers and palm readers, it started life in the mid-nineteenth century as a shrine by the sea: the scholar Hung Sheng is a patron saint of fishermen because of his reputed skill in forecasting the weather.

Opposite the temple, over the main road, **Tai Wong Street West** runs through to Johnston Road, the bottom half of the alley filled with bird cages, the air thick with the calls of songbirds, budgies and their dinner – crickets tied up in little bags. It's not as big as Mongkok bird market (p.136), but if you haven't seen one before, take a slow stroll through. A couple of streets further up is **Gresson Street**, which has a produce market where you can buy freshly peeled bamboo shoots and **preserved eggs** (see the box below) among the more usual items, while over the road at the junction of Johnston Road and Fenwick Street, the red-brick **Chinese Methodist Church** nods towards the Orient with a rooftop pagoda. Johnston Road itself is a handy place to finish up, because you can catch the tram from here, either back to Central or on to Causeway Bay.

Causeway Bay

HONG KONG ISLAND

Completing the short list of Hong Kong Island's major tourist destinations, everyone spends half a day or so in **CAUSEWAY BAY**, one of the original areas of settlement in the mid-nineteenth century. It's a small district, but it manages to pack in more shops and businesses than just about anywhere else in the territory. Indeed, shopping – or at least window-shopping – is the only real reason to come, although once here there are a few low-key attractions which help pad out your day, and the rattling tram ride from Central is pleasant enough to warrant the journey in the first place.

The Bay and the Noon Day Gun

Before land reclamation, Causeway Bay was just that – a large, natural bay, known as *Tung Lo Wan* in Chinese, that stretched back into what's now Victoria Park and the surrounding streets. The British settled here in the 1840s, erecting warehouses along the waterfront and trading from an area they called East Point. Filled in since the 1950s, all that's left of the bay is the **typhoon shelter**, with its massed ranks of junks and yachts, and **Kellet Island**, now a thumb of land connected to the mainland and harbouring the *Hong Kong Yacht Club*. Development around here really got under way with the opening of the two-kilometre-long **Cross-Harbour Tunnel** in the early 1970s, which runs under Kellet Island to Kowloon. With the greater access that this brought (though massive congestion at peak hours threatens its benefit these days), hotels, shops and department stores moved in, effectively making Causeway Bay a

---

Tram Routes from Causeway Bay

From Causeway Bay to Central: Yee Wo St, Hennessy Rd, Johnston Rd Queensway, Des Voeux Rd.

From Causeway Bay to Happy Valley: Percival St, Wong Nai Chung Rd, Morrison Hill Rd, Ting Lok Lane, Hennessy Rd.

From Causeway Bay to Shau Kei Wan: Causeway Rd, King's Rd, Shau Kei Wan Rd.

---

self-perpetuating tourist ghetto. White high-rises now girdle the typhoon shelter, but if it's not the prettiest of the territory's harbour scenes, there's something stirring about the hundreds of masts and bobbing boats that carpet the water.

In front of one of the modern hotels, the **Excelsior** on Gloucester Road, stands one of Hong Kong's most well-known monuments, the **Noon Day Gun**, made famous by one of Noel Coward's better lyrics:

> *In Hong Kong*
> *They strike a gong*
> *And fire off a noonday gun*
> *To reprimand each inmate*
> *Who's in late*
> (from *Mad Dogs and Englishmen*)

Apart from a few local street names, this is the only relic of the influence that the nineteenth-century trading establishments wielded in Causeway Bay, in particular *Jardine, Matheson & Co*, which had its headquarters here. The story is suitably vague, as all legends should be, but it's said that the small ship's gun was fired by a Jardine employee to salute one of the company's ships, an action which so outraged the Governor – whose traditional prerogative it was to fire off salutes – that he ordered it to be fired every day at noon for evermore. Some of the short harbour cruises (see "Organized Tours", p.62) take in the daily noon firing of the gun, and there's a more elaborate ceremony every New Year's Eve, when impeccably dressed Jardine's managers fire the thing off at midnight. The whole story is recorded on a plaque by the gun, which you reach by crossing Gloucester Road: the easiest way is to go through the underground *Wilson* car park on Gloucester Road, next to the *Excelsior*; a tunnel runs under the road and emerges right next to the gun. After all the fuss in print, though, it's simply a rather tiresome gun in a railed-off garden.

Proposed land reclamation means that the Causeway Bay typhoon shelter is slated for redevelopment; the junks and sampans won't be there much longer.

From the gun, you can walk further up the tatty promenade towards Victoria Park, where you can negotiate the hire of a **sampan** with the women from the typhoon shelter who'll be hanging about. Settle on a price and you'll be paddled into the shelter, whereupon other sampans will appear to sell you fresh seafood and produce, which is cooked in front of you and washed down with beer bought from other boats – not a bad way to spend an evening, though hardly the bohemian night out it once was. You'll need to bargain every step of the way.

Victoria Park

The eastern edge of Causeway Bay is marked by the large, green expanse of **Victoria Park**, one of the few decent open-air spaces in this congested city. Built on reclaimed land, it's busy all day, from the crack-of-dawn *tai chi* practitioners to the old men spending an hour or so strolling with their songbirds in little cages along the paths. There's a swimming pool and sports facilities here, too, and if you wander through you might catch a soccer match or something similar, while a couple of times a year the park hosts some lively festivals – a flower market at Chinese New Year, and a lantern display for the Mid-Autumn Festival.

At the park's eastern corner, up Tin Hau Temple Road (by the Tin Hau MTR station), lies Causeway Bay's **Tin Hau Temple**, a couple of centuries old, sited on top of a little hill which once fronted the water. These days it's surrounded by tall apartment buildings, but the temple is one more indication of the area's strong, traditional links with the sea.

Shopping in Causeway Bay

Doing your shopping in Causeway Bay means splitting your time between two main sections. The grid of streets to the north, closest to Victoria Park, contains the modern shops and businesses, many of them owned by the Japanese who moved in here in the 1960s. There are large **Japanese department stores** on and around the main Yee Wo Street – *Mitsukoshi* in the Hennessy Centre, *Sogo* on Hennessy Road, *Daimaru* on Great George Street and *Matsuzakaya* on Paterson Street – stuffed with hi-tech, high-fashion articles, open late and normally full of big-spending customers. The other main store here is *China Products*, on Yee Wo Street, one of the biggest of the stores specializing in products from the PRC, another Aladdin's Cave of bargains. For designer clothes and shoes, visit **Vogue Alley**, a covered, Art-Nouveau-style mall with fountains running between Kingston Street and Gloucester Road.

For lunch, try the Sogo or Daimaru supermarkets, which have cheap takeaway sushi and sit-down Japanese snack bars; each store has a coffee shop, too. Or there's good dim sum at Maxim's Chinese Restaurant; see p.238 for a review.

The area **south** of Yee Wo Street is immediately different. It's the original Causeway Bay settlement and home to an interesting series of interconnected markets and shopping streets. **Jardine's Bazaar** and **Jardine's Crescent**, two narrow, parallel lanes off Yee Wo Street, have contained a street market since the earliest days of the colony (their names echoing the trading connection) and they remain great places to poke around: cheap clothes abound, while deeper in you'll find *dai pai dongs*, a noisy little market and all manner of traditional shops and stalls selling herbs and provisions. There are similar sights the further back into these streets you go: **Pennington Street**, **Irving Street**, **Fuk Hing Lane** and others all reward making a slow circle through them, perhaps stopping for some tea or to buy some herbal medicine.

Times Square and Lee Theatre Plaza

The most startling addition to the Causeway Bay shopping scene is the beige blockbuster of a building that is **Times Square**, at Matheson and Russell streets. It's a towering conceit, a vertical shopping mall supported by great marble trunks and featuring a cathedral window and outsize exterior video advertising screen. From the massive open-plan lobby, silver bullet elevators whizz up to the various themed shopping floors; levels nine to thirteen, *Food Forum*, are devoted to restaurants and bars, the best of them reviewed in Chapters 7 and 8; at ground level there's a cinema and access to Causeway Bay MTR station.

Times Square is paradigmatic of late twentieth-century Hong Kong architectural style, where space can only be gained by building upwards and distinction attained by unexpected design. There's another fine example nearby, at the end of Percival Street, where the architect of the **Lee Theatre Plaza** – faced with an awkward corner on which to build – obviously took New York's Flatiron Building as a starting-point. Up soars the steel, glass and marble tower of shops, offices and restaurants, presenting its sharp rib to the front – which is then chopped out above atrium level, leaving the building resembling a face without a nose.

Aw Boon Haw Gardens

The last stop in Causeway Bay is at the gross **Aw Boon Haw Gardens** (daily 9.30am–4pm; free), a landscaped nightmare also known as the "Tiger Balm Gardens" and which is another of Hong Kong's accredited "sights". It's not strictly in Causeway Bay, though you could easily walk here, up Tai Hang Road. Direct from Central Bus Terminal, the #11 bus takes about twenty minutes, stopping right outside the gardens by a row of souvenir stalls.

The person responsible for the gardens was Mr Aw Boon Haw, a millionaire who made his money by manufacturing *Tiger Balm* ointment (hence the gardens' other name), which you'll see on sale everywhere in Hong Kong and used for soothing aches and pains. Aw Boon Haw blew his cash in 1935 on this landscaped concoction of coloured statues from religious tales, pagodas, garish staircases, animals and grottos; there are bilingual signs on most explaining their significance. There's a good view from the top of the Tiger Pagoda (which alone cost a cool million dollars in the 1930s), but otherwise what charm the place had is entirely lost under the daily deluge of visitors. The only vaguely interesting part, the Haw Par Mansion at the gates, which the founder's family still owns, is closed to the public.

HONG KONG ISLAND

Happy Valley

Travel south on the branch tram line from Causeway Bay and you're soon in **HAPPY VALLEY** (or Pau Ma Tei in Cantonese). After Western district, which was soon discovered to be rife with malaria, Happy Valley was one of the earliest parts of the island to be settled, in the hope that it would be healthier and more sheltered. Plenty of houses were built before the "yellow mud stream" that gave Happy Valley its original Chinese name (Wong Nai Chung) appeared with a vengeance – the settlers had unknowingly built on a fever-ridden swamp. Everyone moved out, the land was drained and the flattest part turned into a racecourse in 1846, which survives and thrives famously today.

There's not a great deal to see in Happy Valley apart from the racecourse, though a walk up the main **Sing Woo Road** reveals a small market and plenty of good restaurants. The area is very much an expat haunt, many of whom live locally, which explains the preponderance of shoe shops and design galleries on Wong Nai Chung Road, quite apart from the **Craigengower Cricket Club** at the junction with Leighton Road. Ride on the top deck of the tram past here and you'll discover that there is, in fact, no cricket pitch inside the walls, crown-green bowling being the preferred sport.

Happy Valley Racecourse

The only legal gambling allowed in Hong Kong is on horseracing, and the **Happy Valley Racecourse** is the traditional centre of this multimillion-dollar business (though there's a second racecourse now, in Sha Tin in the New Territories). It's controlled by the (formerly Royal) Hong Kong Jockey Club, one of the colony's power bastions since its foundation in 1884, with a board of stewards made up of the leading lights of Hong Kong big business. A percentage of the profits go to social and charitable causes – you'll see Jockey Club schools and clinics all over the territory – and such is the passion for betting on horses in Hong Kong (or indeed betting on anything) that the money involved defies comprehension: the racing season pulls in over HK$45 billion. Jan Morris recounts how even the stabled horses have air-conditioned quarters and swimming pools: "Happy Valley on race day . . ." she maintains "is a bitter, brilliant, grasping place."

The Happy Valley tram terminus (for trams to Causeway Bay or back towards Wan Chai/Central) is at the back (southern end) of the racecourse, on Wong Nai Chung Road.

The season at Happy Valley runs from September to May and there are meetings on the synthetic surface twice a week, on Wednesday night and at the weekend. Entrance to the public enclosure is $10, and bilingual staff at the various information desks can help make some sense of the fairly intricate accumulator bets that Hong Kong specializes in. Or give the HKTA's **racing tour** a whirl. They'll take you there, feed you before the races, get you into the members' enclosure and hand out some racing tips: you need to be over 18, have been in Hong Kong for less than three weeks, and take your passport to any of the HKTA offices at least a day before the race.

You can book the racing tour at any of the HKTA offices; see p.46 for addresses. It costs around $500 per person.

The cemeteries

It's tempting to think that the series of **cemeteries** staggered up the valley on the west side of the racecourse is full of failed punters. In fact, they provide an interesting snapshot of the territory's ethnic and religious mix: starting from Queen's Road East and climbing up, the five mid-nineteenth-century cemeteries are officially Muslim, Catholic, Protestant Colonial (the largest, with a berth for Lord Napier, the first Chief Superintendent of Trade with China), Parsee and Jewish. For a quick look, the #15 bus (to The Peak from the Central Bus Terminal) runs past them, up Stubbs Road, though the best views are the virtually airborne ones from Bowen Road, the path that runs to Wan Chai Gap (see "Wan Chai Gap", p.93). If you want to explore them at closer quarters (most are open 8am–7pm), take the Happy Valley tram around Wong Nai Chung Road; there's a stop close to the Catholic and Colonial cemeteries, from where you can walk around to further entrances on Stubbs Road.

HONG KONG ISLAND

The South Side

Apart from The Peak, the other great escape from the built-up north side of Hong Kong Island is to the **south side**, a long, fragmented coastline from Aberdeen to Stanley punctured by bays and inlets. Unfortunately, everyone in Hong Kong escapes there, too, particularly at the weekend, but it's worth braving the crowded buses and roads for some of the territory's best **beaches** and a series of little villages which pre-date the arrival of the British in the mid-nineteenth century – though none of them are exactly traditional or isolated these days. Most have somewhere to eat and you needn't worry about getting stuck as the **buses** are all very regular, and run until late in the evening.

The quickest and most obvious trips are to **Aberdeen** and **Repulse Bay** in the west, and most will find time to move on to **Stanley**, too, which is probably the most interesting place to aim for if you've only got the time for one excursion. If you have children in tow, then **Ocean Park** – Hong Kong's biggest theme and adventure park – is a must.

Aberdeen

ABERDEEN was one of the few places on the island already settled when the British arrived in the 1840s, the bay here was used as a shelter for the indigenous local people – the Hoklos and Tankas who fished in the surrounding archipelago. It's still really the only other large town on the island, with around sixty thousand people, several hundred of them living as they've done for centuries, on sampans and junks tied up in the harbour (though they're gradually being moved into new housing estates). The British named the town that grew up here after their Colonial Secretary, the Earl of Aberdeen, but the Chinese name – *Heung Gong Tsai* – gives the better hint as to its water-based character: "Little Hong Kong", reflecting the attractions of its fine harbour.

The harbour and town

Arriving by bus, you'll either be dropped at the Bus Terminal or on Aberdeen Main Road, but it makes no difference since the central grid of streets is fairly small. It's best to make your way down to the **harbour** first, if you want to understand the importance of the water to the town. Cross the main road by the pedestrian footbridge to the long waterfront and you'll soon be accosted by women touting **sampan rides** through the typhoon shelter, a good way to take a closer look at the floating homes that still clog the water. A bit of bargaining should get you a twenty- or thirty-minute ride for around $50 a head. More sampans and ferries at the harbour take you to other nearby destinations: to Lamma Island (p.183) and the Po Toi group of islands (see below).

If you're especially interested, sampans also run across to the large island just offshore, **Ap Lei Chau** (Duck's Tongue Island) – there's also a connecting bridge – which is one of the main boat-and junk-building centres in the territory. Wandering around the yards is fascinating, particularly if you can find someone to tell you what's going on. The workshops here are mostly family-owned, the skills handed down through generations, with only minimal reliance on proper plans and drawings. To come here directly, take bus #90 from Central's Exchange Square.

Back in town, the small centre is worth a look around, over-touristed these days but with some interesting shops and businesses that can enliven a spare hour or so. At the junction of Aberdeen Old Main Street and Aberdeen Main Road, the **Hung Hsing Shrine** is dedicated to a local god who protects fishermen and oversees the weather. Towards the top of town, at the junction of Aberdeen Main Road and Aberdeen Reservoir Road, a hollow in the ground contains the more important **Tin Hau Temple**, built in 1851, with circular-cut doorways inside leading to the furnace rooms. From here, the energetic can continue up the main Aberdeen Reservoir Road, looking for a left turn, **Peel Rise**, which climbs up over the town to the stepped terraces of an immense **cemetery**, offering fine views of the harbour and Ap Lei Chau. The path continues ever upwards from the cemetery, eventually reaching The Peak, though this is really only a climb for those with their own oxygen tents.

Practicalities

It's around half an hour by **bus** to Aberdeen from Central: take the #7 from Central Piers (via Kennedy Town, getting off on Aberdeen Main Rd) or the #70 (via Aberdeen Tunnel, getting off at the end of the line) from the Central Bus Terminal; or bus #72 from Yee Wo Street in Causeway Bay. Aberdeen's **Bus Terminal** is off Wu Nam Street at its eastern end, close to the water.

There's plenty of choice if you want **something to eat** in Aberdeen. The traditional thing to do here is to take the free shuttle ferry from the harbour front across to the two **floating restaurants**, the *Jumbo* and the *Tai Pak*, which are moored in the yacht bays over to the east of the harbour; see p.241 for details. Or you can take the *kaido* across to **Lamma** and its seafood restaurants (p.186): the regular service stops in the early evening, but it's always easy to find a sampan to take you across and pick you up again after a couple of hours, something that shouldn't cost more than $120 for the boat. There are, of course, restaurants in Aberdeen town, too, though they're nothing special. For something more traditional, look out for the *Tse Kee*, a basic fishball noodle shop, where you can get a tasty and inexpensive bowl of food: it's at 82 Old Main Street (just up from the bus terminal) and open from 10.30am to 6pm.

The Po Toi Islands

Aberdeen harbour is the jumping-off point for a visit to the southerly **Po Toi Islands**, an hour's ferry ride away. Like all the minor outlying islands, their population is dwindling, but the main island, with its prehistoric rock carvings, is good for an isolated stroll and some secluded swimming. There's a small Tin Hau **temple** near the ferry pier at Tai Wan, and a few, simple seafood restaurants that only really see any business on a Sunday. Fans of John Le Carré will know that this island is where the denouement to his *The Honourable Schoolboy*, a thriller largely set in Hong Kong, takes place.

Ferries leave Aberdeen on Tuesday, Thursday and Saturday at 9am, but unfortunately they come straight back again and there's nowhere to stay on the island. Come instead on Sunday, when there are several departures, including return services to St Stephen's Beach near Stanley; phone ☎2554 4059 for more details.

Deep Water Bay and Ocean Park

East of Aberdeen, the road cuts across a small peninsula to **DEEP WATER BAY**, one of Hong Kong Island's better beaches, offering views of the cable cars strung across the Ocean Park headland; you can get there on bus #73 from Aberdeen or the #6A or #260 from Exchange Square in Central. Hong Kong suffered one of its periodic shark scares at Deep Water Bay in 1989, when two people were pulled out of the water with flesh wounds. Investigations revealed that they had actually been attacked by moray eels, which usually live among rocks and don't encroach upon sand beaches. The area was subsequently cleared of eels, some of them more than a metre long. It was, no doubt, all fairly unpleasant for the people attacked, but the signs erected on the beach at the time, "Danger: Eel Attack!", didn't quite have the fearful ring about them that was intended. *

Ocean Park

The adjacent peninsula is wholly taken up by **OCEAN PARK** (Mon–Sat 10am–6pm, Sun 9.30am–6pm; $150, under 11s half-price; ☎2555 3554), a thoroughly enjoyable open-air theme park, funfair and oceanarium which is adding new rides and attractions every year. It opened in 1977 and the massive complex is divided into three sections joined by a cable-car and outdoor escalator – big enough in fact to take up most of a day.

The **ticket** price seems steep but includes all the rides, shows and displays on offer. A couple of **warnings**, though: there's food on sale inside, but it's plastic and pricey (hot dogs, burgers and the like), so you might want to take your own picnic; and try to go early if you're determined to get your money's worth. It'll take a good

---

* The last real shark attack in Hong Kong was in the summer of 1993, when two people died from their injuries. Before that, in August 1979, an illegal immigrant from China made the dangerous mistake of trying to swim across Mirs Bay, in the northeast of the territory, to freedom: he never made it. In addition, in 1986 there was a barracuda attack on a surfboarder off Shek O beach, and in 1985 and 1986 several people were stung by Portuguese Men O'War at Clearwater Bay.

four hours to see all parts of the park, wait in line for a couple of rides and see the marine shows – with kids, and in the busy summer season, expect it to take longer, and expect to have to wait for all the popular rides. If you possibly can, avoid going on Sundays and public holidays.

The first section, the **Lowland** area, is a landscaped garden with greenhouses, a butterfly house, various parks, a theatre and a kiddies' adventure playground. It's also the departure point for about the scariest ride in the complex, the **cable-car**, which hoists you a kilometre-and-a-half up the mountainside, high above Deep Water Bay in a flimsy capsule, to the **Headland** section. Here, there's a mix of rides (including a truly frightening roller-coaster that travels at 80km per hour) and marine displays – a massive aquarium, a seal, sea lion and penguin sanctuary, and Ocean Theatre, where the performing sharks and whales are put through their paces a couple of times a day. Looming over the lot is the **Ocean Park Tower**, 200m above sea level, giving superb views from its viewing platform. After this, you can head down the other side to the **Tai Shue Wan** area, by way of the world's longest outdoor escalator. There are more fine views on the way down, more rides at the bottom, and access to **Middle Kingdom**, a Chinese theme park with pagodas, traditional crafts and all the associated entertainment, including Chinese opera performances.

Back at the main entrance to the Lowland site, you'll find a separate entrance for the adjacent **Water World** (April, May, Sept & Oct daily 10am–5pm; June 10am–10pm; July & Aug 9am–10pm; $70, children $45). This is a water-based fun park – slides and chutes – which gets incredibly packed in the summer, but is just the place to cool down after tramping around Ocean Park.

Bus Routes to Ocean Park

Unless otherwise shown, buses run every ten to fifteen minutes right up until around midnight, though check the Ocean Park opening times above.

From Aberdeen
#48, #70 and #73 from Aberdeen Main Rd run past the park.

From Admiralty MTR
Citybus to Ocean Park every 30min (8.40am–3.40pm). You can also buy an all-in-one bus and entrance ticket for around $160 (children half-price) on this route.

From Causeway Bay
#72 from Yee Wo St; get off just after emerging from Aberdeen Tunnel and follow the signs along

Ocean Park Rd; on Sun the bus stops right outside Ocean Park.

From Central Bus Terminal
#6A, #64, #70 or #260: get off just after emerging from Aberdeen Tunnel and follow the signs along Ocean Park Rd.

From Hong Kong-side Star Ferry/ Edinburgh Place
#6 minibus (daily except Sun and public holidays).

From Repulse Bay/Stanley
Bus #73 runs past the park en route to Aberdeen.

Repulse Bay

The next bay along, **REPULSE BAY**, has lost whatever colonial
attraction it once had, when the grand *Repulse Bay Hotel* stood at
its centre, hosting graceful tea dances and cocktail parties. The
hotel was torn down without ceremony in the 1980s (the only
surviving portion is the ludicrously expensive *Verandah* restaurant,
at 109 Repulse Bay Rd) and the hill behind the bay is now lined with
flash apartments contained with a high-rise curvilinear wall washed
in pink, yellow and blue. The **beach** itself is clean and wide, though
the water quality isn't all it could be, and it's backed by a concrete
promenade containing some unmemorable cafés and a garish
two-in-one *McDonalds* and *KFC*. It's all fairly nasty and you needn't
worry about missing out on anything if you skip it, though kitsch
connoisseurs will want to amble down to the little Chinese garden at
the end of the prom, where a brightly painted group of goddesses,
Buddha statues, stone lions and dragons offer some tempting
photo-opportunities. All in all, it doesn't take great imagination to
work out the derogatory, locally inspired tag the bay has acquired
over the years – Repulsive Bay.

The people packing the beach are mostly oblivious to Repulse
Bay's fairly grim history during World War II. The old hotel was
used as a base by British troops, but the Japanese stormed straight
through in 1941, capturing and executing many of the defenders
and sticking the rest in Stanley prison camp to the east. The bay
here had always been an attractive target for new arrivals: the name
itself comes from the ship *HMS Repulse*, from which the nineteenth-century British mopped up the local pirates operating out of
the area. If the beach is too crowded for comfort you can try the
nearby beaches at **MIDDLE BAY** and **SOUTH BAY**, fifteen minutes'
and thirty minutes' walk around the bay respectively.

*For Repulse
Bay, take bus
#6, #6A, #61,
#64, #66 (not
Sun) or #260
from the
Central Bus
Terminal; or
the #73
from Aberdeen/
Stanley. Buses
#6 or #260,
and the #73,
continue
through
Repulse Bay to
Stanley, a fine
ride.*

Stanley

The major attraction on the south coast is the village of **STANLEY**,
sited on its own little peninsula and with much more appeal than all
the other villages along the coast of the island. If you have the time,
you could fill a day here, certainly if you're planning to do any shopping in the market.

Stanley has been one of the main areas of settlement throughout the island's history, and in 1841 there were two thousand
people living here, earning a decent living from fishing. Today, it's
very much a small residential place, popular with Westerners as
it's only 15km from Central, and fairly lively at most times of the
year. The name, incidentally, is down to another nineteenth-
century Colonial Secretary, Lord Stanley, but as with Aberdeen the
original Chinese name is much more evocative – *Chek Chue* or
"robber's lair", after the pirates who once used the village as a
base.

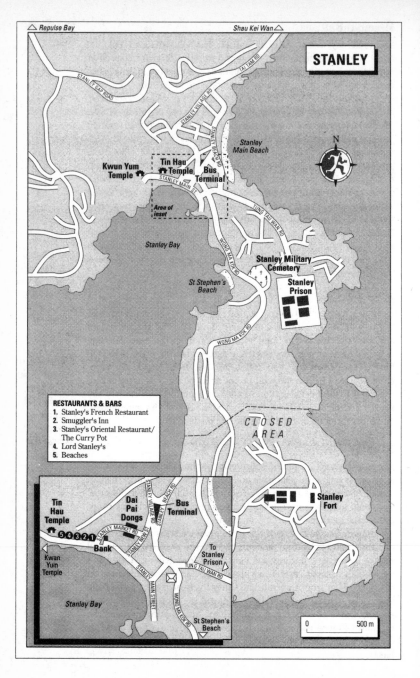

RESTAURANTS & BARS
1. Stanley's French Restaurant
2. Smuggler's Inn
3. Stanley's Oriental Restaurant/
   The Curry Pot
4. Lord Stanley's
5. Beaches

Around the village

The bus will drop you at the **bus terminal** on Stanley Village Road, and the **main beach** is just a couple of minutes' walk away, down on the eastern side of the peninsula. This is narrow and stony, ringed by new development, and for swimming there's actually a much better one, St Stephen's Beach, about ten minutes out of the centre in the opposite direction (see below).

Much of Stanley's attraction lies in its **market** (daily 10am– 7pm), which not surprisingly straddles the streets and alleys around Stanley Market Road, just a step over from the bus terminal. It's famous for its cheap clothes (though they're not actually that cheap), and rooting around turns up all sorts of fake designer gear, silk, T-shirts, cashmere, good sportswear and jeans, as well as the more usual market items – food, household goods, crockery and the rest. When you've done, you can follow Stanley Main Street around the bay to the small **Tin Hau Temple**, which overlooks the western side of the peninsula. It's old by Hong Kong standards, built in 1767, and survived the Japanese bombing of Stanley in the last war, though a large tiger, the skin of which hangs on the wall inside, was less fortunate: killed by an Indian policeman in 1942. Lanterns and model ships decorate the rest of the inside, reminding you of Tin Hau's role as protector of the fishermen, though there's precious little fishing done from Stanley any more.

Past the temple, a path leads through the construction surrounding the redeveloped **MA HANG VILLAGE**, site of the original Chinese settlement here, and up to the **Kwun Yum Temple** gardens, whose main feature is the six-metre-high statue of the Goddess of Mercy, Kwun Yum (or Kuan Yin), set in a pavilion from where you can look out over the bay.

To St Stephen's Beach and Stanley Fort

The other route through Stanley is to follow Wong Ma Kok Road south through the village, down the peninsula. After about ten minutes (just after the playing field), steps lead down to **St Stephen's Beach**, a nice stretch of clean sand with a watersports centre, barbecue pits and decent swimming. If you miss the steps to the beach, you can take the side road on the right a little further on, by St Stephen's School.

A few minutes on down the main road, the **Stanley Military Cemetery** has some graves dating back to the mid-1840s, but is mostly full of those killed defending Hong Kong from the Japanese in 1941 and later in the war. It's a poignant spot to stop and remember the brave stand that many of the soldiers took, especially since the other significant landmark, **Stanley Prison** – where hundreds of civilians were interned in dire conditions by the Japanese during the war – is just over the way. Nowadays, it's a maximum-security prison, housing among others forty convicted murderers who were on Hong Kong's death row until 1993, when capital punishment was finally removed from the statute books. The death sentence hadn't been carried out since 1966 – it was always commuted to terms of imprisonment – but the worry was that China might have carried out the penalty after 1997 if it had remained in law. The prison gallows are destined for one of the territory's museums.

The road continues past the cemetery, climbing up to **Stanley Fort**, base of a British regiment and closed to the public (signs here say "Caution – Troops Marching"), though there's nothing to stop you going as far as you're allowed for the views over Stanley Bay.

Stanley's restaurants are reviewed on the following pages:

Practicalities

Stanley isn't far beyond Repulse Bay, reached on **buses #6, #6A** or **#260** (an express) from the Central Bus Terminal, the **#73** from Aberdeen/Repulse Bay, or – coming around the other side of the island – minibus **#40** from Causeway Bay or bus **#14** from Shau Kei Wan (which is on the MTR and tram route; see below). The journey takes about forty minutes from Central and is a terrific ride, the road sometimes swooping high above the bays.

You can get something cheap **to eat** at the *dai pai dongs* on both sides of Stanley Market Road – noodles and the like, though there's fresh fruit on sale, too. More formally (and expensively), there are several good **restaurants**, reviewed in Chapter 7. Stanley being the *gweilo* hangout it is, there's also a couple of **pubs** on Stanley Main Street; the rather unpleasant *Smuggler's Inn* and, more attractively, with seats by the pavement, *Lord Stanley's Bar* – both serve pub food too. You'll also find a **post office** in Stanley (2 Wong Ma Kok Rd), a couple of **banks** and a **supermarket**.

*Curry Pot
(p.252)*
*Il Mercato
(p.255)*
*Stanley's
French
Restaurant
(p.251)*
*Stanley's
Oriental
Restaurant
(p.254)*
*Tables 88
(p.254)*

The East Coast

HONG KONG ISLAND

There's little incentive to travel much further **east** than Causeway Bay, although the tram ride is fairly entertaining – along King's Road, through **North Point**, the northernmost point of Hong Kong Island, and the residential areas of **Quarry Bay** and **Taikoo Shing** before reaching **Shau Kei Wan** at the end of the line. Once, this whole stretch was lined with beaches, but the views these days are of high-rise apartments. The various developments here have increased in popularity with improvements in the transport system: the **Eastern Island Corridor** is a highway built above and along the shoreline, providing some impressive views if you're speeding along it in a car; the tunnelled **MTR** link across the harbour gives much quicker access to Kowloon. Probably the best combination is to go out on the tram, which will take around half an hour from Causeway Bay to the end of the line, and return by MTR; each place along the tram route also has its own MTR station.

Beyond Shau Kei Wan, heading south, you soon escape into more rural surroundings. Some of the island's best beaches are those on its east coast, the ones around **Shek O** particularly recommended, while you've a better chance of avoiding the crowds if you take one of the high hill walks from **Tai Tam Reservoir** which run over the centre of the island.

North Point

If you're going to jump off the tram anywhere before Shau Kei Wan, **NORTH POINT** is as good a place as any. Home to many of Shanghainese descent, it doesn't get many tourists, which isn't surprising since the apartment buildings and busy main road don't hide any real attractions, but there is a good **market** on Marble Street, a couple of blocks up from North Point Ferry Pier. It sells very cheap T-shirts and light summer clothes, and has the usual alluring produce section. Down at the ferry pier, there's a fresh fish market, too, while the **ferries** run across to Hung Hom or Kwun Tong in Kowloon. The ferry pier is also good for picking up a couple of buses: the #10 through Central to Kennedy Town and the #65 (Sun only) to Stanley.

Quarry Bay, Taikoo Shing and Sai Wan Ho

Further east, the tram runs through **QUARRY BAY**, where the second cross-harbour tunnel comes up on the island. The MTR link under the water means that you can switch lines here if you wish, crossing to Kowloon and the Kwun Tong Line.

If you're on the tram, the only other stop you might want to make is at **TAIKOO SHING**, a massive new development just beyond Quarry Bay. If you don't have time to see one of the New Territories' sparkling, instant cities that have sprung up over the last few years, then Taikoo Shing will do just as well – a large-scale residential city with its own monster shopping and entertainment complex, **Cityplaza**, featuring shops, skating rinks (ice- and roller-), restaurants, free children's shows and lots more indoor entertainment. It's not a bad place for a wet day, and decked out in the glossy, hi-tech fashion loved by the Hong Kong Chinese. Taikoo Shing has its own MTR station, from which you can walk straight into *Cityplaza*.

A few minutes' further on, at **SAI WAN HO**, you can catch a ferry across the Lei Yue Mun channel to Sam Ka Tsuen ferry pier, near which is one of the more renowned places in Hong Kong to eat fresh seafood, Lei Yue Mun. For more details see pp.141–142.

Shau Kei Wan

The tram finishes its run in **SHAU KEI WAN**, which is an important transport terminus as well as somewhere you could profitably spend an hour before heading back. Close to the tram terminus you'll find a Taoist **Shing Wong Temple**, dedicated to the local City God, while further up by the water – close to the fish market – there's the **Tam Kung Temple**, dedicated to a lesser-known fishermen's god. The temple was built at the turn of this century and is the venue of a lively festival, usually at the beginning of May, when it's decorated and there are processions around the whole area. You could take a look around Shau Kei Wan's market stalls, too, before either catching the tram or the MTR back into Central. The **bus terminal** is outside the MTR station; from here the #2 runs into Central.

Shek O and around

The easternmost limb of land on the island holds the enjoyable beach and village of **SHEK O**, reached by taking bus #9 from Shau Kei Wan bus terminal (see above), a glorious half-hour ride down a winding road, taking in splendid views of Tai Tam reservoir, as well as Stanley and the south coast.

The bus drops you at the small bus station in Shek O village. Walk down the road to the roundabout and the **beach** is ahead of you, behind the car park. It's one of Hong Kong's best: wide, with white sand and fringed by shady trees, though it can get very full at the weekend. There's a mini-golf course next to the beach to help while away the afternoon; bikes for rent from the back of the car park; and a few **restaurants** in the village, including a decent one right on the roundabout and a recommended Thai place (see p.259). There's a pub here, too, and on Sunday extra shops and stalls open up, serving food and snacks to the crowds who come down to swim.

The bucket-and-spade shops and basic restaurants in the village don't give the game away, but Shek O is actually one of the swankiest addresses in Hong Kong, and there are some rich houses in the area. You can get a flavour of things by walking through the village and following the path up to **Shek O Headland**, where you'll be faced with yet more sweeping panoramas. To the right is **Cape D'Aguilar**, and to the left, **Rocky Bay**, a nice beach, though with heavily polluted water – which means the sand is generally empty.

Heading back to Shau Kei Wan from Shek O, you don't have to return to the bus station but can instead take a **minibus** from the car park: they're more frequent and a little quicker.

Big Wave Bay

A smarter move if you want more space and less people is to head further north to **Big Wave Bay**, where there's another good beach (that, unlike Rocky Bay, you can swim from), barbecue pits and a refreshment kiosk. You'll have to walk from Shek O, which will take you about half an hour: if you're heading straight here, get off the bus on the way into Shek O at the fork in the road just before the village.

Turtle Cove and Tai Tam Reservoir

The second of the bus routes which operate down the **east side of the island**, the #14 (also from Shau Kei Wan), runs down the other side of Tai Tam Harbour to Stanley, calling at **TURTLE COVE**, a popular beach with all the usual facilities.

On the way back you could call at **Tai Tam Reservoir**, the first in Hong Kong and starting-point for several excellent **hill walks**. The easiest is northwest to Wong Nai Chung Gap, a two-hour walk along Tai Tam Reservoir Road to the Gap, just beyond which is Happy Valley (walk on to Stubbs Road and you can pick up the #15 bus into Central). Longer is the walk due north along Mount Parker Road, between Mount Butler and Mount Parker, to Quarry Bay, from where you can pick up the MTR or tram back into Central.

Chapter 3

Kowloon

The peninsula on the Chinese mainland, which became part of Hong Kong in 1860 – almost twenty years after the British nabbed the island over the water – is called **Kowloon**, an English transliteration of the Cantonese words, *gau lung*, "nine dragons". The dutiful historical explanation of the name is that the fleeing boy-emperor of the Song Dynasty, who ran to the Hong Kong area to escape the Mongols in the thirteenth century, counted eight hills here, purported to hide eight dragons – a figure which was rounded up to nine by sycophantic servants who pointed out that an emperor is also a dragon. Since that flurry of imperial attention, Kowloon's twelve square kilometres have changed from a rolling green peninsula to one of the most built-up areas in the world.

There was an unruly Chinese village here, at the tip of the peninsula, since the very earliest days of the fledgling island colony across the harbour, alongside fortified walls and battlements protecting a Chinese garrison. But after the peninsula was ceded to the British, development gathered pace, and colonial buildings and roads were laid out as the growing population spread across from Hong Kong Island. Today, that gradual development – from village to colonial town – has been subsumed into the packed, frenetic region of Kowloon that is **Tsim Sha Tsui**, which takes up the tip of the peninsula. This is where many visitors stay, eat and – almost Tsim Sha Tsui's *raison d'être* – shop, finding endless diver-

---

KOWLOON: TOP TEN ATTRACTIONS

Hong Kong Cultural Centre and
  Museum of Art (pp.123–126)
Hong Kong Science Museum
  (p.130)
Jade Market (pp.133–134)
Kowloon Park (pp.129–130)
Lei Yue Mun Village (pp.141–142)

Mongkok Bird Market (p.136)
Shopping on Nathan Road
  (pp.128–129)
Peninsula Hotel (p.127)
Temple Street Night Market
  (p.134)
Wong Tai Sin Temple (p.139)

---

sion in a commercial pack of streets that has few equals anywhere in the world.

But there's also a more traditional side to Kowloon, seen in the areas to the north – **Yau Ma Tei** and **Mongkok** – where there are older, explorable streets and buildings. There are similar sights and smells over to the east, around **Kowloon City**: if you fly into Hong Kong, this is the first area you'll see, the plane banking and turning between the buildings in order to straighten up for its descent into nearby **Kai Tak** airport.

Kowloon proper ends at **Boundary Street**, about 4km north of the harbour. In 1860, before the New Territories were added to the colony (in 1898), this formed the frontier between Hong Kong and China. Nowadays, although officially part of the New Territories, the areas immediately above Boundary Street are more usually known as **New Kowloon**, and have a few attractions for the visitor. Mostly, they're densely populated shopping and residential areas, but people ride out here for the amusement park and Chinese cultural village at **Lai Chi Kok**, to the west; for a scattering of temples and minor museums; and to the seafood-eating village of **Lei Yue Mun**, to the east.

Tsim Sha Tsui

If lots of tourists think Hong Kong Island is the only place in the territory worth seeing, then an equal number swear that **TSIM SHA TSUI** is the only place to shop – both mistakes, but both understandable given the HKTA's virtual encouragement of such beliefs in all its literature. Even beyond the brochures, though, Tsim Sha Tsui works hard to maintain the myth that all tourists like nothing better than to spend money: most of its notable monuments are swish commercial developments, and in the kilometre or so from the waterfront to the top of Kowloon Park a devoted window-shopper could find every bauble, gadget and designer label known to humanity – as well as a few pirated by the locals for good measure.

If it all sounds gruesomely commercial, well, it is. But it would be churlish to knock it, since the enterprise and endeavour shown in Tsim Sha Tsui are the main reason Hong Kong exists at all. There's an infectious vibrancy in the "get rich, get ahead" mentality that pervades the streets, and it rubs off in the markets, restaurants, bars and pubs that make Tsim Sha Tsui one of the best places in Hong Kong for a night out. Look close enough, and amid the morass of consumerism are pockets of culture – an excellent Cultural Centre and a museum or two – that can provide a bit of serious relief. It's all a long way, though, from the "sharp, sandy point" that gave Tsim Sha Tsui its Chinese name. Hard to believe now, but in 1860, when the peninsula was ceded to Britain, Chatham Road was a beach and the point of Tsim Sha Tsui an abandoned sandy spit.

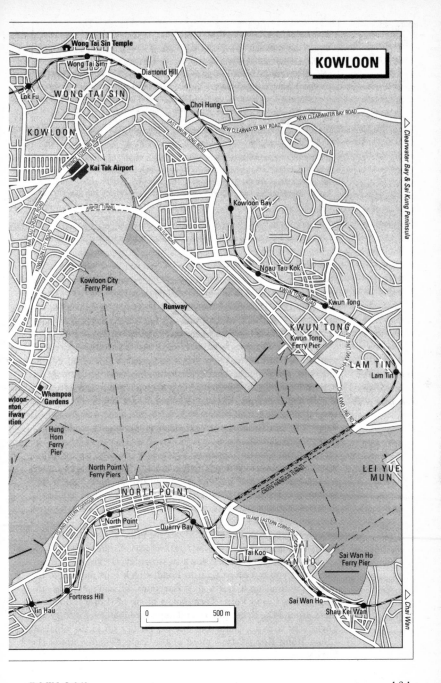

KOWLOON

The Tsim Sha Tsui Skyline

Major land reclamation and redevelopment projects are changing the face of the neighbourhoods immediately to the north (see "Yau Ma Tei" and "Mongkok", pp.131–136), a process which Tsim Sha Tsui has largely escaped. What is set to change. however, is the skyline. Until now, views of Tsim Sha Tsui have, understandably, been compared unfavourably to the megalopolis of Central over the water: the reason why the buildings of Tsim Sha Tsui are so dull – in short, so small – is entirely because of the height restrictions enforced due to the location of Kai Tak airport. It's scary enough landing in the middle of Kowloon without the pilots also having to circumnavigate towers the size of the Bank of China. However, with the construction of the new airport at Chek Lap Kok, Kowloon building restrictions are set to be relaxed. The first shot has already been fired by the *Peninsula* hotel, whose new central tower is easily the most dominant feature of the southern point of Tsim Sha Tsui. In a decade, there will be a forest of towers, spires and needles as developers beat the space restrictions by building ever upwards.

Around the Star Ferry

Walk down the gangway off the **Star Ferry** into its Kowloon-side terminal, and you're in the best possible starting place for a tour of Tsim Sha Tsui. The Concourse is full of newspaper sellers and hawkers; there's an HKTA office (Mon–Fri 8am–6pm, Sat & Sun 9am–5pm), and outside there's a major bus terminal and taxi rank.

On the waterfront, next to the Star Ferry terminal, tour boats are tied up, and beyond here steps and escalators lead up into an immense, gleaming, air-conditioned shopping centre, reputedly the biggest in Asia (although that's not a unique claim in Hong Kong) – all marble, fountains, swish shops and bright lights. It's actually several interconnected centres which run along the western side of Tsim Sha Tsui's waterfront, with luxury apartments studding the upper levels and commanding priceless views over the harbour. The first section, **Ocean Terminal**, which juts out into the water, is where the cruise ships dock; there's a passport control here for the passengers, who usually spend a night or two in Hong Kong before sailing on. Exclusive boutiques line the endless and confusing galleries that link Ocean Terminal with the adjacent **Ocean Centre**, and, the next block up, **Harbour City** – more shops, a couple of swanky hotels, and clothes and shoes the price of a small country's defence budget.

For bus routes from the Star Ferry, see p.53.

If you want to get back down to street level, signs everywhere will direct you out on to **Canton Road**, which runs parallel to the water. Continue up it, north, past Harbour City, and you'll pass the **Hong Kong China Ferry Terminal**, a block of shops and restaurants around the ticket offices and departure lounges for ferry and hoverferry trips to China and Macau; further up is the adjacent **China Hong Kong City** – more of the same though without the ferries.

The Hong Kong Cultural Centre

Back at the Star Ferry, over Salisbury Road, the slender **clock tower**, 45m high, dates from 1921, the only remnant of the grand, columned train station that once stood on the waterfront here, the beginning of the line that stretched from Hong Kong to Beijing. The station was demolished in 1978 to make way for a new waterfront development, whose latest stage, the **Hong Kong Cultural Centre**, was officially opened in late 1989 by the Prince and Princess of Wales. Its construction put the cat firmly among the architectural pigeons. Given six hundred million Hong Kong dollars and *the* prime harbourside site in the territory, the architect managed to come up with a building that, originally at least, had few friends and – astonishingly – no windows. The plain exterior is shaped like a vast winged chute which, among other interpretations, is said to be a bird's wings enshrouding the egg that is the adjacent Space Museum. A brick skirt runs around the entire complex, forming a sort of wedge-shaped cloister, while out in the landscaped plaza, a line of palm trees sit either side of a man-made water channel.

Whatever you think of it, it's certainly bold, and the contentious design aside, the Cultural Centre represents a welcome commitment to making Hong Kong one of Asia's major cultural centres. Inside, the smart, state-of-the-art interior contains three separate venues – a concert hall, grand theatre and studio theatre – while adjacent blocks harbour a superb new art museum, a library, cinema and restaurants. If you're unable to catch a performance inside the Cultural Centre, consider instead taking one of the daily **guided tours** of the complex – in English at 12.30pm (adults $10, children and senior citizens $5). Tickets are available in advance from the Enquiries Counter in the main foyer (☎2734 2009). The box office is here, too, if you want to call in and pick up an events brochure.

There are free foyer programmes and exhibitions at the Cultural Centre most days; also see Chapter 10 for other events and box office details.

The Museum of Art

With the opening of the Cultural Centre came the eagerly awaited establishment of Hong Kong's **Museum of Art** (Mon–Wed, Fri & Sat 10am–6pm, Sun 1–6pm; $10, children and senior citizens $5), six beautifully appointed galleries on three floors, behind the main building. For years, most of the exhibits were crammed into unsuitable, temporary galleries in Central's City Hall, but now they have surroundings equal to their undoubted artistic value. As well as the galleries described below, there's space for touring exhibitions and a fine **museum shop**, by the entrance, with an adjacent gallery for sales of contemporary Hong Kong art and sculpture.

The museum galleries begin on the second floor with the **Xubaizhai Gallery of Chinese Painting and Calligraphy**, primarily featuring a series of hanging scrolls of ink on silk, some up to 4m high. Many depict rural Chinese scenes, though there are simpler representations, too – Jin Nong's podgy and overweight "Lone

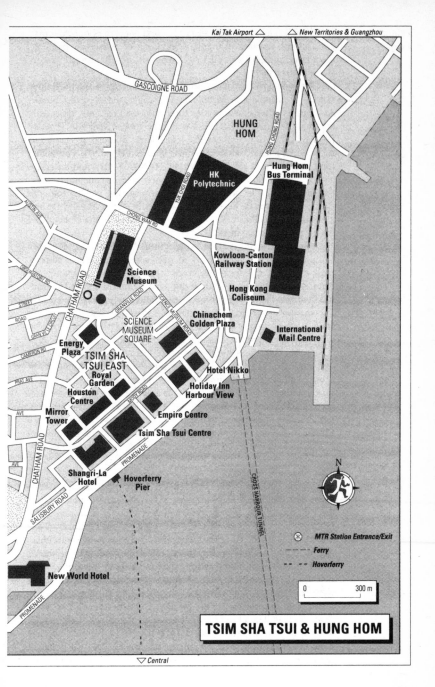

Horse" (1761) an appealing example. Next door, the **Contemporary Art Gallery** features changing exhibitions of silkscreen painting, modern calligraphy, ceramics, and Western and Chinese painting by Hong Kong artists.

These galleries are captivating enough, but up on the third floor are the museum's real highlights. The gallery devoted to **Chinese Antiquities** alone contains over three thousand exhibits, from daily artefacts and decorative items to burial goods. The Han Dynasty (206 BC–220 AD) ceramics are particularly interesting – look out for a green-glazed watchtower, just over a metre high. Pot-bellied tomb figures from the Tang Dynasty (618–907 AD), and an entire side gallery of carved bamboo brush pots and ornamental figures, complete the collection. The Antiquities section shades into the **Chinese Decorative Arts** gallery, laden with carved jade, ivory and glassware, as well as a series of Ming Dynasty ceramics unearthed from a pit on Lantau in 1990.

Also on the third floor, you'll find the **Historical Pictures Collection**, a fascinating array of over a thousand oils, watercolours, drawings and prints that trace the eighteenth- and nineteenth-century development of Hong Kong, Macau and Guangzhou as trading centres. The first painting in the gallery is in fact the earliest known painting of Hong Kong, dated 1816 and executed by William Havell – it depicts a waterfall near Aberdeen. Other works are by army draughtsmen, traders and local professional painters (called "China trade painters") and have acute historical interest: an 1854 oil painting of Victoria, as Central was then called, shows just a few score buildings ranged along the empty waterfront; while contemporary paintings of Guangzhou show it as a thriving centre of warehouses and junks, its buildings sporting the flags of various trading nations. The museum ends on the fourth floor with the **Chinese Fine Art** gallery, rounding up a selection from three thousand works, including modern Chinese art, animal and bird paintings.

The Space Museum

The **Space Museum** (Mon & Wed–Fri 1–9pm, Sat & Sun 10am–9pm; $10, children and senior citizens $5) marked the first stage of the Cultural Centre, built in 1980 and devoted to a hands-on display of space- and astronomy-related objects and themes; the entrance is on Salisbury Road. The *Exhibition Hall* is well laid-out, with push-button exhibits, video presentations, telescopes and picture boards which take you through astronomical and space history, with a perhaps understandable Chinese bias – you learn that the Chinese were the first to spot Halley's Comet, the first to plot star movements and the first to use gunpowder. Upstairs, the *Hall of Solar Sciences* is duller, a brief introduction to all things solar, with explanations of eclipses, sun spots and the like. Most people (certainly most children) want to catch one of the regular daily showings at the *Space Theatre* ($28; 6–15-year-olds, students and senior citizens $14), which has a choice of films shown on the massive Omnimax screen, providing a thrilling sensurround experience – worth going to if you've never seen one before. Call ☎2734 2722 for show times.

Along Salisbury Road

Over the road from the Space Museum stands an equally recognizable monument, though this time it's one of Tsim Sha Tsui's few throwbacks to colonial times: the **Peninsula Hotel**. Built in the 1920s, its elegant wings reaching around a fountain, it used to lord it over the water before land reclamation robbed the hotel of its harbourside position – a high, new central tower, boasting top-floor picture windows and the splendid *Felix* restaurant (see pp.253–254), has rescued its erstwhile views. It was the *Peninsula* that put up the travellers who had disembarked from the Kowloon–Canton railway, and for decades the glitterati frequented it as they also frequented the other grand Asian colonial hotels, the *Taj Mahal* in Bombay and *Raffles* in Singapore. It's still one of the most expensive places to stay in Hong Kong, certainly the hotel with the most social clout, and even if your budget won't stretch to a room here, you can drop into the opulent lobby for afternoon tea – serenaded by a string quartet. It's worth knowing that if you're dressed "inappropriately" (no shorts or sandals) you'll be gently steered to the door whatever the size of your bank balance.

If you book far enough in advance (see "Accommodation", p.224), you can get a room at the **YMCA** building, next door to the *Peninsula*, which apes the grand hotel in its solid design but is a fraction of the price. Stay anywhere else along Salisbury Road and you're still going to spend an enormous amount, from the *Sheraton* at the bottom of Nathan Road to the *New World* and the *Regent* over the road, the latter two part of the waterfront **New World Centre** – a hotel and shopping complex built on reclaimed land. Actually, the New World Centre isn't a bad place to linger: the lobby of the *Regent* has twelve-metre-high windows looking out over the harbour, which make a humble drink there a spectacular affair; and if you work your way outside to the waterfront **promenade**, you can walk all the way up to Hung Hom.

Nathan Road

Between the *Peninsula* and the *Sheraton* hotels, **Nathan Road** is Tsim Sha Tsui's – and Kowloon's – main thoroughfare, running north from the waterfront right the way to Boundary Street. This is the commercial artery for the whole area, buildings crowding to a point in the distance, festooned with neon signs so bright and numerous that they're not allowed to flash at night in case incoming planes mistake Nathan Road for the airport runway. It's always packed and noisy, split by fast-moving traffic which stops occasion-

Buses that head up and down Nathan Road include the #1, #1A, ##2, #6, #6A, #7 and #9. The **MTR** is less useful for short hops; the five stops on Nathan Rd are Tsim Sha Tsui (for Chungking Mansions and Kowloon Park), Jordan (at Jordan Rd), Yau Ma Tei (Waterloo Rd), Mongkok (Argyle St) and Prince Edward (Prince Edward Rd) – with around 3km between the first and last.

ally at the periodic lights to allow an ocean of people to cross from side to side.

Turn-of-the-century photographs show Nathan Road as a tree-lined avenue, with grass verges and no traffic. Built originally in 1865 (and called Robinson Road), there was little prospect of its development until Sir Matthew Nathan, a professional engineer, took up the Governorship of Hong Kong in 1904. Under his orders the road was widened and extended as far north as Yau Ma Tei, but even with the gradual enlargement of Tsim Sha Tsui, the road remained so underused it gained the soubriquet "Nathan's Folly". In 1950 there was only one building more than ten storeys high and not until the 1960s was there real development, when large hotels began to appear in Tsim Sha Tsui and the shopping arcades sprouted.

Shopping on Nathan Road

Today, other than eating and drinking in the surrounding streets, most pedestrians on Nathan Road are intent on trawling the **shops** that have provided the road with its modern tag, the "Golden Mile". It's not just the neon along here that glitters, but the windows too – full of gold and silver, precious stones, hi-fi and cameras, watches and calculators, clothes, shoes and fine art. Window-shopping can be more of a struggle than usual since, apart from the crowds, you also have to contend with the pavement hawkers, who are selling goods at knock-down (and knock-off) prices – you'll soon tire of the insistent offers of a "copy watch".

For full shopping details in Tsim Sha Tsui and elsewhere, see Chapter 12.

As well as the mainstream jewellery and hi-fi shops, Nathan Road has its own **shopping centres**, some of which – in the hotel galleries, like that of the *Hyatt Regency* – are as impressive as those anywhere else. It also has a selection of fairly grim mansion blocks, whose crumbling corridors contain numerous shops and stalls – fun to browse through even if you don't find a real bargain. The best known is **Chungking Mansions**, at nos. 36–44, on the east side before the *Holiday Inn*, which is notorious for its plethora of guest houses, and Indian and Pakistani cafés and restaurants, as well as some great places to buy cheap silk, T-shirts and other clothes; all the shops are on the ground and first floors. **Mirador Mansion**, further up on the same side of the road (nos. 56–58), is more of the same.

The side streets off both sides of Nathan Road are alive with similar possibilities – just saunter around and take your pick. On the east side, **Granville Road** in particular is famous for its bargain clothes shops, though you'll also find clothes, accessories and jewellery stores all the way along **Canarvon**, **Cameron** and **Kimberley** roads. On the west side of Nathan Road, department stores and shopping centres reign: there's a large *Yue Hwa Chinese Products* store at the corner of Peking Road and Kowloon Park Drive; while *HMV*'s megastore, nearby, is one of the latest additions.

The Antiquities and Monuments Office

Opposite Kowloon Park, at 136 Nathan Road, the former Kowloon British School – built in 1902 – is now an exhibition hall for the **Antiquities and Monuments Office** (Mon–Fri 9.30am–12.30pm & 2–4.30pm, Sat 9.30am–noon). The two-storey Victorian villa, with wrap-around verandahs and high ceilings, puts on temporary displays relating to Hong Kong's history – and you can call in and pick up a full set of brochures detailing various archeological and historical sites around the territory. You might also ask here about visiting the Royal Observatory, behind the school, another colonial building, though one which doesn't always take kindly to speculative visits by tourists.

Kowloon Park

There's breathing space close by in **Kowloon Park** (daily 6am–midnight), which stretches along Nathan Road between Haiphong Road and Austin Road. Typically, for such a built-up territory, it's not actually at ground level, but suspended above a "Shoppers' Boulevard"; steps lead up into the park from Nathan Road. Although it's lost a few hundred metres around the edges recently to new buildings, it remains a handy place to rest your legs, parts of it landscaped and styled as a Chinese garden with fountains, rest areas, children's playground, chess garden and an aviary (daily 7am–7pm; free). There's an indoor swimming pool here, too, while a Sculpture Walk (illuminated at night) features work by local artists.

The most obvious focus, though, is the large **Kowloon Mosque** in the southeastern corner, built in the mid-1980s for nearly $30 million to serve the territory's fifty thousand Muslims (of whom about half are Chinese). It replaced a mosque orginally built in 1894 for the British army's Muslim troops from India, and retains its classic design, with a central white marble dome and minarets – surprisingly, it doesn't look out of place, standing above the street. However, sadly, unless you obtain permission in advance (☎2724 0095), you're not allowed in for a further investigation of the mosque and Islamic Centre it encompasses.

You'll have to make do with visiting the park's other building, a converted colonial barracks which does duty now as the informative **Museum of History** (Mon–Thurs & Sat 10am–6pm, Sun 1–6pm; $10, children and senior citizens $5). Exhibitions here attempt to show a cross-section of the museum's enormous archeological and ethnographical collection, and displays cover the story of Hong Kong, from Neolithic times to the present day. Highlights include a model sampan (which you can board), a Hakka house and costumes, even a street reconstruction from the mid-nineteenth century with its medicine shops and opium dens. Old photographs, prehistoric finds and other cultural relics, and video displays on various periods in the colony's history all add up to an hour or so well spent here. There's a full range of public activities held at the museum, which you might find interesting – lectures and film shows particularly – though most are conducted in Cantonese: check at the reception desk for details.

Leave the park at the southern end and you can drop down to Haiphong Road and its covered **market** at the Canton Road end (daily 6am–8pm).

Tsim Sha Tsui East

After the rambling streets and businesses of Tsim Sha Tsui, **TSIM SHA TSUI EAST** couldn't be more different. Starting at the New World Centre, all the land east of Chatham Road is reclaimed, and the whole of the district has sprung up from nothing over twenty years. It is almost exclusively a wedge of large hotels, connected shopping centres and expensive restaurants and clubs, which you can bypass by sticking to the **waterfront promenade** that follows the harbour around from the Cultural Centre. You can get good views of the dragon boat racing from here in June (see "Hong Kong's Festivals", p.282), year-round photo-opportunities across the harbour to the island, and the chance to be horribly fascinated by whether or not the people fishing off the promenade are actually going to eat what they haul out of the vile water. Halfway up, outside the *Shangri-La* hotel, there's a small pier from where you can catch a **hoverferry** over to Queen's Pier on Hong Kong Island.

Minibus #1M runs from Star Ferry to Tsim Sha Tsui East. For the Science Museum, take bus #5 or #5C.

The Hong Kong Science Museum

The only accredited sight in Tsim Sha Tsui East is Hong Kong's newest museum, worth setting aside a few hours for – certainly if you have children to amuse. The **Hong Kong Science Museum** (Tues–Fri 1–9pm, Sat & Sun 10am–9pm; $25, children, students and senior citizens $12.50), at 2 Science Museum Road, is an enterprising venture comprising three floors of hands-on exhibits designed to take the mystery out of all things scientific. Since this includes things like explaining how kitchen and bathroom appliances work, as well as going into the finer points of robotics, computers, cellular phones and hi-fi equipment, even the most Luddite of visitors should be tempted to push buttons and operate robot arms with abandon. Avoid Sundays if you can, and try to go early or late in the day, since the attraction palls if you have to wait in line for a turn at the best of the machines and exhibits.

Hung Hom

Keep to the Tsim Sha Tsui East promenade, past the line of hotels, and eventually (beyond the International Mail Centre) steps take you up into the labyrinthine corridors and overhead walkways which feed into one of several destinations in **Hung Hom**, the next neighbourhood to the north. All told, it's a fifteen- to twenty-minute walk from the beginning of the promenade.

The most noticeable building is the **Hong Kong Coliseum**, completed in 1983, an inverted pyramid which contains a 12,000-seater stadium, used for sports events and concerts. Remarkably, it's built over the concourse and platforms of the **Kowloon–Canton Railway (KCR) Station**, relocated here in 1975 once it had been decided to demolish the old station down by the Star Ferry. This is where you have to come if you want to take the train to China, a route which has been in existence since 1912 and which provides a link with London, through the trans-Siberian railway. From here there are KCR trains to the New Territories, as well as to China.

Heading directly for the KCR Station, take buses #5C, #8 and #8A from the Star Ferry.

Land reclamation has been continuing in earnest in this area for several years now, filling in a kink in the shoreline. A signposted walkway leads you around the relocated **Hung Hom Ferry Pier**, another ten minutes' walk from the station, for services across to Central, Wan Chai or North Point.

If you're coming down this way, it's worth taking the time to look at **Whampoa Gardens**, near the ferry pier, a housing and commercial development built around an old dry dock; bus #8A runs directly from Star Ferry/KCR Station. The Kowloon Dockyard operated on this site from 1870 to 1984, but with the land filled in around it, the dock now supports an impressive hundred-metre-long concrete "ship", open to the public and stacked with more shops, restaurants and recreational facilities. Climb up to the top deck for a surreal view of the surrounding buildings – across to tenth-floor apartments from a ship that looks like it could sail at any minute. North of here is the main Hung Hom shopping area, with **factory outlets** selling clothes and jewellery in the block of streets between Man Yue Street and Hok Yuen Street. You can reach these directly on bus #5C from Star Ferry/KCR Station.

The UCC Coffee Shop, in the Whampoa Gardens ship, serves 23 different types of coffee, as well as iced tea and snacks.

Yau Ma Tei

North up Nathan Road, beyond Jordan MTR, you enter an older part of Kowloon, **YAU MA TEI**, one of the first areas to be developed after 1860 and, with a pleasing symmetry, now at the heart of Hong Kong's most wide-ranging development programme. The name of the district recalls the sesame seed farming that the first inhabitants made their living from (*ma* is sesame). The most interesting streets are the long straight ones north of Jordan Road, on the west side of

Yau Ma Tei

Yau Ma Tei is a 20-minute walk up Nathan Rd; or take the bus (#1, #1A, #2, #6, #6A, #7 or #9 from Star Ferry), the MTR to Jordan, or the cross-harbour ferry from Central Piers to Jordan Rd Ferry Pier.

Nathan Road, which – like Western district on Hong Kong Island – conceal a wealth of traditional shops, businesses, markets and *dai pai dongs*, even a temple of some repute: in particular, Yau Ma Tei is site of the **Jade Market** and the **Temple Street Night Market**, both places not to be missed.

The streets

Starting from Jordan Road, it barely matters which street you follow north. Most are a pot-luck mix of endless fascination, though certain blocks and areas are devoted to specific trades.

One block south of Jordan Road, **Bowring Street** has an outdoor clothes market; you can exit Jordan MTR directly onto the street. To the north, **Canton Road** features just about every kind of business, from jade and ivory shops (*mahjong* sets a speciality) at the bottom end, to a section (Dundas St to Soy St, near Yau Ma Tei MTR) lined with mechanical and electrical shops – ships' chandlers' goods, hardware, engines and engineering works piled high at the side of the road. At no. 627, at Public Square Street, the old colonial **police station** is still in service; while from Waterloo Road as far as Dundas Street, Canton Road becomes a varied street produce market – the wholesale market trade encamped around the Pitt Street junction, with twitching fish and shrimp in shallow plastic buckets near Dundas Street. **Shanghai Street** is similarly eclectic, with shops and stalls selling items as diverse as bright red Chinese wedding gowns, embroidered pillow cases, wedding decorations, laquered shrines, statuettes, chopping blocks, incense, cutlery and kitchenware. To the east, down **Saigon Street**, there's a small enclave of pawn shops and *mahjong* schools.

One of the most intense street markets is that along **Reclamation Street**, between Nanking and Kansu streets. This is very definitely a walk on the wild side at times: fish and turtles cut up on slabs while still alive, calf's heads on the pavements, trays of chicken hearts and livers, and butchers wielding blood-riven cleavers. It does little for the appetite, but there are *won ton* makers scattered here and there and *dai pai dongs* between Ningpo and Saigon streets. At the end of the open-air market, at Kansu Street, the **Yau Ma Tei Covered Market** is a more sober affair.

Further north, at the junction of Waterloo Road and Reclamation Street, there's a large wholesale **fruit market**, with wicker baskets and tiered boxes of oranges stacked under shelters, the interior alleys echoing to the clack of *mahjong* tiles. This is destined to move some time soon because of the work on the nearby West Kowloon Reclamation Project (see below). Reclamation Street itself, immediately north of the market, is clogged with traders and workers handling steel rods, metal drums, and heavy-duty kitchen equipment. The odd shop here specializes in Buddhist utensils and decorations – shrines, joss sticks, urns and pictures by the windowful.

West Kowloon Reclamation Project

Some of the most ambitious development work in the entire territory is taking place in Yau Ma Tei as part of the **West Kowloon Reclamation Project**, a scheme closely associated with the new airport at Chek Lap Kok. Ferry Street used to mark the water's edge, beyond which lay the old Yau Ma Tei typhoon shelter. Now, the entire area has been reclaimed from the water, with the breakwater, **typhoon shelter** and cargo docks shifted several hundred metres further west. The new land in between is earmarked for residential, office and retail buildings, though the linchpin of the entire district is the proposed West Kowloon **rail terminal**, from which the *Airport Express* and *Lantau Line* rail lines will head out west to the new airport. The airport rail link isn't expected to be operational until late 1998, but eventually West Kowloon will be the first downtown stop for air passengers who will change there on to onward transport.

Tin Hau Temple

That Yau Ma Tei was once a working harbour is clear from the presence of the **Tin Hau Temple** (daily 8am–6pm); following successive bouts of land reclamation it's now way inland, just back from Nathan Road, between Public Square Street and Market Street. A small park fronts the complex, usually teeming with men gambling at backgammon and *mahjong*, and the line of low buildings is heralded by people seeking alms as you enter. The main temple, around a century old, is dedicated to Tin Hau, but there are three other temples here, too: the one to the left is dedicated to Shea Tan, protector of the local community; to the right are ones to Shing Wong, the City God, and Fook Tak, an Earth God.

Jade Market

You'll find the **Jade Market** (daily 10am–4pm) underneath the Gascoigne Road flyover on Kansu Street (Jordan or Yau Ma Tei MTR). Several hundred stalls display an enormous selection of coloured jade, from earrings and jewellery to statues, and though there's some serious buying and bargaining going on here between dealers, it's a lot of fun just to poke around the stalls to see what you can turn up. In part, jade owes its value to the fact that as an extremely hard stone, it's very difficult to carve; it's also said by the Chinese to bestow "magical", or at least medicinal qualities to the wearer. Certain shapes represent wealth (deer), good luck (tiger) or power (dragon). All the best stuff goes before lunch, and if you're serious about buying real jade, you should get hold of the HKTA's fact sheet about the market, which tells you what colour and quality to look out for. Basically, there are two kinds: nephrite (which can be varying shades of green) and the rarer jadeite, much of which comes from Burma and which can be all sorts of colours. A rough guide to quality is that the jade should be cold to the touch and with a pure colour which remains constant all the way through; coloured tinges or blemishes reduce the value. However, since the scope for being misled is considerable if you don't know what you're doing, you're best advised simply to pick up small trinkets – rings, pendants, papaperweights, earrings – for just a few dollars if all you want is a souvenir.

Temple Street Night Market

The most famous market in the area unfolds at night up Temple Street (from the junction with Jordan Rd north). From around 6pm to 11pm, **Temple Street Night Market** is alive with activity, its stalls selling cheap clothes (for men particularly), household goods, watches, CDs, cassette tapes and jewellery. If you're lucky, there'll be impromptu performances of Cantonese opera, while fortune tellers and herbalists set up stalls in some of the surrounding streets. About halfway up you'll see stalls laden with an amazing array of shellfish. A couple of plates of sea snails, prawns, mussels or clams, with a beer or two, won't be expensive and it's a great place to stop awhile and take in the atmosphere. More formal meals, hardly more expensive, can be found a little further up, where there's a covered *dai pai dong*. Again, fish and seafood are the speciality and some of the stalls here even have English menus if you want to know exactly what you're getting.

Mongkok

North of Yau Ma Tei is **MONGKOK**, one of the oldest and most dilapidated sections of Kowloon, and – in a territory of extremes – once the most densely populated area in the world. Almost within touching distance across the roads, the decrepit apartment buildings here are stuffed to the gills with people living in some fairly grim conditions, though, as elsewhere in Hong Kong, attempts to move them out of their traditional homes have taken time. Outsiders are unlikely to pick up on the reputed community spirit that keeps many of the inhabitants determined to remain in their peeling apartments, but you might walk through while you can – there's a certain interest in the street markets and day-to-day goings on, though the West Kowloon Reclamation Project will soon change this district, too, beyond recognition.

To the north, at the western end of Argyle Street, you could use the regular cross-harbour ferry to Central from the **Tai Kok Tsui Ferry Pier**. From here, although there's nothing to see, you're within striking distance of **Boundary Street**, which until 1898 and the acquisition of the New Territories marked the boundary with China.

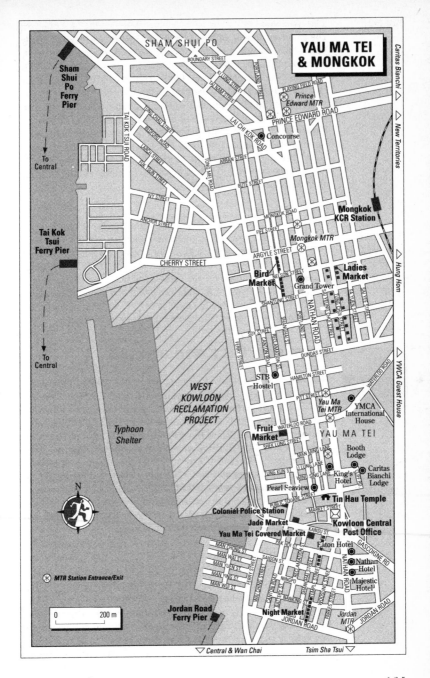

YAU MA TEI
& MONGKOK

SHAM SHUI PO

Sham
Shui
Po
Ferry
Pier

To
Central

Tai Kok
Tsui
Ferry Pier

To
Central

Typhoon
Shelter

N

✳ MTR Station Entrance/Exit

0   200 m

BOUNDARY STREET

PLAYING FIELD ROAD

Prince
Edward MTR

PRINCE EDWARD ROAD

Concourse

Mongkok
KCR Station

Mongkok MTR

ARGYLE STREET

Bird
Market

Grand Tower

Ladies
Market

CHERRY STREET

NATHAN ROAD

DUNDAS STREET

HAMILTON STREET

STB
Hostel

PITT STREET

Yau Ma
Tei MTR

YMCA
International
House

WEST
KOWLOON
RECLAMATION
PROJECT

Fruit
Market

WATERLOO ROAD

YAU MA TEI

SHEK LUNG STREET

Booth
Lodge

King's
Hotel

Caritas
Bianchi
Lodge

Pearl Seaview

Tin Hau Temple

Colonial Police Station

Jade Market

Yau Ma Tei Covered Market

Kowloon Central
Post Office

KANSU ST

Eaton Hotel

Nathan
Hotel

Majestic
Hotel

Jordan Road
Ferry Pier

Night Market

JORDAN ROAD

Jordan
MTR

▽ Central & Wan Chai

Tsim Sha Tsui ▽

Caritas Bianchi ▷

New Territories ▷

Hung Hom ▷

YWCA Guest House ▷

KOWLOON

135

Mongkok

The bird market

The main attraction in the area is the noisy bird market (daily 10am–6pm), down a narrow, fetid alley called Hong Lok Street, between Shanghai Street and Portland Street; from Mongkok MTR take the exit marked Hong Lok Street/Bird Market and cross Portland Street to find the market.

It's filled to the brim with caged songbirds, a fascinating strip which also features crickets tied up in little plastic bags (fed to the birds with chopsticks), birdseed barrels, and men varnishing newly made bamboo cages. You could buy one of these as a souvenir – minus bird they start at $50 or so, though the more elaborate cages run into the hundreds. Little porcelain bird bowls and other paraphernalia cost from around $10.

Ladies' Market

The nearest MTR for Ladies' Market is Mongkok (eastern Nelson St exit).

The one other draw is along **Tung Choi Street**, where a huge women's clothes market (sometimes known as "Ladies' Market"; daily noon–10.30pm) stretches for four blocks between Argyle Street and Dundas Street. It's a good place to pick up bargain skirts, dresses, T-shirts and children's clothes; and there are *dai pai dongs* here, too. You'll find few fixed prices along here, and bargaining is the order of the day. Since the same gear turns up on stall after stall, have a good look around before making a move for anything.

Kowloon City and around

The northeastern edges of Kowloon, beyond the airport, have much less going for them than the shopping streets of Tsim Sha Tsui and Yau Ma Tei, but if you've got the time there are one or two destinations that show a different side of Hong Kong. The airport itself is the limiting factor in this part of Hong Kong, taking up valuable inner-city space and preventing redevelopment and expansion. However, once it's relocated to Chek Lap Kok by 1998, the visionary **Southeast Kowloon Development Plan** will rapidly start to take shape. In construction stages that will last until 2011 it's planned to fill in large chunks of Kowloon Bay on either side of the existing runway in order to create room for a landscaped, waterfront new town with MTR and highway links, capable of housing 250,000 people.

For more on the construction of the new airport, see pp.204–205.

Kowloon City

Boundary Street, Prince Edward Street and Argyle Street all run west from Mongkok, converging on **KOWLOON CITY**, the area immediately surrounding Kai Tak airport. There's been an airport here since the 1930s, though it wasn't until 1956 that the impressive runway was built right into the middle of Kowloon Bay: almost 4km long, it stretches down as far as Kwun Tong. It's an odd sensation to hear and feel the planes just a few metres overhead, though you might bear in mind a report which estimated that a "worst case scenario" plane crash over Kowloon City would kill up to five thousand people – one of the reasons that the new airport on Chek Lap Kok is so eagerly awaited. Currently 350,000 people live under the Kowloon flight path and suffer 300–400 daily take-offs and landings. Night flights aren't allowed though that's scant compensation for the locals who will only rest easy once the new airport comes on stream. That's unlikely to be operational until 1998, so in the meantime Kai Tak – the world's fourth busiest airport – retains one of the world's most demanding runway approaches. It requires pilots to make a manual descent from 200m up above the city, with a final 47-degree turn to line up with the runway – what British journalist Mark Lawson has called "the 747 pilot's equivalent to running with the bulls at Pamplona".

Kowloon Walled City

For years, one of the more notorious districts of Hong Kong lay close to the airport, down Carpenter Road. Beyond Boundary Street and strictly in the New Territories, **Kowloon Walled City** was a slum of gigantic proportions, which had occupied an anomalous position in Hong Kong since 1898, when the Chinese retained judicial control over it by a legal sleight of hand. Originally the site of a Chinese garrison, and walled in (hence the name), it developed into a planned village, rife with disease but thriving from the trade that a nearby wharf brought. There was constant friction between the British authorities and the residents, who felt able to call on the Chinese government whenever they were threatened with resettlement, and the Walled City became a bizarre enclave, virtually free from colonial rule. During the Japanese occupation of Hong Kong, the walls were dismantled and used to extend the airport, and many of the buildings were destroyed. But any hopes the British had of taking over the district were dashed after the end of the war, when thousands of refugees from the Chinese mainland moved into the Walled City and made it their own. Compromise plans came to nothing and for years the Walled City remained a no-go area for the police, becoming a haunt of Triad gangs and fugitive criminals, leading some to call it the "cancer of Kowloon".

Sweat-shops and unlicensed factories employed the refugees, who never left the Walled City in case they were arrested; wells were sunk to provide water and electricity was tapped from the mains; every inch of its tattered surface was covered with wire cages tacked on by the inhabitants to create extra space; there was even a temple and basic restaurants. But life in the city took place amid the most primitive surroundings imaginable: in gloomy, wet corridors, lined with festering rubbish, and with little semblance of order, let alone law. Things improved slightly in the 1970s and 1980s, when residents' associations got together and began to clean up the brothels, abortion clinics, unlicensed medical and dental shops, drinking, drugs and gambling dens that infested the six-hectare site. Finally, in 1987 a planned evacuation programme was agreed with the thirty thousand residents, and by 1991 all of them had been rehoused elsewhere and compensated. The site was levelled and turned into a park, ending one of the more unsavoury of the territory's historical quirks.

*For details of
Kowloon City's
Thai
restaurants, see
pp.257–259.*

With time on your hands at the airport, the best place to head for is the main Prince Edward Road: you can get there by walking through the lobby of the *Regal Meridien* airport hotel and dropping down a couple of floors to the hotel's *China Coast Pub*; the main road is out the main door, on your left. In the streets nearby (particularly Kai Tak Rd) there are several excellent **Thai restaurants**, which sometimes put tables outside so that you can wave at the people in the planes as they lurch past. There's a small **bird market** on Prince Edward Road itself (between the hotel and Kai Tak Rd), and a *dai pai dong*, too, so you should be able to occupy yourself for an hour or two if you're waiting for a flight.

Lok Fu

Just to the northwest of the airport, the district of **LOK FU** sees few tourists, but a couple of offbeat attractions might tempt you away from Kowloon's more usual draws. It's a large-scale residential area with huge apartment buildings towering close to the Lok Fu MTR station. Leave the station by exit A and aim for **Wang Lok House** (above the bus terminal), where – on level 1 – the Government Housing Department has constructed a series of model, single-room apartments open to the public. It's a rare opportunity to delve behind the tourist facade of Hong Kong and examine the cramped conditions in which much of the population lives; the sixteenth floor provides the best view over the **Chinese Christian Cemetery**, spread across a pyramid-shaped hill, that you'll see just before you land in Hong Kong at Kai Tak airport.

A map at the MTR station also directs you to Junction Road, behind the Lok Fu Shopping Centre, and up to **Lok Fu Park**, the green, wooded hill behind the station. This is a terrific place to come and watch the planes landing at Kai Tak, so close to the aiport that one side of the hill has been shaved off to accommodate a red-and-white chequered sign to guide the pilots in. To reach the viewpoint, walk up Junction Road, take the first left and head up the tree-lined road past the barrier; turn left by the water service reservoir, walk to the end of the road and make your way down the dirt path by the side of the fence.

Kowloon Tong

West of the airport, **KOWLOON TONG** is a wealthy, residential area, packed with English and American kindergartens and expensive schools like *St George's*, while nearby **Broadcast Drive** is home to most of the radio and TV stations in the territory. You are hardly likely to find yourself strolling around here, though Kowloon Tong is the site of the **interchange** between the MTR and KCR train systems. More oddly, Kowloon Tong is also noted for its nest of euphemistically tagged "short-time hotels", though given the area, they're anything but seedy. Drive along Waterloo Road and down the adjacent side streets and you can't miss them: all sumptuously decorated and equipped, sitting behind security cameras and grilles.

Wong Tai Sin Temple

There are more strange goings-on a couple of MTR stops east of Kowloon Tong, about a kilometre north of the airport, where the entrance to the massive and colourful **Wong Tai Sin Temple** (daily 7am–5.30pm; small donation expected) is next to the station exit. Built in 1973, it's one of the territory's major Taoist temples, dedicated to Wong Tai Sin, whose image was brought to Hong Kong in 1915 from the mainland and moved here from a temple in Wan Chai six years later. Over three million people come to pay their respects here every year. The god, a mythical shepherd boy with the power of healing, has an almost fanatical following, primarily because he's famous for bringing good luck to gamblers, and there are always crowds at the temple, which shows no restraint in its decoration and lavish grounds. As you enter, you'll be besieged by women selling lucky cards, paper money and joss sticks; it's considered polite to buy something – they're so insistent, you'll be lucky to get away empty-handed anyway.

You're not always allowed into the main temple building, but you'll be able to see the altar, which supports the portrait of Wong Tai Sin brought from China, through the open doors. After that, the other shrines and halls, and the landscaped Nine Dragon Wall Garden (a copy of the famous mural in Beijing; $1 to enter) are good for an hour or so; just watching people here, making offerings and praying for good luck, is diverting enough. There's even a clinic, near one of the exits, with a Chinese herbalist on the upper floor, open for consultations.

On the way to the main entrance you'll have noticed a covered street of booths, whose occupants are there to tell fortunes, and read palms, bumps and faces. It's a thriving industry in Hong Kong and many of these **fortune tellers** have their testimonials of authenticity and success pinned to the booths, with prices and explanations displayed for the sceptical. Some of the people here speak English, so if you want to find out whether or not you're going to win at the races, this is the place to ask. Busiest days at the temple are around Chinese New Year, when luck is particularly sought, and at Wong Tai Sin's festival, on the twenty-third day of the eighth lunar month (usually in September).

New Kowloon: Cheung Sha Wan to Mei Foo

North of Boundary Street, in so-called **NEW KOWLOON**, there are two or three places close enough to tack onto the beginning or end of a day's sightseeing. All are still firmly in built-up parts of the city, in the districts of Cheung Sha Wan (which means "long, sandy bay", giving you an idea of the land reclamation in this area) and Mei Foo – access is easiest by MTR.

The Lei Cheng Uk Branch Museum

In 1955, between the districts of Sham Shui Po and Cheung Sha Wan, a couple of kilometres north of Mongkok, workmen flattening a hillside in order to build a new housing estate unearthed Hong Kong's oldest historic monument – a Han Dynasty tomb almost two thousand years old. It's been preserved *in situ* and now forms the major part of the **Lei Cheng Uk Branch Museum**, 41 Tonkin Street (Mon–Wed, Fri & Sat 10am–1pm & 2–6pm, Sun 1–6pm; free), an offshoot of the Museum of History in Tsim Sha Tsui.

In all truth, the small museum is a bit disappointing, though you can drop in on the way to Lai Chi Kok (see below) rather than make a specific journey. There's a brief explanation of how the tomb was found, with photographs and a few funerary exhibits, and out in the garden is the glass-fronted tomb itself, encased in concrete under the hill to preserve it. It's simple enough to make out the central chamber, which is crossed by four barrel-vaulted brick niches, but the best idea of what it looked like can be gleaned from the diagrams back inside.

*See the colour
plates for a
map of MTR.*

To reach the museum, either take **bus** #2 from the Star Ferry to Tonkin Street, or the **MTR** to Cheung Sha Wan and walk the five minutes up the street, past grim factories and some fairly dense housing. Heading back to the centre, you could always wheel down through Cheung Sha Wan's waterfront wholesale market district to Sha Shui Po **ferry pier**: it's around a kilometre or so, and there's a ferry from there across to Hong Kong Island.

Lai Chi Kok: Sung Dynasty Village and Amusement Park

The **Sung Dynasty Village** (daily 10am–8.30pm; $120, children $65; weekends and public holidays 12.30–5pm $80, children $40) is an attempt to re-create a Chinese village of Sung Dynasty times – 960–1279 AD. It's a small place, with immaculately reproduced shops, houses, craft workshops and a tea house, based around a village square and a pond, "villagers" milling about in traditional costume and providing entertainment of sorts throughout the day – a wedding parade, martial arts displays and traditional Chinese music and dance. It's aimed squarely at tour groups, who arrive in buses throughout the week and pay handsomely for an introduction to traditional Chinese life that, frankly, you can do without if you're going on into China or even staying any length of time in Hong Kong. Unless you coincide with the free shows you'll be hard pushed to get an hour's worth of entertainment for your steep entry fee. Still, your ticket gets you a discount in the expensive restaurant, and entrance to the dismal **Waxworks Museum** (otherwise daily 10am–9pm; $10, children $5; entry from the amusement park), a cosmetic tour of Chinese history from the dynasties to Mao – who, neutrally, on his name card, was simply "founder of the PRC and a very important figure in Chinese history".

It would be nice to be able to say that the **Lai Chi Kok Amusement Park** (Mon–Fri noon–9.30pm, Sat 11am–10.30pm, Sun 10am–9.30pm; $15, children $10, free entry from the Sung Dynasty Village) next door, raises the spirits a little, but it's a tatty collection of sideshows, tame rides and a small and unpleasant zoo. Even sensible children disdain it, since all the big, scary rides are over at Ocean Park, but there's a certain amount of amusement to be derived from the Chinese roller disco.

From **Mei Foo MTR**, both "attractions" are a fifteen-minute signposted walk away. Or catch bus #6A from the Star Ferry, which stops right outside the village and park.

East: to Lei Yue Mun

The other New Kowloon destination is entirely gastronomic in character – a trip to the village of Lei Yue Mun to eat seafood. You can approach from two directions: either **direct by ferry** from Sai Wan Ho on Hong Kong Island (see p.115), or, more interestingly, by taking the **MTR and bus** southeast through some largely unseen parts of Kowloon.

Getting there

Coming by land, take the MTR as far as **KWUN TONG**, a massive residential and industrial area opposite the end of the airport runway. Follow the signs outside to Kwun Tong Road and pick up bus #14C which runs through the new cross-harbour tunnel site at **LAM TIN**; an MTR station here (with Hong Kong's longest escalator) links Kowloon with the island via the cross-harbour track to Quarry Bay. The bus eventually runs down to **SAM KA TSUEN** typhoon shelter, which is where the ferry from Sai Wan Ho docks. From behind the ferry terminal, you can take a sampan across to the village of Lei Yue Mun, passing through moored and inhabited fishing boats.

The village

LEI YUE MUN sits at the narrowest entrance to the harbour; its name means "carp fish gate". Like Lau Fau Shan in the New Territories, it's more or less a line of restaurants and seafood shops, though Lei Yue Mun is probably the biggest and most commercialized of the places to come and eat seafood in Hong Kong. There are around 25 restaurants in a row, and as many fresh fish shops, the slabs and tanks twitching with creatures shortly to

East: to Lei Yue Mun

be cooked. The recognized procedure is to choose your fish and shellfish from a shop, where it will be weighed and priced, and then take it (or you'll be taken) to a restaurant, where it's cooked to your instructions: you generally pay the bill at the end; one to the fishmonger and one to the restaurant for cooking the fish and for any rice and other dishes you may have had. The strongest warnings possible about **rip-offs** are applicable here. You *must* ask the price of the fish you choose before it's bashed on the head and carted off to a restaurant, or you're just inviting someone to choose the most expensive creature for you. A good way to proceed is to name a price to the fishmonger that you want to spend; or if there's a group of you, get the tourist office or a Chinese friend to ring one of the restaurants before you go, sorting out a set, fixed-price menu, which can work out fairly inexpensively. Evenings are the best time to come, when you can sit at the restaurant windows and look out over the typhoon shelter.

Chapter 4

The New Territories

T oo many visitors miss out on the best that Hong Kong has to offer – namely the 740 square kilometres of mainland, beyond Kowloon, leased to Britain in 1898 and known as the **New Territories**. Around half of the colony's population lives here, in both large new cities and small, traditional villages, and the area is the source of much of Hong Kong's food and water. It's in the New Territories, too, that you'll find the most resonant echoes of the People's Republic over the border. Massive housing estates built around gleaming New Towns don't completely obscure the rural nature of much of the land, and although it's not as easy as it once was to spot water buffalo in the New Territories, some country roads still feature teeming duck farms and isolated houses, while in several corners, decrepit walled villages survive, surrounded by their ancestral lands and with their traditional temples and meeting halls intact. What's more, large parts of the New Territories, east and west, have been designated as Country Parks, and peninsular tracts sustain excellent hiking opportunities. The **Sai Kung peninsula**, to the east, is the best example, though the adventurous could see the whole of the New Territories from a hiker's viewpoint by following the cross-territory **MacLehose Trail** (see pp.178–179) from Sai Kung to the far west.

Don't expect it to be all peace and quiet. Parts are as busy and boisterous as anywhere in Kowloon, though there is at least always the impression of more space. Some of the **New Towns** are sights in their own right, built from bright, white stone on view-laden sites

---

NEW TERRITORIES: TOP TEN ATTRACTIONS

Ching Chung Koon Temple (pp.167–168)

Joss House Bay (pp.173–174)

Kam Tin (pp.169–170)

Lau Fau Shan (p.172)

New Town Plaza, Sha Tin (p.150)

Plover Cove (pp.154–156)

Sai Kung Town (pp.174–176)

Sam Tung Uk Museum (pp.162–163)

Sheung Shui (pp.157–159)

Ten Thousand Buddhas Monastery (pp.150–151)

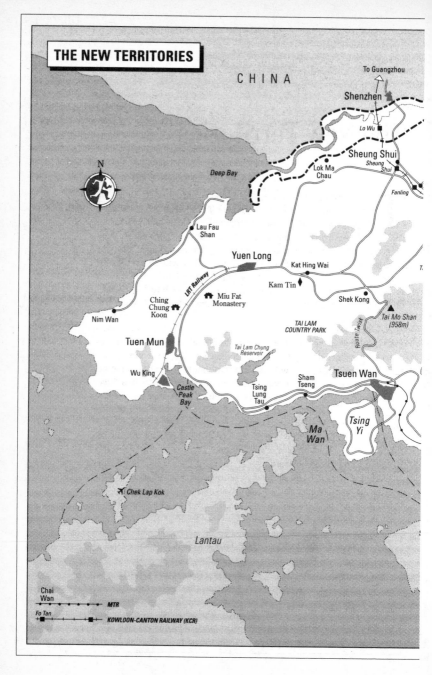

THE NEW TERRITORIES

CHINA

To Guangzhou

Shenzhen

Lo Wu

Sheung Shui

Lok Ma Chau

Sheung Shui

Deep Bay

Fanling

Lau Fau Shan

Yuen Long

Kat Hing Wai

Kam Tin

Shek Kong

LRT Railway

Ching Chung Koon

Miu Fat Monastery

Tai Mo Shan (958m)

Route Twisk

Nim Wan

TAI LAM COUNTRY PARK

Tuen Mun

Tai Lam Chung Reservoir

Wu King

Sham Tseng

Tsuen Wan

Castle Peak Bay

Tsing Lung Tau

Tsing Yi

Ma Wan

Chek Lap Kok

Lantau

Chai Wan

━━━━━ MTR

Fo Tan

━■━━━━■ KOWLOON-CANTON RAILWAY (KCR)

Ping Chau

To Ping Chau

Mirs Bay

CLOSED AREA

Sham Chun River

Sha Tau Kok

Starling Inlet

Luk Keng

PLOVER COVE COUNTRY PARK

PAT SING LENG COUNTRY PARK

Bride's Pool

Fanling

Tai Mei Tuk

Plover Cove Reservoir

Tap Mun Chau

Jones Cove

Tolo Channel

Tai Wo

Tai Po

Tai Po Market

Tolo Harbour

TAI MO COUNTRY PARK

Ma Liu Shui

Three Fathoms Cove

SAI KUNG WEST COUNTRY PARK

University

MA ON SHAN COUNRTY PARK

SAI KUNG EAST COUNTRY PARK

Racecourse

Fo Tan

Shing Mun Reservoir

Sha Tin

Sha Tin

Sai Kung

High Island Reservoir

Tai Wai

Lower Shing Mun Reservoir

LION ROCK COUNTRY PARK

Hebe Haven

Kau Sai Chau

High Island

Kiu Tsui Chau

▲ Lion Rock

Kowloon Tong

MTR

Mongkok

Tsim Sha Tsui

Kowloon

Clear Water Bay

Sheung Wan

Chai Wan

Joss House Bay

Hong Kong Island

0   5 km

THE NEW TERRITORIES

and containing all the energy and industry of the city centre. In between the new structures and roads you'll come across nineteenth-century temples, some fascinating museums and traditional markets – as well as the coastal fishing villages and interior walled villages that have managed to retain an identity amid the rapid development. You can get a glimpse of the modern New Territories by riding the MTR to the end of the line, to **Tsuen Wan**, from where buses connect up with the other major western towns, **Tuen Mun** and **Yuen Long**. Equally rewarding is the **KCR train route** north, through interesting towns like **Sha Tin** and **Tai Po**, to the Chinese border. The last stop on the Hong Kong side, the town of **Sheung Shui**, is currently teetering between a traditional Chinese life and full-blown Hong Kong-style development.

For full transport details, check the text and see "Getting Around", p.48. Useful maps are those of the Countryside Series, available from the Government Publications Centre (see p.47). Bookshops stock maps of the Sai Kung peninsula, worth buying if you're going to spend more than a day in the area.

Public transport is excellent everywhere in the New Territories, by both train and bus. You use minibuses more than usual to get around, but there isn't any one place that you can't get to and back from in a day if you're based in Kowloon or on the island; pick up the HKTA's bus route leaflet for the New Territories, which prints many of the destinations in Chinese characters. There are also some ferry connections between the New Territories and a few of the outlying islands, and hoverferry services between Central and Tsuen Wan and Tuen Mun. Note that you can rent **bikes** at a couple of places, too, particularly at Tai Wai, which is easily reached on the KCR.

In one day, you could tour the greater part of the central and western New Territories on a **circular route** using the KCR and the buses; it would take at least another day to see some of the smaller eastern section, where the going is slower. However, you really need to give yourself more time than this to appreciate the land and its importance to Hong Kong. **Accommodation** is limited to a small number of youth hostels and campsites, which are detailed where appropriate and listed fully in Chapter 6. If you're out for the day, you shouldn't have too much trouble finding somewhere to **eat**. Some of the New Territories' towns have excellent restaurants (especially Sha Tin), though bear in mind that if you're camping or using the youth hostels, you should take plenty of food and a bottle of water with you as the more remote villages and countryside are poorly served as far as eating out is concerned.

The KCR Route: Kowloon to Lo Wu

The best way to see a large chunk of the New Territories quickly is to take the **Kowloon–Canton Railway** (the KCR) from its terminus in Hung Hom north to the Chinese border. The whole trip to Sheung Shui, the last stop you can make on the Hong Kong side as a daytripper, takes around fifty minutes. The route passes through some typical New Towns, like **Sha Tin** and **Tai Po**, which have mushroomed from villages (and sometimes from nothing) in a matter of a few years. In between, there are several temples and markets, while the stop at the Chinese University gives the choice of a scenic ferry ride or a visit to one of the territory's better art galleries. **Sheung Shui** itself is probably the most interesting place at which to break your journey, while from Tai Po and **Fanling** it's only a short bus ride into some quite beautiful countryside to the east, at **Plover Cove** and **Starling Inlet**.

If you're going on into China later, you'll pass through the border crossing at **Lo Wu**, at the end of the Hong Kong part of the KCR line, an otherwise restricted area. Visitors can also peer over the border at a couple of points, particularly **Lok Ma Chau**, where there's been a lookout post for years.

The KCR Route: Kowloon to Lo Wu

For full details and ticket prices on the KCR, see p.50.

Tai Wai

The first stop after the MTR/KCR interchange at Kowloon Tong is TAI WAI, nowadays less a town in its own right (though there's been a village here since the fourteenth century) than an extension of Sha Tin. Its most obvious attraction is easy to spot from the train: **Amah Rock** (*Mong Fu Shek* in Cantonese), to the right across the valley after emerging from the tunnel – though it's debatable to what extent it looks like the human figure it's supposed to be. In legendary times, a woman climbed up the hill with her baby on her back to wait for her husband to return from fishing, but when he failed to appear the gods turned her into stone. There's still a pilgrimage up here by young women at the time of the annual Maiden's Festival (early Aug; see p.283); if you want to clamber up yourself, there's a path from the end of Hung Mui Kuk Road which runs east of the train station.

The other immediately noticeable thing in Tai Wai is the **Happy Dragon Recreation Park** right by the station, which should be open daily but doesn't always bother midweek or during bad weather. There are the usual rides here, and a Water World with chutes.

The huge open space over the way is always busy at the weekend with people renting **bicycles**. Cycle paths start next to the park and run up through Sha Tin, along the river, before skirting Tolo Harbour all the way to Tai Po – a popular route and a good way to get to grips with the New Territories. The bikes cost around $10 an hour, $40 a day, though there's room to bargain at the several stalls which line the park.

Che Kung Temple

A five-minute walk from Tai Wai station, the **Che Kung Temple** is a small Taoist temple dedicated to the Chinese general Che Kung, who is supposed to have beaten off the plague which once stalked this valley. From the KCR station, follow the signs for *Che Kung Miu* to the main road, turn left and then use the subway to cross it; the temple is in a small hollow further up the road, approached over a bridge. The entrance is guarded by extremely persistent old women, who are after your dollars in return for the lucky red paper symbols they'll press into your hand. It can be quite a fight to get through. Che Kung's festival is held on the third day of Chinese New Year, when this temple is packed with people coming here to pray for good luck, which they help along by turning the bronze prayer wheel in front of the altar clockwise.

Come out of the temple and keep on up the main road – Che Kung Miu Road – towards Sha Tin and, after another hundred metres or so on the right, you'll find a little garden containing a **Four-Faced Buddha Shrine**. This is a symbol more commonly found in Thailand: you're supposed to pray to each face, moving around the shrine in an anti-clockwise direction.

Tsang Tai Uk

From the shrine it's only a few more minutes up the main road to one of the New Territories' lesser-known walled villages, **TSANG TAI UK**, curiously dwarfed by the modern apartment buildings on nearby Sha Tin's riverfront. To get there, follow the main road (which becomes Tai Chung Kiu Rd as it approaches Sha Tin) and look for Sha Kok Street on the right: walk down here and the village is behind the recreation ground to the right, under a green bank of hills.

The name Tsang Tai Uk means "Tsang's Big House", though in effect it's a rectangular, greystone walled village, built in the mid-nineteenth century to shelter members of the Tsang family clan. It's survived well and bears comparison with the more frequently visited villages in the Kam Tin area near Yuen Long (see p.169). The thick walls incorporate separate rooms with grilled windows, and at each corner there's a tall, square watchtower, adorned with faded stone decoration. High doorways lead into the "village", based around a central courtyard, with wide alleys running its length split by a network of high-ceilinged rooms and storerooms. Most of the Tsang family have moved out, attracted abroad or by jobs in central Hong Kong, but even so there's a powerful atmosphere here – kids scuttling along the corridors, and washing and cooking going on in corners, much as it has always done.

Sha Tin

Built on both sides of the Shing Mun river in the southern New Territories, **SHA TIN** is one of the most interesting stops on the KCR line. Just 11km out of Tsim Sha Tsui, there's a similar echo in the name, which means "sandy field", a relic of the days when this area consisted of arable land made fertile by the sediment washed down by the river. This productive land supported farming villages, like Tai

TAI WAI & SHA TIN

Sha Tin is one of the few places outside central Hong Kong where you might want to stay; the Regal Riverside *hotel is reviewed on p.227.*

Eating in Sha Tin

You could do worse than plan a day in the New Territories to include lunch or dinner in Sha Tin, since there's a fine selection of local restaurants. Try one of the following:

Laisan Korean BBQ, New Town Plaza, 6th Floor. Korean restaurant with good barbecue.

Lung Wah Hotel and Restaurant, 22 Ha Wo Che. Renowned Cantonese pigeon specialist (see p.245 for more details).

Maxim's Chinese Restaurant, 669–674 New Town Plaza, 6th Floor. Packed and boisterous *dim sum* restaurant.

Regal Riverside, Tai Chung Kiu Rd. Asian buffet lunch and dinner in the hotel restaurant.

Wai, for centuries, though it's only since the 1970s that Sha Tin has taken on its ultra-modern appearance. Much of the New Town building here has occurred on land reclaimed from the mud and sand, which you can still see and smell in the murky channelled river.

The town – due to house seventy thousand people by the end of the 1990s – splits into several distinct areas served by separate KCR stations: Tai Wai is covered above; to the north is Fo Tan, a residential area overlooking the racecourse; while Sha Tin town itself is reached from the central station, also called Sha Tin. From here, signs point you into the **New Town Plaza**, a huge shopping and recreation centre on several floors. It's as good an introduction as any to town life in the New Territories: solidly Chinese, the restaurants here are good value and the shops crowded with local families at all times. There's a big cinema (*UA6*), bowling alleys and swimming pools, and if you're here around noon or in the evening, you can join the crowds of kids who gather to watch the central musical fountain do its stuff with its coloured lights and thirty-foot sprays.

Walk through the plaza, past the *Yaohan* department store, and there are walkway connections to other nearby shopping centres, as well as Sha Tin Town Hall and the riverside park. However, the town is known mainly for **Sha Tin Racecourse**, probably the most modern in the world, and, together with the one at Happy Valley, providing the only legal betting opportunity in Hong Kong. It's packed on race days (the season is from September to May) and the details for entry are the same as at Happy Valley; see p.105. It's even got its own KCR station, Racecourse, to which trains only run on race days. At other times, you can get into **Penfold Park** (closed Mon), in the middle of the track, by taking the KCR to Fo Tan – the track and park are behind the Jubilee Garden estate.

The Ten Thousand Buddhas Monastery

A little way northwest of Sha Tin is the **Ten Thousand Buddhas Monastery**, known locally as *Man Fat Sze*, a stunning temple complex high above the town. The monastery itself is the crowning point of **Po Fook Hill** (daily 9am–5pm; free), a landscaped swathe of gardens, pools, statues and fountains, accessed by an escalator which trundles you up what used to be a stiff climb of four hundred steps; the return journey, back down, is made by an inclined elevator (rather like the Peak Tram), which takes just a couple of minutes. Or you can walk back down the steps through the gardens.

At the top of the escalator, you emerge on a terrace, at the back of which stands the main temple, which actually contains some thirteen thousand small statues of the Buddha. Each is around a foot high, black or gold, and has a different posture; the walls are lined with them, stacked in rows from floor to ceiling. Steps climb on either side of the main temple further up the hillside, where various rooms contain ancestral tablets and terraces sport sparkling views of Sha Tin's skyscrapers, laid out below you in regimented fashion. There's a large central pagoda which houses a seated golden Buddha; other temples contain Hong Kong's tallest standing Buddha statue, and the embalmed body of the monk who founded the monastery, which has been covered in gold leaf and lies preserved behind glass.

To reach the hill and temple, exit Sha Tin KCR following the sign for "Buses/Grand Central Plaza", and go down the ramp to the left of the bus terminal, where there are more signs pointing to the path for the monastery. Turn left when you reach Grand Central Plaza.

Tao Fung Shan

Up the same hillside, but approached from a different path, the **Tao Fung Shan** Christian Centre offers a different perspective over the town. At the bottom of the ramp by the bus terminal, instead of walking straight on for the Ten Thousand Buddhas Monastery, turn sharp left through Pai Tau village: look for the blue arrow on a post. The path leads up above the village, and, after about ten minutes' climb, the main Tao Fung Shan Road. Keep on up the road for another fifteen minutes or so and you can't miss the centre.

It's a complex of buildings built in the 1930s in Chinese style, though this time the pagoda at the top holds a small Christian chapel. A marked path leads through pretty grounds to a large, white stone cross which faces directly out over the river. Away to the left are the blocks of Sha Tin and Fo Tan, while just visible through the apartment buildings at the foot of the hills opposite is Tsang Tai Uk village, a low, grey splash among the towers.

The views aren't the only reason to make the climb. In the grounds you'll find a **porcelain workshop** (Mon–Fri 8.30am–12.30pm & 2–5pm, Sat 8.30am–12.30pm), where you can see good-quality porcelain being hand-painted – a fair proportion of the items on display showing secular themes. The decorated plates run to hundreds of dollars, but you can pick up a souvenir here – a cup and saucer, jug or decorated tile – for around $50.

Steps from the centre lead down to the **cemetery**, below the stone factory, just outside the main entrance, where there's the grave of Tao Fung Shan's founder, a Norwegian evangelist, Karl Ludwig Reichelt (1877–1952), whose idea it was to convert Buddhist monks to Christianity. In part, this explains the centre's orthodox Buddhist look: Reichelt hoped that the buildings would dupe wandering Buddhist monks seeking sanctuary, and it certainly worked – until World War II, Tao Fung Shan was a prosperous Christian centre, although it's struggled to attract devotees in more recent times.

For lunch, or just a drink, drop in at the Yucca de Lac *restaurant, above the Tolo Highway; see p.245 for details.*

University, Ma Liu Shui and Tolo Harbour

Beyond Sha Tin, the train runs upriver before turning to hug the edge of Tolo Harbour. Just before the turn, there's a stop called **UNIVERSITY** (the Chinese characters translate as "Big School"), which serves Hong Kong's **Chinese University**, the campus spread back from the harbour up the hillside.

A shuttle bus from outside the station runs every half-hour up the steep hill to the main campus: if you get off at the second stop, at the top by the Sir Run Run Shaw Hall, the university's **Art Gallery** (Mon–Sat 10am–4.30pm, Sun 12.30–4.30pm; free) is over to the left, in the middle of a block of buildings surrounding a square. The well-lit, spacious split-level galleries usually display items from its own wide collection of Chinese paintings, calligraphy and sculpture, dating from the Ming Dynasty onwards. Mainland Chinese museums often send touring exhibitions here, too, of art and archeological pieces.

Ma Liu Shui

The other reason to get off is for the short walk from the station to the ferry pier at **MA LIU SHUI**: follow the "Ferry Pier" sign out of the KCR, cross the highway by the flyover and descend to the waterfront, a fifteen-minute walk. From here, you can catch the ferry through **Tolo Harbour** and the Tolo Channel, either staying on board for the scenic round trip or jumping off at Tap Mun Chau island or other very minor stops along the way; see the account on p.180 for details.

Ping Chau

Ferries also run from Ma Liu Shui to the island of **Ping Chau**, which is about as far away from central Hong Kong as you can get – which explains why hardly anyone goes there. Way to the northeast, beyond Tap Mun Chau and close to the Chinese coast, it's long been abandoned by its inhabitants, all of whom must have been glad to be off the isolated speck. It's a flat place, its highest point precisely 37m high, but there are some good beaches and the odd overgrown trail along its banana-shaped 4km length. Certainly, you could swim here in the clean water of Mirs Bay; in recent times, people have been known to swim *to* the island, escapees from the Chinese mainland.

There's only a **ferry** at weekends, which leaves Ma Liu Shui on Saturday and Sunday at 9am: buy tickets up to a week in advance from Ma Liu Shui ferry pier. The ferry returns at around 5pm, which is quite long enough on the island, though some people come equipped with **camping gear** and everything else necessary for a pleasant night's stay. Like an enormous bottle of something alcoholic. The campsite is at Kang Lau Shek, at the eastern end of the island, and there's no fresh water source.

Tai Po

At **TAI PO**, on the western point of Tolo Harbour, you're roughly halfway up the KCR line. A market town since the seventeenth century, the manageable town centre is gradually being overwhelmed by the new industrial and housing developments going up all around. Nonetheless, there's enough to warrant a short stroll

THE NEW TERRITORIES

TAI PO MARKET

through Tai Po, and regular buses from the station – called Tai Po Market – give you the first opportunity to escape into the peaceful country surroundings, to the unspoiled hiking and picnic areas around Plover Cove.

The Town

The town's **market** is the principal thing to see, at the end of the main road, Heung Sze Wui Street, a large covered run of stalls that's at its lively best in the morning. On the far side a gate leads up into the **Hong Kong Railway Museum** (Mon & Wed–Sun 9am–4pm; free), which occupies the site and buildings of the old Tai Po Market Railway Station, built in 1913. A small exhibition in the main building includes photographs of the opening ceremony of the Kowloon–Canton Railway, and outside on the preserved tracks you can clamber through a series of coaches dating back to 1911. The only other diversion in the town is the nearby **Man Mo Temple**, on Fu Shin Street, recently restored and dedicated to the Taoist Gods of War and Literature. There are plenty of interesting old shops around here, too, selling dried seafood, religious paraphernalia and all the other usual accompaniments to a Chinese market.

For the rest of Tai Po's points of interest, you have to cross the river which splits the old town from the new industrial developments. Over the bridge, Ting Kok Road leads up to the town's **Tin Hau Temple**, a few hundred metres up on the left – a particularly old relic, built around three hundred years ago, and reflecting Tai Po's traditional importance as a fishing centre. It's also one of the main centres for celebration and devotion around the time of the annual Tin Hau festival (late April/May), when the whole place is decorated with streamers, banners and little windmills: come then and you're likely to catch a Cantonese opera performance on a temporary stage over the road.

Tai Wo

Heading back to town, you could always pick up the train at the next KCR station to the north instead, which you reach from the end of Ting Kok Road. Rather than cross the river again, follow the signs through the new housing estate to your right. TAI WO, a brand new "town" due to hold forty thousand people, was built in just four years, with its own train station, shops and arcades, and is still being finished – giving an idea of the almost indecent haste with which the New Territories are being developed.

Plover Cove

The best thing about Tai Po is its proximity to the nearby countryside, notably **Plover Cove Country Park**, a few kilometres northeast. Bus #75K (roughly every 15–25min) from outside Tai Po Market KCR Station runs there in around thirty minutes, up Ting Kok Road and around the northern shore of Tolo Harbour.

Tai Mei Tuk

The bus terminates at the few houses of **TAI MEI TUK** at the edge of the Plover Cove Reservoir. The bay here was once part of the harbour and has since been dammed to provide a huge fresh water supply for Hong Kong. Close to the terminus there's a line of **bicycle rental** places and a clutch of *dai pai dongs* and drinks stalls: it'll cost $30–40 a day to rent a bike – not a bad idea if your intention is to head straight for Bride's Pool (see below), but cumbersome if you want to tackle some of the excellent walks in the neighbourhood. Over the road, the little peninsula by the main dam shelters a barbecue site, and there's a water sports centre where you can rent rowing boats. If you're going no further into Plover Cove Country Park, you could always try the circular nature trail here, which is signposted and takes approximately an hour to complete.

The KCR Route: Kowloon to Lo Wu

Bradbury Lodge youth hostel is at Tai Mei Tuk. You'll need to book ahead as it's very popular; see p.213 for details.

Local walks

The only road, Bride's Pool Road, heads north, alongside the reservoir past endless barbecue sites, to **Bride's Pool** – around an hour's stroll along a road that gets a fair bit of traffic at the weekend. A

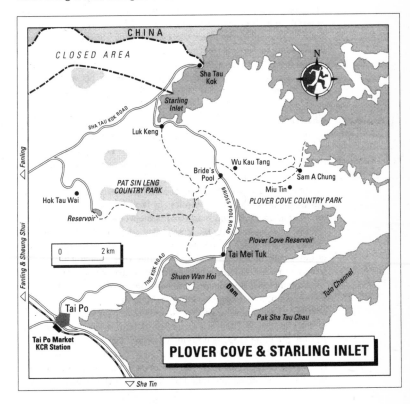

PLOVER COVE & STARLING INLET

series of waterfalls, it's home to more barbecue sites and lots of picnickers, though you can escape the worst of the crowds by taking the trail thirty minutes back downriver to Chung Mei – an abandoned old village of scallop gatherers and vegetable farmers who moved to Tai Po when the reservoir construction destroyed their livelihood.

There are plenty of other local **walks**, and none of them are particularly exacting as long as you carry water. Marked paths lead off the Bride's Pool nature trail to Wu Kau Tang, from where there's a trail to Miu Tin, which leads past some elderly, depopulated villages. Just beyond, there's a very small and basic **campsite** at Sam A Chung, and a circular route back to Wu Kau Tang. Better, if you're just around for the day, to follow the **Pat Sin Leng Trail**, which runs for around 5km between Bride's Pool and Tai Mei Tuk, scrambling above the road for good views of the reservoir. At the Tai Mei Tuk end of the trail, just back from the main road, there's a **Visitor's Centre** (daily except Tues 9.30–11.30am & 1.30–4.30pm) with useful information boards on local flora, fauna and geology, as well as hiking advice and other details.

You can also walk on past Bride's Pool **to Starling Inlet and Luk Keng** (see "Fanling" below). Keep on Bride's Pool Road, past the waterfall, and it's around another 3km to Luk Keng – two hours all told from Tai Mei Tuk – from where you can take the minibus on to Fanling. If you want to cut out the first part of the walk from Tai Mei Tuk, there's a **bus to Bride's Pool** (the #75R from Tai Po Market KCR), though it only runs on Sundays and public holidays between October and April; at other times, you'll have to walk, as described above.

THE NEW TERRITORIES

Fanling

By the time you reach **FANLING**, more than 20km from Tsim Sha Tsui, you're deep in the New Territories and – despite the inevitable new building – it becomes easier to appreciate the essentially rural aspect of the countryside. The people, too, begin to look different. Around Fanling, and especially in Sheung Shui to the north, many families are of **Hakka** descent – traditionally farmers and much in evidence around the area's vibrant markets. It's the women you'll notice most, dressed in simple, baggy black suits and large fringed hats. Besides selling their produce in the markets, they take an active role in what would usually be seen as "male" jobs in the West – hauling barrows on building sites and doing the heavy work in local gardens and fields.

Fanling itself is eminently missable, much of it in the process of being rebuilt and merged with neighbouring Sheung Shui to form another massive new housing development. A couple of destinations might tempt you. There's a large Taoist **temple** opposite the KCR station, the Fung Ying Seen Koon, where you can get a lunch of vegetarian food. Expats come out here to play golf at the swanky *Hong Kong Golf Club*, founded in 1889 (and open to visitors: see p.296), but the tourist attraction touted by the HKTA is the nearby **Luen Wo** market (*Luen Wo Hui*) – certainly worth a visit, but not nearly as good as the one further up the road in Sheung Shui.

To reach the market, take bus #78K or minibus #53K from outside Fanling KCR; they're very frequent and it takes around ten minutes to get there. There's only been a market here since 1948, though Fanling has been a market centre for the local Hakka people for much longer than that. You should get there by 10am to see it at its best; if you do, you'll be able to get **breakfast** very cheaply. The Chinese eat *congee* and a doughnut stick from one of the little noodle stalls around the covered market; for a few dollars more, other places will sell you a plate of duck or pork and rice.

Sha Tau Kok, Starling Inlet and Luk Keng

East of Fanling, the new development peters out into the rural, border area with China. Bus #78K continues past Luen Wo Market to **SHA TAU KOK**, a twenty-minute ride past quiet farming and fishing villages dotted along the valley. It's not an area you can feasibly explore, since Sha Tau Kok itself lies in a restricted area, but it's a pleasant ride. At Starling Inlet, there's a checkpoint on the road, where you'll be politely turfed off the bus: you'll have to wait for the return bus, though the Sha Tau Kok locals have passes which enable them to cross in and out freely.

You can see more of this pretty area by taking a regular maxi-cab instead from Fanling KCR station – the #56K – which turns off the Sha Tau Kok road at **Starling Inlet** and runs around the cove to **LUK KENG**. This is a very peaceful village, with a couple of noodle stalls on the road by the bus stop and two more old Hakka villages in the valley plain behind. If you walk down the main Luk Keng Road, it soon becomes Bride's Pool Road (see "Plover Cove" above); about five minutes from Luk Keng bus stop there's a noticeboard showing the route to Bride's Pool. It also indicates a circular half-hour "Family Walk" which takes you out along the inlet and then cuts back high above the villages and water to regain the main road. There are magnificent views as you go, across to the border village of Sha Tau Kok and China beyond, and down onto the fish farms and junks of Starling Inlet itself.

A much longer hike, though again finishing up at Plover Cove, is accessible by taking the #52K maxicab from Fanling KCR. This drops you at **HOK TAU WAI** (where there's a campsite), around 4km from Fanling, from where a trail runs past a small reservoir over the top of the Pat Sin Leng Country Park and down to Tai Mei Tuk – a lengthy walk but easily done in a day.

Sheung Shui

A few minutes beyond Fanling, **SHEUNG SHUI** is as far as you can go on the KCR without going on into China. It's only 3km from the border and is well worth coming out to visit, one of the most enjoyable of the New Territories' towns, with a centre that's small enough

THE NEW TERRITORIES

to appreciate and a character not yet swamped by new development
– though this will surely come since great apartment buildings are
already encroaching upon the old centre. For the moment, though,
Sheung Shui retains something of its traditional Hakka life.

The town divides into two areas. The main part, just five
minutes on foot from the KCR station, is known as **Shek Wu Hui**,
an interconnected block of streets that can't be bettered as an
example of a down-to-earth New Territories' market town, with its
cheap clothes stalls, *dai pai dongs*, herbalists' shops and hardware stores. Hakka women on their way to the market are laden
down with goods and bags, and it's one of the few places left in
Hong Kong where you still see letter-writers at the roadside at
small tables: for a fee, they'll write a dictated letter for those who
can't manage it themselves. The **food market**, in the alleys behind
San Hong Street (off the main San Fung Avenue), is one of the
best in the territory, certainly the one which comes closest in
appearance to those over the border. The covered stalls are stuffed
with fruit and veg, preserved eggs and beancurd, while in a separate section live fish are picked from the slabs and clubbed on
demand. It's no place for the squeamish, particularly when you
notice the more peripheral trades going on in between the stalls:
vendors selling from buckets of tied crabs and jumping prawns;
the frog-seller who dispatches the beasts with a hatchet across the
back, keeping the legs and throwing the twitching bodies away;
the woman who spends all day wringing the necks of tiny birds,
taken from a squeaking cage, and placing the pathetic plucked
carcasses on a slab.

The other part of Sheung Shui is **Po Sheung Tsuen** – or *Sheung
Shui Wai* (Sheung Shui Village) – the original village over to the
west of the town. Down the main San Fung Avenue from the KCR

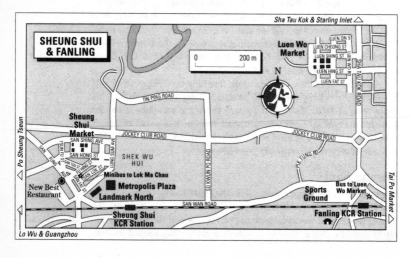

station, take the first left (at the traffic lights) and walk past the *Jockey Club* playground up to the main Po Shek Wu Road, where you'll see the *China Light and Power* building over the way. Cross at the lights and go down the steps straight ahead of you, just to your right. Walk along by the side of the small drainage channel and through the car park, and behind the new apartment buildings is the old village. It's an almost medieval rag-taggle of buildings with dank alleys between the houses, just wide enough for one person to walk down and with open gutters alive with rustling rats. The houses are a strange mixture, some brand new with bright tiling, others just corrugated iron and cheap plaster. It's actually much less alarming than it appears and, though you might be stared at, there's not much to fear. Every house pays protection money to the local "security" group, so opportunistic crime is rare. Foreigners are not entirely unknown here either, since there's a military base nearby. The only thing to see is the large local **ancestral hall**, Man Shek Tong, built in the eighteenth century. Giving directions to this is pointless, since the name and numbering system for the alleys is hopelessly confusing, but you'll stumble across it sooner or later and be glad that you did: unlike many such places in more touristed parts of Hong Kong, this one is firmly in use by the locals and still stands in its original crumbly surroundings, carved and decorated in traditional fashion.

The KCR Route: Kowloon to Lo Wu

Practicalities

Buses use the bays outside the KCR station; the #17 **minibus** to the Lok Ma Chau lookout point (see below) leaves from San Fat Street (see map).

There are lots of **restaurants** in the small centre of Shek Wu Hui, including the rambling *New Best Restaurant*, on San Fung Avenue, good for *dim sum*: head up the escalators and try to attract the attention of the head waiter. The food is great, and very cheap – and you'll be the only tourist in the place. For just a plate of meat and rice, or bowl of noodles, the *Ming Yuen* on the corner of San Fat Street and Fu Hing Street, opposite Watson's, is worth a try. Also on San Fat Street, there's the *Malaysian Restaurant* (no. 26), which serves decent Malaysian food, as well as European lunches and dinners; the *Thai Food Restaurant*, next door, has more good-value Asian cooking. Even cheaper meals are available at the **dai pai dongs** in the town's market – they're all at the eastern end of San Shing Avenue.

The Border: Lo Wu, Lok Ma Chau and San Tin

The **border with China**, which follows the course of the Sham Chun river across the narrow neck of the New Territories' peninsula, has lost much of its erstwhile attraction for tourists since the People's Republic became more receptive to individual travel. There aren't any compelling reasons to go and look – it is only a fence and a river when all's said and done – but if you're in the area anyway, at Sheung Shui particularly, you may want to make the trip just to say you've been.

Lo Wu and the border

The crossing into China used by foreign travellers is the train link through the station of **LO WU**, one stop after Sheung Shui and the last stop on the Hong Kong side of the border. You're only allowed here if you're equipped with valid travel documents to go on into China; otherwise it's a closed area to visitors.

Local people make the crossing at a couple of other points – Sha Tau Kok and Man Kam To, just northeast of Sheung Shui – and with the right documentation, you could cross here as well. But there's no real point without your own transport since onward connections are non-existent.

Lok Ma Chau

For years, **LOK MA CHAU**, 4km west of Sheung Shui, was the place to come and peer over the border at Red China, from a special view-ing platform built above the river. It's a bit anachronistic these days, but still makes for a pleasant hour or two's diversion as Lok Ma Chau lies in some isolated, green surroundings. Even here, though, the jackhammers are falling, as the fields are dug up to accommo-date the new Hong Kong–Guangzhou highway.

The best way here is by **bus**: either the #76K from Sheung Shui KCR station or minibus #17 from San Fat Street (see above). Both take about fifteen minutes to reach the general area: ask the bus driver – you need to get off at the junction of Lok Ma Chau Road and Castle Peak Road, and follow the signposts up the main road to the lookout point, which will take another fifteen to twenty minutes. A steep path leads up between souvenir stalls to a terrace overlook-ing Shenzhen, the Chinese border town; the river marks the boun-dary and the wire fence delineates a sort of no-man's land. There's a map to tell you what you're looking at (not much), a restaurant back down the road, and frequent minibuses heading back to the main road if you can't be bothered to walk.

From the main road, you don't need to head back to Sheung Shui for the return trip. If you set out early enough to get up to this part of the New Territories, flagging down the next #76K bus that runs past takes you into Yuen Long, a New Town around twenty minutes south (see p.170). From here, you can easily circle right around the western New Territories before returning to Kowloon or Central, a couple of hours' travelling all told if you don't linger.

San Tin

If the rural peace and quiet appeals, you could stick around long enough to see the traditional Chinese dwellings at the nearby village of **SAN TIN**, either a thirty-minute walk from Lok Ma Chau or reached on the same buses from Sheung Shui. On foot, return to the main Castle Peak Road (20min) and turn right, heading along the busy main road towards Yuen Long; it's another ten minutes to San Tin. By bus, take the #76K or #17 minibus from Sheung Shui and get off in San Tin by the *Esso* service station.

Walk up the street beside the post office, just off the main road, and within five minutes you'll be at **Tai Fu Tai** (daily except Tues 9am–1pm & 2–5pm; free), a fine example of a nineteenth-century home built for a wealthy Chinese family of the Man clan, who originally settled this area in the fourteenth century. There are some excellent murals inside, terracotta figurines and carvings, and a delightful garden. From here, continue through the maze of quiet streets and eventually you'll stumble on the **Man Lun Fung Ancestral Hall**, built at the end of the seventeenth century, and still in use as a worship and meeting place for local people.

The West: Tsuen Wan, Tuen Mun and Yuen Long

Access to the **western New Territories** is a simple matter, and connecting transport means you can construct a day-trip which runs through all the major towns and villages. There are basically two routes, both of which start at **Tsuen Wan**, a New Town at the end of the MTR line, or reached by hoverferry from Central. You'll want to stop here long enough to see the excellent **Sam Tung Uk Museum**, a restored Hakka village, and there are a couple of other rural diversions, including some good walks in the neighbouring **country parks**. From Tsuen Wan, the quickest and most popular route is the bus run up Route Twisk to **Yuen Long** town, which passes the famous walled villages of the **Kam Tin** area; Yuen Long is also close to the oyster beds at **Lau Fau Shan**, which is one place you might want to break for lunch. Other buses run along the southern shore to **Tuen Mun**, a route which allows you to get off at several excellent **beaches** along the way. Yuen Long and Tuen Mun are connected by bus and train (the LRT), so completing the circle is easy. Alternatively, buses run east from Yuen Long to connect up with stations on the KCR rail line, from where it's an easy trip back to Kowloon.

Tsuen Wan

Approached by bus from the north or west **TSUEN WAN** ("shallow bay") appears as a stack of white high-rises nestling between the hills, overlooking Tsing Yi Island and the greater harbour beyond. Arriving by hoverferry from Central is similarly exhilarating, a short skim across the water providing a rare view of the western side of Kowloon. The only approach that doesn't merit attention is the one that most people are likely to make: taking the tunnel-bound Tsuen Wan MTR line west to its terminal station, leaving you right in the centre of town, and in the midst of some major development. In 1898, there were only three thousand inhabitants, mostly farmers. Now, around a million people live and work in the area, and the town has the futuristic look favoured by planners all over Hong Kong: flyovers and walkways spin off in all directions, and signposts point into interlinking malls and gardens. There's the usual complement of shops and stores, and if it's your first New Town it merits a brief look around. Apart from the **market**, three blocks south of the MTR, the only thing worth seeing in the centre is the first-rate Sam Tung Uk Museum, though there are several attractive **walks** on the outskirts if you've got more time to spare.

The Sam Tung Uk Museum

The Tsuen Wan area was completely depopulated following the orders of the seventeenth-century Manchu government to abandon the coastal villages in response to constant pirate attacks. It wasn't populated again until the end of the century and permanent settlements only developed later, typified by the eighteenth-century Hakka walled village that survives today as the **Sam Tung Uk Museum** (Mon & Wed–Sun 9am–4pm; free). The museum is on Kw Uk Lane; exit left from the MTR and follow the signs along the pedestrian walkway.

Founded by a clan originally from China's Fujian province, who moved into Guangdong, the name of what was a farming village means "three-beamed dwelling" – a reference to the three roofed halls that form the central axis of the village, with new housing added on both sides as the village grew. At the entrance there's an **orientation room** which tells the fascinating story of the village's restoration. There's a particularly revealing photograph that shows Sam Tung Uk surrounded by similar adjacent villages when Tsuen Wan was just a gleam in a planner's eye, as recently as 1977, which indicates the speed of the building here. As the New Town went up around it, the villagers moved out, and in 1980 Sam Tung Uk was declared a monument – cleaned, stripped and renovated to its original condition, with the furniture and most of the exhibits actually collected from two contemporary Hakka villages over the border in Guangdong.

It's a remarkable achievement, although critics might argue that the **buildings** are too pristine to be an authentic representation of life in these villages. The basic layout is of three connected halls: a common room for villagers, with carts and sedan chairs; a central hall for banquets and gatherings; and the Ancestral Hall, which faced the main entrance. Everywhere, the walls are whitewashed and cool, the buildings sporting low lintels and well-crafted beamed roofs. The rooms, connected by narrow streets – corridors really – display traditional farming implements, some beautiful blackwood furniture, as well as more ordinary chairs, tables, cooking and cleaning tools. The Ancestral Hall has been painted in its original bright red and green colours, giving an idea of what you're missing in other parts of Hong Kong, where the halls are often engrained with decades' worth of dust and dirt. Outside, the **gardens** have been landscaped to show how there would have been a threshing ground and a fish pond, and there's a gate house beyond which would have guarded the entrance to the village.

Shing Mun and Kam Shan country parks

Fifteen minutes east of Tsuen Wan by bus, **Shing Mun Country Park** is a fine target if you've got a couple of spare hours and want to get out into more rural surroundings. Minibus #82 from Shiu Wo Street, two blocks south of the MTR, runs straight to the **Country Park Visitor's Centre** (daily except Tues 9.30am–4.30pm), whose exhibition hall highlights the local history – particularly the World War II defensive system (see below) – and the flora and fauna. From the centre, a signposted walk runs around the Shing Mun (Jubilee)

Reservoir, a relatively easy two-hour hike with great views of the surrounding hills, much of the route shaded by trees. Back at the visitor's centre there's a summertime refreshment kiosk and toilets.

A minor detour from the round-reservoir hike takes you to the **Shing Mun Redoubt**, an undergound hilltop fortification built by the British in 1939 as part of the New Territories' defence (known as the "Gin Drinker's Line") against the subsequent Japanese invasion. Based on a series of tuunels – each named after a London street or area – the system was taken by the Japanese after a short and bloody battle in 1941. Large parts of the system still remain intact, covered by undergrowth: if you're intent upon exploring, you'll need a flashlight and you must be careful since the tunnels aren't maintained. To get there from the visitor's centre, walk around the reservoir in an anti-clockwise direction and when you see a big overhead sign marked "MacLehose Trail (Stage Six)", leave the road and join the trail; the tunnels start about ten minutes after the sign.

For more on the MacLehose Trail, see pp.178–179.

This section of the **MacLehose Trail** itself heads south towards Smuggler's Ridge, a ninety-minute climb that takes you into the neighbouring **Kam Shan Country Park**, known for its wild macaque monkeys. The trail section ends at the Kowloon Reservoirs and the park entrance, from where you can pick up buses back to Kowloon: either the #81 to Jordan MTR station or #72 to Sham Shui Po MTR station.

Yuen Yuen Institute

To complete the tour of Tsuen Wan's outskirts, take maxicab #81 from Shiu Wo Street (two blocks south of the MTR) to the **Yuen Yuen Institute**, a ten-minute ride into the green hills overlooking the city; the bus may be marked Lo Wai Village. It's a working temple dedicated to Taoism, Buddhism and Confucianism – which makes for an interesting mix of styles – and there's a dining room where very good vegetarian food can be bought. Lunch should cost around $60.

Practicalities

The **hoverferry** from Central docks down at Tsuen Wan Ferry Pier, a five-minute walk from the Town Hall; see p.56 for details. From the bus terminal next to the pier, you can catch **bus #51 to Kam Tin**, via Route Twisk (see below), though it also makes a stop on the flyover above the MTR station. Also from the Ferry Pier, bus #34B runs along the coastal Castle Peak Road, passing the **beaches** covered in the section below.

The main **bus terminal** in Tsuen Wan is just opposite the MTR station, underneath the shopping centre. From here, you can catch **bus #68M to Tuen Mun/Yuen Long**, which follows the new highway and not the parallel coastal road; this is the bus to take if you're heading for either the Ching Chung Koon Temple or the Mui Fat Monastery. The **taxi/maxicab terminal** along the main road (underneath the multi-storey car park, opposite the Luk Yeung Shopping Centre) is where you catch the #96M minibus, which skirts the coast for the beaches and the goose restaurants at Sham Tseng. **Shiu Wo Street**, a couple of blocks south of the MTR, near the market, has the minibus and maxicab stops for the country parks and the Yuen Yuen Institute.

It's worth noting that Tsuen Wan has one of the New Territories' few **hotels**, the excellent *Kowloon Panda* (see p.227 for details); inside is the *Yuet Loy Heen* **restaurant**, on the second floor, which serves highly rated *dim sum* from 7am to 3pm; the seafood choices are especially good.

The coastal route: Castle Peak Road

Two parallel roads run along the **coast** of the western New Territories: the new, fast highway, Tuen Mun Road, and the quieter and original **Castle Peak Road**. Finished in 1919, this road is the one to follow if you want to see any of the shoreline, as it winds around the **beaches** and small headlands between Tsuen Wan and Tuen Mun, before cutting up through the inland region to Yuen Long, continuing all the way to Lok Ma Chau. The coastal part of the route is best done on minibus #96M or bus #34B from Tsuen Wan: see "Practicalities" above for details.

Tsing Yi Island which dominates the entire first half of the coastline, across Rambler Channel from Tsuen Wan, is home to oil depots and other industrial concerns. The various noxious emissions haven't helped the water quality, which is already hit by the junk flowing out of developing Tsuen Wan's harbour. Consequently, the water hereabouts is off limits for swimming: you'll need to check the latest press reports or watch out for noticeboards at the beaches.

Moreover, this entire coastal area is due some rapid changes over the next few years as the infrastructure for the **new airport** begins to take shape. Tsing Yi island and smaller Ma Wan are set to carry sections of the airport rail line and highway which will run up from Kowloon and then out across the north coast of Lantau.

The beaches and Sham Tseng

The **beaches** nearest to Tsuen Wan are all pretty much affected by the polluted water, but the sands are generally fine. You'll pass **Approach** beach and **Ting Kau**, while further on are **Ho Mei Wan** and **Gemini** beaches; beyond Sham Tseng come **Angler's** and **Dragon**.

If none of these appeal, consider stopping at SHAM TSENG itself, a little roadside village about fifteen minutes out of Tseun Wan. Get off at the stop after the massive *San Miguel* brewery, directly opposite which there's a line of nine or ten **restaurants**, all specializing in roast goose and duck. The *Chan Kee*, right opposite the factory, has an English menu and tables under a marquee where you can spend a very pleasant lunchtime eating goose, swigging the cold, local (*San Miguel*) beer, and avoiding the heavier Chui Chow influenced items on the menu – the rather alarming "pig's ding", as well as intestines and goose blood.

THE NEW TERRITORIES

Tuen Mun and around

For the rest of the ride to Tuen Mun you can sit back and appreciate the views over the water and the increasingly built-up coast. There are a few beaches on the eastern side of town, but again the water quality is dodgy. TUEN MUN itself, a large and straggling town of nearly half a million, doesn't do much to attract you to get off and look around, with only a couple of nearby Chinese temples offering a spark of interest. The name of the town means "Channel Gate", a reminder that this was once an important defensive post, guarding the eastern approaches to the Pearl River Estuary. These days, it's a standard New Town sporting the obligatory shopping and commercial development – **Tuen Mun Town Plaza** – which at least makes an attempt at variation: there's a fake Georgian square around a fountain, planted inside the plaza.

For more on the LRT system and a route map, see "Getting Around", pp.50–52.

If you came from Tsuen Wan on the #68M bus, stick with it as it runs right through the town, passing both temples. Otherwise, get off in the centre and make your way to one of the stations of the **Light Rail Transit** system (LRT), which links Tuen Mun with Yuen

---

New Towns

The dominant feature of the New Territories' countryside is the seemingly ubiquitous **New Town**, each a gleaming forest of residential and commercial towers, shopping centres and flyovers. Borrowing from similar British experiments of the 1950s and 1960s, the first plans were laid in 1972, with the proposed towns designed to provide homes for almost two million people. This resulted in the initial construction of Tsuen Wan, Tuen Mun and Sha Tin, still the three largest developments; Tsuen Wan alone will eventually house around 800,000 people. A second wave of projects saw the rapid rise of Yuen Long, Tai Po and Sheung Shui/Fanling, all of which are now substantially complete. The final wave this century will be the development of sites at Tung Chung (next to the new airport on Lantau), Tin Shui Wai (northwest of Yuen Long) and Tsueng Kwan O (Junk Bay, east of Kowloon City). When finished, all nine new towns will have a capacity of over 3.5 million inhabitants; in 1898, when the New Territories were first leased to Britain, fewer than ten thousand farmers and fishermen lived in the region.

Each New Town is designed to be self-sufficient, in that they feature local employment opportunities, a full range of cultural, civic and leisure services, shops and markets, and co-ordinated transport facilities. For the majority, they're pleasant places to live, certainly more so than the crowded tenement slums of Mongkok or Kowloon City. Residential living space is limited, but much thought was given to enhancing the quality of life outside the home: markets, shops, laundries and sports facilities are provided within apartment buildings; pedestrian and vehicular traffic is segregated as far as possible; cinemas and theatres are on the doorstep.

Long to the north; there are terminals right in the centre, or down at the **Ferry Pier**, where the **hoverferries** from Central arrive and depart. To head back to Kowloon, bus #68X runs to Jordan Road Ferry Pier.

Ching Chung Koon Temple

There's a large Taoist temple complex, the **Ching Chung Koon Temple** (daily 7am–7pm), just out of Tuen Mun. It's a little complicated to find, but worth the effort: the #68M bus stop is on Castle Peak Road, just a few minutes out of the centre (ask the driver), and if you walk to the left over the small hill and cross the river you'll come to Affluence LRT station (line #507 from Tuen Mun Ferry Pier or #612 from the town centre); bear left through the housing estate to the main road, and the temple is visible to your right.

At the entrance, there's a plan which makes sense of the complex of temples, gardens and shrines, built in 1949 and dedicated to Lu Sun Young, an eighth-century "Immortal" blessed with magical and curative powers. The main temple is flanked by separate bell and drum towers, which signal the prayer times. The room to the left of here is where you book your **vegetarian lunch** (a set meal served for a minimum of two people), while next down is the **Ancestral Hall**, unusually large and crammed full of photos and

---

But while they are supposed to be much more than mere "dormitory" towns for central Hong Kong, there is an awareness that to thrive in future the New Towns have to attract inhabitants who work elsewhere in the territory. Consequently, as part of the development programme currently underway in Hong Kong, many New Towns are looking at improved transport links both with each other and with the rest of the territory: Tung Chung forms an integral part of the airport scheme (see pp.204–205) and will be just half an hour from Central once the new rail link is complete; Tsueng Kwan O is scheduled to have its own MTR link by the year 2000; while the proposed 52-kilometre Western Corridor Railway will link Tuen Mun, Yuen Long and Tsuen Wan and connect them with interlinking stations on the MTR and KCR.

It's certainly worth taking the time to look round a New Town, if only to see what remarkable progress can be made where there's a will and a coherent planning programme. Sha Tin (p.149) is perhaps the most attractive since it's splendidly sited and has had time to acquire a certain character. Tuen Mun (see above) has become viable most recently, with its town centre completed only in 1990; while Sheung Shui/Fanling (pp.156–157), close to the Chinese border, is set to change most over the next few years due to its proximity to the free-market antics of the adjacent Shenzhen Special Economic Zone. For visionary building, though, make a date to visit Tung Chung (p.206), across from the new airport, in around ten years' time. It's due to act as the future gateway into Hong Kong and, if early plans are realized, the ride in on the airport train, through the curving sweep of New Town towers, will be as exciting in its way as the old airline swoop into inner-city Kai Tak.

---

records of the dead. People pray here for their ancestors' souls, and occasionally you might catch a commemoration service, when monks chant – accompanied by drums, cymbals and flutes. The best time to see this is at either of the annual festivals which commemorate the dead: Ching Ming or Yue Lan (see "Festivals", p.282). At the end of the buildings, there's an ornamental **garden**, carefully built in traditional style, with imported Chinese rocks, a rock pool and pagodas, setting off perfectly the air of formal prayer and devotion in the complex.

Mui Fat Monastery

The other local temple, this time strictly Buddhist in character, is the **Mui Fat Monastery**, about 4km north of Tuen Mun on Castle Peak Road, halfway to Yuen Long. You can get there on the #68M bus, which stops virtually outside, or on the #68X direct from Jordan Road Ferry Terminal; or ride the LRT from either Tuen Mun or Yuen Long – get off at Lam Tei station, and the temple is just back up the road.

The only part of the monastery you can get into is the tall, square temple set back from the main road, a garish building whose entrance is guarded by two golden dragons, their bodies writhing the whole way up the building. Also outside, on either side of the entrance, sit a toothy lion and an elephant, with pigeons perched everywhere. There are three floors inside, the top one overwhelming in its opulence, with three large golden Buddhas, massive crystal chandeliers, marble tablets and little Buddha images lining the walls, and a bell and a skin drum hanging at either side.

On the middle floor is a decorated dining room which, like Ching Chung Koon, serves **vegetarian lunches** (noon–3.30pm): buy a ticket at the desk on the way in and you'll be brought platefuls of food from the kitchens.

Route Twisk: Tai Mo Shan and Shek Kong

The other bus route through the western New Territories runs anti-clockwise, inland north of Tsuen Wan and around to Yuen Long, on the so-called **Route Twisk**, a high road pass which is sometimes blocked in part by landslides during the typhoon season. Twisk, incidentally, stands for "Tsuen Wan Into Shek Kong". Take the #51 bus (every 12–20min), which you can pick up at Tsuen Wan Ferry Pier or above Tsuen Wan MTR station.

Tai Mo Shan and the MacLehose Trail

It's a splendid climb in the bus up the hillside above Tsuen Wan, with great views back to the sea. The road twists past bamboo groves and banana trees, while the occasional clearing off to the side harbours a picnic site perched on the edge of a hill. After 4–5km, just above the village of Chuen Lung, there's an entrance into the **Tai Mo Shan Country Park**, which contains Hong Kong's highest peak, **Tai Mo Shan**, 958m above sea level. The climb is straightforward enough if you're keen, and it's a nice idea to combine it with a night in the nearby **Sze Lok Yuen youth hostel**, which you reach by getting off the #51 at the junction with the smaller Tai Mo Shan Peak Road – the hostel is signposted, around an hour's walk up the road. There's a Visitor's Centre near the bus stop, too, with details of all the other local trails, including the walk to the magnificent series of waterfalls at **Ng Tung Chai**, in the north of the park.

**The West:
Tsuen Wan,
Tuen Mun
and Yuen
Long**

At the hostel or the peak, you're actually on the **MacLehose Trail** (Stage 8), 22km from its western end at Tuen Mun; there's also a **campsite** here in the Tai Mo Shan Country Park, by the Management Centre, over on the western side of Route Twisk. If you just fancy a short day's hike, join the Trail here and walk west to Tin Fu Tsai (6km), from where you can drop down the 3–4km to the coast at Tsing Lung Tau for buses east or west along the coast.

*See pp.178–179
for more details
on the
MacLehose
Trail.*

Shek Kong

The #51 bus climbs up over the pass and rattles down the winding road into the **SHEK KONG** (pronounced "Sek" Kong) area, through rich forested slopes, offering sweeping views of the plain below. Carved into the plain, and visible from way off, is the runway belonging to Shek Kong's military garrison; as you reach ground level the road passes through neat barracks buildings. Many of the Vietnamese boat people were placed in closed camps at Shek Kong in 1989, creating an impossible situation. Security was limited since the Vietnamese were kept in tents behind wire fences in the military grounds; escapes and mass break-outs into the local area were common and, given the conditions, trouble flared both in the camp and outside in the hard-pressed neighbouring villages.

Kam Tin

The #51 bus ends its ride in **KAM TIN**, an area famous for its surviving **walled villages**. One of them at least is firmly on the tourist map, but there are a couple of others in the area, all displaying the same characteristic buildings and solid defensive walls.

KAT HING WAI is the most obvious walled village, 200m down the main road from the bus stop, opposite a small supermarket. The square walls enclose a self-contained village, encircled by a moat, which has been inhabited for nearly four hundred years by members of the Tang clan, who once farmed the surrounding area. Their ancestors moved here from central and southern China almost a thousand years ago, fortifying villages like these against pirate attacks and organizing their lives with little recourse to the measures and edicts of far-off Imperial China. As late as 1898, this village was one of the ones prepared to see action against the new

British landlords, when local militias were raised to resist the handing over of the New Territories to Britain.

Today, the buildings are as defensively impressive as ever, with guardhouses on each corner and a great wrought-iron entrance gate, but otherwise Kat Hing Wai is a rather sad sight, most of it entirely on show for tourists. Down the main street are tacky souvenir stalls and Hakka women posing for photos in their "costume" (normal wear in many parts of the New Territories). They'll want money if you try and take a photo, and it'll cost you a dollar or so to set foot through the gate in the first place.

You'd do better to make your way to **SHUI TAU TSUEN**, a few hundred metres back down the main road (towards Tsuen Wan) on the right: at the Mung Yeung Public School, follow the lane down and over the bridge. The village is much bigger, though not as immediately promising: there's new building on the outskirts and many of the old buildings are locked or falling down. But the elegant carved roofs are still apparent, and a walk around the tight alleys reveals the local temple and an ancestral hall, and gives at least some impression of normal village life. The other village in the area is **WING LUNG WAI**, up the main road in the opposite direction, beyond Kat Hing Wai, though this is mostly fenced off and inaccessible to visitors. You can, however, get into the market here for the usual mix of noise and activity.

Practicalities

The #51 **bus** stops on the main, traffic-choked Kam Tin Road, opposite the post office and *Hongkong* bank. The road is a virtual bazaar, lined with hardware stores, grocers, restaurants, bars and even discos – slightly surprising in the middle of nowhere until you pass the local military HQ on the way into Yuen Long. The *Naafi* (Navy, Army, Air Force Institute) has a Friday **market** (9am–1pm) at Shek Kong Camp, selling arts and crafts; the #51 bus can drop you close by. There are **cafés** all the way down Kam Tin Road serving noodles and the like. Scarcely any more formal, but providing a change, the *Ghurka Restaurant*, opposite the bus stop and next to the post office, has reasonably priced Nepali and Indian food.

There are a few **onward routes** to consider. As well as bus #51, which runs back to Tsuen Wan, #77K runs down the main road on its way from Yuen Long to Sheung Shui; minibus #18 runs along the same route. You can also catch bus #54 to Yuen Long, while the #64K passes the walled villages on its run between Tai Po and Yuen Long.

Yuen Long

Since it's a major transport hub, you're more than likely to end up in the town of **YUEN LONG** if you've followed any of the routes through the western New Territories. That's about all you'll do there, though; like Tuen Mun, it's not a place to hang around. These days, Yuen Long is unrecognizable as the coastal fishing village it once was – now a built-up New Town of 120,000, it's much like the others, with the LRT train line running right through the middle of the main street. But out in the surroundings there are still visible relics of an older life – small temples and ancestral homes scattered across the fragmented coastline. Unfortunately, they're almost all difficult to reach and mostly run-down, though the government has preserved a series of buildings in nearby Ping Shan which you can visit. The closest you get to tradition in Yuen Long itself are the big annual celebrations of the **Tin Hau Festival**, a throwback to the town's fishing days. If you're around at the time of the Mid-Autumn Festival, it's worth knowing that Yuen Long is also renowned for the quality of its **moon cakes**, the small lotus-seed cakes with a preserved egg yolk that are eaten at this time: some of the best in the territory are the *Wing Wah* moon cakes, made by the *Tai Wing Wah Restaurant*, 11 Tai Lee Street.

Ping Shan Heritage Trail

Opened at the end of 1993, the one-kilometre-long **Ping Shan Heritage Trail** (daily 9am–5pm) passes through an area rich in preserved traditional buildings; the Tang clan has been living in this district of Yuen Long since the twelfth century. The trail – 2km northwest of town – is well signposted, starting at the seventeenth-century Hung Shing temple and then weaving past a study hall and two ancestral halls – of which the Tang Ancestral Hall is among the finest in the territory – before reaching Tsui Shing Lau, a delightfully restored six-hundred-year-old pagoda.

To get here from either Yuen Long itself, or the Tuen Mun ferry pier, take the LRT to Ping Shan station, from where the start of the trail is a twenty-minute walk down Ping Ha Road, opposite a bus stop. By bus, the #276 from Sheung Shui KCR comes this way; get off at the second stop after passing the Ping Shan LRT station. Perhaps the best move is to combine a trip here with a meal at Lau Fau Shan (see below), easily done by hopping on the #655, which passes the trail on the way to and from Yuen Long.

Practicalities

The **bus terminal** is in On Tat Square, just off the main Castle Peak Road down Kik Yeung Road, from where you can catch buses #76K and #77K to Sheung Shui; #68M to Tuen Mun (for Mui Fat Monastery and Ching Chung Koon Temple); #68X to Jordan Road Ferry Pier; or the #64K to Tai Po Market KCR station. Down Castle Peak Road itself, minibus #18 runs into Sheung Shui, and there's a separate **minibus terminal** nearby on Tai Fung Street: to get to it, turn into Kuk Ting Street at 77 Castle Peak Rd (*Bank of East Asia*), follow Sai Tai Street, and Tai Fung Street is over on the right. This is where to come to catch the direct #34 minibus to Lau Fau Shan.

CHINA

THE NEW TERRITORIES

Lau Fau Shan

The main reason to be in Yuen Long is to take the bus out to nearby LAU FAU SHAN, an oyster-gathering and fishing village a few kilometres northwest. It's the most unusual of the places in Hong Kong to come and eat seafood, a ramshackle place literally built on old oyster shells. Even better is the fact that it's the least visited of the seafood villages, which means realistic prices and a meal in basic surroundings without the fear of being ripped off. To **get there**, you need to take minibus #34 or bus #655 from Yuen Long; the minibus leaves from the terminal on Tai Fung Street (see above), the #655 from the main Castle Peak Road

The ride takes around twenty minutes, through some fairly drastic constructions necessary to protect the local villages from floodwater. The bus stop in Lau Fau Shan is right by the only street, Ching Tai Street, which leads down to the water past a succession of small restaurants, fishmongers' stalls and dried seafood provisions stores. The oysters are turned into excellent oyster sauce, which is on sale everywhere, while the fish market is at the very end of the street. The dried foods are interesting – oysters, scallops, mussels and fish used to make soups – but they're something of a delicacy; if you want a packet of dried scallops to take home, you can expect to pay up to $500. Walk through the fish market and you're on the main jetty, on either side of which – stretching a hundred metres to the water and away as far as you can see – are piled millions of old, opened oyster shells, enormous dunes of them hiding fishing pots and wooden skiffs. The village here looks out over Deep Bay and across to the Chinese mainland – a fine aspect.

There are plenty of **restaurants** in the village, all pretty reliable. The *Bond Kee* (9 Ching Tai St; opposite no. 19 and with a Kent cigarette sign to distinguish it) is always good: choose fish and they'll bring it wriggling to your table for inspection before whisking it away to be cooked; the deep-fried oysters are also thoroughly recommended, a massive crispy plateful, easily enough for three.

CHINA

THE NEW TERRITORIES

The East: Clearwater Bay and the Sai Kung peninsula

To visit the eastern limb of the New Territories you'll need to set aside another couple of days: one to take in the popular beaches and magnificent Tin Hau Temple at **Clearwater Bay**; the other to visit the beautiful **Sai Kung peninsula**, with its fishing town, sands and nearby islands. The whole Sai Kung area is about the closest you get in Hong Kong to real isolation, though on weekends and holidays even the large country parks here aren't big enough to absorb all the visitors. Happily, most people stick to two or three spots, and if you're prepared to do some walking, you'll be able to find a bit of space.

Access to both areas is by bus from **Choi Hung** MTR station, on the Kwun Tong line (take the Clearwater Bay North exit). All the buses leave from the bus ranks just outside the station.

To Clearwater Bay

Bus #91 (as well as #91R on Sun) or regular minibuses from outside Choi Hung MTR station run east and then south along **Clearwater Bay Road**, a pleasant half-hour's ride through striking countryside, much of which forms the backdrop to a succession of expensive villas and houses with precarious views over the bays below. About halfway, you'll pass the **Shaw Brothers' Film Studio**, where countless Cantonese movies are churned out every year, before dropping down to **TAI AU MUN**, which overlooks **Clearwater Bay** itself.

There's a bus stop here, where you can get off for the first, smaller **beach** (known as #1 beach), though the bus does continue down the hill to stop at the terminus next to the much bigger #2 beach. You can count on this being packed at the weekend, despite its size, and you should take your own food if you've come for the day as there's only a snack kiosk here. It's no roomier in the adjacent "water world" slide area either. There is a path between the two beaches if you want to check on space at either one.

Joss House Bay and back

Beyond the beaches the road climbs up and across the peninsula giving marvellous views over the sea, passing the tiny village of **PO TOI O** over the other side of a small bay, which is guarded by two temples, one on either side of the bay's headlands. At the end of the road, half an hour away, is the **Clearwater Bay Country Club**, to which the HKTA sells day-passes if you're after a bit of civilized swimming and lounging about (see p.295 for more information).

A marked path to the side leads down to **Joss House Bay**, or Tai Mui Wan, where one of Hong Kong's finest temples is situated. The short path runs past an inscribed rock, the 108-character inscription dating from 1274 (Southern Sung Dynasty) and recording a visit to the area made by an officer in charge of salt administration. Further on is the **Tin Hau Temple** itself – elaborately carved and beautifully sited, with a large terrace overlooking the bay. Built originally in 1266 (though reworked several times since, particularly in 1962 after Typhoon Wanda almost destroyed it), this is *the* major site of the annual Tin Hau celebrations in Hong Kong, and there's a long quay below the terrace where thousands of passengers disgorge from the special chartered junks and ferries to come and pay homage to the Goddess of the Sea. The temple entrance is guarded by two small stone lions with round stones in their mouths: turn the stones three times for luck.

Back at the Country Club, a second path leads, circuitously, back to Clearwater Bay beach, via the village of **SHEUNG LAU WAN**. Bypassing the village, the path heads over the ridge, where you can detour to climb to the nearby summit of **Tin Ha Shan**; or simply drop straight down to the main road, just five minutes from the bus terminal. The whole walk – past Po Toi O, Joss House Bay, the temple and then around the headland – should take three to four hours depending on the heat; take water with you, and be warned that the path is sketchily marked at times – you may spend periods scampering up and down the hill looking for the route.

Tung Lung Chau

Lying just to the south of the peninsula, the small island of **Tung Lung Chau** maintains a restored eighteenth-century Chinese fort on its northern shore. Overlooking the Fat Tong Mun passage, the **Tung Lung Fort** kept a strategic eye on ships sailing from Guangzhou to Hong Kong, but it was finally abandoned to the elements at the beginning of the nineteenth century. It remained overgrown until 1979, when its rectangular walls and interior were restored and opened to the public. There's an **information centre** at the site (daily except Tues 9am–4pm), good for filling in the background to the excavations, and after poking around the fort you can walk on to Tung Lung's other historic attraction, Hong Kong's largest **rock carving**. With dimensions of roughly two by two-and-a-half metres, it represents a dragon: you reach it by taking the path from the fort, back past the ferry pier – around 1500 metres in all.

Despite the island's proximity to the Clearwater Bay peninsula, you can only reach it by **ferry from Sai Wan Ho** on Hong Kong Island, which operates on Saturday, Sunday and public holidays (currently at 8.30am and 3.30pm), and docks roughly halfway between the fort and the rock carving; it returns from the island at 9.30am and 5pm. Call ☎2560 9929 for timetable information, or check with the HKTA.

Sai Kung Town and its beaches

North of Clearwater Bay, beaches and coves spread over a much bigger area, incorporating a series of island retreats, good walking trails, even a folk museum. The whole area is known as **Sai Kung**, and is divided into two main **country parks**, with several approaches and little centres. The main centre (and the destination of all the buses from Choi Hung) is **SAI KUNG TOWN**, a rapidly developing resort that is fast outgrowing its former fishing-village borders. Bus #92 from Choi Hung MTR, or maxicab #1, gets you there in around half an hour, following Clearwater Bay Road before heading north along Hiram's Highway, passing Hebe Haven on the way. There's also a bus from Sha Tin (from the New Town Plaza), the #299.

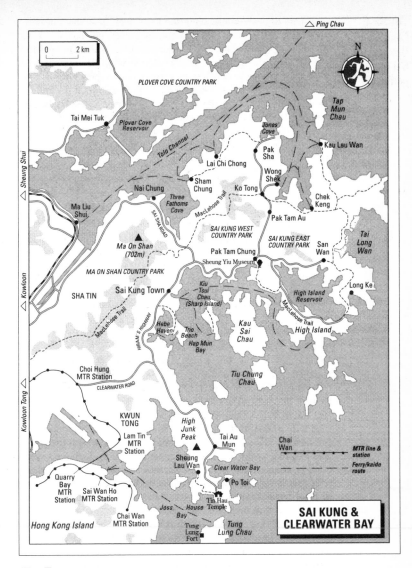

The Town

New building all around is rather dwarfing the little fishing village that Sai Kung once was, but for the moment it remains a pleasant enough seaside port. The bus terminal is just back from the sea, with the whole seafront promenade devoted to fish and seafood **restaurants**, most of which have outside seating overlooking the bay. A walk down the seafront takes you to the **fish market** in the older part of town, overlooking the junks tied up in the harbour. Stroll back, and you can pick up a fishing net, line and bait at one of the stalls, or choose your lunch from one of the slabs and buckets laid out along the quayside. The *Seaside Seafood Restaurant* is a good place to take your fish to be cooked, on the quay towards the fish market; or for a real treat, head for the *San Shui*, at the end of the quayside closest to the bus terminal, where the speciality is "bamboo fish": carp, stuffed with preserved turnip and grilled over charcoal outside on a hand-rotated bamboo pole – pricey but delicious. This is just one of a line of harbourside restaurants here serving excellent fresh fish and seafood.

There's a fairly strong expat presence in town these days, so if you wander through the few streets back from the quay you'll also come across a pub and a pizza place.

Nearby islands and beaches

Along the Sai Kung quayside, you'll be accosted by people selling tickets for *kaidos*, which run across to **islands and beaches** in the vicinity. It's a bit tricky to work out exactly where the boats are going sometimes, as there are no signs and few people speak English, but if you don't really mind and just want to hit a beach, take yourself off with the first that offers itself. They go and return at regular intervals all day, so you won't get stuck anywhere if you don't like it.

The most popular trip is the short run across to **Kiu Tsui Chau** (or Sharp Island), whose main beach at Hap Mun Bay, where the *kaidos* dock, is fine, though it's small and can get mobbed at the weekends. There are barbecue pits, and a snack bar, and a rough trail leads up through thick vegetation to the island's highest point. Most of the rest of the rocky coast is inaccessible, though *kaidos* also run from Sai Kung to Kiu Tsui, a small bay to the north of the island. Be warned that getting back to Sai Kung from Hap Mun Bay can be a bit of a scrum: you have to leave on a boat with the same coloured flag as the one that you came on, and as there's no such thing as a queue in Hong Kong it can be a fight to get on the boat.

Other *kaidos* and ferries run from Sai Kung on the longer route to **High Island**, now actually part of the mainland peninsula since dams linked it to form the High Island Reservoir. *Kaidos* also run from the yachting centre of **HEBE HAVEN** (Pak Sha Wan) across to a peninsular beach, called **Trio Beach**, south of Sai Kung Town: the bus to Sai Kung passes Hebe Haven first, or you can always walk the 2–3km from Sai Kung to the beach.

The Sai Kung peninsula

You need to make a bit more of an effort to get the best out of the rest of the **Sai Kung peninsula**, which stretches all the way north to the Tolo Channel and encompasses some supremely isolated headlands and coves. The whole region is one giant, 7500-hectare

Country Park, split into two sections, Sai Kung East and Sai Kung West, along with neighbouring **Ma On Shan Country Park**, which reaches down to Sha Tin. There have been settlements here since the fourteenth century, mostly fishing villages, though the area was never widely populated: even thirty years ago, you could still only reach most places in Sai Kung on foot. Things changed with the opening of the High Island Reservoir in 1979, and its associated road access, but Sai Kung has still not been spoiled – though it has become mightily popular with weekend-trippers who want a breath of country air. Following the marked paths through the grasslands and planted forests is indeed invigorating after a spell in the city: there's plenty of birdlife, some spectacular coastal geological formations due to the peninsula's volcanic history, and lots of quiet places just to plonk yourself down and tear into your picnic.

The **MacLehose Trail** runs right across the peninsula (see below), while you can see most of the more isolated northern coast from the **ferry** which departs twice daily from Ma Liu Shui in the New Territories to Tap Mun Chau island: there's more on this route below, and see p.152 for information about Ma Liu Shui.

The best place to start any exploration is Sai Kung Town, from where regular buses run out to many of the places covered in this section; though note the alternative approach from Sha Tin on bus #89R, which circles the Ma On Shan Country Park.

The East: Clearwater Bay and the Sai Kung peninsula

Two useful maps for the area are the Countryside Series Sheet 4 (Sai Kung and Clearwater Bay) and the Pak Tam Chung Nature Trail map; both are available from the Govt. Publications Centre; see p.47.

Pak Tam Chung

From Sai Kung Town, bus #94 (hourly) and #96R (Sun only; starts in Choi Hung; every 20min) make the fifteen-minute run around the coast to **PAK TAM CHUNG**, which isn't anything more than a bus terminal and **Visitor's Centre** (daily except Tues 9.30am–4.30pm; ☎2792 7365), where you can pick up local hiking and transport information. However, Pak Tam Chung is the effective start of the MacLehose Trail, and it also attracts visitors to the nearby **Sheung Yiu Folk Museum** (daily except Tues 9am–4pm; free), a twenty-minute walk away from the bus terminal along a nice, shady (signposted) route. The museum is based around an abandoned village, Sheung Yiu, founded 150 years ago by a Hakka family who made their living from the produce of a local lime kiln. The kiln itself is on the outskirts of the village, on the path as you approach, the lime from it used for local agriculture and building purposes. Further on, there's a line of white-washed houses constituting the village, built on a high terrace overlooking the water and defended by a thick wall and gate tower, which kept off the pirates who roamed the area in the nineteenth century. The tile-roofed houses, including an equipped kitchen house, have been restored and filled with farming implements, typical Hakka clothes and diagrams of how the kiln operation worked.

The East:
Clearwater
Bay and the
Sai Kung
peninsula

The MacLehose Trailhead: High Island and Tai Long Wan

Keep on down the Pak Tam Road from Pak Tam Chung, past the turn-off for the museum, and the **trailhead** for the western end of the cross-New Territories **MacLehose Trail** is just a few minutes' walk ahead of you. The first two stages of the hundred-kilometre route run off to the south from here, through the Sai Kung East Country Park, a twenty-kilometre hike around **High Island Reservoir** and then north to Pak Tam Road, from where you can continue the trail or cut back to Pak Tam Chung. This part of the trail would take the best part of a day to complete. There are no less than seven **campsites** along the way, one, at Long Ke Wan, on the southeastern edge of the reservoir, with a fine beach. Less committed hikers could shorten the

---

The MacLehose Trail

The **MacLehose Trail** (named after a former Governor) is a 100-kilometre-long hiking route which stretches from Pak Tam Chung on the Sai Kung peninsula to the new town of Tuen Mun. There's a sketch map of the trail below. It links seven different country parks and is divided into ten different signposted stages, each of which connects with public transport and some of which are provided with campsites, so that you can make a day's hike or complete the whole trail, as you wish. There's one official *IYHF* youth hostel right on the trail at Tai Mo Shan, as well as a couple close to the trail at Wong Shek. You could do the whole trail in four or five days, but most people take it slower, particularly if they're attempting it in the summer, when the going is hot; the most attractive sections are the easternmost ones. An annual charity race sets teams a 48-hour target for the course; the winners usually manage it in well under 24 hours.

Pick up information on the trail from the **Country Parks Division**, Agriculture and Fisheries Department, 12th Floor, 393 Canton Rd, Kowloon (Mon–Fri 9am–5pm, Sat 9am–noon; ☎2733 2132); trail maps – with a scale of 1:10,000 – are available.

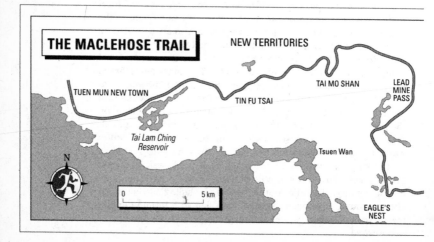

route by just walking around the reservoir and back to the trailhead, as Sai Wan Road branches off the trail about three-quarters of the way round (at Sai Wan), heading directly back to Pak Tam Chung.

If you're looking for a beach at the end of a walk, then a path just beyond Sai Wan leads north to the bay of **Tai Long Wan** – a much better target from Pak Tam Chung if you're not interested in completing any part of the MacLehose Trail for its own sake. It'll still take three to four hours for the round trip (around 12km by concrete path), but the beach is very definitely worth it: unspoiled white sand, among the finest in the territory. The small village of Ham Tin, beside the beach, has a couple of outdoor restaurants serving basic food and drinks, though they're usually only open at the weekend. Note that the last bus back from Pak Tam Road (see above) to Sai Kung is at around 7.30pm; don't miss it.

Wong Shek, Chek Keng and Jones' Cove

Bus #94 (also #95R on Sun from Pak Tam Chung) continues on across the neck of Sai Kung East Country Park to **WONG SHEK** – little more than a pier and a few barbecue pits really, and only worth coming out to if you're going to be staying at one of the nearby youth hostels or catching the *kaido* to the island of **Tap Mun Chau** to the north (see below).

Two of Hong Kong's more remote **youth hostels**, both with over a hundred beds, are in the Wong Shek area. The most popular, *Bradbury Hall*, is at **CHEK KENG**, the next village and bay to the west, which you can either reach directly on the ferry from Ma Liu Shui (see below); or by getting off the bus at the top of the pass, at Pak Tam Au, before you reach Wong Shek, and following the sign-posted path down to Chek Keng – a 45-minute walk. The hostel is right next to the sea (which, for once, is clean enough to swim in),

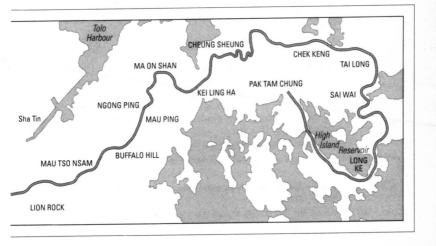

*For booking
details for both
hostels, see
"Accommo-
dation",
pp.212–13.*

and there's space for **camping**, too; you can get cold drinks and basic meals in the village.

The other hostel, *Pak Sha O*, is at **JONES' COVE**, to the north – Hoi Ha Wan on some maps. Again, you could come by ferry from Ma Liu Shui, getting off at either Lai Chi Chong or Wong Shek and following the signs, which will take around an hour to walk. But it's easier to take the #94 bus, getting off just before Wong Shek at Ko Tong. Take Hoi Ha Road, on the left, and it's around a thirty-minute walk to the hostel – though taxis are available if you hang around, and on Sundays and public holidays there's a maxicab service. Hoi Ha **beach** is around another fifteen minutes' walk from the hostel, and again, you can get simple food and cold drinks in the village.

The Northern Coast and the Tolo Channel

The most remote section of the Sai Kung peninsula is its **northern coast**, though you can easily see it by taking the **ferry from Ma Liu Shui** to Tap Mun Chau island (see below). The pier is a signposted fifteen-minute walk from the University KCR station (see p.152) and current departures are at 8.30am and 3.15pm; the return boat from Tap Mun Chau leaves at 5.20pm, with an additional lunchtime return service on Sunday.

Ma Liu Shui lies at one end of the **Tolo Channel**, which basically splits the New Territories' two most rural areas, Plover Cove and Sai Kung. The eighty-minute **ferry** ride makes for a fine half-day trip if all you're going to do is stay on board and soak up the views: the early morning departure runs up the channel for Tap Mun Chau calling on the way at isolated bays along Sai Kung's northern coast. In the order reached from Ma Liu Shui, these are: Shap Sze Heung, Sham Chung, Lai Chi Chong (for *Pak Sha O* hostel), Tai Tan (for Wong Shek), Chek Keng (for *Bradbury Hall* hostel) and Kau Lau Wan. All of these places, which are in **Sai Kung West Country Park**, are connected by paths and rougher trails, and there are campsites along the way, but you'll need to be well equipped with a tent, food and water if you're to explore the area properly.

One place on the northern coast you can visit without too much difficulty is **NAI CHUNG**, only a ten-minute bus ride from Sai Kung Town (#99; hourly). It's one of a dozen similar places in the area, where you'll find barbecue sites, picnic areas, drinks stalls and rowing boats for rent. The others can be seen (or stopped off at) if you take the opportunity to return using **bus #89R** instead from Nai Chung. It only runs on Saturday and Sunday (every 20–30min), but connects Sai Kung Town with Sha Tin on the KCR line, following the coast north around the neighbouring **Ma On Shan Country Park**.

Incidentally, if you fancy the climb to the top of **Ma On Shan** itself – Hong Kong's second highest mountain at 702m – access is by the #99 bus from Sai Kung Town. About five minutes out of Sai Kung, get off at the top of the ridge by the picnic area and follow the signposts for the MacLehose Trail – most of the steep, five-kilometre route, apart from the final peak, is part of Stage 4 of the trail. A great deal of the climb can be very tough, though the extraordinary views make the effort more than worthwhile. A few words of warning, though: you'll need decent footwear, plenty of water, and don't even think of attempting the walk in bad weather.

Tap Mun Chau

Right up in the northeast of the territory, at the mouth of the Tolo Channel, **Tap Mun Chau** is an awkward island to reach, but it is becoming an increasingly popular alternative with Hong Kong's inhabitants. Chartered boats make stops here and though there's not a great deal to see, it's the relative isolation that's the main draw.

The quickest way to **get there** is by *kaido* from Wong Shek (see above), a twenty-minute crossing: currently, departures are Monday to Saturday at 8.20am and then every two hours until 4.20pm, hourly on Sunday from 8.20am to 5.20pm. The **return** *kaidos* from Tap Mun Chau to Wong Shek leave every two hours Monday to Saturday from 7.45am to 3.45pm (with the last one at 6pm); hourly on Sunday from 8am to 5pm. The alternative approach is by ferry from Ma Liu Shui ferry pier (details above under "The Northern Coast and Tolo Channel"), and perhaps the best option for both seeing the island and enjoying a long ferry trip is to cross from the Sai Kung peninsula by *kaido* and pick up the return ferry to Ma Liu Shui (which currently departs at 5.20pm).

Both ferry and *kaido* dock in a sheltered inlet on the island's west side which contains the only **village** – a single line of crumbling houses and small shops overlooking the fish farms that constitute the only industry. It's a run-down, ramshackle kind of place, nice and quiet, with the houses on the only street open to the pavement. There's a Tin Hau temple along here, too (to the left of the pier), the venue for a large annual festival, while to the right of the pier, a fishermen's quarter straddles the low hill – nets and tackle stacked and stored in the huts and houses, many built on stilts over the water.

A couple of paths spread across the island, which is surprisingly green, leading to its English name of "Grass Island". After you've ambled around, the only thing to do is to head back to the main street and its one good **restaurant**, the *New Hon Kee*; left from the ferry pier and it's on the first corner. There's no English sign, but there is an English menu which offers reasonable seafood, fried rice and beer in a room overlooking the water.

Don't miss the last ferry whatever you do – be at the pier in plenty of time. There's no accommodation on Tap Mun Chau, and even the restaurant owners don't live on the island but back in the New Territories.

Chapter 5

The Outlying Islands

H ong Kong island is only one of 230-odd other islands scattered in the South China Sea that, together with the Kowloon peninsula and New Territories, make up the territory of Hong Kong proper. The vast majority of these **outlying islands** are tiny, barren and uninhabited; one, Chek Lap Kok, has been completely transformed by the reclamation work neccessary for it to house Hong Kong's new airport. Others are restricted areas, used as detention centres or for rehabilitating drug addicts, but the few you can visit form some of the territory's less cluttered reaches. The main destinations – the southwestern trio of **Lamma**, **Cheung Chau** and **Lantau** – are very popular with locals and tourists alike: Lantau is actually much bigger than Hong Kong Island, and staying overnight here is a distinct and attractive possibility.

None of the islands are exactly uncharted territory. The easily accessible ones have suffered from the attentions of the developers over the years, and an increasing number of Hong Kongers – *gweilos* especially – choose to live on islands like Lantau and Cheung Chau. Some of the other islands were inhabited way before Hong Kong Island itself, but their fishing communities have been abandoned and the buildings left to rot after the people moved to new cities and jobs on the mainland. Since then things have become much more developed, but some stretches of the islands can still feel relatively deserted – especially if you're lucky enough to be invited onto a private (or chartered) boat, when you can reach some supremely isolated spots.

The main reason that most people head out to any of the islands is for their **beaches**, not a bad idea given the crowded state of the sands on Hong Kong Island. However, even the fine beaches on Lantau are packed if you go at the weekend or on a public holiday, and pollution

---

OUTLYING ISLANDS: TOP FIVE ATTRACTIONS

Cheung Chau Village (pp.190–191)

Cheung Sha beach, Lantau (p.201)

Po Lin Monastery, Lantau (pp.203–204)

Tai O Village, Lantau (p.202)

Yung Shue Wan, Lamma (pp.185–186)

---

often puts many other island beaches out of bounds – at least as far as swimming goes. Luckily, there are other reasons why you might want to come. Lantau is a popular target for **hiking**, and its cross-island trail, old villages and monasteries make it easily the most interesting place to head for. Lamma and, to a lesser degree, Cheung Chau are noted for their **seafood restaurants** and food stalls; while the quieter and less visited islands – including Peng Chau – still offer a slice of the traditional Chinese life that was once lived all over the territory. You may want to stay over at one or two of the places: there are **hotels** on Cheung Chau and Lantau, and a couple of **hostels** on Lantau, all picked out in the text – you'll need to turn to the "Accommodation" chapter (p.227) for reviews and booking details.

There's a good **map** of the southwestern islands – Lantau, Cheung Chau, Peng Chau and Lamma – which is part of the *Countryside Series*, available from the Government Publications Centre, Queensway Government Offices, 66 Queensway, Admiralty. The HKTA dishes out printed **ferry and hoverferry timetables** for all the major routes, which are well worth picking up, particularly since the prices and times given below are all subject to change.

Lamma

The closest island to Hong Kong – Aberdeen is only around 3km from its northern point – **Lamma** is perhaps the best to visit if your time is limited. Its elongated fourteen square kilometres are

Island Practicalities

Getting there

Regular **ferries** run from Hong Kong Island to Lamma, Cheung Chau and Lantau. Faster (and more expensive) **hoverferries** also serve a few main destinations – like Peng Chau, or Silvermine Bay and Discovery Bay on Lantau. Most services depart from the **Central Piers** on Hong Kong Island, just west of the Star Ferry. There are exceptions, though, so check the "Travel Details" at the end of each island account for specific information. Access to a couple of places is by **kaido**, a licensed, motorized sampan or converted fishing boat; some **inter-island connections** are also made by *kaido*. These are less frequent than the ferries and though there are timetables on some of the routes, they are often impossible to track down: you'll just have to ask around.

There are also weekend **excursion ferries** to some of the most popular destinations from the Star Ferry Pier in Tsim Sha Tsui: you have to reserve ahead for these, with the *HYFCO Travel Agency*, Shop 3, Star House, Salisbury Road, Tsim Sha Tsui (☎2730 8608). Or, if you don't mind splashing out, arranging a **charter boat** is easy enough: enquire at ferry piers on the islands. For organized **tours** of the islands by boat, see p.62.

The islands covered in this chapter are the main ones in the southwest of the territory, to which there are regular ferries from Central and Kowloon. However, other, **minor islands** are accessible from various points on Hong Kong Island and in the New Territories and are covered elsewhere in the text:

Ap Lei Chau p.107   Ping Chau p.152

Po Toi Islands p.108   Tap Mun Chau p.181

Tung Lung Chau p.174

Using the ferries

You can't reserve seats on the ferries: it's first come, first served, so get there early at busy times. **Tickets** to all main destinations cost around $8

---

still largely unspoiled and you can round off a trip with a meal in one of the fine seafood restaurants there. There's no motorized traffic on the island, something which attracts many expats to live on Lamma, in search of a rural existence within commuting distance of Hong Kong. By and large they've found it: what development there is is fairly low-key, and some of the more outrageous recent planning proposals have been defeated by conservationists. Much of Lamma's northern region was designated to be the site of an oil refinery in the early 1970s. Opposition, and the recession of 1974, put paid to that, though nothing could prevent the later building of the power station at Po Lo Tsui, on the northwestern coast. This is the island's major eyesore, though it's gradually being rivalled by the quarrying operations on the other side of the island, overlooking Sok Kwu Wan. Still, once you're on the hilltops following the well-marked paths and trails, Lamma regains its peace and quiet.

one-way for "ordinary class" and around $14 for "de luxe class" (upstairs, on the air-conditioned top deck). These fares virtually **double after noon on Saturday** for the duration of the weekend; children under 12 pay half-price at all times. All return tickets are double the price of a single. **Hoverferry** tickets cost around $20–25 one-way: adults and children pay the same price. If you can, especially at the weekend, buy a return ticket on all services so you won't have to queue on the way back.

None of the journeys are very long – around an hour maximum on all the main routes – and if you can't get a seat, you can always lounge on deck; coming back into Hong Kong, especially, the views are fabulous. Each ferry also has a small **bar** selling coffee, sandwiches, hot noodles, cold drinks and beer.

On a *kaido*, you generally pay the fare to the person operating the boat. It will usually only be around $5–10, though tourists can expect to pay more than the locals on some routes. Sometimes, when there's no regular service, you'll need to charter the whole boat – the text tells you when it's necessary and roughly how much it will cost.

When to go

Services to all the main islands are more frequent on **Sunday** for a good reason: the entire territory swaps its packed vertical apartment blocks for packed horizontal beaches. There are enormous queues at the piers, and, after noon on Saturday and all day Sunday, the fares shoot up, too. If you are planning to stay **overnight** on any of the islands, be prepared to pay vastly inflated prices at the weekend, and think about booking well in advance.

Midweek is much better for a quieter visit anywhere, when some places can seem positively secluded. Note that a major annual disruption to the timetables occurs during the **typhoon season** (May–Oct), when ferry services can be abandoned at very short notice. Listen to the bulletins and check with the harbour office if you want to avoid being stranded.

Yung Shue Wan

Ferries run to the two villages on the island, Yung Shue Wan in the northwest and Sok Kwu Wan at the island's squeezed middle. As it's an easy walk between the two, and the best seafood is at Sok Kwu Wan, you're best off aiming first for **YUNG SHUE WAN** ("Banyan Bay"), which is also connected to Hong Kong Island by regular *kaido* service from Kennedy Town. The ferry trip takes forty minutes to the little village, huddled around its harbour, and with just one street, **Yung Shue Wan Main Street**, at the end of which is a typically gloomy, century-old **Tin Hau temple** overlooking the water. The expat presence in the village is manifest in the new bars and restaurants, and the apartment buildings spreading up behind the village, but it remains small-scale enough to be pleasant. Really, the only things that spoil the village atmosphere are the two huge chimney stacks of the power station that glare down from behind the hill.

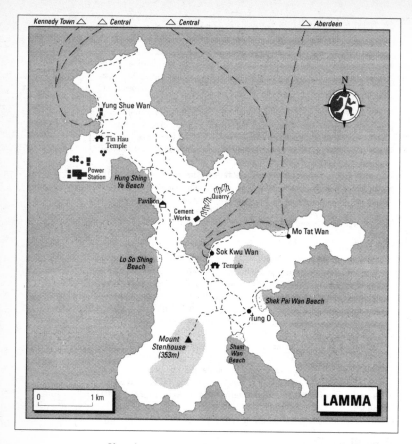

Kennedy Town △ △ Central △ Central △ Aberdeen

Yung Shue Wan

Tin Hau
Temple

Power
Station

Hung Shing
Ya Beach

Pavilion

Cement
Works

Quarry

Mo Tat Wan

Sok Kwu Wan

Temple

Lo So Shing
Beach

Shek Pai Wan Beach

Tung O

Mount
Stenhouse
(353m)

Sham
Wan
Beach

N

0   1 km

LAMMA

If you've come intending to walk across the island, there's nothing much to stop you heading straight off, though the narrow seafront street has a scattering of **restaurants**, a couple with terrace tables outside. Good places here include the *Banyan Café*, 22 Main St, a budget-rated, laid-back café serving a mix of Asian dishes; the *Waterfront* at no. 58, with views and similarly eclectic food on different floors; the *Lancombe*, at no. 47, with no-nonsense fish specialities and decent prices; and the *Man Fung Seafood Restaurant*, at no. 5, one of the better of Yung Shue Wan's terrace restaurants, with *dim sum* in the morning, fresh fish and a long list of budget rice or noodle combination dishes, which will set you up for an afternoon's walk.

Lamma's accommodation is detailed on p.227.

If you made the trip the other way, or if you just fancied the island air, there is **accommodation** in the village, too, including the *Lamma Vacation House*, down Main Street on the left-hand side.

The walk to Sok Kwu Wan

It's around 3–4km on foot to Sok Kwu Wan, across the hill from the northern half of the island and down through the narrow waist of land at Lo So Shing. It'll take an hour or so: from Yung Shue Wan, take the left turn off Main Street, before the Tin Hau temple; the signs say "Hung Shing Ye".

Along a good concrete path, it's a twenty-minute walk to HUNG SHING YE, where there's a tiny sand beach with first-hand views of the power station. It's nice enough when it's empty and there are barbecue pits, a couple of places to get a drink and holiday apartments stretching back up the hillside from the sand. There's another hotel, too, the *Han Lok Yuen*, where you can also eat pigeon or seafood at the terrace tables.

From Hung Shing Ye a clear footpath continues around the beach and up the hill on the other side, now signposted to "Sok Kwu Wan". It's quite a climb on a hot day, but it's not long until the path levels out and you reach a viewing point marked by a Chinese pavilion, roughly halfway between the two villages. Carry on down the hill and views of Sok Kwu Wan gradually unfold – as do those of the vast cement works and quarry away to your left. The path reaches down to the island's waist, and, at the small village school, there's a diversion to LO SO SHING, to the right, a bigger and sandier beach than at Hung Shing Ye, with changing rooms and showers, a snack kiosk and more barbecue pits. It's usually all right for swimming, too, though check the information board first for the current condition of the water. Back onto the main path, it's only another twenty minutes to the other village on the island, Sok Kwu Wan.

Sok Kwu Wan

The bay at SOK KWU WAN is entirely devoted to fish farming. Floating wooden frames cover the water, interspersed with rowing boats, junks and the floating canvas shelters of the fishermen and women. A concrete path runs the length of the village, from the obligatory Tin Hau temple to the main pier, along which Sok Kwu Wan's seafood restaurants form a line. They're the only real reason to come, though what was once a low-key array of simple eating houses has turned into a range of polished restaurants, with outdoor tables overlooking the bay and large fish tanks set back on the street. Some restaurants have special set menus in English posted on the walls, and these are worth investigating – *always* ask the price first, certainly if you're choosing your fish straight from the tank.

The only drawback to eating on the terraces is the view over the bay: the whole hillside opposite has been quarried, scarred and despoiled by storage containers, corrugated-iron huts and a large conveyor belt; and the bay itself – sometimes known by its alternative name, Picnic Bay – is rapidly becoming soiled by the refuse generated by the intensive fish farming in the area. It's illegal for the fishermen to live on the floating rafts, but many do: they use the polystyrene floats at the pier to row themselves across to the fish frames, where they erect canvas shelters, from which they dump sewage and rubbish.

Mo Tat Wan and Mount Stenhouse

If you arrive early enough in the day, there are a couple of other targets around Sok Kwu Wan that can fill in the time before dinner. It's a 25-minute walk (left as you step off the ferry pier) to **MO TAT WAN**, another small beach village and usually quieter than the others on the island. It's one of the oldest villages in Hong Kong, here in some shape or form for over three hundred years, though there's not much to show for it. The *Coral* restaurant provides one reason to hang around, with reasonably priced seafood; and the **kaido** service to Aberdeen from Sok Kwu Wan calls in regularly every day; there's a timetable posted at Sok Kwu Wan pier.

A path from Mo Tat Wan leads the kilometre or so to the bigger beach of **Shek Pai Wan** on the southeastern coast, from where you can continue on – past Tung O – to the smaller **Sham Wan** beach. This is perhaps the remotest beach on the island, and is worth heading to if only for that reason.

Cast around a bit, either in Sok Kwu Wan or at Shek Pai Wan and Sham Wan, and it's not difficult to find one of the paths that lead eventually up to the summit of **Mount Stenhouse**, 353m up in the middle of the island's southwestern bulge. Also known as Shan Tei Tong, it's quite a climb, particularly since the paths aren't wonderful, but you'll be rewarded with some fine views. It should take just under two hours from Sok Kwu Wan to climb up and down again; make sure you take plenty of water along if you're going to tackle it.

Lamma Travel Details

Central Piers
to Yung Shue Wan (14–15 daily; first at 6.45am, Sun at 8.15am, last at 12.30am);
Sok Kwu Wan (7–9 daily; first at 8am, last at 11pm).

Kennedy Town
to Yung Shue Wan (regular *kaido* service).

Aberdeen
to Mo Tat Wan/Sok Kwu Wan (Mon–Sat 6–8 daily, Sun every 45min; first at 6.50am, Sun at 8am, last at 7.15pm).

Yung Shue Wan
to Central (13–14 daily; first at 6.20am, Sun at 6.50am, last at 10.35pm);

to Kennedy Town (regular *kaido* service).

Sok Kwu Wan
to Central (7–8 daily; first at 6.50am, Sun at 8.20am, last at 10pm); to Mo Tat Wan/Aberdeen (6–8 daily, last at 6.45pm, Sun at 6.30pm).

For ticket prices and other ferry details, see pp.184–185. For up-to-date ferry information, call the Hong Kong Ferry Co. ☎*2542 3081.*

Cheung Chau

An hour southwest of the city, **Cheung Chau** is the most congested of the outlying islands, the central waist of its dumb-bell shape crammed with buildings, its harbour and typhoon shelter busy day and night. However, unlike some of the other islands, it's not an artificial development caused by invading outsiders seeking peace and quiet – though certainly these exist on Cheung Chau. Rather, the island is one of the oldest settled parts of Hong Kong, with a prosper-

THE OUTLYING ISLANDS

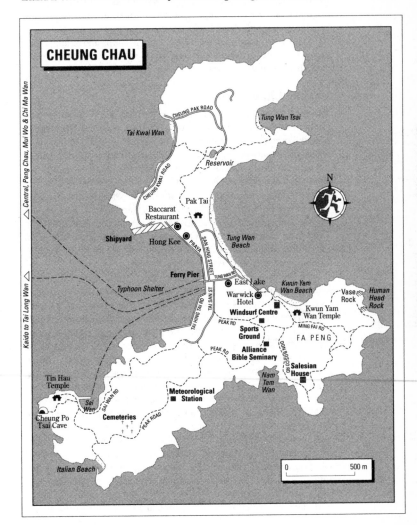

ity based on fishing, supplemented in the past, with smuggling and piracy. There's a life here that's independent of the fortunes of Hong Kong, manifest in a surviving junk shipyard, several working temples and one of Hong Kong's best annual festivals.

Concrete **paths** cover the entire island, and, despite the name, which means "long island" in Cantonese, you can whip around the place fairly quickly. Like Lamma, no cars are allowed here, though you'll have to listen out for the buzz of the motorized scooter-like work vehicles as you walk along – the paths aren't really wide enough for you both. Much of the relatively undeveloped parts of the island are taken up by youth camps, and the two or three fine beaches are regularly crowded. But for all that, the paths repay a dawdle: traditional life thrives in the main village, with its shops and fishing boats and stalls; there are some excellent views as you go; and – as ever – sampling Cheung Chau's seafood is a major reason to visit.

Cheung Chau Village

The ferry from Central picks its way through the breakwaters and junks to dock at **CHEUNG CHAU VILLAGE**, where all the population and activity is concentrated. The waterfront road, or **Praya**, is where the fishermen still lay out their catch in water-filled trays and buckets, and early morning and mid-afternoon this develops into a small market, with the fishermen joined by fruit and veg and clothes sellers. There's not much to the crowded few streets that make up the centre of the village but it invites a leisurely stroll. From opposite the ferry pier, Tung Wan Road leads across the island's waist to Tung Wan Beach (see below), a short walk through a couple of twists and turns lined with stalls and shops, the place to snap up bamboo hats and other essential beach gear.

One block in from the water, **San Hing Street** is the main street, leading up about 500m to the **Pak Tai Temple**, built in 1788 and set in its own little square. Not surprisingly, on an island once totally dependent on fishing, the inhabitants deemed it prudent to dedicate a temple to Pak Tai, the protector of fishermen and "supreme emperor of the dark heaven". Inside, there are relics appropriate to Pak Tai's status: an 800-year-old iron sword, fished out of the sea; a golden crown; a gilded nineteenth-century sedan chair, made to carry the god's image during festivals; and a plaque recording the 1966 visit of Princess Margaret.

The temple is also the venue for the annual four-day **Cheung Chau Bun Festival**, or "Tai Chiu", in late April/early May, held since the ravages of a series of eighteenth- and nineteenth-century plagues that supposedly appeased the vengeful spirits of those wrongly killed by Cheung Chau's pirates. Outside the temple, several sets of bamboo scaffolding are erected, each around twenty metres high and topped with pink and white buns. Up until 1978, at midnight on a designated day, people were encouraged to clamber up the frames to grab the buns, which would bring good luck – the higher the bun, the

better the luck. This particular activity was stopped after what the
tourist authorities refer to darkly as "an unfortunate accident"*, and
these days the buns are just handed out from the bottom of the
frames. The festival's other great draw is the teams of costumed children riding on floats through the streets, some of their peers
strapped onto stilts on which they glide over the crowds. The village
is packed for the four days of the festival – extra ferries are laid on
from Hong Kong – and it's a fascinating time to come: as well as the
high-profile displays, there are a whole host of religious services,
Chinese opera performances, unicorn and lion dances, and all the
bluster and bustle that the Cantonese bring to any celebration.

North of the village

Just down from the temple, at the water, are the **boatyards**, where
junk-builders still work entirely by hand, using no plans and skills
that haven't changed much in five hundred years – though electric
drills and saws have been introduced. Even more unusually, you may
also catch sight of blocks of ice being shipped out of the adjacent ice-
making factory, and loaded onto boats for removal to Hong Kong.

Beyond here, the **northern** stretch of the island only has views
to offer but they're worth the effort. On the seafront, just after the
fire station, some steep steps on the right lead up to a new housing
estate, from where you can look down over the village and harbour.
Or continue around the headland, following the waterfront Cheung
Kwai Road: there's a path off to the left after a few hundred metres
(marked "Family Trail") which leads up to a hilltop **reservoir**, from
where there are splendid views right over the whole island. From
the reservoir, you can descend straight back down into the village,
past a small cemetery – you'll come out close to the Pak Tai Temple.

The East Coast: Tung Wan and Kwun Yam Wan

Across the waist of land from the ferry pier, a few minutes' walk up
Tung Wan Road, is the island's main beach, **Tung Wan Beach**, 700–
800m of fine sand and as popular as anywhere in the territory at the
weekend. There are a couple of restaurants by the beach, as well as
Cheung Chau's bid for the weekend set, the *Warwick* hotel, at the
southern end. Just past here, around the little headland, there's
another sweep of sand, **Kwun Yam Wan Beach** (or Afternoon
Beach), probably the best on the island. The **Windsurf Centre** here
rents out all the relevant bits and pieces and the bar/café at the
centre is a good place for a beer.

A walk around the island

If you've got a couple of hours and fancy something more strenuous
than loafing on a beach, the **southern** part of the island lends itself to

---

*In fact, a couple of the towers collapsed and 24 people were injured.

a good, circular walk along tree-shaded paths. From the waterfront in the village, close to the ferry pier, jump on a *kaido* to **SAI WAN**, across the harbour at the southwestern tip of the island: you'll hear the name of the village being called by the *kaido* operators, or just ask someone on the quayside. It's a five-minute crossing and on the way the *kaido* sometimes calls at one or two of the junks in the harbour, depositing people laden with shopping at their floating homes.

From Sai Wan's pier, a path leads up to one of the island's several **Tin Hau** temples, where there's a pavilion overlooking the harbour. A path runs over the brow of the hill to a rocky bluff, part of which has been landscaped with barbecue pits. Follow everyone else scrambling over the rocks and you'll come to the so-called **Cheung Po Tsai Cave**, touted as the HQ of a notorious Cheung Chau pirate. Whether it was or wasn't, the adventurous and agile can climb through the underground passage here: unless you follow someone else, you'll need a flashlight, which you can buy from a woman sitting at the entrance: it'll cost around $30, though make it clear that you're only renting it and you'll get $20 or so back when you return it. The climb is fairly hard going, though faint hearts will be shamed by the queue of elderly women risking the drop into the abyss with their grandchildren.

Back at Sai Wan pier, follow the only road (Peak Rd) for several hundred metres and detour right down to Pak Tso Wan, known as **Italian Beach** – small and sandy, though a little grubby. The road climbs up through a series of **cemeteries**, with occasional pavilions providing views over the sea, into Lung Tsai Tseun, once a separate village but now a southern outpost of the main village. Just after the Alliance Bible Seminary building, take Fa Peng Road to the right and then follow Don Bosco Road, which leads down to Salesian House, a religious retreat, before doubling back to **Fa Peng Knoll**, the island's eastern bulge. Turn left here and the path runs down past the **Kwun Yam Temple**, at which point you're back at Kwun Yam Wan beach and only a short walk from the centre. Alternatively, you can follow a path from Fa Peng that will take you around the eastern headland, climbing down the cliffside to view a series of weirdly shaped **rocks** that have supposedly self-explanatory names – Vase Rock, Human Head Rock and Loaf Rock; in fact, they could equally be called Big Splodge Rock, Amorphus Rock and Vague Shape Rock.

Practicalities

There are **bike rental** shops on the road between the Pak Tai Temple and the Praya, as well as at the northern end of the Praya itself. There's no shortage of **holiday apartments** to let, either, complete with bathroom and kitchen and many overlooking the beach. During midweek, they're reasonably cheap, even more so if you can get three or four people together. The only time to avoid, or book months in advance, is the period of the Bun Festival, though staying at weekends is relatively pricey, too. Try one of the agencies opposite

Cheung Chau Travel Details

Ferries: daily

Central Piers to Cheung Chau (at least hourly; first at 6.25am, last at 12.30am).

Tsim Sha Tsui to Cheung Chau (Sat at 4pm, Sun at 8am &10am).

Cheung Chau to Central Piers (at least hourly; first at 5.35am, last at 11.30pm); Tsim Sha Tsui (Sun at 12.45pm).

Hoverferries: Mon–Fri only

Central to Cheung Chau (at 9am, 10.15am, 12.15pm, 2.15pm & 4.05pm).

Cheung Chau to Central (at 9.40am, 10.50am, 12.50pm, 2.50pm & 4.50pm).

Inter-Island Ferry Service: daily

Cheung Chau to Chi Ma Wan and Mui Wo (both on Lantau) and on to Peng Chau (roughly every 2hr; first at 7am, last at 10.10pm; not every departure calls at every stop, so check the timetable at the pier).

For ticket prices and other ferry details, see pp.184–185. For up-to-date ferry information, call the Hong Kong Ferry Co. ☎2542 3081.

the ferry pier: you'll see the photo-boards, with details, as you disembark and will pay around $300 a night (for two people); more like $500 at the weekend. Of the **hotels**, the obvious – if most expensive – place to stay is the *Warwick*, overlooking Tung Wan Beach.

For details of hotels on Cheung Chau, see p.227.

For **eating**, most of the village's waterfront Praya is lined with small restaurants, both north and south of the ferry pier. At night, the whole street is decked out with tables and chairs as the *dai pai dongs* arrive to dish out cheap and excellent seafood; take your pick of places and point to what you want. If you need a place with an English menu, try the *East Lake Restaurant*, up Tung Wan Road, on the way to the main beach; or check out those at the northern end of the Praya, nearest the Pak Tai Temple, especially the *Baccarat* or the *Hong Kee*, which serve very tasty things like garlic fried prawns or scallops, and Yang Chow fried rice. For **bottled water** and cold **beer**, there's a *Wellcome* supermarket opposite the ferry pier.

Note that if you're on Cheung Chau during the Bun Festival, the island goes **vegetarian** for a few days – no great hardship since the food on offer remains excellent.

Peng Chau

Some ferries and hoverferries on their way to Lantau (see below) call first at **Peng Chau**, a tiny horseshoe-shaped blob of land fifty minutes from Hong Kong and just twenty minutes from its larger neighbour. It's firmly part of the little southwestern archipelago of islands and is relatively densely populated, but few tourists bother to get off the hoverferry. In truth, there's no real reason why they

Peng Chau Travel Details

Ferries

Central Piers to Peng Chau (hourly; first at 7am, last at 12.30am).

Peng Chau to Central Piers (hourly; first at 6.30am, last at 11.30pm).

Hoverferries: Mon–Fri only

Central Piers to Peng Chau (at 9.40am, 11.20am, 2.25pm & 4.25pm).

Peng Chau to Central Piers (at 10.30am, 12.20pm, 3.20pm & 5.20pm).

Inter-Island Ferry Service: daily

Peng Chau to Mui Wo/Chi Ma Wan/Cheung Chau (roughly every 2hr; first at 5.40am, last at 7.50pm; check the timetable at the pier).

Kaido

Peng Chau to Tai Shui Hang (Trappist Monastery, Lantau; roughly hourly; 5.30am–9.45pm).

For ticket prices and other ferry details, see pp.184–185. For up-to-date ferry information, call the Hong Kong Ferry Co. ☎2542 3081.

should, though the quiet streets are a pleasant alternative to the busy antics of Mui Wo. You could see the whole of Peng Chau in the hour or so that you'll have to wait for the next connection; there are inter-island ferries to Peng Chau from Mui Wo throughout the day.

Wing On Street, just back from the pier, is a typical island street, part market, part residential, with its eighteenth-century Tin Hau temple, noodle shops, Chinese herbalists and no traffic. Some shops here sell hand-painted porcelain, a local cottage industry. Signs point you in the direction of **Tung Wan**, the island's only real beach. It's five minutes' walk away and the bay is pretty enough, with a barbecue site at one end and a few fishing boats. Really, though, you won't want to hang around, unless you've been tempted into one of the **seafood restaurants**, where the food is as good and as cheap as on any of the islands.

Hei Ling Chau

A fairly frequent service runs from the quayside to **Hei Ling Chau**, an island south of Peng Chau and around twice its size, though don't get on the ferry by mistake, since part of the island is used as a drug rehabilitation centre – the chattering trippers are actually visiting relatives.

THE OUTLYING ISLANDS

Lantau

Since it's by far the biggest island in the territory, you could spend three or four days exploring **Lantau**'s fairly obvious charms. The name means "broken head" in Cantonese, though it looks more like the shape of a dog when viewed on a map. Twice the size of Hong Kong Island, Lantau is wild and rugged enough in parts to make real hiking

an attractive option; some of the beaches are among the best in Hong
Kong, and for once there's a full set of cultural diversions, including
several monasteries and Southeast Asia's tallest seated Buddha statue.

Sooner rather than later, too, most people's first glimpse of
Hong Kong will be of Lantau once the new **airport** (see pp.204–
205) on neighbouring Chek Lap Kok is in operation. Over the next
few years Lantau's north coast will change beyond recognition as
the the new highway and airport rail line will prompt urban expansion along what was previously one of the more isolated stretches of
the territory's coastline.

Nevertheless, there should still be plenty of room to get away
from it all, since much of the island is preserved as a country park.
The circular seventy-kilometre-long **Lantau Trail** loops around the
southern half of the island, passing campsites and the island's two
youth hostels along the way. We've marked the trail on our map, but if
you want more detailed information, pick up the free leaflet *Lantau
Trail*, published by the Country Parks Authority (CPA), which lists
the route stages and picks out the relevant camping and local transport details; there's a staffed CPA booth at the ferry pier in Mui Wo,
and for anything more than an afternoon's stroll you'll need camping
equipment and all the related gear. You don't have to tackle the whole
thing at once: there are a couple of easy stages and other half-day
walks accessible from Mui Wo, the village where the ferries dock.

If you're not going to take in any of the Lantau Trail, you're
going to have to rely on some form of **transport** on the island.
Lantau has a small **bus** network (see "Travel Details" at the end of
the account for routes and timetables), which will get you to nearly
all of the places covered below, and there are **taxis**, too.

Mui Wo (Silvermine Bay)

The large ferries from Hong Kong all dock at **MUI WO** ("five petal
flower"), generally known by its English name "Silvermine Bay",
after the silver mine which once brought prosperity to the village
but has long since been boarded up. The walk to the site of the mine
is pleasant enough, about a kilometre inland from the village and
close to a waterfall. The village itself is actually about the least interesting place on the island and most people head from the ferry
straight to the **bus terminal** outside, where queues build up quickly
for buses to the most popular destinations on the island. **Taxis** leave
from the same square and travel information (on ferries back to
Central, etc) is posted on boards at the pier building.

To the right of the bus terminal is the **Cooked Food Market**
(6am–midnight) – a dozen or so covered stalls with outside tables that
overlook the bay itself. They're all fairly cheap, serving bowls of
noodles, seafood and the like. A little more salubrious, and not much
more expensive, is the welcoming *Sang Lee*, a simple **restaurant** with
a terrace overlooking the bay – it's a little way beyond the market on

the way to the beach. Other options are nearby: a *Wellcome* super-market and a *Park 'N' Shop* around the main square, and the *Rome* cake shop, across the square from the ferry pier.

Beyond the Cooked Food Market, a path leads around to the long, curving **beach**, backed by restaurants, barbecue pits, showers and toilets. Unfortunately, the water here has been considered too polluted for safe swimming for the last few years, though that doesn't seem to stop the locals fishing in it, or dredging the sands for shellfish. Still, it looks an attractive stretch of sand from a distance, and there are two **hotels** which capitalize on the nice views across the bay: the large *Silvermine Beach Hotel* (which has a reservations booth at the ferry pier and a terrace café with bay views) and the smaller, more pleasant *Mui Wo Inn*, further along.

For details about all Lantau's hotels, turn to p.227.

Also along the beach at Mui Wo you can **rent bicycles** for around $30 an hour, though given the steep hills between Mui Wo and everywhere else and the excellent bus service, it's difficult to see why you would want one. Mui Wo is also the starting and finishing point of the **Lantau Trail**: section 1 (outwards) runs southwest down the road towards Nam Shan, while section 12 (return) cuts up from the Chi Ma Wan peninsula to the ferry pier.

North: to the Trappist Monastery and Discovery Bay

One of the best short hikes you can make from Mui Wo is over the hills to the Trappist Haven Monastery in the next bay north. It takes around an hour and a half: head along the seafront Tung Wan Tau Road (past the hotels) and take the path on the left by the river, at the end of the beach; keep going straight up, with the river to your left, and the path loops round eventually to the right, steep and very overgrown in parts and signposted only once, right at the very end. There are some excellent views as you go, over Peng Chau and to Hong Kong in the distance, and – if you wish – you can detour to the peak on your left, from where you'll get a view over the golf course above Discovery Bay. Otherwise, stick to the path to the right of the peak, which brings you out at the dairy farm above the **Trappist Haven Monastery**. Founded by refugees from mainland China, the monastery supports itself by selling milk to various outlets in Hong Kong. There's a **kaido** service across to Peng Chau (from where you can return directly to Central) from the small pier at the end of the road beyond the monastery. There are only a few daily crossings, the last one at 4.30pm, so if you miss it, you'll have to walk back to Mui Wo in order to return to Hong Kong.

Discovery Bay and the North

The alternative is to press on to **NIM SHUE WAN**, a couple of kilometres away; there's a path from the Trappist Monastery or a *kaido* service from the monastery's pier. There's a small beach here, at which you should be able to swim, and a road which leads down into **DISCOVERY BAY** ("Disco Bay" to the *gweilo* locals), a fast-growing residential New Town with its own beach, water sports facilities, shops, markets and banks. The main attraction for visitors is the route back to Hong Kong Island that Disco Bay offers: a 24-hour hoverferry service (every 20min during peak hours) provides a half-hour ride to the pier next to the Star Ferry in Central.

North of Discovery Bay there's a network of hiking trails, though nowhere particularly exciting to hike to and nowhere – other than camping in the rough countryside – to stay. Moreover, what destinations there are – principally the inlets of Chek Ko Wan (Penny's Bay) and Yam O Wan – will soon be overwhelmed forever by construction work associated with the airport highway and rail line, due to be routed along Lantau's north coast.

Chi Ma Wan peninsula

The other short walk from Mui Wo is to the **Chi Ma Wan peninsula**, a foot of land around 4km south of the ferry pier. The most direct route there is to follow the first section of the Lantau Trail as far as Nam Shan (where there's a **campsite**) and then switch to the last section of the trail, following it south to the peninsula: you'll come out on Chi Ma Wan Road, which runs east–west across the neck of the peninsula.

East along the road it's only a short walk to **Chi Ma Wan** itself, the bay giving its name to the detention centre there for Vietnamese awaiting resettlement. From the pier, there's a handy **ferry** service, either back to Mui Wo or on to Cheung Chau to the south. With a good map you could make your way around the peninsula clockwise

Lantau

from Chi Ma Wan (there's another campsite right at the peninsula's easternmost point), but it's more rewarding to take in the **western side**. There's a youth hostel there to aim for, and you can cut out the walk from Mui Wo by taking the bus (#1 or #7) from the Mui Wo ferry pier to **PUI O**, where there's an excellent beach. It's one of the most popular on the island, with barbecue pits here, a campsite at its eastern end and, back on the main road, a few simple restaurants, like the Thai *Nam On*. You might find an apartment for rent if you ask around, or try the reasonable *Sea Breeze Hotel* on the main road.

From the bus stop on the main road at Pui O, follow the signpost (on the left) to **HAM TIN**. A concrete footpath leads you across the fields and alongside the river to a small temple, from where another signpost points up towards **Mong Tung Wan** – just under an hour's walk, with lovely views over Pui O beach. The quiet bay has a **youth hostel**, made up of white bungalows set back from the harbour – a nice, clean place, though packed to the gills on Saturday nights from June to August. The warden serves breakfast ($5–15) and dinner (around $30) and camping is allowed here, too; there's a shop selling beer and soft drinks, and barbecue pits outside. The path from the hostel leads down to a tiny harbour, where you could swim, though it's rocky and a little murky. The hostel warden can arrange for a **kaido** to pick you up from the harbour and take you over to Cheung Chau: it'll cost around $80 for the boat and you'll have to order it the night before.

For reservation details for Mong Tung Wan hostel, see pp.212–213. You can reach the hostel by kaido from the waterfront at Cheung Chau. Ask for Mong Tung Wan; it should cost around $100 for the boat.

Yi Long and Tai Long Wan

A footpath runs on from Mong Tung Wan around the peninsula, climbing steeply above the coast, and you can clamber down to good beaches at a couple of places. At **YI LONG**, there's a swanky new private development, *Sea Ranch*, and if you don't fancy the beach there, the next bay along, **Tai Long Wan**, has some long and usually empty sands. It's hard going, though, especially to reach Tai Long Wan, and an easier way of getting there is by *kaido* from Cheung Chau's waterfront (around $80–100, depending on numbers).

The real attraction at Tai Long Wan is the **Frog & Toad** (☎2989 2300), a splendid bar/restaurant at the back of the tiny village behind the beach. A three-storey village house with a roof terrace, at the weekend it's crowded with expats drinking enormous amounts of beer and tucking in to the pub food. The downstairs bar turns into a sweaty disco after about the fifteenth tequila slammer and the whole thing shuts when the last person leaves. As the only realistic way out is by *kaido*, either arrange for the one that brought you from Cheung Chau to return at a certain time, or get someone at the bar to ring for one when you're ready to go.

The south coast: Pui O to Fan Lau

Lantau's best beaches are all on the **south coast** and most are easily accessible by **bus** from Mui Wo; bus #4 (to Tong Fuk), #5 (to Shek

Pik) and #2 (to Po Lin Monastery) run along the coast, so you can get off wherever you like.

Pui O beach (see above) is the closest to Mui Wo, around a fifteen-minute bus ride away. The next one along, at **CHEUNG SHA**, is considered by many to be the best in the territory. There are a couple of cafés here, serving simple Chinese food and cold drinks; a campsite; and the possibility of renting a **room** at the *Cheung Sha Resort House*.

Cheung Sha beach stretches all the way down to **TONG FUK** (more cheap Chinese cafés as well as *The Gallery*, an English-style pub only open on Sundays), where the road strikes inland to reach the **Shek Pik Reservoir**, an impressive construction whose surroundings have been planted and landscaped to provide picnic areas and walking trails. The reservoir, with a capacity of 5500 million gallons, provides much of Hong Kong with drinking water. Collected here by tunnels and gullies, it swooshes through another tunnel to Mui Wo, where a treatment centre close to the ferry pier cleans the water and pipes it to Hong Kong Island. There's a beach below the reservoir at Tai Long Wan, a short walk away. The road up to Tao O/Po Lin (see below) skirts the reservoir and if you crane your head up to the opposing hilltop, you'll get a first view of the seated Buddha – his back to you at this point.

A longer walk from Shek Pik, following a section of the Lantau Trail, leads past a couple of fairly isolated campsites to **FAN LAU**, 5km away on the southwestern tip of the island. It takes around two hours to walk from Shek Pik, via Kau Ling Chung. There are two excellent beaches here, a large east-facing one and a smaller west-facing one a few minutes' walk away, as well as the remains of a 1300-year-old rectangular **fort**, from which there are fine views across the water. Built to garrison troops, the fort overlooked a strategic sea route into the Pearl River Estuary, but was abandoned at the turn of this century. The Lantau Trail swings

---

The Soko Islands

Several of the much smaller islands around Lantau provide ample evidence of the rapid depopulation of the outlying islands, as people move to Hong Kong Island and the New Territories in search of work. The most extreme example of depopulation is that provided by the little archipelago of the Soko Islands, sometimes visible off the south coast of Lantau. This once supported viable communities, linked to Hong Kong by ferry, but as the inhabitants moved out, the islands became the target of weekenders on private yachts seeking an isolated anchorage. In 1989, the last two inhabitants, an elderly couple living on Tai A Chau, the largest island, moved out, renting their home to the government who turned the Sokos into a Vietnamese "reception" centre – a desperate move to alleviate the chronic accommodation shortage for that summer's newly arrived Vietnamese. There was no shelter or fresh water on the Sokos at the time, and four thousand people were crammed onto an overgrown, rubbish-laden Tai A Chau – a sad way of repopulating the islands.

---

north from Fan Lau, with Tai O village around two to three hours' walk further on.

Tai O and around

The largest village on Lantau, **TAI O**, on the northwestern coast, was once the centre of a thriving salt export trade to China. The salt pans are still visible, though the local fishermen have converted them into fish ponds – an enterprise which hasn't stopped the village population from falling rapidly as people move to the city to look for jobs. There are still around three thousand people left in Tai O, though, and it's a favourite tourist destination, with plenty of interest in the village's old streets, shrines and temples.

The village splits into two halves: a mainland section, where the **bus** stops (#1 from Mui Wo; a 45-min ride), and an island settlement, across a narrow creek. There's a **rope-ferry** between the two, a twenty-second crossing on a wooden, flat-bottomed boat pulled by two villagers, a means of transport that's existed here for fifty years (though a new pedestrian bridge is also open). It costs fifty cents to make the crossing and the ferry operates continuously from 6am to midnight. From the bus stop, walk down to the main street and turn right for the small pier. Women in sampans will also try and inveigle you into making a slightly longer crossing, for a much higher fee – good for photo-opportunities at any rate.

Across the other side, fishermen's houses are built on stilts at the creek, and after you've looked around the small village shops and the market you can visit the local **temples**, sited on the island. One – built originally in the eighteenth century – is dedicated to Kwan Ti, the God of War and Righteousness, to whom people pray for protection; the other, the renovated Hau Wong temple (originally built in 1699), facing the sea, contains the local dragon racing boat, some sharks' bones and a whale's head, found by Tai O's fishermen. This is a five-minute walk along the main street through town – the shacks either side alive with the clack of *mahjong* tiles. At the end of the village, on a small headland, there's a barbecue area and the temple, with a lovely carved roof frieze displaying two roaring dragons.

The number of tourists that descend upon Tai O also means that you'll have no trouble getting something to **eat**. Cross over by the rope-ferry, and at the end of the street you'll see the *Fook Moon Lam* (open 11am–9.30pm), next to the market, whose short English-language menu includes good fresh scallops and prawns.

Kwun Yam, Ng Yuen and Tsz Hing Monastery

On the way to or from Tai O, not far from the village, the #1 and #21 buses make a stop at the **Kwun Yam temple**, where you can get a simple vegetarian meal. If you fancy a walk, there's a half-hour route from here up to **Ng Yuen**, an ornamental garden around a kilometre away, at its best in February and March. Another kilometre beyond is

Tsz Hing Monastery – situated in one of the most islolated spots on the island and guarded by a six-metre-long stone dragon. The monks and nuns here aren't really geared up to receiving visitors, though no one will actually object if you do turn up and have a vague interest in Buddhism: Sunday is the recommended visiting day. There is accommodation available, too, but only for those seriously interested in a meditational retreat. If you're just looking, you can descend from the monastery back through Ng Yuen and then straight down to Tai O on a direct path – about an hour's walk all told.

The Po Lin Monastery and Lantau Peak

Apart from a trip to the beach, the one place that everyone makes for in Lantau is the Po Lin Monastery in the central **Ngong Ping** region, north of the Shek Pik Reservoir. There's always a massive queue for the bus from Mui Wo, especially at the weekend, but it's worth the wait, partly for the fifty-minute ride – past the reservoir and slowly up the valley, with swirling views below to the coast.

Book ahead if you want to stay at Ngong Ping youth hostel; see p.213.

Po Lin Monastery and Tian Tan Buddha

The **Po Lin Monastery** was founded by three monks in 1905 on a plateau surrounded by mountains, including Lantau Peak itself. The temple complex is on a much grander scale than is usual in Hong Kong, more reminiscent of a Thai temple; just to reinforce the fact, on the hill behind the compound is the tallest statue of the Buddha in southeast Asia. The hundred monks and nuns now in residence at the monastery led a relatively peaceful existence until the 1970s, when the main temple and its pavilions were opened, since when they've been regularly besieged by swarms of people posing for photos on the temple steps and in the gardens. The main temple houses a noted group of three statues of the Buddha – fairly restrained under the circumstances, at only around three metres high each. There's nothing at all restrained about the temple itself, though, which is painted and sculpted in an almost gaudy fashion, its surfaces awash with vibrant gold, red, pink, orange and yellow.

All this pales into insignificance besides the gigantic but serene **Tian Tan Buddha** statue, at the top of a flight of 260 steps up the hillside in front of the monastery. A bronze figure 34m high, seated in a ring of outsized lotus petals, it was built at a reputed cost of $68 million and is now Lantau's top tourist attraction. Climb up for supreme views over the surrounding hills and down to the temple complex: inside the base there are four paintings depicting the Buddha's spiritual journeys, while if you've bought a meal ticket (see overleaf), you'll also be allowed into the (rather dull) exhibition galleries underneath the statue.

Access to the Budda statue is only from 10am to 4pm, so if you want to climb up to the top, make sure you set out from Central early enough: it's an hour's ferry ride, plus another 45min on the bus.

Everything else in the temple complex is firmly aimed at the weekly tourist invasion, too. There's a huge and chattering **dining hall**, where you can get a filling meal of inventive vegetarian food ($60, or the "deluxe" meal, served in air-conditioned surroundings, for $120): you need a coupon from the ticket office at the Buddha entrance gate; sit at the table numbered on your ticket. A traditional pagoda outside the dining hall shelters a payphone and a drinks vending machine.

Back out beyond the main gate, a path leads up the few hundred metres to the **Lantau Tea Gardens**, once Hong Kong's only tea-producing estate, though since it was sold in 1993 its future has become uncertain. There used to be roller skating and horse riding, and rooms available – and perhaps in the future there will be again – but for now the only surviving facility is the little *Tea Gardens Restaurant*, where you can sit outside, eat fried rice and drink a beer. It's only 300–400m from the monastery, but it's usually fairly peaceful.

Chek Lap Kok and the New Airport

With the capacity of Kai Tak airport at saturation point, not to mention the acknowledged danger of the city-centre site, it was only a matter of time before Hong Kong planned a **new airport**. After early feasibility studies, initial construction agreements were announced in 1989. What was surprising was the choice of site – isolated Chek Lap Kok island, off the north coast of Lantau – and the sheer scale. Quite simply, the airport and its associated schemes is the single biggest civil engineering project in the world.

The island of Chek Lap Kok, which before development supported a dwindling population of around two hundred, has been completely levelled and more than doubled in size by land reclamation schemes. In the early stages, forty thousand tonnes of explosive were used to blast out 75 million cubic metres of rock. When finished, the airport platform will be 6km long, or about the length of Kowloon peninsula, while dimensions of the **airport buildings** currently taking shape on the reformed island are no less staggering. At peak times, ten thousand workers are involved in the project. The terminal building alone (designed by Norman Foster) is twice the size of London Heathrow and New York's JFK put together, designed to handle 35 million passengers a year upon opening and over 80 million within forty years. Because of the siting of the airport in one of the more inaccessible corners of Hong Kong, the territory's communications and transport infrastructure has virtually had to be redrawn and the new airport sits at the hub of ten major associated Airport Core Programme (ACP) projects.

A bridge across connects Chek Lap Kok and the airport with the site of **Tung Chung New Town**, on Lantau, due to house sixty thousand people and act as a "gateway" into Hong Kong for arriving air passengers. From here, the six-lane **North Lantau Expressway** and 32-kilometre **Airport Express** rail line are routed along the northeast coast of Lantau, crossing the islands of Ma Wan and Tsing Yi on suspension bridges before hitting the mainland and turning south (along the West Kowloon Expressway) into Kowloon, where a new **passenger rail terminal** is under construction in the West Kowloon Reclamation Project (see p.133). Express train services from the airport to the new Kowloon station are expected to take just under twenty minutes; another five minutes via the underwater **Western Harbour Crossing** will see passengers deposited in Central at the new Hong Kong Island transport terminus on the reclaimed land by

---

Lantau Peak

A very steep path leads up from the Tea Gardens to the 934-metre-high peak of Fung Wong Shan, as **Lantau Peak** is properly known, the second highest in Hong Kong, and renowned as an excellent venue for sunrise watching. This will mean a crack-of-dawn start, but the views are justly famous – over as far as Macau on a clear day.

The peak is on the Lantau Trail and, depending on how energetic you feel, the path then heads east, reaching the slightly lower **Tai Tung Shan**, or "Sunset Peak", after about 5km. A fairly sharpish two-hour descent from there puts you on the road at Nam Shan and within shouting distance of Mui Wo.

Central ferry piers. There will be in-town check-in facilities at both Hong Kong and Kowloon stations, giving passengers more time to complete business in town before heading out to the airport. In addition to the express rail line, a complementary **Lantau Line** along the same route is designed as a commuter service: new towns and housing projects are expected to follow along its entire length, in areas like Tsing Yi, Tai Kok Tsui and west Kowloon. This, of course, is only the bare outline of most of the projects: on the site of each new urban development, plans are well advanced for interchanges to existing transport links, brand new MTR stations, ferry piers, commercial and retail outlets, housing and hotels.

Naturally, there have been **objections** to a scheme of such immeasurable import. The residents of old Tung Chung have seen their village, and way of life, transformed, some say ruined; fishermen on nearby Cheung Chau claim that the dumping of mud from the project has killed the fish; while environmental groups have pointed to the detrimental effect on species like the humpbacked dolphin which once inhabited the waters around Chek Lap Kok. More vociferous objections came from the Chinese government, worried – perhaps with some justification – that the airport was a last, grand gesture from a departing British government, which wouldn't have to foot the bill after 1997 if things went wrong. The cost (although a matter of some debate) is indeed astronomical: best estimates put the entire ACP budget at around $160 billion, with the airport site itself accounting for around $70 billion of that. For a while there was real concern that arguments over the cost would derail the entire project, though a final financing package between Britain and China was eventually agreed in June 1995.

Work continues at a merry pace, although the arguments about money have set the project back several months. The initial **planned opening** was for mid-1997 (so that the Governor could leave – symbolically – from the new airport after China takes over). The date has now been put back to April 1998, at which time it's expected that the airport will be ready to receive flights even if all the infrastructure isn't quite in place. The airport rail link should follow within a couple of months; completion of most of the rest of the associated projects is due for 2001; while by 2011 the wheel will have turned full circle when the site of the old Kai Tak airport in Kowloon City will have been turned into a new town with a quarter of a million inhabitants.

Tung Chung

The other main village on the island, **TUNG CHUNG**, on the northern shore below Chek Lap Kok island, was once a trading and fishing port with close links with Tai O. It slipped gradually into twentieth-century obscurity and for decades Tung Chung and its fourteen associated settlements lived an unassuming, though self-sufficient life, dependent on a bit of fish- and pig-farming, some local shallot growing and occasional visits by tourists. Then came the decision to site Hong Kong's new airport (see feature on previous page) on Chek Lap Kok, just 400m to the north, and Tung Chung suddenly found itself at the heart of one of the world's most extensive development programmes. The fish vanished from Chek Lap Kok – indeed, Chek Lap Kok itself vanished; two of the local settlements were torn down to make way for access roads; the bridge from the airport was completed; and Tung Chung New Town began to take shape.

It's impossible to say quite when the old village will disappear entirely, but for now it's still worth the ride out here to see the relics that once made Tung Chung important. Indeed, the bus ride (#3 from Mui Wo) is as good a reason as any to head for Tung Chung. Like the

---

Lantau Travel Details

For up-to-date ferry information, call the Hong Kong Ferry Co. ☎2542 3081.

For Discovery Bay hoverferry service call Discovery Bay Transportation Services Ltd ☎2987 7351.

For bus information call New Lantao Bus Co. ☎2984 9848 *or* ☎2984 8361.

Ferries

Central Piers to Mui Wo (hourly; first at 7am, last at 12.20am, Sun at 11.15pm); Tuen Mun/Sha Lo Wan/Tai O (Sat at 9.15am & 2.15pm, Sun at 8.15am).

Star Ferry Pier, Tsim Sha Tsui to Mui Wo (Sat at 1pm, 2pm, 3pm, 5pm & 7pm; Sun hourly 9am–6pm).

Mui Wo to Central Piers (hourly; first at 6.10am, last at 11.10pm, Sun at 10pm); Tsim Sha Tsui (Sat at 2pm, 3pm, 4pm & 6pm; Sun at 10am & hourly noon–7pm).

Tai O to Tuen Mun/Central (Sat at 11.50am & 5pm, these services terminating at Tuen Mun; Sun at 3pm terminating at Tuen Mun, & 5.30pm terminating at Central).

Tai Shui Hang (Trappist Haven Monastery) to Peng Chau (Mon–Sat at 8.10am, 9.30am, 11.30am, 12.30pm, 2.45pm & 4.30pm; Sun at 8.10am, 10.15am, 12.15pm, 3pm & 4.45pm).

Inter-Island Ferry

Mui Wo to Peng Chau (5–7 daily; first at 6.10am, last at 10.50pm); Chi Ma Wan/Cheung Chau (8 daily; first at 6.05am, last at 9.35pm).

Hoverferries

Central Piers to Mui Wo (Mon–Fri only at 9.40am, 11.20am, 2.25pm & 4.25pm).

Star Ferry Pier, Central to Discovery Bay (24-hr service; every 20–30min at peak times).

---

route to Ngong Ping, it's a slow climb up over the hills, before rattling down the valley to the village. The one road out of Tung Chung leads past the nineteenth-century **Battery**, while a kilometre or so further on, the road winds inland to **Tung Chung Fort**, six cannons lining its northern wall, though these days the fortifications protect a school. There was a fortress here as long ago as the seventeenth century, though this building dates back only to 1817, built on the orders of the Viceroy of Guangdong (Canton province) to defend Lantau's northern coast. Over the road from the fort are two paths, the unmarked one on the right leading back over the fields to Ma Wan Chung, the part of the village where the bus drops you.

A series of good **walks** can be made in the vicinity. The obvious one is down **from Po Lin Monastery**, a pleasant two- to three-hour hike which takes you past several smaller temples scattered along the Tung Chung valley. There's also a **bus** to and from the Po Lin monastery, the #23, running five times each Sunday, a 45-minute ride. Much longer **hikes** are those from Mui Wo and the coastal walk from Tai O, both of which will take you around five hours; don't forget to take water along with you.

Mui Wo to Peng Chau/Central (Mon–Fri only at 10.20am, 12.10pm, 3.10pm & 5.10pm).

Discovery Bay to Star Ferry Pier, Central (24-hr service; every 20–30min at peak times).

Kaidos

Kaido services operate on the following routes with varying degrees of regularity; specific details are given in the text where appropriate.

Tai Shui Hang–Nim Shue Wan.

Tai Long Wan–Cheung Chau.

Mong Tung Wan–Cheung Chau.

Buses

On regular services, fares are between $4 and $9 one-way, paid on board; they're just under double on Sunday. The special air-con bus direct to Po Lin Monastery costs $13.

#1 Mui Wo–Tai O (via Pui O and Kwun Yam Temple); half-hourly until12.30am.

#2 Mui Wo–Ngong Ping (Po Lin Monastery); Mon–Sat hourly until 6.35pm, Sun every 30min. The direct air-con service runs every 5–15min, last departure back to the ferry pier at 5pm.

#3 Mui Wo–Tung Chung; hourly; first at 7.50am, last at 6.35pm.

#4 Mui Wo–Tong Fuk (via Nam Shan and Cheung Sha beach); Mon–Sat hourly until 10.15pm, Sun every 30min until 10pm.

#5 Mui Wo–Shek Pik; Mon–Sat hourly until 6.30pm, Sun every 30min until 7.30pm, with an extra bus at 9pm.

#7 Mui Wo–Pui O (via Nam Shan); Mon–Sat hourly until 11.15pm, Sun every 30min until 7.30pm.

#21 Tai O to Ngong Ping; 7 daily; first at 7.45am, last at 3pm.

#23 Tung Chung–Ngong Ping; Sun only, hourly 10.15am–2.15pm.

Hong Kong Listings

Chapter 6

Accommodation

Accommodation in Hong Kong doesn't have to be a major expense. There are plenty of rock-bottom choices, starting at around $70 a night for a bed in a dormitory room (even cheaper if you stay in an *IYHF* hostel), which are bearable if all you're doing is passing through. However, for extended stays – even just three or four nights – they cease to be an attractive proposition: they're often crowded, dirty and hot. If you can afford a little more, then a room in a guest house with fan or air-conditioning starts at around $200–250 double, slightly more with an attached bathroom; while if money is no object, the territory has some of the world's finest hotels, offering an unparalleled degree of comfort and service.

Hong Kong has the world's highest hotel occupancy rate, and there isn't really a high or a low season as far as hotel bookings are concerned. Nevertheless, given the sheer number of options, **booking in advance** isn't strictly necessary – especially at the cheaper end of the market – if you don't mind a bit of legwork. The only time you will be chasing too few hotel beds is in the middle of Chinese New Year and at the end of March, during the Rugby Sevens weekend, but even then you should find something. Still, for peace of mind (and certainly if you want to guarantee space in one of the plusher hotels) it's as well to have at least your first night's accommodation sorted out before you arrive.

Airport arrivals can reserve rooms through the office of the **Hong Kong**

Hotel Association in the Buffer Hall of Kai Tak airport (daily 7am–midnight; ☎ 2383 8380). There's no booking fee, but they'll only contact hotels which are members of their association, which rules out the bulk of the budget hostels and hotels; the cheapest room you'll get through them is from around $800 double. The HKTA also issues a *Hotel Guide*, which includes maps, contact numbers and prices.

Beware of the **touts** at the airport and elsewhere, who will accost you and offer you a cheap room. The place you're taken to might, in fact, be all right, but if you decide you don't want to take the room having seen it they'll probably try and pin a charge on you for taking you there in the first place. If this happens to you, don't pay, but don't expect them to be happy about it. On the other hand, don't be too paranoid: the people handing out guest house business cards are harmless enough; you can always take the card and go and look on your own later.

The bulk of the very cheapest places – dormitories and guest houses – are Kowloon-side, in and around Tsim Sha Tsui, but with money to burn you can take your pick of the hotels on Hong Kong Island or in the new strip of Tsim Sha Tsui East. There is also a string of YMCAs and equivalent places, on the island and in Kowloon, offering more

The various **Airbuses** from the airport can take most people right to their hotel; see p.45 for more details.

Accommodation

downmarket (but thoroughly decent) hotel-style accommodation; and there's a small network of youth hostels (and a few cheap hotels) in the New Territories and on the outlying islands – both under-used options for the most part.

Dormitory accommodation

The cheapest beds in Hong Kong are those found in **dormitory-style accom-modation**, mostly located in Tsim Sha Tsui. They're rather thinner on the ground than they used to be, due to more toughly enforced health and safety restric-tions, but lots of guest houses still main-tain a few bunk-beds here and there. Typically, you'll pay around $70–80 for a space in a multi-bedded dorm, sharing with other backpackers. There will normally be separate shower and laundry facilities, and sometimes a TV room and cooking facilities. The dorms are generally friendly places, good for meeting people, but can be cramped and some are less than secure. Below is a list of places with dorm space, but check the listings for more specific information.

City Guest House: p.222.

Garden Hostel: p.222.

Golden Crown Guest House: p.218.

New Garden: p.223.

Oriental Pearl Hostel: p.223.

Seaview Guest House: p.223

STB Hostel: p.226.

Travellers' Hostel: p.222.

United Guest House: p.222.

Victoria Hostel: p.224.

Youth hostels

There are seven official *International Youth Hostel Federation (IYHF)* **youth hostels** in Hong Kong though only one, Ma Wui Hall on Hong Kong Island, is readily used by foreign travellers. The others are in fairly remote parts of the New Territories and on Lantau Island, but if you want to escape the cloying atmos-phere of central Hong Kong, it's worth making an effort to stay at them. They are all very cheap – $25–50 per person – and have cooking and washing facilities. You'll need an *IYHF* membership card to use them, available from the national organizations in your home country (see the box below): or you can buy a "Welcome Stamp" ($25 per night) at your first Hong Kong hostel – buying six is the equivalent of having international membership. The **head office** of the *Hong Kong Youth Hostels Association* is Room 225, Block 19, Shek Kip Mei Estate, Sham Shui Po, Kowloon (☎ 2788 1638, fax 2788 3105).

You must book beds at the hostels **in advance**, either by writing to or telephon-ing head office, or by telephoning the

---

Youth Hostel Organizations

Australia *Australian Youth Hostels Association*, Level 3, 10 Mallett St, Camperdown, NSW (☎ 02/565 1325).

Canada *Hostelling International/ Canadian Hostelling Association*, Room 400, 205 Catherine St, Ottawa, ON K2P 1C3 (☎ 613/237 7884 or ☎ 1-800/663 5777).

England and Wales *Youth Hostel Association (YHA)*, Trevelyan House, 8 St Stephen's Hill, St Alban's, Herts AL1 (☎ 017278/45047). London shop and information office: 14 Southampton St, London WC2 (☎ 0171/836 1036).

Ireland *An Oige*, 39 Mountjoy Square, Dublin 1 (☎ 01/363111).

New Zealand *Youth Hostels Association of New Zealand*, PO Box 436, Christchurch 1 (☎ 03/799970).

Northern Ireland *Youth Hostel Association of Northern Ireland*, 56 Bradbury Place, Belfast, BT7 (☎ 01232/ 324733).

Scotland *Scottish Youth Hostel Association*, 7 Glebe Crescent, Stirling, FK8 2JA (☎ 01786/51181).

USA *Hostelling International-American Youth Hostels (HI-AYH)*, 733 15th St NW, Suite 840, PO Box 37613, Washington, DC 20005 (☎ 202/783 6161).

hostels themselves. The HKTA office in the Buffer Hall at the airport has a leaflet on how to reach the Ma Wui Hall hostel; use the free phones to check on space with the warden or the head office. The hostels are **closed** between 10am and 4pm, between 1 and 2pm at weekends (some are also closed one day midweek), and there are separate dormitories for men and women – although couples can sometimes get a dorm together if the hostel's empty. On Friday and Saturday nights throughout the year the New Territories hostels are nearly always packed with groups of young Chinese: go in midweek and you'll often be on your own. Also, you'll need a sheet sleeping bag, which you can rent at the hostel for a few dollars.

Mount Davis

Ma Wui Hall, Mount Davis, Hong Kong Island ☎2817 5715. The most popular – and central – hostel in Hong Kong, above Kennedy Town on top of Mount Davis, with superb views. It's open 7–11pm, there are cooking facilities, lockers and 112 beds, but it fills quickly. Take bus #5B (destination "Felix Villas") from Des Voeux Road Central, or bus #47 from Central Bus Terminal and Connaught Road, to beyond Kennedy Town; get off on Victoria Road at the junction with Mount Davis Road, walk back to Mount Davis Path and follow the signs up the very steep access road to the hostel – a tough, two-kilometre, half-hour climb with luggage. Or take a taxi from the Macau Ferry Terminal (around $70) or Kennedy Town (around $50).

New Territories

Bradbury Hall, Chek Keng, Sai Kung Peninsula ☎2328 2458. 100 beds; see p.179.

Bradbury Lodge, Tai Mei Tuk, Tai Po ☎2662 5123. 94 beds and 5 family rooms; see p.155.

Pak Sha O, Hoi Ha (Jones' Cove), Sai Kung Peninsula ☎2328 2327. 112 beds; see p.180.

Sze Lok Yuen, Tai Mo Shan, Tsuen Wan ☎2488 8188. 92 beds; see p.169.

Lantau

Mong Tung Wan, Chi Ma Wan peninsula ☎2984 1389. 88 beds; closed 1–2 days a week, advance booking essential; see p.200.

S.G. Davis, Ngong Ping ☎2985 5610. 48 beds; see p.203.

Guest houses, YMCAs and hotels

Most budget travellers end up in one of Tsim Sha Tsui's **guest houses**. Given the high rents in Hong Kong, most of them are shoe-box sized, with paper-thin walls and a turnover that's fast and furious (qualities shared by many of the owners). Often the decor looks as if someone has tried to swing a cat in the room – and failed. However, if you're prepared to spend a little more than you'd perhaps planned, you should be able to find somewhere reasonable.

Most guest houses are contained inside large mansion blocks on and **around Nathan Road** in Tsim Sha Tsui, most notoriously **Chungking Mansions** (36–44 Nathan Rd), where there are dozens of relatively cheap places – although many are not that inviting. Instead, you might want to try one of the other slightly more appealing blocks, like the nearby **Mirador Mansion** (56–58 Nathan Rd) or the **Lyton Building** (42–48 Mody Rd). After years of procrastination, Chungking Mansions and other similar buildings recently underwent a major redevelopment programme following repeated warnings that they were massive fire risks. Things have improved immeasurably inside most, though you may find this hard to believe on a first viewing since Chungking especially is still an endlessly confusing warren of fairly dingy corridors. It's up to you whether you stay here or not: certainly there are other alternatives. On the other hand, Chungking Mansions has developed a reputation among travellers as a place to meet people and swap information.

When **renting your room**, *always* ask to see it first, and don't be afraid to try and bargain the price down. If you're

Accommodation

Accommodation

staying a few days, you'll often be able to get a reduction, but be wary about paying out the whole lot at once: if the guest house turns out to be roach-infested or noisy, or both, you'll have a hard job getting your money back if you want to leave early. The best advice is to take the room for a night and see what it's like before parting with your cash.

Check that the **air-conditioning** unit works – some places will make an extra charge ($20–30 per night) for air-conditioning; other rooms simply come equipped with a ceiling fan. **Bathrooms** are rarely that: rather, a tiny, very musty additional room with toilet and hand-held shower. But this is usually better than sharing what can be fairly grim communal bathrooms. Most rooms also come with TV, though the reception in places like Chungking Mansions can leave a lot to be desired. Guest houses nearly all charge for the room, which usually sleeps two (sometimes three) people, so **single travellers** will find themselves paying over the odds – the best you can do is ask for the smallest available room, but it will often be terribly claustrophobic.

There are several **YMCAs** and **religious organizations** offering accommodation somewhere in between the most expensive of the guest houses and the cheapest of the regular hotels. The rooms are all well appointed (with air-conditioning and TV) and comparatively spacious; most places add a ten percent service

charge. Most importantly, at these prices, you can start to pick and choose the area that you want to stay in; some of the places below are in excellent locations. Rooms at all of them can be booked at the airport's accommodation office.

Hong Kong has some of the world's finest and most expensive **hotels**, competing for the massive business custom that passes through the colony. The *Peninsula* is the most famous and longest-established, an elegant colonial hotel on the Tsim Sha Tsui waterfront; of the others, the *Mandarin Oriental* is considered to be in the running for the title of the world's best hotel. There are some cheaper, mid-range hotels around if you want to avoid guest houses, though often in these you're just paying for the official designation, "hotel" – the YMCAs might prove better value. With most hotels, the only choice to be made is location since most are fitted with everything that you could possibly want – business centres, gyms and restaurants, hair stylists and gift shops.

Lots of hotels don't distinguish between singles and doubles; you're just charged for the room; breakfast is not usually included. It pays to shop around, since most places offer discounts and deals at odd times of the year. You won't find any real bargains, but you might save a couple of hundred dollars here and there. Count on adding a ten percent **service charge** and a five percent govern-

---

Price Categories

Accommodation in this guide is classified in eight price categories. **Dormitory beds** (①) are classified according to the cost **per person per night**; the **guest house and hotel** categories refer to the amount you can expect to pay for a **double room**, *excluding taxes*. Guest houses tend to have a range of rooms on offer – singles, doubles, with and without air-conditioning or bathroom – and some reviews have multiple price categories to reflect this. In hotels (roughly speaking category ④ and upwards), you can count on rooms coming with a bathroom, air-conditioning and TV. Again, most have a range of available rooms and the price categories sometimes reflect this (eg. ⑥–⑦).

① Under $80 per person	⑤ $500–800 per room
② Under $200 per room	⑥ $800–1200 per room
③ $200–300 per room	⑦ $1200–2000 per room
④ $300–500 per room	⑧ Over $2000 per room

---

ment **tax** to the quoted room price. It's worth remembering, too, that many hotels work out better value if booked as part of an **inclusive tour**. And if you want a **harbour view**, you'll always pay much more than the standard room rate.

Central and Admiralty

On the whole, this is the most expensive area in Hong Kong to look for a room. There are no guest houses and the few hotels are of international quality and price – the locations, though are superb. The big surprise is that the *Hilton* disappeared, though rumours are rife that a new harbourfront site is in the offing. The #A2 Airbus from the airport passes most of the Central hotels; otherwise, take the MTR to either Central or Admiralty (for Pacific Place).

Conrad, Pacific Place, 88 Queensway ☎2521 3838, fax 2521 3888. Spiffy modern hotel which takes full advantage of its position in the upper floors of one of the Pacific Place towers. Great views, but a slightly sterile environment. ⑧.

Garden View International House, 1 Macdonnell Rd ☎2877 3737, fax 2845 6263. The only vaguely budget option in Central, this YWCA-run hotel has an excellent location, near the botanical gardens and handy for the Peak Tram terminal. Book well in advance. Take the Airbus to Central Bus Terminal and bus #12A from there, which runs nearby. ⑤.

Furama Kempinski, 1 Connaught Rd ☎2525 5111, fax 2845 9339. Thoroughly modern hotel, with harbour or Peak views (provided you're above the 16th floor), revolving restaurant, and a faithful business clientele. ⑦–⑧.

Island Shangri-La, Pacific Place, 88 Queensway ☎2872 3838, fax 2521 8742. Completes the selection of classy hotels at Pacific Place and, if anything, this has the best Peak or harbour views of the lot, particularly from the top-floor *Cyrano's* bar. ⑧.

Mandarin Oriental, 5 Connaught Rd ☎2522 0111, fax 2810 6190. The *Mandarin* is considered by many to be the best in the world: there's no faulting

the service (the staff run into hundreds), facilities (the rooms have antiques and balconies, the corridors eighteenth-century Chinese textiles) or location (close to the Star Ferry). You don't need to stay here to appreciate its marvels – pop into the coffee shop, eat in the *Man Wah* restaurant (see p.240) or have a drink in the *Captain's Bar* or maritime *Clipper Lounge*. If you really want to put them through their paces, they claim that the restaurants will prepare any dish that has ever appeared on the menu over the last thirty years. ⑧.

Marriott, Pacific Place, 88 Queensway ☎2810 8366, fax 2845 0737. Part of the flash Pacific Place complex (the first to open here) and exuding Hong Kong luxury and hi-tech – even the lobby has a waterfall. Harbour views are $200 more expensive than the standard rooms. ⑧.

Ritz-Carlton, 3 Connaught Rd ☎2877 6666, fax 2877 6778. Central's ritziest newest hotel, in a prime city centre location; while there's no *Hilton*, it's probably the best alternative to staying at the *Mandarin Oriental*. Rooms (just over 200 of them) are eminently comfortable and there's a high staff-guest ratio; check out the café with harbour views and *Cossacks*, the basement Russian bar. ⑧.

Wan Chai

Again, there are no real bargains here, except for the *Wesley* and *International House*, which are popular enough to warrant booking well in advance. Mostly, the hotels here are patronized by business people: you certainly don't need to stay in Wan Chai to get the best out of its nightlife and the Arts Centre. Access is by Airbus #A2; Wan Chai MTR puts you close to most, too, while from Wan Chai Ferry Pier it's an easy stroll to *Grand Hyatt, New World Harbour View* and *International House*.

Century Hong Kong Hotel, 238 Jaffe Rd ☎2598 8888, fax 2598 8866. Modern, not completely outrageously priced hotel, handy for access to the Convention and Exhibition Centre and Wanchai's nightlife. It's at the bottom of this price range and

Accommodation

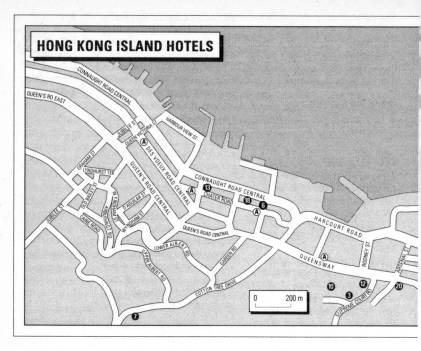

HONG KONG ISLAND HOTELS

boasts a surprising guest list: Bobby Brown and Whitney Houston stayed here when they played Hong Kong. ⑦.

Empire Hotel, 33 Hennessy Rd ☎ 2866 9111, fax 2861 3121. Convenient for Wanchai's nightlife and featuring a small lounge which looks onto Lockhart Road, Two levels of basement food outlets. ⑦.

Grand Hyatt, 1 Harbour Rd ☎ 2588 1234, fax 2802 0677. Part of the Convention and Exhibition Centre (along with the neighbouring *New World*), and bulging with fine harbour views, this is a prime example of the territory's bid for the business trade – massively expensive, hugely luxurious, and bristling with bars, restaurants, pools, gardens and health club. ⑧.

Harbour View International House, 4 Harbour Rd ☎ 2802 0111, fax 2802 9063. One of the best-value Hong Kong Island locations, and good views to boot, right next door to the Arts Centre and handy for Wan Chai ferry pier. It's operated by the YMCA, and the doubles, complete

with all facilities, come at the bottom of this category. ⑥.

Luk Kwok Hotel, 72 Gloucester Rd ☎ 2866 2166, fax 2866 2622. Recently refurbished, this is one of the city's landmark hotels – famous as the hotel name and location used in the film *The World of Suzie Wong* (see p.95). Not that you'd recognize it anymore, with its sleek, brown-marble-and-glass designer treatment. ⑦.

New Harbour, 41–49 Hennessy Rd ☎ 2861 1166, fax 2866 7615. Pretty good value for its location, though the rooms and public areas are quite small – and it's on one of the busiest (read noisiest) routes in Hong Kong. ⑦.

New World Harbour View, 1 Harbour Rd ☎ 2802 8888, fax 2802 8833. More splendid views, as the name suggests, and the same expense-account business clientele as the *Grand Hyatt*, though the rooms are a shade cheaper (and smaller) – you get to use the *Grand Hyatt's* facili-

① *Under $80 per person*
② *Under $200 per room*
③ *$200–300 per room*
④ *$300–500 per room*
⑤ *$500–800 per room*
⑥ *$800–1200 per room*
⑦ *$1200–2000 per room*
⑧ *Over $2000 per room*

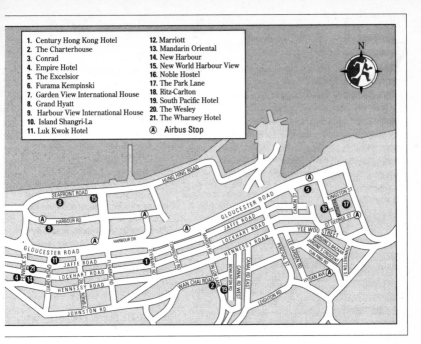

1. Century Hong Kong Hotel	**12.** Marriott
2. The Charterhouse	**13.** Mandarin Oriental
3. Conrad	**14.** New Harbour
4. Empire Hotel	**15.** New World Harbour View
5. The Excelsior	**16.** Noble Hostel
6. Furama Kempinski	**17.** The Park Lane
7. Garden View International House	**18.** Ritz-Carlton
8. Grand Hyatt	**19.** South Pacific Hotel
9. Harbour View International House	**20.** The Wesley
10. Island Shangri-La	**21.** The Wharney Hotel
11. Luk Kwok Hotel	Ⓐ Airbus Stop

ties, too. The breakfast is particularly good here. ⑧.

The Wesley, 22 Hennessy Rd ☎ 2866 6688, fax 2866 6633. Knock-down room rates in a quiet and comfortable modern hotel with coffee shop close to the Arts Centre. The restaurant isn't all it could be though – eat elsewhere. ⑥–⑦.

The Wharney Hotel, 57–73 Lockhart Road ☎ 2861 1000, fax 2865 6023. Nice guest quarters and facilities – gym, whirl-pool, subterranean bar (from where you look up through plate-glass windows to Lockhart Rd) and daily papers delivered to your room. An extra $105 gets you the buffet breakfast. ⑦.

Causeway Bay

Hong Kong's premier shopping district isn't well endowed with decent hotels. Of those listed below, the *Excelsior* and *Park Lane* often feature as part of package tours, and are worth asking about if that's how you're travelling to the territory, since room rates will then be eminently afforda-

ble. Causeway Bay does have several cheap guest houses in its back streets, though most are the sort of places you rent by the hour – worth avoiding on the whole. Access is by Airbus #A3, tram or Causeway Bay MTR.

The Charterhouse, 209–219 Wan Chai Rd ☎ 2833 5566, fax 2833 5888. One of the island's newer choices, with good services and catering. Some rooms have a good view of the Happy Valley race-course. Coming by MTR, take the Times Square exit. ⑦.

The Excelsior, 281 Gloucester Rd ☎ 2894 8888, fax 2895 6459. Best sited of Causeway Bay's major hotels – with many rooms overlooking the water – though it's getting on in years and doesn't feature the same up-to-the-minute facilities of other similar places. Rooms are better value than at most large hotels though. ⑦.

Noble Hostel, 7th Floor, C1, Paterson Building, 37 Paterson St ☎ 2576 6148.

Accommodation

This is the contact address and number for a series of budget-rated air-con rooms in Causeway Bay run by the same owner. Well worth trying first for good, central accommodation, with and without private bathroom. ④.

The Park Lane, 310 Gloucester Rd ☎2890 3355, fax 2576 7853. With views over Victoria Park, this is the most convenient hotel for the department stores, with a wide variety of rooms on offer. ⑦.

South Pacific Hotel, 23 Morrison Hill Rd ☎2572 3838, fax 2893 7773. Architecturally, one of the most striking hotels in Hong Kong, the style continues inside the green cylinder: rooms are well sized and quiet and the tram runs right past the door. Coming by MTR, take the Times Square exit. ⑦.

Tsim Sha Tsui

Most visitors – and nearly all those travelling on a budget – stay in Tsim Sha Tsui, which breaks down into several specific areas, though wherever you end up, you're supremely well sited for all the shops, bars, restaurants and nightlife. The main road, Nathan Road, runs the gamut from high-class hotels like the *Sheraton* and *Miramar* to the myriad cheap guest houses in Chungking Mansions and other buildings. In the streets east and west of Nathan Road, there's a similar mix: it's just to the west of the road that you'll find possibly the two best-sited hotels in the territory, the colonial *Peninsula* and the affordable *Salisbury YMCA*. The #A1 Airbus runs through the area, though it only stops on Nathan Road itself and along the streets on the east side of Nathan Road. Tsim Sha Tsui MTR also puts you within walking distance of all the places listed below.

ALONG NATHAN ROAD

Golden Crown Guest House, 5th Floor, Golden Crown Court, 66–70 Nathan Rd ☎2369 1782. Golden Crown Court is about the least awful of the blocks along Nathan Road, and this is a very friendly place, though there's not much space in the dorms and the other rooms smell musty; a couple have showers, otherwise communal bathroom. Clean, though, and with laundry facilities, China visas available and soft drinks for sale. Dorms ①, rooms ③.

Holiday Inn Golden Mile, 46–52 Nathan Rd ☎2369 3111, fax 2369 8016. Right next door to Chungking Mansions, which must annoy the owners, the rooms here are typically good value from the *Holiday Inn* chain, relatively spacious and with plenty of single rooms, too. There's also a pool and several restaurants. ⑧.

Hyatt Regency, 67 Nathan Rd ☎2311 1234, fax 2739 8701. Fully refurbished, with a spectacular lobby and ground-floor shopping arcade. Perfectly positioned for shopaholics: seventeen floors and over 700 rooms, all very decently equipped with marble bathrooms and hair dryers. ⑧.

Imperial Hotel, 30–34 Nathan Rd ☎2366 2201, fax 2311 2360. A surprising bargain if you're looking for a proper hotel on Nathan Road itself, though you'll need to book ahead – and don't expect too many frills. Prices tend to fluctuate throughout the year. ⑥–⑦.

Kowloon Hotel, 19–21 Nathan Rd ☎2369 8698, fax 2739 9811. Regular hotel comfort (mostly to business travellers) at fairly reasonable rates in a large (700-room) sleek building whose jagged glass facade soars off Nathan Road. You're paying for the location, however, since the rooms are among the smallest on offer in any hotel of this standard, though some have fine Wan Chai and harbour views. ⑦.

Miramar Hotel, 130 Nathan Rd ☎2368 1111, fax 2369 1788. Right opposite Kowloon Park, this is a fairly garish hotel, dating from the 1950s and bursting with shops. It's enormous (the rooms are larger than average too), and pricey, but for all that it's often full. If you want a view over the park, you'll need to be in a more expensive room at the top. ⑦.

Sheraton, 20 Nathan Rd ☎2369 1111, fax 2739 8707. Lording it over the bottom of Nathan Road, the *Sheraton* is swanky and expensive, though for the price of a cocktail you can ride the exterior elevator

TSIM SHA TSUI HOTELS

TAK SHING ST.
AUSTIN ROAD
AUSTIN ROAD
NATHAN ROAD
HILLWOOD ROAD
AUSTIN AVENUE
CHATHAM ROAD
Kowloon Park
OBSERVATORY RD
GRANVILLE ROAD
SCIENCE MUSEUM ROAD
KIMBERLEY ROAD
KOWLOON PARK DRIVE
KIMBERLEY STREET
GRANVILLE ROAD
GRANVILLE CIRCUIT
CAMERON ROAD
PRAT AVE
MODY ROAD
SALISBURY ROAD
HAIPHONG ROAD
HUMPHREY'S AVE
CARNARVON RD
HART AVE
HANKOW ROAD
ASHLEY ROAD
HANOI ROAD
NATHAN ROAD
MODY ROAD
CHATHAM ROAD
MINDEN AVE
MINDEN ROW
CANTON ROAD
KOWLOON PARK DRIVE
PEKING ROAD
MIDDLE ROAD
SALISBURY ROAD

N

0   200 m

1. Chungking Mansions
2. Guangdong Hotel
3. Golden Crown Guest House
4. Holiday Inn Golden Mile
5. Holiday Inn Harbour View
6. Hong Kong Renaissance
7. Hyatt Regency
8. Imperial Hotel
9. International Hotel
10. Kowloon Hotel

11. Kowloon Shangri-La
12. Lee Garden Guest House
13. Lyton Building
14. Mirador Mansions
15. Miramar Hotel
16. New World Hotel
17. Nikko
18. Omni Hong Kong
19. Omni Marco Polo
20. Omni Prince

21. On Sun Tat
22. The Peninsula
23. The Regent
24. Royal Garden Hotel
25. Shamrock
26. Sheraton
27. Victoria Hostel
28. YMCA: The
      Salisbury

Ⓐ Airbus Stop

to the *Sky Lounge* for superb harbour views; yuppies congregate in the basement *Someplace Else* bar. Rooms and public areas are nicely turned out; the lobby, incidentally, is one of the easiest places in Tsim Sha Tsui from which to make a phone call. ⑨.

Chungking Mansions, 36–44 Nathan Rd
Chungking House, Block A, reception 4th Floor ☎ 2366 5362. The only real hotel in the Mansions, its "de luxe" single and double rooms come with air-con, bath and TV, though the decor is rather institutional. There's also a dining room serving

a $20 breakfast and the rooms are actually reasonably spacious though, frankly, with this much money to spend, you can do better than Chungking Mansions. ④.

Fortunate Guest House, Block A, 11th Floor ☎2366 5900. Clean, modern guest house that would do well for a group of friends or family: two of the rooms have four beds. Otherwise the doubles come with air-con and TV but shared bathroom. ③–④.

Happy Guest House, Block B, 10th Floor, B3 ☎2368 1021. Popular and friendly, you'll have to go to "reception" on the 9th floor (B3) first. Singles available, as well as doubles with fan and TV, some with bath. You'll pay extra for air-con. ②–③.

Harbour Guest House, Block B, 4th Floor ☎2368 1428. Only four floors up, which saves a lot of elevator trouble. Relatively pricey double rooms with own toilet and air-con. ③.

Hawaii Guest House, Block A, 14th Floor ☎2366 6127. One of the bargains in the Mansion, with en-suite air-con rooms the same price however many people occupy it – though three would be pushing it. ②.

Hong Kong Guest House, Block B, 12th Floor, no phone. Shabby but acceptable place with rooms with air-con and bath, though some of the "double" rooms contain bunks rather than beds. ③.

Jinn's Ti Guest House, Block B & C, 7th Floor ☎2366 6742. Long-standing cheapie with a range of rooms spread across two blocks. Not great at the less expensive end; worth splashing out on air-con and bath. ③.

Kamal Guest House, Block B, 6th Floor ☎2739 3301. Rooms in two apartments on this floor, including some very cheap ones without air-con or bath; unless you're absolutely broke, it's worth paying double for the ones with facilities. ②–③.

London Guest House, Block A, 6th Floor, A1 ☎2366 5975. Slightly down-at-heel, but with friendy, conscientious staff. Basic doubles, some with shower and TV, and one room with a bathtub. ③

Marria Guest House, Block C, 11th Floor ☎2724 3788. Your money gets you a large and comfortable double with bath and air-con, plus fridge, lots of natural light, a half-decent view and helpful English-speaking staff. ④.

New Carlton Guest House, Block B, 15th Floor, ☎2721 0720. Basic place where all the rooms have private bathroom. It's friendly and good value. ②–③.

New Chungking Mansion, Block C, 7th Floor ☎2368 0981. Well-kept, decent rooms, and a management willing to discount prices. ④.

New Grand Guest House, Block A, 14th Floor ☎2368 6520. Clean and slightly larger-than-usual rooms with their own bathroom. ④.

New Harbour Guest House, Block C, 9th Floor ☎2367 2777. Reasonable doubles with air-con; shared bathroom. ③.

New International, Block A, 11th Floor, A7 ☎2366 7972. Fairly standard doubles and singles with bath, though each room has a fridge and TV. The staff are very helpful and speak good English; laundry service available. ③.

New Washington Guest House, Block B, 13th Floor ☎2368 2228. Not terribly well maintained rooms, but if you can manage without air-con and private bathrooms (or, let's face it, windows), you'll be hard pushed to beat the price. ②.

Park Guest House, Block A, 15th Floor, A1 ☎2368 1689, fax 2366 7936. A guest house you can rely on, this has been renting out rooms for years. Clean, very tidy box-like singles and doubles, some with fridges and shower, some claiming a mythical "sea view"; rooms on the 14th floor too. ③.

Payless Guest House, Block A, 7th Floor ☎2723 0148. You only do if you opt for a longer stay, in which case there'll be $20 knocked off the price per night. Clean and comparatively spacious rooms. ③.

Peking Guest House, Block A, 12th Floor, A2 ☎2723 8320. Bargain-priced but small, doubles with air-con and TV, some with shower. The best rooms face Nathan Road, which can be a bit noisy for some. Welcoming manager. ③–④.

A Chungking Checklist

If you're going to stay in **Chungking Mansions** (36–44 Nathan Rd), it's as well to know what you're letting yourself in for. Despite new licensing restrictions and renovations, which dealt with the most extreme of the Mansions' health and saftey shortcomings (and closed no less than 61 guest houses), it still remains a fairly alarming place: seventeen storeys high, a gloomy collection of apartments housing dimly lit accommodation, gift shops, basic restaurants and loitering locals.

Accommodation

Located next to the *Holiday Inn*, the ground and first floors are shopping arcades; the guest houses are on the floors above. Wander around and you'll find five sets of **elevators**, labelled A to E, two for each block – one for the even floors, one for the odd floors. Noticeboards tell you which guest houses are on each floor: the numbers, A3, B4, etc, are the address on that floor for each guest house. Confusingly, once you're up in the Mansions, some of the **blocks** connect with each other by corridors: one wrong turn through a swing door and you could be coming down Block C having gone up Block B.

Searching for a room, it's best to leave one person downstairs with the luggage as the elevators are very small. When they get overloaded, an alarm sounds and the last one in has to get out. If you're really going to shop around, go straight to the top floor of a block and work your way down: the lists below have been drawn up on that principle. Big queues form for the elevators (especially Blocks A and B), and if you're staying on the 16th floor, walking up the stairs instead isn't always an option.

Most of the **guest houses** themselves are all right and some are really good. A few owners run more than one place, so don't worry if you're packed off to another block or another floor when you try to check in: just make sure to see the room first and establish the price. The **lists** below let you check out the possibilities block by block, and floor by floor; cross-check with the reviews for more detailed information.

① *Under $80 per person*
② *Under $200 per room*
③ *$200–300 per room*
④ *$300–500 per room*
⑤ *$500–800 per room*
⑥ *$800–1200 per room*
⑦ *$1200–2000 per room*
⑧ *Over $2000 per room*

Block A
17th Floor: *United Guest House.*
16th Floor: *Travellers' Hostel.*
15th Floor: *Park Guest House.*
14th Floor: *Hawaii Guest House, New Grand Guest House, Tokyo Guest House.*
12th Floor: *Peking Guest House.*
11th Floor: *Fortunate Guest House, New International, Rhine Guest House.*
8th Floor: *Tom's Guest House.*
7th Floor: *Payless Guest House, Welcome Guest House.*
6th Floor: *London Guest House.*
4th Floor: *Chungking House.*

Block B
16th Floor: *Tom's Guest House.*
15th Floor: *New Carlton Guest House.*
13th Floor: *New Washington Guest House.*

12th Floor: *Hong Kong Guest House.*
10th Floor: *Happy Guest House.*
7th Floor: *Jinn's Ti Guest House.*
6th Floor: *Kamal Guest House.*
4th Floor: *Harbour Guest House.*

Block C
16th Floor: *Tom's Guest House.*
11th Floor: *Marria Guest House.*
9th Floor: *New Harbour Guest House*
7th Floor: *Jinn's Ti Guest House, New Chungking Mansion.*
4th Floor: *Ranjeet Guest House.*
3rd Floor: *Taj Super Deluxe.*

Block D
5th Floor: *Royal Inn, Royal Inn Plaza.*

Block E
8th Floor: *Yan Yan Guest House.*

Accommodation

Ranjeet Guest House, Block C, 4th Floor, C1 ☎ 2368 9943. Cramped rooms done out in lurid pink, though undeniably cheap; Indian movies shown every night. ③.

Rhine Guest House, Block A, 11th & 13th Floor ☎ 2367 1991 or 2721 6863. Very friendly, family-run place with basic doubles with and without bath. ②–③.

Royal Inn/Royal Inn Plaza, Block D, 5th Floor ☎ 2366 2121 or 2367 1424. Slightly more upmarket places under the same management that usually have room, though they're not greatly attractive. ④.

Taj Super Deluxe, Block C, 3rd Floor ☎ 2366 4466 or 2366 4455. Slightly worn out, but with doubles with bath and air-con that could sleep three, and helpful staff. Not bad value (at the bottom of this price range). ④.

Tokyo Guest House, Block A, 14th Floor, A1 ☎ 2367 5407. Nice big doubles ($50–100 more for one with a bath) and a welcoming owner; the single rooms are less impressive though. ②–③.

Tom's Guest House, Block A, 8th Floor, A5; ☎ 2722 4956; Block B & C, 16th Floor, C1 ☎ 2367 9258 or 2722 6035, fax 2366 6706. Pleasant sets of rooms with a friendly owner flitting between them, though the cool doubles with air-con and TV fill quickly. Not surprisingly: it feels safe, you get the use of a fridge, there's chilled water on demand, and the bathrooms are clean and decent. The Block A rooms are more expensive, but come with en-suite shower. ②–③.

Travellers' Hostel, Block A, 16th Floor ☎ 2368 7710. Best known of the backpackers' hostels, with mixed dorm beds, and a few singles, as well as regular doubles. Also with kitchen, TV, lockers, showers and good noticeboard. However, the wierdos the hostel sometimes attracts make it one to avoid for a long-term stay. China visas sorted out at the travel agency next door. Dorms ①, rooms ②–③.

United Guest House, Block A, 17th Floor ☎ 2312 1424. Cramped dorm beds and some basic, shabby rooms with air-con but separate bathroom. Dorms ①, rooms ③.

Welcome Guest House, Block A, 7th Floor, A5 ☎ 2721 7793. A recommended first choice; air-con doubles with and without shower. Nice clean rooms, luggage storage, laundry service and China visas available. ③.

Yan Yan Guest House, Block E, 8th Floor ☎ 2366 8930. Helpful staff renting out doubles with all facilities; you could sleep three in some at a squeeze, making them pretty good value. ④.

Mirador Mansions, 56–58 Nathan Rd

City Guest House, 9th Floor, F2 ☎ 2724 2612. The reasonably friendly *City* has cheaper-than-usual dorm beds (though the room's very dark) as well as regular air-con rooms with TV. Discounts offered for longer stays; laundry service available. Dorms ①, rooms ③.

Dzin Hun Guest House, 11th Floor, A6 ☎ 2301 3018. English-speaking staff offering clean double rooms with air-con and shower (at the bottom of this price category) – not much space in them, however. ④.

First Class Guest House, 16th Floor, D1 ☎ 2722 4935. A popular place in the Mansion, with clean but cramped singles and doubles. The manager isn't the cheery soul he might be, however. ③.

Garden Hostel, 3rd Floor, F4; entrance on Mody Road; ☎ 2721 8567. The dorms in this well-run travellers' hostel attract small discounts if you stay more than one night; the doubles are as cheap as you'll find, with shared bathroom. Also cooking facilities, lockers, TV and noticeboard. Try to book a few days ahead since it's very popular. Dorms ①, rooms ③.

Kowloon Hotel, 13th Floor, F1 and 10th Floor, E10; reception at 13th Floor, F4 ☎ 2311 2523. A guest house, despite the name, the smart, well-kept rooms are looked after by a friendly set. The F1 rooms all have shower, TV and air-con – and there are fridges and an iced-water dispenser, too. The 10th floor rooms are slightly cheaper, but not as nice. Recommended. ③.

Man Hing Lung Guest House, 14th Floor, F2 ☎ 2722 0678 or ☎ 2311 8807. The rooms here are very small and clean (there's barely room to dirty anything), but all come with shower, TV and air-con – the very cheapest don't have a window. The owner speaks good English and has several other rooms scattered around the block, so it's not a bad first choice. ③.

Mei Lam Guest House, 5th Floor, D1 ☎2721 5278. The nice English-speaking owner here has very presentable singles and doubles, all spick-and-span and with full facilities. Worth the higher-than-usual prices. ④.

New Garden, 13th Floor, D1 ☎2369 6132. Cut-price dorm beds (which get cheaper if you're staying a few days) and a range of rooms of varying size and acceptability. Dorms ①, rooms ②–③.

Oriental Pearl Hostel, 6th Floor, A3 & A4 ☎2723 3439 or 2723 1344. The dorm looks like an overstuffed furniture warehouse, or there are air-con doubles too. If you want the luxury of a window, you'll pay another $50. Dorm ①, rooms ③.

Seaview Guest House, 16th Floor ☎2721 3096. Dorms and very inexpensive doubles in a place that attracts a long-staying clientele. Dorms ①, rooms ②.

EAST OF NATHAN ROAD

Guangdong Hotel, 18 Prat Ave ☎2739 3311, fax 2721 1137. CTS-owned hotel that's no real bargain, but within staggering distance of some of the better bars and restaurants. Rooms with street views are pricier the higher up the building you go. ⑤.

International Hotel, 33 Cameron Rd ☎2366 3381, fax 2369 5381. A drab building with large, but dark, rooms and hardly overladen with facilities, but reasonable value if you're looking for hotel-standard comfort. Ask for a room overlooking Cameron Road. ⑥.

Lee Garden Guest House, 8th Floor, 34–36 Cameron Rd ☎2367 2284 or 2367 5872. Renovations have taken this place slightly upmarket and the decent singles, doubles and triples have bath, air-con and TV; prices are in the middle of this category. ④.

Lyton House Inn, Lyton Building, 42–48 Mody Rd, 4th & 6th Floor ☎2367 3791. The Lyton Building (on the south side of Mody Road, beyond Blenheim Ave) has a few guest house options. This is one of the longest-standing, with rooms on two floors, whose big doubles with shower are modern and clean. ④.

On Sun Tat, 7th Floor, Flat F, Champagne Court, 16 Kimberley Rd ☎2723 9143. The pleasant people here have well-kept rooms with shower, air-conditioning and TV (ask in the travel agency). A good first call, since the rooms are cool and quiet, if not enormous; most of them have a window. ③.

Rich Shekel Guest House, 5th Floor, James Lee Mansion, 33–35 Carnarvon Rd ☎2369 6535 or 2739 6434. No English bar the price is spoken here – negotiate your way in, and you'll get a reasonable double room with air-con and shower for the money. ④.

Star Guest House, 6th Floor, 21 Cameron Rd ☎2723 8951. Small, reasonably well-equipped rooms that can accommodate one or two people; under the same management as the *Lee Garden*. ④.

Tourist House, Lyton Building, 42–48 Mody Rd, 6th Floor; use lift no.3; ☎2721 8309. Chinese-run place with doubles with shower and TV, though the small rooms are nothing special. It might also be "full" to Westerners. ③.

WEST OF NATHAN ROAD

Hong Kong Renaissance, 8 Peking Rd ☎2375 1133, fax 2375 6611. Serious prices for rooms for jaded business travellers – there are even fax machines provided, as well as TVs and all the usual comforts, including a pool. It's at the Canton Road end of the street and you'll pay more for a harbour view. ⑧.

Omni, Harbour City, Canton Rd; *The Hongkong* ☎2736 0088, fax 2736 0011; *Marco Polo* ☎2736 0888, fax 2736 0022; *Prince* ☎2736 1888, fax 2736 0066. The massive Harbour City development houses three different hotels under the same *Omni* umbrella. They're all fairly fancy, at least in the public areas – the rooms aren't overwhelming – and you can use

Accommodation

① *Under $80 per person*
② *Under $200 per room*
③ *$200–300 per room*
④ *$300–500 per room*
⑤ *$500–800 per room*
⑥ *$800–1200 per room*
⑦ *$1200–2000 per room*
⑧ *Over $2000 per room*

Accommodation

each hotel's facilities at will; the rest of the time, you'll spend lost in the endless shopping mall corridors. Only the *Hongkong* (the largest) has harbour views; those at the *Prince* overlook the park. ⑧.

Park Guest House, 1st Floor, Haiphong House, 53–55 Haiphong Rd ☎2366 4982. Decent prices for quiet double rooms with air-con and shower. ④.

The Peninsula, Salisbury Rd ☎2366 6251, fax 2722 4170. Far and away the grandest hotel in Hong Kong, the *Pen*, as it's known, has been putting visitors up in unrivalled style since the late 1920s. Its elegant colonial wings have been over-shadowed by the new central tower, which provides harbour views to match the style and quality – the top-floor bar-restaurant, *Felix*, is the work of hotshot designer Philippe Starck. Service everywhere is impeccable, as you might expect; the hotel's restaurants among the best places in the territory to eat. At least drop in for afternoon tea, which lets you gawp at the splendid lobby. See p.127 for more on its history. ⑧.

Victoria Hostel, 33 Hankow Rd ☎2376 0621. Small, mixed dorms (cheaper without air-con), cooking facilities, lockers and a little sitting-out area. The paintwork's peeling, though, and the pushy management isn't to everyone's taste. Double rooms too, are not the bargain they might be. Dorm ①, rooms ④.

YMCA: The Salisbury, 41 Salisbury Rd ☎2369 2211, fax 2739 9315. Spruced up and expanded, this is the best semi-cheap hotel location in this part of town, next to the *Peninsula* and in the middle of Tsim Sha Tsui. It may be a Y, but the facilities are excellent, including two indoor pools, fitness centre, squash court and a good café. The air-con doubles with TV and shower are booked up weeks in advance – try making a reservation *two months* ahead. Harbour-view rooms are an extra $250 and nearly push into the next price category. There are also 56 budget beds available in four-bedded rooms ($165 per person), though you can't book in advance for these: get there early. ⑥.

Tsim Sha Tsui East and Hung Hom

Thirty years ago, Tsim Sha Tsui East didn't exist, but extensive land reclamation allowed the developers to run riot with a spate of high-class hotels sporting harbour views. A couple are as posh as anything in Hong Kong and, accordingly, probably worth the ludicrous expense if you're a style guru. Otherwise, you're a little far from the action in Tsim Sha Tsui itself to make most worth the bother, though inclusive tour holidays often put up in this part of town. The Airbus runs close, but it's easiest to take a taxi.

Holiday Inn Harbour View, 70 Mody Rd ☎2721 5161, fax 2732 2233. *Holiday Inn*'s other location, pricier than the Nathan Road branch because of the harbour views from its fair-sized rooms; there's also a good pool. ⑧.

Holy Carpenter Guest House, 1 Dyer Ave ☎2362 0301, fax 2362 2193. Easily best value in this district, this small church-run guest house only has fourteen rooms; it's close to Whampoa Garden and Hung Hom ferry pier. Modern furnishings, TV and attached bathroom. You'll need to book a good two weeks in advance. ⑤.

Kowloon Shangri-La, 64 Mody Rd ☎2721 2111, fax 2723 8686. The hover-ferry from Central stops right outside, though the mainly business clientele doesn't get much use out of it, holed up in the entire floor given over to "executive" use. Elsewhere inside, the design makes the usual extravagant use of marble, crystal and splashing fountains. ⑧.

New World Hotel, 22 Salisbury Rd ☎2369 4111, fax 2369 9387. One of Tsim Sha Tsui East's earliest fixtures, the sprawling red-brick *New World* has already been completely renovated and it's not even twenty years old. ⑧.

Nikko, 72 Mody Rd ☎2739 1111, fax 2311 3122. Plush Japanese-owned business hotel, with all the contemporary luxury you'd expect, and only a step away from the KCR station – which makes it quite a hike from Tsim Sha Tsui's restaurants, though naturally it has it's own excellent Japanese restaurant. ⑧.

The Regent, Salisbury Rd ☎2721 1211, fax 2739 4546. The only real rival to the *Peninsula* on this side of the water, the *Regent* has an extraordinary glassed-in lobby (in which mere mortals can take a drink) and a twisting marble staircase that pops up in fashion shoots. It has its own pool, a top-rated Cantonese restaurant (the *Lai Ching Heen*) and is connected to the New World Centre, a huge shopping mall; with a fistful of credit cards, you need never leave. ⑧.

Royal Garden Hotel, 69 Mody Rd ☎2721 5215, fax 2369 9976. Hong Kong is notoriously short of green space, so the *Royal Garden* incorporates its own – an interior garden-atrium, overlooked by room terraces and serviced by wall-hugging elevators. It's an extraordinary conceit, even by Hong Kong standards. ⑧.

Jordan

Staying up around Jordan Road, just north of Kowloon Park, is no great hardship. You're still within walking distance of the shops and restaurants of Tsim Sha Tsui (and the streetlife of lower Yau Ma Tei), and although there's no let up in noise you usually get a little more for your money. Jordan MTR for all those listed below.

Anglo-Chinese Guest House, 13th Floor, Lucky House, 18–24 Jordan Rd ☎2735 1122, fax 2377 2606. Clean but slightly musty smelling guest house run by a Hong Kong Chinese owner, educated in Australia. Rooms with air-con and shower. ④.

City Guest House, 6th Floor, Cumberland House, 227 Nathan Rd ☎2730 0212, fax 2730 0336. A large variety of rooms, all at reasonable prices, overseen by a friendly, helpful manager. ④.

Eaton Hotel, 380 Nathan Rd ☎2782 1818, fax 2782 5563. On the fringes of Yau Ma Tei, this large, modern hotel features all the facilities you'd expect at the price. There's a good coffee shop (with dinner buffet). It's also very close to the Jade Market and some interesting street life. ⑦.

Evergreen Hotel, 42–52 Woo Sung St ☎2780 4222, fax 2385 8584. Cramped

chain-style hotel catering largely to overseas Chinese tour groups, so spoken English is limited. ⑤.

International House, 5th Floor, Cumberland House, 227 Nathan Rd ☎2730 9276, fax 2375 5301. As long as you don't expect a sumptuous room like those in the pictures outside, you'll be happy with your clean, nicely furnished room with bath. Prices are at the bottom of this category. ⑤.

Majestic Hotel, 348 Nathan Rd ☎2781 1333, fax 2781 1773. One of the better hotels in this area, recently renovated throughout, with a shopping complex and two-screen cinema beneath it. ⑦.

Nathan Hotel, 378 Nathan Rd ☎2388 5141, fax 2770 4262. Sitting between the *Eaton* and *Majestic*, this doesn't have the character of either, which explains why there's room to spare. However, it's comfortable enough, slightly cheaper, and has a high proportion of single rooms. ⑥.

Prudential Hotel, 222 Nathan Rd ☎2311 1100, fax 2311 8222. Great city views and a swimming pool on the roof do a lot to attract custom, and the MTR exit couldn't be closer. Staff are very helpful, too. ⑦.

San Diego Hotel, 169–189 Woo Sung St ☎2735 3855, fax 2736 0297. Modern and slightly garish hotel block tucked into the street parallel to Temple Street. Perfect for early morning and late-night market bustle; less charming for a quiet break. ⑥.

Shamrock, 223 Nathan Rd ☎2735 2271, fax 2736 7354. Old-style hotel with a bit of character, typical of the first wave of building along Nathan Road in the 1950s. Renovations over the years have made the rooms personable, if not exactly stylish; there's an inexpensive restaurant, with a lunch buffet, and a clientele that's mostly Asian. ⑥.

Siu Hing Hostel, 4th Floor, Siu Hing Building, 230 Temple St ☎2770 9798, fax 2388 6901. Good-value rooms with air-con and shower, though you may feel you should get a window for that price. ③.

Accommodation

① *Under $80 per person*
② *Under $200 per room*
③ *$200–300 per room*
④ *$300–500 per room*
⑤ *$500–800 per room*
⑥ *$800–1200 per room*
⑦ *$1200–2000 per room*
⑧ *Over $2000 per room*

Accommodation

Yau Ma Tei

Comparative hotel prices start to drop
once you get up around Waterloo Road
and you can pick up some bargains this
far north up Nathan Road, especially at
the hotels operated by religious
organizations. Regular buses run up and
down Nathan Road, or you can get to all
those listed below via Yau Ma Tei MTR.
Each one is marked on the map on
p.135.

Booth Lodge, 7th Floor, 11 Wing Sing
Lane ☎2771 9266, fax 2385 1140. A
smart, modern (built in the mid-1980s)
Salvation Army hotel just off Nathan Road,
close to the Jade Market and Temple
Street night market. Not exactly brimming
with comforts, it's at the bottom of this
category; adding an extra bed to a
double room costs around $120. ⑤.

Caritas Bianchi Lodge, 4 Cliff Rd ☎2388
1111, fax 2770 6669. Almost next door to
Booth Lodge, and around twice as big,
the air-conditioned rooms in this Roman-
Catholic-run hotel have bath and TV.
Continental breakfast is included and
there's a restaurant serving cheap
lunches and dinners. There's also a
second branch, further north on Boundary
St (see "Mongkok" below). ⑤.

King's Hotel, 473–475a Nathan Rd
☎2780 1281, fax 2782 1833. A budget
hotel with passable rooms (at the bottom
of this category) and a splendid Thai
restaurant on the premises. Ask for a
room at the back; the rooms above
Nathan Road can be very noisy. ⑤.

Pearl Seaview Hotel, 262 Shanghai St
☎2782 0882, fax 2388 1803. Excellent
location, next to Temple Street night
market, and all the comforts of a proper
hotel at relatively reasonable prices.
Worth venturing beyond the confines of
Tsim Sha Tsui. ⑥–⑦.

STB Hostel, 2nd Floor, Great Eastern
Mansion, 255–261 Reclamation St; junction with Dundas St; ☎2710 9199, fax
2385 0153. Terrific bustling environment
outside; inside, segregated dorm beds
(slightly pricier than in Tsim Sha Tsui), and
very small twin-bedded rooms and triples.
Newish, clean and pleasant, with a

common room. Book in advance if you
can. ④.

YMCA International House, 23 Waterloo
Rd ☎2771 9111, fax 2388 5926. Smart
and well-equipped YMCA guest house
with some budget single rooms for men:
you can't book these in advance, just turn
up early. Otherwise, standard singles and
doubles come with air-con, bath and TV;
laundry service too. The restaurant serves
a good buffet breakfast. ⑥.

Mongkok

To be honest, not many tourists choose
to stay this far north in Kowloon, with
many of the hotels solely the preserve of
Chinese businessmen and tour groups.
But certain places have a tempting proximity to attractions like the Bird Market or
Ladies' Market and you won't have to
look far for something decent to eat. Each
hotel is marked on the map on p.000.

Caritas Bianchi, 134 Boundary St,
Mongkok, Prince Edward MTR ☎2339
3777, fax 2338 2864. Second branch of
the religious-run lodge, though this one is
too far out to be of any use other than as
a standby if everywhere else is full.
Rooms are pleasant enough, though. ⑤.

Concourse, 20 Lai Chi Kok Rd, Prince
Edward MTR ☎2397 6683, fax 2381
3768. Large (over 400 rooms), fairly new
CTS-owned hotel, with good prices. You're
a fair way from any downtown action, but
there are a two restaurants, a bar and
coffee shop on the premises. ⑤.

Grand Tower, 627–641 Nathan Rd,
Mongkok MTR ☎2789 0011, fax 2789
0945. Not exactly a stand-out hotel, but
well sited, right by the MTR station (and
Bird Market), and with a free shuttle bus
to Tsim Sha Tsui. Rooms (many at the
bottom of this range) are comfortable, if
on the small side, and triples are good
value. There's a very good *dim* sum
restaurant on the 5th floor (see p.238);
reception is on the 6th. ⑦.

Lucky Hostel, 13th Floor, Chun Yee
Building, 731 Nathan Rd, Mongkok MTR
☎2308 1264, fax 2787 6948. Good
rooms in a Chinese-spoken-only hostel.
③.

YWCA Guest House, 5 Man Fuk Rd, Waterloo Hill Rd, Mongkok MTR/KCR ☎2713 9211, fax 2761 1269. Basic singles and doubles with shower at pretty good rates; men can stay here, too, now. It's a little bit off the beaten track, though only a short walk from Mongkok KCR station which puts you in easy touch of New Territories' day trips. ⑤.

The New Territories

Most people tend to see the New Territories on a day trip, but if you want a night away from the manic centre, either stay at one of the youth hostels (for which see p.213) – which are fairly remote – or either of the two major hotels.

Kowloon Panda, 3 Tsuen Wah St, Tsuen Wan, Tsuen Wan MTR ☎2409 1111, fax 2409 1818. Easily accessed on the MTR (though admittedly at the end of the line), the enormous, 1000-roomed *Panda* has plenty of space, some rooms with water views, masses of facilities (including a pool and two good restaurants) and offers the chance to see a bit of New Town life at first hand. ⑦.

Regal Riverside, Tai Chung Kiu Rd, Sha Tin ☎2649 7878, fax 2637 4748. The New Territories' best hotel – though there's not a lot of competition – close to Sha Tin and all its New Town amenities. This comfortable hotel often appears on holiday packages; there's a fine Asian lunch buffet served here, too. ⑦.

The Outlying Islands

If you want to get away from the city and stay on any of the outlying islands, you'll need to book rooms in advance – especially if you're planning to go at the weekend, when half of Hong Kong heads out of the urban areas. As well as the places listed below, there are two youth hostels on Lantau, for details of which, see p.213.

LAMMA

Han Lok Yuen, Hung Shing Ye ☎2982 0608. Eight double rooms near the beach available; or they'll rent you a two- to three-roomed apartment – though you'll

really need to book in advance. The restaurant is terrific, serving famous roast pigeon. Rooms ③, apartment ⑤.

Lamma Vacation House, Main St, Yung Shue Wan 2982 1886. Down the street from the ferry pier, on the left-hand side. Pleasant rooms (which sleep two), with a separate bathroom and kitchen; the price almost doubles at the weekend. ③.

CHEUNG CHAU

Warwick, East Bay ☎2981 0081, fax 2981 9174. Overlooking Tung Wan Beach, this is the obvious – if most expensive – place to stay, a concrete box whose singles or doubles have balconies. Sea-view rooms are pricier than others, though there's a thirty percent discount on rooms from Monday to Friday and during winter. ⑥.

LANTAU

Cheung Sha Resort House, Cheung Sha ☎2980 2872. Self-contained apartments big enough to sleep six (the price doubles at the weekend). ⑤–⑥.

Mui Wo Inn, Mui Wo ☎2984 8597. Further along from the *Silvermine Beach*, this small hotel has attractive rooms with a balcony and cheaper rooms at the back. ④.

Sea Breeze Hotel, Pui O ☎2984 7977. On the main road and popular with weekenders who pack out the nearby beach. ④.

Silvermine Beach Hotel, Mui Wo ☎2984 8295. Overlooking the beach at Silvermine Bay, this is comfortable, almost luxurious, and great value for money compared to the hotels back in the centre. Rooms are discounted from Sunday to Thursday. ⑤–⑥.

Camping

There are around forty official **campsites** throughout the territory, most in the various Country Parks. There are large concentrations on Lantau Island and on the Sai Kung Peninsula in the New Territories; several of the most usefully sited are detailed in the text. All of them

Accommodation

① *Under $80 per person*
② *Under $200 per room*
③ *$200–300 per room*
④ *$300–500 per room*
⑤ *$500–800 per room*
⑥ *$800–1200 per room*
⑦ *$1200–2000 per room*
⑧ *Over $2000 per room*

Accommodation

cost just a few dollars and you can't reserve a space, making getting there early at the weekend or on a public holiday a good idea. All the sites have basic facilities: toilets, barbecue pits and a water supply. But generally you'll need to take your own food and equipment, and be prepared to walk to most of them as they're often well away from shops and villages. There's a free combined informa-tion sheet/map of the sites called *Campsites of Hong Kong Country Parks*, available from the HKTA.

You can sometimes **camp at the youth hostels** on Lantau and out in the New Territories; see the list at the begin-ning of this chapter and call first to check before setting out. Camping this way, you'll be able to use the hostel facilities, too.

THE MTR & KCR ROUTE MAP

Kowloon-Canton Railway (KCR)
MTR Island Line
MTR Tsuen Wan Line
MTR Kwun Tong Line
Kowloon Tong (MTR & KCR Interchange)
MTR Interchange

MTR Enquiries ☎ 2750 0170
KCR Enquiries ☎ 2602 7799

Guangzhou

Lo Wu
Sheung Shui
Fanling
Tai Wo
Tai Po Market

NEW TERRITORIES

University
Fo Tan
Racecourse
Sha Tin
Tai Wai

N

Tsuen Wan
Tai Wo Hau
Kwai Hing
Kwai Fong
Lei King
Mei Foo
Lai Chi Kok
Cheung Sha Wan
Sham Shui Po
Prince Edward
Mongkok
Yau Ma Tei
Jordan
Tsim Sha Tsui

Wong Tai Sin
Lok Fu
Kowloon Tong
Shek Kip Mei
Mongkok

Diamond Hill
Choi Hung
Kowloon Bay
Ngau Tau Kok
Kwun Tong
Lam Tin

Kowloon

North Point
Quarry Bay
Fortress Hill
Sheung Wan
Central
Admiralty
Wan Chai
Tin Hau
Causeway Bay
Tai Koo
Sai Wan Ho
Heng Fa Chuen
Shau Kei Wan
Chai Wan

HONG KONG ISLAND

Ferry
Piers

Central
Piers

Hang
Seng
Bank
Building

CONNAUGHT ROAD

TUNG MAN ST

TING LUNG ST

JUBILEE STREET

Central
Market

QUEEN VICTORIA STREET

3

CONNAUGHT ROAD

Exchange
Square

2

Central Bus
Terminal

1

Central
Mid-Levels
Escalator

MAN WA LANE

POTTINGER STREET

DES VOEUX ROAD

Wing-On
House

COCHRANE ST

CRC Dept.
Store

STANLEY ST

POTTINGER ST

WELLINGTON STREET

LI YUEN ST W

LI YUEN ST E

QUEEN'S ROAD

General
Post
Office

Taxis

Jardine
House
ⓘ

Worldwide
Plaza

DOUGLAS LANE

CHIU LUNG ST

St George's
Building

High
Block

Lane
Crawford

WO ON LANE

THEATRE LANE

Central
MTT

PEDDER ST

Swire
House

Pedder
Building

PEDDER ST

Mandarin
Oriental
Hotel

STATUE
SQUARE

Entertainment
Building

Gloucester
Tower

The
Landmark

Alexandra
House

ICE HOUSE ST

Prince's
Building

CHATER ROAD

STATUE
SQUARE

D AGUILAR ST

LAN KWAI FONG

WYNDHAM ST

ON LAN ST

ON NING TERR

Central
Tower

QUEEN'S ROAD

LEGCO
Building

JACKSON RD

D AGUILAR ST

ZETLAND STREET

Edinburgh
Tower

ICE HOUSE ST

Standard
Chartered
Bank

HK &
Shanghai
Bank

Old
Bank of
China

WYNDHAM ST

GLENEALY

Old Dairy Farm
Building
(Fringe Club &
FCC)

RUDDELL ST

QUEEN'S ROAD

Beaconsfield

BATTERY PATH

St John's
Cathedral

ARBUTHNOT RD

LOWER ALBERT ROAD

LOWER ALBERT ROAD

LOWER ALBERT ROAD

GARDEN ROAD

Zoological &
Botanical
Gardens

ALBANY ROAD

UPPER ALBERT ROAD

Government
House

US Consulate

Lower Peak
Tram Terminal

To Tsim Sha Tsui

To Disco Bay → To Hung Hom

CENTRAL

— Tram route
● MTR Station Entrance/Exit
▨ Reclaimed land

To Tsim Sha
Tsui East

N

**Queen's
Pier**

EDINBURGH PLACE

**Urban Council
Chambers**

City Hall Low Block | Car Park

CONNAUGHT ROAD

**Prince of Wales
Barracks**

Hong Kong Club

**Hutchison
House**

CLUB ST

**Prince of Wales
Building**

Ritz
Carlton | Furama
Hotel

LAMBETH WALK

**Bank of
America
Tower**

**Far East
Finance
Centre**

HARCOURT ROAD

Wan Chai ▷

Chater
Garden

MURRAY ROAD

DRAKE ST

Tower 1

Admiralty
MTT

**Tower
2**

QUEENSWAY

**Bank of
China**

**Lippo
Centre**

TAMAR ST

**Queensway
Plaza**

**Admiralty
Centre**

RODNEY ST

Wan Chai ▷

Citibank
Plaza

COTTON TREE DRIVE

**Flagstaff House
(Museum of Tea Ware)**

**United
Centre**

QUEENSWAY

**Hong Kong
Park**

Aviary

0   100 m

**Supreme
Court**

**Queensway
Govt.
Offices**

**Island
Shangri-La**

**One Pacific
Place**

**Marriott
Hotel**

SUPREME COURT RD

**Conrad
Hotel**

**Two Pacific
Place**

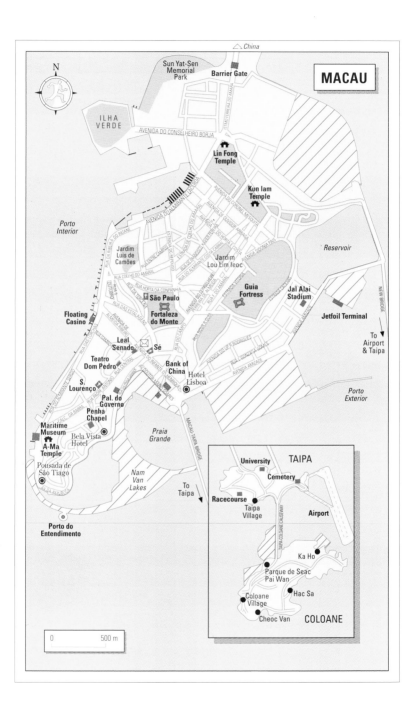

Chapter 7

Eating

Don't underestimate the importance of
food in Chinese culture. Meals are a
shared, family affair, full of opportunity to
show respect for others – by the way the
food and drink is served, accepted and
eaten. Although they're generally informal
in tone, there's a structured form to each
meal which reflects the importance of the
food being eaten. As a visitor, especially
as a foreigner, the nuances might pass
you by, but it will soon become apparent
that the Hong Kong Chinese live to eat –
every café and restaurant is noisy and
packed, the shrill interiors more reminiscent of school cafeterias than fancy eater-
ies. On the street, too, stalls and stands do
a brisk trade in snacks and cheap meals.

Almost everyone eats out regularly and
the vast Chinese restaurants organize their
opening hours around the long working
days of most of the population. You can
also pick and choose from one of the
world's widest selections of cuisines.
Quite apart from the **regional Chinese**
variations on offer – of which the local
Cantonese cooking is the most familiar to
foreigners – there isn't any kind of **Asian**
food you can't sample, from Burmese to
Vietnamese. Probably the biggest surprise
is the number of excellent **Indian** and
Pakistani restaurants in the territory.
American and **European** food is well
represented, too, though it's cooked with
varying degrees of skill: generally speak-

Eating

Children are welcomed in most Chinese restaurants; see "Children"s Hong Kong", p.302 for more details.

ing, the high-class hotel, French and Italian restaurants are good, but other food can often leave a lot to be desired. There's also a catch-all category of **international** restaurants and bars, where you can eat anything from burgers and steaks to nouvelle cuisine. At the other end of the scale, most pubs put on **British**-style food of the pie-and-chips variety.

Food needn't be expensive, certainly if you stick to Chinese and Asian restaurants. The important thing is to retain your spirit of adventure at all times: some of the best dining experiences in Hong Kong are in the most unlikely-looking places, and some of the best food is eaten almost in passing, on the street or taken quickly in a *dim sum* restaurant or café.

The **listings and reviews** below should help you decide where and what to eat in Hong Kong. We've started with cafés, coffee shops, delis and street food, followed by *dim sum* restaurants and Chinese food in its various guises, succeeded by all the other cuisines available in the territory, listed in alphabetical order. At the end of the chapter are details for buying your own food in markets and supermarkets.

You'll find **descriptions** of Cantonese food, including *dim sum*, as well as other regional Chinese food and Asian cuisines

in the introductions to the various sections. **Vegetarian** restaurants, and those that serve vegetarian meals, are included throughout, though bear in mind that the only solely vegetarian places are either Cantonese or Indian/Pakistani – there's a round-up on p.258. To go straight to the listings for the kind of food you want to eat, check the **food index**.

The **opening hours** given throughout are daily, unless otherwise stated. Don't count on being able to use **credit cards** everywhere. Many restaurants – especially the smaller ones – will only take cash, so always check first if you're unsure.

Cafés, coffee shops, delis and fast food

Whether it's breakfast, coffee and cake, sandwich, burger or ice cream you want, Hong Kong isn't going to present you with any difficulty. **Cafés** and **hotel/department store coffee shops** are ubiquitous, while all the familiar Western **burger and pizza joints** are represented in Hong Kong, though *McDonald's* seems to have a stranglehold on the market. Burgers here are the same as anywhere else in the world, though prices are around half (or less) of what you'd pay at

---

Tea, Coffee and Soft Drinks

You can sometimes get non-Chinese **tea** in cafés and snack bars (but not in Chinese restaurants): it's generally *Liptons* and comes hot or cold on request. It's common to drink it with lemon; tea with milk is much more rare – if you want milk, it will normally be the condensed variety. For real milk and tea, venture into one of the big hotels for **afternoon tea**, something which is well worth doing at least once for the atmosphere. **Coffee** is the more usual hot drink, but in a Chinese café it's invariably weak and instant and again served with condensed milk, and sugar unless you specify otherwise. However, there's a fast-growing band of European and American **coffee shops** and stands, where you can get espresso, cappuccino, mocha, latte and all the other caffeine drinks that civilization demands. You'll also get a decent cup of coffee in most of the larger hotels and many European restaurants.

Coke and all the usual international fizzy **soft drinks** are available from stalls and shops everywhere, as are a variety of **fruit juices** – though the small boxed ones are packed with sugar and additives. Fresh fruit juice is always expensive. Try the **local soft drinks**: *Vitamilk* is a plain or flavoured soya milk drink – a few dollars a carton – while lemon tea, chocolate milk and lots of other infusions all come cold and in cartons. Regular **milk** isn't drunk very much by the Cantonese (who have a lactose intolerance), but you can buy it in supermarkets.

Breakfast

The traditional Chinese breakfast is **congee**, a gruel made from rice boiled for a long time in lots of water, served with chopped spring onions or morsels of meat or fish. It's available from some early opening restaurants or street stalls (*dai pai dongs*), and often comes with long sticks of fried dough – a bit like doughnuts. Congee is an acquired taste, but it's something that Chinese kids get used to from a very early age, since it's virtually force-fed to babies and sick children. It's more appealing to breakfast on **dim sum**, served from selected restaurants, many of which erect stalls outside to sell takeaway *dim sum* to passers-by – though the stalls have usually disappeared by 9am or so. **Western breakfasts** – cooked and Continental – are available in most of the bigger hotels, and in cafés, coffee shops and some pubs. Check the reviews under "Cafés, Coffee Shops, Delis and Fast Food" and "Dim Sum" for full details of where serves what.

Eating

home – kept low in order to establish American fast-food in a culture that has been producing its own more appetizing version for thousands of years. Burger bars are now terribly popular with Chinese kids; they are also, incidentally, the cheapest places to get a cup of coffee and a welcome blast of air-conditioning. Other Western delights include a growing number of **sandwich bars** and **delis**, a few specialist **ice-cream shops**, and some fine independent **coffee shops**.

A couple of Chinese chains sell Asian-influenced snacks (radish cake, chicken wings and the like) and there are some excellent Chinese **cake shops**, too. **Chinese cafés**, often just hole-in-the-wall jobs, dish out polystyrene and foil boxes of more substantial food – rice and meat, noodles, etc – which you can generally eat perching on a stool or take away, for around $20–40 a go.

Territory-wide

Burger King. Outlets at 59 Des Voeux Rd, Central, and 26 Granville Rd, Tsim Sha Tsui.

Café de Coral. Chinese takeaway snacks from a bright, plastic interior. Chicken wings, radish cakes, salads and sandwiches at low prices, and shops on every corner.

Delifrance. Pseudo-French deli-cafés selling croissants, French bread sandwiches and decent cakes and coffee. Rapidly expanding, with branches (among others)

at Worldwide Plaza, Central; 1st Floor, 16–18 Queen's Rd, Central; A1–A3 Queensway Plaza (at the entrance to the Lippo Centre), Admiralty.

Häagen-Dazs. Hong Kong's best ice cream, with branches (among others) at 1 Lan Kwai Fong, Central; Shop C1, World Wide Plaza, Pedder St, Central; The Forum, Exchange Square, Central; Shop B209, Times Square, Causeway Bay; *Hyatt Regency*, Nathan Rd, Tsim Sha Tsui.

Ka Ka Lok. Ubiquitous, bargain Chinese takeaway snacks and meals.

KFC. Branches at 6 D'Aguilar St, Central; 40 Yee Woo St, Causeway Bay; 28 Beach Rd, Repulse Bay; 2 Cameron Rd, Tsim Sha Tsui; 241 Nathan Rd, Yau Ma Tei.

Maxim's. BBQ chicken legs, hamburgers, salads, roast meat dishes, drinks and sandwiches. Good cake shops, too, at MTR and KCR stations, and at the Star Ferry terminals.

McDonald's. Two 24-hour restaurants at 21 Granville Rd and 12 Peking Rd (both in Tsim Sha Tsui), plus many other branches.

Oliver's Super Sandwiches. Reliable deli and sandwich shop chain (most open Mon–Sat 8am–6pm), also serving breakfast, afternoon tea and baked potatoes. Branches at: Shop 104, Exchange Square II, 8 Connaught Place, Central; Shop 201–205, Prince's Building, 10 Chater Rd, Central; Shop 8, Lower Ground Floor, The Mall, Pacific Place, 88 Queensway, Admiralty; Shop A, Fleet House, 38 Gloucester Rd, Wan Chai; Shop G,

Eating

Windsor House, 311 Gloucester Rd, Causeway Bay; 28 Hankow Rd, Tsim Sha Tsui; 100 Nathan Rd, Tsim Sha Tsui.

Pizza Hut. The many branches include: B1, Edinburgh Tower, The Landmark, 11–19 Queen's Rd, Central; Goldmark, Jardine's Bazaar, Causeway Bay; Beach Centre, 33 Beach Rd, Repulse Bay; Shop 22, Basement, Silvercord, 30 Canton Rd, Tsim Sha Tsui; Shop 008, Ocean Terminal, Harbour City, Canton Rd, Tsim Sha Tsui.

Starlight Express. Cantonese café chain with budget breakfasts, Western and Chinese meals and snacks. Handiest branch is in the Cultural Centre Restaurant Block, Salisbury Rd, Tsim Sha Tsui (Mon–Sat 8am–10pm, Sun 9am–10pm).

Central and Admiralty

Café Chater, *Furama Kempinski*, 1 Connaught Rd. Hotel coffee shop which prepares pretty much anything, at a price: fresh fruit and eggs, Japanese breakfasts, the full American and British works, or just coffee and pastries – from around $80–150. Breakfast served 6–11am.

Cafe Piatti: at Exchange Square; 108 Prince's Building; Far East Finance Centre, Harcourt Rd; Lippo Centre, Queensway; and *Seibu Food Court*, The Mall, Pacific Place, 88 Queensway. Five stands dotted around Central, whose range of real coffees frees the masses from the tyranny of *Nescafé*. Experts recommend the chocolate chip cookies. Open 8am–6pm.

Cappucci, Government Offices Lower Block, 66 Queensway. Popular Italian coffee bar/sandwich kiosk, an enterprise run by people with disabilities. Open 8am–5.30pm.

La Cite, Basement, Pacific Place, 88 Queensway. Smart bistro-cum-café that pushes all the right buttons – soup, snacks, set lunches, or just teas and coffees while you take the weight off your shopping feet. Open 11am–11pm.

Dan Ryan's Chicago Bar and Grill, 114 The Mall, Pacific Place, 88 Queensway. American restaurant (see p.249) serving classic breakfasts at weekends – eggs, pancakes and all the fixings. Served Sat & Sun 7.30–11am.

Giants Sandwiches, 53 Wellington St. Recommended sandwiches; there's a small seating area. Open 7.30am–7.30pm.

Joyce Café, The Galleria, 9 Queen's Rd. In a league of its own for stylish café surroundings, this is an expensive place to eat, though there are set breakfast menus (8am–noon) and afternoon tea is served. Otherwise it's soups, sandwiches, pastas, salads and a definitive club sandwich for Central's smart set. Open Mon–Sat 10am–7.30pm, Sun noon–6.30pm.

Mandarin Oriental Hotel, 5 Connaught Rd. *The* serious hotel breakfast (served 7–11am in the Grill Room, where around $230 gets you unlimited stabs at an enormous buffet, from fresh fruit juice and cereals, eggs and all the works, through to strudels and cheese. Sunday brunch (11am–3pm) is similarly stylish, though costs a whopping $350. For coffee, all-day snacks and light meals the *Coffee Shop* (7am–1am) is the favoured moneyed haunt.

Marriott Café, *Marriott Hotel*, Pacific Place, 88 Queensway. Good Western/Asian snacks and meals in an elegant hotel coffee shop whose long hours are a boon in this district. Open 7am–1am.

Pacific Coffee Company, Ground Floor, Shop 1C, Bank of America Tower; (Mon–

Food Courts

Hong Kong has several Food Courts – areas in shopping malls devoted to inexpensive takeaway shops serving different types of food. Pick and mix your cuisine and sit at one of the central tables. The best food courts are:

IFJ Food Plaza, 2nd Floor, Chungking Mansions, 36–44 Nathan Rd, Tsim Sha Tsui (open 24hr).

The Majestic Centre, 348 Nathan Rd, Tsim Sha Tsui.

Shop 029, Marine Deck, Ocean Terminal, Basement, Harbour City, Canton Rd, Tsim Sha Tsui.

Seibu, The Mall, Pacific Place, 88 Queensway, Central.

Afternoon Tea

If you're gasping for a real cup of tea, British-style with proper milk and all the trimmings, then some of Hong Kong's most splendid hotels do the honours. The lobby lounges are generally the places to head for, among which the **Peninsula** (Salisbury Rd, Tsim Sha Tsui) is the most magnificent – all gilt and soaring pillars and a string quartet playing as you sip tea and munch scones. Other marvellous venues for afternoon tea are the **Regent** (Salisbury Rd, Tsim Sha Tsui); the **Omni Hongkong Hotel** (3 Canton Rd, Tsim Sha Tsui), the *Tiffin Lounge* at the **Grand Hyatt** (1 Harbour Rd, Wan Chai) and the **Mandarin Oriental** (5 Connaught Rd, Central). At all these places, expect to pay around $130 per person for a set tea.

Sat 7.30am–6pm); Shop 404, Pacific Place II, Admiralty (Mon–Sat 7.30am–1pm, Sun 8am–9pm); Star Ferry Pier (Mon–Fri 8am–8pm, Sat & Sun 8am–10pm). Stylish little coffee dispensers at strategic Central locations; great coffee, good fruit juices and cookies.

La Rose Noire, 301, Pacific Place, 88 Queensway. One of the best French cafés in town, serving cakes, pastries and sandwiches from breakfast onwards: what's more, you can nearly always get a seat and it's not half as dear as it could be. Highly recomended. Open 7.30am–11pm.

Tiffany Delicatessen, 13–14 Connaught Rd (Ground Floor of Euro Trade Centre). Takeaway sandwiches; freshly baked European-style bread, cooked meats, smoked fish, cakes and wines. Open 8am–5pm.

Uncle Russ, California Tower, 30 D'Aguilar St, Lan Kwai Fong. Stand-up booth serving excellent filter coffee in various incarnations and cookies too. Open 7.30am–11pm. Branches with similar hours, too, at Shop B216, Times Square, Causeway Bay; and Ground Floor, 2 Canton Rd, Tsim Sha Tsui.

Wan Chai

Grand Hyatt Coffee Shop, *Grand Hyatt*, 1 Harbour Rd. Some of the finest window seats in the territory and stylish, elegant surroundings. The food matches these step for step – always pricey, but top quality. Open 6.30am–1am.

USA Deli, 8–12 Hennessy Rd. Massive sandwiches as well as standard coffee shop offerings – omelettes to salads. Open 11am–11pm.

Causeway Bay

Martino, 68 Paterson St. Japanese-style coffee shop serving a variety of freshly ground coffees and snacks. Open noon–midnight.

New York Deli, 17 Lan Fong Rd. You'll know what to expect from the name, and servings are up to scratch – just don't expect the food to be terribly authentic. Eat in, takeaway service available. Open noon–11pm.

Panash, *Daimaru*, Household Square, Kingston St. Superb bakery with adjacent café for speciality breads, cakes, sandwiches, fresh fruit juices and good coffee. Open 10.30am–9.30pm; closed Wed.

Pokka, *Daimaru*, Household Square, Kingston St. Coffee by the cup in the department store coffee shop, or buy the beans from a fine variety on offer. Open 10am–7pm.

Phoenix Congee and Noodle, 13–15 Cleveland St. Congee and all the trimmings for a real Cantonese breakfast; noodles too. Open 7.30am–11.30pm.

Zumtobel, 2 Hysan Ave. A little hole-in-the-wall that serves various coffees with an Austrian twist, as well as tempting pastries – try the carrot cake. Open 8am–8pm.

Happy Valley

Superbowl, 21 King Kwong St. Congee as an art form and as tasty as it comes, but relatively pricey. Open 11am–11pm.

Tsim Sha Tsui

An American Place, Carnarvon Plaza, 20 Carnarvon Rd. Coffee, bagels and muffins for homesick Americans. Open 9am–6pm.

Eating

Cherikoff, 184 Nathan Rd. Good, budget Western breakfasts, and coffee and cakes served all day. Open 8am–6pm.

Chungking Mansions, 36–44 Nathan Rd. Cheap curried breakfast, for those with cast-iron constitutions, at *Kashmir Fast Food* (Ground Floor, no. 17) and *Lahore Fast Food Centre* (Ground Floor, no. 19); served from around 8am.

Delicatessen Corner, 1st Basement, *Holiday Inn Golden Mile*, 46–52 Nathan Rd. Lunch boxes, soups, salads and sandwiches. Open 7.30am–11.30pm

Mall Café, Ground Floor, *YMCA*, 41 Salisbury Rd. Favourite Tsim Sha Tsui spot for a leisurely breakfast – Continental, English or Chinese for $30–40 – set lunch or sandwich. The Hong Kong daily papers are available. Open 7am–midnight.

Street food: dai pai dongs

You'll find it hard to resist the **street food** in Hong Kong: a short walk through some of the most densely populated parts of the territory gives you the choice of dozens of different snacks, all sold at incredibly cheap prices. If you're worried about **hygiene**, most of the snacks are fairly innocuous anyway, made out of fresh or preserved ingredients, while more elaborate food – noodles and the like – is freshly cooked in front of you.

The street stalls you'll see all over the territory are called **dai pai dongs**. Most are mobile mini-kitchens and you just point to what you want and pay, usually just a few dollars for most things. Common snacks are fish, beef and pork balls (threaded onto bamboo sticks and dipped in chilli sauce), fresh and dried squid, spring rolls, steamed buns, won ton (stuffed dumplings), simple noodle soups, pancakes, congee (rice gruel served with a greasy, doughnut-type stick), cooked intestines, tofu pudding and various sweets. In some places – open-air and indoor markets and on a couple of the outlying islands – *dai pai dongs* are more formal affairs, grouped together with simple tables and chairs, and with more elaborate food: seafood, mixed rice and noodle dishes, stews and soups, and

bottled beer. There'll rarely be a menu, but everything will still be dirt cheap, and you should be able to put together a decent meal for around $30–40.

The following central Hong Kong and Kowloon locations are the most accessible places to sample *dai pai dong* food. Every New Territories town has its own particular area for *dai pai dongs*, as do various of the outlying islands; see the text for more details.

Graham St market, at the bottom of Stanley St, Central.

Haiphong Rd, bottom of Kowloon Park, Tsim Sha Tsui.

Hau Fook St, Tsim Sha Tsui. Off Carnarvon Road, between Cameron Road and Granville Street, the street tables here serve basic Cantonese and Shanghai food, especially seafood.

Luard Rd, opposite Southorn Playground, Wan Chai.

Sheung Wan Market, Urban Council Complex, 345 Queen's Rd, Central. The Cooked Food Market on the second floor is one of the more exhilarating culinary experiences in town: no frills, no foreigners. Open 6am–2am.

Sutherland St and Hing Lung St, off Des Voeux Rd, Sheung Wan.

Temple St, Yau Ma Tei. Reliable seafood-based street food at the Temple Street Night Market, from 7pm; see p.134.

Dim sum

Some of the most exciting of all Cantonese food is **dim sum**, which, literally translated, means "to touch the heart". Basically, it's steamed or braised stuffed dumplings, small cakes and other appetizers served in little bamboo baskets. This might not sound like much, but there are scores of different varieties. There's a list of the most common dishes given overleaf, but everyday items include pork, prawn, crab, beef or shark's fin dumplings, as well as spring rolls, prawn toast, rice and cooked meats in lotus leaves, curried squid, chicken feet, turnip cake, stuffed peppers, pork and chicken buns, custard tarts and steamed sweet buns.

Restaurants that specialize in *dim sum* **open early** in the morning, from around 7am, and serve right through lunch up until around 5pm; nearly all regular Cantonese restaurants also serve *dim sum*, usually from 10–11am until 3pm. If you can't make breakfast, the best time is before the lunch rush – say around noon; after lunch there won't be much left. The opening hours given in the reviews below (daily, unless otherwise stated) are the *dim sum* hours for that particular restaurant: most of the places convert into regular restaurants for the evening session.

Central

City Hall Chinese Restaurant, 2nd Floor, City Hall Low Block ☎2521 1303. Harbour views and a good range of *dim sum* served by friendly types throughout the day. You'll have to wait for a lunchtime table; take a ticket at the door. Open Mon–Sat 10am–3pm, Sun 8am–3pm.

Jade Garden, 1st Floor, Swire House, 11 Chater Rd ☎2526 3031. One of a chain (with two more in Causeway Bay); dependable *dim sum* meals served by staff who are used to novice *gweilo* visitors. Open Mon–Fri 2.30–6pm, Sat 11.30am–6pm, Sun 10am–6pm.

Luk Yu Teahouse, 24–26 Stanley St ☎2523 5464. Excellent, if rather pricey, *dim sum* from this traditional wood-panelled and screened Chinese tea-house, with service by white-coated waiters. You order from a Chinese order-paper, but a waiter will choose a selection for you if you ask – though don't expect the service to be particularly welcoming. You really need to book, or be prepared to wait if you're not a regular, but it's worth persevering for the experience. Open 7am–6pm.

Tai Woo, 15–19 Wellington St ☎2524 5618. All-day *dim sum* ordered from a short English menu – a lunchtime favourite with local office workers and shoppers. Open 11am–4pm.

Tsui Hang Village Restaurant, 2nd Floor, New World Tower, 16–18 Queen's Rd ☎2524 2012. Get there early for the good *dim sum* in splendid, traditional surroundings. Open Mon–Sat 2.30–6pm, Sun 10am–6pm.

Yung Kee Restaurant, 32–40 Wellington St ☎2522 1624. Classic Cantonese restaurant which gets mobbed for its fine *dim sum*. Open 2–4.30pm.

Zen, LG1, The Mall, Pacific Place, 88 Queensway ☎2845 4555. Sharp designer-style and expertly cooked *dim sum*, which means considerably higher prices than usual. Expect to pay $150 a head. Open Mon–Fri 11.30am–3pm, Sat 11.30am–4.30pm, Sun 10.30am–4.30pm.

Sheung Wan

Diamond Restaurant, 267–275 Des Voeux Rd ☎2544 4708. A swarming Cantonese diner on several floors, you may have to wait (or share a table), but it's loud, authentic and cheap. Trolley women shout out their wares and you'll have to speak up if you want to eat anything – learn the names of a few dishes before you go. It's near Western Market. Open 6.30am–5pm.

Mythical China, 2nd Floor, Western Market, 323 Des Voeux Rd ☎2815 3212. Galleried, lantern-hung restaurant trying hard for that traditional look. Order from the cards left at the table: the food isn't bad, though the restaurant is slightly pricier than normal and not overwhelmingly friendly. Open 11am–3pm.

Wan Chai

Canton Room, 1st Floor, *Luk Kwok Hotel*, 72 Gloucester Rd ☎2866 2166. Weekend only *dim sum* hours in this rather splendid hotel dining room with wood panelling and Deco touches. Open Sat & Sun 11am–3pm.

Dynasty Restaurant, 3rd Floor, *New World Harbour View*, 1 Harbour Rd ☎2584 6971. Harbour views from one of Hong Kong's best hotels and excellent, if pricey, *dim sum*. Open Mon–Sat noon–3pm, Sun 11.30am–3pm.

Round Dragon Chinese Restaurant, 60th Floor, Hopewell Centre, 183 Queen's Rd East ☎2861 1668. *Dim sum* sixty floors up, with views to match, which on the whole is what you're paying for, since the

Eating

For more details about restaurants – etiquette, the bill and service charges – see "Restaurants", p.239.

Dim Sum Restaurants

Most *dim sum* restaurants are enormous, often with tables on several floors; in the smarter places, staff with two-way radios check on space before letting you through. Also, many are decorated in a completely over-the-top fashion: they're used for wedding receptions and parties, and so are covered in dragons, swirls and painted screens, ornate backgrounds that can easily cost millions of Hong Kong dollars.

Going in, you'll either be confronted by a *maître d'*, who'll put your name on a list and tell you when there's space, or often you can just walk through and fight for a table yourself. It's busiest at lunchtime and on Sunday when families come out to eat, when you'll have to queue. This is not an orderly concept: just attach yourself to a likely looking table where people appear to be finishing up, and hover over the seats until they leave. Any hesitation and you'll lose your table, so keep an eye out.

It's best to **go in a group** if you can, in order to share dishes. As all the tables seat about ten or more, you'll be surrounded by others anyway, which is fun if the experience is new to you.

How to order, how to pay

Sit down and you'll be brought **tea** – apt since if you're Chinese you don't go just to eat *dim sum*, but to *yam cha* ("drink tea"). You don't pay for this, though in some places there'll be a small cover charge. Foreigners will generally be given jasmine tea (*heung ping*), which is light and fragrant, but the Chinese mostly drink *bo lay*, a strong black or fermented tea which is particularly suited to cutting through the oil and stodge. If you

Dim Sum Terms

If you can't find what you want, try approximating the following sounds to order *dim sum*.

Savouries

Steamed prawn dumplings	*har gau*	蝦餃
Steamed beef ball	*au yuk*	牛肉丸
Steamed spare ribs in spicy sauce	*pai gwat*	排骨
Steamed pork and prawn dumpling	*siu mai*	燒麥
Steamed bun stuffed with barbecued pork	*cha siu bau*	叉燒包
Gelatinous rice-flour roll stuffed with shrimp/meat	*cheung fun*	長粉
Steamed glutinous rice filled with assorted meat, wrapped in a lotus leaf	*nor mai gai*	糯米雞
Deep-fried stuffed dumpling served with sweet and sour sauce	*won ton*	餛飩
Half-moon shaped steamed dumpling with meat/shrimp	*fun gwor*	粉角
Congee (thick rice gruel, flavoured with shredded meat and spring onion)	*djuk*	粥
Spring roll	*chun kuen*	春卷
Turnip cake	*law bak go*	羅蔔糕
Chicken feet	*fung jao*	鳳爪
Stuffed beancurd	*yeung do fu*	釀豆腐

want this (and hot water too, to dilute it), ask for *bo lay gwan soy*. When you want a refill, just leave the top off the teapot and it'll be replaced for free.

At this stage, if you're Chinese you'll have already started to wash your chopsticks and rinse your bowls in the hot tea or water: everything's clean anyway, but it's almost an obsession with some people.

In most places you'll see **trolleys** being wheeled through the restaurant. They contain the bamboo baskets which, typically, contain three or four little dumplings or similar-sized bites to eat. Somewhere, too, there'll be people frying stuffed vegetables at mobile stands, others with trays of spring rolls and cakes, and different trolleys dispensing noodle soups, congee and other food. Just flag down the trolleys as they pass and see what you fancy by lifting the lids. Each time you pick something, the basket or plate will be dumped on the table, and a mark made on a card left at your table when the tea was brought. In some of the more upmarket *dim sum* restaurants, you'll have to order your dishes from the kitchen, in which case there'll invariably be a short menu in English on the table.

When you've finished, cross your chopsticks over the pile of rubble left on your table and flag down a waiter, who will take your card. He or she counts the number of empty baskets/plates on the table, checks it off against the ticks on your card and goes away to prepare the bill. Most things **cost** the same, just $25–35 a basket. Even if you absolutely stuff yourself on *dim sum*, you'll find it hard to spend more than $80–100 a head, perhaps as much as $130 if you eat in one of the fancier, famous *dim sum* places. On top of this, you'll nearly always pay a ten percent service charge.

Taro/yam croquette	*woo kok*	蕃薯糊角
Crabmeat dumplings	*hie yuk gau*	蟹肉角
Shark's fin dumplings	*yu chi gau*	魚鰭餃
Curried squid	*gar li yau yu*	咖喱魷魚
Steamed, sliced chicken wrapped in beancurd	*gai see fun kuen*	雞絲粉卷
Fried, stuffed green pepper	*yeung chen jiu*	釀青椒
Deep-fried beancurd roll with pork/shrimp	*seen chuk guen*	鮮春卷
Steamed dumpling with pork and chicken	*guon tong gau*	豬肉雞水餃
Steamed chicken bun	*gai bau tsei*	雞包仔
Barbecued pork puff	*cha siu so*	叉燒酥
Mixed meat croquette	*ham shui kok*	咸水角

Sweets

Water chestnut cake	*ma tai go*	馬蹄糕
Sweet beancurd with almond soup	*do fu fa*	豆腐花
Sweet coconut balls	*nor mai chi*	糯米池
Steamed sponge cake	*ma lai go*	馬來糕
Mango pudding	*mango bo din*	芒果布丁
Sweet lotus seed paste bun	*lin yung bau*	蓮蓉糕
Egg-custard tart	*daan tat*	蛋撻

Eating

food is unremarkable. There's an English menu to help you out. Open 11.30am–3pm.

Causeway Bay

Jade Garden, branches at 1 Hysan Ave ☎2577 9332 and 1st Floor, Hennessy Centre, 500 Hennessy Rd ☎2895 2200. Part of the *Maxim's* chain, these mainstream Cantonese restaurants serve reliable *dim sum*. Hysan Ave branch open 7.45am–6pm, Hennessy Rd 8am–6pm.

Maxim's Chinese Restaurant, 1st & 2nd Floors, 1 Yee Wo St (entrance on Gt. George St) ☎2894 9933. Not many tourists find themselves in this refeshingly down-to-earth *dim sum* palace, where the relatively cheery trolley-pushers muster up the odd word of English. Open 8am–5pm.

Happy Valley

Dim Sum, 63 Sing Woo Rd ☎2834 8893. Old-style wooden booths make this a nice, cosy place to experiment with *dim sum* – the food is top quality too. Open 11am–11pm.

Aberdeen

Jumbo Floating Restaurant, Shum Wan, Wong Chuk Hang ☎2553 9111. The famous floating restaurant (see "Cantonese" below) serves *dim sum* from breakfast onwards, as does its neighbouring sister ship, the *Jumbo Palace*. It's the cheapest way to have a meal aboard, so worth considering. Open 7.30am–4pm.

Tsim Sha Tsui

Beijing Restaurant, 34–36 Granville Rd ☎2366 9968. A Beijing restaurant that trots out northern-style *dim sum* at lunchtime – stodgy dumplings a speciality. There's not a huge choice and it's very meat-orientated: the noodle soups and mixed cold cuts of meat are the local choice. Open 10.30am–2.30pm.

The Chinese Restaurant, 2nd Floor, *Hyatt Regency*, 67 Nathan Rd ☎2311 1234. Extremely elegant traditional Tea House surroundings, complete with booth seating and deferential waiters, make for one of the finer *dim sum* experiences. Pricey,

but worth every cent. Open 11.30am–3pm.

Fontana Restaurant, 6–8a Prat Ave ☎2367 2452. *Dim sum* palace, where *maitre d's* with two-way radios find you a table in the bowels of the restaurant. There's a wider range of dishes than usual, served from trolleys, but get there early as it attracts a bustling local clientele. Open 11am–5pm.

Jade Garden, 4th Floor, Star House, 3 Salisbury Rd, by the Star Ferry terminal ☎2730 6888. Part of the *Maxim* chain, serving *dim sum* with harbour views. There's another branch, also with reasonable *dim sum*, at 25–31 Carnarvon Rd ☎369 8311. Open 7.30am–5pm.

Orchard Court, 1st & 2nd Floors, 37 Hankow Rd, Tsim Sha Tsui ☎2317 5111. Hidden away, this is a rather nice spot with framed prints and window grilles in the shape of fans. Mark your choices on the order card – fried beancurd skin roll or dumpling with shrimp and cabbage are both splendid – and they'll be delivered quickly. Open 11am–5pm.

Tao Yuan, 1st Floor, China Hong Kong City, 33 Canton Rd ☎2736 1688. Authentic Cantonese *dim sum* for a clientele that couldn't be more critical: Chinese travellers from the adjacent Departure Level for China ferries. It's usually packed. Open 11am–5pm.

Mongkok

Orchid Garden, 5th Floor, *Grand Tower Hotel*, 627–641 Nathan Rd ☎2789 0011. Extremely handy for Bird/Ladies' Market visitors. There are no English menus or trolleys but enough English spoken for you to assemble a good lunch, which arrives steaming hot from the kitchen. Rather elegant, but not overpriced. Try the *char siu bau*. Open 11am–3pm.

Vegetarian dim sum

Bodhi Vegetarian Restaurant. A reliable vegetarian restaurant chain that usually has a takeaway/stand-up *dim sum* section as well as waiter service. Worth trying at least once even for committed carnivores. Branches include: 56 Cameron

Rd, Tsim Sha Tsui ☎2739 2222; 36 Jordan Road, Yau Ma Tei ☎2735 4686; 32–34 Lock Rd/81 Nathan Rd, Tsim Sha Tsui ☎2366 8283. All branches open for *dim sum* 11am–5pm.

Healthy Mess, Ground Floor, 51–53 Hennessy Rd ☎2527 3918. Stylish little place with veggie *dim sum* and snacks served all day – take a look in the window first to see what you fancy. Open 11am–11pm.

Lotus Garden, 60 Yee Wo St, Causeway Bay ☎2895 4333. Small vegetarian restaurant, with *dim sum* to eat in or take away. Open 8.30am–11pm.

Natural Vegetarian Food, Ground Floor, 36 Lyndhurst Terrace, Central ☎2851 6811. Convenient stop for veggie *dim sum* and other snacks and meals, though the selection is a bit limited. Open 8am–noon.

Pak Bo Vegetarian Kitchen, Ground Floor, 106 Austin Rd, Tsim Sha Tsui ☎2380 2681. Point to what you want from the window and eat inside; it's all cheap and very tasty.

Vegi-Food Kitchen, 8 Cleveland St, Causeway Bay ☎2890 6660. One of Hong Kong's best-known vegetarian restaurants (p.241) serves *dim sum*, too. Open 11am–5pm.

Restaurants

If you've mastered the *dim sum* palaces, no Chinese or Asian **restaurant** in Hong Kong need hold any fears. Almost everywhere will have a **menu** in English and the only real problem is that often the

translations leave a lot to be desired. Also, the English-language menu is generally much less extensive and exciting than the Chinese one: you may have to point at what other Chinese diners are eating if you want seasonal, traditional food rather than the more bland tourist menu.

Most Cantonese restaurants are **open all day**, from early in the morning until midnight or beyond – until 3–4am in certain parts of the city, like Tsim Sha Tsui and Wan Chai. The ones that serve *dim sum* start serving their regular menu from mid- to late afternoon onwards. Other regional Chinese and Asian restaurants keep pretty much the same long hours, though perhaps not opening up until around 11am or so. Western restaurants generally have shorter hours, but you'll never have a problem finding somewhere to eat up until around midnight.

For the intricacies of **eating and ordering** in a Chinese restaurant, see the box below. To ask for **the bill** you say *mai dan*, which – with the wrong intonation – can also mean to "buy eggs". Sign language works just as well. Nearly all restaurants will add a ten percent **service charge** to your bill; if there are nuts and pickles on your table, you'll often pay a small cover charge, too. In places where there is no charge, leaving ten percent is fine, though you can just leave the few dollars or coins from your change. Even if you've paid service, the waiter may wave your change airily above your head in the leather wallet that the bill came in; if you want the change, make a move for it or that will be deemed a tip, too.

Eating

These restaurants serve solely vegetarian food: you can be sure there's no minced pork or prawn lurking in the dumplings, even if they look exactly like their meaty counterpart.

Restaurant Price Categories

The restaurants reviewed in this book have been given price categories as follows:

Inexpensive under $120	Expensive $250–400
Moderate $120–250	Very Expensive $400–750

The prices are for a **three-course meal**, or Asian equivalent, **per person excluding drinks and service**. Alcohol in Hong Kong is expensive: count on an extra $25–45 for each beer, and from $200 for a bottle of house wine. It's also worth noting that anything sold at the market rate – shark's fin and abalone dishes, and fresh fish and lobster plucked from restaurant fish tanks – can be wildly expensive. If you make them part of your Chinese meal, expect to nudge into the Expensive or Very Expensive category nearly every time.

Eating

The restaurants reviewed in this book have been given price categories as follows:

Inexpensive under $120

Moderate $120–250

Expensive $250–400

Very Expensive $400–750

Chinese

Lots of Chinese restaurants offer a set tourist menu, which can be good value but are unlikely to be very adventurous. Also, if you're going on into China, you'd do best to sample all the foods first in Hong Kong: on the whole the quality and choice here is infinitely better than in most cities on the mainland.

CANTONESE

Central and Admiralty

Fat Heung Lam, 94 Wellington St ☎2593 0404. It's hard to fault this small, cheap and cheerful vegetarian restaurant. Inexpensive.

House of Canton, Century Square, 1 D'Aguilar St ☎2868 2988. Showpiece branch of the small *House of Canton* chain – traditional dishes with a nouveau twist, upmarket surroundings but reasonable prices. Open 11am–11.30pm. Moderate.

Jade Garden, 1st Floor, Swire House, 11 Chater Rd ☎2526 3031. Reliable member of the *Maxim* restaurant chain with a decent – if unsurprising – menu. There'll be plenty that's recognizable, all well cooked, and served by English-speaking staff. Mon–Sat 11.30am–11pm, Sun 10am–midnight. Moderate.

Man Wah, 25th Floor, *Mandarin Oriental Hotel*, 5 Connaught Rd ☎2522 0111. If you've got the cash for one extravagantly priced Cantonese meal, blow it here on some beautiful food (which follows a seasonal menu) and spectacular views. If they don't take your breath away, the bill will. Reservations are essential. Open noon–3pm & 6.30–11pm. Very Expensive.

Metropol Restaurant, 4th Floor, United Centre, 95 Queensway ☎2865 1988. A veritable ballroom of a restaurant, though the available space doesn't stop them packing in the tables. The food comes up to scratch, though it's a trifle expensive, but don't count on a romantic night out – you'll be lucky if you can hear yourself above the clatter of the *mahjong* tiles. Open 8.30am–midnight. Moderate.

Tsui Hang Village Restaurant, 2nd Floor, New World Tower, 16–18 Queen's Rd ☎2524 2012. Named after the home town of Sun Yat-sen, the restaurant is well thought of – the food and decor traditional and prices not too bad for this part of the city. Open Mon–Sat 11am–11pm, Sun 10am–10pm. Moderate.

Yung Kee Restaurant, 32–40 Wellington St ☎2522 1624. Impressive four-storey eating-house into whose nether regions you're led by walkie-talkie-wielding staff. Diners are presented with "hundred-year-old eggs" and preserved ginger as they sit down – traditional Cantonese appetizers – and the house speciality is roast goose (there's a roaring trade in takeaway roast goose lunch boxes during the week). You can also try frog served in several forms and hot pot dishes. Open 11am–11.30pm. Moderate.

Zen, LG1, The Mall, Pacific Place, 88 Queensway ☎2845 4555. Designer-led, new Cantonese cuisine – which means hi-tech surroundings, imaginative Cantonese food which borrows influences extensively from the rest of Asia and competent, English-speaking staff. Open Mon–Fri 11.30am–3.30pm & 6–11pm, Sat 11.30am–3.30pm & 6–11pm, Sun 10.30am–3.30pm & 6–11pm. Expensive.

Wan Chai

China Restaurant, 18 Johnston Rd ☎2520 0282. Plenty of choice on the menu – ask about the daily specials, which are not always listed – and friendly enough staff make this a decent pit-stop. Open 9am–midnight. Inexpensive–Moderate.

Fook Lam Moon, 35–45 Johnston Rd ☎2866 0663. Among Hong Kong's finest – and most famous – Cantonese restaurants, this is no place to come if you're skimping on costs. Classic cooking, pricey ingredients (shark's fin, bird's nest) and consistently reliable quality. Open 11.30am–11.30pm. Expensive–Very Expensive.

Healthy Mess, Ground Floor, 51–53 Hennessy Rd ☎2527 3918. Bright and busy mock-traditional Cantonese vegetarian restaurant that specializes in *tofu* (beancurd) dishes. It's next to the *New*

Harbour Hotel. Open 11am–11pm. Inexpensive.

Man Yu, 159 Johnston Rd ☎572 0337. Long-standing and unusually quiet Cantonese restaurant that comes recommended, though the prices might seem high for the rather uninspired surroundings. Open 7.30am–11pm. Inexpensive–Moderate.

One Harbour Road, *Grand Hyatt*, 1 Harbour Rd ☎2588 1234, x7338. The high-ranking Chinese businessmen's favourite, and they know a thing or two about quality food. Superb meals and spot-on service. Reservartions advised. Open noon–2.30pm & 6.30–10.30pm. Very Expensive.

Steam & Stew Inn, Hing Wong Court, 21–23 Tai Wong St East ☎2529 3913. Typical Cantonese family cooking: soups, stews and braised dishes, guaranteed MSG-free. Open 11.30am–11.30pm. Inexpensive.

Causeway Bay

Ah Yee Leng Tong, Basement, Hang Lung Centre, 2–20 Paterson St ☎2576 8385; 503–505 Lockhart Rd ☎2834 3480; and Lai Chi Building, 42 Leighton Rd ☎2895 0192. Old-style Cantonese cafés serving warming soups and casseroles, and simple family-style meat dishes, all guaranteed MSG-free. Open 11.30am–11.30pm. Inexpensive.

Lotus Garden, 60 Yee Wo St ☎895 4333. Small vegetarian restaurant, with a takeaway counter too. Open 8.30am–11.30pm. Inexpensive.

Vegi-Food Kitchen, 8 Cleveland St ☎2890 6660. A sign at the entrance warns "Please do not bring meat of any kind into this restaurant", which gives you an inkling of what to expect – inventive Cantonese vegetarian food at very fair prices. Open 11am–11.30pm. Moderate.

Street Food

For the very cheapest Cantonese food, you'll need to head for the nearest *dai pai dong* (street stall); see p.234 for locations.

Happy Valley

Pigeon Club Seafood Restaurant, 5a Sing Woo Rd ☎2591 0298. An unassuming location, but the food is wonderful and very good value – don't neglect the delectable pigeon dishes. Open 11.30am–11.30pm. Moderate.

Aberdeen

Floating restaurants, Shum Wan, Wong Chuk Hang. Docked in Aberdeen harbour, Hong Kong's famous floating restaurants are, in truth, a bit of a disappointment. You can eat better, cheaper seafood at various other venues around the territory. But you can't eat it floating aboard something that looks like it fell off the set from Bertolucci's *The Last Emperor* anywhere else. There are three: the *Jumbo* ☎2553 9111; the *Jumbo Palace* ☎2554 0513; and the *Tai Pak* ☎2552 5953. Each has its own private boat that will run you there across the harbour. The two *Jumbos* are open 7.30am–11.30pm, the *Tai Pak* 11.30am–11.30pm. Moderate–Expensive.

Tsim Sha Tsui

Bodhi Vegetarian Restaurant, 32–34 Lock Rd/81 Nathan Rd ☎2366 8283. Possibly the best branch of this territory-wide chain, serving inventive vegetarian food. There are appealing set menus, too, if you're not sure what to order. Open 11am–11pm. Inexpensive.

East Ocean Seafood Restaurant, B1, East Ocean Centre, 98 Granville Rd ☎2723 8128. Noisy basement dining with excellent seasonal cooking and approachable waiters. Open 11am–3pm & 6pm–midnight. Moderate–Expensive.

Lai Ching Heen, *Regent Hotel*, 18 Salisbury Rd ☎2721 1211. Reckoned one of Hong Kong's best for cutting-edge Cantonese cooking – and for the excellent service and amazing harbour views. Count on $800 a head for the works, though a $600 set menu relieves the pain a little. Reservations essential. Open noon–2.30pm & 6–11pm. Very Expensive.

New Year Seafood Restaurant, 8 Ashley Rd ☎2376 0926. One of Tsim Sha Tsui's

Eating

Eating

Eating Chinese Food

Don't be unnecessarily intimidated by the prospect of eating in a Chinese restaurant in Hong Kong. The following tips will help smooth the way – telling you how, and what, to eat.

Chopsticks and other utensils

You eat, naturally enough, with **chopsticks**, which – with a bit of practice and patience – are easy enough to master.

The basic idea is to use them as pincers, between thumb and forefinger, moving the bottom one to get a grip on the food; but really, any method that gets the food into your mouth is acceptable. If you can't manage, use the china spoon provided, or shrink with shame and ask for a fork and spoon – many restaurants will have them. You eat out of the little **bowl** in front of you (the smaller cup is for your tea), putting your rice in and plonking bits of food on top. Then, raise the bowl to your lips and shovel it in with the chopsticks (much easier than eating with chopsticks from a plate), chucking bones and other grungy bits onto the tablecloth as you go. They'll change the cloth when you leave, so it's no problem if your table looks like culinary Armageddon.

Etiquette demands that you don't stick your chopsticks upright into your bowl when you're not eating (it's a Taoist death sign); place them across the top of the bowl, or flat on the table, or on the chopstick rests.

There may well be one or two tiny **dishes** laid at your place too: at some stage someone will come round and fill one of them with soy sauce, the other with chilli sauce, and you dip your food into either.

Ordering food and drink

For **ordering Chinese food**, you're best off in a group; as a rough guide, order one more dish than there are people. The idea is that you put together a balanced meal, including the "five tastes" – acid, hot, bitter, sweet and salty – best achieved by balancing separate servings of meat, fish and vegetable, plus rice and soup. **Soup**, incidentally, is drunk throughout the meal rather than as a starter – normally meat, fish or vegetable stock that will come in a tureen – though if you want your individual bowl of chicken and sweetcorn soup you'll usually be able to get that too. **Rice** with food is white and steamed; fried rice comes as a fancier dish as part of a large meal. It's bad manners to leave rice, so don't order too much. The food will either come with various **sauces** (like plum sauce or chilli sauce), which are poured into the little dishes provided, or you can use the soy sauce and sesame oil on the table to flavour your food. Bear in mind that you use the sauces as dips: sloshing soy sauce over your rice and food will pick you out as an uncouth foreigner straight away. **Dessert** is rarely served (maybe ice cream in some places), though you'll often get a sliced orange with which to cleanse the palate.

The classic **drink** with your meal is tea (for which see "*Dim Sum*", above), and you'll always be brought this as a matter of course. Beer also goes well with most Chinese food. Wine is generally prohibitively expensive in Hong Kong's restaurants, and in any case isn't as suitable an accompaniment; if you must drink wine, go for a dry white so as not to kill the taste of the food. Other than beer, Chinese people drink very little alcohol with their food: if it's a party or a celebration, they're most likely to drink neat brandy or whisky.

The Cuisines

Cantonese cuisine is the most common cooking style in Hong Kong, but most types of Chinese food can be eaten, if not in specialist **regional restaurants**, then as individual dishes in places that are otherwise firmly Cantonese – the waiter should always be able to point you towards the house speciality. One thing common to most of the regional cuisines is the inclusion of things that Westerners often baulk at eating at all. Chinese food over the centuries has been essentially a starvation food: nothing can ever afford to be wasted, and intestines, bone marrow, fish heads, chicken feet and blood are all recycled as food in various forms. Some are not as disgusting as they sound; others – like braised chicken blood – can challenge even the most robust palates.

Eating

Cantonese

Cantonese cuisine, from China's southeastern Guangdong (or Canton) province, is that which has been exported in bastardized forms to virtually every country in the world by Cantonese immigrants, and it is at its supreme best in Hong Kong. Throw away all your ideas of "Chinese" food when you sit down at a good Cantonese restaurant: apart from the cooking methods – mainly stir-frying and steaming – there's little similarity, and no self-respecting Chinese person would eat what they dismiss as the "foreign food" served up in restaurants and takeaway shops at home.

Ingredients are based around fish and seafood, pork, beef and vegetables, either lightly fried with a little oil, or steamed, or braised, and flavoured with fresh ginger, spring onion, soy and oyster sauce. Everything is bitingly fresh and full of natural flavour, as a walk around any market proves – too fresh for some sensibilities, who can't bring themselves to choose their dinner from a restaurant fish tank. The **fish and seafood** is excellent: garoupa, mullet and bream (which are often steamed whole), prawns, scallops, crayfish, mussels, clams, crabs, oysters, abalone, squid, octopus and lobster. In particular, prawns and crabs, served in spicy black bean sauce, are classic dishes.

Chicken is the most widely eaten meat, and duck is popular too: commonly, it'll either come sliced and stir-fried with vegetables, or marinaded and braised with things like lemon and soy or black bean sauce. Other **specialities** are *dim sum* (for which, see above), and roast and barbecued meats, especially pork and duck, as well as pigeon, all of which you'll see hanging up in restaurant windows, served with plain rice. Frog's legs are eaten, too; snake (see p.82) is one of the territory's more notorious delicacies, along with various intestinal dishes, and (more appealing) preserved eggs (p.100). For some Cantonese recipes, turn to p.393.

Hakka

The **Hakka** people originated in northern China, but migrated south over the years and have been farming in what are now the New Territories for centuries. Their food is often taken to be Cantonese, and although there are few Hakka restaurants in Hong Kong, most Cantonese restaurants serve some Hakka dishes. These use beancurd a lot, and salted and preserved food, deriving from the days when the Hakka carried their food with them as they moved: salted, baked chicken, pork and preserved cabbage, intestines and innards cooked in various ways are staple dishes. One real speciality is boned duck, stuffed with rice, meat and lotus seeds.

Chiu Chow

Another southeastern cuisine (from the Swatow district of Guangdong), **Chiu Chow** food is strong on seafood, including thick shark's fin soup and eel, and also encompasses the famous (and very expensive) bird's nest soup – made from the dried saliva which binds the nests of the sea swallow. The food uses much the same ingredients but is oilier than Cantonese (roast goose is another favourite), and you assist the digestion with a drink of bitter tea, known as "Iron Maiden" or "Iron Buddha".

The restaurants reviewed in this book have been given price categories as follows:

Inexpensive under $120

Moderate $120–250

Expensive $250–400

Very Expensive $400–750

continued over page

Eating

better Cantonese choices – it may have only a basic menu with few surprises, but the restaurant is always busy. Open 11am–11.30pm. Inexpensive.

Orchard Court, 1st & 2nd Floor, 37 Hankow Rd ☎ 2317 5111. If you liked the *dim sum*, come back at night for good-value seasonal Cantonese cuisine, dishes cooked with fruit in the summer, casseroled in winter. Open 11am–midnight. Moderate.

Shang Palace, Basement 1, *Kowloon Shangri-La Hotel*, 64 Mody Road, Tsim Sha Tsui East ☎ 2721 2111. Marvellous restaurant with over-the-top Imperial decor, which seems to cook everything well, including pigeon. It's busy at lunchtime – go early. Open Mon–Sat noon–3pm & 6.30–11pm, Sun 11am–3pm & 6.30–11pm. Expensive–Very Expensive.

Sun Tung Lok, Shop 63–64, Ocean Galleries, Harbour City, 17–19 Canton Rd ☎ 2730 0288. Famous shark's fin restaurant, serving the (wildly expensive) delicacy in several different ways, alongside other excellent food. For a cheaper meal try the eel in black bean sauce and one of the chicken or pigeon dishes – all authentically Cantonese. (There's a second branch at Sunning Plaza, 1–5 Sunning Rd, Causeway Bay ☎ 2882 2899). Open 11am–midnight. Expensive.

The Sweet Dynasty, 88 Canton Rd ☎ 2375 9119. Decorative Chinese tea house which specializes in Cantonese desserts – there's inventive use of *tofu*, exotic fruits and nuts, and the red bean soup is a house speciality. Savoury dishes are available, too. Open 11.30am–midnight. Inexpensive.

New Territories

Lung Wah Hotel and Restaurant, 22 Ha Wo Che, Sha Tin ☎2691 1594. The best place in Hong Kong to eat hot, greasy pigeon – a Cantonese speciality. It's tricky to find, but the effort is worth it for this traditional New Territories' restaurant, with a garden full of *mahjong* players and outdoor tables, which gets packed at the weekend. Get there by taxi or minibus #60X from Sha Tin KCR, or bus #48 – from Tsuen Wan ferry to Wo Che – to Sha Tin Police Quarters, then take the footbridge at the end of Wo Che Street. Open 11am–11pm. Inexpensive.

Yucca de Lac, Ma La Shui ☎2692 1835. Long-established open-air restaurant in the hills overlooking the Chinese University and Tolo Harbour. There's an extensive menu – the pigeon is recommended, as are the beancurd dishes. It's on the old Tai Po Road, above Tolo Highway – take a taxi from Sha Tin and walk back down on foot to University KCR; or take bus #70, from Jordan Rd Ferry Terminal to Sheung Shui, which passes the restaurant. Open 11am–11pm. Moderate.

HAKKA

Chuen Cheung Kui, 108 Percival St, Causeway Bay ☎2577 3833. Large portions of family style cooking make this a popular place with locals – weekends are always packed. Not much English spoken; you may have to point. Open 11am–11pm. Moderate.

Kowloon Tsui King Lou, 7–9 Saigon St, Yau Ma Tei ☎2384 8593. A traditional Hakka restaurant on three floors. The staff don't speak much English but are genuinely very helpful. Open noon–11pm.

New Home Hakka & Seafood Restaurant, 19–20 Hanoi Rd, Tsim Sha Tsui ☎2366 5876. Fairly austere tile and mirror decor, but attentive service and authentic Hakka food. The tangy salt-baked chicken is excellent (and half a bird is big enough for two), as are the beancurd dishes and soups. Open 11am–11pm. Moderate.

CHIU CHOW

Carrianna Chiu Chow Restaurant, 151 Gloucester Rd, Wan Chai ☎2511 1282. Large servings and good value for money – consequently, it's always noisy and busy. Try the goose. Open 11am–11.30pm. Moderate.

Chiu Chow Garden, Basement, Jardine House, 1 Connaught Place, Central ☎525 8246; 3rd Floor Vicwood Plaza, 199 Des Voeux Rd, Central ☎2545 7778; 2nd & 3rd Floor, Hennessy Centre, 500 Hennessy Rd, Causeway Bay ☎2577 3391. Chiu Chow food from the *Maxim* people. Always reliable and not expensive; goose is a speciality. All open 11.30am–3pm & 5.30pm–midnight. Moderate.

City Chiu Chow Restaurant, 1st Floor, East Ocean Centre, 98 Granville Rd, Tsim Sha Tsui East ☎2724 5383. One of a chain (look for the words "City Chiu Chow" in the name) selling reasonably priced food, even if the cooking doesn't always inspire. Open 11am–midnight. Moderate.

Hot Yuet Chui Chow Restaurant, Basement, 63 Peking Rd, Tsim Sha Tsui ☎2368 9688. One of the few specifically Chiu Chow places this side of the harbour, with presentable food and staff used to customers ignorant about what's best to order. Open 11.30am–midnight. Moderate.

Kornhill Chiu Chow Restaurant, Kornhill Plaza, 1 Kornhill Rd, Quarry Bay ☎2885 1992. The roast goose on display is the best thing to have here, but other dishes are equally authentic and the prices are very fair. Open 11am–3pm & 5.30pm–midnight. Inexpensive–Moderate.

Pak Lok, 25 Hysan Ave, Causeway Bay ☎2576 8886. An enormous Chiu Chow menu features wildly expensive shark's fin soup, amongst other politically incorrect dishes of the endangered kind. Avoid this and the rest of the food is reasonably priced, given the restaurant's high reputation. Open noon–1am. Moderate–Expensive.

Tsui Hung Restaurant, 15 Saigon St, Yau Ma Tei ☎2385 4947. Noisy, crowded local restaurant, where you can just pop

Eating

The restaurants reviewed in this book have been given price categories as follows:

Inexpensive under $120

Moderate $120–250

Expensive $250–400

Very Expensive $400–750

Eating

Shark's Fin

If there's one dish that epitomizes both the Chinese propensity to eat unlikely parts of an animal's body and pay through the nose for the privilege, it's shark's fin. Many Cantonese restaurants offer it up as thick, fibrous shark's fin soup, not so much an acquired taste but an outrageously expensive one: suffice it to say, that if there's a cheap bowl of shark's fin on the menu, it isn't the real thing.

Quite how and why it came to be eaten in the first place is unclear, though – as with most obscure animal parts – the Chinese claim medicinal properties for the fin. Modern medical thought is sceptical to say the least, though the wider concern is that eating shark's fin soup is putting the various fish species at risk. Economic growth in Southeast Asia and the Pacific Rim is fuelling demand for shark's fin and consequently, shark fishing is now very big business. Numbers are declining rapidly and since the shark is an important part of the food chain, the destruction of large numbers of them has disturbing implications for the marine environment.

For this reason alone, there's a growing move to boycott the eating of shark's fin products. If you need any more convincing, it's worth noting that shark flesh is not usually eaten in the Far East, so the fish are killed just for their fins. These are cut off while the shark is still alive and then the fish is thrown back into the sea, where – without its fins to give it mobility – it drowns.

The restaurants reviewed in this book have been given price categories as follows:

Inexpensive under $120

Moderate $120–250

Expensive $250–400

Very Expensive $400–750

---

in for a plate of roast goose or eat more lavishly. One of the staff members speaks English, but most will help you out with sign language if you're unsure about what to order. Open 11am–midnight. Inexpensive–Moderate.

BEIJING (PEKING)

American Restaurant, 20 Lockhart Rd, Wan Chai ☎2527 7277. Misleadingly named, averagely priced Beijing restaurant with a large menu that's a favourite with tourists. Open 11.30am–11.30pm. Inexpensive–Moderate.

Beijing Restaurant, 1st–3rd Floor, 34–36 Granville Rd, Tsim Sha Tsui ☎2366 9968. Peking duck buffet dinners served from 7–9pm for around $120 a head, plus a full menu too. Reservations advised for the buffet. Open 10.30am–11pm. Moderate.

Cheung Kee, 1st Floor, 75–79 Lockhart Rd, Wan Chai ☎2529 0707. Despite the unprepossessing entrance, and the lack of an English menu, this place is highly recommended for delicious Beijing-style food – try the smoked fish. Open 11.30am–11pm. Inexpensive.

Peking Garden, branches at Basement, Alexandra House, 6 Ice House St, Central ☎2526 6456; Shop 003, The Mall, Pacific Place, 88 Queensway, Central ☎2845 8452; and 1st Floor, *Excelsior Plaza*, East Point Rd, Causeway Bay ☎2577 7231. High culinary standards in all three restaurants, with particularly renowned Peking duck and interesting desserts. Tourist side shows include nightly noodle-making displays and the occasional impromptu cookery demonstration. Open 11.30am–3pm & 6pm–midnight. Moderate–Expensive.

Peking Restaurant, 227 Nathan Rd, Jordan MTR ☎2730 1315. Don't be put off by the fairly glum decor: this place serves some of the best Beijing food in Hong Kong, with the duck especially recommended. Open 11am–2.30pm & 6–10pm. Moderate–Expensive.

Pine and Bamboo Restaurant, 30 Leighton Rd, Causeway Bay ☎2577 4914. A large and well-located restaurant that always has space. The duck's good here, and try the dumplings; in winter, hot pots are on offer, which make for useful party dishes. For other meals, two people can easily share the "small size" dishes. Open 11am–11pm. Moderate.

Spring Deer, 1st Floor, 42 Mody Road, Tsim Sha Tsui ☎723 3673. Long-established place noted for its Peking duck (which is carved at the table), among a barrage of authentic dishes. The duck starts at $250, so single diners are in trouble, but the rest of the food is magnificent and filling – and served in three dish sizes. Try the smoked chicken, and the beancurd with minced pork. Open noon–2.30pm & 6–11pm. Moderate.

SHANGHAINESE

Andy's Kitchen, 25 Tung Lo Wan Rd, Causeway Bay ☎2577 1819. Despite the name, this small, local restaurant serves terrific and affordable Shanghai cooking. The smoked fish is worth trying – dry pieces of aromatic fish – and you'll get a plate of nuts and pickled cabbage to nibble on while you make up your mind about the rest. Open 11am–10pm. Moderate.

Great Shanghai, 26 Prat Ave, Tsim Sha Tsui ☎2366 8158. One of the most reliable of Hong Kong's Shanghai restaurants, with well-presented food (fine fish and seafood) served in small or large portions. A good choice for a first Shanghai meal. Open 11am–11pm. Moderate.

Kung Tak Lam, 45–47 Carnarvon Rd, Tsim Sha Tsui ☎2367 7881; 31 Yee Wo St, Causeway Bay ☎2890 3127. Shanghai vegetarian resturants, owned by Lau-Wo Ching, whose wife was a 1960s' Cantonese movie star. Very reasonably priced food – beancurd, thick soups and dishes that mock their meat and fish counterparts. Open 11am–11pm. Inexpensive.

Shanghai Garden, Hutchison House, 10 Harcourt Rd, Central ☎2524 8181. More upmarket than the Tsim Sha Tsui Shanghai eating places, the *Shanghai Garden* also mixes in dishes from other regions. But the scrumptious food is authentic and prices aren't too extreme for Central (though they are higher than all the other places listed in this section). Open 11.30am–3pm & 5.30pm–midnight. Moderate–Expensive.

Shanghai Number One, 5 Hart Ave, Tsim Sha Tsui ☎2316 2517. A fairly standard menu, but good prices and fair-sized

portions leave you feeling satisfied. Open 11am–2pm & 5–11pm. Inexpensive.

Shanghai Restaurant, 24 Prat Ave, Tsim Sha Tsui ☎2739 7083. Lashings of old-time style in this large, recommended restaurant. The food is a cut above average, though go with a friend or two if you want to experiment fully with the menu. And be prepared to point at other diners' food, since very little English is spoken. Open 11am–11pm. Moderate.

Shanghai Tai Woo, 10 Ashley Rd, Tsim Sha Tsui ☎2376 0225. Poor service and little character, but the portions are ample, which comes as some compensation. Open 11am–11pm. Inexpensive.

Wu Kong Shanghai Restaurant, Basement, Alpha House, 27 Nathan Rd, Tsim Sha Tsui ☎2366 7244; and *Food Forum*, 12th Floor, Times Square, Causeway Bay ☎2506 1018. Popular restaurants with a wide menu, and – given their handy positions – not destined to break the bank either. There are some challenging specialities alongside more mainstream dishes like chicken with garlic and chilli or beancurd with sliced pork. Fish is pricier. In Tsim Sha Tsui, go early for dinner or expect to wait in line. Open 11.30am–11pm. Moderate.

SZECHUAN (SICHUAN)

Fung Lum, 1st Floor, 23 Prat Ave, Tsim Sha Tsui ☎2367 8686. Popular with tourists and with English-speaking staff, but don't let that put you off – there's plenty worth investigating on the menu, with dishes split into "small" and "medium" sizes; stick with the small dishes (which feed two in any case) and increase your choices. Try the chicken in garlic and chilli oil. Open 11am–11pm. Inexpensive–Moderate.

Kam Kong Restaurant, 60 Granville Rd, Tsim Sha Tsui ☎2367 3434. Good, no-nonsense food, highly spiced and coming with lashings of hot green and red chillis. Try the "green fish", the dumplings (*won ton*) and the smoked fish; the dishes come in three sizes so you don't need to over-order. Open 11am–11pm. Inexpensive–Moderate.

Eating

Eating

The restaurants reviewed in this book have been given price categories as follows:

Inexpensive under $120

Moderate $120–250

Expensive $250–400

Very Expensive $400–750

The Red Pepper, 7 Lan Fong Rd, Causeway Bay ☎2577 3811. The name says it all – a good choice for devilishly hot food and a favourite with expats, which means higher-than-warranted prices and pushy staff. The smoked duck and beancurd are standard favourites here. You might want to book in advance, since it can get very busy. Open noon–midnight. Moderate.

Szechuan Lau, 466 Lockhart Rd, Causeway Bay ☎2891 9027. Classic Szechuan food, with all the best-known dishes served in relaxed, old-style surroundings. The chilli prawns are great, and there are more elaborate (and expensive) seafood dishes, too. The waiters keep the beer coming – go easy if you're trying to cut costs. Open noon–midnight. Moderate.

OTHER CHINESE REGIONS

Forever Green Taiwanese Restaurant, 93 Leighton Rd, Causeway Bay ☎2890 3448; 16 Cheong Lok St, Yau Ma Tei ☎2332 7183. Despite the OTT decor and traditionally dressed staff, there's more than just curiosity value at these late-opening Taiwanese restaurants. Both have interesting and comparatively cheap menus. Open noon–3pm & 6pm–4.30am. Moderate.

Hunan Garden, 3rd Floor, The Forum, Exchange Square, 8 Connaught Place, Central. ☎2868 2880. Hunan province features spicy dishes akin to those from Szechuan; the menu points out what's hot and what isn't, though ask first and read between the lines since some dishes disappoint. An attractive place with harbour views (though land reclamation is slowly robbing these of their erstwhile attraction). Open 11.30am–3pm & 5.30pm–midnight. Expensive.

Tien Hung Lau, 18c Austin Ave, Tsim Sha Tsui. ☎2368 9660. Food from the south-western city of Hangzhou, including the famous "Beggar's Chicken", a whole chicken baked and covered in mud and lotus leaves (which you must order in advance), and West Lake fish with vinegar sauce. You'll need to book. Open noon–2pm & 6–10pm. Moderate–Expensive.

Yunnan Kitchen, 12th Floor, Times Square, 1 Matheson St, Causeway Bay ☎2506 3309. Yunnan province specialities make for a change after the Canto dishes on offer in most of Hong Kong's restaurants, but they don't come particularly cheap and you have to endure the usual Times Square thematic shennanigans and costumed staff. Open 11.30am–3.30pm & 5.30–11.30pm. Moderate–Expensive.

African

Cafe Afrikan, 7 Glenealy St, Central ☎2868 9299. One of Hong Kong's latest culinary experiments, the *Afrikan* dishes up a mean *couscous*, as well as more exotic creations – including soup served in a bread shell and some highly rated desserts. There's also terrific coffee and other drinks available; and thumping good-time music, too. Open Mon–Sat noon–midnight. Inexpensive–Moderate.

American

Al's Diner, 39 D'Aguilar St, Lan Kwai Fong, Central ☎2869 1869. Straightforward diner food – burgers, dogs, chilli and sandwiches – and late opening at weekends for ravenous clubbers. Open Mon–Thurs noon–1am, Fri & Sat noon–3am. Inexpensive–Moderate.

American Pie, 4th Floor, California Entertainment Building, 34–36 D'Aguilar St, Lan Kwai Fong, Central ☎2877 9779. Forget the overpriced meals in this rather chic, if cramped, restaurant and come instead for the excellent Sunday brunch; if you book ahead, you can eat out on the terrace. Or simply call in for a coffee and hog out on the superb desserts and cakes. Open Mon–Thurs 11.30am–2.30pm & 6.30pm–midnight, Fri–Sun noon–midnight. Moderate–Expensive.

Bostonian, *Hong Kong Renaissance Hotel*, 8 Peking Rd, Tsim Sha Tsui ☎2375 1133. American-style hotel restaurant which excels in meat dishes. If you can eat the 46oz rib of beef, they'll tear up your bill (and if you were wondering, the record is *seven minutes* . . .). Good salads, too, and desserts to die for. Open noon–3pm & 6–11pm. Expensive–Very Expensive.

California, 30–32 D'Aguilar St, Lan Kwai Fong, Central ☎ 2521 1345. Restaurant/café/bar that oozes Americana and serves a classic menu – burgers, potato skins, salads and barbecues. Pricey and flash. Mon–Sat noon–1am, Sun 6pm–1am. Expensive.

Dan Ryan's Chicago Bar and Grill, 114 The Mall, Pacific Place, 88 Queensway, Central ☎ 2845 4600; Ocean Terminal, Harbour City, Canton Rd, Tsim Shga Tsui ☎ 2735 6111. Bumper American-size portions of ribs, burgers, steaks, salads and homemade desserts. You'll get enough food to sink a battleship, but it doesn't come cheap. Open Mon–Sat 8.30am–midnight, Sun 9.30am–midnight. Expensive–Very Expensive.

Hard Rock Café, Ground–3rd Floor, 100 Canton Rd, Tsim Sha Tsui ☎ 2377 8118; Basement–Ground Floor, Swire House, 11 Chater Rd, Central ☎ 2377 8168. Twin branches of the burger-and-rock emporiums, with menus short on surprises, though portions are decent enough. There are live bands at the Kowloon branch, dancing every night at both after 10.30pm, and a daily 3–7pm Happy Hour. Open noon–midnight. Moderate.

LA Café, Ground Floor, Lippo Centre, Admiralty ☎ 2526 6863. The *LA Café* sports a *Harley Davidson* above the bar, Californian cuisine and international beer served by staff with attitude. Open noon–midnight, later at the weekend. Moderate–Expensive.

Planet Hollywood, 3 Canton Rd, Tim Sha Tsui ☎ 2377 7888. Sly, Bruce and Arnie's venture heads East: burgers, fries, Tex-Mex specials and ice cream, with some Asian additions, in regulation movie-heaven surroundings. Open 11.30am–2am. Moderate.

Prince's Tavern, Mezzanine Floor, Prince's Building, 10 Chater Rd, Central ☎ 2523 9352. Surprisngly good Cajun and Creole cooking as well as American standards and appetizing set lunches. Open Mon–Fri 11am–10pm, Sat 11am–7pm. Moderate.

Top Dog, 5 Lan Kwai Fong, Central ☎ 2868 9196. Chic, retro, hole-in-the-wall café serving hot dogs with all the trimmings and other snacks. Open 11am–late. Inexpensive.

Australian

Brett's Seafood, 72 Lockhard Rd, Wan Chai ☎ 2866 6608. Seafood café/takeaway joint doing good business in fish and seafood platters (the raw ingredients flown in from Australia) served with rice or fries. Open Mon–Thurs & Sun 7.30am–2am, Fri & Sat 7.30am–4am. Inexpensive–Moderate.

Ned Kelly's Last Stand, 11a Ashley Rd, Tsim Sha Tsui ☎ 2376 0562. Laid-back Aussie bar with live jazz (see "Live Music") and a filling range of tucker – meat pies much in evidence. Open 11.45am–1.45am. Inexpensive.

British

For no-nonsense portions of fish and chips, steak and kidney pie or an all-day English breakfast, most pubs can do the honours; see the next chapter for full pub and bar listings.

Bentley's Seafood Restaurant & Oyster Bar, B4 Basement, Prince's Building, 3 Des Voeux Rd, Central ☎ 2868 0881. British fish and seafood/oyster restaurant serving classic grills alongside a smattering of Southeast Asian-inspired dishes. Open Mon–Sat 11.30am–3pm & 6–10.30pm. Expensive.

Harry Ramsden's, Wu Chung House, 213 Queen's Rd East, Wan Chai ☎ 2832 9626. The famous British fish-and-chip shop moves out East – and remains remarkably true to its origins. The best fish and chips for thousands of miles, served under imported Yorkshire chandeliers. Full takeaway service too. Open 11.30am–11pm. Moderate.

Buffets and set meals

Most of the larger hotels put on a self-service **buffet** lunch and dinner; often, there will be a three-course **set meal**, too, which is the most inexpensive way to eat in the grander hotel restaurants. Check

Eating

Eating

the "Hotel Fare" section on the *What's On* page of the daily *South China Morning Post* for special deals. Buffet lunch (around $110) is usually noon–2.30pm, dinner ($160–250) 6.30–10pm, but ring for exact times; ten percent service will be added in all cases and drinks are extra.

Century, 238 Jaffe Rd, Wan Chai 2598 8888. Daily Western/Asian buffet lunch and dinner in the *Century Café*; Sunday brunch, too.

Excelsior, 281 Gloucester Rd, Causeway Bay ☎ 2894 8888. Daily buffet lunch and dinner in the *Coffee Shop*; set lunch in *The Grill*.

Furama Kempinski, 1 Connaught Rd, Central ☎ 2525 5111. Expensive lunch and dinner buffets in the revolving, top-floor *La Ronda*; superb views while you eat.

Island Shangri-La, Pacific Place, 88 Queensway, Central ☎ 2877 3838. High-class breakfast, lunch and dinner buffets in the *Island Café*.

Kowloon, 19–21 Nathan Rd, Tsim Sha Tsui ☎ 2739 9811. Daily buffet lunch in *Window Café*; set Italian lunch in *The Pizzeria*.

Marriott, Pacific Place, 88 Queensway, Central ☎ 2810 8366. International buffet lunch and dinner in the *Marriott Café*; Sunday brunch too.

New World Harbour View, 1 Harbour Rd, Wan Chai ☎ 2802 8888. Health-conscious buffet lunch in the 8th floor *Oasis* (weekdays only) and carvery buffet in the *Lobby Lounge*.

Omni Prince, Harbour City, Canton Rd, Tsim Sha Tsui ☎ 2736 1888. Southeast Asian lunch and dinner buffet in the *Spice Market*. The other *Omni* hotels also have a good choice of well-priced buffets and set meals.

Regal Riverside, Tai Chung Kiu Rd, Sha Tin, New Territories ☎ 2649 7878. Excellent daily Southeast Asian buffet served in the *Asian Delights* restaurant.

Ritz-Carlton, 3 Connaught Rd, Central ☎ 2877 6666. Very expensive, very classy Italian set meals in the *Toscana*, buffet

breakfast in *The Café*, seafood buffet nightly, and weekend champagne brunches.

Sheraton, 20 Nathan Rd, Tsim Sha Tsui ☎ 2369 1111. Dinner buffet in the *Coffee Shop* and set Indian lunch at *Bukhara*.

Windsor, 39–43 Kimberley Rd, Tsim Sha Tsui ☎ 2739 5665. Daily dinner buffet that has a loyal local clientele.

Burmese

Rangoon, Ground Floor, 265 Gloucester Rd, Hoi Kung Mansion, Causeway Bay ☎ 892 1182 or ☎ 893 0778. This quiet Burmese restaurant – the only one in Hong Kong – is a real treat, with a high-quality menu (with vegetarian dishes) that's not particularly expensive. Subtly spiced curries predominate. The food is beautifully presented and comes in hefty portions. Open 11.30am–11.30pm. Moderate.

Filipino

Chungking Café, Ground Floor, no. 24, Chungking Mansions, 36–44 Nathan Rd, Tsim Sha Tsui, no phone. Cheap, filling stews and rice-based dishes at a café at the back of the Mansions' ground floor. Open 10.30am–10.30pm. Inexpensive.

Cinta Restaurant, Basement, *Hotel New Harbour*, 6 Fenwick St, Wan Chai ☎ 2527 1199. Extensive Filipino menu (as well as Malaysian standbys and an Indonesian *rijstafel*): portions are gratifyingly large and the atmosphere nice and laid-back. As the lounge bar features Filipino singers after 9pm, it's worth turning up just for a drink, too. Open 11am–3pm & 6pm–1am. Moderate.

Cinta-J, 69–75 Jaffe Rd, Wan Chai ☎ 2529 6622. Just around the corner from the associated *Cinta*, this has good-value meals (and a long Happy Hour) – soups, casseroles and seafood. Open 11am–midnight. Inexpensive.

Mabuhay, 11 Minden Ave, Tsim Sha Tsui ☎ 2367 3762. Crispy fried pig's intestines is fairly typical of the authentic dishes offered here, but there are plenty of other choices – hearty soups, garlicky baked clams (actually green mussels) and grilled fish. Basic, bustling canteen dining accompanied by Western pop and cheap schooners of beer. Thoroughly recommended. Open 9am–11.30pm. Inexpensive.

French

Au Trou Normand, 6 Carnarvon Rd, Tsim Sha Tsui ☎ 2366 8754. This long-standing restaurant dishes up fine provincial French food in rustic surroundings, with Calvados to wash it all down. Open noon–3pm & 7–11pm. Moderate.

Gaddi's, 1st Floor, *Peninsula Hotel*, Salisbury Rd, Tsim Sha Tsui ☎ 2366 6251. One of the most respected Western restaurants in Hong Kong. Extraordinary food, extraordinary prices (at least $800 per person for a full meal); advance booking and smart dress essential. Open noon–2.30pm & 7–11pm. Very Expensive.

Papillon, 8–13 Wo On Lane, Central ☎ 2526 5965. Extensive and not overly expensive menu of French bistro classics in a pleasing little place, close to Lan Kwai Fong. Best value is the three-course set meal for $260 or so; the desserts are wantonly attractive. Open noon–2.30pm & 7–11pm. Moderate–Expensive.

Stanley's French Restaurant, 86 Stanley Main St, Stanley ☎ 2813 8873. Chic French restaurant in Stanley village which is winning a lot of friends with its imaginative, regularly changing menu and bay views. You'll need to book in advance at weekends. Open noon–3pm & 7pm–midnight. Expensive.

W's Entrecote, 13th Floor, Times Square, 1 Matheson St, Causeway Bay ☎ 2506 0133. Not exactly a thoroughbred Fench restaurant, but it does serve the one thing that matters – steak (it's the only dish on the menu) which comes with a green salad and unlimited *frites*. Open noon–midnight. Moderate.

German, Austrian and Swiss

Baron's Table, 1st Floor, *Holiday Inn Golden Mile*, 46–52 Nathan Rd, Tsim Sha Tsui ☎ 2369 3111. Grand and expensive German meals, including smoked specialities. Servings are enormous, while the

Teutonic surroundings are absurdly out of place in Hong Kong. Open noon–2.30pm & 7–11pm. Very Expensive.

Chesa, 1st Floor, *Peninsula Hotel*, Salisbury Road, Tsim Sha Tsui ☎ 2366 6251. The *Pen*'s top-price Swiss restaurant with great fondue and superb meat and fish dishes. Reservations essential. Open noon–2.30pm & 6.30–11pm. Very Expensive.

Mozart Stub'n, 8 Glenealy St, Central ☎ 2522 1763. Meat dishes predominate in this small Austrian restaurant. If you're looking for filling central European food, this is about the best value on offer in the territory – book ahead for dinner. Open Mon–Sat noon–2pm & 7.30pm–11pm. Moderate–Expensive.

Greek, Turkish and Lebanese

Bacchus, Basement, Hop Hing Centre, 8–12 Hennessy Rd, Wan Chai ☎ 529 9032. There are Greek dishes on the extensive Mediterranean menu, and now that the *Bacchus* is more of a bar it makes for a fun evening out. Open noon–2.30pm & 6pm–midnight. Moderate–Expensive.

Beirut, Shop A, Winner Building, 26–39 D'Aguilar St, Central ☎ 804 6611. A chic setting for Lebanese food, kebabs and mixed grills – though the bar gets just as much custom as the restaurant. Open noon–3pm & 6.30–11.30pm. Moderate.

Midnight Express, 3 Lan Kwai Fong, Central ☎ 2525 5010. Pitta bread stuffed with all kinds of fillings at bargain prices. Just the place after a drinking bout in Lan Kwai Fong. Open Mon–Sat 11.30am–3am, Sun 6pm–12.30am. Inexpensive.

Indian and Pakistani

For related restaurants, see also "Burmese" and "Sri Lankan".

CENTRAL

The Ashoka, 57–59 Wyndham St ☎ 2524 9623. A very popular, comfortable restaurant serving highly recommended Northern Indian food. There are very good-value set lunches and dinners, and several vegetarian choices. A second branch in Wan Chai (185 Wan Chai Rd

Eating

The restaurants reviewed in this book have been given price categories as follows:

Inexpensive under $120

Moderate $120–250

Expensive $250–400

Very Expensive $400–750

Eating

2891 8981) also gets rave reviews. Open noon–2.30pm & 6–10.30pm. Moderate.

Gunga Din's Club, Lower Ground Floor, 59 Wyndham St 2523 1276. Among the very best of Hong Kong's small, club-like Indian restaurants. Meals – served in pastel surroundings – can be memorable and the prices are extremely reasonable; booking recommended. Open 11.30am–2.30pm & 6–10.30pm. Moderate.

India Curry Club, 3rd Floor, 10 Wing Wah Lane, Winner Building (off D'Aguilar St) 2523 2203. A very limited menu, but fine food (always some vegetarian) and friendly service in basic, cramped surroundings. Open 11.30am–2.30pm & 6.30–10.30pm. Inexpensive.

The Mughal Room, 1st Floor, Carfield Commercial Building, 75–77 Wyndham St 2524 0107. Upmarket Northern Indian restaurant, with costumed staff, historical notes on a decent-looking menu that's strong on tandoori dishes. The food can be a bit hit-and-miss though, but the surroundings are worth paying for. Open noon–3pm & 6–11.30pm (evening only on Sun). Moderate.

Shalimar Club, 2nd Floor, 28a Stanley St 2522 8489. A wider menu than usual, including kebabs and tandoori food. A small place with friendly service. Open 11.30am–3pm & 6–10.30pm. In-expensive.

WAN CHAI

Club Aparmar, 1st Floor, 16 Lee Tung St, Wan Chai 2574 2643. Cheap and extremely good food in a small, badly lit restaurant. If it's quiet the owner himself may talk you through the choices. Open 11am–2.30pm & 5.30–11pm. In-expensive.

Jo Jo Mess Club, 1st Floor, 86–90 Johnston Rd, Wan Chai (entrance on Lee Tung St) 2527 3776. Hardly luxury surroundings, but a deservedly popular spot with tandoori specialities and views out onto the busy street. Open 11am–3pm & 6–11pm. Inexpensive.

Vicaroy, 2nd Floor, Sun Hung Kai Centre, 30 Harbour Rd, Wan Chai 2827 7777.

Food from all parts of India and terrace dining, too, with harbour views. The lunch buffet is particularly well regarded. Open noon–2.30pm & 6pm–midnight. Moderate.

STANLEY

The Curry Pot, 6th Floor, 90B Stanley Main St 2899 0811. Very friendly little restaurant with ocean views from its sixth-floor windows and delicately judged Indian food from all regions. The set lunch is remarkable value, but you can't go wrong choosing a la carte either. There are two other branches (at 68–70 Lockhart Rd, Wan Chai 2865 6099; and Lot 522, DD.210, near Pak Sha Wan ferry pier, Sai Kung 2358 2038), but the Stanley one is most attractive. Open noon–3pm & 6–10.30pm. Inexpensive–Moderate.

TSIM SHA TSUI

Delhi Club Mess, Block C, 3rd Floor, C3, Chungking Mansions, 36–44 Nathan Rd, no phone. A curry house par excellence, once you ignore the spartan surroundings and slap-down service. The ludicrously cheap set meal would feed an army. Open noon–2.30pm & 6–11.30pm. Inexpensive.

The Gurkhas, 2nd Floor, Haiphong Mansion, 53–55 Haiphong Rd 2724 2014. Clean, mess-type operation with friendly staff serving Indian and Nepalese cuisine. Open noon–3pm & 6–11pm. Inexpensive.

Khyber, 2nd Floor, Wing Lok Building, 16b Peking Rd (entrance on Lock Road) 2368 9014. Despite an unprepossess-ing entrance, this is one of the best Indian restaurants in town, with an unusually broad selection of vegetable dishes, served in brasserie-style surround-ings. Open noon–2.30pm & 6–11pm. Moderate.

Koh-i-Noor, 1st Floor, 16c Mody Rd, 3–4 Peninsula Apartments (on corner with Minden Row) 2368 3065. The garish, upmarket decor hides fairly average food, though it does have a tandoori menu and all the usual snacks, breads and accompaniments. There's a second branch in Central. Open 11.30am–2.30pm & 6–10.30pm. Moderate.

Maharaja, 1–3a Granville Rd ☎2574 9838. Fine food (including halal options) and even better prices; a good first choice for a budget Indian meal. Open noon–2.30pm & 6.30–10.30pm (Sun, evening only). Inexpensive.

Nanak Mess, Block A, 11th Floor, A4, Chungking Mansions, 36–44 Nathan Rd ☎2368 8063. Punjabi-style food served in a spacious (for Chungking Mansions) dining room. Open noon–3pm & 6pm–midnight. Inexpensive.

Woodlands, Mirror Tower, 61 Mody Rd ☎2369 3718. Part of an international chain, this is a mainly southern Indian restaurant serving strict vegetarian food, with a menu that describes each dish in detail. Snacks as well as full meals, including biryani and excellent thalis, the portions large enough to share. Always popular, with friendly service. Open noon–3.30pm & 6.30–11pm. Inexpensive.

YAU MA TEI

Ah Long, Ground Floor, 95B Woo Sung St, Jordan MTR ☎2782 1635. Chinese-run place cooking halal curries. Usually busy and worth a look if you're in the market for a cheap and cheerful meal. Open 11am–11pm. Inexpensive.

Indonesian

Bali Restaurant, 10 Nanking St, Yau Ma Tei ☎2780 2902. Affordable, but often fairly unimaginative, Indonesian food (though the fish in chilli sauce is very tasty) served in extremely kitschy surroundings – lanterns, bamboo and drapes as far as the eye can see. Open noon–11pm. Inexpensive–Moderate.

Cinta Restaurant, Basement, *Hotel New Harbour*, 6 Fenwick St, Wan Chai ☎2527 1199. Filling *rijstafel* among other reliable meal choices; does good business with tourists. Open 11am–2am. Moderate.

Indonesia Padang Restaurant, 85 Percival St, Causeway Bay ☎2576 1828. An unassuming spot with better-than-usual food and highly recommended

desserts, which are also sold as take-away snacks. Open 11am–11pm. Moderate.

Indonesian Restaurant, 28 Leighton Rd, Causeway Bay ☎2577 9981. Recommended place with canteen-style surroundings and staff who'll help you get the best out of the extensive menu – the curries or spicy eggplant are great. Open 11.30am–11.30pm. Inexpensive.

Indonesian Restaurant, 500 Lockhart Rd, Causeway Bay ☎2892 0328; 9 Keswick St, Causeway Bay ☎2881 0103; 1st Floor, Cameron Centre, 57 Chatham Rd, Tim Sha Tsui ☎2366 0918. A little chain of restaurants, all with pretty good food served in downbeat surroundings. Open 11am–10.30pm. Inexpensive.

Java Rijstafel, 38 Hankow Rd, Tsim Sha Tsui ☎2367 1230. Bang in the middle of Tsim Sha Tsui and consequently popular; you might want to book ahead since it's a tiny place. The *rijstafel* ("rice table") – a buffet of ten or more little dishes – is certainly worth considering, though it's only served for a minimum of two people; the satay scores highly, too. Open noon–10.30pm. Moderate.

Restaurant Indonesia, 514 Lockhart Rd, Causeway Bay ☎2831 0101. Restaurant with a good local reputation and a take-away counter. Open 11.30am–11.30pm. Inexpensive–Moderate.

International

Cafe Deco Bar & Grill, Level 1 & 2, Peak Galleria, 118 Peak Rd, The Peak ☎2849 5111. Superbly located restaurant with unrivalled views and a stylish Art Deco interior that extends to the rest-rooms. The menu ranges over gourmet pizzas, curries, Thai noodles, grilled meats and oysters; prices, surprisingly, are not too high. Or just call in for a drink, or cake and coffee; the bar stays open an hour or so after the kitchen closes (until 1am on Fri & Sat) and there's often live jazz. Kitchen open Mon–Thurs & Sun 10am–10.45pm, Fri & Sat 10am–11pm. Moderate–Expensive.

Felix, 28th Floor, *Peninsula Hotel*, Salisbury Rd, Tsim Sha Tsui ☎2366 6251.

Eating

The restaurants reviewed in this book have been given price categories as follows:

Inexpensive under $120

Moderate $120–250

Expensive $250–400

Very Expensive $400–750

Eating

The restaurants reviewed in this book have been given price categories as follows:

Inexpensive under $120

Moderate $120–250

Expensive $250–400

Very Expensive $400–750

The *Pen's* latest dining-and-sluicing emporium is as chic as can be, with a Philippe Starck-designed bar, supreme aerial views, and a guest list that's pure Hollywood. Oh, and the Eurasian food's good, too, but it costs a packet. Reservations required. Open 6–11pm. Very Expensive.

Jim's Euro Diner, Ground Floor, Tak House, 5–11 Stanley St, Central ☎2868 6886. Spotless, modern diner serving three-course set meals comprising Italian, French, German and British dishes: few thrills or surprises, but honest enough food. Open 8am–10pm. Inexpensive–Moderate.

Jimmy's Kitchen, Basement, South China Building, 1–3 Wyndham St, Central ☎2526 5293; 1st Floor, Kowloon Centre, 29 Ashley Rd, Tsim Sha Tsui ☎2376 0327. Old European restaurant, popular with expats and serving a menu of standards from French onion soup to steak pie. It's relatively cheap given its decent-sized portions, but the cooking isn't always greatly accomplished. Open 11.30am–3pm & 6.30–11pm. Moderate-Expensive.

M at the Fringe, 2 Lower Albert Rd, Central ☎2877 4000. Stylish restaurant much favoured by the glitterati (and the Governor) for its boldly flavoured, health-conscious dishes – meat, fish and veggie – whose influences range the world. Reservations advised. Open Mon–Sat noon–2.30pm & 7–10.30pm. Expensive.

Peak Café, 121 Peak Rd, The Peak ☎2849 7868. Refurbished in Californian designer-style, the East–West food at the *Peak* is spot on, as are the views out to sea from one of Hong Kong's finest vantage points. Set meals are good value and there are weekend barbecues and vegetarian choices, too. Open 10.30am–10.45pm. Expensive.

Parc 27, 27th Floor, *Park Lane Hotel*, 310 Gloucester Rd, Causeway Bay ☎2890 3355, x3344. It's having to work harder now there's more competition but people still come for the views and the food – both are worth the admittedly high tab. Open noon–3pm & 6–11pm. Expensive.

Post 97, 1st Floor, 8–11 Lan Kwai Fong, Central ☎2810 9333. Relaxed, brasserie surroundings for an eclectic menu of Mediterranean-American food, with a daily vegetarian choice. There's also real coffee and herbal teas, while an imaginative list of brunch specials is served all day on Sunday. Open Mon–Thurs 8.30am–1am, Fri 8.30am–4am, Sat 24hr, Sun 8.30am–1am. Moderate-Expensive.

Roy's at the New China Max, 11th Floor, Times Square, 1 Matheson St, Causeway Bay ☎2506 2282. The "Roy" in question is Hawaiian superchef Roy Yamaguchi, whose Pacific Rim cookery leaves pale imitators standing: a massive menu of pasta with Asian sauces, satays, ribs, seared and blackened fish, stuffed chicken, you name it, served with gusto in a highly funky, split-level Asian-South Seas-style restaurant and bar. Thoroughly recommended. Open noon–2am. Moderate-Expensive.

Stanley's Oriental Restaurant, 90b Stanley Main St, Stanley ☎2813 9988. Excellent location, with a terrace overlooking Stanley's bay, and featuring an enterprising mix of Indian, Thai, Cajun and Chinese cooking. Daily specials are always worth trying, including a set vegetarian menu and a set lunch. Open 9am–11pm. Moderate-Expensive.

Tables 88, 88 Stanley Village Rd, Stanley ☎2813 6262. Bizarrely furnished, upmarket village restaurant serving mainly, but not only, Mediterranean-style food. It has its fans, though charges fairly high prices for Sticksville. Open 11.30am–2.30pm & 7–10pm.

Italian

La Boheme, 2nd Floor, 151 Lockhart Rd, Wan Chai ☎2511 7717. Value-for-money restaurant with classic, northern Italian dishes; the *risotto* is particularly well regarded. It also hosts rave dance parties on occasional Saturdays. Open noon–2.30pm & 7–10.30pm. Moderate-Expensive.

Jaffe's, 1st Floor, *Century Hong Kong Hotel*, 238 Jaffe Rd, Wan Chai ☎2598 8888. An excellent bet for lunch; there's a fine salad bar as well as pasta and pizza. Open noon–2.30pm & 6.30–10.30pm. Moderate.

Marco Polo Pizza, 23 Lan Kwai Fong, Central ☎2868 1013. Great takeaway pizzas and free deliveries in Central. Open Mon 11am–9pm, Tues–Thurs 11am–midnight, Fri & Sat 11am–12.30am, Sun 3–10.30pm. Inexpensive.

Il Mercato, Basement, 34–36 D'Aguilar St, Central ☎2868 3068. Fine pizzas, or spend a little more and dine out on fresh, superior Italian food. Set lunches help keep the costs down. *Marco Polo* (see above) will deliver their food, too. Open noon–3pm & 6.30pm–midnight (Central branch closed Sun lunch). Moderate.

The Pizzeria, 2nd Floor, *Kowloon Hotel*, 19–21 Nathan Rd, Tsim Sha Tsui ☎2369 8698. Smart and highly rated pizzeria (takeaway available too), with pricier pasta dishes and main courses. Open noon–3pm & 6–11pm. Moderate.

Rigoletto's, 14–16 Fenwick St, Wan Chai ☎2527 7144. Established Italian restaurant whose decent food draws lots of visitors. Open Mon–Sat noon–2.30pm & 6–11.30pm, Sun 6–11.30pm. Moderate.

Tivoli, 130 Austin Rd, Tsim Sha Tsui ☎2366 6424. A cosy, candlelit, checked-tablecloth joint, serving good pasta and authentic thin-crust pizzas. Open noon–midnight. Moderate.

Toscana, *Ritz-Carlton*, 3 Connaught Rd, Central ☎2877 6666. Fashionable Tuscan restaurant in one of the fanciest of the city's hotels. Surprisingly, you can eat well here at almost-decent prices: the anti-pasto buffet is excellent ($175) and there are set lunches and dinners, too, from around $320. Open noon–2.30pm & 7–10.30pm. Expensive.

Tutto Meglio, 33 D'Aguilar St, Central ☎2869 7833. Just about every Italian region gets a look-in around Lan Kwai Fong – the food from Florence served in this tile-floor-cork-wall restaurant is perhaps a tad less well known than its neighbours, but it's just as good. You can usually just turn up and get a table, too, though maybe there'd be more of a queue if they turned the music down. Open Mon–Sat noon–2.30pm & 7–10.30pm. Moderate.

Va Bene, 58–62 D'Aguilar St, Central ☎2845 5577. Stylish Venetian restaurant that requires a full wallet (and a reservation) – authentic Italian cuisine like this (including great fresh pasta) doesn't come cheap in Hong Kong. Open noon–2.30pm & 7pm–midnight. Expensive.

Japanese

Department stores. For informal, cheap Japanese food, try the supermarkets in the *Sogo* (555 Hennessy Rd) and *Daimaru* (Household Square, Kingston St) department stores, which feature takeaway *sushi* and Japanese snack bars. Inexpensive.

Genroku, 27a Chatham Rd, Tsim Sha Tsui ☎2369 9728. The S-shaped conveyor belt delivers your food – about the cheapest way to eat Japanese in Hong Kong. There are a dozen other branches too. Open 11am–11pm. Inexpensive.

Kiku Express, Lower Ground Floor, Jardine House, Connaught Rd, Central ☎2845 9541. Popular Japanese café serving *sushi*, noodles and other dishes, as well as takeaway lunch boxes. Open Mon–Sat 7.30am–7pm. Inexpensive.

Ichizen, Level LG1, Seibu, The Mall, Pacific Place, 88 Queensway, Admiralty ☎2523 0185. Plenty of Japanese diners attest to the quality here, with *teppanyaki* and *sashimi* dishes all in constant demand. Open Mon–Sat 11.30am–3pm & 6–11pm, Sun 12.30–9.30pm. Moderate–Expensive.

Momoyama, Shop 15, Lower Ground Floor, Jardine House, Connaught Rd, Central ☎2845 8773. Jardine House's other Japanese option, this time for the flash and speedy business-lunch brigade. Medium to pricey set meals. Open Mon–Sat 11am–3pm & 6.30–10pm. Moderate–Expensive.

Nadaman, Basement 2, *Kowloon Shangri-La*, 64 Mody Rd, Tsim Sha Tsui East ☎2721 2111, x8371. Traditional, minimalist Japanese dining room where most of the Japanese business clientele tucks

Eating

Eating

in at the *sushi* bar or spends big on the other house specials – like the *kaiseki*, a set dinner of various small, beautifully presented dishes. Open noon–3pm & 6.30–11pm. Expensive.

Orba, Ground Floor, 99 Hennessy Rd, Wan Chai ☎2528 3853. Japanese counter lunches providing excellent value for money, particularly the *sashimi*. Open noon–2.30pm & 5.30–11.30pm. Moderate.

Tokio Joe, 16 Lan Kwai Fong ☎2525 1889. The designer-refectory look hits Hong Kong: great food and set *sushi* meals served at large pine tables. Meals are quick and cheap. Open noon–2.30pm & 6.30pm–midnight. Inexpensive–Moderate.

Unkai, 3rd Floor, *Sheraton Hotel*, 20 Nathan Rd, Tsim Sha Tsui ☎2369 1111 x2. If you're going to blow your money on one ridiculously expensive meal, it may as well be somewhere fairly true to its Japanese origins. In this case, the chefs are from Osaka and the food is beautifully presented. Open noon–2pm & 6.30–10pm. Very Expensive.

Yorohachi, 5–6 Lan Kwai Fong, Central ☎524 1251. A small restaurant in the trendy heart of Central serving good *sushi* and other delicately prepared dishes. Book in advance. Open 11am–3pm & 6–11pm. Moderate.

Korean

Nearly all Korean restaurants in Hong Kong feature a "barbecue" (*bulgogi*) as part of the menu – the table contains a grill, over which you cook marinated slices of meat, fish or seafood; assorted pickles (including *kimchi*, spicy, pickled cabbage), rice and soup come with the meal. One odd feature of many restaurants is the ginseng-flavoured chewing gum handed out when you leave.

Jindian Chuang Korean Restaurant, United Mansions, 37K Jordan Rd, Jordan MTR ☎2374 4339. Fairly standard Korean food, but worth noting for the set lunch which is one of the cheapest in town. Open 12.30–2.30pm & 6–11pm. Inexpensive.

Korean Restaurant, 1st Floor, 8 King Kwong St, Happy Valley ☎2573 6662. Spacious restaurant, well used to *gweilos* who fill the place up at weekends. Ginseng chicken is a speciality, though most stick with the budget-rated barbecues – there's chicken, beef, shrimp and squid, though frog's legs, deer and offal get a look in too. Open 11am–2.30pm & 6–11pm. Inexpensive–Moderate.

Koreana, 55 Paterson St, Causeway Bay ☎2577 5145. Decently priced barbecue restaurant with all the standard dishes as well as some interesting vegetable choices and good noodles. Open 11am–11pm. Moderate.

Laisan Korean BBQ, New Town Plaza, 6th Floor, Sha Tin ☎2606 7711. New Territories' restaurant that's popular with Sha Tin youth. The combination barbecue meals for two are excellent value. Open noon–11pm. Inexpensive.

Manna Korean Restaurant, Basement, 83b Nathan Rd, Tsim Sha Tsui ☎2721 2159. Cavernous place, whose smoke funnels over the tables make it look like a ship's engine room. No frills, plenty of clatter and great food; get a plate of Korean noodles to soak up the barbecue sauce. Open 11am–11pm. Inexpensive.

Malaysian and Singaporean

Banana Leaf Restaurant, Lockhart House, 440 Jaffe Rd, Wan Chai ☎2573 8187; 3rd Floor, Golden Crown Court, 68 Nathan Rd, Tsim Sha Tsui ☎2721 4821; 3rd Floor, 440 Prince Edward Rd (at Lung Kok St), Kowloon City ☎2382 8189. Malaysian and Singaporean standards, served on banana leaves, as is traditional. Curries are notable, too, particularly fish-head curry; pad out your meal with satay, samosas and breads. Note that no alcohol is served at any of the restaurants, but there's plenty of fresh fruit juices. Open 11am–3pm & 6pm–midnight. Inexpensive.

Satay Hut, 1st Floor, Houston Centre, Mody Rd, Tsim Sha Tsui East ☎2723 3628. Authentic satay dishes and other Singaporean staples in a friendly restaurant. Open 11.30am–10.30pm. Moderate.

Seefah Restaurant, 1–3a Hart Ave, Tsim Sha Tsui ☎721 3270. A large restaurant with budget Malaysian dinners, and other Asian dishes, too. There's little English spoken, but the staff are tolerant enough of first-timers. Open 11am–11pm. Inexpensive.

Mexican

Casa Mexicana, Ground Floor, Victoria Centre, 15 Watson Rd, North Point ☎2566 5560. Ropey Mexican food but everyone comes to get blind on the *margheritas* and beer. Open 11.30am–midnight. Moderate.

Mexican Mess, 11th Floor, Hankow Centre, 1c Middle Rd, Tsim Sha Tsui ☎2367 4535. The food's just about OK here, though most concentrate their attention on the frozen pitchers of *margheritas*, the best in town. The building is behind the YMCA. Open noon–midnight. Moderate.

La Placita, 13th Floor, Times Square, 1 Matheson Rd, Causeway Bay ☎2506 3308. With an arcaded interior modelled on a Mexican village square, staff in ponchos, and pastel paint thrown about like it was on special offer, you know you're in themeland. It's the best Mexican food in town (not much of a recommendation, admittedly) and the bar is a good place for a drink. Open noon–midnight. Moderate–Expensive.

Mongolian

Kublai's, 1st Floor, 151 Lockhart Rd, Wan Chai ☎2511 2287; 3rd Floor, One Capitol Place, 18 Luard Rd, Wan Chai ☎2529 9117; 55 Kimberley Rd, Tsim Sha Tsui ☎2722 0733. Mongolian "barbecue" restaurant: pick your own ingredients – noodles, spices, vegetables, sliced meat and fish, and sauces – and then take it to be cooked. Highly entertaining if there's a crowd, and you can keep going back for more – though the whole affair can be a little rushed at busy times. Open noon–3pm & 6.30–11pm. Inexpensive.

Spanish

La Bodega, 31 Wyndham St, Central ☎2877 3101. Stylish bar-restaurant that specializes in "Nueva Cocina Espanola",

which means fancy cooking, fancy decor and fancy prices. Daily specials are always worth investigating, and there's a grand wine list. Open noon–midnight. Moderate–Expensive.

Rico's, 44 Robinson Rd, Mid-Levels ☎2840 0937. It's always busy at this homely tapas bar, where you can put together a meal from a choice of a score of different bits and pieces – shrimp, croquettes, meatballs, fried squid, spicy potatoes and tortilla. Wash it down with the house wine, not bad and relatively cheap for once. Open noon–midnight. Moderate.

Sri Lankan

Club Sri Lanka, Basement, 17 Hollywood Rd ☎2526 6559. Sri Lankan restaurant (at the Wyndham St end) with some fine vegetarian dishes and a different bread baked every day; the food is similar to southern Indian, although it can be highly spiced. There's a help-yourself buffet meal as well as a limited menu. Extra friendly staff and nice surroundings make this one of Central's better choices. Open noon–2.30pm & 6–11pm. Inexpensive.

Thai

There are some classy Thai places about, especially in Central, but almost without exception the best places are the cheaper restaurants in Kowloon City, near the airport – take buses #11 (from Jordan Rd Ferry), #5, #5C and #9 (Star Ferry), or #5K and #5C (Kowloon Station) and get off at Carpenter Road, opposite the airport.

Baan Thai, 4th Floor, Causeway Bay Plaza 1, 489 Hennessy Rd, Causeway Bay ☎2831 9155. Lots of Thai style and spice make this one of the most authentic of Hong Kong's Thai restaurants – a good place to splash out on the more expensive fish dishes. Steer clear of those and a meal can be a bargain, given the slick service and quality food, though the overbearing staff can dull the experience on occasion. Open noon–3pm & 6–11.30pm. Moderate.

The Chili Club, 88 Lockhart Rd, Wan Chai ☎2527 2872. A shade too popular for its

Eating

The restaurants reviewed in this book have been given price categories as follows:

Inexpensive under $120

Moderate $120–250

Expensive $250–400

Very Expensive $400–750

Eating

own good these days, full of in-the-known *gweilos*, the *Chili Club* continues to knock out splendid meals on the spicy side. Booking – especially at night – is wise. Open noon–3pm & 6–10.30pm. Inexpensive–Moderate.

Her Thai, Shop 1, Promenade Level, Tower 1, China Hong Kong City, 33

Canton Rd, Tsim Sha Tsui ☎2735 8898. High-class restaurant with harbour views, outdoor tables, and a nice line in interior decor. The food's extremely good – especially the green curries or seafood – but expect to pay more than usual. Open noon–3pm & 6–11pm. Moderate–Expensive.

The restaurants reviewed in this book have been given price categories as follows:

Inexpensive under $120

Moderate $120–250

Expensive $250–400

Very Expensive $400–750

Vegetarian Food

The main problem with being **vegetarian** in Hong Kong is the language barrier in restaurants; often, even when the waiters do speak English, they will insist that things like chicken or pork aren't really meat. In Chinese restaurants, it's better to say "I eat vegetarian food" (*ngor sik tzai*), or Buddhist monk's food as it's thought of, which is an accepted concept. Even committed Chinese meat-eaters eat strictly vegetarian meals fairly regularly in order to clean out the system and balance their diet, while a fair number of the population are vegetarian for religious reasons, either permanently or on certain religious holidays.

It's fairly easy to stick to vegetarian Chinese food, either eating the mainstream vegetable, mushroom and beancurd (*tofu*) dishes on the menu or ordering a regular noodle dish without the meat. Bear in mind, though, if you're a purist, that many Chinese dishes start off life with a meat stock. Some strictly vegetarian **dishes** to order are *lo hon tzai* ("monk's vegetables"; a mixture of mushrooms, vegetables and beancurd) and *bak choy* (Chinese cabbage), usually stir-fried and served with oyster sauce.

To avoid any problems, it's easiest to eat in one of the excellent **Cantonese vegetarian restaurants**, where the food is based on *tofu*, which can be shaped into – and made to taste of – almost anything. Several places also specialize in **vegetarian dim sum**, where all the food looks exactly like its meaty counterpart (you even call it by the same names), but is all strictly vegetarian. In regular *dim sum* restaurants, you'll have a much harder time eating widely and well unless you eat prawns, though the various cakes and puddings are usually harmless enough.

Other than these places, you're best off in the territory's **Indian and Pakistani restaurants** (p.251), which have lots of non-meat choices, at a **pizza** (see "Italian" p.254) place, or a hotel buffet (p.249), which will always have a good salad bar and other vegetarian options. A meal at one of the **Buddhist monasteries** in Hong Kong will also consist of strictly vegetarian food; see especially Lantau (Chapter 5) and the various temples in the New Territories (Chapter 4).

Vegetarian restaurants
The places listed below are completely vegetarian, and are reviewed elsewhere in this chapter.

Bodhi Vegetarian Restaurant: several locations in Hong Kong and Kowloon; see "Chinese: Cantonese", above.

Dim Sum: for vegetarian *dim sum*, see p.239.

Fat Heung Lam, 94 Wellington St, Central; p.240.

Healthy Mess, Ground Floor, 51–53 Hennessy Rd, Wan Chai; p.239.

Kung Tak Lam, 45–47 Carnarvon Rd, Tsim Sha Tsui; 31 Yee Wo St, Causeway Bay; p.247.

Vegi-Food Kitchen, 8 Cleveland St, Causeway Bay; p.239.

Woodlands, Mirror Tower, 61 Mody Rd, Tsim Sha Tsui; p.253.

Phukets Seafood Grill, 30–32 Robinson Rd, Mid-Levels ☎2868 9672. Upmarket Thai place with beach-party decor, fine seafood (try the hotpot) and grilled garlic shrimp. The drinks menu is a shade more interesting than usual, too. Open noon–3pm & 6–11pm. Moderate.

Shek O Chinese Thai Seafood Restaurant, near the bus stop, main corner, Shek O ☎2809 4426. On Hong Kong Island's east coast (see p.116 for transport details), this open-air café gets crowded quickly, and deservedly so. Excellent food from an extensive menu, and a fine atmosphere. Open noon–10pm. Inexpensive.

Supatra's, 50 D'Aguilar St, Lan Kwai Fong, Central ☎2522 5073. Chic setting and decor, as befits the trendy end of town (which you can view from the window-side tables), though the food doesn't always live up to its promise. Open noon–11.30pm. Moderate.

Thai Delicacy, 44 Hennessy Rd, Wan Chai ☎527 2598. Compact, eat-and-go diner with a large, varied menu of low-budget, high-quality Thai food. Open 11.30am–11.30pm. Inexpensive.

Thai Food Restaurant, 1st Floor, *King's Hotel*, 473 Nathan Rd, Yau Ma Tei ☎2780 1281. The large pictorial menu makes this plain-looking restaurant a good choice if you're unsure what to order. The spicy, tasty dishes are keenly priced; you won't spend a fortune whatever you order. Open 7.30–11pm. Inexpensive.

Thai Wah, 24 Kai Tak Rd, Kowloon City ☎2716 7432. A small restaurant serving all the classic dishes, including a fiery *tom yam* in three sizes (the middle-sized bowl is enough for two or three people). Check out the daily specials – and be sure to have the prawn cakes. Open 11am–midnight. Inexpensive-Moderate.

Wong Chun Chun Thai Restaurant, 70–72 Nga Tsin Wai Rd, Kowloon City ☎2383 4680; 21–23 Prat Ave, Tsim Sha Tsui ☎2721 0099. Bright and clean Thai places that serve a reasonably priced meal. Open noon–2am. Inexpensive.

Vietnamese

Golden Bull Restaurant, Level 1, 17, New World Centre, 18 Salisbury Rd, Tsim Sha Tsui ☎369 4617; 11th Floor, Times Square, 1 Matheson St, Causeway Bay ☎2506 1028. Impressive, top-of-the-range Vietnamese restaurants with approachable staff and a fair choice of dishes. The barbecued prawns are always good or try one of the specials – the "seven kinds of beef", the house platter, or best of all, the mixed meat satay, actually a hot pot in which you cook thinly sliced squid, shrimp, fish, beef, chicken and rice noodles. Open noon–11.30pm. Moderate-Expensive.

Indochine 1929, 2nd Floor, California Tower, Lan Kwai Fong, Central ☎2869 7399. The very elegant *Indochine* serves up some of the tastiest Vietnamese food in the territory. There's a whiff of French colonial style about the place – stuffed snails feature on the menu – and every dish is a winner. Reservations advised. Open Mon–Sat noon–2.30pm & 6–11pm, Sun 6–11pm. Moderate-Expensive.

Myer, 10 Cheung Lok St, Kowloon ☎2771 2401. North of Jordan MTR, down the second street on the right, this cheap café has excellent spring rolls (which you wrap in lettuce leaves and dip in sauce) and other snacks. Open 11.30am–10.30pm. Inexpensive.

Perfume River, 89 Percival St, Causeway Bay ☎2576 2240. Ignore the owner's tendency to cover everything in the interior in green paint and this is one of the better Vietnamese restaurants in town. Open 11am–11pm. Inexpensive.

Saigon Beach Restaurant, 66 Lockhart Rd, Wan Chai ☎2529 7823. Good little restaurant that's a draw with young travellers and locals because it sticks to the basics and cooks them well. Open noon–3pm & 6–10pm. Inexpensive.

Vietnam City, Lower Ground Floor, Energy Plaza, 92 Granville Rd, Tsim Sha Tsui ☎2518 0801. More upmarket Vietnamese place, with French and Chinese influences apparent in the menu. Open noon–11.30pm. Moderate.

Eating

Eating

Special Diets

Some of the Pakistani restaurants in Chungking Mansions advertise themselves as serving **halal** food (see p.000), as does the occasional Chinese Muslim restaurant.

For **kosher** food, enquire about the kosher kitchen and restaurant at the Ohel Leah synagogue, 76 Robinson Road, Mid-Levels ☎ 2559 4820, or contact *King David at the Jewish Club*, 33 Queen's Rd, Central ☎ 2801 5440, a dinner-only, members-only, kosher dining room. Visitors can buy temporary membership for $150, and the buffet costs $190. There's also the *Shalom Grill*, 2nd Floor, 61 Connaught Rd, Central ☎ 2851 6300, serving kosher Middle Eastern food and couscous.

Any other dietary requirements can probably be catered for by the biggest hotel restaurants; it's always worth a phone call. Or check the list of **supermarkets** given under "Markets, supermarkets, bakeries and barbecues" (below), if you want to play safe and buy your own provisions.

Markets, supermarkets, bakeries and barbecues

With hot food and snacks so cheap in Hong Kong, there isn't much incentive to buy **picnic food**. However, you'll probably want to buy bread, cakes and fruit from the **markets**, and more elaborate food if you're going to use any of the hundreds of **barbecue sites** throughout the territory. If you're on any kind of special diet – or simply want to know exactly what you're eating – there are **supermarkets** right across Hong Kong. Be warned, though, that for anything recognizably Western, you'll pay a lot more than you would at home.

Markets

A walk around a Cantonese **market** is a sight in itself, and several are detailed in the text, including Hong Kong Island's Central Market (p.75), Sheung Wan market (p.82) and Luen Wo (p.157) and Sheung Shui markets (p.158) in the New Territories. A market is where the bulk of the population buys its fresh food, shopping at least once a day for meat, fish, fruit and vegetables. All the towns and residential buildings, especially in the developments in the New Territories, have a market hall.

They can look a bit intimidating at first, but no one minds you wandering around and checking out the produce. Most food is sold by the **catty**, which equals 1.3lb or 600g. Prodding and handling **fruit and veg** is almost expected: just pick out the items

you want and hand them over. They'll invariably be weighed on an ingenious set of hand-held scales, and, although the metric system is in official use, will almost certainly be priced according to traditional Chinese weights and measures. No one's out to cheat you, but it can help to know some Cantonese numbers and prices. Some stallholders will let you sample some of the more obscure fruit: one to watch for is the durian, a yellow, spiky fruit shaped like a rugby ball, that is fairly pricey and decidedly smelly – very much an acquired taste.

Buying **meat and fish** is also straightforward, though if you're going by sight alone make sure that the pretty fish you're pointing at isn't extremely rare and very expensive. It's perfectly all right to have several things weighed until you find the piece you want. For the best fish, either get to the market early in the morning, or come back in the mid-afternoon when the second catch is delivered. Every market will also have a **cooked meat** stall, selling roast pork, duck and chicken, which can perk up a picnic lunch no end.

Supermarkets

There are plenty of **supermarkets** around, but apart from a couple of notable exceptions they're pricey and concentrate on tinned and packet foods. Territory-wide **supermarket chains** include *Wellcome* and *Park 'N' Shop*. For addresses of these, and other specialist supermarkets, see below; they're generally open daily from around 8am to 8pm, though stores throughout the territory vary their hours.

TERRITORY-WIDE SUPERMARKETS

Park 'N' Shop: including branches at Pedder St, Central; Admiralty Centre, Central.

Wellcome: including branches at The Forum, Exchange Square, Central; 78 Nathan Rd, Tsim Sha Tsui.

SPECIALIST STORES

Asia Provisions Co. Ltd, 14 Pottinger St, Central; 31 Granville Rd, Tsim Sha Tsui. Despite the name, this is full of British and European brand names – the place to get jams, baked beans and cornflakes.

Daimaru, Household Square, Kingston St, Causeway Bay. Excellent Japanese supermarket inside the department store; takeaway food, too.

Indian Provision Store, Ground Floor, nos. 65–68, Chungking Mansions, 36–44 Nathan Rd, Tsim Sha Tsui. Indian spices, sweets and pickles as well as tins and dairy products.

Mok Po Food Co, 16th Floor, Korean Centre, no. 7, Sheung Wan. Korean supermarket.

Sogo, East Point Centre, 555 Hennessy Rd, Causeway Bay MTR. There's a Japanese supermarket inside the department store – takeaway Japanese snacks and food as well.

Thai Corner, 1A, Level 3, Sha Tin Plaza, Sha Tin, New Territories. Thai spices and sauces, noodles and pickles.

Yaohan, New Town Plaza, 18 Sha Tin Centre Rd, Sha Tin, New Territories. The ground floor of this department store has a huge Japanese supermarket, fresh meat and fish, alcoholic drinks, takeaway *sushi* and a Japanese snack bar.

Bakeries

The bread sold in supermarkets tends to be white and horrible, and you're better off buying it from the **bakeries** you'll find in every market and on most street corners. It'll be substantially the same – brown and wholemeal are virtually unknown – but will at least be fresher, and costs only a couple of dollars for a small sliced loaf. **Cakes** from bakeries are cheap, too, only a dollar or two for very sweet and very addictive creations. More elaborate cream cakes and buns are sold from the *Maxim's* chain of shops, which you'll find in most MTR and KCR stations, as well as at the Star Ferry terminals.

Barbecues

Almost everywhere of scenic interest you go in Hong Kong (and at some youth hostels and campsites) there are special **barbecue pits** provided in picnic areas. They're inordinately popular and getting the ingredients together for a barbecue isn't difficult. Supermarkets sell fuel, barbecue forks and all the food, as do kiosks at some of the more enterprising sites; either buy ready-made satay sticks or pick up cuts of meat and fish from the market.

Eating

Chapter 8

Nightlife: Bars, Pubs and Clubs

If you're not making eating your sole evening's entertainment, then Hong Kong has plenty to occupy you, lots of it carrying on until the small hours. There's no shortage of **bars, pubs and clubs** in which you can while away the night and allthough several of the pubs are, as you might expect, British in style – complete with homesick expats, horse brasses and dartboards – lots of other bars are either American or Australian, with food and drink to match. And because Hong Kong doesn't have that desperately trendy edge that bedevils London and New York, most of them are good, down-to-earth fun. That doesn't mean they're scruffy. Some are, but plenty are expensively decorated and dripping with sophistication, so if you're planning some extensive investigation, bring (or buy) clothes that won't wilt under a supercilious Hong Kong glare. Most of the newer, trendier bars and clubs are in Central, especially **Lan Kwai Fong**, while **Tsim Sha Tsui** has some long-standing pubs and discos much favoured by travellers staying in the nearby guest houses. Traditionally, **Wan Chai** has played host to the less refined, late-opening, hard-drinking dens, though as high rents push promoters out of Central, this area is currently enjoying something of a renaissance, with several new bars opening recently.

Most bars are **open** from around lunchtime until well after midnight; some, especially in Lan Kwai Fong and Wan Chai, stay open until breakfast time, and a few keep serving drinks right around the clock, most noticeably at the weekend. If there's a DJ or it's a **club** night, you might have to pay to get in; from around $60 at the smaller places to $150–200 for entry to the flash designer clubs. Some include a drink or two in the entry price, and lots only charge an entrance fee on the busy Friday and Saturday nights. Many bars also put on **live music**, mostly folk (singer-guitarists mangling "Yesterday") and jazz: these are picked out in the lists below, but for fuller details of live music, turn to the following chapter.

The **music** played is generally mainstream European and American pop and dance music, although there's a miniscule Indie scene, while plenty of places also play Canto-pop (see "Live Music", p.273), and others have Japanese-style karaoke lounges. **Rave culture** made a belated appearance in Hong Kong, but is going strong now with several bars and other venues hosting seasonal and one-off party nights – keep an eye out for flyers and check local **listings magazines** (*BC* and *HK Magazine*) for an accurate rundown of what's happening where.

The main drawback is that pubbing and clubbing – or at least drinking – is comparatively **expensive** and you'll need a fairly substantial amount of money to party every night (see the box

Alcoholic Drinks

The most readily available alcoholic beverage is **beer** – lager style and served ice cold. For years, the main brews were *San Miguel* (brewed in the territory for fifty years) and (better) *Tsingtao*, the latter a sharp Chinese beer made originally from a German recipe; where these weren't available, there was locally brewed *Carlsberg*. However, changes to the duty charged on imported alcohol in 1994 opened the floodgates and bars and restaurants (and lots of supermarkets) now sell British bitter, *Guinness* and untold other foreign beers, designer or otherwise, draft or bottled, Belgian to Venezuelan. There's even a Hong Kong-based microbrewery, selling decent unadulterated, locally produced ale: look for *Crooked Island Ale* in bars. **In a supermarket**, beer costs from around $7–8 a small can. In most **restaurants**, it's around $20–25 for the same small can; while in **bars and pubs**, this can rise dramatically – anything from $35 upwards for a small bottle, $45–60 for a draft pint.

Drinking **wine** in a bar or restaurant is similarly expensive, starting at around $25–45 a glass, $200 a bottle, for even the most average of wines – considerably more for anything halfway decent. Buy your own in a supermarket, and you'll pay at least $70–100 for basic French plonk – the alternatives are often South African, though Australasian wine is fairly well represented. You can get wine from the Chinese mainland but it's not common, and is unspectacular. Most internationally known **spirits** are available in bars and restaurants, again at a price. Cheaper, though much nastier and guaranteeing a miserable morning-after, are the various brands of Chinese **rice wine**, some of the cheaper examples of which are best left for cooking.

Nightlife: Bars, Pubs and Clubs

above). The main thing to watch out for in this respect is the prevalence of **Happy Hour**, where you'll get two-for-one drinks. They generally last a lot more than an hour: some time between 5pm and 8pm is usual (though some places sell cheap drinks all afternoon); many places also try to lure you back in with same deal at around 11pm–1am. Blackboards and notices in pubs and bars have details, and check the reviews below. Finally, it's worth noting that in the newer, trendier bars you're expected to **tip the barstaff**; ten percent will cover it.

Lan Kwai Fong

Beirut, Shop A, Winner Building, 27–39 D'Aguilar St ☎ 2804 6611. Lebanese restaurant with a downstairs bar that opens onto the street. There's enough elbow space and style to attract a more-sophisticated-than-usual LKF crowd. Open noon–midnight.

Bit Point, 31 D'Aguilar St ☎ 2523 7436. German bar with decent beer and schnapps. It throws its doors open on summer evenings; otherwise, it can be a claustrophobically male hang-out. Open noon–2am.

Cactus Club, Ground Floor, 13 Lan Kwai Fong ☎ 2525 6732. Fashionable bar which mixes a mean *margherita* for a young crowd; good beer selection too, and *mescal* to knock your socks off. Open Mon–Thurs noon–1am, Fri & Sat noon–4am.

California, Ground Floor, California Tower, 24–26 Lan Kwai Fong ☎ 2521 1345. Expensive American bar and restaurant with a tiny dance floor on which the local yuppies strut their stuff three times a week. It's been around for too long to be at the cutting edge of anything, but can still be fun on occasion. Open Mon–Thurs noon–11pm, Wed, Fri & Sat until 4am.

Club 64, Ground Floor, 12–14 Wing Wah Lane ☎ 2523 2801. Down-at-heel, back-alley drinking den playing blues and rock to an enthusiastic, vaguely Indie crowd most nights, many of whom spill out onto the pavement later. Drinks are affordable and Happy Hour is a long 11am–8pm. Open 11am–2am.

Club 97, 9 Lan Kwai Fong ☎ 2810 9333. A popular ground-floor disco, with a small

Nightlife: Bars, Pubs and Clubs

dance floor and good Western rock and pop. Mobbed at the weekend, when there's a cover charge, but free and emptier during the week. Mon–Thurs 9pm–3am, Fri & Sat 6pm–5am, Sun 9pm–3am.

La Dolce Vita, 9 Lan Kwai Fong, ☎2810 9333. Too-happening-for-words Italian bar open to the street, this is very much where the beautiful people, their hangers' on and aspirants congregate, sipping coffee and grappa, and contemplating the bizarre red satin, nippled backdrop. Late-night dancing is rather less chic, with 70s' and 80s' disco trash the usual ticket. Happy Hour 4–8pm. Open Sun–Thurs 11am–2am, Fri & Sat 11am–4am.

F-Stop, 14 Lan Kwai Fong ☎2868 9607. Self-consciously cool place with regular live bands and beer promotions. Open 11.30am–2.30pm & 4.30pm–12.30am.

Hardy's, 35 D'Aguilar St ☎2522 4448. Popular pub with folk singers and a decent, party atmosphere, particularly on Fridays – make sure you know the words

to "American Pie". Happy Hour 5–9pm and midnight–1am. Open Sun–Thurs 5.30pm–2am, Fri & Sat 5.30pm–3am.

Le Jardin, 10 Wing Wah Lane ☎2526 2717. Cosy bar with hit-and-miss service and a small sitting out area, set back from the hustle of Lan Kwai Fong. Given its removed location and the fact that after dark this is a difficult place to find, it's surprising that it's nearly always full. Mon–Thurs 9am–2am, Fri & Sat 9am–4am.

The Jazz Club, 2nd Floor, 34–36 D'Aguilar St ☎2845 8477. The narrow bar is open to non-members, who can drink to the jazz sounds coming from the video CD provided for customers' use. Happy Hour 6–9pm. Open Mon–Thurs 5pm–2am, Fri & Sat 5pm–3am, Sun 7pm–2am; also see "Live Music", p.000.

Mad Dogs, Century Square, 1 D'Aguilar St ☎2810 1000. Unashamedly British pub, with pictures of Queen Victoria, British beer on draught and comfy seating. It mostly attracts a business district clien-

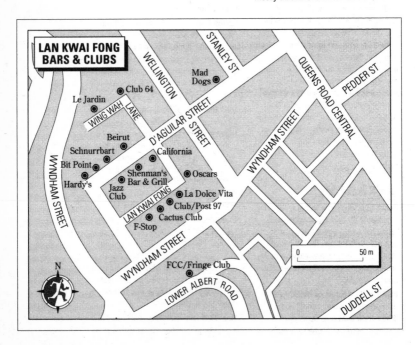

LAN KWAI FONG BARS & CLUBS

STANLEY ST · WELLINGTON · QUEENS ROAD CENTRAL · PEDDER ST · WYNDHAM STREET · D'AGUILAR STREET · WING WAH LANE · WYNDHAM STREET · LAN KWAI FONG · WYNDHAM STREET · LOWER ALBERT ROAD · DUDDELL ST

Mad Dogs ● · Club 64 ● · Le Jardin · Beirut ● · Schnurrbart ● · California · Bit Point ● · Shenman's Bar & Grill ● · Oscars ● · Hardy's ● · Jazz Club ● · La Dolce Vita ● · Club/Post 97 ● · Cactus Club ● · F-Stop ● · FCC/Fringe Club ●

N

0   50 m

tele, all of whom pack in for the 4–8pm and 10–11pm Happy Hours. Open Mon–Thurs 7am–2am, Fri & Sat 7am–3am, Sun 10am–2am.

Oscars, 2 Lan Kwai Fong ☎2804 6561. Crush-box bar-restaurant with propellor blade fans and a few stools and seats for the early arrivals. Everyone else piles outside for the Fong's most good-natured street party, where it's standing room only and barely that at times. Open Mon–Sat 11.30am–2am, Sun 11.30am–midnight.

Post 97, Upper Ground Floor, 9 Lan Kwai Fong ☎2810 9333. The upstairs brass-erie-bar in the *Nineteen 97* complex features sink-in-and-slouch chairs, arty surroundings, great coffee, all-day Sunday brunch and a decent list of beers and wines. Not a lot more to ask of life really. Happy Hour is 5–7pm. Open Mon–Thurs 8.30am–1am, Fri 8.30am–4am, Sat 24hr, Sun 8.30am–1am.

Schnurrbart, Ground Floor, Winner Building, 29 D'Aguilar St ☎2523 4700. German bar with bar stools, herring and sausage snacks, and some of the best beer around. Serious headaches are available courtesy of the 25 different kinds of schnapps – try the butterscotch. Open Mon–Thurs noon–12.30am, Fri & Sat noon–1.30am, Sun 6pm–12.30am.

Shenman's Bar & Grill, Ground Floor, California Building, 34–36 D'Aguilar St ☎2801 4946. Stylish open-fronted bar; cool but not pretentious. Open Mon–Sat noon–midnight.

Central

Bank Bar at Portico, Basement, Citibank Plaza, 3 Garden Rd ☎2523 8893. High-priced pub for city execs who seem content with the less-than-scintillating atmosphere and half-hearted arty surroundings. Open noon–11pm.

Cossacks, Basement, *Ritz Carlton*, 3 Connaught Rd ☎2869 0328. Full marks for a hotel bar actually worth drinking in. Russian theme bar with vodka, naturally enough, playing a significant part in most people's downfall. Good one-nighter club events, too. Mon–Fri 12.30pm–1am, Sat 6pm–1am.

The Gallery & Pier One, Shop 12, Basement, Jardine House, 1 Connaught Rd ☎2526 3061. Dark, nautical surround-ings – oak barrels, ropes and maritime bric-a-brac – for this basement British pub with a city clientele and Filipino musicians struggling with "Smoke on the Water". Open Mon–Sat 8am–midnight.

Godown, Upper Basement, *Furama Hotel*, 1 Connaught Rd ☎2524 2088. Traditional expat haunt with regular live jazz sessions – which is the only time it's worth going. Open 10am–2am.

The Jockey, 1st Floor, Swire House, 11 Chater Rd ☎526 1478. Long-in-the-tooth British-style pub which attracts the suits and portable phones. Open Mon–Sat 11am–11pm.

Judgement AD, Bank of America Tower, 12 Harcourt Rd ☎2521 0309. Cavernous late-opening club playing techno to a free-spending city crowd; Tuesday nights can be wild. Open 5pm–4am.

LA Café, Ground Floor, Lippo Centre, Queensway ☎2526 6863. American designer bar: Harley Davidson in the bar, TVs in the toilets, trendies lurking in the corners. Friday and Saturday are club nights – usually some mix of retro, grunge, indie and alternative sounds. Open daily 10.30am–1.30am, Fri & Sat 9.30am–3.30am.

Pomeroy's, Level 3, 349 Pacific Place, 88 Queensway ☎2523 4772. Not a bad stab at a London wine bar (though it lacks the genteel shabbiness of the

Nightlife:
Bars, Pubs
and Clubs

Nightlife: Bars, Pubs and Clubs

Rumpole of the Bailey original). There's a decent, if predictably expensive wine list, and British food and salad bar on offer all day. Open 9am–midnight.

Wan Chai

BB's, 114–120 Lockhart Rd ☎ 2529 7702. Part of the Wan Chai new wave, *BB's* wouldn't look out of place in Lan Kwai Fong: open-fronted, mirror-and-marble bar packed with city types and cool dudes, microbrew beers on tap, decent Cal-Ital food, and dance and jazz after hours upstairs. Happy Hour 4–9pm. Open 9.30am–3am.

Beer Castle, 15–19 Luard Rd ☎ 2527 7211. A barn of a drinking den with friendly staff but an unpredictably rambunctious clientele whose main interest is the maintenance of high alcohol levels. Open Mon–Sat 11am–6am, Sun 6pm–4am.

Big Apple, 20 Luard Rd ☎ 2529 3461. The hippest place in town at 4am on Sunday morning, when spaced-out socialites, chemically fuelled stockbrokers and Eurotrash mix it on the crowded dance floor – most of them are still there at 7am. During daylight, and up until midnight, it's a rather tame bar. Open Mon–Fri noon–5am, Sat & Sun 2pm–6am.

Carnegies, 53–55 Lockhart Road ☎ 2866 6289. Noise level means conversation here is only possible by flash cards, and once it's packed hordes of punters keen to revel the night away fight for dancing space on the bar. Home of the much talked about topless barman on a Wednesday night; occasional riotous club nights, too, and regular live music. Open 11am–3am, often later.

Delaney's, 2nd Floor, One Capital Place, 18 Luard Road ☎ 2804 2880. Take the elevator up to the second floor to reach this extremely popular re-creation of a Dublin pub, complete with live traditional music every night, *Guinness* flowing like

Bars With Views

The places below all offer views while you drink – mostly of the harbour, though the *Flying Machine* gives you a great vantage point over the airport runway. Some have already been covered in the listings, but where they haven't (especially if they're hotel bars), you can expect to pay more than usual for your drink.

Cafe Deco, Level 1 & 2, Peak Galleria, 118 Peak Rd, The Peak ☎2849 5111.

Cyrano's, *Island Shangri-La*, Pacific Place, 88 Queensway, Central ☎2872 3838.

Harbour View Lounge, 1st Floor, *Holiday Inn Harbour View*, 70 Mody Rd, Tsim Sha Tsui East ☎2721 5161.

Harlequin, 25th Floor, *Mandarin Oriental*, 5 Connaught Rd, Central ☎2522 0111.

Flying Machine, 14th Floor, *Regal Airport Hotel*, 38 Sa Po Rd, Kowloon City ☎2718 0333.

Peak Café, 121 Peak Rd, Victoria Peak ☎2899 7868.

La Ronda, 30th Floor, *Hotel Furama*, 1 Connaught Rd, Central ☎2525 5111.

Sky Lounge, 18th Floor, *Sheraton*, 20 Nathan Rd, Tsim Sha Tsui ☎2369 1111.

Tiffin Bar, *Grand Hyatt*, 1 Harbour Rd, Wan Chai ☎2588 1234.

Nightlife:
Bars, Pubs
and Clubs

water and loud, red-faced expats. Drinks are very expensive. There's a second branch at 3–7 Prat Ave in Tsim Sha Tsui. Open Mon–Thurs & Sun noon–2am, Fri & Sat noon–3am.

Flying Pig, 2nd Floor, 81–85 Lockhart Rd ☎2865 3730. Extremely boisterous and young, weekend Wan Chai party venue with more whizz than Billy. A must if you've ever wondered what dancing in an overcrowded aeroplane to disco trash would be like. Weekdays are much quieter and, dare it be said, much nicer. Open Mon–Thurs 11.30am–3am, Fri & Sat 11.30am–4am, Sun 3.30pm–2am.

Horse and Carriage, 117 Lockhart Rd ☎2529 6914. Old-style Wan Chai hang-out with very cheap food and budget drinks during the 11am–8pm Happy Hour. Open Mon–Sat 11am–6am, Sun 7.30pm–6am.

Horse and Groom, 161 Lockhart Rd ☎2519 7001. Recently smartened-up pub serving drinks any time of the day or night; worth visiting for the inexpensive pub food. Open Mon–Sat 10.30am–4.30am, Sun 7pm–4am.

JJ's, *Grand Hyatt*, 1 Harbour Rd ☎2588 1234. Classy mainstream disco with a smart dress code, two bars, snooker and darts. There's live music every night from

the (usually not bad) house band except Sunday and a stiff cover charge. Open Mon–Thurs 5.30pm–2am, Fri until 3am, Sat 4am.

Joe Bananas, 23 Luard Road ☎2529 1811. Lively, unsophisticated American bar with a late disco, occasional live music and marathon weekend opening hours; Happy Hour 11am–9pm. You need to be (or look) 21 and there's a strict door policy – men need a shirt with a collar; non-drinkers will require tolerance and understanding. Open Mon–Thurs 11.30am–5am, Fri & Sat 11.30am–6am, Sun 5pm–5am.

Neptunes, Basement, 62 Lockhart Rd ☎2527 5276. Dingy but good-natured club, the backdrop for mostly Western pop, interspersed with bouts of the Filipino house band playing cover versions. The clientele is mainly Filipina, too – which means significant numbers of sad Western men on the prowl. Open 6pm–7am.

Old China Hand, 104 Lockhart Rd ☎2527 9174. Pub for hard-core drinkers, hung-over clubbers (who come for breakfast), and those with a taste for formica surfaces. Open Mon–Thurs 7am–2am, Fri & Sat 24hr, Sun 9am–1am.

Rick's Café, 78–82 Jaffe Rd ☎2528 1812. Rowdy bar with a reputation – primarily, it

Nightlife: Bars, Pubs and Clubs

seems, for being a cattle market and playing naff music. Open 11am–2am, Fri & Sat until 5am.

Ridgways, 1st Floor, 81–85 Lockhart Rd ☎ 2866 6608. Basically an overspill from the *Flying Pig*, upstairs, and as such considered prime pick-up territory by the more Neanderthal element in town. If you don't want a one-night stand, a fight or a hangover, you're in the wrong place. Open 11am–3pm.

The Wanch, 54 Jaffe Rd ☎ 2861 1621. Another venue for all those party animals who know the words to various 1960s' song classics – and want to sing along, loudly. Open daily 11am–1am, Fri & Sat until 4am.

Westworld, 4th Floor, *New World Harbour View*, 1 Harbour Rd, Wan Chai ☎ 2824 0380. Glitzy dance club that's visually and financially extravagant – a decidedly non-Canto-pop experience. Open 9.30pm–3am, Thurs–Sat until 4am.

Causeway Bay

Brecht's, 123 Leighton Rd ☎ 2577 9636. Intimate joint that's a hit with the creative types who perch at the ludicrously uncomfortable suspended stainless steel tables and peruse metal menus that can barely be lifted. The bar serves food and

has a good selection of imported beers, including Belgian ones. Open Mon–Thurs 4pm–2am, Fri & Sat till 4am.

Dickens Bar, Lower Ground Floor, *Excelsior Hotel*, 281 Gloucester Rd ☎ 2894 8888. One of the few decent hotel bars, this also features regular jazz sessions. Mon–Thurs & Sun 11am–2am, Fri & Sat 11am–3am.

The Jump, 7th Floor, Plaza Two, 463 Lockhart Rd, Causeway Bay ☎ 2832 9007. If you make it past the self-opinionated fashion police masquerading as bouncers, then entertainment is split between the small dance floor and the performance art of the bar tenders. Escapes being a cattle market by the skin of its teeth. Open Mon–Wed noon–2am, Thurs–Sat noon–5am.

La Placita, 13th Floor, Times Square, 1 Matheson St ☎ 2506 3308. The domed, horseshoe-shaped bar in this Mexican restaurant (see p.257) is a decent Times Square venue. Prices are spot on at Happy Hour (5–7.30pm) for splashing out on Mexican beers or *margheritas*, and included are free chips and salsa and the dulcet tones of the Filipino *mariachi* band. Open noon–midnight.

Roy's at the New China Max, 11th Floor, Times Square, 1 Matheson St

☎2506 2282. This has been through so many name changes recently the staff are getting dizzy, but the theme remains the same: in-your-face, funky Asian interior where Thai elephants and Vietnamese statues rub shoulders, great central bar, good restaurant (see p.254) and dance floor. Live bands and wired DJs complete the set-up. Open noon–2am.

Shooters 52, 13th Floor, Times Square, 1 Matheson St ☎2506 2626. Ersatz American bar and grill, mightily popular with young execs. There's NFL on TV, but no good reason to drink here except at Happy Hour (Mon–Sat 4.30–8pm): no self-respecting bar-keep would wear the "humourous" buttons sported by all the staff. Open Mon–Thurs & Sun 11am–midnight, Fri & Sat 11am–2am.

Tsim Sha Tsui

Bahama Mama's, 4–5 Knutsford Terrace ☎2368 2121. Beach-bar theme and outdoor terrace that prompts party crowd antics. It's all right as a mere bar, but for the best crack, stump up the cover charge and come along on club nights where a mixed music policy sees Garage to World get a look in. Open Mon–Thurs 6pm–3am, Fri & Sat 6pm–5am, Sun 6pm–2am.

The Catwalk, *New World Hotel*, 22 Salisbury Rd ☎2369 4111. Mirrors and chrome and bland Western pop, or salsa and funk, depending on the night – which doesn't seem to have prevented it from acquiring a reputation as a Triad hang-out. Free midweek; steep cover charge Thurs, Fri & Sat. Open 9pm–3am.

Falcon, Basement, *Royal Garden Hotel*, 69 Mody Rd ☎2721 5215. Posh surroundings and mainstream Canto-pop for the well-heeled clientele. Open Mon–Thurs 9.30pm–2am & Sun, Fri & Sat 9pm–3am.

Hard Rock Café, 100 Canton Rd ☎2377 8118. Live bands playing cover versions and mainstream rock and pop keeps the dance floor busy. The music starts at 10.30pm and there's a cover charge. Open 10.30pm–2am.

Jousters II, 19–23 Hart Ave ☎2723 0022. Ludicrous drinking venue – mock medi-eval interior, suits of armour, coats of arms and other baronial trappings, washed down with loud rock music and very cheap drinks right up until 9pm. Open Mon–Thurs 3pm–2am, Fri & Sat 3pm–3am, Sun 6pm–2am.

Kangaroo Pub, 1st Floor, 35 Haiphong Rd ☎2376 0083. An old favourite, popular with travellers – split-level Australian pub, with windows overlooking the bottom of Kowloon Park.. Australian beer, sports on the video, a fine-juke box and snacks or a

Nightlife: Bars, Pubs and Clubs

Hostess Clubs

Hong Kong is notorious for its plethora of hostess clubs, or "girlie bars", which the HKTA tries hard to push as a tourist experience. Frankly, they're pathetic places for pathetic patrons, exploitative in every way, whose sleazy offers of "one drink $50" are distinctly worth resisting.

Still, whatever your feelings about them, some have almost entered into Hong Kong legend. *Bottoms Up* (14 Hankow Rd, Tsim Sha Tsui) is a case in point, famous simply because parts of the James Bond film *The Man With the Golden Gun* were shot there. *Red Lips* (1a Lock Rd, Tsim Sha Tsui) is notorious for the advanced age of its host-esses, most of whom are over sixty. And *Club BBoss* (New Mandarin Plaza, 14 Science Museum Rd, Tsim Sha Tsui East) is reputedly the largest hostess club in the world, an enormous, super-plush haunt, where a full-sized Rolls Royce-shaped model car drives you to your table. It was forced to change its name – from *Club Volvo* – after losing a court action brought by Volvo cars about the use of the name. The club argued, unsuc-cessfully, that the name was merely a transliteration of its Chinese name, Dai Fu Ho, or "big wealthy tycoon".

Nightlife: Bars, Pubs and Clubs

full menu in the restaurant. Happy Hour 4–7pm. Open 11am–3am.

Mad Dogs Kowloon, 32 Nathan Rd ☎ 2301 2222. More entertaining than the Central branch, this basement pub elevates serious drinking to an art form. Live musicians kick off the evening proceedings, which degenerate later on as guest DJs whip up the beer monsters. Great fun. Happy Hour 4–7pm, plus two-for-one deals most nights on selected drinks. Mon–Thurs 8am–2am, Fri–Sun 8am–4am.

Ned Kelly's Last Stand, 11a Ashley Rd ☎ 2376 0562. Dark Australian bar with great live trad jazz after 9pm; good beer and meaty Aussie food served at the tables. It's a real favourite with travellers and good fun – after 9pm you'll be lucky to get a seat. Open 11.45am–1.45am.

Sky Lounge, 18th Floor, *Sheraton Hotel*, 20 Nathan Rd ☎ 2369 1111. Marvellous city and harbour views in stylish surroundings; dress up for the impeccable service, and free nibbles, accompanied by nightly crooners and instrumentalists. It's cheaper before 8pm, after which there's a steep minimum charge per person. Open Mon–Thurs & Sun 4pm–1am, Fri & Sat 11am–2am.

Someplace Else, Basement, *Sheraton Hotel*, 20 Nathan Rd ☎ 2721 6151. The *Sheraton*'s other bar (entered at the junction with Middle Rd) is much more accessible – an upmarket singles' bar, whose large, rowdy two-floor bar-restaurant has live music, free popcorn nibbles, Tex-Mex and Asian snacks and a good cocktail list. Happy Hour 5–7pm. Open 11am–2am.

TSIM SHA TSUI BARS & CLUBS

Elsewhere

Beaches, 92b Stanley Main St, Stanley Village ☎ 2813 7313. Expat bar-restaurant-disco haunt which pounds out 60s' and 70s' sounds nightly. Open until 2am.

Cafe Deco, Level 1 & 2, Peak Galleria, 118 Peak Rd, The Peak ☎ 2849 5111. Stupendous views from the picture windows and great Deco surroundings make this one of the island's highlights. Come for a meal, or just a drink; stop and listen to the jazz band. Open Mon–Thurs 10am–midnight, Fri & Sat 10am–1am, Sun 10am–midnight.

Visage Too, 411–413 Shek O Village ☎ 2809 2129. The coolest bar on the island's south side, with staff as laid-back as the customers, snacky food, and flexible opening hours. Live music, too, on occasions. Mon–Fri 8pm–1am, Sat 3pm–1am, Sun noon–1am.

Nightlife: Bars, Pubs and Clubs

Chapter 9

Live Music: Rock, Pop, Folk and Jazz

Hong Kong is never the first place that touring Western bands think of, but even so the **live music** scene has picked up considerably over the last couple of years. Venues, however, remain few: apart from the *Hong Kong Coliseum*, *Hong Kong Stadium* and the *Queen Elizabeth Stadium*, where the megastars play, there's no real middle-ranking concert hall for rock and pop music. If you're in Hong Kong during a quiet period for Western bands, check to see if any of the big names in the homegrown pop music scene are playing: **Canto-pop**, a Chinese-language variety of ballads and disco music, is easily the most popular music in Hong Kong – there are more details in the feature below.

There's a thriving local **jazz** scene, based around regular gigs in pubs and clubs, while many bars offer evening punters what is euphemistically referred to as **folk** music. You'll never see anyone very exciting, but if all you want to do is drink to the strains of Eagles cover versions, there's plenty of opportunity. Finally, most of the large **hotels** feature resident bands and visiting "international artists" in their bars – invariably mood music and crooning as an accompaniment to expensive cocktail-sipping.

To find out **what's on**, look in the free listings magazines *BC* and *HK Magazine*, available at many of the venues listed below and at bars and restaurants, partic-

For details of where to hear classical music in Hong Kong, see the following chapter.

ularly in and around Lan Kwai Fong. The *South China Morning Post* also has a daily "What's On" page (which lists the hotel-bar music in detail) and a weekly "Gig Guide".

Rock and pop

Outside the big venues, less well-known bands tend to appear in bars and pubs, or are served up as PAs ("personal appearances" singing or miming to backing tapes) in one or two of the clubs. You'll find details of forthcoming events in the local press, or contact the places listed below direct. Ticket prices vary, but you'll usually pay from $50–100 for local bands and visiting second-rank groups and artists, more like $400–700 for someone famous.

Academic Community Hall, Baptist College, 228 Waterloo Rd, Kowloon Tong ☎2339 5182. Major pop concerts by Chinese and international stars.

Carnegies, Ground Floor, 53–55 Lockhart Rd, Wan Chai ☎2866 6289. Regular gigs by local acts; usually no cover charge.

China Max, 11th Floor, Times Square, 1 Matheson Rd, Causeway Bay ☎2506 2282 or ☎2506 4471. Mixed music, but generally enough R & B and rock and roll (with bands every night) to keep things moving; no cover charge either.

Fringe Club, 2 Lower Albert Rd, Central ☎2521 7251. Occasional rock and pop

Canto-pop

The origins of **Canto-pop** lie in the Cantonese movie musicals of the 1950s and 1960s, whose soundtracks became enormously popular in postwar Hong Kong. But until the 1970s, most true pop music in Hong Kong was either imported from the West or from Taiwan, whose Mandarin pop singers were among the first to receive star treatment. **Sam Hui**, in the mid-1970s, was the first Hong Kong-based artist to mix Cantonese lyrics with Western pop music – a style that quickly became known as Canto-pop. To Western ears, it's often fairly bland stuff – ballads are easily the most popular song form – but to the practitioners it's anything but straightforward. The nine tones in the Cantonese language cause major problems, since they limit the expressiveness that singers can put into the songs; singing in Mandarin is actually much easier.

Hui – the "Elvis Presley of the Orient" – retired in 1992, but by then he had been superseded by a phalanx of young (and not so young) hopefuls, including **Alan Tam**, **Jacky Cheung**, **Andy Lau**, **Leon Lai** and **Aaron Kwok**. It's largely a male-dominated scene, though there are notable women singers, too. For years, undisputed Canto-pop Queen was **Anita Mui**, unearthed in a TVB talent contest in 1982. Mui, too, has recently announced her "retirement", but there are several others hoping to follow her – **Sally Yeh**, **Sandy Lam**, **Sammy Cheung**, **Vivian Chow**, **Faye Wong** and **Shirley Kwan** are among the best known.

And let there be no doubt about how popular these singers are. Michael Jackson or Madonna would be able to fill the 12,000-seater *Coliseum*, but Sam Hui's retirement concerts saw 41 sold-out nights there; Paula Tsui performed 43 sell-outs in 1992, while Alan Tam has played at the *Coliseum* 121 times in his career. If you get the chance to see one of the big names live in Hong Kong, it's an experience worth catching – more cabaret than pop concert.

Live Music: Rock, Pop, Folk and Jazz

gigs by local bands; Saturday night is open-mike night when anyone can have a go, using the club's equipment – this is not always as entertaining as it sounds.

Hard Rock Café, 100 Canton Rd, Tsim Sha Tsui ☎2377 8118. A live band every night from 10.30pm, with an occasional name act to thrill the crowds.

Hong Kong Coliseum, 8 Cheong Wan Rd, Hung Hom, Kowloon ☎2355 7234. Fairly regular performances by major international rock and pop bands, and lengthy concert series by Canto-pop superstars.

Hong Kong Stadium, 55 Eastern Hospital Rd, Causeway Bay ☎2895 7895. Very occasional gigs by megastars.

Queen Elizabeth Stadium, 18 Oi Kwan Road, Wan Chai ☎2591 1346. Major rock and pop bands.

Folk

Entrance to all these bars and pubs is free, but you must expect to buy a drink or two.

Cinta Restaurant and Lounge, *Hotel New Harbour*, 8–10 Fenwick St, Wan Chai ☎2527 1199. Filipino singers after 9pm.

Delaney's, 2nd Floor, One Capital Place, 18 Luard Rd ☎2804 2880; 3–7 Prat Ave, Tsim Sha Tsui ☎2301 3980. Genuine traditional Irish folk, every night at both venues. Sunday afternoon in Wan Chai sees a jam session.

Hardy's, 35 D'Aguilar St, Central ☎2522 4448. Inoffensive folk singers (and enthusiastic, drunk amateurs) every night doing cover versions. Starts at 9.30pm.

Mad Dogs, Century House, 1 D'Aguilar St, Central ☎2810 1000; 32 Nathan Rd, Tsim Sha Tsui ☎2301 2222. Early evening singer-guitarists most nights at both pubs, and occasional bands too.

Someplace Else, Basement, Sheraton Hotel, 20 Nathan Rd, Tsim Sha Tsui ☎2369 1111. Regular live singers doing all the regular cover versions.

The Wanch, 54 Jaffe Rd, Wan Chai ☎2861 1621. Solid folk and pub rock

**Live Music:
Rock, Pop,
Folk and
Jazz**

venue, with live music seven nights a week from 9pm to 2am.

Jazz

Mostly, entrance to pub and bar jazz gigs is free (except where stated below), and the standard of playing is very high. Visiting name acts play at the *Jazz Club*, while August sees the annual two-day *Select Live Under the Sky* **jazz festival**, which attracts some top people, though it's become less jazz-orientated and more middle-of-the-road of late; details from the HKTA.

Cafe Deco, Level 1 & 2, Peak Galleria, 118 Peak Rd, The Peak ☎2849 5111. Regular jazz and cool sounds in the Peak's Art Deco extravaganza (with occasional cover charge); ring for current performances.

Dickens Bar, Lower Ground Floor, *Excelsior Hotel*, 281 Gloucester Rd, Causeway Bay ☎2894 8888. Jazz sessions every Sun 3–6pm.

The Godown, Upper Basement, *Furama Hotel*, 1 Connaught Rd, Central ☎2524 2088. Jazz night with the resident band Wed after 8pm.

Fringe Club, 2 Lower Albert Rd, Central ☎2521 7251. Occasional jazz gigs; cover charge for non-members.

The Jazz Club, 2nd Floor, 34–36 D'Aguilar St, Central ☎2845 8477. A unique venue in Hong Kong. Live jazz nightly at 10pm. Admission varies from free to around $100, with more expensive tickets for big-name bands and soloists throughout the year.

The Jump, 7th Floor, Causeway Bay Plaza 2, 463 Lockhart Rd, Causeway Bay ☎2832 9007. Jazz brunch with the pianist Larry Allen (Sun 11am–4pm).

Ned Kelly's Last Stand, 11a Ashley Road, Tsim Sha Tsui ☎2376 0562. Trad and Dixieland jazz every night after 9pm from the stomping resident band, the "Kowloon Honkers". Recommended.

Chapter 10

The Arts and Media

For years Hong Kong has had a poor cultural reputation among visitors, though it's not for want of trying: the **Cultural Centre** in Tsim Sha Tsui, a conglomeration of theatre, studios and concert hall, and the **Hong Kong Arts Centre** and the adjacent **Academy for Performing Arts**, in Wan Chai both put on high-quality work. Nevertheless, it's true that the formal, mostly Western arts, remain limited in scope in Hong Kong. The only art form that commands a mass audience is **film**, with the cinemas packed for every new Hollywood release, and – more pertinently – for every new Chinese film. Local **Chinese culture** is less formally presented in the territory, though, as you might expect, there's much more of it around. The main venues host traditional dance, opera and music performances, but you're just as likely to see something exciting in the night markets, or during religious holidays at temples and on the street.

Cantonese might be the language of the overwhelming majority in Hong Kong, but for tourists it's the preponderance of the English-language **media** that makes the territory such an easy place to come to terms with. Television, radio and newspapers are immediately accessible to English-speaking visitors.

Information, listings and tickets

Information about cultural events and performances can be picked up at any of the venues listed below. For detailed list-ings of forthcoming events, there are three free magazines: the Urban Council's dual-language monthly *City News* (available in City Hall and other government buildings); the Hong Kong Arts Centre's monthly *Artslink* magazine; and the weekly *HK Magazine* (available at bookshops, bars, clubs and restaurants throughout the centre). Take a look, too, at *BC*, a monthly reviews magazine (from outlets all over Hong Kong); at the weekly *TV & Entertainment Times*; as well as in the English-language daily newspapers, the *Hong Kong Standard*, *Eastern Express* and the *South China Morning Post*, whose weekend editions have good reviews and listings.

Tickets for most events can be bought at any of the main venues, and from offices called **URBTIX** outlets; there's a list below of venues and outlets. Cultural events are very good value in Hong Kong. Many are subsidized by the government and accordingly, you won't pay anything like the prices you would at home. Generally, expect to pay $50–120 for seats for most local productions, rising to $250–650 for anything international.

Main venues

Academy for Performing Arts, 1 Gloucester Rd, Wan Chai ☎ 2584 1500. Six separate stages for local and international drama, modern and classical dance. Box office 10am–6pm.

Alliance Française, 123 Hennessy Rd, Wan Chai ☎ 2527 7825; and 52 Jordan

The Arts and Media

Rd, Kowloon ☎ 2730 3257. Films and culture at the French Cultural Institute. Box office 8.30am–9.30pm.

City Hall, 7 Edinburgh Place, Central ☎ 2921 2840. Drama, concerts, recitals, exhibitions and lectures. Box office 10am–10pm.

Fringe Club, 2 Lower Albert Rd, Central ☎ 2521 7251. Offbeat venue for local performance art, jazz, concerts, poetry and drama, as well as exhibitions, classes and workshops. Pick up the schedule from the venue; temporary membership available. Box office 5–11pm.

Goethe Institute, 14th Floor, Hong Kong Arts Centre, 2 Harbour Rd, Wan Chai ☎ 2802 0088. Films and events at the German Cultural Institute.

Hong Kong Arts Centre, 2 Harbour Rd, Wan Chai ☎ 2877 1000. Local art, drama, concerts and film screenings, galleries and exhibitions. Box office 10am–8pm.

Hong Kong Coliseum, 9 Cheong Wan Rd, Hung Hom ☎ 2765 9234. Hong Kong's largest venue (12,000 seats) for concerts,

dance and sports events. Box office 10am–6.30pm.

Hong Kong Convention and Exhibition Centre, 1 Harbour Rd, Wan Chai ☎ 2582 8888. Major conventions, exhibitions, concerts and performances. Box office varies according to the promoter; check press for details.

Hong Kong Cultural Centre, 10 Salisbury Rd, Tsim Sha Tsui ☎ 2734 2009. Dance, drama and concerts in Hong Kong's newest and most controversial building, drawing on local and international performers. See p.123 for more details about the building. Box office 10am–9.30pm.

Ko Shan Theatre, Ko Shan Rd (off Chatham Rd North), Hung Hom ☎ 2740 9212. Hong Kong's first open-air theatre, located in a disused quarry. Film, theatre, Chinese opera and concerts.

Ngau Chi Wan Civic Centre, 2nd Floor, Ngau Chi Wan Complex, 11 Clearwater Bay Rd, New Territories ☎ 2726 0854. Drama, dance and film. Box office 10am–6.30pm.

Queen Elizabeth Stadium, 18 Oi Kwan Rd, Wan Chai ☎ 2591 1346. Stadium with 3500 capacity for large concerts and sports events. Box office 10am–8pm.

Sha Tin Town Hall, 1 Yuen Wo Rd, New Town Plaza, Sha Tin, New Territories ☎ 2694 2536. Drama, dance and concerts. Box office 10am–9.30pm.

Sheung Wan Civic Centre, 345 Queen's Rd, Sheung Wan ☎ 2853 2689. Drama, concerts, lectures and exhibitions. Box office 10am–6.30pm.

Tsuen Wan Town Hall, 72 Tai Ho Rd, Tsuen Wan, New Territories ☎ 2414 0144. Large venue for concerts, dance and drama. Box office 10am–9.30pm.

Tuen Mun Town Hall, 3 Tuen Hi Rd, Tuen Mun, New Territories ☎ 2452 7328. Local venue for concerts, dance and drama. Box office 10am–9.30pm.

URBTIX outlets

Telephone bookings can be made on ☎ 2734 9009 (10am–8pm). Otherwise, central URBTIX outlets include: City Hall, the Cultural Centre and the Hong Kong Arts Centre.

Chinese cultural performances

Chinese cultural performances are widespread in Hong Kong, every town and village having its hall, theatre or outdoor space where traditional opera and dance can take place. All performances are highly theatrical; coming across one by accident can be a real highlight of your stay.

The best known is the **Chinese opera**, which you'll see performed locally at festivals, on religious holidays, and in some of the larger venues by visiting and local troupes. In Hong Kong, the style is mostly Cantonese (though visiting mainland Chinese groups perform Peking Opera on occasion, too) – a highly stylized affair, a musical drama with mime, set songs and responses based on well-known legends and stories. The costumes and garish make-up are magnificent, and while the strident operatic singing and percussion is decidedly awkward to untuned Western ears, it becomes compelling after a while

– particularly as the story is interspersed with bouts of elaborate, skilful swordfighting and acrobatics. Performances often go on for three hours or more, but the ones held in or near temples at festivals are usually informal, people walking about, chatting and eating right the way through.

Other cultural shows you might catch include traditional Chinese **music**, **puppet theatre**, folk **dancing**, **acrobatics** and tumbling, magic and **martial arts** – all things that are soon evident if you're in Hong Kong for any length of time. Street markets and festivals are good places to look; or check in the local press for specific performances at some of the main venues listed above.

Obviously, it's most rewarding to stumble on performances as you travel around the territory: **religious festival events** (see pp.281–284) and cultural shows out in the New Territories (often listed in the press) are put on for the locals and have few pretensions. But if you want to ensure you see at least something of the traditional culture during your stay, the HKTA organizes free hour-long shows every week at various places in the territory. Main venues are in the New World Centre (Tsim Sha Tsui) and Cityplaza (Taikoo Shing), where there'll usually be a bit of everything on display from opera extracts to glove puppetry. For more information, contact any of the HKTA offices (see p.46).

There are also daily Chinese craft and culture displays at the **Sung Dynasty Village** in Lai Chi Kok (p.140) and events and performances in **Middle Kingdom**, Ocean Park (p.110). And make an effort to visit the **Temple Street Night Market** (p.134), where you can see enthusiastic amateurs performing Cantonese opera – pay a few dollars, and you'll be allowed into a seated enclosure and served tea while you watch.

Film

There are at least thirty **cinemas** in Hong Kong, with the current trend firmly towards multi-screen complexes, which show a mixture of new Hollywood and Cantonese releases. Going to the movies is inexpensive and it's worth taking in one of the

The Arts and Media

The Arts and Media

Chinese-language films if you can: most are lightweight pot-boiler films, slapstick comedies, gangster movies and martial arts thrillers, though increasingly some very interesting films from the mainland are on view, too. There are English subtitles, and reviews of current films in both English-language daily newspapers to help you choose which to see. All the major **English-language films** make it to Hong Kong soon after release, and are shown in their original language, with Chinese subtitles.

You'll often have to queue to get into cinemas, and all the major venues are computer-controlled: you pick your seat from the available ones left, shown on the video monitor by the box office, and pay the cashier. Entrance is around $55 a ticket (the *loge*, incidentally, is equivalent to the dress circle).

Films are participatory experiences in Hong Kong. There's plenty of clapping and booing, and as the Hollywood films are subtitled, the Chinese audience talks right through them. It can be hard to concentrate as the couple in front of you argue heatedly and the chicken feet snacks fly overhead, but it's undeniably fun.

The **major cinemas**, and a few interesting minor ones, are listed below, but for a full rundown of what's on where, consult the local press. If you're just wandering and fancy a movie, the biggest concentration of cinemas is in Causeway Bay. There are also regular film shows (often free) sponsored by the *Alliance Française* and *Goethe Institute*; see "Main Venues" above for addresses.

Real film buffs will want to try to coincide with the annual **film festival**, which always has an excellent and entertaining international programme, though it can be hard to get seats (see "Arts Festivals" feature, above, for more details).

Astor Classics, 380 Nathan Rd, Jordan ☎2781 1833. Sister cinema of *Columbia Classics*, below, with a similar programme of new releases.

Cine-Art House, Sun Hung Kei Centre, Harbour Rd, Wan Chai ☎2827 4820. Arty foreign films in two mini-cinemas.

Columbia Classics, Great Eagle Centre, 23 Harbour Rd, Wan Chai ☎2827 8291.

Usually an interesting programme of non-blockbuster films as well as new releases.

Hong Kong Arts Centre, 2 Harbour Rd, Wan Chai ☎2582 0200. Seasons of alternative film and Chinese cinema.

New Majestic Cinema, 348 Nathan Rd, Jordan ☎2782 0272. Long runs for new releases – it's at Saigon St.

New York Cinema, 463–483 Lockhart Rd, Plaza ll, Causeway Bay ☎2838 7380. Plush cinema for new Western and Chinese releases.

Silvercord Cinema, Silvercord Plaza, 30 Canton Rd, Tsim Sha Tsui ☎2317 1083. A double-screen cinema offering both Hollywood blockbusters and art-house movies.

United Artists, One Pacific Place, 88 Queensway, Central ☎2869 0322; Times Square, Causeway Bay ☎2506 2822; Level 2, Whampoa Plaza, Hung Hom ☎2303 1040; New Town Plaza, Sha Tin, New Territories ☎2698 0651. Modern multi-screen venues for all new releases. Note that you can also book tickets by phone at all four with *Ticketmaster* ☎2317 6666

Windsor, Windsor House, 311 Gloucester Rd, Causeway Bay. ☎2882 2621. Well-located two-screen cinema with smoochy double-seats at the back.

Music: classical and Chinese

The main exponent of **Western classical music** is the *Hong Kong Philharmonic Orchestra*, formed in 1975, whose season runs from September through to June, and which regularly employs guest conductors and soloists. Performances are at a variety of venues, including the Cultural Centre; information on ☎2832 7121. Look, too, for performances by the *Asian Youth Orchestra*, which performs an annual summer programme. Less formally, there are free lunchtime concerts every Wednesday in St John's Cathedral, Garden Rd, Central, from around 1.15pm to 2pm; details on ☎2523 4157.

For **Chinese orchestral music**, watch for performances by the *Hong Kong*

Chinese Orchestra, founded in 1977, the territory's only professional Chinese music group. The orchestra plays at City Hall and the Cultural Centre. Its repertoire takes in traditional Chinese instruments and reworkings of Western classical music, a combination which is not to everyone's taste but is certainly worth hearing. For other types of Chinese music, see "Chinese Cultural Performances", above.

Television and radio

You may end up watching more **television** than you'd bargained for. Every hotel and most guest houses lay them on for their guests, and you're hard pushed to escape them in bars and restaurants.

There are four main domestic channels, two English-language and two Chinese, operated by two companies. *Television Broadcasts* (TVB) runs Jade (Chinese) and **TVB Pearl** (English); *Asia Television* (ATV) runs Home (Chinese) and **ATV World** (English). In addition, domestic and hotel TVs can often receive cable and satellite channels, including ESPN and a relayed BBC channel.

Much of the domestic **English-language programming** is imported – documentaries, soaps and sitcoms – while on the whole, the homegrown product is unbelievably bad. Indeed, English-language broadcasting (in both TV and radio) is becoming ever more marginalized. It's of distinct minority appeal in a territory where almost six million of the inhabitants speak Chinese as a first language – the way forward has already been signalled by *TVB*, which now carries Mandarin news, weather and financial reports on its English-language Pearl channel. In the meantime, however, the saving grace of both English-language channels is that each features at least one **film** every night, some made for TV but plenty of recent Hollywood productions too. Also, they're fairly good on **sporting events** and you can count on getting live coverage of important soccer matches, as well as tennis, rugby and other sports – though often shown here in the early hours because of the time

---

Radio Stations

RTHK Radio 3 (567 kHz, 1584 kHz). News, finance and current affairs.

RTHK Radio 4 (97.6 to 98.9 mHz). Western and Chinese classical music.

RTHK Radio 6 (675 kHz). The BBC World Service relay station.

Quote AM (864 kHz). 24-hour commercial radio; pop and easy listening.

Metro Plus (1044 kHz AM). Local and Asian news and finance, interspersed with music. Half-hourly news and weather.

BFBS (96.6, 102, 104.8, 107.4 mHz FM). The British Forces Broadcasting Service – soon to become obsolete.

---

difference. Be warned, though, that the constant commercials are no respecter of film plot or goalmouth action.

If you speak Cantonese, try the **Chinese channels** which put on a lot more locally produced stuff – including some good Cantonese and mainland Chinese feature films – but on the whole it's a diet of soaps and variety shows.

On the **radio**, there's plenty in English to tune in to. Stations include those operated by the main broadcasting outfit, *Radio Television Hong Kong* (*RTHK*); there's a commercial station too, as well as British Forces radio and the BBC World Service.

Full **programme details** for TV and radio are contained in the daily newspapers and in the week's *TV & Entertainment Times*.

Theatre and the performing arts

Hong Kong has recently become the home of excellent local **drama and performance art**, alongside the usual international touring companies and artists who enliven the cultural year. There's a wealth of **venues** to check for forthcoming performances (details above), most dominant of which is the Cultural Centre. Most of the other main venues host drama and perfor-

---

The Arts and Media

For details of Hong Kong's daily newspapers, see p.307.

The Arts and Media

mance art throughout the year, too: the only thing to check is whether the **productions** are in English or Cantonese.

Other than straight drama, some of the most exciting local performances are **dance**-orientated, which don't have the disadvantage of a language barrier and often mix Western and Chinese forms very successfully. **Fringe events** are common, too: the *Fringe Club*, especially, hosts its fair share of mime, magic, cabaret and tumbling.

Some interesting **local companies** to watch out for, who play at venues all over the territory, include:

Actor's Rep. A professional group covering English-language drama.

Agitprop. Hong Kong's first all-women theatre company, operating as a co-operative and producing consistently challenging new work.

American Community Theatre. Performances of American classics.

Chung Ying Theatre Company. English and Cantonese performances, including Chinese opera.

City Contemporary Dance Company. Full-time professionals who usually perform at the Arts Centre.

Hilton Hotel Dinner Theatre. Light comedy from visiting British West End stars; now looking for a new home since the *Hilton* closed down.

Hong Kong Ballet Company. Classical and contemporary ballet performances at various venues.

Hong Kong Dance Company. Modern and classical Chinese dance.

Hong Kong Singers. Musical comedy of the Gilbert and Sullivan variety.

Stage Renegades. Trendy PC productions which merit a look.

Zuni Icosahedron. Avant-garde theatre-dance in Cantonese and English.

Visual arts: galleries and exhibition space

Some of the main venues listed above have **gallery and exhibition space** that's

worth checking for current displays. Otherwise, keep an eye on all the territory's **museums**, which host occasional lectures and exhibitions based around their subject. Also, the Urban Council's district **libraries** put on year-round lectures, displays and exhibitions that might be of interest; full details in each month's *City News* magazine (available from City Hall).

There are many **private galleries** in Hong Kong which display art and fine art. The *South China Morning Post* highlights a good selection of current exhibitions in its daily *What's On* section, as does the monthly *BC* magazine. The places listed below are always worth dropping in on:

Alisan Fine Arts, 315 Prince's Building, 10 Chater Rd, Central ☎2526 1091.

Artland Gallery, 3rd Floor, Lockhart Centre, 301–307 Lockhart Rd, Wan Chai ☎2511 4845.

Fringe Club: *Fringe Gallery* and *Heineken Gallery*, 2 Lower Albert Rd, Central ☎2537 1482.

Galerie La Vong, 13th Floor, One Lan Kwai Fong, Central ☎2869 6863.

Gallery 7, 1 Glenealy, Central ☎2526 7183.

Hanart TZ Gallery, 5th Floor, The Old Bank of China Building, Bank St, Central ☎2526 9019.

LKF The Gallery, 1st Floor, Lan Kwai House, 5–6 Lan Kwai Fong, Central ☎2524 8976.

Plum Blossoms Gallery, 305–307 Exchange Square One, Central ☎2521 2189.

Pottery Workshop, 2 Lower Albert Rd, Central ☎2525 7634.

Wagner Art Gallery, 7th Floor, Lusitano Building, 4 Duddell St, Central ☎2521 7882.

Wattis Fine Art, 2nd Floor, 20 Hollywood Rd, Central ☎2524 5302.

Zee Stone Gallery, 11 The Forum, Exchange Square Three, Central ☎2845 4476.

Chapter 11

Festivals

Timimg your trip to coincide with one of Hong Kong's traditional **Chinese festivals** can greatly add to its interest. Below is a round-up of the year's events, with details of what to expect and where to see the associated celebrations. We've given the likely months and dates for the festivals (as well as the lunar dates), but for the exact dates look in one of the HKTA's free publications, which should summarize them. (The *South China Morning Post* records each lunar day on its daily listings page.) The festivals below are dealt with **chronologically**, starting with the Chinese New Year.

Chinese New Year

Most famous and most important of the Chinese festivals, **Chinese New Year** falls some time between the end of January and the end of February. Decorations go up everywhere, there's a huge **flower market** in Victoria Park on Hong Kong Island (and in Fa Hui Park and Cheung Sha Wan playground in Kowloon), where locals buy lucky flowers – peach and plum blossom – fruit, lanterns and sweets. You might also catch an impromptu **lion dance**. These are mostly held in residential areas, but ask the tourist office which large hotels are likely to put on a dance display. The most obvious manifestation of New Year is the red scrolls and posters that are pasted to walls and houses all over the territory: the Chinese characters wish long life, prosperity and happiness.

This aside, though, there's not actually a great deal to see at Chinese New Year.

It's a family festival, when people will settle debts, visit friends and relations, buy new clothes and generally ensure a fresh start for the year. Married couples hand out lucky money in red envelopes (*lai see*) to their families and tip dustmen and cleaners in the same way; people on salaries get a bonus; and shop assistants and waiters are feasted by their employers. Traditionally, services like hairdressing cost double in the run-up to the festival. Lots of shops, businesses and restaurants close down for three days or even longer (traditional New Year celebrations last fifteen days), but plenty stay open since families also eat out to celebrate. To wish someone a "Happy New Year", you say **kung hay fat choi**.

Arriving in Hong Kong and trying to find a room during Chinese New Year is something you should avoid. And don't even think about travelling to China during the festival: everything is jam-packed solid as the Hong Kong Chinese stream across the border to visit relatives.

Yuen Siu (Lantern) Festival

The **Yuen Siu Festival** marks the last official day of the Chinese New Year celebrations (the fifteenth day of the first moon), when traditionally designed and brightly coloured lanterns are hung in restaurants, shops, temples and houses. It falls a couple of weeks after the start of the New Year – and is also known as "Lovers' Day", a kind of Chinese Valentine's Day. There's a second lantern festival in September; see "Mid-Autumn Festival" over page.

Not all the Chinese festivals are also public holidays. For a full rundown of public holidays in Hong Kong, see p.28.

Festivals

Ching Ming Festival

Generally held in April, **Ching Ming** is when families visit their ancestral graves to perform traditional rites. The day – the beginning of the third moon, a public holiday – signals the beginning of spring and a new farming year, but it's more noted for the sweeping of graves at the territory's cemeteries. Whole families take along joss sticks, incense and food offerings (roast pork and fruit), which are left for the dead at the graves while prayers are said for the departed souls and blessings sought for the latest generations of the family. Extra public transport is laid on for trips to the cemeteries, on Hong Kong Island and out in the New Territories, as well as extra ferries to carry people to the outlying islands: it's one enormous scrum.

Tin Hau Festival

A traditional fishing festival, this is one of the most spectacular of the year's events. Falling in late April or May (on the 23rd day of the third lunar month), it is in honour of **Tin Hau**, a legendary fisherman's daughter of a thousand years ago, who could forecast the weather, calm the waves and generally assist the fishermen to a decent catch; not surprisingly, she is regarded as the Goddess of Fishermen and protector of those at sea. Fishing boats are colourfully decorated with flags, streamers and pennants as fishermen and others who follow the goddess gather at the various Tin Hau temples throughout the territory to ask for luck in the coming year and to offer food, fruit and pink dumplings as a mark of respect. The main temple is the one at **Joss House Bay** in Sai Kung (p.173), where massive crowds congregate every year, and there is always a good celebration in **Yuen Long** in the New Territories, another large centre of Tin Hau worship. Special ferry services run out to some of the temples; the temples themselves are brightly decorated and there are usually Chinese opera displays, dances and parades at most of them.

Tam Kung Festival

The second patron saint of the fishing people is **Tam Kung**, whose festival is celebrated in May (eighth day of the fourth lunar month) at the temple in Shau Kei Wan on Hong Kong Island (p.115).

Birthday of the Lord Buddha

A low-key celebration in May when the Buddha's statue is taken out of the various Buddhist monasteries in the territory and "bathed" in scented water. The monasteries on Lantau are an obvious place to head for to see the rites being performed, but there are important monasteries in the New Territories, too, at Sha Tin and Lam Tei (see Chapter 4).

Tai Chiu (Cheung Chau Bun) Festival

A week-long extravaganza in May (starting on the eighth day of the fourth moon) on Cheung Chau Island, the **Tai Chiu Festival** is one of the highlights of the festival year. The buns that give the festival its English name are distributed for luck at the end of the celebrations, which consist of dances, operas, parades – and the famous "floating children" and bun towers. See "Cheung Chau" (p.190) for more details; and expect the island and all the transport there and back to be in a state of siege during this time.

Tuen Ng (Dragon Boat) Festival

The **Tuen Ng Festival** is one of the oldest of Cantonese festivals, held to commemorate the Chinese hero Ch'u Yuen, an advisor to the king who committed suicide by jumping in a river in Hunan Province and drowning, in protest against a corrupt third-century-BC government. The local people tried to save him in their boats, while others threw rice dumplings into the water to feed the fish that would otherwise have eaten his body.

Today, the festival is celebrated in early June (fifth day of the fifth moon) with noisy dragon boat races – narrow rowing boats with a dragon's head and tail – throughout the territory, while rice dumplings are eaten, too. The boats are crewed by anything up to eighty people (though most are smaller), the oar-strokes set by a drummer, and the races are accompanied by cymbals and watched from scores of junks and launches. You can see **races** in many places, particularly on the Tsim Sha Tsui East waterfront, where it's become a major spectacle; there are races, too, at Tai Po, Stanley and Yau Ma Tei – watch the local press for details or ask the tourist office. Since 1976 there's been an annual International Dragon Boat Race, with teams from all over the world competing.

Birthday of Lu Pan

Held in July, this is a holiday for anyone connected with the building trades. **Lu Pan** was a Master Builder in around 600 BC, a skilled carpenter and possessor of miracle powers. Banquets are held in his honour on his festival day (the thirteenth day of the sixth moon) and there are ceremonies at the Lu Pan Temple in Kennedy Town (p.87).

Maiden's Festival

Also known as the Seven Sister's Festival, the **Maiden's Festival** is held in mid-August, on the seventh day of the seventh moon. It is observed mostly by young girls and lovers, and prayers and offerings are made to the six sisters of Chih Nu, separated from her lover by the Queen of Heaven – a celebration that dates back more than 1500 years. One

place you can see the devotions and offerings is at the Bowen Road Lover's Stone Garden at Wan Chai Gap (p.94).

Yue Lan Festival

The **Yue Lan Festival** is held in late August (the fifteenth day of the seventh moon). It's known as the "Festival of the Hungry Ghosts", commemorating the lunar month when ghosts are released from the underworld to roam the earth. It's generally seen as an unlucky day, when accidents or sinister events can happen. To forestall that, people give offerings to the ghosts in the form of paper models of food, cars, houses, money, furniture, etc – which are then ceremoniously burnt so that the ghosts can take them back to the underworld with them. It's not a public holiday, but you may see fires on the pavements and at the roadside during this time where the elaborate models are burnt. See the account of the Pak Tai Temple in Wan Chai (p.97) for more details about the dying craft of making paper models.

Mid-Autumn Festival

Another major festival, the **Mid-Autumn Festival** is also called the **Moon Cake Festival** after the sweet cakes eaten at this time – mostly made from sesame and lotus seeds and stuffed with a duck egg. The festival takes place in September (on the fifteenth day of the eighth moon), is roughly similar to the Western Harvest Festival, and purportedly commemorates a fourteenth-century revolt against the Mongols, when the call to arms was writ-

Festivals

The Maiden's Festival: the Legend

While you're considering the wonderful views from Lover's Stone Garden, over Wan Chai and the harbour beyond, you can muse on the **legend** commemorated by the festival. A cowhand stole the clothes of a weaving girl, a daughter of the Kitchen God, while she was bathing, and having seen her naked, had to marry her, after which they lived together happily. But the gods ordered her to return to heaven to continue her weaving, and said that the couple could meet only once a year. The cowhand died and became an Immortal, but to prevent the couple meeting in heaven, the Queen of Heaven created the Milky Way, leaving the weaving girl on one side and the cowherd on the other. Although they can see each other, they only meet on the seventh day of the seventh moon, when magpies form a bridge so that they might cross to each other.

Festivals

ten on pieces of paper, stuffed inside the cakes and distributed to the population. Today, there are various kinds of moon cake (yuek beng) on sale around this time, all wonderfully sickly: you will see them stacked up in bakeries, costing from around $100 for a box of four, though the better, more elaborate double-yolk cakes are pricier. The festival also combines with lantern displays, which take place on hillsides throughout the territory. The Peak and various spots in the New Territories are favourite places to go and light your lantern while watching the moon rise – at which point you scoff the cakes. There's a lantern display, too, in Victoria Park on Hong Kong Island. The day after the festival is a public holiday, and expect transport to anywhere near a hill (like the Peak Tram) to be packed the night before.

Birthday of Confucius

The **birthday of Confucius**, in September, is marked by low-key religious ceremonies at the Confucius Temple in Causeway Bay.

Cheung Yeung Festival

A public holiday in October (on the ninth day of the ninth month), the **Cheung Yeung Festival** relates to a tale from Han Dynasty times, when a soothsayer advised an old man to take his family to the mountains for 24 hours to avoid disaster. On his return, everything else in the village had died. The same trip to high places is made today in remembrance, with the result again that all transport to hilly areas is packed. Lots of people also take the opportunity to visit family graves.

Chapter 12

Shopping

The stories you've heard about bargain-basement prices for electrical goods, clothes and other items are broadly accurate – the only imported goods to attract duty in Hong Kong are alcohol, tobacco, perfumes, cosmetics and cars. However, don't be misled into thinking that you're going to pick up goods for next to nothing. The picture has changed over recent years as other Southeast Asian countries have begun to rival the territory: clothes from Bangkok are better value these days, while prices for hi-fi and photographic equipment are not the steal they once were. Approach your shopping as you would at home: buy something because you like it, shop around, and always check the small print on the never-to-be-repeated special offers.

You shouldn't need our help to find designer gear or hi-fi and electrical equipment in Hong Kong: all the big names are sold absolutely everywhere and specific addresses, if you need them, are given in the HKTA's *Shopping* guide and a dozen other publications and leaflets. We've

listed more mainstream places – markets, bookshops and department stores – that should be useful for anyone stopping in Hong Kong, as well as a selection of miscellaneous shops, any of which can occupy a spare half-hour or so, or provide an offbeat souvenir.

Shop opening hours vary according to what part of Hong Kong you shop in. Mostly, shops are open seven days a week; some department stores close on Sunday, while Japanese department stores open on Sunday but close for one day mid-week instead. Otherwise, the only time that shops close is for two to three days around Chinese New Year, and even then by no means all do so. Shops mostly stay open during Western holidays like Christmas and Easter. Opening hours for street **markets** are even longer – open daily until 11pm or midnight, though with a couple of exceptions which are dealt with in the text.

Antiques, arts and crafts

There are great opportunities to buy Chinese antiques, arts and crafts in Hong Kong, in hundreds of specialist stores and markets, but you'll rarely come across bargains. If you're looking for something specific, be prepared to pay for it. Art and antiques more than one hundred years old should come with a certificate of authenticity; such items are also allowed into most countries duty-free, though check first with your consulate if unsure (there's a list on pp.304–305).

Shopping Hours

Central and Western: daily 10am–7pm.

Wan Chai and Causeway Bay: daily 10am–10pm.

Tsim Sha Tsui, Yau Ma Tei and Mongkok: daily 10am–10pm.

Tsim Sha Tsui East: daily 10am–7.30pm.

Shopping

Shopping: A Survival Guide

Although it may sometimes seem like it, not everyone's out to rip you off, but there are some rules to follow and dodges to be aware of before you part with any cash. The most important ground rule is to **shop around** to get an idea of what things cost: pirate goods are common, so if you see something that's spectacularly cheap, always check it out elsewhere. Obviously, buying a calculator or cheap digital watch from a vendor on the street, you're not going to expect it to work for ever. But with expensive hi-fi gear you need to be more circumspect; take your time, ask for demonstrations, and don't buy the first one you see.

Choosing a shop

For expensive items, it's often recommended that you use shops that are **members of the Hong Kong Tourist Association (HKTA)**; they pay an annual membership fee and identify themselves by a sign in the window of a red junk within a red circle. Obviously, only a fraction of the territory's shops and stores are in the HKTA and the ones that aren't aren't necessarily all villains – far from it. But it's a starting point if you're worried.

All the registered shops are listed in the HKTA's *Shopping* guide (available free from HKTA offices), which has plenty of information on shopping for various items and goods. Look, too, at the newspaper *Hongkong* and the monthly *Hong Kong Guide*, both available from HKTA offices, for their articles on shopping and factory outlets.

For questions about shopping in Hong Kong, or **complaints against HKTA members**, ring ☎ 2807 6134 (Mon–Fri 9am–5pm, Sat 9am–1pm).

Agents and importers

Many of the products sold in Hong Kong are handled by a sole **agent or importer**, who can give you reliable information about the particular model you're interested in if the shop is vague or unhelpful. The agents' and importers' names and telephone numbers are given in the HKTA *Shopping* guide.

Guarantees

Always check the **guarantee** you're given for photographic, electronic or electrical goods. Some are international guarantees, in which case they should carry the name of the sole agent in Hong Kong for that product; others are purely local guarantees, which are **only valid in Hong Kong**, usually for a period of twelve months. All guarantees should carry a description of the product, including a model number and serial number, as well as the date of purchase, the name and address of the shop you bought it from and the shop's official stamp.

Deposits and refunds

You don't need to put down a **deposit** on anything unless it's being made for you. For tailored clothes for example, expect to put down up to fifty percent of the price. On other items, if the shop insists (to secure the item, or to order a new one because they're "out of stock"), go somewhere else – there are always plenty of alternatives. Generally, goods are not returnable or **refundable**, though if something is faulty or missing, the better shops will replace your goods. To make sure, always have your receipt itemized and go straight back to the shop if there's something wrong.

Compatibility

It's important to check that electrical goods are compatible with your domestic mains voltage, and that television sets and VCRs are compatible with each other, and with your domestic broadcasting system.

Customs, shipping and insurance

Before making large puchases, check with the relevant consulate (there's a list on pp.304–305) or the HKTA about **customs** regulations for the country you want to import the goods to. Most shops can arrange to have your purchase packed and sent overseas, but make sure you have it **insured** to cover damage in transit as well as loss. To send items home yourself, you need to go to a main post office (see p.307), where you can also arrange insurance (though check to see if you're covered by your own travel insurance). Parcels usually take at least six weeks by surface mail and one week by airmail to reach Europe or North America.

Avoiding rip-offs

Having checked all the main points, you still need to be armed against the out-and-out bad guys – or simply against the shopkeepers who see their chance to make a little extra cash from a tourist.

•**Always ask the price**.

•**Bargaining**: for most large items in the bigger shops and department stores, the price will be fixed and you won't be able to bargain, though you might be able to wangle extra accessories and the like before completing the sale. However, you can bargain in markets and smaller shops, though bear in mind that the seller always wins.

• **Switching goods**: if you've paid for goods, don't let them out of your sight as it's not unknown for bits and pieces to have mysteriously vanished by the time you get home, or for cheaper gear to have been substituted. Either pack your purchases yourself, or check everything before you leave the shop. If things like camera cases or electrical leads are part of the package, make sure they're there and itemized on the receipt: otherwise, return later to complain and you may be told that they're "extras" which you now have to pay for.

• **Fake and pirate gear**: sometimes you know that goods are fakes and it doesn't matter. Hong Kong's ubiquitous fake Rolex watches, for instance, are definitely worth the money, and fake designer-label gear from markets has a certain cachet. But if you want the real McCoy, don't buy anything from anyone on the street; also, don't be tempted by stupid bargains – pay the going rate and get receipts and guarantees. Lots of the traffic in pirated things like watches and cameras has been stamped upon recently by the customs authorities in any case, although there's a major trade in pirate computer gear and CDS.

Boycotting products

There's nothing you can't buy in Hong Kong, which means that there are markets in several products you may not feel entirely happy about – **furs, leather and skin** goods made from rare and exotic or endangered species and, most importantly, **ivory**. There are huge stocks of ivory in Hong Kong, one of the world's largest markets in the product and, while lots of countries have recently placed import bans on the stuff, the British government initially refused to ban sales in Hong Kong because stocks were so great and the ivory lobby so powerful – Hong Kong is home to the biggest ivory processing centre in the world and employs about three thousand people in the business. However, the government is a party to CITES (the Convention on International Trade in Endangered Species) and since 1990, the Hong Kong authorities have abided more stringently by the rules of the worldwide ban. But, without compensation paid to the merchants here, it seems likely that illegal trading will continue, further undermining the efforts to save the elephant from exploitation.

The trade in endangered species also rears its head in **traditional Chinese medicine**, much of which utilizes the body parts of animals like tigers and rhinos. A lot of the medicines (surprisingly) carry bilingual ingredient lists – if you're going to buy anything, check first.

Shopping

Shopping

A few ideas

Art Galleries. There's a list of art galleries with regular exhibitions and sales on p.280.

Chinese Products Stores. See "Department stores" below for a list of stores specializing in arts, crafts and goods from the Chinese mainland.

Hollywood Road, Central. The main venue for antique, art and craft shops, with scores of shops open Mon–Sat 10am–6pm.

Markets. Check the list on p.292 for the addresses of markets specializing in arts and crafts.

Specific stores

Amazing Grace Elephant Company, 348–349 Ocean Centre, Harbour City, Canton Rd, Tsim Sha Tsui. Assorted Asian handicrafts, collectibles and knick-knacks.

Banyan Tree, 214–218 Prince's Building, Chater Rd, Central; 257 Ocean Terminal, Canton Rd, Tsim Sha Tsui. Antiques and reproduction furniture, pricey Asian handicrafts.

Chinese Arts and Crafts Bazaar, Level II, New World Shopping Centre Mall, 18–24 Salisbury Rd, Tsim Sha Tsui East. Displays of traditional arts and crafts – painting, seal carving, calligraphy, doll-making and tea-making. Closed Mon.

Creative Hands, Shop 34, Western Market, 323 Des Voeux Rd, Sheung Wan. Original paintings, prints, watercolour materials.

Mountain Folkcraft, 12 Wo On Lane (off D'Aguilar St), Central. Beautiful handmade folk art and crafts from Southeast Asia and elsewhere.

Museum Shop, Hong Kong Arts Centre, Cultural Centre, Salisbury Rd, Tsim Sha Tsui. Art books and supplies, calligraphy materials, prints, postcards, gifts and stationery.

The Pottery Workshop, 2 Lower Albert Rd (entrance on Wyndham St), Central. Small gallery for locally produced pottery and ceramic art. Affordable and interesting.

Welfare Handicrafts, Shop 7, Jardine House, 1 Connaught Place, Central; Salisbury Rd, Tsim Sha Tsui. Store selling arts and crafts on behalf of charities.

Bookshops

All the **bookshops** below sell English-language books, and in some you can buy foreign-language newspapers and magazines, too. There are, of course, hundreds of other bookshops that only sell Chinese-language books.

Age of Aquarius, 2–6 Foo Ming St, Causeway Bay. New Age hippy-dippy books, tapes and gifts.

Bookazine, 102–103 Alexandra House, Chater Rd, Central; Basement, Jardine House, 1 Connaught Rd, Central; Room 229–230, Princes Building, Central; Room 117, Shui On Centre, Harbour Road, Wan Chai; Shop 8 & 9, 3rd Floor, Hopewell Centre, Queens Rd East, Wan Chai; Shop 208, Caroline Centre 2 Yun Ping Rd, Causeway Bay; Shop UG34, Tsim Sha Tsui Centre, Tsim Sha Tsui East. Excellent selection of foreign magazines and books, especially good for cookery books and novels.

Cosmos Books, 1st Floor, 30 Johnston Rd, Wan Chai. Good for travel, novels and history.

Data Bank, The Goldmark, 502 Hennessy Rd, Causeway Bay; Shop 206 & 313A Mongkok Computer Centre, 8 Nelson St, Mongkok. Specialist shops for computer books, magazines and accessories.

Government Publications Centre, Queensway Government Offices, Low Block, Ground Floor, 66 Queensway, Admiralty. Official government publications, Hong Kong maps, exhibition catalogues, and books on local flora, fauna, politics, environment, industry and anything else you can think of.

Hong Kong Book Centre, Basement, On Lok Yuen Building, 25 Des Voeux Rd, Central. Cramped, library-like interior, but well stocked with novels and travel books, and good on Chinese history and politics. Foreign newspapers, too.

Joint Publishing, 9 Queen Victoria St, Central. Sole agent/distributor for mainland Chinese publications, with a good stock of Marxist-Leninist works, foreign-language books and magazines, and books published in Hong Kong and Taiwan.

Kelly and Walsh, Shop 348, Pacific Place Shopping Mall, 88 Queensway, Central. Big, central, general bookshop, good on travel and art.

Museum Shop, Hong Kong Museum of Art, Cultural Centre, Salisbury Rd, Tsim Sha Tsui. Books on art and artists, as well as art supplies, stationery and postcards.

South China Morning Post Family Bookshop, 2nd Floor, Times Square, 1 Matheson St, Causeway Bay; Star Ferry Concourse, Central; 313 Ocean Centre, Harbour City, Canton Rd, Tsim Sha Tsui; Basement One, New World Centre, 18–24 Salisbury Rd, Tsim Sha Tsui East. Fine selection of English-language novels, travel guides, dictionaries, maps and books on Hong Kong and China, and foreign newspapers.

Swindon Book Co. Ltd, Star Ferry Concourse, Tsim Sha Tsui; 13–15 Lock Rd, Tsim Sha Tsui; 249 Ocean Terminal, Harbour City, 3 Canton Rd, Tsim Sha Tsui; 310 Ocean Centre, Harbour City, 5 Canton Rd, Tsim Sha Tsui. A general bookshop with a fairly large travel section; the Star Ferry branch is particularly good for books on Hong Kong.

Shopping

Clothes

For the addresses of the big-name **designers** – from Armani to Valentino, as well as local Hong Kong whizz-kids – look no further than the HKTA *Shopping* guide, which lists them all in exhaustive detail. Otherwise, it's best simply to check out all the options as you wend your way around the city. Typically, you'll save up to 25 percent by buying designer gear here rather than in its country of origin.

For cheaper clothes shopping, check out the main **local fashion chain stores** – *Giordano, U2, 2000* and *Bossini* – for decent-quality, value-for-money everyday wear, from shirts and jeans to jackets and socks. There are countless branches in all

Clothing and Shoe Sizes

Dresses

USA	8	10	12	14	16	18	20
UK	10	12	14	16	18	20	22
Continental	40	42	44	46	48	50	52

Women's shoes

USA	4.5	5.5	6.5	7.5	8.5	9.5
UK	3	4	5	6	7	8
Continental	35.5	36.5	37.5	38.5	39.5	40.5

Men's suits/coats

USA	36	38	40	42	44	46
UK	36	38	40	42	44	46
Continental	46	48	50	52	54	56

Men's shirts

USA	14	15	16	17
UK	14	15	16	17
Continental	36	38	41	43

Men's shoes

USA	6	7	8	9	10	11
UK	6	7	8	9	10	11
Continental	39	41	42	43	44	46

Shopping

areas of the city. Or track down the **factory outlets** (see below), where designer shirts and jackets with snipped-out labels really start to save you money. For other ideas, visit the various **markets** (p.292) that specialize in clothes – Stanley Market is famous for its **silk** – and don't neglect the department stores (see below), either. The Japanese department stores are particularly good on designer labels; the Chinese products stores are excellent for fabrics.

Factory outlets

One unusual aspect of shopping in Hong Kong is the chance to buy something from a wide variety of **factory outlets** – in commercial buildings selling clothes, fabrics and jewellery direct to the public. Prices here are very competitive, either because there's no retail mark-up, or because you're buying seconds whose imperfections are minimal. The HKTA puts out a brochure, *Factory Outlets*, which details all the main clothing and jewellery businesses that deal in this way, as well as opening times and the average prices of the goods on offer. Some of the shops provide free transport, so if you know what you want, ring first and see if it's worth the trip.

Two areas to browse in are along **Granville Road** in Tsim Sha Tsui (off Nathan Rd), which has a long run of cheap, discount clothing shops; and around **Man Yue Street/Man Lok Street** in Hung Hom, where there are lots of jewellery and clothing businesses. Also try Johnston Road in Wan Chai; the shops near the Caroline Centre in Causeway Bay; and the many stores around Lai Chi Kok MTR station.

Tailors

Hong Kong has always been famous for the speed and good value of its **tailors**, but whatever you've heard, if you're foolish enough to buy a suit made in 24 hours, it either won't fit, will fall apart, or both. You'll need at least two or three fittings for a decent tailor to make you a decent suit, spread over several days, and though it won't be spectacularly cheap it will be considerably better value than the same suit made at home. Personal recommendation is the best way to find a tailor in Hong Kong, but if you are willing to spend the money, it's safe to go to one of the long-established tailors in the arcades of the main hotels. Or visit *Sam's Tailors*, 94 Nathan Road, Tsim Sha Tsui; almost a Hong Kong institution.

Computers

Hong Kong is an excellent place to stock up on hardware and software, but be warned that there's a huge piracy problem. Always check that what you're buying is compatible with your country's electrical system. You'll need to check customs' requirements for some purchases, too. The main places to head for include:

Asia Computer Plaza, Lower Ground Floor, Silvercord, 30 Canton Rd, Tsim Sha Tsui; and 2nd Floor, Star House, Salisbury Rd, Tsim Sha Tsui. Reliable computer malls with specialist computer bookshop, too.

Golden Shopping Arcade, 156 Fuk Wah St, Sham Shui Po, Kowloon. Famous for its supply of cheap computer goods, but notorious as a centre for pirate gear.

Windsor House, 311 Gloucester Rd, Causeway Bay. Useful Hong Kong-side computer arcade.

Department stores

One of Hong Kong's great joys is the diverse selection of mammoth, air-conditioned **department stores**, owned by parent companies from different countries; pick your culture and dive in. Most have cafés and coffee shops inside, too.

Chinese products stores

All the following department stores specialize in products made in mainland China – clothes, silk, furniture, antiques, herbal medicines, fine art, porcelain, electrical goods, jewellery – and there are some occasional bargains to be had.

China Products, 19–31 Yee Wo St, Causeway Bay; 488–500 Hennessy Rd, Causeway Bay.

China Resources Artland Centre Department Store, China Resources Building, Low Block, 26 Harbour Rd, Wan Chai.

Chinese Arts and Crafts, Shell House, 24 Queen's Rd, Central; 230 The Mall, Pacific Place, 88 Queensway, Central; Ground Floor, Prince's Building, 3 Des Voeux Rd, Central; Star House, 3 Salisbury Rd, Tsim Sha Tsui; Silvercord, 30 Canton Rd, Tsim Sha Tsui; 233–239 Nathan Rd, Yau Ma Tei.

Chinese Merchandise Emporium, Chiao Shang Building, 92–104 Queen's Rd, Central.

Chung Kiu Chinese Products Emporium, 17 Hankow Rd, Tsim Sha Tsui; 528–532 Nathan Rd, Yau Ma Tei; 47–51 Shan Tung St, Mongkok.

Shanghai Tang, Pedder Building, Pedder St/Theatre Lane, Central.

Yue Hwa Chinese Products Emporium, Mirador Mansion, 54–64 Nathan Rd, Tsim Sha Tsui; Park Lane Shoppers' Boulevard, 143–161 Nathan Rd, Tsim Sha Tsui; 301–309 Nathan Rd, Yau Ma Tei.

Hong Kong stores

Lane Crawford, 70 Queen's Rd, Central; Levels 1–3, The Mall, One Pacific Place, 88 Queensway, Admiralty; Ground Floor, Windsor House, 311 Gloucester Rd, Causeway Bay; Ground Floor, 74 Nathan Rd, Tsim Sha Tsui; Shop 100, Ocean Terminal, Harbour City, 3 Canton Rd, Tsim Sha Tsui. Hong Kong's oldest Western-style department store – the first branch listed is the main one.

Sincere, 173 Des Voeux Rd, Central; 83 Argyle St, Mongkok. A more downmarket store, though with the same range of products; the Argyle St branch is good for shoes.

Wing On, 26 Des Voeux Rd, Central; 211 Des Voeux Rd, Central; 183 Queen's Rd East, Wan Chai; Cityplaza I, 1111 King's Rd, Taikoo Shing; 361 Nathan Rd, Yau Ma Tei; Wing On Plaza, 62 Mody Rd, Tsim Sha Tsui East; Site 11, Whampoa Garden, 6 Tak Hong St, Hung Hom. Standard department store with branches all over the territory, good for day-to-day items.

Japanese stores

Daimaru, Household Square, Kingston St, Causeway Bay; Fashion Square, Paterson St/Great George St, Causeway Bay. The first branch has a Japanese supermarket and snack bar and specializes in household goods, the second is mainly fashion and sportswear. Closed Wed.

Matsuzakaya, Hang Lung Centre, 2–20 Paterson St, Causeway Bay. Good for clothes; closed Thurs.

Mitsukoshi, Hennessy Centre, 500 Hennessy Rd, Causeway Bay; Sun Plaza, 28 Canton Rd, Tsim Sha Tsui. Flashest of all the Causeway Bay stores.

Seibu, Pacific Place, 88 Queensway, Admiralty. Perhaps the most upscale Japanese store, just the place to kit out your company apartment.

Sogo, East Point Centre, 555 Hennessy Rd, Causeway Bay. Ten floors' worth of consumerism, including a good Japanese supermarket.

Yaohan, Ground Floor, Whampoa Garden, Hung Hom; New Town Plaza, 18 Sha Tin Centre Rd, Sha Tin, New Territories; Tuen Mun Town Plaza, Tuen Mun, New Territories. Useful New Territories chain of department stores.

Other stores

Marks & Spencer, Shop 120 & 229, The Mall, Two Pacific Place, 88 Queensway, Admiralty; Ground–2nd Floor, Excelsior Plaza, East Point Rd, Causeway Bay; Shop 313–316 & 418–421, Times Square, 1 Matheson St, Causeway Bay; Shop 102 & 254, Ocean Centre, Harbour City, 5 Canton Rd, Tsim Sha Tsui. Classic British department store selling sensible underwear, even in the Far East.

Food and drink

For a list of **bakeries**, **delicatessens**, **takeaways** and **supermarkets**, consult the relevant sections of Chapter 7. You'll find accounts of **markets** where you can buy food throughout the book. The main ones

Shopping

Shopping

Learn to say gay dor chin? (how much is it?), the numbers (see p.397), the word for dollar (mahn), catty (gan) and ounce (onsi), and you might just be able to buy something in a Hong Kong market.

are Central and Sheung Wan markets (Chapter 2); Temple Street Night Market (Chapter 3); and Luen Wo Market and Sheung Shui Market (both Chapter 4).

For **wines and spirits** and other drinks, most of the supermarkets have adequate selections: *Yaohan* in Sha Tin and *Wellcome* in The Forum, Exchange Square, Central, are particularly well stocked. A good specialist shop is *Remy Fine Wines* (117 Swire Arcade, Swire House, Central; and elsewhere), worth checking for bin end sales and other offers.

For buying food in markets, you need to know that **Chinese weights and measures** are different from Western ones. Most things (vegetables, beansprouts, rice, dried foods) are sold by the **catty**, which is the equivalent of 1.3 lb or 600g; the smaller unit is the **tael**, equivalent to 1.3 oz or 38g. That said, unless you can speak and read Chinese, you'll probably find that simply picking up the amount you want and handing it to the stallholder is the best way to go about things. Fruit is sold by the piece or the pound, meat and fish by the ounce.

Jewellery

Jewellery prices are relatively low in Hong Kong (since precious stones can be imported without paying duty) and there are probably more jewellers' shops in the territory than any other kind. If you're going to buy, first get hold of the HKTA's free *Shopping Guide to Jewellery*, which explains about the different quality and grade of various precious stones sold in Hong Kong. This is particularly important if you're buying **jade**, which is very popular here: there's a special Jade Market in Kansu Street, Yau Ma Tei (see p.133).

If you need help or information on buying **diamonds**, you can contact the *Diamond Importers' Association Ltd*, Room 1707, Parker House, 70 Queen's Rd, Central ☎ 2523 5497.

For **opals**, a fun place to visit – without any pressure to buy at all – is *The Opal Mine* (Burlington House, Ground Floor, 92 Nathan Rd, Tsim Sha Tsui), an informative exhibition on the mining of opal in Australia, where ninety percent of the world's opal comes from. It also describes its manufacture as jewellery, and details how to distinguish between the various types.

Markets: clothes, fabrics and bric-a-brac

You'll get the cheapest clothes and fabrics in markets, but shop around and haggle. You'll not be able to try anything on and you'll never be able to take anything back, but be sensible and you shouldn't go too far wrong. The list below is just a round-up; full details appear in the text at the given page number.

Jade Market, Kansu St, Yau Ma Tei. Jade jewellery, artefacts and statues; p.133.

Jardine's Bazaar, Causeway Bay. Clothes and household goods; p.103.

Li Yuen Street East and West, Central. Women's and children's clothes; p.75.

Man Wa Lane, Sheung Wan. Traditional Chinese seals; p.81.

Marble Street, North Point. Shirts and shorts; p.115.

Stanley Market, Stanley Village. Clothes, silk, cashmere, fake designer labels a speciality; p.113.

Temple Street, Yau Ma Tei. The best night market: clothes, tapes, watches, jewellery, digital bits and pieces, everything; p.134.

Tung Choi Street, Mongkok. Women's and children's clothes and accessories; p.136.

Upper Lascar Row, Central. Flea market; p.84.

Western Market, Sheung Wan. Fabrics, arts and crafts; p.81.

Music: CDs and tapes

You'll be able to buy most mainstream CDs and tapes (laser discs too) in Hong Kong: prices are generally around twenty to thirty percent lower than in the UK (and slightly higher than in the US). Check out the locally produced Canto-pop releases, as well as recordings of mainland Chinese artists. Note that artists are almost always filed under first names.

Chick's Collection, 2nd Floor, 22 Wood Rd, Wan Chai. Rare and retro stuff, with a large stock of vinyl, too.

Chungking Mansions, 36–44 Nathan Rd, Tsim Sha Tsui. Cheap tapes and CDs at various stalls inside Nathan Road's most labyrinthine shopping centre.

DoReMi Records, D16, Queensway Plaza, 93 Queensway, Admiralty. A bit limited in range, but with the odd bargain.

Good Times Music Store, Shop 109, Ocean Centre, Harbour City, 5 Canton Rd, Tsim Sha Tsui. You can listen to your selection before buying here.

Hong Kong Records, Shop 252, The Mall, Pacific Place, 88 Queensway, Admiralty. Good mixture of styles and prices; no vinyl in sight, despite the name.

HMV, Swire House, Connaught Rd, Central; Windsor House, Great George St, Causeway Bay; Sand Building, Peking Rd, Tsim Sha Tsui. Megastores with listening stations and a mammoth choice, as good for World and Canto-pop as Western releases.

Satellite Record Co, B9–10, United Centre, Queensway Plaza, 93 Queensway, Admiralty. Good for classical music.

Tower Records, 7th Floor, Times Square, 1 Matheson St, Causeway Bay. Huge selection of music (often a few dollars less than *HMV*), with in-store appearances to pull in the punters.

Works Record Company, 38 Hankow Rd, Tsim Sha Tsui. Mainly Canto-pop and classical, though a fair amount of Western pop and rock, with lots of bootleg CDs.

Shopping malls

Even if you hate shopping, it's impossible to avoid walking through a **shopping mall** on any visit to Hong Kong, since half the pedestrian overpasses and walkways in Central and Tsim Sha Tsui East pass straight through one or more of them. You're not even immune in hotels – most of the larger ones have ground-floor arcades so that you run the gauntlet on every trip in and out. You may as

well accept that you're going to see the inside of more shopping malls than you thought existed; you may even enjoy them, since they are at least air-conditioned.

The main concentrations are in Central, Tsim Sha Tsui and Tsim Sha Tsui East, with a few in Causeway Bay and a couple of other major malls in the New Territories. They are almost sights in themselves, gleaming, climate-controlled consumer paradises, filled with slick, chic shops, serviced by state-of-the-art elevators and computer directories, enlivened by galleries, lights and fountains, and sustained by bars, cafés and restaurants. All the important ones are covered in the text, but a quick checklist of the best includes:

Cityplaza, 111 King's Rd, Taikoo Shing.

The Landmark, Des Voeux Rd, Central.

New Town Plaza, Sha Tin, New Territories.

New World Centre, 20 Salisbury Rd, Tsim Sha Tsui.

Ocean Terminal (incorporating *Harbour City* and *Ocean Centre*), Canton Rd, Tsim Sha Tsui.

Pacific Place Mall, 88 Queensway, Admiralty.

Prince's Building, Chater Rd, Central.

Shun Tak Centre, 200 Connaught Rd, Sheung Wan.

Swire House, Connaught Rd, Central.

Times Square, 1 Matheson St, Causeway Bay.

Tea shops

Buying **Chinese tea** in little tins and boxes is a nice idea for a souvenir, and Hong Kong has lots of specialist tea shops, some of which are listed below. Buy in small amounts, from any of a hundred different types, since tea loses its flavour over long periods of time, and don't be afraid to ask if you can taste various varieties. Not all shops will oblige, but some are quite prepared to let you taste before you make your choice.

Shopping

Shopping

Best Tea House, 3 Lock Rd, Tsim Sha Tsui; Unit 201, Causeway Bay Plaza II, 463–483 Lockhart Rd, Causeway Bay.

Chan Chuan Lan Tea Co., 26 Cochrane St, Central.

Chinese Merchandise Emporium, 92–104 Queen's Rd, Central.

Fook Ming Tong Tea Shop, Ground Floor, Shop 5C, Prince's Building, Ice House St, Central; Western Market, 323 Des Voeux Rd, Sheung Wan; LG3, *Mitsukoshi*, Hennessy Centre, 500 Hennessy Rd, Causeway Bay; Shop 200A, Ocean Terminal, Harbour City, Canton Rd, Tsim Sha Tsui.

Kee Heung Chun Tea Co., 67 Wellington St, Central.

Tea Zen, 290 Queen's Rd, Sheung Wan.

Ying Kee, 151 Queen's Rd, Central; 170 Johnston Rd, Wan Chai; LG1, Two Pacific Place, 88 Queensway, Admiralty; 139 Shanghai St, Yau Ma Tei; 446A Nathan Rd, Yau Ma Tei.

Chapter 13

Sport

The only drawback to Hong Kong's varied range of **sporting opportunities** is the inevitable lack of space for such things. **To play** some sports – particularly racquet sports – you'll have to book well in advance, or just be lucky with vacancies, which is why so many residential buildings have private sports facilities. Still, as a tourist, you will be able to find something energetic to do, and all the possibilities are detailed below in alphabetical order, with advice on how to participate. **Spectator sports** are more limited, primarily because the territory's available space restricts the number of stadiums and sports grounds, not to mention teams. That said, there are events throughout the year – some of them of international standard – and again, you'll find details below.

The major municipal stadiums and sports grounds are run by the Urban Council, whose free monthly magazine *City News* (from City Hall) carries a "Sports Diary" listing current events and competitions. For more information, contact the **Sports Promotion Office** at the territory's main sporting venue, the **Queen Elizabeth Stadium**, 18 Oi Kwan Rd, Wan Chai ☎ 2591 1346.

One privately run sports centre is the **Hong Kong Sports Institute** in Sha Tin (☎ 2681 6188), which has excellent facilities and is open to non-members during off-peak hours (Mon–Fri 8am–6pm). Ring for information if you're interested, and see the various sports listings below. A second centre offering visitor's passes for $30 is the **South China Athletic Association**

(Caroline Hill, Causeway Bay; ☎ 2577 6932, membership enquiries ☎ 2577 4427), founded in 1904 and with facilities for all kinds of sports and keep-fit activities.

Finally, you can let someone else do the organizing by signing on for the HKTA's **sports and recreation tour** (information from any HKTA office). Around $400 gets you a day-return trip to the Clearwater Bay Golf and Country Club, in the Sai Kung peninsula, which includes admission, lunch and transport. On top of this, you'll pay $45 for swimming, sauna and jacuzzi, $70 an hour for squash, badminton and tennis; and a much heftier charge if you want to play golf. You have to book a day in advance (departures are at around 7.30am). There's a bar and restaurants there, too.

Badminton

You can rent **badminton** courts for $60–80 an hour at the two places listed below, or play at the *Clearwater Bay Golf and Country Club* (see introduction, above). More general information is available from the **Hong Kong Badminton Association** ☎ 2504 8318.

Hong Kong Sports Institute, Sha Tin ☎ 2681 1688. Off-peak hours only for visitors; Mon–Fri 8am–6pm, Sat 8am–1pm.

Queen Elizabeth Stadium, 18 Oi Kwan Rd, Wan Chai ☎ 2591 1346.

Bowling

For **ten-pin bowling**, try one of the bowling alleys below. At either, you'll pay

Sport

around $50 an hour; avoiding weekends is a good idea, as alleys are extremely popular. For **lawn bowls**, which also costs from around $50 an hour, try the green at Victoria Park, Causeway Bay (☎2570 6186).

South China Bowling Centre, 88 Caroline Hill Rd, Causeway Bay ☎2890 8528. Open 10am–midnight.

Top Bowl Ltd, Whampoa Garden, Hung Hom ☎2764 0811. Open 9am–1am.

Fishing

The **fishing** season in Hong Kong's reservoirs lasts from September to March; if you're over thirteen, you can get a licence from the Water Supplies Department, 7 Gloucester Rd, Wan Chai (☎2824 5000). They'll also give you information about what you can and can't catch.

Golf

Golf is a pricey sport in Hong Kong, and you'll have to be keen to make the arrangements to play at the various clubs in the territory. The **Hong Kong Open Golf Championship** is held every February. Less serious golf is catered for by the **minigolf** course at Shek O, right by the beach, and a similar set-up, with a driving range, at Sha Tin's New Town Plaza.

Clearwater Bay Golf and Country Club ☎2335 1271. The HKTA runs an inclusive day trip to this club. Green fees on the *Executive Nine* course are around $450, golf cart and clubs extra; playing the 18-hole championship course starts at $1000.

Discovery Bay, Lantau ☎2987 7273. Among the newest of Hong Kong's golf clubs, with a course spectacularly laid out on top of the island's hills. Fees

> You can't play **golf** on a whim in Hong Kong. Clothes specifically banned from the greens include tracksuits, T-shirts, collarless shirts, shorts which are more than four inches above the knee, jeans, vests and bathing gear. If you're going to play, pack or buy accordingly.

here are around $900 from Monday to Friday, weekends around $1600, plus extras.

Hong Kong Golf Club, Fanling, New Territories ☎2670 1211. The territory's major club, and site of the HK Open, there are three 18-hole courses at which visitors can play on weekdays for around $1400 per person (Hong Kong residents $1200), plus caddies and clubs. The *RHKGC* also operates a course at Deep Water Bay on Hong Kong Island (☎2812 7070), which costs visitors around $450 plus extras, again on weekdays only (9.30am–1.30pm). You should book well in advance for all these courses.

Shek O Golf and Country Club ☎2809 4458. The swishest golf course, on the south side of Hong Kong Island, open to members only – with membership restricted to only three hundred people.

Horses: racing and riding

The only sport in Hong Kong to command true mass appeal, **horse racing** is a spectating must if you're here during the season, which runs from September to May. There are two courses, both run by the **Hong Kong Jockey Club**: the original one at Happy Valley (☎2966 8111) and a much newer, state-of-the-art affair at Sha Tin in the New Territories (☎2692 0542), to which the HKTA can organize tours and tickets for the enclosures. If you want to go on your own, and not as part of a package, then take your passport to the racecourse a couple of days before the races (over-18s only) and the *HKJC* will sell you a guest badge for $50; or you can just turn up and pay $10 to get into the public stands. See p.105 and p.150 for full details of each course.

If you want to get on the back of one of the beasts, then there are a couple of places where you can go **horse riding**, though it's necessarily a limited option given the terrain. Contact **Tuen Mun Riding**, Lot 45, Lung Mun Rd, Tuen Mun (☎2461 3338), where lessons start from $275 per hour, or the **Pokfulam Public Riding School**, at 75 Reservoir Rd,

Pokfulam, Hong Kong Island Sept–June only; closed Mon (☎ 2550 1359), which costs around $340 an hour for lessons – book well in advance. This also has riding facilities designed for disabled people, and long waiting lists, especially for beginners.

Indoor sports: snooker, billiards, pool and darts

There are dozens of private clubs at which you can play table games like **billiards**, **snooker** and **pool**. You usually have to join, though sometimes you only need pay a nominal fee, and then pay for your games. Look in the Yellow Pages (under "Billiards") for a club near you and ring for opening hours and membership details before setting out. You can also usually get a game at *Top Bowl*, Whampoa Garden, Hung Hom (☎ 2764 0811).

Less formal is a game of **darts** in one of the pubs. Several have boards (including the *Kangaroo Pub* in Tsim Sha Tsui); check the pub listings in Chapter 8 for more possibilities.

The best place for all these games is *Jimmy's Sports Bar & Grill*, the **sports bar** at the Hong Kong Stadium (55 Eastern Hospital Rd, So Kon Po, Happy Valley; ☎ 2882 2165). As well as pool and darts, there's table soccer and hockey, and big-screen action for all the major sports events.

Martial arts

As in China, **martial arts** are phenomenally popular in Hong Kong, where every second film released features combat of some sort or other. Though born in the United States, **Bruce Lee** (1940–73) spent the later part of his childhood in Hong Kong, and every kid still wants to be him, or one of the dozens of other movie practitioners who have emerged since. Bruce's actor son, Brandon Lee, died tragically young like his father, in an accident on a film set in 1993; meanwhile Jackie Chan remains one of the most prolific of the current stars – you'll see his name everywhere in magazines and on film posters.

The martial art you see most of in Hong Kong outside the cinema, however, is **tai chi**, also known as shadow boxing – a series of slow, balletic exercises designed to stimulate both the mind and the body. Early morning in most of the parks and gardens is the best time to watch or participate in this extraordinarily uplifting exercise. Popular venues include Kowloon Park, Victoria Park, Chater Gardens and the Botanical and Zoological Gardens.

Hong Kong Chinese Martial Arts Association, 687 Nathan Rd ☎ 2394 4803.

Hong Kong Tai Chi Association, 60 Argyle St, Mongkok ☎ 2395 4884.

Rugby

Rugby (Union, not League) is generally of a good standard and each Easter a couple of days are devoted to a series of Rugby Sevens matches, with international teams competing for the prize – though this is largely an excuse for the expats to get drunk. The event is organized by the **Hong Kong Rugby Football Union** (Room 2003/ 4, Sports House, 1 Stadium Path, So Kon Po, Happy Valley; ☎ 2504 8300), which can provide more information and tell you how to go about joining a team in Hong Kong.

Running: jogs, runs and marathons

You'll see people **jogging** at dozens of places throughout the territory, some of

Sport

Sport

which have marked routes and exercise stops along the way. A few of the most popular spots are along Bowen Road in Mid-Levels; around the roads at the top of Victoria Peak; along the Tsim Sha Tsui East waterfront; around Victoria Park, Causeway Bay; and in Kowloon Park, off Nathan Road. If you do run or jog, remember that the summer heat and humidity are crippling; run in the early morning or evening and take some water along.

Two annual **races** to watch out for are the **Hong Kong Marathon**, held in January, and the **Coast of China Marathon**, which takes place in the first week of March. You can get information, and entry forms, for the HK Marathon from the *Hong Kong Amateur Athletic Association* (☎ 2504 8215); for the Coast of China from *Athletic Promotions Ltd* (☎ 2573 5292). Both events start early, and in the past the Hong Kong Marathon has attracted a large contingent of disabled athletes in wheelchairs.

More offbeat running is provided by the **Orienteering Association of Hong Kong** (Room 1014, Sports House, 1 Stadium Path, So Kon Po, Happy Valley; ☎ 2504 8111), which runs an orienteering course in Pokfulam Country Park on Hong Kong Island. The Association issues a map showing the course, which you can get by writing to them.

Skating

There are two **ice-skating** rinks in Hong Kong and a fairly central **roller-skating** rink, too. On the streets, the pedestrian walkways in Central and the Tsim Sha Tsui East waterfront are alive with **skateboarders and rollerbladers**.

Ice-skating

Cityplaza Ice Palace, Cityplaza, Taikoo Shing ☎ 2885 4697; Taikoo Shing MTR. Open 7am–10pm (closed Sun morning); $45 all day during the week, $55 for two hours at the weekend, including the skates.

Whampoa Super Ice, Whampoa Garden, Hung Hom ☎ 2774 4899. Open 10am–

11pm; two-hour sessions $40 weekday, $50 weekend, including skates.

Roller-skating

Sportsworld Association, Telford Gardens, Kowloon Bay ☎ 2757 2211. Open 9am–11pm; $40 a session.

Soccer

Soccer is widely played throughout the territory, Hong Kong's First Division littered with has-been or never-were players from other countries (mostly Britain) – teams are allowed five overseas players. Good local talent is fairly thin on the ground, but games can be entertaining, not least because the foreign players tend to be bought as strikers – and consequently face local defences comprised of people much shorter than themselves.

If you're sufficiently interested, teams to watch are Happy Valley, South China and Eastern. The "national team", such as it is, usually has a torrid time in the World Cup qualifying matches, making heavy weather against such footballing giants as Bahrain and Lebanon. The best advice for soccer fans is to find a TV on Saturday evenings during the English soccer season, when you get an hour's worth of the previous week's top English matches; most major cup and international matches are televised live, too.

Squash

Squash is about the most popular indoor racquet sport. You'll need to book well in advance, and you'll pay around $50 an hour at the public courts listed below – or you can play at the *Clearwater Bay Golf and Country Club* (see introduction, above). For beginners, the Urban Council (☎ 2529 7960) organizes courses, and the **Hong Kong Squash Association** (☎ 2869 0611) has private lessons for intermediate players.

Hong Kong Sports Institute, Sha Tin ☎ 2681 6188; off-peak hours only Mon–Fri 8am–5.45pm, Sat 8am–1pm.

Hong Kong Squash Centre, Cotton Tree Drive, Central ☎ 2521 5072; book up to ten days in advance in person.

Lai Chi Kok Sports Hall, Lai Chi Kok, Kowloon ☎2745 2796.

Queen Elizabeth Stadium, 18 Oi Kwan Rd, Wan Chai ☎591 1346.

Victoria Park, Causeway Bay ☎2570 6186.

Swimming

If you don't want to risk the water at any of the territory's **beaches** – the best of which are covered in the text – then you'll have to take your dip in one of the few, and crowded, **swimming pools** operated by the Urban Council: call the Urban Services Department for information (Hong Kong ☎2832 2616; Kowloon East ☎2320 6542; Kowloon West ☎2309 1058). Some of the bigger hotels have pools, though these are usually open to residents only.

Aberdeen, 2 Shum Wah Rd, Aberdeen ☎2553 3617. Daily 7am–9pm; adults $15, children $7. Good facilities for the disabled.

Hong Kong Sports Institute, Sha Tin ☎2681 6188. You can use the pool in the off-peak hours – Mon–Sat 7–8.30am & noon–2pm, Sun 7–9am. Call first; $40 per person.

Kowloon Park, Nathan Rd, Tsim Sha Tsui ☎2724 3577. Open 6.30am–9pm; adults $17, children $8.

Kowloon Tsai, Inverness Rd, Hung Hom ☎2336 5817. Daily 7am–9pm; adults $17, children $8.

Morrison Hill, Oi Kwan Rd, Wan Chai ☎2575 3028. Daily 6.30am–9pm; adults $17, children $8.

Victoria Park, Hing Fat St, Causeway Bay ☎2570 4682. Daily 7–11.15am & 1–9.45pm; adults $17, children $8.

Tennis

Public **tennis** courts are often solidly booked, but if you can get a court you'll pay around $50 an hour. Try at one of the following places, or play at the *Clearwater Bay Golf and Country Club* (see introduction, above). The Queen Elizabeth Stadium also has the facilities for **table tennis**, which costs about half as much per hour.

Hong Kong Sports Institute, Sha Tin ☎2681 6188. Off-peak hours only for visitors; Mon–Fri 9.30am–5.45pm.

Tennis Centre, Wong Nai Chung Gap Rd, Happy Valley ☎2574 9122.

Victoria Park, Causeway Bay ☎2570 6186.

Watersports

As you might expect, there's plenty of choice for watersports in a territory of 230 islands. **Sailing** enthusiasts, who are members of an overseas club, can contact the prestigious *Hong Kong Yacht Club* on Kellet Island, Causeway Bay (☎2832 2817), which has reciprocal arrangements with many foreign clubs. The *Hong Kong Yachting Association* (☎2504 8160) operates intensive instruction courses at Clearwater Bay. For plain **boating and pleasure cruising**, contact any of the tour companies listed under "Organized Tours", p.62, or ask the HKTA for recommendations.

You can rent **windsurfing** equipment at quite a few of the territory's beaches: there are government-funded centres at Tai Po and Sai Kung where you can learn the basics fairly cheaply, or try the *Windsurf Centre* (☎2981 8316) on Kwun Yam Wan Beach on Cheung Chau (p.191), which also offers courses and rental. The *Hong Kong Windsurfing Association* (PO Box 1083, Central) can help with other enquiries.

Some beachside operations also offer **water-skiing** and **canoeing** (particularly at the Cheung Chau *Windsurf Centre*); you can get more information from the *Water-Skiing Association* (☎2504 8168).

Sport

Chapter 14

Children's Hong Kong

It's some kind of achievement in itself to have got the children unscathed through a long-haul flight, so once here it's nice to know that in many ways Hong Kong is made for them. Not that there's an enormous amount in the way of specialized activities and events, but the territory itself can be a playground. Most of the things that you'll want to do anyway – from visiting island beaches to trawling through space-age shopping malls – are of sufficient general interest to keep everyone amused. The transport, particularly the trams and ferries, is exciting, most of the views and walks more so; and there is a hard core of venues with a real family slant – Ocean Park is only the best known. The sections below should give you some ideas for day-to-day **activities**. You'll need to follow the

page references for the full accounts of each sight, activity or sport. There's also a round-up of **dangers** to be aware of if you're travelling with small children.

Outings

Base a day trip around the places and activities below, all of which can occupy several hours with kids in tow.

Hong Kong Park, Central (p.78). Enormous aviary, greenhouses, gardens, picnic areas, restaurant and excellent play areas. Also close to the pedestrian walkways that snake off into the hi-tech buildings of Central.

KCR train to Sheung Shui and back, New Territories (Chapter 4). A train ride, with stops at traditional markets, brand-new

---

Babysitting

Most large hotels can organize **babysitting** for you if you contact reception; the HKTA has a full list of ones that will oblige, if you want to check before you leave.

Playgroups and information

Playgroups and parent-toddler groups are run by a variety of organizations. Information from – among others – the *Pre-School Playgroups Association* (Mon–Fri 9am–12.45pm, term-time only; ☎ 2523 2599); *St Andrew's Church*, 138 Nathan Rd, Tsim Sha Tsui (☎ 2367 1478; playgroups every Tues & Fri); *St John's Cathedral*, Central (☎ 2523 4157; parent and childrens' group every Tuesday). There's also a bi-monthly *Mother and Baby* magazine published in Hong Kong, available in many kids' clothes stores and toddler shops.

Clothes and supplies

Hong Kong has branches of specialist store *Mothercare* (Shop 338–340, Prince's Building, Chater Rd, Central; Shop 137, Ocean Terminal, Harbour City, Canton Rd, Tsim Sha Tsui); for details of kids' clothes shops, check the listings in HKTA's *Shopping* guide (available free at HKTA offices).

---

towns and shopping centres, and a railway museum.

Ocean Park and Water World, Deep Water Bay, Hong Kong Island (pp.109–110). Multi-ride amusement and theme park, with marine animals, shows, gardens, and an adjacent slide-and-splash park.

Outlying islands (Chapter 5). Ferry rides to all the main islands, where there are beaches, walks, temples and watersports.

Sea cruises (see "Organized tours", p.62). Cruises lasting anything from an hour to a whole day through the harbour and around the outlying islands; many include a picnic lunch.

Stanley Village, Hong Kong Island (pp.111–114). Beaches, watersports, a market, rest-aurants, and a good bus ride there and back.

Sung Dynasty Village and Lai Chi Kok Amusement Park, Lai Chi Kok, Kowloon (pp.140–141). Historical Chinese theme park, waxworks museum, a small-scale amusement park and zoo.

Victoria Peak (pp.88–92). A trip up on the Peak Tram; walks around the Peak, panoramic views and picnic areas.

Whampoa Gardens, Hung Hom (p.131). Huge concrete ship-shaped shopping mall, with musical fountain, coffee shop, ice-skating rink, cinema and children's play area.

Museums and temples

The following places will interest an inquisitive child. The museums are ones where participation is encouraged – operating robots, clambering on old train carriages, walking through a renovated village – and while nearly all the temples in Hong Kong are unusual enough for most visitors, the ones listed below are particularly large and colourful.

Ching Chung Koon Temple, Tuen Mun, New Territories (pp.167–168).

Po Lin Monastery, Lantau (pp.203–204).

Railway Museum, Tai Po Market, New Territories (p.154).

Sam Tung Uk Folk Museum, Tsuen Wa New Territories (pp.162–163).

Science Museum, Science Museum Rd, Tsim Sha Tsui East (p.130).

Space Museum, Salisbury Rd, Tsim Sha Tsui (pp.126–127).

Wong Tai Sin Temple, Kowloon (p.139).

Sport

Consult Chapter 13, "Sport", for details of all **sporting activites** in Hong Kong. You should be able to persuade even the most slothful child that there's something there that they'd enjoy, whether it's bowling, skating or swimming. If you want your sport self-contained, think about the HKTA trips to the *Clearwater Bay Golf and Country Club*, where there's a variety of activities on offer in one well-equipped complex.

Entertainment

Obvious ideas include **cinemas**, which show the latest films in English; the HKTA-organized **cultural shows**, with song, dance and mime in various venues; and a visit to a **Chinese opera** for the singing and costumes. Some places, like the Arts Centre and local libraries, organize **special events** for children throughout the school summer holiday: the HKTA will have current information, or call into City Hall and look at the noticeboards, and pick up the *City News* magazine. There's more information on all these activities and events in Chapter 10.

Coinciding with one of Hong Kong's **festivals** (see pp.281–284 for details) is another way to expose kids to a bit of cultural entertainment. They'll particularly enjoy the Cheung Chau Bun Festival, the dragon boat racing, and any of the colourful Tin Hau celebrations.

Shopping

Shopping can keep children amused, too, especially when it's raining, since if you pick one of the huge shopping malls you don't have to set foot outside for hours on end, even to eat.

There's a list of the main malls on p.293; while specific **shops** that you might want to take in include the enor-

Children's
Hong Kong

Children's Hong Kong

mous *Toys R Us* (Shop 003, Basement, Ocean Terminal, Harbour City, Canton Rd, Tsim Sha Tsui; 3rd Floor, The In Square, Windsor House, 311 Gloucster Rd, Causeway Bay; Shop A197–199, Level I, New Town Plaza, Sha Tin, New Territories), and the Japanese department stores in Causeway Bay (see p.291), which feature games, toys, comics and cafés. The *Pre-School Playgroups Association* (see box on p.300) has a shop at 12 Barrett Rd, Mid-Levels, which stocks educational toys.

Eating

It's good to know that **restaurants** in Hong Kong (certainly Chinese restaurants) generally welcome kids with open arms; nearly all have high chairs available. Eating is a family affair, as a trip to any *dim sum* restaurant shows, and you don't need to worry about children running up and down the aisles and shrieking: they'll be considered abnormal if they don't.

Chapter 7 details all the eating possibilities. You can get fish and chips in Hong Kong (Yorkshire's famous *Harry Ramsden's* has a branch here), as well as pizzas, hamburgers and all manner of calorific junk, so no one needs to starve. For more of an occasion, visit one of the specialist **fish restaurants** in Lau Fau Shan (Chapter 4) or Lei Yue Mun (Chapter 3) or on one of the outlying islands (Chapter 5), where youngsters can pick dinner out of the fish tanks.

Chapter 15

Directory

AIRLINES All the airlines in Hong Kong are listed in the Yellow Pages under "Air Line Companies". The main ones include:

Aeroflot, 2nd Floor, New Henry House, 10 Ice House St, Central ☎ 2537 2611.

Air India, 42nd Floor, Gloucester Tower, The Landmark, 11 Pedder St, Central ☎ 2521 4321.

Air New Zealand, Room 601, Fairmount House, 8 Cotton Tree Drive, Central ☎ 2524 9041.

British Airways, 30th Floor, Alexandra House, 7 Des Voeux Rd, Central ☎ 2868 0303.

Cathay Pacific, 4th Floor, Swire House, 9 Connaught Rd, Central, and *Sheraton Hotel*, D1, 2nd Floor, 2 Nathan Rd, Tsim Sha Tsui ☎ 2747 5577

China Airlines, Ground Floor, St George's Building, 2 Ice House St, Central ☎ 2868 2299.

Dragon Air, 904 World Wide House, 19 Des Voeux Rd, Central ☎ 2868 6777

Emirates, 37th Floor, Room 3707–3708, Gloucester Tower, The Landmark, Central ☎ 2526 7171.

Japan Air Lines, 20th Floor, Gloucester Tower, The Landmark, 11 Pedder St, Central ☎ 2523 0081.

Korean Air, Ground Floor, St George's Building, 2 Ice House St, Central ☎ 2523 5177, and Ground Floor, Tsim Sha Tsui Centre, 66 Mody Rd, Tsim Sha Tsui East ☎ 2369 7151.

Lufthansa, 6th Floor, Landmark East, 12 Ice House St, Central ☎ 2868 2313.

Philippine Airlines, Room 1801, Swire House, 9 Connaught Rd, Central ☎ 2722 7723.

Qantas, Room 1443, Swire House, 9 Connaught Rd, Central ☎ 842 1430.

SAS, Room 1401, Harcourt House, 39 Gloucester Rd, Wan Chai ☎ 2865 1370.

Singapore Airlines, 17th Floor, United Centre, 95 Queensway, Admiralty ☎ 2520 2233.

Swissair, 8th Floor, Tower II, Admiralty Centre, 18 Harcourt Rd, Admiralty ☎ 2529 3670.

Thai International, Shop 122, 1st Floor, World Wide Plaza, Pedder St, Central ☎ 2529 5601.

United Airlines, 29th Floor, Gloucester Tower, The Landmark, 11 Pedder St, Central ☎ 2810 4888.

AIRPORT ENQUIRIES Hong Kong International (Kai Tak) Airport ☎ 2769 7531. For *Airbus* routes and times, call ☎ 2745 4466.

AMBULANCE Call ☎ 999, or the St John's Ambulance Brigade, which runs a free ambulance service – on ☎ 2576 6555 (Hong Kong Island), ☎ 2713 5555 (Kowloon) or ☎ 2639 2555 (New Territories).

AMERICAN EXPRESS Ground Floor, New World Tower, 16–18 Queen's Rd, Central (Mon–Fri 9am–5.30pm, Sat 9am–noon; ☎ 2811 7000); report stolen cheques on ☎ 2885 9366.

AMNESTY INTERNATIONAL The local branch of the campaigning organization is

Directory

at 3rd Floor, Besto Best Building, Unit C, 32–36 Ferry St, Kowloon ☎ 2300 1251.

BANKS AND EXCHANGE There are banks of every nationality and description throughout Hong Kong, seemingly on every street corner. Opening hours are Mon–Fri 9am–4.30pm, Sat 9am–12.30pm, with small fluctuations – half an hour each side – from branch to branch. Most charge commission for exchanging travellers' cheques (around $50 per transaction), though generally, the *Hang Seng Bank, Wing Lung Bank, Wing On Bank* and the *Union Bank of Hong Kong* don't. There's no commission either if you change *American Express* or *Thomas Cook* cheques at their respective offices (see above and below). You can also change money and cheques at a licensed money changer – there are several in Tsim Sha Tsui which are open late (and on Sun). They won't rip you off, but they do charge a big commission (around 9 percent of the sum changed). The signs on the windows of the moneychangers which say "No Commission" only apply if you're *selling* Hong Kong dollars. Otherwise, you can change travellers' cheques and cash at the big hotels and in some stores, but the rates will be lower than at the bank.

BIKE RENTAL Not an option in central Hong Kong, though possible on the islands and in the New Territories. Check with the HKTA, or contact the *Hong Kong Cycling Association*, at the Queen Elizabeth Stadium, 18 Oi Kwan Rd, Wan Chai ☎ 2573 3861, fax 2834 3715.

BRITISH COUNCIL At 255 Hennessy Rd, Wan Chai ☎ 2879 5145; bus #11 stops outside. There's a lending library on the first floor (Mon, Tues, Thurs & Fri 9.30am–8.30pm, Wed noon–8.30pm, Sat 10am–5pm) which costs $160 a year to join, a reference library with the same opening times, and British newspapers available. For French and German equivalents, see "Cultural Groups" below.

CAR PARKS The biggest garaging firm is *Wilson*, which, among other places, has car parks at Kowloon (Hung Hom) Station, City Hall (Central), 310 Gloucester Rd and 475 Lockhart Rd; other central car parks are at Exchange Square and Prince's Building.

CAR RENTAL You'll pay from around $620 a day, $2900 a week, for the smallest available car. You need to be over 18 (25 with some firms), have been driving for at least a year, and have a valid overseas driving licence (with which you can drive in Hong Kong for a year) or an international driving licence. Remember that you drive on the left. Agencies include: *Avis*, Ground Floor, Bonaventure House, 85 Leighton Rd, Causeway Bay ☎ 2890 6988 and Zung Fu Car Park Building, 50 Po Loi St, Hung Hom ☎ 2334 6007; and *Intercontinental Hire Cars Ltd*, 21st Floor, Lane Crawford House, 70 Queen's Rd, Central ☎ 2532 1388.

CONSULATES AND EMBASSIES British citizens who need consular assistance, particularly with regard to passport issues, should contact the *Hong Kong Immigration Department*, 7 Gloucester Rd, Wan Chai ☎ 2829 3000. The other main consulates and embassies are:

Australia, Harbour Centre, 23rd Floor, 25 Harbour Rd, Wan Chai ☎ 2827 8881.

Canada, 14th Floor, One Exchange Square, Central ☎ 2810 4321.

China, 5th Floor, China Resources Building, Lower Block, 26 Harbour Rd, Wan Chai ☎ 2827 1881.

India, 16th Floor, 16D, United Centre, 95 Queensway, Central ☎ 2528 4028.

Indonesia, 127 Leighton Rd, Causeway Bay ☎ 2890 4421.

Ireland, 22nd Floor, Prince's Building, 10 Chater Rd, Central ☎ 2826 2798

Japan, 46th Floor, One Exchange Square, Central ☎ 2522 1184.

Korea, 5th Floor, Far East Financial Centre, 16 Harcourt Rd, Central ☎ 2527 2724.

Malaysia, 50 Gloucester Rd, Malaysia Building, 23rd Floor, Wan Chai ☎ 2527 0921.

New Zealand, Room 2705, Jardine House, Connaught Rd, Central ☎ 2525 5044.

Philippines, 22nd Floor, Wah Kwong Regent Centre, 88 Queen's Rd, Central ☎ 2866 8738.

Portugal, 10th Floor, Two Exchange Square, Connaught Place, Central ☎ 2523 1338.

Singapore, Admiralty Centre Tower One, Unit 901, 9th Floor, 18 Harcourt Rd, Admiralty ☎ 2527 2212.

South Africa, 27th Floor, Sunning Plaza, 10 Hysan Ave, Causeway Bay ☎ 2577 3279.

Thailand, 8th Floor, Fairmont House, 8 Cotton Tree Drive, Central ☎ 2521 6481.

Taiwan, 4th Floor, East Tower, Lippo Centre, 89 Queensway, Admiralty ☎ 2525 8315.

USA, 26 Garden Rd, Central ☎ 2523 9011.

Vietnam, 15th Floor, Great Smart Tower, 230 Wanchai Rd, Wan Chai ☎ 2591 4510 or ☎ 2591 4517.

CONTRACEPTION Condoms are available in supermarkets, the Pill on prescription from pharmacists. For anything else, contact a Family Planning Clinic: the HQ is at Ground Floor, 8B, Wing Lot House, Fu Loi Estate, Cheung Wan ☎ 2493 3318. There's a more central clinic at 130 Hennessy Rd, Wan Chai ☎ 2575 4477.

COUNSELLING AND ADVICE *Community Advice Bureau*, St John's Cathedral New Hall, 8 Garden Rd, Central ☎ 2815 5444 (Mon–Fri 9.30am–4pm), deals with day-to-day problems and advice for newcomers and tourists. The *AIDS Concern* counselling service is on ☎ 2898 4422 (Thurs & Sat 7–10pm); *Alcoholics Anonymous* on ☎ 2522 5665 (daily 6–7pm). The *Samaritans* have an English-speaking 24-hour service; call ☎ 2896 0000.

COUNTRY PARKS The *Country Parks Division*, Agriculture and Fisheries Dept, 12th Floor, 393 Canton Rd, Kowloon (Mon–Fri 9am–5pm, Sat 9am–noon; ☎ 2733 2132) has information and trail maps for all Hong Kong's country parks.

COURIER FLIGHTS For international courier flights, contact *Cathay Pacific* ☎ 2735 2163, *Airtropolis Express* (for *Singapore Airlines*) ☎ 2751 6186, *Bridges Worldwide* ☎ 2305 1412, or *Jupiter Air* ☎ 2735 1946.

CULTURAL GROUPS *Alliance Française*, 123 Hennessy Rd, 2nd Floor, Wan Chai (Mon–Fri 10am–1pm & 2–6pm; bus #11

passes by) has a French-language library and films; there's a second branch at 52 Jordan Rd, Kowloon ☎ 2730 3257. The *Goethe Institute*, 14th Floor, Hong Kong Arts Centre, 2 Harbour Rd, Wan Chai (Mon–Fri 9.30am–7.45pm; ☎ 2802 0088) has a general-purpose German-language library (as well as some English-language books), and also newspapers and a video library.

DENTISTS Dentists are listed in the Yellow Pages (under "Dental Practitioners"); or you can ring the *Hong Kong Dental Association* (☎ 2528 5327) for a list of qualified dentists. Treatment is expensive.

DEPARTURE TAX Airport departure tax is $50 for anyone over 12.

DISABLED TRAVELLERS For a full rundown of services, pick up a copy of the *Guide to Public Transport Services in Hong Kong for Disabled Persons*, issued by the Transport Department (41st Floor, Immigration Tower, Gloucester Rd, Wan Chai). In particular, a special twelve-seater bus service, *Rehabus*, operates a scheduled service on 34 routes in the territory, as well as a dial-a-ride service; phone the *Hong Kong Society for Rehabilitation* on ☎ 2817 8154 in advance to make a reservation. Other useful numbers include: *Hong Kong Red Cross* ☎ 2802 0021 (wheelchair loans and other services); *Hong Kong Society for the Blind* ☎ 2778 8332; *Hong Kong Society for the Deaf* ☎ 2527 8969.

DOCTORS Look in the Yellow Pages (under "Physicians and Surgeons"), or contact the reception desk in the larger hotels. Most doctors speak English. You'll have to pay for a consultation and any medicines they prescribe, which will cost around $350 for anything fairly basic; pick up the medicine at the doctor's surgery and ask for a receipt for your insurance. It's cheaper to visit the nearest local government clinic (often with the words "Jockey Club" in the title, since that's who partly funds them): they stay open late, and you'll only pay a few dollars if you need a basic prescription or treatment at the casualty desk – though you may have to queue. All the clinics are listed in the

Directory

Directory

Hong Kong phone book (at the beginning, in the Government directory).

DRESS As you would in any city where it's usually hot and humid, though bear in mind that a lot of the smarter hotels and restaurants insist on some kind of dress code: no shorts, sandals or flip-flops if you're going for tea at the *Peninsula* and a jacket and tie if you're eating in an expense-account restaurant. For formal dinners, you'll need the penguin suit and tie rental services of *Tuxe Top Co. Ltd,* 1st Floor, 18 Hennessy Rd, Wan Chai & 3rd Floor, 16 Peking Rd, Tsim Sha Tsui (both branches open daily 10am–7pm).

DRY CLEANING There are shops inside the MTR stations at Jordan, Admiralty, Causeway Bay, Central and Tsim Sha Tsui.

ELECTRICITY Current is 200 volts AC. Plugs are either square three-pin or two round pins, so a travel plug is useful.

EMERGENCIES Call ☎999 for Fire, Police or Ambulance; also see "Ambulance", "Counselling and Advice" and "Doctors" above, and "Hospitals" below.

ENVIRONMENTAL MATTERS Contact *Friends of the Earth* (2nd Floor, 53–55 Lockhart Rd, Wan Chai ☎2528 5588) for details of local issues and campaigns.

GAY LIFE Until very recently, homosexuality was completely illegal; the statutes carried a maximum penalty of life imprisonment for committing a homosexual act. The law was brought into line with Britain's in 1990, but there is still only a very limited gay scene in the territory. Few people are prepared to speak about their homosexuality, and there's no open, obvious place for gay men and women to meet people. There's an advisory service, *Horizons* (☎2815 9267) for gays and lesbians; other than that, you'll have to rely on one of a very few places where you might meet other gay people, listed in the box on p.265.

GOVERNMENT PUBLICATIONS CENTRE Queensway Government Offices, Low Block, Ground Floor, 66 Queensway, Admiralty (Mon–Fri 9am–5pm, Sat 9am–1pm; ☎2537 1910). For maps of the islands, New Territories and other useful publications.

HOSPITALS Government hospitals are the cheapest; they're listed in the Hong Kong phone book. Hong Kong ID Card and British passport holders pay $60 per day if admitted; everyone else will have to pay around $2800 a day, though casualty visits are free – the government hospitals below have 24-hour casualty departments. Private hospitals are more expensive, but the standard of care much higher.

Government Hospitals *Princess Margaret Hospital,* 2–10 Lai King Hill Rd, Lai Chi Kok, Kowloon ☎2990 1111; *Queen Elizabeth Hospital,* Wylie Rd, Kowloon ☎2958 8888; *Queen Mary Hospital,* Pokfulam Rd, Hong Kong Island ☎2855 3838; *Tang Shiu Kin Hospital,* Queen's Rd East, Hong Kong Island ☎2831 6800.

Private Hospitals *Baptist Hospital,* 222 Waterloo Rd, Kowloon ☎2337 4141; *Canossa Hospital,* 1 Old Peak Rd, Hong Kong Island ☎2522 2181; *Hong Kong Adventist Hospital,* 40 Stubbs Rd, Hong Kong Island ☎2574 6211; *Matilda Hospital,* 41 Mount Kellett Rd, The Peak ☎2849 6301; *St Teresa's Hospital,* 327 Prince Edward Rd, Kowloon ☎2711 9111.

ID CARDS Available to long-term residents from the Immigration Department at Wan Chai Tower, Gloucester Rd, Wan Chai ☎2829 3000.

LAUNDRY There's a same-day laundry service in most hotels (though it's usually fairly expensive); guest houses generally have a cheaper service. Otherwise, try *Man Kee Laundry Service,* 24 Hankow Apartment, 49 Hankow Rd, Tsim Sha Tsui; *Fabric Care,* 87 Kimberley Rd, Tsim Sha Tsui; or *Singclean,* 1st Floor, Room 114, Worldwide Plaza, Pedder St, Central. Places charge by the weight of your washing.

LEFT LUGGAGE There's an office in the departure lounge at the airport (daily 6.30am–1am); or leave luggage at various guest houses in Chungking Mansions and elsewhere – though you'll have to be happy with the owners/general security to leave anything valuable here.

LIBRARIES The main English-language library is in the City Hall High Block in

Edinburgh Place, Central, open Mon–Fri 10am–9pm, Sat 10am–5pm, Sun 10am–1pm; Junior Library (2nd Floor), Lending Library (3rd Floor), Reference Library (4th Floor), Newspaper Reading Room and Record Library (5th Floor); to join, you need a passport and $100 deposit (ID card holders free). There's also the British Council library (see above) and the *American Library*, 1st Floor, United Centre, 95 Queensway, Admiralty (Mon–Fri 10am–6pm), which is free to join; apply in person with your passport/ID card.

LOST PROPERTY Police ☎ 2860 2000; MTR, Admiralty station (daily 11am–6pm); KCR, 8th Floor, KCR House, Sha Tin, NT ☎ 2606 9392 (Mon–Sat 9am–noon).

NEWSPAPERS There are five English-language newspapers published in Hong Kong. The *South China Morning Post* is the most reliable, a firmly centrist publication that's the best thing to read on the various problems that face Hong Kong. It carries a good, daily "what's on" listings section. The *Hong Kong Standard* is the *Post's* main rival, duller and notable only for its reasonable daily listings section. Newest is the *Eastern Express*, good on features and photos, weak on hard news, particularly business news. The other two papers are the *Asian Wall Street Journal* and the *International Herald Tribune* – the first business-led, the second culled mostly from American newspapers. Published in China, but widely available in Hong Kong, the *China Daily* makes interesting reading in an Alice-in-Wonderland kind of way – straight-down-the-line government propaganda. There are also over forty Chinese newspapers published daily in Hong Kong of various political hues. Beijing objects to the hard reporting of several of them, though there are a few pro-China papers as balance.

British, European and American newspapers are widely available too, normally a couple of days late. They're on sale at both Star Ferry concourses; or try inside the *South China Morning Post Family Bookshop* in Central's Star Ferry concourse. For magazines, check the newsstand in Theatre Lane, just off

Queen's Rd Central, or – again – either of the Star Ferry concourses. For local listings magazines and freesheets, see p.275.

PHARMACIES The largest Western-style pharmacy is *Watson's*, which has branches all over Hong Kong (open daily 9am–6pm) and stocks toiletries, contact lens fluid and first-aid items. For the nearest branch to you, phone ☎ 2606 8833. Hong Kong branches are at Shop 31, Paterson Plaza, Paterson St, Causeway Bay ☎ 2895 4008, Melbourne Plaza, 33 Queen's Rd, Central ☎ 2523 0666, and Shop 301–307, 1st Floor, Prince's Building, 10 Chater Rd, Central; in Tsim Sha Tsui there are branches at 101 Nathan Rd ☎ 2369 2011 and 18 Carnarvon Rd ☎ 2723 3802.

PHOTOCOPYING There's a photocopy service in the City Hall library (see "Libraries" above for address).

POLICE Main police stations are as follows: *Hong Kong Island HQ*, Arsenal St, Wan Chai ☎ 2860 2000 and *Kowloon Regional HQ*, 190 Argyle St, Mong Kok ☎ 2760 5500. For lost property, call ☎ 2860 2000 and you'll be given the address and telephone number of the local police station that will deal with your loss. For Crime Hotline and Taxi Complaints, call ☎ 2527 7177, and for Complaints Against the Police, call ☎ 2862 9697.

POST OFFICES The main General Post Office (GPO) building is at 2 Connaught Place, Central (Mon–Fri 8am–6pm, Sat 8am–2pm ☎ 2921 2222), just behind the Star Ferry on Hong Kong Island, to the right as you get off: the ground floor is for collecting registered letters and parcels, and there are public pay phones there as well; the first floor is for stamps, sending registered letters and other counter services. Kowloon-side, the Kowloon Central Post Office is at 405 Nathan Rd (Yau Ma Tei MTR; same hours as above). Letters sent poste restante will go to the Central GPO building, where you can collect them Mon–Sat 8am–6pm: take your passport.

TELEPHONES For local calls, you'll find phones at public transport terminals, in

Directory

Directory

shops, hotels, restaurants and bars – local calls are free, except for a $1 charge in coin-operated phones. For long-distance calls, either use an IDD pay phone – many accept phone cards or credit cards – or go to a *Hong Kong Telecom Service Centre*: Ground Floor, Century Square, 1 D'Aguilar St, Central (open 24hr); 3 Gloucester Rd, Wan Chai (Mon–Fri 8am–9pm, Sat 8am–3pm); 3 Hennessy Rd, Wan Chai (Mon–Fri 9am–6pm, Sat 9am–4pm); Hermes House, 10 Middle Rd, Tsim Sha Tsui (open 24hr); Unit D37, Kai Tak Airport, Kowloon (daily 8am–11pm). See pp.29–30 for more information.

Useful telephone numbers include:

Collect calls ☎010

Directory Enquiries (English) ☎1081

Emergencies (ambulance, police or fire) ☎999

IDD and Cardphone enquiries ☎013

International Operator ☎013

Telefax operator ☎014

Telephone problems/repair ☎109

Time and temperature ☎18501

Tourist information (multi-lingual) ☎2801 6177

Weather (English) ☎187 8066

THOMAS COOK Changes travellers' cheques at 18th Floor, Vicwood Plaza, 199 Des Voeux Rd, Central (Mon–Fri 9am–5.30pm, Sat 9am–1pm; ☎2545 4399); Ground Floor, Mirador Mansion, 58a Nathan Rd, Tsim Sha Tsui (daily 8am–10pm; ☎2366 9687).

TIME Eight hours ahead of the UK (seven in summer), sixteen hours ahead of Los Angeles, thirteen hours ahead of New York, and two hours behind Sydney.

TIPPING Large hotels and most restaurants will add a ten percent service charge to your bill. In restaurants where there's no service charge, they'll expect to pick up the dollar coins change. In taxis, make the fare up to the nearest dollar. Porters at upmarket hotels and at the airport aren't carrying your bags for the love of the job – tip at your discretion.

TOILETS You'll find public toilets at all major beaches, sights and country parks – there's usually no paper, though there might be an attendant on hand to sell you a couple of sheets. Public toilets are more scarce in the centre, but that's no problem given the number of restaurants and hotels in Tsim Sha Tsui and Central. The swankier the place, the less likely you'll be challenged; indeed some of the very top hotels have rest rooms incorporated into their high-class ground-floor shopping arcades. The finest (and most intimidating) toilet experience is in the arcade of the *Peninsula* hotel: attendants turn on the taps, hand over the soap and retrieve the towels amid brass and marble elegance; you're expected to tip.

TRANSPORT ENQUIRIES See "Getting Around", pp.48–60, for public transport information.

TRAVEL AGENCIES As well as flights to the rest of Southeast Asia and beyond, most of the places below can help with travel to China, including organizing visas.

China Travel Service (CTS), 4th Floor, CTS House, 78–83 Connaught Rd, Central ☎2853 3533; 2nd Floor, China Travel Building, 77 Queen's Rd, Central ☎2525 2284; 1st Floor, Alpha House, 27–33 Nathan Rd, Tsim Sha Tsui ☎2721 1331; 10–12, 1st Floor, China Hong Kong City, 33 Canton Rd, Tsim Sha Tsui ☎2736 1863. China visas, tours and tickets.

Global Union Express Ltd, Room 96A, New Henry House, Ice House St, Central ☎2845 4232. Trans-Siberian train specialists.

Hong Kong Student Travel Ltd, 10th Floor, Room 1021, Star House, Salisbury Rd, Tsim Sha Tsui ☎2730 3269; right by the Kowloon-side Star Ferry. Very popular place for flights, package tours, boats and trains to China, visas, ISIC and YIEE cards. Open Mon–Fri 9.30am–7pm, Sat 9.30am–6pm, Sun noon–5pm. Branches at 1812 Argyle Centre, 688 Nathan Rd, Mongkok; 11th Floor, Circle Plaza, 499 Hennessy Rd, Causeway Bay; 305 Entertainment Building, 30 Queen's Rd, Central.

Honour Tourist Company, Room 807, Universal Commercial Building, 69 Peking Rd, Tsim Sha Tsui ☎2311 4211. Worth trying for flights.

Phoenix Services, Milton Mansions, 6th Floor, Room B, 96 Nathan Rd, Tsim Sha Tsui ☎ 2722 7378. Chinese visas, train tickets, and flight and hotel booking services.

Shoestring Travel, 4th Floor, Alpha House, 27–33 Nathan Rd, Tsim Sha Tsui ☎ 2723 2306 (entrance on Peking Rd). Flights, visas and bus tickets to Guangzhou.

Time Travel, Block A, 16th Floor, Chungking Mansions, 36–44 Nathan Rd, Tsim Sha Tsui ☎ 2366 6222. Helpful place with visas, tickets, passport photos and telex/fax service.

Wah Nam Travel, Room 602, Sino Centre, 582–592 Nathan Rd, Kowloon ☎ 2332 0367. Visas, boat and train tickets.

VACCINATION CENTRES At Room 903–905, Kowloon Government Office, 393 Canton Rd, Tsim Sha Tsui ☎ 2368 3361 (Mon–Fri 9am–1pm & 2–4.30pm, Sat 9am–12.30pm); 18th Floor, Wu Chung House, 213 Queen's Rd East, Wan Chai

☎ 2961 8840 (Mon–Fri 9am–1pm & 2–4.30pm, Sat 9am–12.30pm).

WESTERN UNION Agencies include: Budget Finance Ltd, Shop 2038, 2nd Floor, United Centre, Hong Kong ☎ 2528 5631; and Amel Express Ltd, Unit F, 4th Floor, Freder Centre, 3 Mok Cheung St, Kowloon ☎ 2362 7171.

WOMEN'S HONG KONG The main women's organization is the Hong Kong Council of Women (PO Box 819, Hong Kong, or 4 Jordan Rd, Yau Ma Tei, Kowloon), dominated by expats and not overtly radical. It does, however, maintain a library, support groups and a refuge – Harmony House (☎ 2522 0434) – for battered women and their children; the telephone number is a 24-hour hotline. It's also worth knowing that there's a long-term residential hotel/club for women in Hong Kong, the Helena May, but you'll have to book well in advance: more information from the Helena May, 35 Garden Road, Mid-Levels ☎ 2522 6766.

Directory

Macau

Chapter 16

Introducing Macau

The territory (or enclave, as it's often called) of **Macau** is 60km west of Hong Kong and 145km south of Guangzhou. It's split into three small, distinct parts – a peninsula and two islands – and the whole enclave covers less than nineteen square kilometres (making it the fourth smallest country in the world), in which lives a population of roughly half a million.

The **city** of Macau itself is built on a **peninsula** of the Chinese mainland, about 4km by 2km at its widest points and easy to negotiate on foot. It's here that you'll find most of the real sights, colonial buildings and historical interest, lots of restaurants and the bulk of the casinos, for which Macau is famous. Two bridges link the peninsula with **Taipa** island, from where a slightly shorter causeway runs across to the southernmost **Coloane** island. Both islands are small, easily reached by bus, and feature more good restaurants and the odd church and temple; Coloane also has the enclave's only beaches.

See colour plates for a map of Macau, Taipa and Coloane.

Although the bulk of the population is Chinese, at times it's easy to imagine yourself in the Mediterranean. The pace of life is slower than in Hong Kong: there's time to have a drink at an outdoor café and as you climb up to old fortresses through hilly, cobbled streets, you pass small squares lined with pastel-coloured mansions and cracked, whitewashed Catholic churches.

But Macau is gradually losing its sleepy colonial image with the completion of a series of **construction projects** designed to allow it to compete with the other burgeoning Southeast Asian economies. The face of the peninsula itself has been changed markedly by the enclosing of the Praia Grande bay, while plans have just been unveiled for a huge trade-and-entertainment project on reclaimed land between Taipa and Coloane islands. Macau's new international airport – in operation well before Chek Lap Kok in Hong Kong – and container port are designed to attract trade and investment, challenging Hong Kong's current dominance. A planned highway from Macau and the neighbouring Chinese Special Economic Zone of Zhuhai will run up to Guangzhou, joining with the Hong Kong–

Guangzhou highway – firmly linking the territory with the rapidly expanding southeastern Chinese economy.

For Macau's visa regulations, customs and currency matters, turn to the relevant sections of Basics.

If you're really pushed for time, a day trip from Hong Kong can take in most of the interesting things in the whole of Macau, but it really warrants a longer visit. Three or four days is enough time to get around everything comfortably and gives you the chance to sample a few of the excellent restaurants. It's also worth considering leaving for China from Macau – you don't need to return to Hong Kong to move on, since there are regular bus and ferry connections.

Getting to Macau

If you're travelling on to Macau directly on arrival in Hong Kong, take the #A2 airport bus (daily every 15–20min, 7am–midnight) which runs from Kai Tak airport to the Macau Ferry Terminal.

Although the airport is now operational, the majority of visitors still arrive by sea from Hong Kong, the journey taking from 55 to 100 minutes, depending on the vessel. Most departures are from the Macau Ferry Terminal in Central, on Hong Kong Island, though there are links with Kowloon, too. From China, there's a straight

---

Hong Kong–Macau by Sea

The Hong Kong government charges a **departure tax** of $26 per person on sea journeys to Macau, which is included in the price of your ticket; if you buy a return ticket, you'll also be charged a Macau departure tax of $22. At the Macau Ferry Terminal, you can book same-day and advance tickets for all services, as well as tickets for the Jetfoils up to 28 days in advance. Advance Jetfoil and High-speed Ferry tickets are also available from *MTR Travel Services Centres*, which you'll find in Hong Kong at the MTR station concourses of Tsim Sha Tsui, Mongkok, Tsuen Wan, Kwun Tong, Causeway Bay, Central and Admiralty.

Try to **book in advance** for all crossings, especially at the weekend and on public holidays, when all the transport is packed; buying a return ticket is also recommended since it saves time at the other end. Standby tickets are available, but you'll have to join the queue – though frequent departures from the Macau Ferry Terminal mean you shouldn't have too long a wait. All **prices** given below are for one-way fares; returns are double. All tickets are for a specific **departure time**; aim to be at the ferry terminal at least thirty minutes before departure as you'll have to fill in immigration forms before boarding; also allow extra time if you have to pick up pre-booked tickets. **Carry-on luggage** on the jetfoils is limited to hand luggage. You'll be allowed on with a suitcase or rucksack, but anything more and you'll have to check it in at the counter on the third floor of the Shun Tak Centre at least thirty minutes before departure – you'll pay an extra $20–40 depending on weight. Alternatively, take the High-speed Ferry instead, which has baggage racks.

Jetfoils

Run by the *Far East Jetfoil Company* (☎2859 3333), **Jetfoils** provide the quickest ride to Macau, getting there in 55 minutes. There's a daily 24-hour service from the Macau Ferry Terminal, with **departures** every

---

land route from Guangzhou, which allows you to take the bus into Macau, and there are also boat services from cities in Guangdong province, though these are rarely used by foreigners. For all **arrival details**, see the following section.

By air

Macau International Airport, which became operational in late-1995, is located at the eastern end of Taipa island. Services are still somewhat limited, though there are currently flights from Beijing, Shanghai, Taipei, Kuala Lumpur and Singapore, and provisional service agreements with a score of other countries: it's hoped that eventually there will be direct flights from elsewhere in China, Asia, Europe and North America.

In addition, there's a **helicopter service** between Hong Kong and Macau, with flights every hour (10am–10pm) operated by *East Asia Airlines* (information in Hong Kong on ☎2859 3359), which costs around $1250 one-way ($1350 at the weekend) – the journey takes

---

fifteen to thirty minutes during the day, less frequently (though still regularly) at night. **Tickets** are priced according to class and departure time, but broadly day services from 7am to 6pm cost around $97 for economy class (lower deck) and $110 first-class (upper deck); weekend prices are around $108 and $120 respectively. Night services, from 6pm to 7am, cost around $126 (economy) and $140 (first-class).

Telephone credit-card bookings in Hong Kong for Jetfoil services can be made on ☎2859 6596; *Visa, Mastercard, American Express* and *Diners Club* are all accepted.

Catamarans
CTS-Parkview (☎2789 5421) has 28 crossings a day by either **Turbocat** or **Jumbo-cat**, the journey taking an hour. There are services from either Macau Ferry Terminal, roughly every thirty minutes – weekdays $97 (economy) or $191 (first-class), weekends $108/$208, and nights $120/$220; or six daily from the China Ferry Terminal – weekdays $85/$185 and weekends $100/$200. Both types of cat also have six-seater VIP cabins available, for around $1200 each way. Holders of *American Express* and *Visa* cards can reserve by phone on ☎2559 9255.

Hoverferries and High-speed Ferries
Hong Kong Ferries' (☎2516 9581) **Hoverferries** run twelve times daily from the China Ferry Terminal between 8.30am and 6pm (two night services, too). They take around seventy minutes, for a fare of around $85 Monday to Friday, $100 at weekends and $118 at night.

Despite the name, **High-speed Ferries** (*Hong Kong Hi-Speed Ferries Ltd*; ☎2815 3034) take longer – around ninety to a hundred minutes. There's more room for luggage, though, and there are five daily departures (6 at weekends) between 8am and 8pm from the Macau Ferry Terminal. Tickets cost $38 economy ($58 weekend), $55 tourist class ($79 weekend) and around $71 first-class ($95 weekend).

---

twenty minutes. Departures are from the helipad at Hong Kong's Macau Ferry Terminal (see above), where you can buy tickets from a window adjacent to the jetfoil ticket offices; see "Directory", p.366, for telephone number of *East Asia Airlines* in Macau.

By sea

Most departures by sea **from Hong Kong** – by Jetfoil, High-speed Ferry or catamaran – are from the **Macau Ferry Terminal** (☎2859 3359), in the Shun Tak Centre, 200 Connaught Road, Central, Hong Kong Island (Sheung Wan MTR). Other, less frequent departures – by catamaran – are from the **China Ferry Terminal** at 33 Canton Road, Tsim Sha Tsui. All the ticket details are covered in the boxed feature on pp.314–315: Jetfoils provide the quickest service, High-speed Ferries the longest and cheapest.

By land

Two daily **buses** operate from Guangzhou direct to Macau, a six-hour trip. They cross the border at Gongbei, the town immediately over the border from Macau, in the Zhuhai Special Economic Zone; if you get off in Gongbei for a look around, the Barrier Gate border into Macau is open daily 7am–9pm; otherwise the buses run right through to the centre of Macau.

Arriving in Macau

All Jetfoils, catamarans, Hoverferries and High-speed Ferries dock at the **Macau Maritime Terminal** on Avenida da Amizada in the Outer Harbour (Porto Exterior), on the eastern side of the Macau peninsula; the helicopter service from Hong Kong lands on a pad above the terminal. The terminal is most commonly known as the **Jetfoil Terminal**, which is what it says on the buses that run past there. If you're only staying for the day, use the **left-luggage office** on the second floor of the terminal building (daily 6.30am–midnight), or the luggage lockers on the ground and first floors (24hr). There's also a money-exchange office here, though you can spend Hong Kong dollars in Macau.

For details about the peculiarities of the Macanese currency, see p.26.

Pick up a map at the Visitor Information Centre inside the terminal (see below) and you can **walk into central Macau**: it takes around twenty minutes to reach the *Hotel Lisboa*. Otherwise, **buses** from the stops right outside the terminal run into the centre, past several of the main hotels and out to the outlying islands: #3, #3A, #28A, #28B and #32 all go past the *Lisboa*; #28A goes on to Taipa island. Other transport options from the terminal are taxis and pedicabs, for details see "Getting Around" below.

From the airport, the **airport bus**, the #AP1 (3.50ptcs) runs across the new Macau–Taipa bridge and makes a stop outside the Jetfoil Terminal, before heading on to the *Hotel Lisboa*. **Ferries** from Shekou and Kongman in Guangdong Province dock at the pier next to the Floating Casino, from where it's a short walk to the main avenue, Avenida de Almeida Ribeiro; buses run down here towards the *Lisboa*.

The **bus from Guangzhou** stops outside the *CTS* office on Rua de Nagasaki, midway between the Jetfoil Terminal and the *Hotel Lisboa*. If you break your journey in Gongbei, walk over the **border with China** and jump on a #5 which will take you to Avenida de Almeida Ribeiro and to Rua da Praia Grande.

For all departure details from Macau, see "Directory", pp.366 and 367.

Arriving in Macau

Information

It's easy to pick up information on Macau before you arrive: there's an office of the **Macau Tourist Information Bureau** (*MTIB*) in **Hong Kong** at the Shun Tak Centre, Room 3704, 200 Connaught Road (Mon–Fri 9am–1pm & 2–6pm, Sat 9am–1pm; ☎2540 8180), which has lots of useful leaflets and maps. Otherwise, **in Macau**, you can pick up the same information at various *MTIB* offices, including the Visitor Information Centre at the Jetfoil Terminal (daily 9am–6pm; ☎726416). The main office is central, at Largo do Senado 9 (daily 9am–6pm; ☎315566), and there are smaller information counters at a few of the fortresses in Macau.

Free **literature** to look out for includes separate leaflets on Macau's churches, temples, outlying islands and walks; a bus timetable; hotel brochures; and the free monthly newspaper, *Macau Travel Talk*, which lists forthcoming cultural events and entertainment, and carries useful reviews of hotels and restaurants.

Getting around

You'll be able to **walk** almost everywhere in Macau, though to reach the outlying islands and a couple of the more far-flung sights, you'll need transport. **Buses and minibuses** are run by two companies, *Transportes Colectivos de Macau* (*TCM*) and *TRANSMAC*, and operate on circular routes from 7am daily until 11pm–midnight; a few stop running after 6–8pm, though the short distances mean you shouldn't get stuck. **Fares** are low: 2ptcs for any single trip on the city routes, 2.50ptcs to Taipa, 3.50ptcs to Coloane Village and 4ptcs to Hac Sa; the airport bus costs 3.50ptcs – pay the driver as you get on with the exact fare.

Main **terminals** and stops for the buses are outside the Jetfoil Terminal; in front of the *Hotel Lisboa;* at Barra (near the Maritime Museum and A-Ma temple); along Avenida de Almeida Ribeiro; and at Praça Ponte e Horta (for the Floating Casino). The main routes from these places are listed in the box below, while the text gives details of buses for particular destinations where appropriate.

Bus Terminals and Routes

Jetfoil Terminal: #AP1 to *Hotel Lisboa*/*Hyatt* hotel/airport; #1A to Floating Casino/Rua do Almirante Sergio/Barra; #3 and #3A to *Hotel Lisboa*/Avda. de Almeida Ribeiro; #28A to *Hotel Lisboa*/*Hyatt* hotel/ Taipa village; #28B to *Hotel Lisboa*/Rua de Praia Grande/*Bela Vista* hotel; #32 to Lisboa/Avda. de Horta e Costa.

Hotel Lisboa: #AP1 to airport; #3 and #3A to Jetfoil Terminal; #11 to *Hyatt* hotel/Taipa village; #21 to Taipa village/Coloane village; #21A to Coloane village/Parque de Coloane/Hac Sa beach; #26A to Taipa/Coloane village; #28A to *Hyatt* hotel/Taipa village; #33 to Taipa/Coloane village.

Avenida de Almeida Ribeiro: #3 to Jetfoil Terminal; #3A to Jetfoil Terminal (eastbound) or Floating Casino (westbound); #5 to Rua do Campo/Avda. de Horta e Costa/ Barrier Gate; #10 to *Hotel Lisboa* (eastbound) or Barra (south-bound); #11 to Barra (south-bound) or *Hotel Lisboa*/Taipa (eastbound); #21 to Barra (south-bound) or *Hotel Lisboa*/Taipa/ Coloane (eastbound).

Barra: #1A to Jai Alai stadium; #2 to Rua de Praia Grande/Avda. de Ferreira Almeida; #5 to Avda. de Horta e Costa/Portas do Cerco; #9 to Lisboa/Avda. de Ferreira Almeida/Avda. de Horta e Costa/ Portas do Cerco #10 to *Hotel Lisboa*; #11 to Taipa; #21 to Taipa/Coloane; #18 to M. Russa; #21A to Hac Sa beach.

Praça Ponte e Horta (close to Floating Casino): #3A, #11, #21 and #21A all pass through.

Taxis, pedicabs, car and bike rental

It's cheap enough to get around Macau by **taxi**, and you'll find ranks outside all the main hotels and at various points throughout the enclave. All rides are metered: minimum charge is 8ptcs (for the first 1500m), after which it's 1ptca for every 250m, plus 1ptca for each piece of luggage. Going by taxi to the islands of Taipa and Coloane, there's a 5ptcs and 10ptcs surcharge respectively, though there's no surcharge if you're coming back the other way.

Outside the Jetfoil Terminal and the *Hotel Lisboa* you'll be accosted by the drivers of **pedicabs** – three-wheeled bicycle rick-shaws. They're more suited for short tourist rides – say around the Praia Grande – than for serious getting around, since Macau's hills prevent any lengthy pedalling. You're supposed to bargain for the ride, which will will cost around 30ptcs for a short turn along the harbour, around 100ptcs for an hour's sightseeing.

Renting a car doesn't make an awful lot of sense in Macau, simply because it's so easy to get around cheaply by public trans-port and on foot. Moreover, it's extremely difficult to find parking spaces in central Macau. But you might want to pay for the novelty of driving a **moke** – a low-slung jeep – particularly if you intend to see a bit of the two outlying islands where transport is less common. See "Directory" for driving details.

Renting a **bicycle** is the best bet if you want a little more mobil-ity, though be warned that the traffic in the centre is as manic as in

Hong Kong, and that you're not allowed to ride over the Macau–Taipa bridge. Bike-riding is most enjoyable on the islands: on Taipa, you can rent bikes either from the *Hyatt Regency* hotel, the shop in the main square where the buses stop, or from Largo do Camões, next to the Pak Tai temple; in Coloane, the bike rental shop is at the bottom of Coloane village's main square, towards the water. They cost around 15ptcs an hour, depending on the bike, or 50ptcs a day. Note that if you want a bike for Coloane it's better to rent one there than ride over the causeway from Taipa.

Getting around

For organized tours of Macau, see "Directory", p.368.

Festivals and holidays

Macau's mostly Cantonese population celebrates the same Chinese religious and civil **holidays and festivals** as in Hong Kong: there's a round-up of the events and celebrations associated with the festivals on pp.281–284. But the enclave also celebrates several holidays and festivals lent to Macau by Portugal, often marked by parades, special exhibitions and concerts. The major ones are:

February: procession of Our Lord of Passos. An image of Christ is carried in procession from Santo Agostinho to the Sé for an overnight vigil and then returned via the stations of the cross.

Lent (first Sunday): procession of Our Lord of Passion. The statue of Christ is carried in procession from Santo Agostinho church to the Sé, with stations of the cross set up as it goes.

April 25: anniversary of the 1974 Portuguese revolution. A public holiday.

May 13: procession of Our Lady of Fatima, from São Domingos church to the Penha chapel to commemorate a miracle in Fatima, Portugal, in 1913. The biggest annual Portuguese religious celebration, though not a public holiday in Macau.

June 10: Camões Day (Portuguese Communities Day). A public holiday to commemorate Portugal's national poet.

June 24: procession in honour of St John the Baptist (the patron saint of Macau), with a special Mass in the cathedral. Also in June is a procession in honour of St Anthony of Lisbon.

July 13: holiday on Taipa and Coloane celebrating the defeat of pirates in 1910.

October 5: Portuguese Republic Day; a public holiday to mark the establishment of the Portuguese Republic in 1910.

December 1: Portuguese Independence Day; a public holiday.

Language and addresses

Roughly 95 percent of the population of Macau is Chinese, three percent Portuguese and two percent of other origins. Nevertheless, as in Hong Kong, the colonial power has retained the primacy of its **language** and Macau's two official languages are Portuguese and Cantonese. In practice, for visitors, this means becoming familiar

Language and addresses

with Portuguese street and office signs, which are explained throughout the text if there's any confusion; a few useful Portuguese words are given below to help decipher signs and maps. Otherwise, you won't need Portuguese to get around, though you may find the menu reader on pp.355–356 useful. Although taught in schools, English is patchily spoken and understood – and a few words of Cantonese will always help smooth the way (for which see "Language", pp.397–399).

Addresses are written in the Portuguese style: street name followed by number. Abbreviations to be aware of are Av. or Avda. (Avenida), Est. (Estrada), Calç. (Calçada) and Pr. (Praça).

Some Useful Portuguese Words			
Alfandega	Customs	*Largo*	Square
Avenida	Avenue	*Lavabos*	Toilets
Baia	Bay	*Mercado*	Market
Beco	Alley	*Museu*	Museum
Bilheteira	Ticket office	*Pensão*	Guest house
Correios	Post office	*Ponte*	Bridge
Edifício	Building	*Pousada*	Inn/Hotel
Estrada	Road	*Praça*	Square
Farmácia	Pharmacy	*Praia*	Beach
Farol	Lighthouse	*Rua*	Street
Fortaleza	Fortress	*Sé*	Cathedral
Hospedaria	Guest house	*Travessa*	Lane
Jardim	Garden	*Vila*	Guest house

Chapter 17

Macau, Taipa and Coloane

O ver four hundred years of foreign trade and colonial rule have shaped **MACAU** into arguably the most intriguing of the southern Chinese settlements ceded to European powers over the centuries. When the **Portuguese** arrived off the southern Chinese coast at the turn of the sixteenth century, they were looking for trading opportunities to add to their string of successes in India and the Malay peninsula. In particular, they were hoping to break the Venetian monopoly of the Far Eastern spice trade, something that had seemed possible since the seizure of the Malay port of Malacca in 1510. Three years later, the first European to set foot in southern China, Portuguese explorer Jorges Álvares, opened up trade with the Chinese Empire. Later, with the Portuguese "discovery" of Japan in 1542 – accidentally, as it happens, by a ship blown off course – it became vital for the Portuguese to find a base from where they could direct trading operations between China and Japan, as well as between both countries and Europe. This base was Macau, first settled in 1557, and by the end of the sixteenth century nine hundred Portuguese settlers were living here. The area was already well known to the local Chinese, who knew it as **A-Ma-Gao** ("Bay of A-Ma"), after the goddess of the sea A-Ma, who was reputed to have saved a ship from a storm off the Macau coast. From A-Ma-Gao is derived the modern name, Macau, linking it firmly with the territory's seafaring and trading history.

Most of the interest is contained on the fist-shaped **peninsula** of land that reaches south from the Barrier Gate and the border with China. You can easily walk around the central streets, making separate visits to various points of interest further north and south – all of which can also be reached by bus or taxi if you run out of puff. It's harder going than you might at first think: Macau's hills make for tiring climbing in the heat of the day, though you're always rewarded by excellent views from the churches and fortresses that crown the summits, most notably the ruined church of **São Paulo** and the adjacent **Fortaleza do Monte**. Other attractions include a couple of **temples** that are the equal of any of the better known ones in Hong Kong; an excellent **Maritime Museum**, which illuminates the enclave's long associations with fishing and trade; and a series of quiet **gardens** and squares reflecting the enclave's more laid-back approach to life. Spare time, too, for trips out to the two islands: **Taipa**, best known for the fine restaurants in its one village, and Coloane, which sports a couple of good **beaches**, including the black sands at Hac Sa.

A little history

Following the intitial Portuguese settlement, a city soon grew up on the peninsula, becoming influential as a centre for sending Christian **missionaries** to China and Japan. The Jesuit Francis Xavier had visited Japan from 1549 to 1551 and he was followed by a series of missionaries, who travelled through Macau and left an indelible mark on the settlement. The **Jesuits** were pioneers, using the vast trading funds to build great churches in a European Baroque style, the most notable of which was the church of São Paulo. Given city status in 1586, Macau's civil and religious importance to the Portuguese was confirmed in a decree which named it as *Cidade do Nome de Deus de Macau*: "City of the Name of God, Macau".

Throughout the sixteenth and early seventeenth century Macau prospered, but from 1612 onwards the authorities were forced to build **fortifications** on the city's hills to ward off attacks from the **Dutch**, who had their eyes on the valuable trade which emanated from the city. The Dutch came close to taking Macau in 1622, but were beaten off, only to move in elsewhere in the Far East, encouraged by the failing Spanish Empire, which since 1580 had incorporated Portugal. Before long, the Dutch had gained a foothold in Japan, turning the Japanese against the Jesuit missions there, and by 1639 Japan was closed to the Portuguese for trade, removing one of Macau's vital links. Another disappeared in 1641 with the Dutch capture of Malacca, and although Portugal regained its independence from Spain at around the same time, it was too late to restore the country's – and Macau's – trade with the Far East. From the end of the seventeenth century onwards Macau became impoverished, adversely affected by the loss of trade and its proximity to a meddling Imperial Chinese authority. At its lowest political point, in the mid-eighteenth century, it was known rather contemptuously as the "City of Women", a reference to the number of child slaves and prostitutes abandoned in what was rapidly becoming a miserable backwater.

Ironically, it was the growing importance of other foreign traders in the South China Sea during the eighteenth century that saved Macau. Forced to spend the summers away from the trading "factories" in Guangzhou by the Chinese, who wouldn't allow permanent foreign settlement on their soil, the British, Americans, Dutch, French and others moved to Macau instead. The city became a sort of halfway house for foreign companies, whose merchants built fine mansions to live in – a time recalled in Timothy Mo's novel *An Insular Possession*. However, even this position was undermined after 1841, with the **founding of Hong Kong** as a British colony and free port, and the opening up of the other Chinese Treaty Ports in 1842 for direct trade.

The **nineteenth century** saw modern Macau begin to take shape. A new Governor, João Ferreira do Amaral, arrived in 1846 to stake a claim for Portuguese sovereignty over the peninsula; he annexed the neighbouring island of Taipa, expelled the Chinese customs officials from Macau, and built new roads – although sovereignty wasn't ceded by China until 1887. Macau prospered again in a minor way, yet it was always clear that it was second-best to Hong Kong, whose rapidly expanding infrastructure now attracted all the direct trade with China that Macau once monopolized. The enclave became renowned for less salubrious methods of money-making, notably with the advent of **gambling** and prostitution rackets, which existed alongside the well-established opium trade that had been run through Macau since the very earliest days.

Lurching on in its down-at-heel way, Macau's last great upheavals came with the great **population movements** in Southeast Asia earlier this century. The population increased rapidly after the Sino-Japanese War in the 1930s; many Europeans moved in during World War II as the Japanese respected Portuguese neutrality; and it was the turn of Chinese refugees, after 1949 and the Communist victory in the civil war, to migrate to Macau in massive numbers. The fairly cordial relations between Portugal and China were strained in 1966 when the Chinese **Cultural Revolution** led to a series of riots in Macau, during which demonstrators were shot dead. Yet even this failed to provide the impetus for China to take back the land it had claimed for so long. In fact, since the late 1960s China has had complete political control over Macau, finding a benefit in Portugal's sovereignty not frightening away Western business and investment. This position became clear in 1974, after the **revolution in Portugal**. The new left-wing government there began to disentangle itself from its remaining colonial ties in Mozambique, Angola and elsewhere, yet was told firmly by the Chinese that they'd prefer things to remain as they were, with the Portuguese holding nominal sovereignty while it continued to make money for China. By now, a tourist-industry infrastructure in Macau was well in place, with new hotels and sports facilities going hand-in-hand with the vast amounts of money generated by the gambling industry.

With Britain and China reaching agreement in 1984 over the future of Hong Kong, it was only a matter of time before Macau would also be **returned to China** – something that, following the **Joint Declaration** of 1987, is now due to happen on 20 December 1999, when the last chapter in the long history of colonialism in the South China Sea will be closed. Officially, the agreed Basic Law (promulgated in 1993) means that Macau – like Hong Kong – will get to keep its capitalist structure intact for at least fifty years. In practice, though, Macau has always been far more under China's influence than Hong Kong. Local liberals and pro-democracy activists are in the minority and on the defensive, concerned that the enclave will rapidly lose its Portuguese heritage once it returns to China. They point – with some justification – to the way the conservatives in government accede to China's every wish, citing, most noticeably, the removal of a long-standing statue of a former Macau governor, which Beijing regarded as too "colonial". The conservatives, for their part, talk of the need for "convergence" with China if Macau is to continue to be economically viable after 1999. Quite how Macau will develop as a "Special Administrative Region" (SAR) of China is literally anyone's guess, though the pace of infrastructural **development** (see feature on pp.328–329) suggests that the die has already been cast in favour of close economic cooperation with China.

Around the Peninsula

In the early days of the Portuguese settlement at Macau, a thriving town emerged at the bottom half of the **PENINSULA**. Grand buildings were erected around a network of streets which still exists, including a fine central avenue which ran across the peninsula. The central focus of the town was the Praia Grande, a large, handsome bay from which all the streets radiated, and around which the locals worked and rested, promenading in the evenings along the waterfront much as they would have done back home in Portugal.

Along the Praia Grande

The **Praia Grande** – once the colonial heart of Macau – now sits at the heart of a redevelopment programme (see below) that will radically transform the face of the entire enclave. What was formerly a fine banyan-planted sweep today echoes with the sound of jackhammers as work continues on the plan to enclose the bay, forming two artificial lakes (the Nam Van Lakes) and reclaiming land for residential and commercial building – losing its classic simplicity for ever but catapulting the Macau cityscape into the twenty-first century.

New buildings will eventually line the revised parameters of the bay, but for now the northern edge sports two prominent landmarks, both at odds with much of colonial Macau. The modern snub-nosed **Bank of China** building, and its adjacent second phase, is the latest addition to an increasingly built-up waterfront, while just to the east sits the orange polka-dot bulk of the **Hotel Lisboa**, whose low flanks are fronted by a multi-storey circular drum done up like a wedding cake and lit to extravagant effect at night. No one should miss a venture into the hotel's 24-hour casinos, or a wander through the hotel's gilt and marble surroundings, past the gift shops, and the ten restaurants and bars inside. Outside the hotel is a good place to pick up a pedicab around the bay.

Around the Peninsula

Just back from the *Lisboa*, on Rua da Praia Grande, stand the old colonial São Francisco **barracks**, washed in pink and highlighted with white trim. The public are allowed into the dining room of the *Clube Militar* (see p.357), contained within, but no further. The building itself dates from 1864: before that, on the same site, stood the original São Francisco fortress, which guarded the edge of the old Praia Grande – giving you some idea of how far land reclamation has changed this part of the city over the years. The fine round tower in the upper level of the ornate gardens behind the barracks was built to honour those from Macau who saw service in World War I.

The Lisboa's casinos are covered on p.362.

Along Avenida de Almeida Ribeiro

Macau's central avenue stretches from the *Hotel Lisboa* right across to the Inner Harbour on the west side of the peninsula. The first section is known as **Avenida do Infante d'Henrique**, changing its name as it crosses Rua da Praia Grande to **Avenida de Almeida Ribeiro**. It's a fine thoroughfare, shops and banks tucked into shady arcades on either side of the road, and there's plenty to stop off for as you make your way up it.

On the right, the steps of Rua da Sé climb past some graceful balconied houses before dipping down into a large square which holds the squat **Sé** itself – Macau's Cathedral, hidden from the rest of town in a natural hollow. It's not a particularly distinguished church, rebuilt in stone in the mid-nineteenth century on top of its original sixteenth-century foundations, and completely restored again in 1937, though it's spacious enough inside, with some fine stained glass, and flanked by some rather pretty colonial buildings. What must once have been a handsome cathedral square now serves as a market and car park.

From the Sé, a side road drops down into the rather grander **Largo do Senado** or Senate Square, though it's better approached from the main avenue. Like the avenue, the square is arcaded, its elegant buildings painted pale pink, yellow or white and set off by a small fountained park with benches and flowers. In the arcade on one side sit fortune tellers and newspaper vendors, while off to one side, down Rua Sul do Mercado de São Domingos and adjacent streets, is a **market**: a quadrangle of clothes stalls and *dai pai dongs* around a covered building which deals mostly in fish and meat.

To the local Chinese, the avenue is known as San Ma Lo ("new road").

At the bottom of Largo do Senado, the arcaded buildings peter out in the adjacent Largo São Domingos, which holds the fine seventeenth-century Baroque church of **São Domingos** (usually open afternoons; ring the bell at the side gate). Built for Macau's Dominicans, its restrained cream and stucco facade is echoed inside

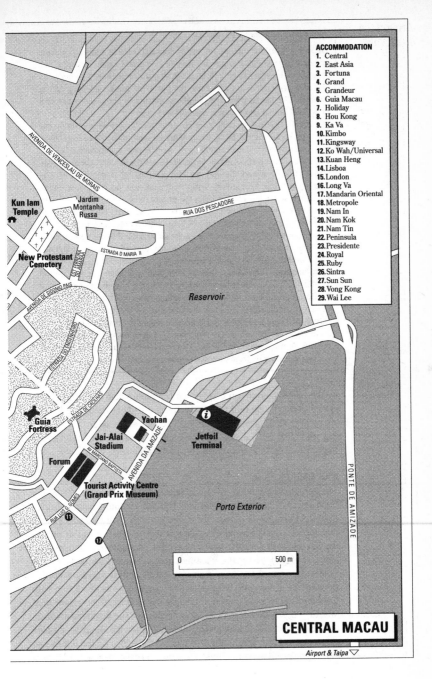

ACCOMMODATION
1. Central
2. East Asia
3. Fortuna
4. Grand
5. Grandeur
6. Guia Macau
7. Holiday
8. Hou Kong
9. Ka Va
10. Kimbo
11. Kingsway
12. Ko Wah/Universal
13. Kuan Heng
14. Lisboa
15. London
16. Long Va
17. Mandarin Oriental
18. Metropole
19. Nam In
20. Nam Kok
21. Nam Tin
22. Peninsula
23. Presidente
24. Royal
25. Ruby
26. Sintra
27. Sun Sun
28. Vong Kong
29. Wai Lee

CENTRAL MACAU

Airport & Taipa ▽

The Redevelopment of Macau

There's a startling amount of **redevelopment** taking place in Macau, much of it occupying huge swathes of reclaimed land: for once, it's strictly accurate to say that given a ten-year absence from the enclave, a visitor would simply not recognize the place. To put it into perspective, consider that the land area of the Macau peninsula alone is already two-and-a-half times bigger than it was 150 years ago.

All the impetus for change derives from Macau's close relation to the booming economies of Hong Kong, Guangzhou and the Pearl River estuary, and the new constructions are an obvious manifestation of the enclave's determination not to be left behind. The Joint Declaration with China of 1987 paved the way for the planning of new infrastructures which would link Macau very firmly with economic developments on the mainland, and in the last few years the progress has been rapid.

The most obvious new construction is the **airport**, built at a cost of US$975 million off the east coast of Taipa, with a potential capacity of six million passengers a year. Both the terminal and the 3.5-kilometre runway were built on reclaimed land, while a second, four-kilometre-long **Macau–Taipa bridge** provides a direct road route to the Macau mainland and the new **Maritime Terminal** (built a little way up from the old Jetfoil Terminal). The construction of the airport and the huge **container port** at Ka Ho on Coloane prompted further development plans, which – perhaps most extraordinarily – include the filling in of the water between the islands of **Taipa and Coloane** (at present linked by causeway) and building a trade centre and theme park there. With this completed, it will be possible to run a road and rail line into mainland China, so that goods can be freighted directly from port and airport.

by the pastel colours on display, on the pillars and walls and on the statue of the Virgin and Child which sits on top of the altar. There's a small museum of sculpture and church art at the back of the building, and on May 13 every year the church is the starting point of the major procession in honour of Our Lady of Fatima.

The Leal Senado

The Senate House itself, the **Leal Senado** ("Loyal Senate"), faces the main square on Avenida de Almeida Ribeiro, earning its name from a grateful Portuguese monarchy in recognition of the loyalty Macau had shown to the crown during the Spanish occupation of Portugal in the seventeenth century; alone of all the Portuguese dependencies, Macau refused to fly the Castilian flag. Founded as early as the 1580s, it's one of the truly great buildings in Macau, of traditional Portuguese design and with interior courtyard walls decorated with *azulejo* tiling. These days it's used by the municipal government of Macau, whose powers are a shadow of those of the democratic forum that once met here. But as a public building it's open to visitors (Mon–Sat 1–7pm; free), and if you ask in the office on the left as you enter, you're allowed to climb the main staircase, past a little formal

If this is ambitious, the ongoing work designed to close the **Praia Grande** is positively visionary. Prompted in part by the gradual silting up of the Pearl River estuary, it was decided to link the pockets of land reclamation on the Macau peninsula by running four-lane roads on causeways around them, thus forming two artifical lakes. The almost two million square metres of reclaimed land this scheme has produced will be occupied by hotels, shops, office space, leisure complexes and pedestrian precincts. The outline shape is already visible, and the lake enclosures almost complete: buildings are rising rapidly, too, though the most striking addition so far are the towers of the **Gate of Understanding** monument, towards the southern end of the peninsula.

For tourists, the transformation of Macau is most obviously reflected in the expanding range of facilities. Nine **new hotels** came on stream in 1993 alone, many in the intensively developed strip of land between the Maritime Terminal and the *Hotel Lisboa*. In the same area, the new **Tourist Activity Centre**, next to the Forum, houses a Grand Prix Museum and will soon sport two restaurants; a new Cultural Centre is on the drawing board; while a new museum building is currently being established in the ruins of São Paulo.

It's an undeniably impressive achievement, with more to follow, though the development comes at a price. Matching the economic expansion of its neighbours has not only changed the very geography of Macau, but arguably affected its soul as well. It's already a noticeably busier and noisier place, with traffic levels set to increase once all the new roads are in place. The colonial peace of the once elegant Praia Grande has been lost for ever, while new building is rapidly encroaching upon the remaining old-town pockets in the centre. Twenty-first-century Macau will undoubtedly be an impressive Southeast Asian city, but along the way it will have sacrificed much of its colonial charm.

garden, to the **Senate Chamber** on the first floor – a rich, grand room with panelled walls and ceiling and excellent views out over the square. Adjacent is the **library**, two-tiered and elaborately carved, whose wooden chambers house musty sixteenth-century books.

The Inner Harbour and surrounding streets

The main avenue ends on the peninsula's western side, at the **Inner Harbour** or Porto Interior – the main harbour of Macau for centuries until the new terminals were built over on the Porto Exterior on the eastern side. The overriding attraction here is the so-called **Floating Casino** (properly called the *Casino Macau Palace*), a moored wooden vessel that was once a floating restaurant in Hong Kong. It replaced an even shabbier casino that had been moored here for years, and remains incredibly popular, filled with all kinds of different ways to lose money, and punters who stay in the nearby cheap hotels so as not to waste any valuable gambling time.

The harbourside retains a turn-of-the-century atmosphere that's worth sampling. Rua das Lorchas leads down past **Praça Ponte e Horta**, an elongated square that was obviously once grand though its central expanse has been filled by a produce **market** and it now

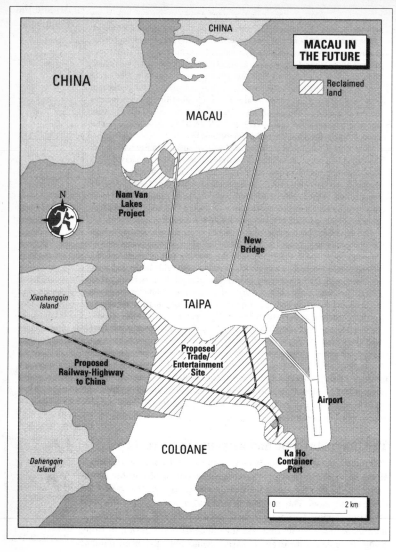

MACAU IN
THE FUTURE

///// Reclaimed
land

CHINA

CHINA

MACAU

Nam Van
Lakes
Project

New
Bridge

N

Xiaohengqin
Island

TAIPA

Proposed
Railway-Highway
to China

Proposed
Trade/
Entertainment
Site

Airport

Dahengqin
Island

COLOANE

Ka Ho
Container
Port

0   2 km

sports only one surviving old building, the green four-storey, balconied house on the left. From the square, **Rua do Almirante Sergio** is
arcaded all the way down to Barra and the tip of the peninsula (see
below), a fascinating twenty-minute walk. The arcade pillars are
painted red with Chinese characters which advertise each shop, and
you'll pass chandlers and fishing-supply shops (selling nets and
great steel hawsers), greasy electrical and hardware stores, pawn

shops, incense sellers, peddlers with jade ornaments, vegetable sellers and *dai pai dongs*. There's a small temple at no. 131, while the side streets around conceal a tumbledown world of dark, peeling, tatty shops and mildewed houses.

Closer to the Floating Casino you'll find similar streets of similar interest. Some, like **Rua da Felicidade** – almost parallel with the main avenue – have been spruced up, and what was once a red-light district of sordid repute is now a fairly endearing run of small guest houses, shops selling luridly coloured strips of cured beef and pork (a local Cantonese speciality), seafood restaurants and cake shops. It was still considered suitably rough to double as old Shanghai, when scenes in *Indiana Jones and the Temple of Doom* were filmed here.

More basic in every way are the streets over on the other side of the main avenue, which can have changed little since last century. Turn down **Rua de Cinco de Outubro** for its traditional tea houses, one at no. 126–130, another at no. 159, and the splendid *Farmacia Tai Neng Tong* on the left at no. 146, which has a remarkable decorated facade and sculpted interior. Beyond, the street opens out into **Largo do Pagode do Bazar**, a small market square and site of the **Hong Kung temple**, past which things become more intense as the very old surrounding streets degenerate into a noisome wholesale market: wicker baskets full of vegetables and roots, chickens in coops waiting to be killed and plucked, and whole side alleys turned over to different trades – one full of ironmongers, another of street barbers. In a similar vein, **Rua das Estalagens**, **Rua da Tercena** and the parallel **Rua dos Ervanarios** are also worth investigating. Along these you'll find smiths beating metal, jade carvers, carpenters working wood and various stores selling joss sticks, wedding dresses, antiques, blackwood furniture, medicines, silk and shoes.

São Paulo and the Fortaleza do Monte

Macau's most enduring monument – and its most famous image – is the imposing facade of the church of São Paulo, which stands high above the nest of streets to the north of the main avenue. Building began in 1602 on a Jesuit church here, known as Madre de Deus ("Mother of God"), and its rich design reflected the precocious, cosmopolitan nature of early Macau. Designed by an Italian, it was built largely by Japanese craftsmen who produced a stunning Spanish-style retable-facade that took twenty-five years to complete. The church and adjacent Jesuit college became a noted centre of learning, while the building evoked rapture in those who saw it: "I have not seen anything that can equal it, even in all the beautiful churches of Italy, except St Peter's" wrote one visitor in the 1630s. However, following the expulsion of the Jesuits from Macau, the college did duty as an army barracks and on a fateful day in 1835 a fire, which had started in the kitchens, swept through the entire complex leaving just the carved stone facade.

Approaching up the impressive wide swathe of steps (floodlit at night), you can just about convince yourself that the church still stands, but on reaching the terrace the **facade** is revealed, like a misplaced theatre backdrop, rising in four tiers and chipped and cracked with age and fire damage. The statues and reliefs carved on the facade over 350 years ago have lost none of their power and are worth a cricked neck to study more closely: a dove at the top (the Holy Spirit) is flanked by the sun and moon; below is Jesus, around whom reliefs show the implements of the crucifixion – a ladder, manacles, a thorn crown, a flail. Below are the Virgin Mary and Angels, flowers representing China (a peony) and Japan (chrysanthemum), a griffin and a rigged galleon, while the bottom tier holds four Jesuit saints, and the crowning words "Mater Dei" above the central door.

In what was the nave and crypt, behind the facade, a new **museum** is destined to open during 1997, detailing the building and design of the church. The architects took great care to tailor the museum building to the extraordinarily elegant facade, which rather begs the question of why the square below the steps was not afforded the same protection. What was once a harmonious cobbled expanse is now disfigured by a shopping centre, of all things.

Fortaleza do Monte

To the right of the church, a path and steps lead up the few hundred metres to the solid **Fortaleza do Monte** (daily 9am–5.30pm; free), a fortress that was part of the Jesuit complex of São Paulo and dates from the same period. It saw action only once, when its cannon helped drive back the Dutch in 1622, and like São Paulo fell into disuse after the Jesuits had gone. From the ramparts (made from a hardened mixture of earth, shells, straw and lime, packed in layers between strips of wood) you can appreciate its fine defensive position, cannon still pointing out to the water and giving fine views around almost the whole peninsula – only the Guia fort and lighthouse to the east is higher. The well-kept grounds contain a meteorological station (in the pale yellow colonial building), and, most welcome after the climb, a small bar at the entrance; there's a tourist information counter here, too.

The Camões Garden and Museum; the Old Protestant Cemetery

From São Paulo, Rua de São Paulo and Rua do Santo António run northwest towards the Camões Garden, past the church of **Santo António**. This is rather plain in appearance, though given that it was wrecked by fire in 1809, 1874 and 1930 it's perhaps surprising that it survives at all. Each St Anthony's Day (June 13), the saint – a mili-

tary figurehead – is presented with his wages by the President of the
Senate, and then his image paraded around the city to inspect
Macau's battlements.

Beyond is **Praça Luís de Camões** (buses #17, #18 & #19 all
run past), at the head of which the **Jardim Luís de Camões** is a
garden of banyans, ferns and flowers commemorating the sixteenth-
century Portuguese poet who is supposed to have visited Macau and
written part of his epic *Os Lusías* (about Vasco de Gama's voyages)
in the vicinity. There's a bust of Camões, encircled by rocks, and
although there's no real evidence that he ever did come to Macau,
the Macanese have awarded themselves an annual holiday in his
name, just in case. The garden was once part of the grounds of the
adjacent building, a stylish late eighteenth-century country villa,
originally called the **Casa Garden**, and later the headquarters of the
British East India Company in Macau. Now known as the Fundação
Oriente, it contains the **Museu de Luís de Camoes** (daily 11am–
5pm; 1ptca), whose historical and art collection pertaining to
Macau is wide-ranging, and includes some attractive old prints of
the enclave.

The Old Protestant Cemetery
To the side of the museum, you might need to knock in order to
gain entrance to the **Old Protestant Cemetery**, established in
1814 as a plaque above the door records. In here lie many of the
non-Portuguese traders and visitors who passed through Macau,
some of them shifted to this cemetery in later years as the pre-
1814 gravestones show. This was because for decades Protestants
who died in Macau had no set burial place: the Catholic
Portuguese didn't want them cluttering up the city and the
Chinese objected if they were interred on ancestral lands. The
older graves were moved here from various resting places outside
the city walls after the East India Company bought the land to set
up their own cemetery.

The most famous resident is the artist **George Chinnery** (on
the cemetery's upper tier), who spent his life painting much of the
local Chinese coast; a plaque on his tomb recounts how he
proclaimed the Christian message of Goodwill Towards All Men
"by word and by brush". There's also real interest in roaming
around to seek out the various poignant graves, many belonging
to ordinary **seamen** who died in the seas nearby. It was a dangerous, uncomfortable time to be at sea: Samuel Smith "died by a fall
from aloft"; the cabin boy of ship's master Athson similarly met
his end "through the effects of a fall into the hold"; while poor
Oliver Mitchell "died of dysentery". There's also the grave of the
missionary Robert Morrison, who translated the Bible into
Chinese, and his wife who died in childbirth. The small **Morrison
Chapel** in the grounds, formerly the British Chapel, was conse-
crated in 1822.

*For the full
rundown of
grave
inscriptions,
the MTIB sells a
fascinating
book called* The
Protestant
Cemeteries of
Macau *by
Manuel
Teixera, which
covers both this
cemetery and
the New
Protestant
Cemetery –
over by the Kun
Iam temple, off
Avenida do
Coronel
Mesquita.*

MACAU

East: across to the Outer Harbour

The largest cemetery on the peninsula is over to the east from here, the otherwise undistinguished **Cemeterio São Miguel** (daily 8am–6pm), from where Avenida do Conselheiro Ferreira de Almeida – with its fine colonial mansions set back from the road – takes you to the quiet **Jardim Lou Lim Ieoc** (daily 6am–10pm; 1ptca, free on Fri). A formal Chinese garden enclosed by a high wall, with the usual grottoes, pavilions, carp ponds, shrubs and trees, it was built in the nineteenth century and modelled on the classical gardens of Suzhou, in China. It's known locally as Lou Kau, after the nineteenth-century Chinese merchant who funded its construction; his son was Lou Lim Ieoc.

Around the corner, on Avenida de Sidonio Pais (at the junction with Rua de Silva Mendes), the granite **Sun Yat-sen Memorial Home** (Mon & Wed–Sun 10am–1pm & 2.30–5pm; free), a Moorish-style building, was built by the republican leader's family to house relics and photos. Sun Yat-sen lived in Macau for a few years, practising as a doctor, before developing his revolutionary beliefs, and while there's no massive interest here, you could spend half an hour quite happily in this odd building. There's a Chinese reading room on the ground floor, while upstairs Mrs Sun-Yat-sen's former bedroom opens onto a balcony with green twisted pillars. Rooms off here are lined with photocopied manuscripts of less-than-thrilling content ("Dr Sun narrating the beginning of revolutionary activities") and some very poor copies of old photos of Dr Sun and various comrades and committees. Things pick up slightly on the top floor where there's a photographic record of the war against the Japanese, led by the "Great Man", Chiang Kai-Shek. Here scenes of Japanese atrocities (like the newspaper report of two soldiers engaged in a beheading competition) sit uneasily alongside pictures of Chiang hobnobbing with Roosevelt, Churchill, Gandhi and Mountbatten.

Guia Fortress

North of here, the steep hill leads up to the nearby **Guia Fortress**, built in 1638 on the highest point in the territory. It was originally designed to defend the border with China, though it's seen most service as an observation post given its extraordinary perch above the whole peninsula. It's a long, hot walk up the quiet lane to the fort, but you'll be rewarded by the pick of the views in Macau and a small seventeenth-century chapel within the walls dedicated to Our Lady of Guia, which contains an image of the Virgin that local legend says left the chapel and deflected Dutch bullets with her robe during the Dutch attack of 1622. You can only get into the chapel once a year, on August 5 (6–9am), the saint's day. The chapel's other function was to ring its bell to warn of storms, something now taken care of by the fortress's lighthouse, built in 1865 and crowning the hill. From the fortress walls, among other sweeping views are those over the **Outer Harbour**, the Porto Exterior, where you probably arrived.

Within the ramparts (daily 9am–5.30pm), there's a small tourist information office whose most useful function is to provide much-needed drinks in an adjacent bar.

The Maritime Terminal to the Hotel Lisboa

There's been a phenomenal amount of new development on the eastern side of the Guia hill, between the new **Maritime Terminal** and the *Hotel Lisboa*, much of it on land reclaimed from the sea. For the most part, it's office and hotel buildings, though attractions around the terminal include the old **Jai Alai Stadium** (now full of casino games) and a massive *Yaohan* department store.

Further down Rua Luis Gonzaga Gomes the so-called **Tourist Activity Centre**, in front of the Forum, is the latest draw, basically a complex housing exhibition space and the **Museu da Grande Prémio** (daily 10am–6pm; 10ptcs, children 5ptcs). This, the city's Grand Prix Museum was established to commemorate the fortieth anniversary of the Macau Grand Prix in 1993 – a race now considered one of the highlights of the Formula 3 calendar. The subterranean hall displays vintage and modern racing cars and backs up the vehicles with race videos and information boards – all frankly rather dull and rescued only by the opportunity of spending a few minutes strapped into a race simulator which brings you face to face with the twists and turns of the Formula 3 circuit.

North to the Barrier Gate

There are a couple of stops worth making on the way north to the Barrier Gate, though you're going to have to be very energetic to want to do it all on foot. By public transport, the best way is to use bus #5, which you can catch on the main Avenida de Almeida Ribeiro, getting off about halfway down Avenida Horta e Costa.

Kun Iam Temple

A couple of blocks north on the parallel Avenida do Coronel Mesquita is the splendid **Kun Iam Temple** (daily 7am–6pm), entered through a banyan-planted courtyard. Dedicated to the Buddhist Goddess of Mercy (Kwun Yum or Kuan Yin in Hong Kong), and venue of the signing of the first ever Sino-American treaty in 1844, the temple complex is around four hundred years old and one of the most interesting in both Hong Kong and Macau. There's an overpowering smell of incense inside, and from the formal gardens outside you can look up to the porcelain tableaux that decorate the eaves and roofs of the main buildings. A flight of stone steps approaches the three altars of the main temple, one behind the other, the third one dedicated to Kun Iam herself, dressed in a Chinese bridal suit. She is surrounded by other statues of the eighteen wise men of China; the figure on the left, nearest the fortune teller's desk, with the moustache, round eyes and pointy beard, is Marco Polo, said to have become a Buddhist during his time in China. If you want your fortune told, shake one of the cylinders on the fortune teller's desk in the main temple until a bamboo sliver falls out, when it's matched with the "correct" fortune hanging behind the desk – the Chinese characters are explained to you and you hand over a few *patacas* in return. Elsewhere in the complex, there are plenty of other opportunities to bring yourself good luck, though you'll probably have to join a queue each time. You can touch the miniature tree shaped like the Chinese character for "long life", and turn the stone balls in the mouths of the lions on the main steps three times to the left for luck.

Lin Fong Temple

Pick up the #5 bus again and it runs on, up Avenida do Almirante Lacerda, past a second temple, the **Lin Fong Temple** (daily 7am–6pm), or Lotus Temple – smaller than the Kun Iam and Taoist rather than Buddhist. Built in 1592 in order to provide overnight accommodation for mandarins travelling between Macau and Guangzhou, it has a fine nineteenth-century facade, and altars dedicated to a variety of Chinese deities.

The Barrier Gate

The #5 bus from Lin Fong Miu runs through the less edifying parts of the Macau peninsula, primarily apartments and roadworks, before stopping right outside the imposing stucco **Barrier Gate**, built in the late nineteenth century and marking the border with China. Called the *Portas do Cerco* in Portuguese (or "Siege Gate"), a gate here has always marked the entrance to Portuguese territory, even when the old city walls were much further south. Once upon a time, all you could do was peer through the gate at the other side, but these days it's possible to walk or bus across if you've got the right documents – though you'll join the queue of bulging goods trucks that line up all day in both directions. The **Sun-Yat-sen Memorial Park**, just to the west, sits against the canal that marks the border; there's a statue of the man outside, aviary, greenhouse and café inside.

South to Barra: the A-Ma Temple and the Maritime Museum

MACAU

From the **Leal Senado**, following Rua Central, the route south down the finger of the peninsula to the area known as Barra shouldn't take more than half an hour to walk. Up a small side street, on the right, you pass the peppermint-coloured **Teatro Dom Pedro V**, built in 1873, across from which is the early nineteenth-century church of **Santo Agostinho**, whose pastel walls are decorated with delicate piped icing – the monthly accounts are pinned to the inside of the door, showing expenditure on flowers and "Liturgical Comestibles". Further down Rua Central, the square-towered **São Lourenço** on Rua de São Lourenço also dates from the early nineteenth century, though like Santo Agostinho it's built on much older foundations, both parishes having existed since the very early Portuguese days.

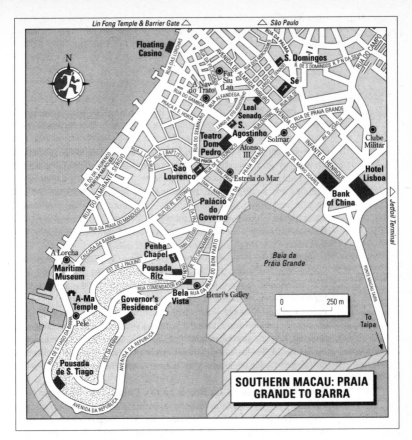

SOUTHERN MACAU: PRAIA GRANDE TO BARRA

Beyond the churches lies the **Barra district** of Macau, the road lined
with cheap Chinese cafés, clothes-making workshops, car repairers
and the work spaces of various craftsmen.

A-Ma Temple

By the water, turn left for the **A-Ma Temple** (*A-Ma Miu* in Cantonese),
built underneath Barra Hill and probably the oldest temple in Macau,
parts of it dating back six hundred years. A-Ma, the Goddess of the Sea
and Queen of Heaven (known in Hong Kong as Tin Hau), is supposed
to have saved a ship from a storm; where the ship landed, the goddess
ascended to heaven and a temple was built on the spot. She subsequently gave her name to the whole territory and is honoured here in a
convoluted complex of temples and altars dotted among the rocks.
Red is the predominant colour, in the buildings and in the characters
painted on the grey and green rocks. Paths lead you above the carved

roof joints, curved like prows and topped by dragons; inside the cluttered pavilions are fortune tellers and incense burners. The busiest time to come is during A-Ma's festival (late April/May; the 23rd day of the third moon), when alongside the devotions there's Cantonese opera in a temporary theatre erected at the site.

The Maritime Museum

Over the road from the temple, in new purpose-built premises designed to look like wharf buildings, is Macau's superb **Maritime Museum** (*Museu Maritimo de Macau*: daily except Tues 10am–5.30pm; 5ptcs, children 3ptcs), a place where you could easily spend an hour or so. Ranged across three storeys is an engaging and well-presented collection relating to local fishing techniques and festivals, Chinese and Portuguese maritime prowess and boat building. Poke around and you'll find navigational equipment, a scale model of seventeenth-century Macau, traditional local clothing used by the fishermen, even a small collection of boats moored at the pier, including a naval tug and a dragon racing boat. The whole collection is made eminently accessible with the help of explanatory English-language notes, video displays and boat models. There's an outdoor café where you can get a beer, and it's possible to take a half-hour **junk ride** from the museum around the Inner Harbour, which is very definitely worth doing – giving you a different perspective of the enclave's comings and goings by water as you chug past warehouses, floating homes, dredgers and tug boats. Daily departures are at 10.30am, 11.30am, 3.30pm and 4.30pm (15ptcs); buy tickets in the museum (which then allows you free entry into the museum).

From the Fortaleza da Barra to the Palácio do Governo

Keep on past the museum and the road swings around the tip of the peninsula past the swanky **Pousada de São Tiago**, built over the ruins of arguably the most important of Macau's fortresses, the **Fortaleza da Barra**. The fortress was finished in 1629, designed to protect the entrance to the Inner Harbour, a function it achieved by hiding two dozen cannon within its ten-metre-high walls. Over the centuries, it fell into disrepair along with all Macau's other forts, and was rescued in 1976 when it was converted into a *pousada* or inn. Don't worry if you can't afford the outlandish prices to stay here, since if you've a genuine interest in seeing the foundations and eighteenth-century chapel inside, no one will mind if you have a look. The *pousada*'s terrace bar is reasonably priced too, and makes a good venue for a pot of tea, overlooking the water.

For full details of the pousada, *see "Accommodation", p.353.*

At this point you're at the edge of the southernmost of the lakes formed by the closing of the bay. A road runs from the tip of the peninsula, skirting the lake to the newest of Macau's monuments the unintentionally bleak **Porta do Entendimento** erected in 1993. Three interlocking black marble fingers, forty metres high, reaching up from a little circular platform supposedly symbolize the "spirit of Macau":

what's hardest to understand, at the "Gate of Understanding", is who'd want to eat whatever it is that the rows of fishermen on the flanks of the monument are intent upon catching from the filthy water.

Continue around the Praia Grande and the energetic can detour up to the left via **Penha Hill**, another steep climb, this time rewarded by the nineteenth-century Bishop's Palace and **Penha chapel** (daily 9am–4pm) – with more grand views over the city. The restored, colonial **Bela Vista** hotel (see pp.352–353) is close by and has an excellent restaurant, with bay views – you'll need to reserve in advance if you want to stop here for lunch. Dropping down again to the harbourside road, Rua da Praia Grande, and heading back to the centre, you'll pass the pink **Palácio do Governo** (Government House), built in the mid-nineteenth century and as graceful as any of the colonial buildings already seen.

Taipa

In the eighteenth century the island of **TAIPA** – just to the south of the peninsula – was actually two adjacent islands, whose sheltered harbour was an important anchorage for trading ships unloading their China-bound cargo at the mouth of the Pearl River. Silting of the channel between the two islands eventually caused them to merge, providing valuable farming land. With the emergence of Hong Kong and the development of the Macau peninsula, Taipa was left to get on as best it could, and for decades it was a quiet, laid-back sort of place, with little industry – just a couple of fireworks factories – and not much to it.

That all changed once it had been decided to build the new airport off the island's east coast, following which construction became almost frenzied in character. A second bridge now crosses to Taipa from the peninsula to cope with the increased traffic, and the modern business and residential area on the edge of old Taipa village is expanding daily. It's the original village that provides the only real attraction these days, with its fine restaurants and colonial waterfront houses, one of which has been turned into a museum.

Across the bridge: the north coast

Buses from the *Hotel Lisboa* cross the 2.5-kilometre **Macau–Taipa bridge**, and going either way there are terrific views from its highest section about halfway across. The **new bridge**, further to the east, is of a similar design, though even longer at around 4km; if you come into the city on the airport bus you'll cross on this one.

The first bus stop on the island is outside the **Hyatt Regency** hotel, a little way beyond the end of the bridge, from where some buses continue to Taipa village, five minutes beyond. Up from the hotel on the left, on the hill overlooking the water, is the **University of Macau**, just down from which – on a ledge east of the bridge – is

Take the #11, #22, #28A or #33 if you're heading directly for Taipa village. All the other buses to Taipa (#14, #21, #21A, #26 and #26A) stop outside the Hyatt Regency, at the roundabout outside Taipa village itself (a 15-min walk away) and at a stop close to the Taipa House Museum, before running on to Coloane.

Taipa

a small **Kun Iam Temple**, with an image of the goddess in a tiled altar. Further back towards the bridge, on the other (western) side of the hotel, is the more interesting **Pou Tai Un Temple** (daily 9am–6pm). Brightly painted, it's the largest temple on the island and is still being added to, with gardens and pavilions, and a large dining room which serves up vegetarian Chinese meals.

Taipa village

Buses pull up in **TAIPA VILLAGE**'s main square, the **Largo Governador Tamagnini Barbosa**, just back from the sea – a big name for such a half-pint place. There are a couple of cafés here, a bike rental shop and – next to the restaurant, to the side of the garage – the local **Tin Hau Temple**, a small grey-brick building whose doorway is lined with painted red paper.

There are only a few streets to the village and a wander through them takes in a couple of faded squares and some pastel-painted houses in narrow, traffic-free alleys. Largo do Camões, a more spacious square just behind the main one (off Rua Regedor) could

TAIPA VILLAGE

be straight out of rural Portugal, with its peeling, balconied houses and shady trees, if it wasn't for the large **Pak Tai Temple** here. Inside, there's a carved altar whose figures are echoed in the impressive carved frieze above the entrance.

The half an hour it'll take to stroll around all this can be finished off by walking to the older waterfront area of the village, where the Portuguese gentry of Taipa used to live. Head down Rua Correia da Silva from the main square and look for a flight of steps on the right by a bus stop, across from Rua do Cunha. A cobbled road leads up to Taipa's hundred-year-old **Igreja do Carmo** (daily except Tues 8am–5pm), below which, on the banyan-planted waterfront Avenida da Praia, are several late nineteenth- and early twentieth-century **mansions**, built with shutters and verandahs and commanding fine views over the sound to Coloane.

One of the houses has been opened to the public as the **Taipa House Museum** (*Casa Museu*: daily except Mon 9.30am–1pm & 3–5.30pm; free), which shows off the house as it appeared a century ago. Its airy, wooden interior is filled with period blackwood and rosewood furniture, an equipped kitchen, and assorted chinoiserie and Portuguese-influenced bits and bobs. This is only the first house to be restored along the Praia; the others, once spruced up and open, are intended to form a complete cultural and historical exhibition for Taipa.

For reviews of Taipa village's best eating places, see p.358; check their locations on the map opposite.

Back in the centre of the village, narrow Rua do Cunha has evolved into a sort of "Food Street" over the years, and it now incorporates an impressive array of **restaurants** – indeed this is one of the main reasons to come. Lunchtime is especially good, when you'll be sharing the restaurants with the expat Portuguese businessmen who come here for authentic Portuguese food.

The rest of the island

Rent a bike from one of the shops in the village square and you can cycle around the **eastern half** of Taipa in under an hour. Retrace your route back to the main junction outside Taipa village and head straight over, following Estrada Coronel Nicolau de Mesquita, which leads uphill, past the university and above the island's north coast. At the top of the rise is the **United Chinese Cemetery**, with stepped rows of graves leading down to the water. The whole coast below is in the process of being reclaimed and as you move on, what would once have been fairly nice beaches are now disfigured by water drainage pipes, dumper trucks and foundation works. Still, it's an exhilarating ride as the road swoops down the other side of the island, passing the causeway to Coloane and the Avenida da Praia before reaching the main road junction again.

To the **west** of Taipa village, the only draw is the **racecourse**, operated by the Macau Jockey Club. It used to host horse-trotting races, no serious rival to the money-making horse racing in Hong Kong, until a new grass track was laid here at the end of 1989 and regular horse racing started up; the season runs from September to June. A satellite dish beams out the racing to other Asian countries, giving Hong Kong a run for its money at last. The **Four-Faced Buddha Shrine** outside the stadium is meant to bring luck to the punters. Incidentally, most of the buses come this way on their way back to Macau from Taipa village.

Direct from the Macau peninsula, take buses #21, #21A, #26 or #26A which run over the causeway to Coloane village. Moving on from Taipa, either take the same buses from the stop near Taipa House Museum, or the #14, which leaves every 20min from Taipa village's main square.

Coloane

COLOANE island is around twice the size of Taipa, a base for pirates as late as the turn of this century who hid out in the cliffs and caves, seizing the cargoes of trading ships passing between Macau and Guangzhou. Like Taipa, there's little specifically to attract you, other than some eminently peaceful surroundings and a village with the same mix of temples and colonial leftovers. There's been massive land reclamation on the eastern side of the island at the Ka Ho container port, and ongoing reclamation near the causeway, but for now much of Coloane remains relatively enticing, especially as the island has a couple of good sand **beaches** and – with bike rental possible – the means to waste time gently in some fairly isolated bays and hills. Things are set to change beyond all recognition, however, if plans go ahead to build a huge US$300-million trade-and-entertainment **project** on reclaimed land between Taipa and Coloane islands, where the causeway currently stands. The scheme is still awaiting final approval from the Macanese and Chinese authorities, but consists of erecting a World Trade Centre, trade fair building, oriental theme park and up to ten hotels, all to be completed by 1999.

Parque de Seac Pai Wan

On the way around the west coast of the island, the buses from the peninsula and Taipa pass the **Parque de Seac Pai Wan** (Tues–Sun summer 8am–9pm, winter 9am–5pm; free), a twenty-hectare site with gardens, ponds, pavilions and views out over the water. It's probably best visited for the *Balichão* restaurant (see p.358), but there's an aviary (5ptcs) here, too, with peacocks and pheasants, and a display of the local flora and fauna, as well as picnic and barbecue areas. Trails also provide good walking in the park, including one to the 170-metre heights of **Alto de Coloane**.

Coloane village

Most of the buses end their run in **COLOANE VILLAGE**, in a little central square surrounded by shops and cafés; a small covered market stands on one side. Signs point off to the few local attractions, down roads that are all cobbles and cart-tracks. There's little traffic, chickens scratching around the pot-holes, and a ramshackle air about the low, crumbling Chinese houses, mouldering shrines and temples.

Walk down to the bottom of the square and turn left along an alley of shops which winds around to the tiny, pale yellow chapel of

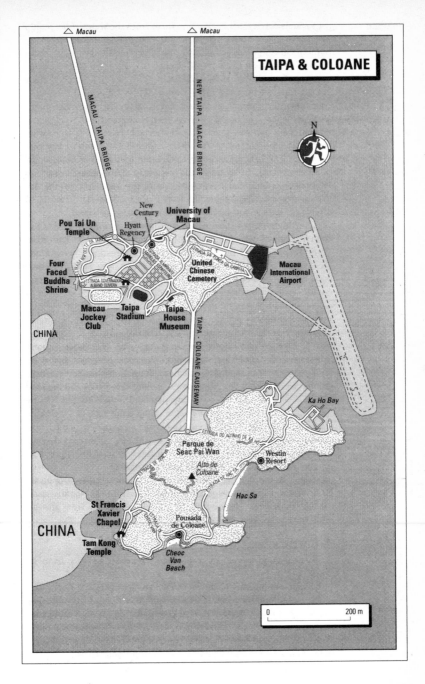

TAIPA & COLOANE

△ Macau
△ Macau

MACAU · TAIPA BRIDGE
NEW TAIPA · MACAU BRIDGE

N

New
Century
**Pou Tai Un
Temple**
Hyatt
Regency
**University of
Macau**
**Four
Faced
Buddha
Shrine**
**United
Chinese
Cemetery**
**Macau
International
Airport**
**Macau
Jockey
Club**
**Taipa
Stadium**
**Taipa
House
Museum**

CHINA

TAIPA · COLOANE CAUSEWAY

Ka Ho Bay

ESTRADA DO ALTINHO DE

**Parque de
Seac Pai Wan**
**Westin
Resort**
Alto de
Coloane
Hac Sa
**St Francis
Xavier
Chapel**
Pousada
de Coloane
CHINA
**Tam Kong
Temple**
Cheoc
Van
Beach

0 _____ 200 m

Coloane

St Francis Xavier, set back a few yards from the waterfront. Built in the same style as others in Macau, the chapel dates from 1928 and honours the eponymous sixteenth-century missionary who passed through Macau on his way to China and Japan. If the friendly priest is around, you'll be let into the sacristy to see St Francis's elbow and a fine selection of other bones of the "Martyrs of Japan" – seventeenth-century Christians killed in Japan after the missionaries were expelled. The bones were rescued from the fire at São Paulo in Macau, kept in the Sé and then transferred here in 1976, since when an increasing number of Japanese visitors have come to pay their respects. The priest was born in Italy, but speaks excellent English and Cantonese. In front of the chapel, the **monument** with the embedded cannonballs commemorates the repelling of the last pirate attack in Coloane, which took place on 12 and 13 July 1910. The latter date is now an annual celebration on the island.

Further along the waterfront (to the left), past the library, a **Kun Iam Temple** is set back among the houses, though the **Tam Kong Temple** at the end of the road is more interesting, facing China across the narrow channel. The prize piece here is a whalebone shaped into a dragon boat with oarsmen – though the locally caught shark's snout runs it a close second. Like St Francis's chapel, if there's someone around to point out all the exciting religious exhibits you'll probably get stung for 10ptcs or so. Dig deep, as there's not much else to spend your money on in Coloane.

The other way along the harbour, past the junks moored offshore and people loafing around the rocks, it's not far to the village's last temple, the small **Sam Seng Temple**. Beyond here, shops are built out over the water, selling dried fish and seafood, while the road leads on to a tiny pier and police station. On the other side of the hill is Coloane's working **shipyard** – a fascinating place where junk building still takes place. Wooden planks fashioned from tree trunks lie around waiting to be seasoned, while work goes on on the two or three half-finished boat hulls, pervaded by the intoxicating smell of sawdust and grease.

Back in the village, there are simple Chinese **cafés** around the church, the rather more attractive *Alem Mar* in the square, and a decent Portuguese **restuarant**, *O Pescador*, across from the bus stop next to the post office.

Coloane's beaches

Coloane's good **beaches** are all easily reached by bike from the village, or by bus.

The closest sandy beach to the village is at **CHEOC VAN**, just a couple of kilometres east. It's fairly well developed, featuring cafés, the *Pousada de Coloane* (see "Accommodation", p.353) and generally murky seawater – though it's mud from the Pearl River rather than anything unsavoury. There's a swimming pool here, too (daily 9am–1pm), which you'll have to pay a few *patacas* to use.

A few kilometres further east, **HAC SA** is much the better choice, since the grey-black sand beach (*hac sa* means "black sand") is very long and backed by a pine grove, with plenty of picnic places amid the trees. You can rent windsurfers here, and even go horse riding, while if you don't fancy the sea or sands, there's a **Sports and Recreation Complex** behind the beach (daily 8am–9pm, Sat until midnight), where a dip in the pool costs 15ptcs. On the sands there's a beach bar, as well as a couple of **restaurants** near the bus stop (including the excellent *Fernando's*; see pp.358–359), while at the northeastern end of the beach the new, upmarket *Westin Resort* complex sprawls across the headland.

KÁ HO, at the far eastern end of the island, is really only for the curious, since the beach has disappeared under the massive new container port and local cement works. It's a nice ride there and back, though.

Coloane

Bus #14 or #21A, from Taipa every 20–40min, stops in Coloane village before moving on to Cheoc Van beach and Hac Sa; you can also get to Hac Sa on the #26 or #26A. Bus #15 runs every 2hr from Coloane to Ká Ho.

Macau Listings

Accommodation

There is a huge number of places to stay in Macau, but weekends and public holidays are always busy with gamblers coming over from Hong Kong, so think about **booking in advance** if you're travelling to Macau at these times. You can do this through the MTIB office in Hong Kong in the Shun Tak Centre (though not for the cheapest hotels), through the Hong Kong reservations offices of the larger hotels (see the reviews below), or directly with the hotels and guest houses themselves in Macau. To call Macau from Hong Kong dial ☎001 853 followed by the subscriber number. Other busy times are Chinese New Year, Easter and during the Macau Grand Prix in late November. If you've arrived without a booking, there are **courtesy phones** in the Jetfoil Terminal from where you can make reservations at one of the larger hotels.

It's worth noting that there are no youth hostels or campsites in Macau. However, the guest houses and hotels are, for the most part, much better value than in Hong Kong – at the bottom end of the market you'll often be able to find

> All the hotels and guest houses below are **marked on the relevant maps**. For places from the Jetfoil Terminal to the *Lisboa* and across to the inner harbour, see the map of central Macau on pp.326–327; for southern Macau, see p.337; and for Taipa and Coloane see p.343.

a self-contained room for around the same price as a sweatbox Kowloon dormitory bed.

Guest houses and hotels

As development takes a grip, Macau is slowly losing many of its cheap hotels, and what new accommodation there is tends to be firmly mid- and upmarket; the strip of land between the Jetfoil Terminal and the *Hotel Lisboa*, in particular, has seen a frenzy of high-class hotel building in the last few years. For now, though, there's still no great shortage of budget accommodation, though many of the available rooms are small, dark and grubby. They're mostly used by weekend gamblers from Hong Kong who aren't too bothered about where they get their two hours' sleep a night before heading off to lose yet more money.

Most of Macau's **cheap hotels** – called either a *vila*, *hospedaria* or *pensão* – are located in two main areas: around the **Hotel Lisboa and Hotel Sintra** (the area bounded by Rua da Praia Grande, Avda. do Infante d'Henrique, Rua Dr. P. J. Lobo and Avda. de Dom João IV) and around the **Floating Casino** (bus #3A from the Jetfoil Terminal). However, few of the owners speak English, so telephoning in advance isn't always an option. The other problem is that many places are highly prejudiced against Westerners, particularly young ones with backpacks. Often, a place is "full", even when it patently isn't; sometimes you won't even get your foot in the door. Basically you'll

Macau: Accommodation

have to accept that there's no consistency – a hotel that we've said is all right, or you've found to be before, might just change its mind the next time you turn up. The places around the *Hotel Lisboa* are generally a better bet than the ones in the more traditional Chinese streets around the Floating Casino, though there are notable exceptions in both areas. Bear in mind that you may have to grab the first available place you see at busy times, looking around later for something better.

You'll have no such problems with the **mid-range** and **top-of-the-range** places, some of which offer very good value for money, especially during midweek when **discounts** make it possible to undercut the official prices. The most obvious concentration of places is along the strip of land **between the Jetfoil Terminal and the Hotel Lisboa**, where most rooms come with good views; more exclusive are the few luxury hotels, including the two *pousadas*, down in **southern Macau**, at the foot of the peninsula. There are only a few choices out on the **islands** of Taipa and Coloane, and they're all fairly expensive too. Still, it's an attractive idea to stay out of the centre, particularly at one of those hotels right on the beach on Coloane, but bear in mind the extra travel to and from the centre.

Between the Jetfoil Terminal and Hotel Lisboa

Hotel Fortuna, Rua de Cantão ☎786333, fax 786363; Hong Kong reservations ☎2517 3728. New 350-room hotel, behind the *Lisboa*, typical of the latest wave of building to hit Macau; steel and glass outside, Chinese decor inside, and nicer than usual rooms, many with harbour views. ⑤.

Hotel Grandeur, Rua de Pequim 199 ☎781233, fax 781211; Hong Kong reservations ☎2857 2846. Top-notch business hotel with all the trimmings, including a revolving restaurant, sauna, pool, gym and coffee shop. ⑤.

Hotel Guia Macau, Estrada do Eng. Trigo 1–5 ☎513888, fax 559822; Hong Kong reservations ☎2770 9303. Smart choice with views (if your room's up high enough), on the southern fringes of the Guia hill, with an atrium and swish elevators. Decently priced, though, for this sort of style, and with a shuttle bus to the *Lisboa* to save you the walk. ④.

Hotel Kingsway, Rua Luis Gonzaga Gomes ☎702888, fax 702828, Hong Kong reservations ☎2548 0989. One of the newest and most glam of Macau's hotel creations, this bristles with facilities – 24-hour coffee shop, upmarket casino, sauna and health spa, and well-appointed rooms with views of the city or

Taipa. There's a shuttle bus to and from the terminal. ⑤.

Hotel Mandarin Oriental, Av. da Amizade ☎567888, fax 594589; Hong Kong reservations ☎2881 1288, US reservations ☎1-800/526 6566. Swanky comforts, including a pool, tennis courts, restaurants, gym and a casino, costing considerably less than the sister hotel in Hong Kong. The only drawback is that it's a little far out for an evening stroll. ⑥.

Hotel Presidente, Av. da Amizade ☎553888, fax 552735, Hong Kong reservations ☎2857 1533. Just a block from the casinos of the *Lisboa*, this modern tower mostly caters for a business clientele. It has some good restaurants (including a Korean one), decent-priced rooms with harbour views, and a free shuttle bus from terminal to hotel. ④–⑤.

Hotel Royal, Estrada da Vitoria 2 ☎552222, fax 563008; Hong Kong reservations ☎2543 6426. A modern highrise, close to the Guia fortress and some extremely good Thai restaurants. It's well-equipped, with standard and deluxe doubles, suites and a pool. Rooms are at the lower end of this price range. ⑤.

Around the Hotel Lisboa and Hotel Sintra

Vila Kimbo, 1st Floor, Av. do Infante d'Henrique 59 ☎710010. Small, clean rooms with TV, toilet and shower – worth a try even if they might not take you. ②.

Hotel Lisboa, Av. da Amizade ☎377666, fax 567193; Hong Kong reservations ☎2546 6944. A monstrous orange circular drum (with adjacent annexe) that has roughly 1100 rooms and a bundle of 24-hour casinos, shops, bars and restaurants, outdoor pool and sauna – some people never set foot outside the door. Rooms in the rear block don't have the same atmosphere, but are cheaper than those at the front – all have nice bathrooms and decent furnishings. You can also pay considerably more than the price category shown for a superior double or suite. ④–⑤.

Hotel Metropole, Rua da Praia Grande 63–63A ☎388166, fax 330890; Hong Kong reservations ☎2540 6333. *CTS*-owned, this well-placed, central hotel is just back from the Praia Grande, and good value if you're looking for rooms with all the fixings. It also has a "fast food" centre, serving *dim sum*, roast meats and congee 8am–midnight. ④.

Pensão Nam In, Trav. da Praia Grande 3 ☎710008. If the *Nam Tin* over the way is full, try here. Rooms aren't quite as nice, but doubles with bath are good value and there are cheap singles with shared bathroom. ②.

Vila Nam Kok, Rua da Praia Grande 95 ☎555523. Fairly large, bright rooms with bath, although the unprepossessing entrance doesn't particularly encourage investigation. ②.

Hotel Nam Tin, Trav. da Praia Grande 4 ☎711212. A friendly place – recently modernized and smartened up – whose largish, bright rooms come with TV and attached bathroom. The street is off Av. de Dom João IV. ②–③.

Hotel Sintra, Av. de Dom João IV ☎710111, fax 567769; Hong Kong reservations ☎2546 6944. Close to the *Lisboa* and all the action, the *Sintra* has had a recent makeover, outside and in, and many of the smart rooms with bath and TV have views across the bay to Taipa – though the land reclamation opposite may eventually change that. ④–⑤.

Wai Lee Guest House, 1st Floor, Av. de Dom João IV 38 ☎710199. The (rather indistinct) sign outside says *Vila Vai Lei* – nice, quiet and friendly and although the rooms are gloomy, they do have TV and shower. One of the better-value options in this price range. ②.

From Avenida Almeida de Ribeiro to São Paulo

Hotel Central, Av. de Almeida Ribeiro 26–28 ☎372404 or ☎373309, fax 332275. One of Macau's oldest hotels, open since 1928. It's a good location, right on the central avenue, and many of the rooms have a bathroom. But ask to see the room first, since others don't even have windows. ③.

Holiday, Estrada do Repouso 36 ☎361696. Close to the Fortaleza and

Macau: Accommodation

São Paulo and recently renovated. The compact rooms are just about worth the money. ②.

Pensão Ka Va, Calçada de São João 5 ☎574022. Just below the Sé, at the junction with Rua Formosa, this smart *pensão* has affordable rooms with bath. ②.

Pensão Long Va, 8th floor, Av. de Almeida Ribeiro 21 ☎371867. Above *Wing Heng* bank, there are lovely large rooms with bath, though you might well be told it's "full". ②.

Around the Floating Casino

East Asia Hotel, Rua da Madeira 1 ☎922433, Hong Kong reservations ☎2540 6333. In the heart of old Macau, off Rua 5 de Outubro, the *East Asia* is a long-standing gamblers' haunt, recently renovated so that many of the rooms now have attached bath. It has a good restaurant, too. ③.

Hotel Grand, Av. de Almeida Ribeiro 146 ☎921111, fax 922397. Splendid 1930s hotel with soaring Deco facade, featuring several restaurants, nightclub, and useful proximity (at least for most of its clientele) to Kam Pek and Floating Casino. Rooms are reasonably good value and there are lots of them. ④.

Hou Kong Hotel, Travessa das Virtudes 1 ☎937555, fax 338884. On an alley down Rua da Felicidade and off Travessa do Auto Novo. More welcoming than most along here, a real hotel with clean, balconied rooms. ③.

Hotel Ko Wah, 3rd Floor, Rua da Felicidade 71 ☎375599. A reasonably pleasant hotel on one of Macau's most interesting streets. It's seen better days, though most of the largish, refurbished rooms have bath and TV, making this one of the most attractive budget choices. ②–③.

Vila Kuan Heng, 2nd Floor, Rua Ponte e Horta 3–4 ☎573629. The best of the budget options on this square, which is just off Rua das Lorchas. Not much English spoken, but you should be able to snag yourself a spick-and-span room with attached bathroom. ②.

Hotel London, Praça Ponte e Horta 4 ☎937761. Just about warrants the title "hotel", though things are never quite as impressive once you leave the lobby behind. Still, these are well-equipped rooms (singles, doubles and triples) in a decent location; prices tend to increase to the next category at weekends. ②.

Hotel Peninsula, Rua das Lorchas, Ponte Cais 14 ☎318899, fax 344933. Almost next to the Floating Casino, your money buys a modern, clean room in a building overlooking the water. Air-conditioning too, and some good-value suites if you want to blow your winnings. ③.

Ruby Pension, Ru Nova do Comercio 11 ☎923118. Behind the *Grand*, this is slightly fancier than the guest houses on the other side of the avenue. ②.

Hotel Sun Sun, Praça Ponte e Horta 14–16 ☎939393, fax 938822; Hong Kong reservations ☎2517 4273. Smart new hotel with inner harbour views, inoffensively furnished rooms with TV and bath, and plenty of marble and wood in the lobby. ③–④.

Vila Universal, Rua da Felicidade 73 ☎573247. Popular place, midway between guest house and hotel standard. There's a relatively friendly welcome here, some English spoken, and decent rooms for the price. ②.

Hospedaria Vong Kong, Rua das Lorchas 45 ☎574016. Opposite the *Gulf* service station, this is about as cheap as it gets in Macau, with rock-bottom singles and larger doubles; fairly spartan facilities, though. ①.

Southern Macau

Bela Vista, Rua Comendador Kou Ho Neng 8 ☎965333, fax 965588; Hong Kong reservations ☎2881 1288, US reservations ☎1-800/526 6566. The finest colonial hotel in Macau, the *Bela Vista* is a grand building with balconied suites and a high-ceilinged dining room where splendid meals are served on the terrace (see p.357). Renovated using imported Portuguese materials and specialist craftsmen, there are just eight sumptuous suites: book well in advance if you want to stay at the weekend (or you want an unencumbered bay view), at least a few days ahead at other times. It's easily the most pricey choice, with rooms running from 1800 to 5000ptcs. ⑥.

Pousada Ritz, Rua da Boa Vista 2 ☎339955, fax 317826; Hong Kong reservations ☎2739 6993. Above the *Bela Vista*, and accordingly graced with superb views from its terrace and best rooms. There's an indoor pool and billiards room, among other amenities. It's also the one luxury hotel here likely to have room at short notice, since it has five times as many rooms as the other two put together. ⑥.

Pousada de São Tiago, Av. da República ☎378111, fax 552170; Hong Kong reservations ☎2739 1216. A gloriously preserved seventeenth-century fortress now turned into an upmarket hotel with all the creature comforts and an unbeatable location at the foot of the peninsula. Rooms with views cost around 300ptcs extra; there's a swimming pool and terrace bar. Again, book well in advance for one of the 23 rooms. ⑥.

Taipa

Hyatt Regency, Estrada Almirante Marques Esparteiro 2 ☎831234, fax 830195; Hong Kong reservations ☎2559 0168. Just over the bridge from Macau (all the Taipa buses run past it), it's what you'd expect from the *Hyatt* chain: smart rooms, casino, landscaped swimming pool and attentive staff. Rooms overlooking the water cost most; specify when booking if that's what you want. ⑤–⑥.

New Century, Av. Padre Tomás Pereira 889 ☎831111, fax 832222; Hong Kong reservations ☎2581 9863. Enormous five-star hotel across from the *Hyatt*, and with similar high-class comfort levels. Views are good, and the *Silver Court* restaurant here is also highly recommended. ⑥.

Coloane

Pousada de Coloane, Praia de Cheoc Van ☎882143, fax 882251; Hong Kong reservations ☎2540 8180. For years the only choice on Coloane, the *pousada* is surprisingly inexpensive given its location and facilities. It's a small place, whose 22 rooms have balconies overlooking the beach: book in advance. ④.

Westin Resort, Estrada de Hac Sa ☎871111, fax 871122; Hong Kong reservations ☎2803 2015. Coloane's newest hotel, the *Westin* lies at the far end of Hac Sa's fine beach – a white swathe of terraced rooms spread across the hillside. Ideal for a quiet day or two, and offering excellent private sports facilities, including an 18-hole golf course, two pools, and jacuzzi. All rooms have terrace and beach or sea views. You're a little stranded once the sun goes down, though *Fernando's* (see pp.358–359) is within walking distance and the hotel has three other restaurants. ⑥.

Chapter 19

Eating and Drinking

As in Hong Kong, most of the **food** eaten in Macau is Cantonese. If this is all you eat, however, you would be missing out on a lot, since Macau's unique combination of Portuguese and Asian cuisine – called **Macanese** – is well worth trying. A variety of cafés and restaurants serve straightforward and excellent **Portuguese** food – from *caldo verde* (a cabbage and potato soup), through different varieties of *bacalhau* (dried salted cod, Portugal's national dish), to *pudim flan* (egg custard). Staples like steak, rabbit and sausages, grilled chicken, fried fish, sardines and other seafood dishes are also available, all served in huge quantities. From **Africa** and **India** (Goa particularly) the Portuguese took spices and chillis, and Macanese restaurants nearly always serve enormous spicy prawns and "African Chicken" – Macau's most famous dish, chicken grilled with peppers and chillis. Food from Angola, including fine spicy meat and vegetable stews, is served in at least one of Macau's restaurants. From **Brazil**, there is *feijoda*, an elaborate meal traditionally made from meat, beans, sausage and vegetables.

Most restaurants mix and match all these influences, also using local **Cantonese** ingredients and dishes, so that pigeon, quail and duck, as well as seafood (like crab and sole), are all available alongside the Macanese standbys. One result of this cross-fertilization of culinary ideas is that the Cantonese influence in some supposedly Macanese restaurants is very heavy-handed. Thus steaks

are sometimes small, thick and grilled, rather than flat and fried with garlic; Portuguese staples can be inexpertly cooked; and everything comes at once, like in a Cantonese meal. None of this matters very much, but can be annoying if you've taken the trouble to search out a "Portuguese" restaurant.

Eating in a **Portuguese/Macanese restaurant** in Macau is, however, a revelation if you've already spent time in Hong Kong's Cantonese diners. For a start, freshly baked **bread** is common; all meals are washed down with cheap imported **Portuguese wine** – fine, heavy reds, chilled whites and slightly sparkling *vinho verde*, as well as any number of **ports** and brandies; and you can get decent **coffee** too. In most places, the **menu** is in Portuguese and English as well as Chinese; check the lists below for descriptions of the food you don't recognize.

Vegetarians should do well for themselves. Every Portuguese restaurant serves excellent mixed salads; and most places will fry eggs and serve them up with some of the best french fries around. *Caldo verde* is always good (though you might have to fish out the piece of Portuguese sausage); *sopa álentejana* (garlic and bread soup) is harder to come by, but much tastier than it sounds.

People eat out earlier in Macau than in Hong Kong – you should aim to be at the restaurant by 8pm – and they rarely stay open later than 11–11.30pm. As for the **price of a meal**, it's uniformly good value, certainly compared to similar meals in

A Portuguese/Macanese Menu Reader

**Macau:
Eating and
Drinking**

Basics and Snacks

Arroz	Rice
Batatas fritas	French fries
Legumes	Vegetables
Manteiga	Butter
Omeleta	Omelette
Ovos	Eggs
Pimenta	Pepper
Prego	Steak roll
Sal	Salt
Salada mista	Mixed salad
Sandes	Sandwiches

Meat

Almondegas	Meatballs
Bife	Steak
Chouriço	Spicy sausage
Coelho	Rabbit
Cordoniz	Quail
Costeleta	Chop, cutlet
Dobrada	Tripe
Figado	Liver
Galinha	Chicken
Pombo	Pigeon
Porco	Pork
Salsicha	Sausage

Fish and Seafood

Ameijoas	Clams
Bacalhau	Dried, salted cod
Camarões	Shrimp
Carangueijo	Crab
Gambas	Prawns
Linguado	Sole
Lulas	Squid
Meixilhões	Mussels
Pescada	Hake
Sardinhas	Sardines

Soups

Caldo verde	Green cabbage and potato soup, often served with spicy sausage
Sopa álentejana	Garlic and bread soup with a poached egg
Sopa de mariscos	Shellfish soup
Sopa de peixe	Fish soup

Cooking Terms

Assado	Roasted
Cozido	Boiled, stewed
Frito	Fried
Grelhado	Grilled
No forno	Baked

Specialities

African Chicken (Galinha á Africana)	Chicken baked or grilled with peppers and chillis; either "dry", with spices baked in, or with a thick, spicy sauce
Camarões	Huge grilled prawns with chillis and peppers
Cataplana	Pressure-cooked seafood with bacon, sausage and peppers (named after the dish in which it's cooked)
Cozido á Portuguesa	Boiled casserole of mixed meats (including things like pig's trotters), rice and vegetables
Galinha á Portuguesa	Chicken baked with eggs, potatoes, onion and saffron in a mild, creamy curry sauce
Feijoda	Rich Brazilian stew of beans, pork, sausage and vegetables
Pasteis de bacalhau	Cod fishcakes, deep-fried
Porco á álentejana	Pork and clams in a stew
Pudim flán	Creme caramel
Arroz doce	Portuguese rice pudding

Drinks

Água mineral	Mineral water
Café	Coffee
Chá	Tea
Cerveja	Beer
Sumo de laranja	Orange juice
Vinho	Wine (*tinto*, red; *branco*, white)
Vinho do Porto	Port (both red and white)

Macau: Eating and Drinking

Vinho verde	Green wine – ie a young wine, slightly sparkling and very refreshing. It can be white, red or rosé in Portugal but in Macau is usually white	

Meals

Almoço	Lunch
Comidas	Meals
Jantar	Dinner
Prato dia/	Dish/menu of the day
Menu do dia	

Hong Kong: soup or salad, a main course, half a bottle of wine and coffee comes to around 170ptcs almost everywhere; dessert and a glass of port adds another 40–50ptcs – though two courses in most restaurants will fill you to the brim since servings are so large. Eating Macanese specialities – such as curried crab and grilled prawns – pushes the price up a little, since these are charged at the daily market rate. To all restaurant bills, add fifteen percent service charge and tax; it'll usually be included in the total.

There isn't the **bar scene** that there is in Hong Kong, and most of your drinking will be done with your meal – much the most civilized way to while away an evening. There are a couple of late-night bars in the north of the city, though for a relaxed beer or glass of wine, several of the Portuguese cafés and restaurants can accommodate you at outdoor tables, while all the upmarket hotels have their own bars.

Cafés

You'll find small **cafés** all over Macau, many serving a mixture of local Cantonese food and Portuguese-style snacks. Some are known as *Casa de Pasto*, a traditional Portuguese workers' dining room, though in Macau, as often as not, they're thoroughly Chinese in cuisine and atmosphere. For late-night meals and snacks, many hotels have **24-hour coffee shops**, serving bleary-eyed gamblers: the handiest is the one in the *Lisboa*, but there are others in the *Kingsway* and *Holiday Inn*, to name just three.

Bolo de Arroz, Trav. de São Domingos. Near the Largo do Senado, this is a great place for Portuguese pastries and good coffee. Open Tues–Sun 9am–8pm.

Caravela, Rua Comandante Mate e Oliveira 7H. Excellent Portuguese *pastelaria*, with outdoor tables, great cakes and coffee and a dish of the day. Despite the address it's a bit tricky to find: it's actually off the street, on an alley which runs between Avda. Dom João IV and Rua Dr. P. J. Lobo. Open Mon–Sat 10am–11pm.

Casa de Pasto San Pou, Rua de Camilo Pessanha 10. Very cheap snacks and meals in a cake shop-cum-café in the old market quarter. Large portions of Portuguese and Chinese food.

Garden Terrace, *Pousada de São Tiago*, Av. da República. Excellent breakfasts served on the *pousada* terrace: fresh fruit juices, eggs, home-baked pastries and bread and good coffee – a thoroughly civilized way to start the day. Breakfast served 7–11am; open for lunch and afternoon tea, too.

Leitaria I Son, Largo do Leal Senado 7. A dairy-products café, with an endless variety of inexpensive milk puddings, ice cream and milkshakes, as well as fried-egg breakfasts and tea with real milk.

Noite e Dia, *Hotel Lisboa*, Av. da Amizade. The *Lisboa*'s splendid 24-hour coffee shop, serving everything from *dim sum* and breakfast to good-value snacks and meals.

Riquexo, Av. Sidónio Pai 69. Odd site, inside the *Park n' Shop*, but offering very good-value Macanese dishes, snacks and coffee. Open 9am–9pm.

Safari, Patio do Coto Velo 14. Close to the Leal Senado, off the main avenue, this has good-value European breakfasts, plus other snacks, tea and coffee, and regular meals. Open 9am–11pm.

Sopa de Fitas Boa Fortuna, Av. do Infante d'Henrique 41. Late-opening noodle soup specialist. A bowlful for around 20ptcs. Open 11am–4.30am.

Sopa de Fitas Infante, Av. do Infante d'Henrique 65. No English menu in this cheap noodle shop, so you'll have to point. Bowls of noodles for around 20ptcs. Open 11am–4am.

Restaurants

The reviews below concentrate on the excellent Portuguese and Macanese restaurants in Macau, but there are other options in the unlikely instance that you tire of this kind of food. You can buy wine at the same inexpensive prices in all Macau's restaurants, Portuguese or not.

Macanese and Portuguese

All the following restaurants, except the Montanha Russa, are marked on the map of southern Macau on p.337

Afonso III, Rua Central 11A ☎586272. Split-level café-restaurant presided over by Afonso – former chef at the *Hyatt* – who will decipher the Portuguese menu for you. Provincial dishes feature, like a mammoth, oily serving of Álentejo pork with clams, drenched in fresh coriander. Other seafood dishes are pricier. Check the daily list of specials to see what the mainly Portuguese clientele is eating. Open noon–3pm & 7–11pm; closed every other Thurs.

Bela Vista, Rua Comendador Kou Ho Neng 8 ☎965333. Macau's most exclusive hotel has a fine Portuguese-Continental restaurant open to all – make a reservation and ask for a terrace seat. There's a good *cataplana* (pressure-cooked fish and seafood in spicy sauce) and a separate port list that runs from around 50ptcs a glass to 7500ptcs a bottle. It's more expensive than all the other restaurants in this section, though if careful you could still get away for 250ptcs for two courses and wine; more like 350ptcs once coffee, dessert and service have been added. Open noon–3pm & 7pm–midnight.

Clube Militar, Av. de Praia Grande 795 ☎714009. The private club within the São Francisco barracks has a dining room open to the public and, along with the *Bela Vista*, it's one of the colonial dining experiences in Macau – a grand setting with formal staff and sparkling silver service. That said, the food never quite matches the promise: competent Portuguese dishes, on the small side, though there's a very good-value daily three-course set meal. Otherwise, you'll spend 300ptcs for a full meal. Open noon–3pm & 7–11pm.

Estrela do Mar, Travessa do Pavia 11 ☎322074. A small and friendly restaurant, with Portuguese and Macanese specialities, including a selection of *bacalhau* dishes. Not the best food in town by any means, but cheaper than most, though you're probably better off just popping in for a coffee and a brandy – there's a couple of outdoor tables. It's off Rua da Praia Grande, close to the Palácio do Governo. Open 11am–midnight.

Fat Siu Lau, Rua da Felicidade 64 ☎573585. The oldest and most famous of Macau's restaurants, with pigeon the speciality, best eaten with their excellent French fries. Nice, relaxed atmosphere, but – pigeon apart – not the best food in Macau by any means, whatever the adverts say. Open 11am–1am.

Henri's Galley, Av. da República 4 ☎556251. Rather subdued interior, but the spicy prawns are renowned as the best in Macau, or try the curried crab, roast pigeon or quail, or any of the immense chicken dishes – *Galinha á Portuguesa* and African Chicken are both terrific and you'll need the aprons provided. The tables outside overlooking the bay get the traffic noise; go for an indoor window seat instead. Open noon–11pm.

A Lorcha, Rua do Almirante Sergio 289 ☎313193. Just around the corner from the Maritime Museum, this attractive wood-beamed restaurant is always busy – it's best to reserve in advance for lunch when the Portuguese business community are out in force. There's a large menu

Macau: Eating and Drinking

of Portuguese staples, superbly cooked, which the Governor of Macau is reputed to enjoy on regular visits. Open 1–3pm & 7pm–midnight; closed Tues.

Montanha Russa, Jardim da Montanha Russa, Estrada Ferreira de Amaral ☎302731. Highly attractive set-up with outdoor dining under the trees in the little *jardim*. Steak, mullet, cod, pork and clams at reasonable prices, attracting a loyal Portuguese clientele, especially at lunchtime. Go for the daily specials – they rarely miss. It's a bit far out in the north of the city, up near the Kun lam Temple. Open Tues–Sun noon–1pm.

A Nav do Trato, Rua do Gamboa 10A ☎934119. The "Black Ship" is a welcome central addition, with great grilled shrimp and daily specials. It's a relaxed spot with good service and decent wine, and the bonus of one of Macau's few bars downstairs (see p.360). Open noon–3pm & 7–10.30pm.

Pele, Rua de São Tiago da Barra 25 ☎965624. The African Chicken comes swimming in sauce and there are great spicy prawns to start. But there's a funereal café atmosphere and no great surprises on the menu. The restaurant is close to the *pousada*. Open noon–11.30pm.

Solmar Restaurante, Rua da Praia Grande 8–10 ☎574391. Old (since 1961), averagely priced Macanese restaurant with reliable if unadventurous food, including sardines and all the other classics. Open 11am–11pm.

TAIPA

The restaurants below are all marked on the map of Taipa village on p.340.

Galo, Rua do Cunha 47 ☎827318. Decorated in Portuguese country style with the cock (*galo*) – the national emblem of Portugal – much in evidence. The photographic menu is very Portuguese – plenty of boiled meats and pig's trotters – but mainstream dishes include steaks, great grilled squid and large mixed salads. You can eat very well, very cheaply, though the staff are a bit grumpy. Open 11.30am–10pm.

Mocambique, Rua dos Clerigos 28a ☎827471. Small restaurant serving tasty Portuguese colonial food, with various dishes from Goa and Africa – from *samosas* to African Chicken. Standard prices and a popular place, so book ahead. Open 12.45–3pm & 7.30–10pm.

Panda, Rua Carlos Eugénio 4–8 ☎827338. Reasonably priced and with good sardines but betrays its Chinese influence in the kitchen – unless you order your courses separately, everything comes at once, and not always delivered with good grace either. Open Mon–Fri 11am–2.30pm & 6–10.30pm, Sat & Sun 11am–10.30pm.

Pinocchio's, Rua do Sol 4 ☎827128. Good Macanese food served at tables in an outdoor garden – fish cakes, crab and prawns are well regarded. Open noon–11.30pm.

O Santos, Rua do Cunha 20 ☎827508. The best place on Taipa for authentic, traditional café food – *bacalhau*, grilled squid, rabbit, sardines, Portuguese sausage, steak and fries, fried fish and rice. It's great value, and serves huge portions washed down with decent Portuguese wine, port and strong espresso coffee. Open noon–3pm & 6–10pm.

COLOANE

Balichão, Parque de Seac Pai-Wan ☎870098. Well-regarded Portuguese-Macanese food in an attractive restaurant in Coloane's park. This is a nice place for lunch (the buses to Coloane village all pass by the park entrance); at night, you'll probably want to come back in a taxi. Open Tues–Sun noon–11pm.

Caçarola, Rua das Gaivotas 8 ☎882226. Welcoming, popular restaurant with excellent daily specials and very affordable prices. It's off the main village square. Open Tues–Sun noon–3pm & 7–11pm.

Fernando's, Hac Sa Beach ☎882531. The sign is hidden, but this is very close to the bus stop, at the end of the car park, under the *Coca Cola* sign – the nearest to the sea in a small line of cafés. Walk through to the back and there's a huge barn-like dining room, where Fernando explains the menu to novices – clams and crab are house specials, the grilled chicken is enormous and succulent. Slightly pricier than usual, but then it's better than usual, and backs on to the beach. Open noon–10pm.

O Pescador, Rua do Cordoaria 87–91 ☎880197. Village restaurant, next to the post office, that's not at all bad, with daily specials and all the usual standards at fair prices. Open noon–3pm & 7–10pm.

Pousada de Coloane, Praia de Cheoc Van ☎882143. Reserve a table if you want to eat here – deservedly popular for the *cataplana* dishes and other seafood specialities. Often, tables are set on the terrace. Open noon–10.30pm.

Chinese

Dai pai dongs. Along Rua Escola Comercial, off Av. do Infante d'Henrique (to the side of the sports ground between the hotels *Sintra* and *Lisboa*). Cheap and cheerful noodle and seafood dishes, eaten outdoors.

Fook Lam Mun, Av. da Amizade 63 ☎786622. Next to the *Presidente* hotel, this is the place to come for Cantonese seafood specialities. High prices (although more affordable in the morning and at lunchtime for *dim sum*) but considered one of the best in town. Open 7.30am–11pm.

Long Kei, Largo de Senado 7B ☎573970. A huge menu takes in good *dim sum* and Cantonese food. Open 11am–11pm.

Palace, Av. Almeida Ribeiro 24–28 ☎373838. *Dim sum* restaurant on the central avenue. Open 7am–midnight.

Shanghai 456, New Wing, Mezzanine Floor, *Hotel Lisboa*, Av. da Amizade ☎388474. Long-established Shanghai restaurant which does the rounds of other regional cuisines, too, including Szechuan and Beijing dishes. Open 11am–11pm.

Silver Court, *New Century Hotel*, Estrada Almirante Marques Esparteiro, Taipa ☎831111. Wonderful Cantonese seafood

restaurant that's pricier than most, but is fine value compared to equivalents in Hong Kong. Specialities are from the Shun-de region, south of Guangzhou, like carp mousse dumplings and pigeon. Open 9am–3pm & 6–11pm.

Other Asian restaurants

Baan Thai, Rua de Henrique de Macedo ☎344663. Authentic Thai food, which might be too hot for some. It's close to the *Hotel Royal*, one of several Thai places in this district. Open 6.30pm–6am.

Ko Ka, Rua Ferreira do Amaral 21 ☎568993. Across the gardens from the *Hotel Royal*, this late-opening Thai restaurant is one of the most reasonably priced in town, though the cooking isn't always spot on. Open 5.30pm–6am.

Korean, Mezzanine Floor, *Hotel Presidente*, Av. da Amizade ☎569039. Top-quality Korean restaurant with barbecue grills. Open 11am–midnight.

Tee Jei, Estrada Nova, Edifício Va Fai Un, Loja C, Taipa ☎827103. Tandoori Indian cooking; try the mixed grill for a taste of everything. It's at the crossroads on the outskirts of the village. Open noon–3pm & 6.30–11pm.

Thai Restaurante, Rua Abreu Nunes 27E ☎552255. Superb Thai food with portions large enough to defeat most people. Soups are marvellous (especially the mixed seafood) and fish and shellfish are a strong point. Go with a friend – on your own, two dishes is plenty. Open 6pm–3.30am.

Italian

Café Luso, Rua Central 33b ☎570413. A good Italian/Mediterranean restaurant with some interesting daily specials (squid is always excellent, as is the stuffed tiger prawn), and very reasonably priced pasta and pizzas. Friendly staff. Open noon–3pm & 7–11pm.

Mezzaluna, *Mandarin Oriental*, Av. da Amizade ☎567888. Exteremly elegant contemporary Italian cooking in swish surroundings; the wood-fired pizzas are Macau's finest. Open Tues–Sun 12.30–3pm & 6.30–11pm.

Macau: Eating and Drinking

Pizzeria Toscana, Av. da Amizade ☎726637. Genuine Italian food and not just pizzas, though these are superb, as is the coffee. It's out at the Jetfoil Terminal, near the Grand Prix stand. Open 9am–11.30pm.

Buying your own food and wine

Apart from the market on Rua Sul do Mercado de São Domingos, where you can buy fruit and veg, there are branches of the **supermarket** *Park 'N' Shop* at Av. Sidonio Pais 69 and Praça Ponte e Horta 11. *Days and Days*, at Rua da Praia Grande 57b, also sells cheap wine and spirits.

Bars

Bar da Guia, *Mandarin Oriental*, Av. da Amizade. One of the better hotel bars, and every weekday 5–9pm and weekend 11am–9pm, there's big-screen sporting action. Happy Hour is 5–7pm.

Caravela, Rua Comandante Mate e Oliveira 7H. Portuguese *pastelaria*, with beer (and coffee and cakes) served outside in the alley all day (see "Cafés", p.356 too). Open Mon–Sat 10am–11pm.

A Nav do Trato, Rua do Gamboa 10A. Macau's only central bar, and it's not a bad one – juke-box, draft beer (Happy Hour 7.30–8.30pm), friendly staff and a decent restaurant upstairs. Open noon–2am.

Pyretu's, Rua de Pedro Coutinho 106. Macau's liveliest drinking-and-dancing joint, with free-flowing sangria, African and Latin American sounds and a funky clientele. It's a good 25-minute hike from the centre; take a taxi. Open 9pm–3am.

Talker Pub, Rua de Pedro Coutinho 104. Trendy bar with a decent beer list and juke-box, next door to *Pyretu's*; don't go before 11pm. Open 9pm–3am.

Chapter 20

Gambling and other Entertainment

Eating out is one of the two main entertainments in Macau. The other is **gambling** in various shapes and forms, and most people spend their evenings lurching from restaurant to casino. This is no bad thing in moderation – a couple of nights in Macau is all you need to get around the more interesting venues for losing your money. In lots of cases, too, just being a spectator is entertainment enough, particularly at the "sporting" venues – horse- and dog-racing stadiums – which encourage betting (for which, see the next chapter, "Sports and Recreation"). **Cultural** activities of any kind are thin on the ground, though a couple of annual music and arts festivals do their best to bridge the gap.

Gambling

The main thing about **gambling** in Macau is that – with the exception of the casinos in the *Mandarin Oriental, Kingsway* and *Hyatt Regency* hotels – it's a downmarket, no-frills occupation, designed to rake in the largest amount of money in the shortest possible time. If you're expecting the gilt and glitter of Las Vegas (as well as the free drinks and cheap buffet dinners), you're in the wrong town.

The vast majority of the **punters** in Macau's casinos are Hong Kong Chinese, deprived of the legal right to pursue games of chance in their own territory – some deprivation bearing in mind that

gambling is second only in importance to breathing in China. It's not a subdued, high-class operation, and the casinos are noisy, frenetic places – nearly always packed, especially at the weekend, with a constant stream of people who leg it off the jetfoil and into the games.

Given that the sole object of the casinos is to take money off ordinary people, there aren't the **dress restrictions** that you might expect, and in most places you'll be fine as you are. However, **cameras** aren't allowed in any of the casinos and if you've got a bag you'll have to check it in, noting down the serial number of any valuable items in there on a pad provided.

The casinos

The gambling franchise in Macau is held by the *Sociedade de Turismo e Diversoes de Macau (STDM)*, which operates eight **casinos**. Each has its own character and variation of games. To get in, visitors officially need to be (or look) 18; there's no entry fee. Except for the *Victoria*, all the casinos are open 24 hours a day.

Casino Jai-Alai, Outer Harbour, by the Jetfoil Terminal. All-night table action in a stadium that used to host *Jai-Alai* (Basque pelota) games. Also has an off-course betting centre for the dogs.

Casino Kam Pek, Av. de Almeida Ribeiro. Known also as the Chinese Casino on account of the mainly Chinese card and

Macau: Gambling and other Entertainment

How to Win

Basically, you won't win unless you're very lucky, so don't look upon Macau as the way out of your money troubles. You can bet on a series of casino games, some of which are outlined below, or on one of several sporting events which take place regularly throughout the year. Wherever you go, and whatever you do, the same **warnings** apply. Gamble for fun only; *never bet more than you can afford to lose*. It's notoriously easy to get carried away, particularly if you're trying to make up for money that you've already lost. The best advice is to decide beforehand how much you're prepared to lose and then walk away when it's all gone. The same applies if you actually win, since the speed with which you can pour it all back is phenomenal. Remember, too, that the only system that works is the casino's. Recent figures show Macau's casinos pulling in around US$450 million a year.

The Casino Games

There's an astounding number of games on offer in any of Macau's casinos. Lots are familiar: you'll need no coaching to work the **one-armed bandits** or slot machines (called "hungry tigers" locally), which either take Hong Kong dollars or *patacas* and pay out accordingly. Many of the card games are also the ones you would expect, like **baccarat** and **blackjack**.

However, local variations and peculiarly **Chinese games** can make a casino trip more interesting. To sort them all out, ask at the tourist information centres where you can buy the *A-O-A Macau Gambling Guide*, which details all the games, rules and odds. **Boule** is like roulette but with a larger ball and fewer numbers (25) to bet on. **Pai kao** is Chinese dominoes and is utterly confusing for novices. **Fan tan** is easier to grasp, involving a cup being scooped through a pile of buttons which are then counted out in groups of four, bets being laid on how many are left at the end of the count – about as exciting as it sounds. In **dai-siu** ("big-small" in Cantonese) you bet on the value of three dice, either having a small (3–9) or big (10–18) value – this is probably the easiest to pick up if you're new to the games. In all the games, the **minimum bet** is usually $50 ($100 on blackjack).

dice games played here. Very popular and very intense. Also has an off-course betting centre for the dogs.

Casino Macau Palace, Inner Harbour, Av. de Almeida Ribeiro. Otherwise known as the Floating Casino, recently replaced by a new two-decked vessel, though still delightfully downmarket.

Hyatt Regency, Taipa. Among the newest and smallest of the casinos. Very select and for high-rollers only.

Hotel Kingsway, Rua de Luis Gonzaga Gomes. Most recent casino to open, fairly flash and not terribly interesting unless you've come to risk your all – there are very high minimum stakes here.

Hotel Lisboa, Av. da Amizade. The biggest casino in Macau, a four-level extravaganza covering all the possible games.

There are enough comings-and-goings here to entertain you without losing a cent. Bars, restaurants and shops are all within chip-flicking distance and there's also an off-course betting centre for the dog track.

Mandarin Oriental Macau, Av. da Amizade. Upmarket hotel casino, worth popping into for the contrast. Still no Las Vegas, but you'll need decent clothes to play the small range of games.

Victoria, Macau Jockey Club. Over on Taipa, this is only in operation at weekends and on midweek race days.

The arts and culture

The free newspaper, *Macau Travel Talk*, lists the month's **concerts and exhibitions**, the usual **venues** for which are the

Tourist Activity Centre (Rua Luis Gonzaga Gomes) for art displays and exhibitions; the gallery in the **Leal Senado**, which puts on temporary art displays; the **University of Macau** (☎831622) on Taipa, whose auditorium is used for concerts; and – more rarely – the **Jardim Lou Lim Ieoc**, which also hosts recitals and concerts. Other occasional concert venues are a couple of the central churches (like São Lourenço) and the **Macau Forum** (Av. Marciano Baptista ☎702986), which puts on rock gigs now and then.

Cinema

The **Cineteatro Macau**, Rua de Santa Clara (☎572050), near the junction with Rua do Campo, has two screens and four performances a day; there should usually be something in English. Tickets are 35ptcs. There's also a **UA** cinema (☎712622) at the Jai Alai statium, near the Jetfoil Terminal.

Annual arts festivals

Annual arts events worth catching include the **International Music Festival**, held in October, when Chinese and Western orchestras and performers stage concerts at all the above venues over a seven-day period. Tickets go for 100– 300ptcs; check with the MTIB for details. There's also the **Macau Arts Festival**, usually held in February/March, which features a month's worth of events and performances by local cultural and artis- tic groups.

For the last few years, Macau has also held an international **fireworks festival**, when teams compete with each other to produce the biggest and brightest bangs over the Praia Grande. There's no fixed date, so check with the MTIB.

Macau:
Gambling
and other
Entertain-
ment

For a round-up of Macau's religious and national festivals and holidays, see p.319.

Chapter 21

Sports and Recreation

Apart from horse and dog racing, Macau's biggest sporting draw is the annual **Macau Grand Prix**, which takes place on the enclave's streets, part of the circuit following the enlarged shoreline Avenida da Amizade. Accommodation and transport is mobbed over this weekend, and you'll need to book well in advance if you want to see it.

There are various other recreational **sports** on offer too, from squash to horse riding, though most people will probably be content with a swim at one of the good beaches on Coloane.

Spectator sports

Most **spectator sports** take place either at the **Forum** (Av. Marciano Baptista ☎702986) – which hosts things like volleyball, table tennis and indoor athletics meetings – or the new **Taipa Stadium**, a 20,000-seater next to the racecourse, for soccer, track and field events. Major events are listed in *Macau Travel Talk*, and look for posters around the city.

Macau Grand Prix

Held on the third weekend in November, the **Macau Grand Prix** is a Formula 3 event (plus a motorbike race, too). Stand **tickets** for race days run to around $350–600 ($100 on qualifying days) and are available from the Macau Government Tourist Office or from overseas tourist representatives. Be sure to book well in advance.

Horse racing

Horse racing is as popular as it is in Hong Kong, with races held on the enlarged and converted racecourse on Taipa. The *Macau Jockey Club* hosts regular weekend **horse racing** from September to June; more information on ☎821188, and consult the MTIB. The minimum bet on a race is $10. The buses to Taipa (#11, #22, #28A or #33) from close to the *Hotel Lisboa* all return via the racecourse.

Greyhound racing

There's **greyhound racing** at the Canidrome (*Canidromo*; ☎574413) in Av. General Castelo Branco, very close to the Lin Fong Temple; buses #1, #2 and #5 from the Floating Casino go right past it. There are races on Tuesday, Thursday, Saturday and Sunday starting at 8pm, and on Sunday afternoons; entrance is 2ptcs to the public stand, 5ptcs for the members' stand. Again, the minimum bet is $10. You'll find a bar and a restaurant there, alongside the betting facilities.

Participatory sports

Participatory sports available include **squash**, which you can play at the *Hyatt Regency* (☎831234), the *Mandarin Oriental* (☎567888) or the Westin Resort (☎871111) for around 90ptcs a session. Otherwise, head for the *Hotel Lisboa* (☎377666), whose labyrinthine twists and turns conceal a **swimming pool** open to the public and a **snooker and billiards** room.

Macau:
Sports and
Recreation

Hotels With Pools

The following hotels in Macau have swimming pools for the use of guests only:

Hotel Grandeur
Hyatt Regency
Mandarin Oriental
Hotel New Century
Pousada de Coloane
Pousada Ritz
Pousada de São Tiago
Hotel Royal

Hac Sa beach (p.345) on Coloane has a **recreation centre** (Mon–Fri 9am–9pm, Sat & Sun 9am–10pm; 5ptcs) with swimming pool (another 15ptcs), roller-skating, mini-golf, children's playground and tennis courts. You can rent **wind-surfing** equipment on the beach here, too.

Walking/jogging trails criss-cross the land around the Guia Fortress, the most popular a 1700-metre trail reached from the lower car park, just up the hill from the *Guia Hotel*. There are also signposted walking trails on Coloane: the *Trilho de Coloane* and *Trilho Nordeste de Coloane*. The latter is the more accessible, a six-kilometre walk that begins/ends near Ká Ho beach.

In the first week of December the **Macau Marathon** clogs up the enclave's streets, the course running across the peninsula and both islands.

Finally, the **Macau Horse Riding Centre** (Tues–Sun; ☎828303), also at Hac Sa beach, has horses for hire and arranges instruction.

Chapter 22

Directory

AIRLINES Airlines represented in Macau include: *Air France* (c/o *Agencia de Viagens Turisticas Luis Chou*, Av. do Dr. Mário Soares ☎712622); *Air India* (c/o *STDM* Air Travel Dept, *Hotel Lisboa*, new wing, ground floor ☎375068); *Air Macau* (Av. da Praia Grande 639 ☎396 6888); *British Airways* (c/o *Agencia de Viagens Turisticas F. Rodrigues*, Rua Formosa 2A ☎339678); *East Asia Airlines* (Hong Kong helicopter service; ☎725939). For other companies, contact the airport.

AIRPORT Macau International Airport (flight enquiries ☎785448). Current departures are to Beijing, Shanghai and Taipei (with *Air Macau*); Kuala Lumpur (*MAS*); Singapore (*Singapore Airlines*); and Taipei and Kaohsiung (*EVA Airways*).

BANKS AND EXCHANGE Banks are generally open Monday–Friday 9am–4pm, Saturday 9am–noon, though a bank in the arcade of the *Hotel Lisboa* keeps much longer hours than this. Most of the main banks will exchange travellers' cheques. These include *Banco Nacional Ultramarino* (Av. de Almeida Ribeiro 2); *Banco Comercial de Macau* (Av. Praia Grande 22; Av. Sidónio Pais 69A); *Bank of China* (Av. Dr. Mario Soares, and in *Hotel Lisboa*); *Standard Chartered Bank* (Av. Infante d'Henrique); and *Hongkong and Shanghai Bank* (Rua Praia Grande 75; Av. Horta e Costa 122–124; Av. Ferreira de Almeida 17), which gives cash advances with a *Visa* card. The large hotels will also change money, though obviously at a price; and there are licensed money-changers, too (*casa de cambio*), including one at the Jetfoil Terminal and a 24-hour service in the *Hotel Lisboa* There's also a bank on both Taipa and Coloane.

BOOKSHOPS It's hard to find bookshops in Macau that carry English-language books. However, books about Portugal and Macau are available from the *Portuguese Bookshop and Cultural Centre*, Rua de Pedro Nolasco da Silva (near the Sé).

CAR RENTAL Contact *Avis* (at *Mandarin Oriental* ☎336789 or ☎567888; or in Hong Kong ☎2541 2011) or *Happy Mokes* (Macau Ferry Terminal ☎831212 or Hong Kong ☎2540 8180). For moke rentals, expect to pay 450ptcs for 24 hours, with slightly cheaper midweek rates available; rates are inclusive of vehicle and third-party insurance. You need to be at least 21, to have held a driving licence for two years and have an international driving licence. Remember to drive on the left.

CHINA DEPARTURES There's no longer a ferry to Guangzhou, though there are still departures to Kongman (daily at 1.40pm, arrive 3.40pm; around 80ptcs, reserve 3 days in advance); and Shekou (daily at 2.30pm, arrive 4pm; around 100ptcs). Tickets can be bought from *Yuet Tung Shipping Co.*, next to the Floating Casino on the quayside (daily 8am–noon & 2–5.30pm). The bus to Guangzhou leaves daily at 9am and 2pm from outside the main *CTS* office on Rua de Nagasaki (see "Tour Operators" below). Tickets cost

55ptcs one-way, bought from any *CTS* office.

DEPARTURE TAX 22ptcs per person, included in the price of your jetfoil/ferry ticket.

DOCTORS Go to the hospital casualty departments (see below) or look in the telephone directory Yellow Pages under "Médicos".

DRINKING WATER It comes straight from China and is perfectly all right to drink. It doesn't always taste wonderful, though, and you might be happier with bottled water, sold in shops everywhere.

ELECTRICITY Most of Macau's electricity is supplied at 220V, although some buildings in the older parts of the city still use power at 110V. Plugs use three round pins.

EMERGENCIES Call ☎999 for the police. Other numbers include Fire Brigade ☎572222; Ambulance ☎577199 or ☎378311; Public Security Force ☎573333.

HONG KONG DEPARTURES Jetfoil, catamaran and High-speed Ferry tickets (and *East Asia Airlines* helicopter tickets) can be bought at the Jetfoil Terminal ticket offices; the various companies' windows sell tickets for all immediate sailings. For advance tickets and information, use the Jetfoil ticket office at the *Hotel Lisboa* (Mon–Sat 9.30am–11.30pm, Sun 9.30am–7.30pm) or call the following numbers: Jetfoils (☎859 6596), High-speed Ferries (information only on ☎815 3043); Jumbo-cats (☎559 9255); Turbo-cats (☎853 3533); Catamarans (☎542 3428). Departure frequencies are the same as from Hong Kong (see "Getting to Macau", p.314), as are the prices – though they're expressed in *patacas*.

HOSPITALS There are 24-hour casualty departments at *Centro Hospitalar Conde São Januário*, Calç. Visconde São Januário ☎313731 (English-speaking), and *Hospital Kiang Wu*, Est. Coelho do Amaral ☎371333 (mostly Chinese-speaking).

LAUNDRY Two central laundries (*lavanderia*) are the *Fok Sang*, Rua da Felicidade 55, opposite the *Fat Siu Lau* restaurant,

and *Fai Kit* on Rua Sul do Mercado, close to the market.

NEWSPAPERS You can buy Hong Kong's English-language daily newspapers in Macau, as well as imported copies of foreign newspapers, from the newspaper stands along the central avenida. Macau's local newspapers are, of course, in Cantonese and Portuguese, except for the weekly *Macau Express*, an English-language business-orientated trawl through local and international news.

PHARMACIES *Farmácia Popular*, Largo do Leal Senado 16 ☎573739; *Farmácia Tsan Heng*, Av. de Almeida Ribeiro 7 ☎572888; *Farmácia Lap Kei*, Calç. do Gaio 3D ☎590042; *Farmácia Chun Cheong*, Rua de S. Domingos 8 ☎332252. Each takes it in turn to open for 24hr; details posted on the door.

POLICE The main police station is at Av. Dr. Rodrigo Rodrigues ☎573333.

POST OFFICES The main post office is the large granite building on the central Largo do Leal Senado, just off Avenida de Almeida Ribeiro (Mon–Fri 9am–6pm, Sat 9am–1pm); this is where poste restante mail is sent. There's also a post office at the Jetfoil Terminal (Mon–Sat 10am–8pm). Otherwise, little booths all over Macau sell stamps, as do the larger hotels, and there's a post office on each of the two outlying islands, Taipa and Coloane. *Correios* is Portuguese for "post office"; *selos* is "stamps".

TAXIS To order a taxi by phone, call ☎519519.

TELEPHONES Local phone calls from pay phones cost 1ptca, though like Hong Kong, local calls are free from courtesy phones in hotels and restaurants. There are groups of pay phones around the Largo do Leal Senado and at the Jetfoil Terminal. Some take telephone cards, available from the telephone office at the back of the main post office (open 24hr), from where you can make international calls. See p.30 for details of dialling abroad.

Useful telephone numbers include:

Directory Enquiries ☎185 (Portuguese); ☎181 (Chinese and English)

Macau: Directory

Macau: Directory

Emergencies ☎999

Time ☎140 (English)

Weather Information ☎911 (Portuguese)

TELEVISION You can pick up Hong Kong's television stations in Macau, as well as some from mainland China; there's also a local station, *Teledifusao de Macau (TdM)*, whose programmes are mostly in Cantonese and Portuguese, though a few are in English. *TdM*'s programme listings are carried in Hong Kong's daily newspapers.

TIME Macau is eight hours ahead of GMT, thirteen hours ahead of New York, sixteen hours ahead of Los Angeles, and two hours behind Sydney.

TOUR OPERATORS There's no shortage of companies which will show you the sights by bus. There are endless tour combinations available – half-day whisks around the peninsula and islands, from around 120ptcs a head, to pricey three- or four-day trips that take in Zhuhai and parts of Guangdong province. Most can be booked in Hong Kong as well, though it's generally cheaper to book in Macau. For details, ask at any of the *MTIB* offices in Hong Kong or Macau or contact one of the tour operators, some of which are listed below and all of which offer the same tours at broadly similar prices.

China Travel Service, Rua de Nagasaki ☎700888; *Metropole Hotel*, Rua da Praia Grande 63 ☎782331; Jetfoil Terminal ☎726756.

International Tourism, Trav. do Padre Narciso 9, Ground Floor ☎975183.

Macau Star, Room 511, Tai Fung Bank Building, Av. de Almeida Ribeiro 34 ☎558855.

Macau Tours, Av. Dr. Mário Soares 35 ☎710003.

Sintra Tours, *Hotel Lisboa*, Room 135, Av. da Amizade ☎710361.

VACCINATION CENTRE At *Direcção dos Serviços de Saudé* (Health Dept), Av. Conselheiro Ferreira de Almeida ☎562235.

VISAS For China visas, visit the main office of the *China Travel Service*, on Rua de Nagasaki (see above), which issues visas and tickets (including tickets for the bus to Guangzhou), and organizes tours. Most other tour agencies can sort out a visa for you, too; see "Tour Operators", above, for addresses.

Contexts

Hong Kong: A History

To Western eyes, the history of Hong Kong starts with the colonial adventurers and merchants who began settling on the fringes of southeast China in the mid-sixteenth century. The Portuguese arrived in Macau in 1557; almost three hundred years later, the British seized Hong Kong Island. However, the whole region has a long, if not greatly distinguished, history of its own that is thoroughly Chinese – a tradition that can only intensify with the handing back of both Hong Kong and Macau to China by the end of this century.

Early times

Archeological finds point to settlements around Hong Kong dating back six thousand years, and while there's little hard evidence, it's accepted that the archipelago off the southeastern coast of China was inhabited in these very early times by fishermen and farmers. There was no great living to be made: then, as now, it was a largely mountainous region, difficult to cultivate and with trying, tropical weather. Disease was common, and though the sea was rich in fish, the islands formed a base for bands of marauding pirates. Later, though far from the Imperial throne in Peking, the land became a firm part of the great Chinese Empire, which was unified in 221 BC. Throughout the series of ruling dynasties that dominated the next 1500 years, the area around Hong Kong was governed – after a fashion – by

a magistrate who reported to a provincial Viceroy in Guangdong (Canton province).

The local population was made up of several **races**, including the Cantonese, who were the most powerful and divided into clans; the Hakka people, a peripatetic grouping who had come down from the north; and the Tankas, who mostly lived on the water in boats. Villages were clan-based, self-contained and fortified with thick walls, and the inhabitants owned and worked their nearby ancestral lands. The elders maintained temples and ancestral halls within the villages, and daily life followed something of an ordained pattern, activities and ceremonies mapped out by a geomancer, who interpreted social and religious ideas through a series of laws known as **fung shui** or "wind and water".

Examples of these **walled villages** still survive in the New Territories, most notably at Kam Tin and Tsang Tai Uk (near Sha Tin), while geomancy is a flourishing art in modern Hong Kong, where the design of all new buildings takes into account the ancient principles of favourable location.

This village-based life continued uneventfully for centuries, the small population of the peninsula and islands mostly untroubled by events elsewhere in the empire. Recorded history made its mark only in the thirteenth century AD, when one of the rulers of the **Song Dynasty**, a boy-emperor, was forced to flee to the peninsula of Kowloon in order to escape the Mongols who were driving south. They cornered him in 1279 and he was killed, the last of his dynasty. The Mongol victory caused a great movement of local tribes in southern China, and a general lawlessness and unrest followed, characterized by continuing pirate activity based on Lantau Island.

Trade and the Chinese

The wider Chinese Empire, however, had begun to engineer links with the Western world that were to bring Hong Kong into the historical mainstream. Although the empire considered itself superior to other lands, supreme and self-sufficient, there had been **trade** between China and the rest of the known world for hundreds of years, often conducted under the guise of "tribute" from other countries and leaders, so as to preserve the idea of Chinese pre-eminence. Out from China went silk, tea and fine art; in came horses, cloth and other luxuries.

The concept of superiority was a resilient one, with foreigners seen as "barbarians" by the Chinese and kept at arm's length. Foreign merchants had to petition the authorities to be allowed to trade; they were not allowed to live within the borders of the empire; they were forbidden to learn the Chinese language, and were generally treated with disdain by Chinese officials.

The relationship changed slightly in the sixteenth century, when some of the first of the Western traders, the **Portuguese**, were given a toehold in the Chinese Empire by being granted permission to establish a trading colony at **Macau**, 60km west of Hong Kong. To the Chinese, it was a concession of limited importance: the Portuguese were confined to the very edge of the empire, far from any real power or influence, and when the same concessions were given to other Western nations in the eighteenth century, the Chinese saw things in the same light. As long as the barbarians kept to the fringes of the Celestial Empire, their presence was accepted – and mostly ignored.

For the West, and especially Britain, such trading territories were viewed altogether differently. Allowed to establish trading operations in **Canton** (Guangzhou) from 1714 onwards, many Western countries saw it as a first step to opening up China itself, and by the turn of the nineteenth century, the Dutch, American and French had joined the British in Canton hoping to profit from the undoubtedly massive resources at hand.

For the time being, however, foreign traders in Canton had to restrict themselves to the peculiar dictates of the Chinese rulers. Their **warehouses** (called "factories") were limited to space outside the city walls on the waterfront, and there they also had to live. All their operations were supervised, their trade conducted through a selected group of Chinese merchants, who formed a guild known as a **Cohong** (from which is derived the Hong Kong word *hong*, or company). In the summer, foreigners had to leave for Portuguese Macau, where most of them kept houses (and often, their families). Under these circumstances foreign merchants somehow prospered and trade thrived. The British East India Company was only one of the firms involved, seeing their Chinese enterprises as simply an extension of

the worldwide trade network they'd built up on the back of the British victory over Napoleon and mastery of the seas.

The opium trade

The problem that soon became apparent was that trade took place on eminently favourable terms for the Chinese. Foreigners had to pay for Chinese tea and silk in silver, while the Chinese wanted little that the Westerners had. The breakthrough was the emergence of the trade in **opium**, in demand in China but illegal and consequently little grown. The Portuguese had been smuggling it into Macau from their Indian territories for years, and as it became clear that this was the one product that could reverse the trade imbalance, others followed suit. Most energetic were the British, who began to channel opium – "foreign mud" as the Chinese came to call it – from Bengal to Canton, selling it illegally to corrupt Chinese merchants and officials in return for various goods. Illegal or not, the trade mushroomed and opium became the linchpin of the relationship between the Chinese and the ever-richer foreign merchants.

Familiar Hong Kong names began to appear in Canton, most of whom were connected with the opium trade. **William Jardine** and **James Matheson** were two of the most successful and unscrupulous traders, both Scottish Calvinists who had no qualms about making fortunes from an increasing Chinese reliance on drugs. The trade was also encouraged by the British government, and by corruptible Chinese government officials who ignored what had become an overt smuggling operation. By 1837, around forty thousand chests of the drug were landed annually in China, unloaded at Lin Tin Island in the Pearl River estuary, transferred onto Chinese barges and floated upriver to Canton.

As silver began to flow out of China to pay for the increasing amounts of the drug being imported, the trade imbalance came to the attention of the Chinese Emperor in Peking (Beijing), who also began to show concern for the adverse effect that the opium was having on the health of his population. In 1839, the Emperor appointed an opponent of the trade, the Governor of Hunan province, **Lin Tse-Hsu**, to go to Canton to end the import of opium – something he'd achieved fairly spectacularly in his own province by brute force. Once in Canton, Lin Tse-Hsu ordered the surrender and destruction of all the foreigners' opium chests, twenty thousand in all, and much to the disgust of the enraged merchants, the British Chief Superintendent of Trade, **Captain Charles Elliot**, did just that. His was a difficult position, since he represented the traders, yet personally stood against the opium trade, and his actions did nothing to diffuse the affair. Governor Lin ordered a blockade against the merchants' factories and demanded they each sign a bond, promising not to import opium into China in future. Under Elliot's direction, the traders left Canton and retreated to Macau and their boats, anchored in Hong Kong harbour, fearing further trouble. The situation deteriorated when Lin reminded the Portuguese of their official neutrality, which they upheld by refusing Elliot a secure base on Macau and by forbidding the selling of supplies to the British merchant fleet, which still waited nervously off Hong Kong.

The First Opium War

If it was Governor Lin's intention to force the British back to Canton to trade on his terms, then he miscalculated disastrously. The mood in Britain, where Lord Palmerston was Foreign Secretary in the Whig government of Lord Melbourne, was one of aggressive expansionism. Merchants like Jardine and Matheson had long been urging the government to promote British free trade in China, demanding gunboats if necessary to open up the Chinese Empire. The first Superintendent of Trade in China, Lord Napier, had been given precisely those instructions, but had been humiliated by the Chinese when he had tried to press British claims in the region. Canton had been closed to him and his frigates forced to retreat, a disgrace in British eyes that Palmerston had not forgotten.

Captain Elliot had already begun the skirmishes that would degenerate into the so-called **First Opium War**, having replied to Lin's threats by firing on a Chinese fleet in September 1839 and sinking a number of ships. It was these threats, rather than the protection of the opium trade, that gave Britain the excuse it sought to expand its influence in China. There was opposition to the trade in Britain, particularly among the ranks of the Whigs, who had already made their mark with the abolition of the slave trade. But potential attacks on British personnel and overseas livelihoods couldn't be ignored.

Palmerston ordered an **expeditionary fleet** from India, comprising four thousand men, which arrived off Hong Kong in June 1840 with the express purpose of demanding compensation for the lost opium chests and an apology from the Chinese, and – most importantly – acquiring a base on the Chinese coast, which could be used like Portuguese Macau to open up the country for free trade. Several ports up and down the Chinese coast had been suggested by traders over the years, including Canton itself, and the expedition (led by Admiral George Elliot, a cousin of Charles) was authorized to grab what it could. The British fleet soon achieved its military objectives: it attacked the forts guarding Canton, while other ships sailed north, blockading and firing on ports and cities right the way up the Chinese coast. When part of the fleet reached the Yangtze river, approaching Beijing itself, the Chinese were forced to negotiate.

Governor Lin was dispensed with by the Emperor, who appointed a new official, Kishen, to deal with the British fleet, by now again under the command of Charles Elliot. The fighting stopped and the British withdrew to the Pearl River to negotiate, but after six weeks of stalling by the Chinese, the fleet once again sailed on Canton and knocked out its forts. Kishen capitulated and Elliot **seized Hong Kong Island**; the British flag was planted there on January 26, 1841.

Fighting began again soon after, when in August 1841 Elliot was replaced by Sir Henry Pottinger, who was determined to gain more than just Hong Kong Island. The fleet sailed north, taking ports as they went, which were later recognized as free-trade "Treaty Ports" by the 1842 **Treaty of Nanking**, which halted the fighting. In this way, Shanghai, Amoy (Xiamen), Fuzhou, Canton and others were opened up for trade; the Chinese were forced to pay an indemnity to the British; but most important of all, the treaty ceded Hong Kong Island to Britain in perpetuity.

The new colony

Not everyone was thrilled with Britain's new imperial acquisition. The small island was called Hong Kong by the British, after the Cantonese name (*Heung Gong*), most commonly translated as meaning "Fragrant Harbour". But aside from the excellent anchorage it afforded to the British fleet, Palmerston for one saw Elliot's action as a lost opportunity to gain further parts of China for Britain. It was a move which cost Elliot his job, while at home Queen Victoria was amused by the apparent uselessness of her new out-of-the-way colony.

Nevertheless, the ownership of Hong Kong – which formally became a British Crown Colony in 1843 – gave a proper base for the opium trade, which became ever more profitable. By 1850 Britain was exporting 52,000 chests of opium a year to China through the colony.

Sir Henry Pottinger, who replaced Elliot, became the colony's first **Governor**, a constitution was drawn up, and from 1844 onwards, a Legislative Council and a separate Executive Council were convened – though the governor retained a veto in all matters. In colonial fashion, pioneered elsewhere in the world by the British, government departments were created, the law administered and public works commissioned. At first, though, the colony remained something of a backwater, since the British were still ensconced at Canton and most of the China trade went through the other Treaty Ports. The population of around fifteen thousand was mostly made up of local Chinese, lots of whom were attracted by the commercial opportunities they thought would follow; many of them sold land rights (that often they didn't own in the first place) to the newly arrived British, who began to build permanent houses and trading depots.

The first buildings to go up were around Possession Point, in today's Western district – offices, warehouses (called "godowns") and eventually European-style housing. This area was abandoned to the Chinese when the first colonists discovered it to be malarial and mistakenly moved to Happy Valley – which turned out to be even more badly affected. Gradually, though, sanitation was improved. Happy Valley was drained and turned into a racecourse; summer houses were built on The Peak; and a small, but thriving town began to emerge – called **Victoria**, on the site of today's Central. The number of Europeans living there was still comparatively small – just a few hundred in the mid-1840s – but they at least now existed within a rigid colonial framework, segregated from the Chinese by early governors and buoyed by new colonial style and comforts. Streets and settlements were named after Queen Victoria and her ministers; Government House was finished in 1855; the Zoological and Botanical Gardens laid out in 1864; St John's Cathedral opened in 1849; and the first path up The Peak cut in 1859. As Hong Kong began to come into its own as a trading

port, the British merchants who lived there started to have more say in how the colony was run: in 1850, two merchants were appointed to the Legislative Council.

The Second Opium War and colonial growth

Relations between Britain and China remained strained throughout the early life of the colony, flaring up again in 1856 when the Chinese authorities, ostensibly looking for pirates, boarded and arrested a Hong Kong registered schooner, the *Arrow*. With London always looking for an excuse for further intervention in China, this incident gave Britain the chance to despatch another fleet up the Pearl River to besiege Canton – instigating a series of events sometimes known as the **Second Opium War**. Joined by the French, the British continued the fighting for two years and in 1858 an Anglo-French fleet captured more northern possessions. The **Treaty of Tientsin** (Tianjin) gave foreigners the right to diplomatic representation in Peking, something Palmerston and the traders saw as crucial to the future success of their enterprise. But with the Chinese refusing to ratify the treaty, the Anglo-French forces moved on Peking, occupying the capital in order to force Chinese concessions.

This second, more protracted series of military engagements finally ended in 1860 with the signing of the so-called **Convention of Peking**, which ceded more important territory to the British. The southern part of Kowloon peninsula – as far north as Boundary Street – and the small Stonecutter's Island (which is still restricted to the military) were handed over in perpetuity, increasing the British territory to over ninety square kilometres. This enabled the British to establish control over the fairly lawless village that had grown up on the peninsula at Tsim Sha Tsui, while the fine Victoria Harbour could now be more easily protected from both sides. Almost as a by-product of the agreement, the opium trade was legalized, too.

The period immediately after was one of **rapid growth**. With a more secure base, the colony's commercial trade increased and Hong Kong became a stop for ships en route to other Far Eastern ports. They could easily be repaired and refitted in the colony, which began to sustain an important shipping industry of its own. As a result of the increased business, the **Hongkong and Shanghai Bank** was set up in 1864 and allowed to issue banknotes, later building the first of its famous office buildings. The large foreign trading companies, the **hongs**, established themselves in the colony: Jardine, Matheson was already there, but it was followed in the 1860s by Swire, which had started life as a shipping firm in Shanghai. The town of Victoria spread east and west along the harbour, around its new City Hall, taking on all the trappings of a flourishing colonial town, a world away from the rather down-at-heel settlement of twenty years earlier. One of the major changes was in the size of the **population**: the Taiping rebellions in China greatly increased the number of refugees crossing the border, and by 1865 there were around 150,000 people in the colony. With Hong Kong soon handling roughly a third of China's foreign trade, the colony began to adopt the role it assumes today – as a broker in people and goods.

By **the 1880s**, Hong Kong's transformation was complete. Although the vast majority of the Chinese population were poor workers, the beginnings of today's meritocracy were apparent as small numbers of Chinese businessmen and traders flourished. One enlightened governor, **Sir John Pope Hennessy**, advocated a change in attitude towards the Chinese that didn't go down at all well: he appointed Chinese people to government jobs, there were Chinese lawyers, and even a Chinese member of the Legislative Council. It was an inevitable move, but one that was resisted by the bigoted colonialists, who banned the Chinese from living in the plusher areas of Victoria and on The Peak.

1898: the leasing of the New Territories

Following Japan's victory in the **Sino-Japanese War** (1894–95), China became subject to some final land concessions. Russia, France and Germany had all pressed claims on Chinese territory in return for limiting Japanese demands after the war, and Britain followed suit in an attempt to defend Hong Kong against possible future attack from any foreign source in China. One British gain was the lease of Weihaiwei in Shandong, in the north, to be held as long as the Russians kept Port Arthur (Lushun), on which they'd secured a 25-year lease in 1897.

More significant, though, was the British government's demand for a substantial lease on the land on the Kowloon peninsula, north of Boundary Street. Agreement was reached on an area stretching across from Mirs Bay in the east to Deep Bay in the west, including the water and islands in between, and this territory was **leased from China for 99 years**, from July 1, 1898. It came to be known as the **New Territories**, and provides the legal focus for the return of the whole colony to China in 1997. Although the British undoubtedly thought they'd got a good deal in 1898 – a 99-year lease must have seemed as good as an outright concession – it was to become clear over the years that Hong Kong would never survive as a viable entity once the greater resources of the New Territories were handed back. Thus had the British authorities effectively provided a date for abolition of one of their most dynamic colonies.

The colony of Hong Kong was now made up of just under 1100 square kilometres of islands, peninsula and water, but there was an indigenous Chinese population of around 100,000 in the newly acquired territory which resisted the change. Many villagers feared that their ancestral grounds would be disturbed and their traditional life interfered with, and local meetings were called in order to form militias to resist the British. There were clashes at **Tai Po** in April 1899, though British troops soon took control of the main roads and strategic points. Resistance in the New Territories fizzled out and civil administration was established, but the villagers retained their distrust of the authorities. One further problem caused by the leasing agreement was the anomalous position of **Kowloon Walled City**, beyond the original Boundary Street – a mainly Chinese garrison that had evolved into a fairly unpleasant slum by 1898. For some reason, the leasing agreement didn't include the Walled City, and China continued to claim jurisdiction over it, hastening its degeneration over the years into an anarchic settlement and a flashpoint between the two sets of authorities.

The years to World War II

By the turn of the **twentieth century**, the population of Hong Kong had increased to around a quarter of a million (and more came after the fall of the Manchu Dynasty in China in 1911), and the colony's trade showed an equally impressive performance, finally moving away from opium – which had still accounted for nearly half of the Hong Kong government's finances in 1890. In 1907, an agreement was reached between Britain and China to end the opium trade, and imports were cut over a ten-year period – though all that happened was that the cultivation of poppies shifted from India to China, carried on under the protection of local Chinese warlords. Opium smoking wasn't made illegal in Hong Kong until 1946 (three years later in China).

Alongside the trade and manufacturing increase came other improvements and developments. The **Kowloon Railway**, through the New Territories to the border, was opened in 1910 (and completed, on to Canton, by the Chinese, in 1912); the **University of Hong Kong** was founded in 1911; **land reclamation** in Victoria had begun; and the **Supreme Court** building was erected in the first decade of the new century (and still stands today, in Central, as the Legislative Council building).

Despite this activity, movements outside the colony's control were soon to have their effect, and the years following World War I saw a distinct economic shift away from Hong Kong. Shanghai overtook it in the 1920s as *the* Chinese trading city, and Hong Kong lost its pre-eminence for the next thirty years or so. The polarization in Chinese politics began to have an effect, too. Sun Yat-sen was elected President of the Republic in Canton, and a militant movement on capitalistic Hong Kong's doorstep was bound to cause trouble. Most of Hong Kong's Chinese were desperately poor and there had been the occasional riot over the years, which erupted in 1926 (following Sun Yat-sen's death) into a total **economic boycott** of the colony, organized and led by the Chinese Nationalists (the Kuomintang), based in Canton. There was no trade, few services and – more importantly – no food imports from China, a state of affairs which lasted for several months and did untold damage to manufacturing and commercial activity. Expat volunteers had to keep things going as best they could, while the strike leaders in Hong Kong encouraged many Chinese people to leave the colony so as to press home their demands: a shorter working day, less discrimination against the local Chinese population and a reduction in rent.

The strike didn't last, but the colony's confidence had been badly dented. And although business picked up again, new worries emerged in the 1930s as the **Japanese occupied southern China**. Hundreds of thousands of people fled into the colony, almost doubling the population, and many saw the eventual occupation of Hong Kong itself as inevitable.

Japanese occupation 1941–45

The Japanese had been advancing across China from the north since 1933, seizing Manchuria and Beijing before establishing troops in Canton in 1939 – an advance which had temporarily halted the civil war then raging in China. What was clear was that any further move to take Hong Kong was bound to succeed: the colony had only a small defensive force of a few battalions and a couple of ships, and couldn't hope to resist the Japanese army.

Some thought that the Japanese wouldn't attack, and certainly, although Hong Kong had been prepared for war since 1939, there was a feeling that old, commercial links with the Japanese would save the colony. However, when the Japanese occupied Indo-China, the colony's defences were immediately strengthened. A line of pillboxes and guns was established across the New Territories, the so-called Shing-mun redoubt, which was hoped would delay any advancing army long enough for Kowloon to be evacuated and Hong Kong Island to be turned into a fortress from which the resistance could be directed.

On December 8, 1941 the **Japanese army invaded**, overran the border from Canton, bombed the planes at Kai Tak airport and swept through the New Territories' defences. They took Kowloon within four days, the British forces retreating to Hong Kong Island where they were shelled and bombed from the other side of the harbour. The Japanese then moved across to the island, split the defence forces in hard fighting and finished them off. The **British surrender** came on Christmas Day, after around six thousand military and civilian deaths, with nine thousand more men captured. The soldiers were held in a prisoner-of-war camp at Sham Shui Po, in Kowloon, while those British civilians who had not previously been evacuated to Australia were interned in Stanley Prison on the island.

It was a dark time for the people of Hong Kong, who faced a Japanese army out of control. Although some Chinese civilians collaborated, many others helped the European and Allied prisoners by smuggling in food and medicines, and helping to organize escapes. It wasn't necessarily a show of support for the British, but an indication of the loyalty most Hong Kong Chinese felt towards China, which had suffered even worse under the Japanese. Atrocities faced the Allied prisoners, too: during the short campaign, the Japanese had murdered hospital staff and prisoners, and in prison, beatings, executions for escape attempts and torture were commonplace. Life in Stanley meant disease and malnutrition, and being a civilian was no guarantee of safety: in 1943, seven people were beheaded on the beach for possessing a radio.

The Japanese meanwhile sent a military governor to Hong Kong to supervise the **occupation**, but found the colony to be much less use to them than they had imagined. It wasn't incorporated into the Japanese-run parts of China, and apart from changing the names of buildings and organizations – and adding a few Japanese touches to Government House – nothing fruitful came of their time there. The New Territories became a battleground for bandits, various factions of the Chinese defenders and the Japanese invaders; towns and villages emptied as many of the local Chinese were forcibly repatriated to the mainland; food and supplies were run down; the cities on either side of the harbour were bombed out. As the Japanese gradually lost the battle elsewhere, Hong Kong became more and more of an irrelevance to them, and when the **Japanese surrendered to the Allies** in August 1945, colonial government picked itself up surprisingly quickly.

Postwar reconstruction: the 1950s and 1960s

The immediate task in Hong Kong was to rebuild both buildings and commerce, something the colony undertook with remarkable energy. In 1945, the population had been reduced to around 600,000 people, who were faced with an acute housing shortage. Within five years the population had risen to over two million, the harbour had been cleared and the trading companies were back in business. This was, however, achieved at a price, and Hong Kong lost out on the democratic reforms that were sweeping the rest of the world. There had been suggestions that the colony become a free-trading "international" state after the war, or that it be handed back to China, but quick thinking by the imprisoned British leaders on Japan's surrender – who declared themselves the acting government – ensured that Hong Kong remained a British colony. Liberal measures designed to introduce at least some democratic reforms into the running of the colony were treated with virtual disdain by the population, which was interested only in getting its business back on its feet.

The boost the economy needed came in 1949–50, when the **Communists came to power in China**, unleashing a wave of new immigration across the border. The civil war in China had been fought in earnest since the end of World War II, and with the fall of Nationalist China, traders and businessmen were desperate to escape. Thousands arrived, many from Shanghai, to set up new businesses and provide the manufacturing base from which the colony could expand. By 1951, the population had grown to around two-and-a-half million, and Hong Kong had moved from being a mere entrepôt to become an industrial centre. New, lucrative industries – directly attributable to the recent refugees – included textiles and construction. A further incentive for a change in emphasis in the colony came with the American embargo on Chinese goods sold through Hong Kong during the **Korean War**, so that the territory was forced into manufacturing goods as a means of economic survival.

The new immigrants unleashed new problems for the colony, not least the fact that there was nowhere for them to live. **Squatter settlements** spread like wildfire and faced with a private housing sector that couldn't build new homes fast enough, the government established approved squatters' areas throughout the territory. In addition, virtually all of the new immigrants were ardently anti-Communist, many supporting the Kuomintang, and they took every opportunity during the 1950s to unsettle the relationship between Hong Kong and China. This resulted in **riots** in the colony between Communists and Nationalists, pointing the way towards future conflict. In an attempt to solve the problem thousands of ex-Kuomintang soldiers and their families – who had been unable to join the bulk of their colleagues in Taiwan – were forcibly moved to the village of Rennies Mill, on Hong Kong Island, which remains today a bastion of Nationalist support.

This uneasy link with China was exploited by both sides throughout the 1960s, each action emphasizing Hong Kong's odd position as both a British colony and a part of China, prey to the whims and fortunes of the Chinese leadership. In 1962, the point was made by the Chinese government in the so-called **trial run**, which allowed (and encouraged) upwards of sixty thousand people to leave China for Hong Kong. The border was flooded, and though the British authorities were determined to keep such an influx out, there was little they could do in the face of blatant provocation from the Chinese army, which was directing the flow of people.

Things finally got out of hand in 1966–67, as the worst excesses of the Chinese **Cultural Revolution** began to spill over into the colony. There had already been serious rioting in Hong Kong in April 1966, ostensibly against a price rise in the first-class Star Ferry fare. Against the background of increasing political turmoil in mainland China (where the Red Guards emerged in Beijing in August 1966), local strikes and unrest began to dominate the colony in spring of the following year. After deaths and rioting in neighbouring Macau, where the Portuguese authorities were overrun by Red Guard agitators, the situation in Hong Kong deteriorated, and May and June 1967 saw the worst violence yet: Government House was besieged by pro-China activists, there were cases of Europeans being attacked in the streets, and some policemen were killed on the Hong Kong–Chinese border. There were also riots and strikes, and a curfew was imposed; and in July a bomb exploded on Hong Kong Island, injuring nine people. However, apart from supportive and vociferous press reports in the pro-China newspapers, and a virulent anti-Imperialist/British poster campaign taken directly from the mainland, the organizers of the riots and unrest took little comfort from the attitude of Beijing. Chairman Mao was intent upon pursuing the Cultural Revolution to its fullest extent in China and had little time for what was happening in Hong Kong. Mao was also keen to avoid destabilizing the colony, as it was an important source of revenue – a pragmatic attitude that determined the Chinese approach towards Hong Kong throughout this period. Although there were more disturbances throughout the rest of 1967, the protests fizzled out as tourism and confidence in the local economy gradually picked up again.

The 1970s: social problems

The economic gains of the postwar period were accompanied by the growth of a number of social problems that still trouble the colony today. The **population** continued to grow, bolstered by the ever-increasing number of immigrants, legal and (mostly) illegal, from China. There had been a housing shortage since the end of World War II, which this growth exacerbated, and **squatter settlements** evolved throughout Hong Kong. A fire

in 1953 in Shek Kip Mei, Kowloon, had already demonstrated the inherent danger of such settlements: over fifty thousand people were made homeless in just one night. An emergency housing programme – taking people out of wooden huts and into fairly basic resettlement estates – went some way to addressing the problem, though it wasn't until the development of the New Town programme in the early 1970s that the problem of adequately housing Hong Kong's burgeoning population was fully addressed. The first **New Town**, Tuen Mun, opened in 1973, was a prototype of the gleaming cities that now spread across the New Territories, housing hundreds of thousands. Eight others are either completed or in the process of being built and, in the process, have made the Hong Kong government the world's largest landlord – roughly half the population lives in public housing. For more on the development of the New Towns, see the feature on pp.166–167.

The rise in population caused concern in Hong Kong for other reasons. Although there was no unemployment, there were water and power shortages over the years, limited welfare facilities and poor public services, all of which had to be shared by more and more people. Resentment against the new arrivals was nothing new but was to have an importance after 1975, when the first of the **Vietnamese boat people** – fleeing their country after the North Vietnamese victory – fetched up in the colony. Although no one was turned away (a credit to the Hong Kong authorities even now), the numbers involved soon soared to frightening proportions – 65,000 refugees in 1979, many of whom had no chance of subsequent resettlement in other parts of the world.

The other major problem during this period was that of **crime and corruption**, endemic in Hong Kong since the founding of the colony. In modern times, crime was fuelled in particular by the number of Chinese illegal immigrants, who had little else to turn to once the Hong Kong authorities began to make it harder for them to secure official papers and earn a living. This was mirrored by the emerging scale of **official and police corruption** throughout the 1960s, which touched most aspects of life, from accepting bribes from street traders through to police cover-ups of serious illegal activity – a state of affairs only partly redeemed by the setting up in 1974 of the **Independent Commission Against Corruption**.

The Triads

Behind much of the major crime and corruption in Hong Kong were the various secretive **Triad** organizations, akin to the Sicilian Mafia in scale and wealth, though probably unrivalled in terms of sheer viciousness. Triads (so called because their emblem was a triangle denoting harmony between Heaven, Earth and Man) were first established in the seventeenth century in China, in an attempt to restore the Ming Dynasty after its overthrow by the Manchus. They moved into Hong Kong early in the colony's history, where they were able to organize among the new immigrants, splitting up into separate societies with their own elaborate initiation rites and ceremonies. The Triad organizations relied on a hierarchical structure, with ranks denoted by numbers which begin with 4 – representing the four elements, compass points and seas.

After World War II, with the colony in tatters, refugees and immigrants from newly Communist China moved into Hong Kong, many to the Walled City in Kowloon, which became a notorious criminal haven, protected by the Chinese assertions of legal rule over this small enclave on Hong Kong territory. The Walled City became a no-go area for the Hong Kong police, while the number of groups operating throughout the colony rose to around fifty – with possibly 100,000 members in all, operating everything from street gangs upwards to organized crime.

Towards 1997: the political moves

As China began to open up to the wider world in the early 1970s, Hong Kong's relationship with its neighbour improved dramatically. Trade between the two increased, as did Hong Kong's role as economic mediator between China and the West. Chinese investment in Hong Kong became substantial – in Chinese-owned banks, hotels, businesses, shops – and Hong Kong was a ready market for Chinese food products, even water. This shift in relationship was recognized in the mid-1970s, when the word "colony" was expunged from all official British titles in Hong Kong: in came the concept of Hong Kong as a "territory", which sounded much better to sensitive Chinese ears.

Against this background came the realization that 1997 – and the handing back of the New Territories – was fast approaching. There was a general belief that it would be absurd to pretend that Hong Kong could survive without the New Territories, and that it was unlikely that China would want them without the money-making parts of Kowloon and Hong Kong Island.

It hasn't always been so clear cut to observers. Ian Fleming, author of the James Bond books, visiting in the 1950s, thought that "when the remaining forty years of our lease on the mainlands territory expire, I see no reason why a reduced population should not retreat to the islands and the original territory which Britain holds in perpetuity."

The first tentative moves towards finding a solution occurred in **1982**, when British Prime Minister Margaret Thatcher visited China and Hong Kong. Certain injudicious remarks by her on that tour, concerning British responsibility to Hong Kong's citizens and the validity of the original treaties ceding the territory to Britain, caused the Chinese to make an issue of the sovereignty question. As far as they were concerned, Hong Kong and its people were Chinese, so any responsibility was that of Beijing. To the Chinese government, historically the treaties had been "unequal" (that is, forced by a strong nineteenth-century Britain on a weak China) and therefore illegal. After Thatcher had gone home, and the dust had settled, talks continued, with both sides agreeing that their aim was the "prosperity and stability" of a future Hong Kong, while arguing about the question of sovereignty. It became clear during 1983 that Britain would eventually concede sovereignty to China, and that Britain would abandon all claims to Hong Kong, not just the New Territories.

After two years of debate and uncertainty, which had a negative influence on business and confidence in the colony, the **Sino-British Joint Declaration** was signed in September 1984, with Britain agreeing to hand back sovereignty of the entire territory to China in 1997. In return, Hong Kong would continue with the same legal and capitalistic system for at least the next fifty years, becoming a "Special Administrative Region" (SAR) of China, in which it would have virtual autonomy – a concept the Chinese labelled as "one country, two systems". Almost immediately, the declaration haunted the British government: no changes to the document were allowed after it was signed and, as people began to point out in the colony, with virtually no democratic institutions in place in Hong Kong, the Chinese would effectively be able to do what they liked after 1997. Only the economic necessity to retain Hong Kong's wealth-producing status would limit their actions, and even that wouldn't be enough in the face of any radical change in leadership in Beijing.

The declaration was followed by the publication in Beijing in 1988 of the **Basic Law**, a sort of constitutional framework for explaining how the SAR of Hong Kong would work in practice. Again, in theory, the Basic Law guaranteed the preservation of the existing capitalist system in Hong Kong, along with various freedoms – of travel, speech, the right to strike – that were deemed necessary to sustain confidence. But, in spite of this, concern grew steadily in Hong Kong. Only a third of the Legislative Council seats were to be directly elected by 1997 (with half elected by 2003); vague references to the outlawing of "subversion" were disturbing to anyone who was even remotely critical of Beijing's actions; and China refused a referendum in Hong Kong on the provisions of the Basic Law. Despite a consultation exercise in Hong Kong, where the Hong Kong government invited direct comment from the public on the Basic Law, confidence wasn't restored. Liberals in Hong Kong, in the Legislative Council and elsewhere, accused the British government of a sell-out, and of failing to implement democratic reforms that would at least provide some guarantee of stability after 1997. The **brain drain** of educated, professional people leaving Hong Kong for new countries, which had been picking up ever since 1984, began to increase more rapidly.

1989: shattered confidence

1989 was a grim year for Hong Kong. On June 4, following student-dominated pro-democracy demonstrations in China, Deng Xiaoping sent in the tanks to **Tiananmen Square** in Beijing to crush the protest – an act which killed hundreds, possibly thousands, of people, with many more arrested, jailed and executed in the following weeks. This put China on show as never before, and confirmed the worst fears of almost the entire Hong Kong population that the British government had indeed sold them out to a dangerous and murderous regime. No one now doubted that with the People's Liberation Army due to be stationed on Hong Kong territory after 1997, any future dissent in the colony against Chinese authoritarian rule could be stamped upon as easily as in Beijing, whatever the Basic Law said. And to indicate the seriousness of this view, the Hang Seng Index, the performance indicator of

the Hong Kong Stock Exchange, dropped 22 percent on the Monday following the massacre.

Tiananmen Square was a particularly galling experience for Hong Kong's own **pro-democracy movement**, which had staged extraordinary rallies in support of the Beijing students – and which spirited several dissident Chinese students out of China to safety in the following months. Successive protest rallies in Hong Kong had brought out up to a million people on to the streets – almost twenty percent of the population – to demand democracy in China, and more significantly, more democracy in Hong Kong itself. A copy of Beijing's Goddess of Liberty was erected in Hong Kong after the massacre; Cantonese pop stars recorded a song, For Freedom, in support of the Chinese students; while in typical Hong Kong fashion, manufacturers cashed in on the protests with stores selling democracy armbands, headbands and T-shirts. Everywhere, the point was being made loudly and angrily that without democratic institutions in place well before 1997, the territory and its people would be entirely at the mercy of the whims of the leaders in Beijing.

If there had been a brain drain from Hong Kong before June 4, it was now a flood. Embassies and consulates were swamped by people desperate for an escape route should things go wrong in the future. Singapore's announcement that it would be taking up to 25,000 Hong Kong Chinese over the next five to eight years led to scuffles for application forms. Surveys and opinion polls showed that sixty percent of the population wished (and expected) to qualify for a foreign passport, and that one in six people would leave anyway before 1997.

On top of all this, the territory was enduring the worst problems yet caused by the continuing influx of the **Vietnamese boat people**. The summer sailing season saw the numbers top fifty thousand, the highest for a decade – and with fewer countries prepared to accept new immigrants, most Vietnamese arrivals were doomed to a protracted and unpleasant stay in Hong Kong's closed camps. As the camps filled and then burst, isolated and uninhabited outlying islands were used to hold the boat people. Shelter was in makeshift tents, conditions were unsanitary, food was poor, and, not surprisingly, trouble followed. There were disturbances in some of the camps – fighting between rival groups of Vietnamese, break-outs into the local villages, a few attempted suicides and the occasional murder – all of which the Hong Kong authorities could see no end to, given the numbers still arriving daily from across the South China Sea.

Into the 1990s

The turn of the decade brought no respite for Hong Kong. The two main problems were still the question of what would happen in 1997 and what to do with the Vietnamese. They were complicated and, in many ways, related questions, attracting emotional debate both in the territory and in Britain. Both matters affected the quality of life in Hong Kong, with many feeling that there was no assured future. Yet certain features of life in Hong Kong, like the **economy**, were still to be envied. The territory ranks eleventh in the world league of trading nations; it's the biggest container port in the world, the largest exporter of watches and radios (second largest of clothes and toys), and the fourth most important financial centre. Its economic growth has averaged eight percent a year for a decade; there's full employment; and it has a per capita income of around US \$10,000 (second only to Japan in Asia). In addition, sixty percent of all China's exports pass through Hong Kong, while the territory accounts for seventy percent of foreign investment in China. It's a formidable record for a place that was devastated only fifty years ago, and founded just a century earlier.

Domestic troubles

However, to pretend that everything else was rosy in this capitalistic garden would be naive in the extreme. **Crime** was on the increase throughout the period – although the Triads seemed intent upon moving out of Hong Kong before 1997, setting up shop in places like London and Amsterdam, Australia and Canada – while **drug addiction** was a major worry, with estimates of around forty thousand active drug users, 96 percent of them heroin addicts. And though the Far Eastern **sex trade** had shifted substantially to Thailand during the 1980s, the combination of prostitution and needle-sharing contributed to marked increases in the AIDS figures.

Most disturbing of all, however, was that despite Hong Kong's long association with Britain, and British protestations that she had a duty to the territory's citizens, Hong Kong had few of the **rights and privileges** that people in Britain enjoyed and expected. There was no democracy

worth the name; citizens could be stopped and searched by the police at any time, and forced to carry an ID card; public welfare provision was limited; while over the years, the citizens of Hong Kong had been stripped of the right of abode in Britain by successive Immigration Acts. Told to consider themselves British for a century and a half for the purposes of government and administration, the vast majority of the Hong Kong Chinese – having given up Chinese nationality in order to become subjects of the British Crown – were effectively stateless.

The passport question

The problem of the duty of the British government to the territory's population was crystallized into the **passport question**. Since the events in Tiananmen Square, increasing numbers in Hong Kong had sought a second passport so that if China went back on the promises enshrined in the Joint Declaration they would have an "insurance policy" – the right to leave the territory and live elsewhere.

The issue was not strictly whether or not people were able to get hold of such passports. Many countries, from Paraguay to The Gambia, were willing virtually to sell passports (and thus citizenship) to the large numbers of Hong Kong Chinese wishing to leave. All it took was money. However, this was obviously an option open only to the wealthy and the well connected. The moral question faced by the British government was whether or not to grant the **right of abode** to all the citizens of Hong Kong, so that people would have a choice of where to live after 1997.

After 1997, anyone without a foreign passport automatically becomes a citizen of the PRC and eligible for a Special Administraive Region (SAR) passport. The view **in Hong Kong** was that Britain had a duty to the territory's people, which involved overturning the various Immigration Acts passed in Britain and restoring their right of abode in Britain by giving them full British passports. It was argued that most people wanted to stay in Hong Kong anyway, and that, given the choice, most certainly wouldn't want to come to Britain – by far the most popular destinations for Hong Kong Chinese leaving the territory are Canada and Australia, where there are large Chinese populations. But the right to a passport would give the residents of Hong Kong more security, and thus lend the territory more stability.

The view of the **British government** was confused from the start. Having effectively made many Hong Kong people stateless through the provisions of the 1981 British Nationality Act (Hong Kong people hold a British "dependent territories" or "overseas national" passport), the government argued that insurance policies exist to be used. It claimed all those with passports would in fact come to Britain, which would be disastrous for housing and social security measures, and for race relations in the UK. The figures were uncertain (it depends whether you count the whole Hong Kong population or just those with dependent territory passports), but the spectre of between three and a half million and five million people flooding into Britain was raised. Instead, the government – by way of the British Nationality (Hong Kong) Act – offered full passports and space in Britain for fifty thousand "key personnel", in effect, high-ranking civil servants and police officers, technical and professional people, businesspeople and the wealthy, plus their families – a figure of around 225,000 in all. This was designed to ensure that these people stayed in Hong Kong, unless things became intolerable; placements were determined by a points system and the governor had the final judgement on the matter.

This was clearly a tokenistic offer, and although it's arguable whether anything like three and a half million people would have come in any case, there was fierce opposition in the UK to the plan. In fact, with 1992 and the single European market looming, those who did come would have had the right to settle anywhere in the European Community, not just Britain (which most Hong Kong Chinese people find cold and economically backward).

The situation was further confused by the **attitude of the British people**, who in opinion polls said that they opposed letting any substantial number of Hong Kong Chinese settle in Britain. The opposition Labour Party particularly was torn between its moral heart and its political head: it knew that to call for a large influx of non-white immigrants into Britain would cost it dear in terms of support from the very people it needed to put it back into power.

The Chinese government, too, started to criticize Britain for supposedly reneging on the terms of the Joint Declaration, saying that whatever happened, it wouldn't honour the full British passports issued, as the people in Hong Kong would be Chinese citizens after 1997 – and thus not entitled to leave or enter the territory on so-called "foreign" passports.

The Vietnamese

There was an ironic twist to the nationality debate for the people of Hong Kong regarding the fate of the **Vietnamese boat people**, who had been landing in the territory since 1975. These were part of a mass exodus from Vietnam of over 800,000 people, fleeing in the wake of the Communist takeover. While seeking overseas passports themselves, the people of Hong Kong were increasingly adamant that the unfortunate refugees from Vietnam should not be allowed to stay in the territory. From having initially offered sanctuary to the boat people – the only Southeast Asian state to do so – Hong Kong now felt inclined to tow the Vietnamese back out to sea. Partly it was frustration with the lack of any progress in finding an international solution to the problem – successive Geneva conferences failed to come up with sufficient quotas from countries prepared to take the boat people. But it was a little rich from a people which one day hoped to seek sanctuary itself.

The situation became even more ironic once the British government decided upon its course of action towards the boat people in Hong Kong. Those deemed "economic migrants" were to be repatriated to Vietnam – forcibly if necessary – while long screening procedures would sort out the genuine refugees, thought to be ten percent of the total, who would be guaranteed resettlement in a third country. The first **forced repatriation** took place in December 1989, and a pathetic sight it was, as 51 men, women and children were herded into trucks by armed police and forced on to an aeroplane back to Vietnam. It drew worldwide condemnation, but was supported in Hong Kong at most levels – though quite what the distinction was between Vietnamese economic migrants and those Chinese who fled China in the 1950s to set up in Hong Kong, or those who now seek to flee Hong Kong for whichever third country will have them, was never satisfactorily explained.

Britain's tougher stance led to a marked decrease in the numbers sailing to Hong Kong, though there is considerable evidence that the Vietnamese simply headed to other nearby countries instead, like Thailand and Malaysia – shifting rather than alleviating the problem. There was also an upturn in the Vietnamese economy at the turn of the decade, which perhaps persuaded many would-be migrants to stay. Whatever the truth, the last boat recorded as entering Hong Kong was in late 1991 (with only the odd refugee adding to the total since).

Meanwhile, in Hong Kong, conditions deteriorated in the nine **camps** in which the Vietnamese were held. At its peak, the camps' population was just over 64,000 people – conditions were basic and exacerbated by violent clashes between the different Vietnamese factions contained within. In the worst incident, 21 people died at Shek Kong camp in a fire set during a fight between north and south Vietnamese groups.

By mid-1993, the camps' population had diminished to around 42,000 as the number of **voluntary returnees** steadily increased, following agreement between Britain and Vietnam on the method of return. Overseen by the United Nations High Commission for Refugees (UNHCR), those who volunteer to return to Vietnam receive a US\$50 bonus and US\$30 a month during their first year back; forced returnees are supervised by the Orderly Return Programme and get the \$30 a month but not the bonus. With the average rate of return running at around a thousand per month, at the start of 1996 the number of Vietnamese people still detained in camps in Hong Kong was down to under twenty thousand, with hopes that all would be gone by the time of the handover to China in mid-1997. This, however, has become something of a political football of late: China has demanded Britain take note of its "unshirkable responsibility" for any Vietnamese left in the colony after the handover. Britain, not surprisingly, will make no such commitment, keen to avoid the impression that all the remaining boat people have to do is hold out until 1997 to be accepted into Britain (or any other country) by the back door.

The new politics

The **Basic Law** – the projected "constitution" for Hong Kong as a Special Administrative Region of China after 1997 – was finally approved by China's National People's Congress in April 1990, and immediately provided a focus around which people in Hong Kong began to question the lack of democratic progress in the territory.

Leaders in Hong Kong were particularly outraged by the attitude of the British govern-

ment, which – in their eyes – during the consultations on the Basic Law had capitulated every step of the way to the Chinese. China, for obvious reasons, was keen to have as little democracy as possible in place in Hong Kong by 1997, and the final draft of the Basic Law as passed had worrying implications for the future – a promise of eventual universal suffrage was deleted, Beijing maintained the power to declare martial law in Hong Kong, and an anti-subversion clause was added.

Out of the protests against the Basic Law grew a new **political awareness**, which expressed itself in a number of emerging pressure groups and fledgling political parties. The **Hong Kong Alliance in Support of the Patriotic and Democratic Movement** organized a 10,000-strong rally in April 1990, defying warnings from China to stop this kind of "provocation". One of the leading liberal activists in Hong Kong, Martin Lee, a barrister, became head of a new pro-democracy party, the United Democrats of Hong Kong, now known as the **Democratic Party**; the other main grouping was the conservative, business-led (and confusingly named) **Liberal Democratic Federation**.

In **elections in September 1991** – the territory's first direct elections – United Democrat candidates swept the board, winning sixteen of the eighteen seats on the sixty-seat Legislative Council (Legco) that were up for grabs. It was a limited exercise in democracy – 21 other candidates were selected by so-called "functional constituencies", consisting of trade and professional groups, while the rest were appointed by the governor – but it sent a powerful message to Beijing that Hong Kong people were dissatisfied with the provisions of the Basic Law. Even more alarming for Beijing was the fact that pro-China candidates failed to win a single seat.

Despite the advance of the United Democrats, the governor, David (later Sir David) Wilson refused to appoint liberals to his Executive Council (Exco) – a move welcomed in Beijing, though denigrated in Hong Kong. Indeed, Wilson's role in Hong Kong's government became increasingly suspect in the eyes of many, who accused him of giving in too readily to the Chinese. His fate was sealed when new British prime minister John Major was forced to travel to Beijing to sign the agreement for Hong Kong's new airport. Major's presence at the signing ceremony was virtually a condition of the

For more on the colonial system of government, see the feature on pp.72–73.

agreement, and it was seen very much as an embarrassment for the British that Wilson, with his diplomatic skills, should have avoided.

Fortuitously, as it turned out for the prime minister, his close ally **Chris Patten** – Conservative Party chairman – lost his parliamentary seat in Britain's April 1992 elections, even as his party was returned to power. Major offered him the governorship, which he eventually accepted, ushering in a new political era in Hong Kong.

The last governor

Chris Patten was the 28th – and last – **governor** to be appointed, but uniquely he was the first career politician to take the post. His arrival caused consternation all round: among the local population, who complained about having Britain's cast-off politicians imposed upon them, and among the Chinese leadership who – rightly as it turned out – feared Patten's motives for taking the job.

Any thoughts that Chris Patten was there to make up the numbers until 1997 soon disappeared. He quickly jettisoned much of the colonial paraphernalia associated with his position, while in talks with Beijing it became clear that he – and Britain – sought an extension in the franchise for Hong Kong before the handover to China, that went beyond the provisions made in the Basic Law. New Legco elections were due in 1995, which – under the provisions of the Basic Law – would see the number of elected members rise from eighteen to twenty (and to thirty by 2003). This had already been dismissed by Hong Kong liberals as too slow a move towards democracy: the Democratic Party wanted fifty percent of Legco directly elected in 1995, rising to a hundred percent by 2003. Patten's proposal was to stick to the number of directly elected members agreed with China, but to **widen the franchise**, by lowering the voting age from 21 to 18; by increasing the number of indirectly elected council members; and by creating extra "functional constituencies", which would effectively enfranchise 2.7 million Hong Kong people – as opposed to the roughly 200,000 voters that the previous system allowed.

The Chinese government began a loud campaign against the new governor and his proposals, and **relations between Britain and China** worsened considerably. Patten has been personally branded a "serpent", a "prostitute", a "sinner for all millennia" and – most intriguingly – a "tango dancer" by the mainland Chinese press, reflecting the (correctly held) view of the Chinese government that his attempts to meddle with the franchise were a Western attempt to import democracy into China by the back door. As talks dragged on, and relations soured, new threats were made to Hong Kong's stability. China vowed to renege on all contracts and commercial agreements signed by the Hong Kong government without its consent as soon as the colony was returned to its control in 1997 – something that threatened the future of several major projects, including the new Chek Lap Kok airport. The Hang Seng Index reflected a general lack of confidence in the territory's future by recording massive falls; and rumours of destabilization by the Chinese government caused huge runs on two of Hong Kong's largest banks, Citibank and the Standard Chartered. China also reiterated its non-recognition of the UK passports offered to the fifty thousand key Hong Kong personnel and their families. In the meantime, Britain announced a new British National Overseas (BNO) passport to replace the British Dependent Territories passport after 1997 – the BNO passport would grant British consular protection outside China, and visa-free entry to, but not the right of abode in, the UK.

The situation reached something of a stalemate, with both sides playing a nerve-wracking poker game with the territory's future. Meetings throughout 1993 consistently failed to provide any breakthrough with China hostile to Governor Patten's very presence in any negotiations and Britain adamant that its limited democratic proposals should prevail.

In the end, the governor prevailed, simply by ignoring the threats and gambling that the Chinese government wouldn't abandon its commercial agreements, thus cutting off its nose to spite its face. **Elections in September 1995** marked the first time that each of Legco's sixty seats was contested and brought gains for the Democratic Party, which could, for the first time, count on the support of almost half of Legco's members. The main pro-Beijing grouping, the Democratic Alliance for the Betterment of Hong

Kong, came a distant second, despite vociferous Chinese backing. However, come 1997, Beijing, for its part, has no intention of honouring a contest it dismissed as mere "Patten elections".

The governor's firm line continues to command respectable support in Hong Kong, although pro-democracy Legco members have recently changed their stance from supporting his electoral reforms to complaining now that the reforms don't go anywhere near far enough. In particular, faced with China's insistence on its right to veto any "subversive" legislators appointed before 1997, Democratic Party members propose a "through train", whereby legislators in place by 1997 should be allowed to remain.

It's unlikely to happen, though all sides sport weaknesses in their **negotiating positions**. China itself needs the Western investment that Hong Kong provides and is desperate to retain Most Favoured Nation (MFN) status with the USA; above all, it's keen to re-establish itself in the eyes of the world following the break in relations that occurred after the events in Tiananmen Square in 1989. In Hong Kong, conservative business groups press for an accommodation with China, arguing that the territory's future prosperity rests on co-operation and not confrontation, but the various conservative and pro-Beijing factions have commanded little popular support so far. Conversely, the Democratic Party and other liberals see full democracy by 1997 as the only safeguard against future Chinese clampdowns – but privately concede that there is little hope of this happening, given the constraints of the Basic Law within which they have to operate.

However, in many ways the most indefensible position is that adopted by the **British government** and its representative in Hong Kong, the governor. Adopting the high moral ground and arguing forcefully for democracy now, Britain conveniently forgets the past. For 150 years, there has been no real democracy in Hong Kong. Successive governments have shown no interest in establishing a democratic forum, and liberal reforms – like the abolition of the death penalty and the legalization of homosexuality – have only occurred in the past few years, decades after similar reforms were enacted in Britain itself. In April 1992 the International Commission of Jurists (ICJ) claimed that Britain had broken the law when deciding to give only fifty thouand key citizens the right to settle in Britain. The ICJ maintained that the people of Hong Kong had a right

to self-determination which should have been tested in a referendum before the Joint Declaration was signed in 1984. It concluded that all three million British Dependent Territory citizens should be given the right of abode in the UK – something that the British government has never had any intention of doing. Moreover, Governor Patten's movements are circumscribed by Britain's long-term wish to maintain cordial relations with China because of the trading opportunities that are involved.

The final throw of the British dice was made by Prime Minister John Major, on his visit to the territory in **March 1996**. Pushed by Governor Patten, who had been making disturbing noises about granting full British citizenship to Hong Kong's residents, he announced **visa-free entry** into the UK for the 2.2 million people who, after 1997, will hold Special Administrative Region (SAR), ie Chinese, passports; they will be able to stay for up to six months at a time without applying for a visa, but will not be entitled to British residency or allowed to work or study in Britain. The three million holders of the British Nationals Overseas (BNO) passports already have this visa-free entry right. In addition, Major promised British residency rights to the seven thousand Indians and other non-Chinese who, technically stateless after 1997, might feel forced to leave Hong Kong. The announcement was clearly designed as a confidence-building measure and received support in Hong Kong, but in reality it's no more than cosmetic in effect. Visa-free travel to the UK is expected to be taken up by no more than fifteen thousand or so a year out of the two million people enabled (since those eligible for SAR passports are those who don't have travel documents anyway and have, presumably, never left Hong Kong). In addition, if push came to shove and China made life so intolerable for Hong Kong citizens that there was a sudden flood of visa-free travel and asylum applications, Britain would simply withdraw the right – it has no permanent force in law. Out of Hong Kong's six million citizens, only 250,000 are entitled to visa-free access *and* residency.

Endgame: the handover and beyond

Despite the posturings on all sides, it's accepted that China holds all the aces: in simple terms, the Chinese government can afford to wait until midnight on **30 June 1997**, when – once back in control of Hong Kong – they can do what they please. With this realization, relations between Britain and China have improved somewhat of late, enabling firm commitments to be made about the completion of the Chek Lap Kok airport (now due in mid-1998) and progress on the question of Hong Kong's new container port, which China had previously blocked.

Politically, however, China is making all the running and with time running out, there is seemingly little that Governor Patten or the Hong Kong democrats can do. Patten has been sidelined by the Chinese leadership, which refuses to invite him to Beijing; moreover, the senior Chinese official responsible for the handover, Lu Ping, comes and goes in Hong Kong without ever feeling the need to talk to the governor directly. Since 1993, there's effectively been a government-in-waiting in Beijing, following the establishment of the **Preliminary Working Committee** (PWC), a body of Communist Party officials and conservative (ie. rich) Hong Kong citizens appointed by the National People's Congress. The Committee has countered every proposal by the governor with pronouncements of its own that do little to build confidence in the territory. The level of welfare spending in Hong Kong has been criticized, while lately the PWC has proposed a "watering down" of the **Bill of Rights**, promulgated in 1991 as a confidence-building measure after the events of Tiananmen Square, leading to fears that human rights and civil liberties in the territory may be threatened after 1997. Moreover, having been affronted by Patten's widening of the franchise in Hong Kong, which it claimed violated previous agreements, Beijing now maintains that it will simply **dissolve Legco** as soon as the territory reverts to Chinese rule.

It's becoming clearer by the day what is intended to replace Hong Kong's existing government. A 150-member **Preparatory Committee**, established in January 1996, was handpicked in Beijing and granted the task of setting up Hong Kong's first "Chinese" government. Although 94 of the 150 members were from Hong Kong, most were millionaires (and billionaires) and not surprisingly there was no place on the committee for pro-democracy liberals, whose influence looks more and more likely to stop abruptly in mid-1997. In turn, the Preparatory Committee will establish a 400-strong selection committee – again, made up of pro-Beijing and conservative supporters – whose job it will be to nominate a **Chief Executive**, who will become, in effect, the first post-colonial governor. Less dramatically, but no less symbolically, various venerable Hong Kong institutions are changing their names: the "Royal" will be dropped from the police force, the yacht club, the golf club and all the other bastions of colonial rule and privilege.

The **lead-up to the handover** has been highly tense, with both sides talking more and more bluntly about domesday scenarios. Things reached fever-pitch in Hong Kong during the **Taiwan crisis** in March 1996, when China undertook extensive and threatening missile trials and military manoeuvres during the run-up to Taiwan's first democratic presidential elections. China has a long-standing policy aim of reincorporating Taiwan into its fold and the military threat, while hardly new, was a direct reminder to Hong Kong of what might be expected there in the years after 1997.

Yet there are signs of hope for the future of Hong Kong, not least in the massive **development programme** that is currently touching most parts of the centre. On the face of it, Hong Kong doesn't look like a place in peril, as the new airport, transport and communications infrastructure, land reclamation schemes, New Town housing projects and commercial ventures attest: locally, at least, there's still some confidence that a revitalized Hong Kong will thrive in the burgeoning economy of southeastern China. As they were for centuries, the stability and prosperity of Hong Kong are once again dependent on China.

See the features on p.122, p.133, pp.166–167 and pp.204–205 for more details on the massive development programme currently underway in Hong Kong

Books

There's no shortage of **books** written about Hong Kong and Macau, and you'll find that you can get most of them in Hong Kong, too; for a list of main bookshop addresses in Hong Kong, see pp.288–289. What there is a lack of – certainly in translation – is books about both territories written by Chinese authors. In the reviews below, the UK publisher is listed first, followed by the publisher in the US – unless the title is available in one country only, in which case we've specified the country; o/p signifies out of print.

Hong Kong

History and politics

Nigel Cameron *Power* (OUP East Asia, o/p). Immensely detailed history of the *China Light & Power Co*, one of Hong Kong's biggest economic successes. More interesting, though, for the insight it offers into one of the territory's main power-broking families, the Kadoories.

Austin Coates *Myself a Mandarin* (OUP East Asia, UK). Light-hearted account of the author's time as a magistrate in the colonial administration during the 1950s. For more from the prolific Coates, see "Macau" below.

Maurice Collis *Foreign Mud* (Faber, o/p). Useful coverage of the opening up of China to trade and of the opium wars.

Robert Cottrell *The End of Hong Kong: The Secret Diplomacy of Imperial Retreat* (John Murray, UK). One of the most recent perusals of the manoeuvrings between Britain and China, this is a lucid enough account for anyone interested in how Hong Kong will be handed over to the Chinese. Well written and perceptive.

E. J. Eitel *Europe in China* (OUP East Asia, UK). First published in 1895, this is an out-and-out colonial history of early Hong Kong – lively, biased and interesting.

G. B. Endacott *A History of Hong Kong* (OUP, UK), *Hong Kong Eclipse* (OUP, UK). Hong Kong's most important postwar historian, Endacott is still the standard authority. *Hong Kong Eclipse* deals with the fraught period 1941–45, the Japanese occupation, and is a comprehensive, general account relying on first-hand accounts and official records.

Jean Gittins *Stanley: Behind Barbed Wire* (HK Univ. Press/State Mutual, US). Well-written and moving eyewitness account of time spent behind bars at Stanley Prison during the internment of civilians by the Japanese in World War II.

Kevin Rafferty *City on the Rocks: Hong Kong's Uncertain Future* (Penguin, UK & US). One of the more recent surveys of Hong Kong's history, people and institutions. Wide-ranging and knowledgeable, this big book marshals all the usual views and looks to the future, putting Hong Kong firmly on the world's economic and political stage.

Gerald Segal *The Fate of Hong Kong* (Simon & Schuster/St Martin's Press). Excellent current round-up of the various interests at work in deciding Hong Kong's future, and incorporating informed accounts on what the effects of 1997 are likely to have on the rest of the region.

Peter Wesley-Smith *Unequal Treaty 1898–1997* (OUP, o/p). Sound and detailed review of the leasing of the New Territories to Britain in 1898, recording the reaction of both the British and Chinese authorities along the way. Written before the Joint Declaration, but full of pertinent comment about the future difficulties concerning the expiry of the lease.

Gavin Young *Beyond Lion Rock* (Penguin, UK). Dismal account of the history of *Cathay Pacific Airways*, which although started in Shanghai after World War II, came to international prominence from its later base in Hong Kong under the wing of the Swire company. On the whole a full-blown apology for some fairly unappealing characters.

Travel, architecture, reference and contemporary life

Emily Hahn *China to Me* (Virago, o/p/Da Capo). A breathless account of pre- and postwar jinks in (mainly) Shanghai and Hong Kong, including time when the American author and her child lived under Japanese rule in the territory while her friends were interned.

Susanna Hoe *The Private Life of Old Hong Kong* (OUP East Asia, UK & US). A history of the lives of Western women in Hong Kong from 1841 to 1941, re-created from contemporary letters and diaries. A fine book, and telling of the hitherto neglected contribution of a whole range of people who had a hand in shaping modern Hong Kong.

Hong Kong (Hong Kong Government Press). The HK government's official yearbook, published annually, and a detailed – if uncritical – mass of photos, statistics, essays and information. Available in most HK bookshops.

Vittorio Magnago Lampugnani (ed). *Hong Kong Architecture: The Aesthetics of Destiny* (Prestel, UK). Beautifully produced, large-format account of Hong Kong's most important and innovative architectural projects, with fine colour pictures and sketches and an informative background history.

John and Kirsten Miller (ed). *Hong Kong* (Chronicle Books, UK). A nice little compendium of extracts from novels and travelogues based in Hong Kong, encompassing all the usual suspects: Somerset Maugham, Jan Morris et al.

Jan Morris *Hong Kong: Epilogue to an Empire* (Penguin/Vintage). Hong Kong – historical, contemporary and future – dealt with in typical Morris fashion: which means an engaging mix of anecdote, solid research, acute observation and lively opinion. One of the best introductions there is to the territory.

Jackie Pullinger *Chasing the Dragon* (Hodder & Stoughton/Servant Publications). The missionary author spent the best part of two decades – the 1970s and 1980s – grubbing around in the Walled City and saving souls. Fine on Hong Kong low-life, but you soon get tired of the proselytizing and doubt her success rate with hardened heroin addicts and Triad members. Her *Crack in the Wall* (Hodder & Stoughton, UK) details Triad

life in the Walled City and makes more interesting reading.

Madelaine H. Tang (and others) *Historical Walks: Hong Kong Island* (The Guidebook Company). An invaluable little book detailing five walks through parts of Hong Kong Island, with clear maps and directions. Available in most Hong Kong bookshops.

Fiction

James Adams *Taking the Tunnel* (Signet, o/p). Ruthless Hong Kong-based Triad members hold a trainload of passengers hostage on the Channel Tunnel – a pacy thriller that ticks along nicely, incorporating authentic background touches throughout.

James Clavell *Tai-Pan* (Coronet/Dell), *Noble House* (Coronet/Dell). Big, thick bodice-rippers set respectively at the founding of the territory and in the 1960s, and dealing with the same one-dimensional pirates and businessmen. There's no real Hong Kong atmosphere in either. A much better read, incidentally, is his *King Rat*, set in Changi prisoner-of-war camp in Singapore where Clavell was a POW.

John Le Carré *The Honourable Schoolboy* (Coronet/Bantam). Taut George Smiley novel, with spooks and moles chasing each other across Hong Kong and the Far East. Accurate and enthusiastic reflections on the territory and the usual sharp eye trained on the intelligence world.

Elizabeth Darrell *Concerto* (Michael Joseph/St Martin's Press). Blockbuster novel set against the background of the Japanese invasion of Hong Kong in 1941.

Somerset Maugham *The Painted Veil* (Mandarin/ Viking Penguin). Colonial story of love, betrayal and revenge which unfolds in Hong Kong and moves on to cholera-ravaged mainland China. First published in 1925.

Timothy Mo *An Insular Possession* (Pan/Random House o/p). A splendid novel, re-creating the nineteenth-century foundation of Hong Kong, taking in the trading ports of Macau and Canton along the way. Mo's ear and eye for detail can also be glimpsed in *The Monkey King* (Vintage/ Double day, o/p), his entertaining first novel about the conflicts and manoeuvrings of family life in postwar Hong Kong, and his filmed novel *Sour Sweet* (Vintage/Random House, o/p) – an endearing tale of an immigrant Hong Kong family setting up business in 1960s London.

For a rundown of useful Cantonese **cookery books**, see the section in Cantonese recipes on p.396.

Macau

C. R. Boxer *Seventeenth Century Macau* (Heinemann, US, o/p). Interesting survey of documents, engravings, inscriptions and maps of Macau culled from the years either side of the restoration of the Portuguese monarchy in 1640. An academic study, but accessible enough for some informative titbits about the enclave.

Daniel Carney *Macau* (Corgi/Kensington Pub. Corp.). Improbable characterization in a Clavell-like thriller set in the enclave.

Austin Coates *Macao and the British* (OUP East Asia, UK), *A Macao Narrative* (OUP East Asia, UK), *City of Broken Promises* (OUP East Asia, UK). Coates has written widely about the Far East, where he was Assistant Colonial Secretary in Hong Kong in the 1950s. *Macao and the British* follows the early years of Anglo-Chinese relations and underlines the importance of the Portuguese enclave as a staging post for other traders. *A Macao Narrative* is a short but more specific account of Macau's history up to the mid-1970s; *City of Broken Promises* is an entertaining historical novel set in Macau in the late eighteenth century.

Cesar Guillen-Nunez *Macau* (OUP, UK & US). Decent, slim hardback history of Macau, worth a look for the insights it offers into the churches, buildings and gardens of the city.

Books about China

David Bonavia *The Chinese* (Penguin, o/p/Viking Penguin). Excellent introduction to the Chinese – their lives, aspirations, politics and problems. Intended as a discussion of the Chinese of the People's Republic, it remains useful and instructive for all travellers to Asia.

John King Fairbank *The Great Chinese Revolution 1800–1985* (Pan/HarperCollins). Readable and enjoyable account of the opening up of China since the turn of the nineteenth century. Good for straightforward explanation of the tricky manoeuvring before and after the Revolution in 1949.

Michael Fathers and Andrew Higgins *Tiananmen: the Rape of Peking* (Doubleday UK & US, o/p). Eyewitness account of the events leading up to the massacre in and around Tiananmen Square in 1989.

Christopher Hibbert *China and the West 1793–1911* (Penguin/Viking Penguin). Superbly entertaining account of the opening up of China to Western trade and influence. Hibbert leaves you in no doubt about the cultural misunderstandings that bedevilled early missions to China – or about the morally dubious acquisition of Hong Kong and the other Treaty Ports by Western powers.

Astrology: the Chinese Calendar and Horoscopes

Most people are interested to find out what sign they are in the Chinese zodiac system, particularly since – like the Western system – each person is supposed to have characteristics similar to those of the sign which relates to their birthdate. There are twelve signs of the Chinese zodiac, corresponding with one of twelve animals, whose characteristics you'll find listed below. These animal signs have existed in Chinese folk tradition since the sixth century BC, though it wasn't until the third century BC that they were incorporated into a formal study of astrology and astronomy, based around the device of the lunar calendar. Quite why animals emerged as the vehicle for Chinese horoscopy is unclear: one story has it that the animals used are the twelve which appeared before the command of Buddha, who named the years in the order in which the animals arrived.

Each **lunar year** (which starts in late January/ early February) is represented by one of the twelve animal symbols. Your sign depends on the year you were born – check the **calendar chart** below – rather than the month as in the Western system, but beyond that the idea is the same: born under the sign of a particular animal, you will have certain characteristics, ideal partners, lucky and unlucky days. The details below will tell you the basic facts about your character and personality, though it's only a rough guide: to go into your real Chinese astrological self, you need to be equipped with your precise date and time of birth and one of the books listed below, which can explain all the horoscopical bits and pieces. The **animals** always appear in the same order so that if you know the current year you can always work out which one is to influence the following Chinese New Year.

The Rat

Characteristics: usually generous, intelligent and hard-working, but can be petty and idle; has lots of friends, but few close ones; may be success-ful, likes challenges and is good at business, but is insecure; generally diplomatic; tends to get into emotional entanglements.

Partners: best suited to Dragon, Monkey and Ox; doesn't get on with Horse and Goat.

Famous Rats: Wolfgang Amadeus Mozart, William Shakespeare, Marlon Brando, Doris Day, Yves St Laurent, Leo Tolstoy, Jimmy Carter and Prince Charles.

The Ox

Characteristics: healthy; obstinate; independent; usually calm and cool, but can get stroppy at times; shy and conservative; likes the outdoors and old-fashioned things; always finishes a task.

Partners: best suited to Snake, Rat or Rooster; doesn't get on with Tiger, Goat or Monkey.

Famous Oxen: Walt Disney, Adolf Hitler, Napoleon Bonaparte, Richard Nixon, Vincent Van Gogh, Peter Sellers, Dustin Hoffman, Robert Redford, Margaret Thatcher, Shirley Bassey, Jane Fonda, Pieter Paul Rubens.

The Tiger

Characteristics: adventurous; creative and idealis-tic; confident and enthusiastic; can be diplomatic and practical; fearless and forward, aiming at impossible goals, though a realist with a forceful personality.

Partners: best suited to Horse for marriage; gets on with Dragon, Pig and Dog; avoid Snake, Monkey and Ox.

Famous Tigers: Karl Marx, Queen Elizabeth II, Alec Guinness, Stevie Wonder, Ludwig van Beethoven, Marilyn Monroe, Princess Anne, Diana Rigg, Charles de Gaulle, Rudolf Nureyev.

The Rabbit

Characteristics: peace-loving; sociable but quiet; devoted to family and friends; timid but can be good at business; needs reassurance and affec-tion to avoid being upset; can be vain; long-lived.

Calendar Chart

Date Of Birth	Animal	Date Of Birth	Animal
1.2.1900–18.2.1901	Rat	29.1.1949–16.2.1950	Ox
19.2.1901–7.2.1902	Ox	17.2.1950–5.2.1951	Tiger
8.2.1902–28.1.1903	Tiger	6.2.1951–26.1.1952	Rabbit
29.1.1903–15.2.1904	Rabbit	27.1.1952–13.2.1953	Dragon
16.2.1904–3.2.1905	Dragon	14.2.1953–2.2.1954	Snake
4.2.1905–24.1.1906	Snake	3.2.1954–23.1.1955	Horse
25.1.1906–12.2.1907	Horse	26.1.1955–11.2.1956	Goat
13.2.1907–1.2.1908	Goat	12.2.1956–30.1.1957	Monkey
2.2.1908–21.1.1909	Monkey	31.1.1957–17.2.1958	Rooster
22.1.1909–9.2.1910	Rooster	18.2.1958–7.2.1959	Dog
10.2.1910–29.1.1911	Dog	8.2.1959–27.1.1960	Pig
30.1.1911–17.2.1912	Pig	28.1.1960–14.2.1961	Rat
18.2.1912–5.2.1913	Rat	15.2.1961–4.2.1962	Ox
6.2.1913–25.1.1914	Ox	5.2.1962–24.1.1963	Tiger
26.1.1914–13.2.1915	Tiger	25.1.1963–12.2.1964	Rabbit
14.2.1915–3.2.1916	Rabbit	13.2.1964–1.2.1965	Dragon
4.2.1916–22.1.1917	Dragon	2.2.1965–20.1.1966	Snake
23.1.1917–10.2.1918	Snake	21.1.1966–8.2.1967	Horse
11.2.1918–31.1.1919	Horse	9.2.1967–29.1.1968	Goat
1.2.1919–19.2.1920	Goat	30.1.1968–16.2.1969	Monkey
20.2.1920–7.2.1921	Monkey	17.2.1969–5.2.1970	Rooster
8.2.1921–27.1.1922	Rooster	6.2.1970–26.1.1971	Dog
28.1.1922–15.2.1923	Dog	27.1.1971–14.2.1972	Pig
16.2.1923–4.2.1924	Pig	15.2.1972–2.2.1973	Rat
5.2.1924–23.1.1925	Rat	3.2.1973–22.1.1974	Ox
24.1.1925–12.2.1926	Ox	23.1.1974–10.2.1975	Tiger
13.2.1926–1.2.1927	Tiger	11.2.1975–30.1.1976	Rabbit
2.2.1927–22.1.1928	Rabbit	31.1.1976–17.2.1977	Dragon
23.1.1928–9.2.1929	Dragon	18.2.1977–6.2.1978	Snake
10.2.1929–29.1.1930	Snake	7.2.1978–27.1.1979	Horse
30.1.1930–16.2.1931	Horse	28.1.1979–15.2.1980	Goat
17.2.1931–5.2.1932	Goat	16.2.1980–4.2.1981	Monkey
6.2.1932–25.1.1933	Monkey	5.2.1981–24.1.1982	Rooster
26.1.1933–13.2.1934	Rooster	25.1.1982–12.2.1983	Dog
14.2.1934–3.2.1935	Dog	13.2.1983–1.2.1984	Pig
4.2.1935–23.1.1936	Pig	2.2.1984–19.2.1985	Rat
24.1.1936–10.2.1937	Rat	20.2.1985–8.2.1986	Ox
11.2.1937–30.1.1938	Ox	9.2.1986–28.1.1987	Tiger
31.1.1938–18.2.1939	Tiger	29.1.1987–16.2.1988	Rabbit
19.2.1939–7.2.1940	Rabbit	17.2.1988–5.2.1989	Dragon
8.2.1940–26.1.1941	Dragon	6.2.1989–26.1.1990	Snake
27.1.1941–14.2.1942	Snake	27.1.1990–14.2.1991	Horse
15.2.1942–4.2.1943	Horse	15.2.1991–3.2.1992	Goat
5.2.1943–24.1.1944	Goat	4.2.1992–22.1.1993	Monkey
25.1.1944–12.2.1945	Monkey	23.1.1993–9.2.1994	Rooster
13.2.1945–1.2.1946	Rooster	10.2.1994–30.1.1995	Dog
2.2.1946–21.1.1947	Dog	31.1.1995–18.2.1996	Pig
22.1.1947–9.2.1948	Pig	19.2.1996–6.2.1997	Rat
10.2.1948–28.1.1949	Rat	7.2.1997–27.1.1998	Ox
		28.1.1998–15.2.1999	Tiger

Partners: best suited to Pig, Dog and Goat; not friendly with Tiger and Rooster.

Famous Rabbits: Fidel Castro, Bob Hope, Harry Belafonte, David Frost, Martin Luther King, Josef Stalin, Queen Victoria, Ali McGraw and Albert Einstein.

The Dragon

Characteristics: strong, commanding, a leader; popular, athletic; bright, chivalrous and idealistic, though not always consistent; likely to be a believer in equality.

Partners: best suited to Snake, Rat, Monkey, Tiger and Rooster; avoid Dog.

Famous Dragons: Joan of Arc, Ringo Starr, Mae West, John Lennon, Frank Sinatra, Salvador Dali, Jimmy Connors, Kirk Douglas, Che Guevara, Shirley Temple Black and Yehudi Menuhin.

The Snake

Characteristics: charming, but possessive and selfish; private and secretive; strange sense of humour; mysterious and inquisitive; ruthless; likes the nice things in life; a thoughtful person, but superstitious.

Partners: best suited for marriage to Dragon, Rooster and Ox; avoid Snake, Pig and Tiger.

Famous Snakes: J. F. Kennedy, Abraham Lincoln, Edgar Allen Poe, Mao Zedong, Pablo Picasso, Brahms, Franz Schubert and Ferdinand Marcos.

The Horse

Characteristics: nice appearance and deft; ambitious and quick-witted; favours bold colours; popular, with a sense of humour, gracious and gentle; can be good at business; fickle and emotional.

Partners: best suited to Tiger, Dog and Goat; doesn't get on with Rabbit and Rat.

Famous Horses: Neil Armstrong, Barbara Streisand, Paul McCartney, Theodore Roosevelt, Rembrandt, Raquel Welch, Leonid Brezhnev and Igor Stravinsky.

The Goat

Characteristics: a charmer and a lucky person who likes money; unpunctual and hesitant; too fond of complaining; interested in the supernatural.

Partners: best suited to Horse, Pig and Rabbit; avoid Ox and Dog.

Famous Goats: Andy Warhol, Billie Jean King, Liberace, Mohammed Ali, Michelangelo, Laurence Olivier, James Michener and Diana Dors.

The Monkey

Characteristics: very intelligent and sharp, an opportunist; daring and confident, but unstable and egoistic; entertaining and very attractive to others; inventive; a sense of humour but with little respect for reputations.

Partners: best suited to Dragon and Rat; doesn't get on with Tiger and Ox.

Famous Monkeys: Leonardo da Vinci, Mick Jagger, Bette Davis, Charles Dickens, Julius Caesar, Paul Gauguin, Joan Crawford and Rene Descartes.

The Rooster

Characteristics: frank and reckless, and can be tactless; free with advice; punctual and a hard worker; imaginative to the point of dreaming; likes to be noticed; emotional.

Partners: best suited to Snake, Dragon and Ox; doesn't get on with Pig, Rabbit and Rooster.

Famous Roosters: Michael Caine, Prince Philip, Charles Darwin, Peter Ustinov, Elton John, Katharine Hepburn, Peter O'Toole and Yves Montand.

The Dog

Characteristics: alert, watchful and defensive; can be generous and is patient; very responsible and has good organizational skills; spiritual, home-loving and non-materialistic.

Partners: best suited to Rabbit, Pig, Tiger and Horse; avoid Dragon and Goat.

Famous Dogs: David Niven, Henry Moore, Brigitte Bardot, Liza Minnelli, Zsa Zsa Gabor, Winston Churchill, Elvis Presley, Golda Meir, Sophia Loren and Voltaire.

The Pig

Characteristics: honest; vulnerable and not good at business, but still materialistic and ambitious; outgoing and outspoken, but naive; kind and helpful to the point of being taken advantage of; calm and genial.

Partners: best suited to Dog, Goat, Tiger and Rabbit; avoid Snake and Rooster.

Famous Pigs: Alfred Hitchcock, Ronald Reagan, Maria Callas, Henry Kissinger, Woody Allen, Julie Andrews, Humphrey Bogart, Al Capone, Ernest Hemingway and Johnny Mathis.

Cantonese Recipes

Cantonese cooking is generally quick and simple, and with a few basic utensils and ingredients you can create a tasty, nutritious Cantonese meal in your own home. The recipes given below can either be attempted individually, or eaten as part of a wider meal, making changes and additions as suggested. There's nothing particularly complicated about the recipes; they're examples of good, basic home cooking, the sort of things you'd eat every day in a Chinese home in Hong Kong – though not necessarily in a restaurant, where people take the opportunity to eat more elaborate, expensive food.

Utensils

The main utensil you need is a **wok**, a thin metal frying pan with deep sides and a curved bottom, designed to spread the heat evenly around the whole surface. A normal frying pan is not really a substitute. Woks generally come with either one long handle or two wooden side-handles, the first type for stir-frying, the second for steaming or deep-frying. Bought in Chinatown supermarkets, they're fairly inexpensive – the long-handled sort is best for general use. Fancy ones with plastic fittings, or "non-stick" ones, sold in department stores as "wok sets" are inferior in every way. Once you have your wok, you need to season it before use: rinse it in water, dry it, then heat it slowly for ten minutes or so wiped with a little oil (use a kitchen roll); let it cool, and wipe the wok, repeating the whole process until the paper wipes clean. When in use, the interior surface of the wok will eventually turn black, which is fine: never clean it with detergent; always use plain water and dry thoroughly before rubbing with a little oil and storing it. If it rusts, scrub it off and season the wok again before use.

Really, the only other equipment you need for basic Cantonese cooking is a large **lid** for the wok, for use when steaming, and a **wok stand**, which makes a base for the wok over the gas flame or electric ring (gas is best for Cantonese cooking, since you can turn the heat off immediately; with electricity you have to take a little more care). You can use the **spatulas** and other ordinary kitchen utensils you already have, though if you're going to cook lots of Chinese food, a long-handled metal spatula, a sieve and wooden chopsticks are all useful things to have. You can also buy **bamboo steamers**, which you place on a little metal stand inside your water-filled wok. They come in various sizes, but again, unless you're mad keen, you can make do with steaming fish and the like on a heat-resistant plate, which you place on top of the stand.

Ingredients

If you live near a Chinatown you'll be able to get all the ingredients you need for even the most elaborate of Cantonese meals. But most supermarkets and grocers carry the basics, certainly all the things you'll need to make all the recipes below. The main things to have in large supply are **garlic**, fresh **ginger** root (powdered is no good), **spring onions** (scallions) and **peppers**, both capsicums and chilli peppers. Other flavourings are **soy sauce** (light and dark), **oyster sauce** and **sesame oil**, and **vegetable oil** (or any mild-flavoured oil) to fry in.

Common **vegetables** are Chinese cabbage, baby corn, mushrooms and beansprouts. If you're lucky enough to have a specialist shop near you, stock up whenever you can on tinned (unless you can get fresh) **bamboo shoots**, **straw mushrooms** and **water chestnuts**; fresh **beancurd**; preserved **black beans**; and dried **Chinese mushrooms** – which you need to soak in hot water before use. With all these, a bottle of **rice wine**, some small, **dried shrimps** (dried oysters, scallops and mussels are available in Chinatowns, too) and a selection of **nuts**, **noodles** and **rice**, there's barely a recipe you're not prepared for.

If you can't get all the right ingredients, don't worry. Chinese cooking is nothing if not adaptable. Remember, though, that the ingredients must complement the food being cooked, so don't substitute strong flavours for delicate ones; it's better to leave an ingredient out, than put in one that's overpowering. The most important rule of all is wherever possible to use **fresh food**.

The recipes

All the recipes below will feed four people, unless otherwise stated. The beauty of Chinese food, though, is that since it's eaten communally, you can easily spin out meals to accommodate more, by cooking more of the basic things, like rice and soup. The other rule to follow is that you should aim to cook one more dish than the number of people present, and maintain the general balance between meat, fish and vegetable dishes.

Soup

Soup is an indispensable part of a Cantonese meal, drunk throughout the meal and not just at the beginning as in the West. Mostly the soups are clear, and their basis is a good stock, which you should prepare in advance, keeping it in the fridge or freezing it for future use.

Chicken carcass or bones/spare ribs/root vegetable chunks

4 slices fresh ginger

2 cloves garlic, sliced

Pinch of salt

Put the ingredients in a large saucepan of water (using meat or vegetables, as you like) and boil on a low heat for 2 hours, adding more water if necessary. Skim the pan as it boils and strain at the end, reserving the liquid as the basis for any soup. Heat with diced vegetables, seafood chunks, dried shrimp, slices of meat or beaten egg (or any combination of these) for a clear, hot soup.

Plain rice

The other indispensable part of any meal, rice accompanies the other dishes and is generally eaten just plain boiled. Use only long grain white rice; any other variety is just not the same. Unless you've got an expensive rice cooker, follow these steps for perfect rice. Using one cup of rice per person, place rice in a saucepan and wash and rinse well under a running tap, draining the water off each time until it stops appearing cloudy (about six or seven rinses). To the drained rice, then add just under twice the amount of cups of water to rice. Cover with a tight-fitting lid and bring to the boil; then turn heat down to minimum and simmer for 10 minutes. Then turn off the heat and keep covered for another 10 to 15 minutes. Only now

should you take the lid off – the rice will be ready to eat.

Basic fried rice

In a more elaborate meal, fried rice can become one of the main dishes. In Hong Kong and China, it's always prepared with leftover cooked rice from the day before – if you're starting from scratch, cook the rice well in advance and only use it when cold.

3 tablespoons vegetable oil

1 large onion, thinly sliced

2–3 eggs, beaten

4 bowls cooked rice

2 spring onions (scallions), chopped

Soy sauce

Heat the oil in a wok and stir-fry the onions at high heat for a minute or so. Add the cooked rice and toss well, heating through, adding a little more oil if necessary to prevent sticking. Make a well in the rice and pour in the beaten eggs. Let them set on the bottom, then worry the eggs into the rice, adding splashes of soy sauce as they cook. The rice is ready when the egg is set; garnish with chopped spring onion. For more elaborate fried rice, add shrimp, peas, bacon, strips of meat or mushrooms (or any combination) when you add the onion, making sure they're cooked before you add the rice.

Simple steamed fish

This is the most common way to eat fish, which is cleaned and served whole, with head and tail intact; cut them off if you prefer. Or simply use fillets; chunky haddock is good (and can be used frozen for this recipe).

500–750g/1–1^{1}/$_{2}$lb white fish

4 slices fresh ginger, cut into strips

2 cloves garlic, sliced

Vegetable oil

Salt

Soy sauce

2 spring onions, chopped

3 Chinese mushrooms, thinly sliced

1 tablespoon tinned Chinese preserved vegetables

Prepare the fish and place on a steaming plate or shallow dish. Sprinkle with garlic, ginger and salt, pushing some into the cavities if it's a whole fish. Pour over a little vegetable oil and soy sauce and sprinkle with spring onions, Chinese mushrooms and Chinese preserved vegetables; the last two are not essential. Cover and steam over boiling water in wok for 15–20 minutes.

Easier, and just as common, is to steam the fish on its own, heat the oil in a wok with a dash of soy sauce and serve by pouring the hot oil over the fish – this ensures that the fish is cooked thoroughly and you use the remaining sauce as a dip.

Braised fish in sweet tomato sauce

The Cantonese generally eat their fish steamed, but this is a simple recipe for a dish with plenty of sauce.

1kg/2lb mackerel, cleaned and cut across into 5cm/2in chunks

2 cloves garlic, chopped

4 slices fresh ginger, chopped

3 tablespoons vegetable oil

500g/1lb fresh tomatoes, skinned and halved

2 tablespoons soy sauce

1–2 tablespoons sugar

1 teaspoon cornflour

Heat the oil in a wok and fry the chunks of fish for 5 minutes, turning so that they brown on all sides. Remove and put aside. Add the garlic and ginger to the remaining oil and stir-fry for 30 seconds. Then add the tomatoes and stir-fry on high heat until they break down into a thick sauce, adding water as necessary to prevent sticking. In a cup, mix the soy sauce, sugar and cornflour into a paste and add to the tomatoes. Turn down the heat and cook until the sauce is a fairly thick consistency, adding water as necessary and more sugar to taste – the sweet taste should complement the tomatoes, not overpower them. Finally, add the cooked fish, stir together and serve.

Lemon chicken

A dish with an unusual mix of flavours; good for a dinner party.

1 small chicken, jointed and cut into largish chunks

3 slices fresh ginger, chopped into strips

2 cloves garlic, sliced

3–4 tablespoons vegetable oil

2 large lemons, sliced

3 spring onions, chopped

2 tablespoons chicken stock

1 tablespoon rice wine (or dry sherry)

Cornflour

1 tablespoon soy sauce

Salt

Heat the oil in a wok, add the chicken pieces and stir-fry for 5 minutes until they start to brown. Remove the chicken, add the garlic, ginger and half the spring onion and stir-fry for 1 minute. Then add the stock, rice wine, soy sauce and a pinch of salt and stir. Put the chicken back in, add the lemon slices and a little cornflour and cover. Cook over a low heat until the chicken pieces are cooked through (20–30 minutes), adding a little sugar if the sauce is too sharp. The secret is not to add water: the sauce should not be wet, but cooked in and clinging to the chicken.

Steamed spare ribs in black bean sauce

Spare ribs in Hong Kong are not the long Tex-Mex variety, but cut into short sections 5–8cm/2–3in long. Buy what you can and cut them to size.

500–750g/1–1¹/₂lb pork spare ribs

2 tablespoons black beans

1 onion, finely chopped

¹/₂ teaspoon salt

2 tablespoons vegetable oil

2 tablespoons stock

2 teaspoons sugar

1 tablespoon soy sauce

1 tablespoon rice wine (or dry sherry)

Cornflour

1 tablespoon red chillis, chopped

3 cloves garlic, crushed

Blanch the spare ribs in boiling water for 2 minutes, then drain and put aside in a bowl. Soak the black beans in hot water for 10 minutes, drain and crush lightly with the back of a spoon. Heat the oil in a wok, stir-fry the onion for less than a minute, add the black beans, stock, sugar, salt, rice wine and soy sauce and stir-fry together briefly. Pour onto the spare ribs and mix together, adding cornflour to thicken.

Then put ribs on a dish, sprinkle with chilli and garlic and steam for 30 minutes.

Vegetables in oyster sauce

In Hong Kong this is a standard dish, made with whatever vegetable happens to be in season. Use green vegetables and try, variously, Chinese cabbage, white cabbage, spinach, broccoli; greens and even brussel sprouts (cut them in half to get the best results).

Green vegetable

2 tablespoons vegetable oil

2 cloves garlic, chopped

2 slices fresh ginger, chopped finely

1 teaspoon sugar

1 tablespoon soy sauce

2 tablespoons oyster sauce

$1/2$ teaspoon cornflour mixed in a little water

Wash the vegetable and cut into large strips or separate leaves. Heat the oil in a wok and stir-fry the garlic and ginger for 30 seconds. Then add the vegetable. Continue to cook, stir-frying for 2 minutes. Add the sugar, soy sauce and cornflour mixture and mix in. Add the oyster sauce and heat through before serving. Place on a dish and drip more oyster sauce over before eating.

Cookbooks

Learning by trial and error is the best way to get to grips with the basic recipes; don't be afraid to experiment. However, if you want to improve your Cantonese cooking skills rapidly, get yourself a decent **cookbook**. There are plenty on the market, though if you're a beginner get one with good pictures so that you can see what the end result is supposed to look like. One thing to check is that you're buying a knowledgable book. Most are classed as "Chinese" cookbooks, which generally means that they cull their recipes from all over China – no bad thing, but skimpy if you want to concentrate on Cantonese (ie southern Chinese) cooking. A good book should tell you where in China the recipes come from, so you can make up your own mind; one with Chinese characters next to the recipes can be handy if you're going to Hong Kong and want to test out the genuine article once there.

The first doyen of the Chinese cookbook was **Kenneth Lo**: anything by him is straightforward, informative and inspiring. Of recent publications, **Yan-Kit So**'s *Classic Food of China* is erudite and full of good sense (and includes all the classic Cantonese recipes), while **Ken Hom**'s *Fragrant Harbour Taste: The New Chinese Cooking of Hong Kong* details modern Hong Kong cooking (as dished up in some of the swankier, designer restaurants), which culls its influences from all over Asia as well as the West.

On the subject of recipes and books, two Cantonese foodie **jokes** seem relevant here (both originally noted by the writer and journalist Paul Levy). First, when casting about for suitable ingredients, always bear in mind what the northern Chinese say about their southern neighbours: "The Cantonese will eat anything with four legs except a table and anything that flies except an aeroplane." Second, and hardly any less graphic, is the story of the day that an alien lands on earth and appears before an Indian and a Cantonese person – the Indian prostrates himself before the alien and prays to it, while the Cantonese person hurries off to consult a recipe book.

Language: a Cantonese Survival Guide

The language spoken by the overwhelming majority of Hong Kong and Macau's population is Cantonese, a southern Chinese dialect used in the province of Guangdong – and the one primarily spoken by the millions of Chinese emigrants throughout the world. Unfortunately, Cantonese is one of the world's most difficult languages for Westerners to learn: it's tonal, and the same word can have several different meanings depending on the pitch of the voice; there are nine different tones. To learn to speak it fluently would take years, and even mastering the basics can be fraught with misunderstanding. Things are further complicated by the fact that written Chinese is a different matter altogether –

Cantonese Words and Phrases

Basics

Good morning	*jo san*
Hello/how are you?	*nei ho ma*
Thank you	*m goy*
Goodnight	*jo toe*
Goodbye	*joy gin*
What is your name?	*nei gwei sing ah?*
My name is...	*or sing...*
What time is it?	*cheung mun, gay dim le?*
How much is it?	*cheung mun, gay dor chin?*
Where is the train station/	*cheung mun, for che tjam hay been doe ah/*
bus stop/	*ba-si tjam hay been doe ah/*
ferry pier?	*ma-tou hay been doe ah?*
Hong Kong	*heung gong*
China	*chung kwok*
Britain	*ying kwok*

Transport and Essentials

Train	*for che*
Bus	*ba-si*
Ferry	*do shun*
Taxi	*dik-si*
Airport	*gei-cheun*
Hotel	*lui dim*
Restaurant	*fan dim*
Campsite	*yer ying way ji*
Toilets	*chi sor*
Police	*ging-tchak*

Numbers

1	*yat*
2	*yih*
3	*saam*
4	*sei*
5	*ngh (um)*
6	*luk*
7	*tchat*
8	*baat*
9	*gau*
10	*sahp*
11	*sahp yat*
12	*sahp yih*
20	*yih sahp*
30	*saam sahp*
100	*yat baak*
1000	*yat tin*

Note that the number two changes when asking for two of something – *long wei* (a table for two) – or stating something other than counting – *long mung* (two dollars).

meaningful phrases and sentences are formed by a series of characters, or pictographs, which individually represent actions and objects.

Still, most visitors get by without knowing a word of Cantonese. Hong Kong is officially **bilingual**, and all signs, public transport and utility notices and street names are written in English, as well as Chinese characters; about the only problem is making out the small English script written on the front of the buses. Also, nearly

---

SOME SIGNS

Entrance	入口	No smoking	請勿吸菸
Exit	出口	Danger	危險
Toilets	廁所	Customs	關稅
Gentlemen	男廁	Bus	公共汽車
Ladies	女廁	Ferry	渡船
Open	營業中	Train	火車
Closed	休業	Airport	飛機場
Arrivals	到達	Police	警察
Departures	出發	Restaurant	飯店
Closed for holidays	休假	Hotel	賓館
Out of order	出故障	Campsite	野營位置
Drinking/mineral water	礦泉水	Beach	海灘
		No swimming	禁止游永

PLACE NAMES

Hong Kong	香港	Jordan	佐敦
Hong Kong Island	香港島	Central	中環
Tsim Sha Tsui	尖沙咀	Wan Chai	灣仔
Kowloon	九龍	Causeway Bay	銅鑼灣
New Territories	新界	Aberdeen	香港仔
Happy Valley	跑馬地	Stanley	赤柱
Sha Tin	沙田	Lantau	大嶼山
Tsuen Wan	荃灣	Cheung Chau	長州
Mongkok	旺角	Lamma	南丫島
Yau Ma Tei	油麻地		

everyone you'll have dealings with in Central and Tsim Sha Tsui, as well as most of the other tourist destinations, will speak at least some English. In Macau, the dominant colonial language is Portuguese (for more on which, see pp.319–320), but English is increasingly spoken there, too.

To help out, we've provided a small, basic guide to **everyday Cantonese** on p.397– the sort of things you'll want to say to people on the street and in hotels and restaurants. The problem with it is that the accepted way the Cantonese words are written in English often bears little relation to how they're actually **pronounced** by a Chinese person: the romanized word is at best an approximation of the Chinese sound and, in any case, no one will understand you without the correct intonation. You'll only get it right by listening and practising. As far as the **characters** go, we've provided some examples of the most important **signs and place names**, but that's all – it's incredibly difficult for the untrained eye to read them, and anyway, they don't help with pronunciation.

Glossary of Hong Kong Words and Terms

Lots of strange words have entered the vocabulary of Hong Kong people, Chinese and Westerners alike, and you'll come across most of them during your time here. Some are derivations of Cantonese words, adapted by successive generations of European settlers; others come from the different foreign and colonial languages represented in Hong Kong – from Chinese dialects to Anglo-Indian words. For words and terms specifically to do with Chinese food, see the chapter on "Eating", pp.236–237.

Amah Female housekeeper/servant.

Ancestral Hall Main room or hall in a temple complex where the ancestral records are kept, and where devotions take place.

Cheongsam Chinese dress with a long slit up the side.

Chop A personal seal or stamp of authority.

Dai pai dong Street stall selling snacks and food.

Expat Expatriate; a foreign worker living in Hong Kong.

Feng Shui Literally "wind and water", the Chinese art of geomancy.

Godown Warehouse.

Gweilo Literally "ghost man"; used by the Cantonese for all Westerners (*gweipor*, "ghost woman"); originally derogatory, but now in accepted use.

Hong Major company.

Kaido Small boat used as a ferry, a sampan (also *kaito*).

Junk Large flat-bottomed boat with a high deck and an overhanging stern.

Mahjong A Chinese game played with tiles, like souped-up dominoes.

Miu The Cantonese word for temple.

Nullah Gully, ravine.

Praya The Portuguese word for waterfront promenade (in occasional use).

Sampan Small flat-bottomed boat.

Shroff Cashier.

Tai Chi Martial arts exercise.

Taipan Boss of a major company.

Acronyms

EXCO Executive Council.

HKTA Hong Kong Tourist Association.

KCR Kowloon–Canton Railway.

LEGCO Legislative Council.

LRT Light Rail Transit.

MTR Mass Transit Railway.

SAR Special Administrative Region.

Index

Stay in touch with us!

ROUGHNEWS **is Rough Guides' free newsletter. In three issues a year we give you news, travel issues, music reviews, readers' letters and the latest dispatches from authors on the road.**

I would like to receive ROUGH**NEWS**: please put me on your free mailing list.

NAME . . . .

ADDRESS . . . .

Please clip or photocopy and send to: Rough Guides, 1 Mercer Street, London WC2H 9QJ, England or Rough Guides, 375 Hudson Street, New York, NY 10014, USA.

direct orders from

Amsterdam	1-85828-218-7	UK£8.99	US$14.95	CAN$19.99
Andalucia	1-85828-219-5	9.99	16.95	22.99
Australia	1-85828-220-9	13.99	21.95	29.99
Bali	1-85828-134-2	8.99	14.95	19.99
Barcelona	1-85828-221-7	8.99	14.95	19.99
Berlin	1-85828-129-6	8.99	14.95	19.99
Belgium & Luxembourg	1-85828-222-5	10.99	17.95	23.99
Brazil	1-85828-223-3	13.99	21.95	29.99
Britain	1-85828-208-X	12.99	19.95	25.99
Brittany & Normandy	1-85828-224-1	9.99	16.95	22.99
Bulgaria	1-85828-183-0	9.99	16.95	22.99
California	1-85828-181-4	10.99	16.95	22.99
Canada	1-85828-130-X	10.99	14.95	19.99
China	1-85828-225-X	15.99	24.95	32.99
Corfu	1-85828-226-8	8.99	14.95	19.99
Corsica	1-85828-227-6	9.99	16.95	22.99
Costa Rica	1-85828-136-9	9.99	15.95	21.99
Crete	1-85828-132-6	8.99	14.95	18.99
Cyprus	1-85828-182-2	9.99	16.95	22.99
Czech & Slovak Republics	1-85828-121-0	9.99	16.95	22.99
Dublin Mini Guide	1-85828-294-2	5.99	9.95	12.99
Edinburgh Mini Guide	1-85828-295-0	5.99	9.95	12.99
Egypt	1-85828-188-1	10.99	17.95	23.99
Europe	1-85828-289-6	14.99	19.95	25.99
England	1-85828-160-1	10.99	17.95	23.99
First Time Europe	1-85828-270-5	7.99	9.95	12.99
Florida	1-85828-184-4	10.99	16.95	22.99
France	1-85828-228-4	12.99	19.95	25.99
Germany	1-85828-309-4	14.99	23.95	31.99
Goa	1-85828-275-6	8.99	14.95	19.99
Greece	1-85828-300-0	12.99	19.95	25.99
Greek Islands	1-85828-310-8	10.99	17.95	23.99
Guatemala	1-85828-189-X	10.99	16.95	22.99
Hawaii: Big Island	1-85828-158-X	8.99	12.95	16.99
Hawaii	1-85828-206-3	10.99	16.95	22.99
Holland	1-85828-229-2	10.99	17.95	23.99
Hong Kong	1-85828-187-3	8.99	14.95	19.99
Hungary	1-85828-123-7	8.99	14.95	19.99
India	1-85828-200-4	14.99	23.95	31.99
Ireland	1-85828-179-2	10.99	17.95	23.99
Italy	1-85828-167-9	12.99	19.95	25.99
Jamaica	1-85828-230-6	9.99	16.95	22.99
Kenya	1-85828-192-X	11.99	18.95	24.99
Lisbon Mini Guide	1-85828-297-7	5.99	9.95	12.99
London	1-85828-231-4	9.99	15.95	21.99
Madrid Mini Guide	1-85828-353-1	5.99	9.95	12.99
Mallorca & Menorca	1-85828-165-2	8.99	14.95	19.99
Malaysia, Singapore & Brunei	1-85828-232-2	11.99	18.95	24.99
Mexico	1-85828-044-3	10.99	16.95	22.99
Morocco	1-85828-040-0	9.99	16.95	21.99
Moscow	1-85828-118-0	8.99	14.95	19.99
Nepal	1-85828-190-3	10.99	17.95	23.99
New York	1-85828-296-9	9.99	15.95	21.99
Norway	1-85828-234-9	10.99	17.95	23.99

In the UK, Rough Guides are available from all good bookstores, but can be obtained from Penguin by contacting: Penguin Direct, Penguin Books Ltd, Bath Road, Harmondsworth, West Drayton, Middlesex UB7 0DA; or telephone the credit line on 0181-899 4036 (9am–5pm) and ask for Penguin Direct. Visa and Access accepted. Delivery will normally be within 14 working days. Penguin Direct ordering facilities are only available in the UK and the USA. The availability and published prices quoted are correct at the time of going to press but are subject to alteration without prior notice.

around the world

Pacific Northwest	1-85828-092-3	9.99	14.95	19.99
Paris	1-85828-235-7	8.99	14.95	19.99
Poland	1-85828-168-7	10.99	17.95	23.99
Portugal	1-85828-180-6	9.99	16.95	22.99
Prague	1-85828-122-9	8.99	14.95	19.99
Provence	1-85828-127-X	9.99	16.95	22.99
Pyrenees	1-85828-308-6	10.99	17.95	23.99
Rhodes & the Dodecanese	1-85828-120-2	8.99	14.95	19.99
Romania	1-85828-305-1	10.99	17.95	23.99
San Francisco	1-85828-299-3	8.99	14.95	19.99
Scandinavia	1-85828-236-5	12.99	20.95	27.99
Scotland	1-85828-302-7	9.99	16.95	22.99
Sicily	1-85828-178-4	9.99	16.95	22.99
Singapore	1-85828-237-3	8.99	14.95	19.99
South Africa	1-85828-238-1	12.99	19.95	25.99
Soutwest USA	1-85828-239-X	10.99	16.95	22.99
Spain	1-85828-240-3	11.99	18.95	24.99
St Petersburg	1-85828-298-5	9.99	16.95	22.99
Sweden	1-85828-241-1	10.99	17.95	23.99
Thailand	1-85828-140-7	10.99	17.95	24.99
Tunisia	1-85828-139-3	10.99	17.95	24.99
Turkey	1-85828-242-X	12.99	19.95	25.99
Tuscany & Umbria	1-85828-243-8	10.99	17.95	23.99
USA	1-85828-307-8	14.99	19.95	25.99
Venice	1-85828-170-9	8.99	14.95	19.99
Vietnam	1-85828-191-1	9.99	15.95	21.99
Wales	1-85828-245-4	10.99	17.95	23.99
Washington DC	1-85828-246-2	8.99	14.95	19.99
West Africa	1-85828-101-6	15.99	24.95	34.99
More Women Travel	1-85828-098-2	10.99	16.95	22.99
Zimbabwe & Botswana	1-85828-186-5	11.99	18.95	24.99

Phrasebooks

Czech	1-85828-148-2	3.50	5.00	7.00
French	1-85828-144-X	3.50	5.00	7.00
German	1-85828-146-6	3.50	5.00	7.00
Greek	1-85828-145-8	3.50	5.00	7.00
Hungarian	1-85828-304-3	4.00	6.00	8.00
Italian	1-85828-143-1	3.50	5.00	7.00
Japanese	1-85828-303-5	4.00	6.00	8.00
Mexican	1-85828-176-8	3.50	5.00	7.00
Portuguese	1-85828-175-X	3.50	5.00	7.00
Polish	1-85828-174-1	3.50	5.00	7.00
Spanish	1-85828-147-4	3.50	5.00	7.00
Thai	1-85828-177-6	3.50	5.00	7.00
Turkish	1-85828-173-3	3.50	5.00	7.00
Vietnamese	1-85828-172-5	3.50	5.00	7.00

Reference

Classical Music	1-85828-113-X	12.99	19.95	25.99
European Football	1-85828-256-X	14.99	23.95	31.99
Internet	1-85828-288-8	5.00	8.00	10.00
Jazz	1-85828-137-7	16.99	24.95	34.99
Opera	1-85828-138-5	16.99	24.95	34.99
Reggae	1-85828-247-0	12.99	19.95	25.99
Rock	1-85828-201-2	17.99	26.95	35.00
World Music	1-85828-017-6	16.99	22.95	29.99